FOURTEENTH EDITION

Patterns for College Writing

A RHETORICAL READER AND GUIDE

Laurie G. Kirszner
University of the Sciences, Emeritus

Stephen R. Mandell
Drexel University

bedford/st.martin's
Macmillan Learning
Boston | New York

For Peter Phelps, 1936–1990, with thanks

For Bedford/St. Martin's
Vice President, Editorial, Macmillan Learning Humanities: Edwin Hill
Director of Content Development: Jane Knetzger
Development Manager: Maura Shea
Senior Program Director: Leasa Burton
Program Manager for Readers and Literature: John E. Sullivan III
Developmental Editor: Sherry Mooney
Senior Content Project Manager: Jessica Gould
Media Producer: Rand Thomas
Senior Content Workflow Manager: Jennifer Wetzel
Marketing Manager: Joy Fisher Williams
Associate Editor: Jennifer Prince
Copy Editor: Kathleen Lafferty
Senior Photo Editor: Martha Friedman
Photo Researcher: Sheri Blaney
Permissions Editor: Kalina Ingham
Senior Art Director: Anna Palchik
Text Design: Richard Korab
Cover Design: John Callahan
Cover Art: Autumn Interior, Wheatley, Jenny; Private Collection/Bridgeman Images
Opener Banner Photo: JonnyDrake/Shutterstock
Composition: Lumina Datamatics, Inc.
Printing and Binding: LSC Communications

Manufactured in the United States of America.

2 1 0 9 f e d c b

For information, write: Bedford/St. Martin's, 75 Arlington Street, Boston, MA 02116

ISBN 978-1-319-05664-3 (Student Edition)
ISBN 978-1-319-10667-6 (Instructor's Edition)

Acknowledgments
Text acknowledgments and copyrights appear at the back of the book on pages 786–90, which constitute an extension of the copyright page. Art acknowledgments and copyrights appear on the same page as the art selections they cover.

PREFACE

Since it was first published, *Patterns for College Writing* has been used by millions of students at colleges and universities across the United States. We have been delighted by the overwhelmingly positive response to the first thirteen editions of *Patterns*, and we continue to be gratified by positive feedback from the many instructors who find *Patterns* to be the most accessible and the most pedagogically sound rhetoric-reader they have ever used. In preparing this fourteenth edition, we have worked hard to fine-tune the features that have made *Patterns* the most popular composition reader available today and to develop new features to enhance the book's usefulness for both instructors and students.

What Instructors and Students Like about *Patterns for College Writing*

An Emphasis on Critical Reading

The Introduction, "How to Use This Book," and Chapter 1, "Reading to Write: Becoming a Critical Reader," prepare students to become analytical readers and writers by showing them how to apply critical reading strategies to a typical selection and by providing sample responses to the various kinds of writing prompts in the book. Not only does this material introduce students to the book's features, but it also prepares them to tackle reading and writing assignments in their other courses.

Extensive Coverage of the Writing Process

The remaining chapters in Part One, "The Writing Process" (Chapters 2 through 5), comprise a "mini-rhetoric," offering advice on drafting, writing, revising, and editing as they introduce students to activities such as freewriting, brainstorming, clustering, and journal writing. These chapters also include numerous writing exercises to give students opportunities for immediate practice.

Detailed Coverage of the Patterns of Development

In Part Two, "Readings for Writers," Chapters 6 through 14 explain and illustrate the patterns of development that students typically use in their college writing assignments: narration, description, exemplification, process, cause and effect, comparison and contrast, classification and division, definition, and argumentation. Each chapter begins with a comprehensive introduction that presents a definition and a paragraph-length example of the pattern to be discussed and then explains the particular writing strategies and applications associated with it. Next, each chapter analyzes one or two annotated student essays to show how the pattern can be used in particular college writing situations. Chapter 15, "Combining the Patterns," illustrates how the various patterns of development discussed in Chapters 6 through 14 can work together in an essay.

A Diverse and Popular Selection of Readings

Varied in subject, style, and cultural perspective, the sixty-eight professional selections engage students while providing them with outstanding models for writing. We have tried to achieve a balance between classic authors (George Orwell, Jessica Mitford, E. B. White, Martin Luther King Jr.) and newer voices (Bich Minh Nguyen, Zeynep Tufekci, Marina Keegan) so that instructors have a broad range of readings to choose from.

More Student Essays than Any Comparable Text

To provide students with realistic models for improving their own writing, we include eighteen sample student essays.

Helpful Coverage of Grammar Issues

Grammar-in-Context boxes in chapter introductions offer specific advice on how to identify and correct the grammar, mechanics, and punctuation problems that students are likely to encounter when they work with particular patterns of development.

Apparatus Designed to Help Students Learn

Each professional essay in the text is followed by three types of questions. These questions are designed to help students assess their understanding of the essay's content and of the writer's purpose and audience; to recognize the stylistic and structural techniques used to shape the essay; and to become sensitive to the nuances of language. Each essay is also accompanied by a Journal Entry prompt, Writing Workshop topics (suggestions for full-length writing assignments), and Thematic Connections that identify related readings in the text. Also following each essay is a Combining the Patterns feature that focuses on different patterns of development used in the essay and possible alternatives to these patterns. Each chapter ends with a list of Writing Assignments and a Collaborative Activity. Many of these assignments and activities have been updated to reflect the most current topics and trends.

Extensive Cultural and Historical Background for All Readings

In addition to a biographical headnote, each reading is preceded by a headnote containing essential background information to help students make connections between the reading and the historical, social, and economic forces that shaped it.

An Introduction to Visual Texts

Every rhetorical chapter includes a visual text – such as a photograph, a piece of fine art, or panels from a graphic novel – that provides an accessible introduction to each rhetorical pattern. Apparatus that helps students discuss the pattern in its visual form follows each image.

Thorough Coverage of Working with Sources

Part Three, "Working with Sources," takes students through the process of writing a research paper and includes a model student paper in MLA style. (The Appendix addresses APA style and includes a model APA paper.)

What's New in This Edition

Engaging New Readings

The twenty-five new professional essays treat topics of current interest. Isabel Wilkerson explores the history of "Emmett Till and Tamir Rice, Sons of the Great Migration." Josh Barro explains "Why Stealing Cars Went Out of Fashion." Karen Miller Pensiero shows us the "Photos That Change History." In all cases, readings have been carefully selected for their high-interest subject matter as well as for their effectiveness as teachable models for student writing.

Argumentation Chapter Updated

The argument chapter has been revised to focus on issues of particular importance to college students. It includes two new debates ("Should Public Colleges Be Free?" and "Does It Pay to Study the Humanities?") and one new casebook ("Do College Students Need Trigger Warnings?").

With Bedford/St. Martin's, You Get More

At Bedford/St. Martin's, providing support to teachers and their students who use our books and digital tools is our top priority. The Bedford/St. Martin's English Community is now our home for professional resources, including Bedford *Bits*, our popular blog with new ideas for the composition classroom. Join us to connect with our authors and your colleagues at **community.macmillan.com**, where you can download titles from our professional resource series, review projects in the pipeline, sign up for webinars, or start a discussion. In addition to this dynamic online community and book-specific instructor resources, we offer digital tools, custom solutions, and value packages to support both you and your students. We are committed to delivering the quality and value that you've come to expect from Bedford/St. Martin's, supported as always by the power of Macmillan Learning. To learn more about or to order any of the following products, contact your Bedford/St. Martin's sales representative or visit the website at **macmillanlearning.com**.

LaunchPad for *Patterns for College Writing*: Where Students Learn

LaunchPad provides engaging content and new ways to get the most out of your book. Get an interactive e-Book combined with assessment tools in a fully customizable course space; then assign and mix our resources with yours.

- **Interactive Peer Review Worksheets** allow students to type their responses into a form that is easy to share with fellow students and their instructor.
- **Reading Comprehension Quizzes** for every selection in *Patterns* help you quickly gauge your students' understanding of the assigned reading.
- **Diagnostics and Exercise Central** provide opportunities to assess areas for improvement and assign additional exercises based on students' needs. Eight diagnostic quizzes—pre- and post-tests on sentence grammar, punctuation and mechanics, reading skills, and reading strategies—offer visual reports that show performance by topic, class, and student as well as comparison reports that track improvement over time. Use these reports to target additional practice by assigning quizzes from the Exercise Central question bank.
- **Pre-built units**—including readings, videos, quizzes, discussion groups, and more—are easy to adapt and assign by adding your own materials and mixing them with our high-quality multimedia content and ready-made assessment options, such as **LearningCurve** adaptive quizzing.
- LaunchPad also provides access to a **gradebook** that offers a clear window on the performance of your whole class, individual students, and even results of individual assignments.
- Use LaunchPad on its own or **integrate it** with your school's learning management system so that your class is always on the same page.

LaunchPad for *Patterns for College Writing* can be purchased on its own or packaged with the print book at a significant discount. An activation code is required. To order LaunchPad for *Patterns for College Writing* with the print book, use ISBN 978-1-319-13642-0. For more information, go to **launchpadworks.com**.

Choose from Alternative Formats of *Patterns for College Writing*

Bedford/St. Martin's offers a range of affordable formats, allowing students to choose the one that works best for them.

- *Paperback* To order the paperback edition, use ISBN 978-1-319-05664-3.
- *Popular e-Book formats* For details of our e-Book partners, visit **macmillanlearning.com/ebooks**.

Select Value Packages

Add value to your text by packaging one of the following resources with *Patterns for College Writing*. To learn more about package options for any of the following products, contact your Bedford/St. Martin's sales representative or visit **macmillanlearning.com**.

LaunchPad Solo for Readers and Writers allows students to work on whatever they need help with the most. At home or in class, students learn at their own pace, with instruction tailored to each student's unique needs. *LaunchPad Solo for Readers and Writers* features:

- **Pre-built units that support a learning arc.** Each easy-to-assign unit is composed of a pre-test check, multimedia instruction and assessment, and a post-test that assesses what students have learned about critical reading, writing process, using sources, grammar, style, and mechanics. Dedicated units also offer help for multilingual writers.
- **Diagnostics that help establish a baseline for instruction.** Assign diagnostics to identify areas of strength and areas for improvement on topics related to grammar and reading and to help students plan a course of study. Use visual reports to track performance by topic, class, and student as well as comparison reports that track improvement over time.
- **A video introduction to many topics.** Introductions offer an overview of the unit's topic, and many include a brief, accessible video to illustrate the concepts at hand.
- **Twenty-five reading selections with comprehension quizzes.** Assign a range of classic and contemporary essays, each of which includes a label indicating Lexile level to help you scaffold instruction in critical reading.
- **Adaptive quizzing for targeted learning.** Most units include LearningCurve, game-like adaptive quizzing that focuses on the areas in which each student needs the most help.

- **The ability to monitor student progress.** Use our gradebook to see which students are on track and which need additional help with specific topics.
- **Additional reading comprehension quizzes.** *Patterns for College Writing* includes multiple-choice quizzes, which help you quickly gauge your students' understanding of the assigned reading. These are available in *LaunchPad Solo for Readers and Writers.*

Order ISBN 978-1-319-14527-9 to package *LaunchPad Solo for Readers and Writers* with *Patterns for College Writing* at a significant discount. Students who rent or buy a used book can purchase access, and instructors may request free access at **macmillanlearning.com/readwrite**.

Writer's Help 2.0 is a powerful online writing resource that helps students find answers whether they are searching for writing advice on their own or as part of an assignment.

- **Smart search.** Built on research with more than 1,600 student writers, the smart search in Writer's Help provides reliable results even when students use novice terms, such as *flow* and *unstuck*.
- **Trusted content from our best-selling handbooks.** Choose *Writer's Help 2.0, Hacker Version,* or *Writer's Help 2.0, Lunsford Version,* and ensure that students have clear advice and examples for all of their writing questions.
- **Diagnostics that help establish a baseline for instruction.** Assign diagnostics to identify areas of strength and areas for improvement on topics related to grammar and reading and to help students plan a course of study. Use visual reports to track performance by topic, class, and student as well as comparison reports that track improvement over time.
- **Adaptive exercises that engage students.** Writer's Help 2.0 includes LearningCurve, game-like online quizzing that adapts to what students already know and helps them focus on what they need to learn.
- **Reading comprehension quizzes.** *Patterns for College Writing* includes multiple-choice quizzes, which help you quickly gauge your students' understanding of the assigned reading. These are available in Writer's Help 2.0.

Writer's Help 2.0 can be packaged with *Patterns for College Writing* at a significant discount. For more information, contact your sales representative or visit **macmillanlearning.com/writershelp2**.

Macmillan Learning Curriculum Solutions

Curriculum Solutions brings together the quality of Bedford/St. Martin's content with our expertise in publishing original custom print and digital products. Developed especially for writing courses, our ForeWords for English program contains a library of the most popular, requested content in easy-to-use modules to help you build the best possible text. Whether you are considering creating a custom version of *Patterns for College Writing* or incorporating our content with your own, we can adapt and combine the resources that work best for your course or program. Some enrollment minimums apply. Contact your sales representative for more information.

Instructor Resources

You have a lot to do in your course. Bedford/St. Martin's wants to make it easy for you to find the support you need—and to get it quickly.

Resources for Instructors Using Patterns for College Writing is available as a PDF that can be downloaded from **macmillanlearning.com**. Visit the instructor resources tab for *Patterns for College Writing*. In addition to chapter overviews and teaching tips, the instructor's manual includes sample syllabi, suggestions for classroom discussion, and possible responses for every question in the book.

NEW! *A Student's Companion for Patterns for College Writing*

If your students need a little extra support, consider ordering *A Student's Companion for Patterns for College Writing* (ISBN 978-1-319-12674-2). This text reinforces the most foundational elements in academic writing. While recognizing and respecting students' abilities, this supplement breaks down the steps necessary to excel in college writing, tackling time management; critical reading skills across print, digital, and professional genres; the essay-drafting process; and the essentials of grammar. This companion, meant to supplement the coverage in *Patterns for College Writing*, gives students the additional support they need to get or stay on-level in the composition classroom. It is an ideal solution for accelerated learning programs or corequisite courses, while the deep integration with *Patterns* makes it an ideal resource for any instructor who wants students to build a strong foundation in academic writing.

Acknowledgments

As always, friends, colleagues, students, and family all helped this project along. Of particular value were the responses to the questionnaires sent to the following instructors, who provided frank and helpful advice: Amelia Magallanes Arguijo, Laredo Community College; Victoria Bryan, Cleveland State Community College; Thomas Chester, Ivy Tech Community College; Anne Dearing, Hudson Valley Community College; Jennifer Eble, Cleveland State Community College; Marcus Embry, University of Northern Colorado; Ulanda Forbess, North Lake College; Jan Geyer, Hudson Valley Community College; Priscilla Glanville, State College of Florida; Scott Hathaway, Hudson Valley Community College; Josh Miller, Cape Fear Community College; Janet Minc, University of Akron Wayne College; Jennifer Ravey, Lamar University;

Cheryl Saba, Cape Fear Community College; Ana Schnellmann, Lindenwood University; Dhipinder Walia, Lehman College; and Coreen Wees, Iowa Western Community College. Additional thanks to Cedric Burroughs at Marquette University for his valuable suggestions.

Special thanks go to Jeff Ousborne for his help with some of the apparatus and for revising the headnotes and the *Resources for Instructors*.

Through fourteen editions of *Patterns for College Writing*, we have enjoyed a wonderful working relationship with Bedford/St. Martin's. We have always found the editorial and production staff to be efficient, cooperative, and generous with their time and advice. As always, we appreciate the encouragement and advice of our longtime friend, Nancy Perry. In addition, we thank Joan Feinberg, past president of Bedford/St. Martin's, for her support for this project and for her trust in us. During our work on this edition, we have benefited from our productive relationship with John Sullivan, Program Manager, Readers and Literature, who helped us make this edition of *Patterns* the best it could be. We have been especially lucky to work on this edition with our talented developmental editor, Sherry Mooney, a real star. We are also grateful to Jessica Gould, senior content project manager, and Lisa Kinne, managing editor, for their work overseeing the production of this edition; John Callahan for the attractive new cover; and associate editor Jennifer Prince for her invaluable help with tasks large and small. We are fortunate to have enjoyed our long and fulfilling collaboration; we know how rare a successful partnership like ours is. We also know how lucky we are to have our families to help keep us in touch with the things that really matter.

Laurie G. Kirszner
Stephen R. Mandell

CONTENTS

THEMATIC GUIDE TO THE CONTENTS

Family Relationships

Language

Reading and Writing

Education

Business and Work

Race and Culture

Gender

Nature and the Environment

Media and Society

History and Politics

Ethics

Citizenship

Introduction: How to Use This Book

Patterns for College Writing is a book of readings, but it is also a book about writing. Every reading selection is followed by questions and exercises designed to help you become a thoughtful and proficient writer. The study questions that accompany the essays in this book encourage you to think critically about writers' ideas. Although some of the questions (particularly those listed under **Comprehension**) call for fairly straightforward, factual responses, other questions (particularly the **Journal Entry** assignments) invite more complex responses that reflect your individual reaction to the selections.

The essay that begins on the following page, "'What's in a Name?'" by Henry Louis Gates Jr., is typical of those that appear in this book. It is preceded by a **headnote** that gives readers information about the author's life and career. This headnote includes a **background** section that provides a social, historical, and cultural context for the essay.

HENRY LOUIS GATES JR.

"What's in a Name?"

Henry Louis Gates Jr. was born in 1950 in Keyser, West Virginia, and grew up in the small town of Piedmont. Currently Alphonse Fletcher University Professor and director of the W. E. B. Du Bois Institute for African and African American Research at Harvard University, he has edited many collections of works by African-American writers and published several volumes of literary criticism. He is probably best known as a social critic whose books and articles for a general audience explore a wide variety of issues and themes, often focusing on race and culture. In the following essay, which originally appeared in the journal *Dissent,* Gates recalls a childhood experience that occurred during the mid-1950s.

Background on the civil rights movement In the mid-1950s, the first stirrings of the civil rights movement were under way, and in 1954 and 1955, the U.S. Supreme Court handed down decisions declaring racial segregation unconstitutional in public schools. Still, much of the country — particularly the South — remained largely segregated until Congress passed the Civil Rights Act of 1964, which prohibited discrimination based on race, color, religion, or national origin in businesses (including restaurants and theaters) covered by interstate commerce laws, as well as in employment. This legislation was followed by the Voting Rights Act of 1965, which guaranteed equal access to the polls, and the Civil Rights Act of 1968, which prohibited discrimination in housing and real estate. At the time of the experience Gates recalls here — before these laws were enacted — prejudice and discrimination against African Americans were the norm in many communities, including those outside the South.

> The question of color takes up much space in these pages, but the question of color, especially in this country, operates to hide the graver questions of the self.
>
> —JAMES BALDWIN, 1961

> . . . blood, darky, Tar Baby, Kaffir, shine . . . moor, blackamoor, Jim Crow, spook . . . quadroon, meriney, red bone, high yellow . . . Mammy, porch monkey, home, homeboy, George . . . spearchucker, schwarze, Leroy, Smokey . . . mouli, buck. Ethiopian, brother, sistah.
>
> —TREY ELLIS, 1989

I had forgotten the incident completely, until I read Trey Ellis's essay 1
"Remember My Name" in a recent issue of the *Village Voice* (June 13, 1989). But there, in the middle of an extended italicized list of the bynames of "the race" ("the race" or "our people" being the terms my parents used in polite or

reverential discourse, "jigaboo" or "nigger" more commonly used in anger, jest, or pure disgust), it was: "George." Now the events of that very brief exchange return to mind so vividly that I wonder why I had forgotten it.

My father and I were walking home at dusk from his second job. He 2
"moonlighted" as a janitor in the evenings for the telephone company. Every day but Saturday, he would come home at 3:30 from his regular job at the paper mill, wash up, eat supper, then at 4:30 head downtown to his second job. He used to make jokes frequently about a union official who moonlighted. I never got the joke, but he and his friends thought it was hilarious. All I knew was that my family always ate well, that my brother and I had new clothes to wear, and that all of the white people in Piedmont, West Virginia, treated my parents with an odd mixture of resentment and respect that even we understood at the time had something directly to do with a small but certain measure of financial security.

He had left a little early that evening because I was with him and I had 3
to be in bed early. I could not have been more than five or six, and we had stopped off at the Cut-Rate Drug Store (where no black person in town but my father could sit down to eat, and eat off real plates with real silverware) so that I could buy some caramel ice cream, two scoops in a wafer cone, please, which I was busy licking when Mr. Wilson walked by.

Mr. Wilson was a very quiet man, whose stony, brooding, silent manner 4
seemed designed to scare off any overtures of friendship, even from white people. He was Irish, as was one-third of our village (another third being Italian), the more affluent among whom sent their children to "Catholic School" across the bridge in Maryland. He had white straight hair, like my Uncle Joe, whom he uncannily resembled, and he carried a black worn metal lunch pail, the kind that Riley* carried on the television show. My father always spoke to him, and for reasons that we never did understand, he always spoke to my father.

"Hello, Mr. Wilson," I heard my father say. 5

"Hello, George." 6

I stopped licking my ice cream cone, and asked my Dad in a loud voice 7
why Mr. Wilson had called him "George."

"Doesn't he know your name, Daddy? 8
Why don't you tell him your name? Your name isn't George."

For a moment I tried to think of who 9
Mr. Wilson was mixing Pop up with. But we didn't have any Georges among the colored people in Piedmont; nor were there colored Georges living in the neighboring towns and working at the mill.

"Doesn't he know your name, Daddy? Why don't you tell him your name? Your name isn't George. . . ."

"Tell him your name, Daddy." 10

"He knows my name, boy," my father said after a long pause. "He calls all 11
colored people George."

* Eds. note — The lead character in the 1950s television program *The Life of Riley,* about a white working-class family and their neighbors.

A long silence ensued. It was "one of those things," as my Mom would put it. Even then, that early, I knew when I was in the presence of "one of those things," one of those things that provided a glimpse, through a rent curtain, at another world that we could not affect but that affected us. There would be a painful moment of silence, and you would wait for it to give way to a discussion of a black superstar such as Sugar Ray or Jackie Robinson. 12

"Nobody hits better in a clutch than Jackie Robinson." 13

"That's right. Nobody." 14

I never again looked Mr. Wilson in the eye. 15

• • •

Responding to an Essay

The study questions that follow each essay will help you **think critically** about what you are reading; they will help you formulate questions and draw conclusions. (Critical thinking and reading are discussed in Chapter 1 of this book.) Four types of questions follow each essay:

- *Comprehension* questions help you assess your understanding of what the writer is saying.
- *Purpose and Audience* questions ask you to consider why, and for whom, each selection was written and to examine the implications of the writer's choices in light of a particular purpose or intended audience.
- *Style and Structure* questions encourage you to examine the decisions the writer has made about elements such as arrangement of ideas, paragraphing, sentence structure, and imagery. One question in this category, designated **Vocabulary Project**, focuses on word choice and connotation.
- *Journal Entry* assignments ask you to write a short, informal response to what you read and to speculate freely about related ideas, perhaps by exploring ethical issues raised by the selection or by offering your opinions about the writer's statements. Briefer, less polished, and less structured than full-length essays, journal entries may suggest ideas for more formal kinds of writing.

Following these sets of questions are three additional features:

- *Writing Workshop* assignments ask you to write essays structured according to the pattern of development explained and illustrated in the chapter. Some of these assignments, designated **Working with Sources**, will ask you to cite the essay or an outside source. In these cases, you will be reminded to include parenthetical documentation and a works-cited page that conform to MLA documentation style.
- *Combining the Patterns* questions focus on the various patterns of development – other than the essay's dominant pattern – that the writer uses. These questions ask why a writer uses particular patterns (narration, description, exemplification, process, cause and effect,

comparison and contrast, classification and division, and definition), what each pattern contributes to the essay, and what other choices the writer might have had.

- *Thematic Connections* identify other readings in this book that explore similar themes. Reading these related works will enhance your understanding and appreciation of the original work and perhaps give you material to write about.

Following are some examples of study questions and possible responses, as well as a **Writing Workshop** assignment and a list of **Thematic Connections**, for "'What's in a Name?'" (page 2). The numbers in parentheses after quotations refer to the paragraphs in which the quotations appear.

Comprehension

1. *In paragraph 1, Gates wonders why he forgot about the exchange between his father and Mr. Wilson. Why do you think he forgot about it?*

   Gates may have forgotten about the incident simply because it was something that happened a long time ago or because such incidents were commonplace when he was a child. Alternatively, he may *not* have forgotten the exchange between his father and Mr. Wilson but pushed it out of his mind because he found it so painful. (After all, he says he never again looked Mr. Wilson in the eye.)

2. *How is the social status of Gates's family different from that of other African-American families in Piedmont, West Virginia? How does Gates account for this difference?*

   Gates's family is different from other African-American families in town in that they are treated with "an odd mixture of resentment and respect" (2) by whites. Although other black people are not permitted to eat at the drugstore, Mr. Gates is. Gates attributes this social status to his family's "small but certain measure of financial security" (2). Even so, when Mr. Wilson insults Mr. Gates, the privileged status of the Gates family is revealed as a sham.

3. *What does Gates mean when he says, "It was 'one of those things,' as my Mom would put it" (12)?*

   Gates's comment indicates that the family learned to see such mistreatment as routine. In context, the word *things* in paragraph 12 refers to the kind of incident that gives Gates and his family a glimpse of the way the white world operates.

4. *Why does Gates's family turn to a discussion of a "black superstar" after a "painful moment of silence" (12) such as the one he describes?*

   Although Gates does not explain the family's behavior, we can infer that they speak of African-American heroes like prizefighter Sugar Ray Robinson and baseball player Jackie Robinson to make themselves feel better. Such discussions are a way of balancing the negative images of African Americans created by incidents such as the one Gates describes and of bolstering the low self-esteem the family felt as a result. These heroes seem to have won the respect denied to the Gates family; to mention them is to participate vicariously in their glory.

5. *Why do you think Gates "never again looked Mr. Wilson in the eye" (15)?*

    Gates may have felt that Mr. Wilson was somehow the enemy, not to be trusted, because he had insulted Gates's father. Or, he may have been ashamed to look Wilson in the eye because he believed his father should have insisted on being addressed properly.

Purpose and Audience

1. *Why do you think Gates introduces his narrative with the two quotations he selects? How do you suppose he expects his audience to react to these quotations? How do you react?*

    Gates begins with two quotations, both by African-American writers, written nearly thirty years apart. Baldwin's words seem to suggest that, in the United States, "the question of color" is a barrier to understanding "the graver questions of the self." That is, the labels *black* and *white* may mask more fundamental characteristics or issues. Ellis's list of names (many pejorative) for African Americans illustrates the fact that epithets can dehumanize people; they can, in effect, rob a person of his or her "self." This issue of the discrepancy between a name and what lies behind it is central to Gates's essay. In a sense, then, Gates begins with these two quotations because they are relevant to the issues he will discuss. More specifically, he is using the two quotations – particularly Ellis's shocking string of unpleasant names – to arouse interest in his topic and provide an intellectual and emotional context for his story. He may also be intending to make his white readers uncomfortable and his black readers angry. How you react depends on your attitudes about race (and perhaps about language).

2. *What is the point of Gates's narrative? That is, why does he recount the incident?*

    Certainly Gates wishes to make readers aware of the awkward, and potentially dangerous, position of his father (and, by extension, of other African Americans) in a small southern town in the 1950s. He also shows us how names help to shape people's perceptions and actions: as long as Mr. Wilson can call all black men "George," he can continue to see them as insignificant and treat them as inferiors. The title of the piece suggests that the writer's main focus is on how names shape perceptions.

3. *The title of this selection, which Gates places in quotation marks, is an allusion to act 2, scene 2, of Shakespeare's* Romeo and Juliet, *in which Juliet says, "What's in a name? That which we call a rose / By any other name would smell as sweet." Why do you think Gates chose this title? Does he expect his audience to recognize the quotation?*

    Because his work was originally published in a journal read by a well-educated audience, Gates would have expected readers to recognize this **allusion** (and also to know a good deal about 1950s race relations). Although Gates could not have been certain that all members of this audience would recognize the reference to *Romeo and Juliet,* he could have been reasonably sure that if they did, it would enhance their understanding of the selection. In Shakespeare's play, the two lovers are kept apart essentially because of their names: she is a Capulet and he is a Montague, and the two families are involved in a bitter feud. In the speech from which Gates takes the title quotation, Juliet questions the logic of such a situation. In her view, what a person is called should not determine how he or she is regarded, which, of course, is Gates's point as well. Even if readers do not recognize the allusion, the title still foreshadows the selection's focus on names.

Style and Structure

1. *Does paragraph 1 add something vital to the narrative, or would Gates's story make sense without the introduction? Could another kind of introduction work as well?*

   Gates's first paragraph supplies the context in which the incident is to be read; that is, it makes clear that Mr. Wilson's calling Mr. Gates "George" was not an isolated incident but part of a pattern of behavior that allowed those in positions of power to mistreat those they considered inferior. For this reason, it is an effective introduction. Although the narrative would make sense without paragraph 1, the story's full impact would probably not be as great. Still, Gates could have begun differently. For example, he could have started with the incident itself (paragraph 2) and interjected his comments about the significance of names later in the piece. He also could have begun with the exchange of dialogue in paragraphs 5 through 11 and then introduced the current paragraph 1 to supply the incident's context.

2. *What does the use of dialogue contribute to the narrative? Would the selection have a different impact without dialogue? Explain.*

   Gates was five or six years old when the incident occurred, and the dialogue helps to establish the child's innocence as well as his father's quiet acceptance of the situation. In short, the dialogue is a valuable addition to the piece because it creates two characters, one innocent and one resigned to injustice, both of whom contrast with the voice of the adult narrator: wise, worldly, but also angry and perhaps ashamed, the voice of a man who has benefited from the sacrifices of men like Gates's father.

3. *Why do you think Gates supplies the specific details he chooses in paragraphs 2 and 3? In paragraph 4? Is all this information necessary?*

   The details Gates provides in paragraphs 2 and 3 help to establish the status of his family in Piedmont; because readers have this information, the fact that the family was ultimately disregarded and discounted by some white people emerges as deeply ironic. The information in paragraph 4 also contributes to this **irony**. Here, we learn that Mr. Wilson was not liked by many white people, that he looked like Gates's Uncle Joe, and that he carried a lunch box – in other words, that he had no special status in the town apart from that conferred by race.

4. **Vocabulary Project.** *Consider the connotations of the words* colored *and* black, *both used by Gates to refer to African Americans. What different associations does each word have? Why does Gates use both – for example,* colored *in paragraph 9 and* black *in paragraph 12? What is your response to his father's use of the term* boy *in paragraph 11?*

In the 1950s, when the incident Gates describes took place, the term *colored* was still widely used, along with *Negro,* to designate Americans of African descent. In the 1960s, the terms *Afro-American* and *black* replaced the earlier names, with *black* emerging as the preferred term and remaining dominant through the 1980s. Today, although *black* is preferred by some, *African American* is used more and more often. Because the term *colored* is the oldest designation, it may seem old-fashioned and even racist today; *black,* which connoted a certain degree of militancy in the 1960s, is probably now considered a neutral term by most people. Gates uses both words because he is speaking from two time periods. In paragraph 9, re-creating the thoughts and words of a child in a 1950s southern town, he uses the term *colored*; in paragraph 12, the adult Gates, commenting in 1989 on the incident, uses *black.* The substitution of *African American* for the older terms might give the narrative a more contemporary flavor, but it might also seem awkward or forced – and, in paragraph 9, inappropriately formal. As far as the term *boy* is concerned, different readers are apt to have different responses. Although the father's use of the term can be seen as affectionate, it can also be seen as derisive in this context since it echoes the bigot's use of *boy* for all black males, regardless of age or accomplishments.

Journal Entry

Do you think Gates's parents should have used experiences like the one in " 'What's in a Name?' " to educate him about the family's social status in the community? Why do you think they chose instead to dismiss such incidents as "one of those things" (12)?

Your responses to these questions will reflect your own opinions, based on your background and experiences as well as on your interpretation of the reading selection.

Writing Workshop

Write about a time when you, like Gates's father, could have spoken out in protest but chose not to. Would you make the same decision today?

By the time you approach the Writing Workshop assignments, you will have read an essay, responded to study questions about it, discussed it in class, and perhaps considered its relationship to other essays in the text. Often, your next step will be to write an essay in response to one of the Writing Workshop questions. (Chapters 2–4 follow Laura Bobnak, a first-year composition student, through the process of writing an essay in response to this Writing Workshop assignment.)

Combining the Patterns

Although **narration** *is the pattern of development that dominates " 'What's in a Name?' " and gives it its structure, Gates also uses* **exemplification***, presenting an extended example to support his thesis. What is this example? What does it illustrate? Would several brief examples have been more convincing?*

The extended example is the story of the encounter between Gates's father and Mr. Wilson, which compellingly illustrates the kind of behavior African

Americans were often forced to adopt in the 1950s. Because Gates's introduction focuses on "the incident" (1), one extended example is enough (although he alludes to other incidents in paragraph 12).

Thematic Connections

- "The Myth of the Latin Woman: I Just Met a Girl Named Maria" (page 225)
- "'Girl'" (page 254)

As you read and think about the selections in this text, you should begin to see thematic links among them. Such parallels can add to your interest and understanding as well as give you ideas for class discussion and writing.

For example, one related work is Judith Ortiz Cofer's "The Myth of the Latin Woman: I Just Met a Girl Named Maria." Although Cofer is Latina, not African American, she too faces the stigma of being seen as a stereotype rather than as an individual; she is characterized as "Maria" just as Gates's father was characterized (and dismissed) as "George." Because Cofer's essay was written in 1993 and discusses fairly recent events (in contrast to Gates's essay, which explores an event that took place in the 1950s), it provides a more contemporary – and, perhaps, broader – context for discussing issues of race and class.

Jamaica Kincaid's short story "'Girl,'" by an African-American writer, also has some parallels with Gates's autobiographical essay. Like Gates, Kincaid's protagonist seems to occupy a subservient position in a society whose rules she must obey. The lessons in life skills that are enumerated in the story are also similar to the lesson Gates learns from his father.

In the process of thinking about Gates's narrative, discussing it in class, or preparing to write an essay on a related topic (such as the one listed under Writing Workshop on page 8), you might find it useful to read Cofer's essay and Kincaid's story.

Responding to Other Kinds of Texts

The first selection in Chapters 6 through 14 of this book is a visual text. It is followed by **Reading Images** questions, a **Journal Entry**, and a short list of **Thematic Connections** that will help you understand the image and shape your response to it.

The final selection in each chapter, a story or poem, is followed by **Reading Literature** questions, a **Journal Entry**, and **Thematic Connections**.

NOTE: At the end of each chapter, **Writing Assignments** offer additional practice in writing essays structured according to a particular pattern of development. Some of these assignments, designated **Working with Sources**, will ask you to refer to one or more of the essays in the chapter (or to an outside source). In these cases, you will be asked to include MLA parenthetical documentation and a works-cited page. Finally, a **Collaborative Activity** suggests an idea for a group project.

PART ONE

The Writing Process

Every reading selection in this book is the result of a struggle between a writer and his or her material. If a writer's struggle is successful, the finished work is welded together without a visible seam, and readers have no sense of the frustration the writer experienced while rearranging ideas or hunting for the right word. Writing is no easy task, even for a professional writer. Still, although there is no simple formula for good writing, some approaches are easier and more productive than others.

At this point, you may be asking yourself, "So what? What has this got to do with me? I'm not a professional writer." True enough, but during the next few years, you will be doing a good deal of writing. Throughout your college career, you will compose exams, reports, essays, and research projects. In your professional life, you may write progress reports, proposals, business correspondence, and memos. As diverse as these tasks are, they have something in common: they can be made easier if you are familiar with the stages of the **writing process** — a process that experienced writers follow when they write.

THE WRITING PROCESS

- **Invention** (also called **prewriting**) During invention, you decide what to write about and gather information to support or explain what you want to say.
- **Arrangement** During arrangement, you decide how you are going to organize your ideas.
- **Drafting and revising** During drafting and revising, you write several drafts as you reconsider your ideas and their organization and refine your style and structure.
- **Editing and proofreading** During editing, you focus on grammar and punctuation, as well as on sentence style and word choice. During proofreading, you correct spelling, mechanical errors, and typos and check your essay's format.

Although the writing process is usually presented as a series of neatly defined steps, that model does not reflect the way people actually write. Ideas do not always flow easily, and the central idea you set out to develop does not always wind up in the essay you ultimately write. In addition, writing often progresses in fits and starts, with ideas occurring sporadically or not at all. Surprisingly, much good writing occurs when a writer gets stuck or confused but continues to work until ideas begin to take shape.

Because the writing process is so erratic, its stages overlap. Most writers engage in invention, arrangement, drafting and revision, and editing simultaneously – finding ideas, considering possible methods of organization, looking for the right words, and correcting grammar and punctuation all at the same time. In fact, writing is such an idiosyncratic process that no two writers approach the writing process in exactly the same way. Some people outline; others do not. Some take elaborate notes during the invention stage; others keep track of everything in their heads.

The writing process discussed throughout this book reflects the many choices writers make at various stages of composition. Regardless of writers' different approaches, however, one thing is certain: the more you write, the better acquainted you will become with your personal writing process and the better you will learn how to modify it to suit various writing tasks.

Because much of your college writing will be done in response to texts you read, Chapter 1 of this book introduces you to critical reading; then, Chapters 2 through 5 discuss the individual stages of the writing process. These chapters will help you define your needs as a writer and understand your options as you approach writing tasks in college and beyond.

1

Reading to Write: Becoming a Critical Reader

On a purely practical level, you will read the selections in this book to answer study questions and to prepare for class discussions (and, often, for writing). More significantly, however, you will also read to evaluate the ideas of others, to form judgments, and to develop original viewpoints. In other words, you will engage in **critical reading**.

By introducing you to new ideas and new ways of thinking about familiar concepts, reading prepares you to respond critically to the ideas of others and to develop ideas of your own. When you read critically, you can form opinions, exchange insights with others, ask and answer questions, and develop ideas that can be further explored in writing. For all these reasons, critical reading is a vital part of your education.

Understanding Critical Reading

Reading is a two-way street. Readers are introduced to a writer's ideas, but they also bring their own ideas to what they read. After all, readers have different national, ethnic, cultural, and geographic backgrounds and different kinds of knowledge and experiences, so they may react differently to a particular essay or story. For example, readers from an economically homogeneous neighborhood may have difficulty understanding an essay about class conflict, but they may be more objective than readers who are struggling with such conflict in their own lives.

These differences in readers' responses do not mean that every interpretation is acceptable, or that an essay (or story or poem) may mean whatever a reader wants it to mean. Readers must make sure they are not distorting a writer's words, overlooking (or ignoring) significant details, or seeing things in an essay or story that do not exist. It is not important for all readers to agree on a particular interpretation of a work. It *is* important, however, for each reader to develop an interpretation that the work itself supports.

When you read an essay in this book, or any text that you expect to discuss in class, you should read it carefully, ideally more than once. If a text is accompanied by a headnote or other background material, as those in this book are, you should read this material as well because it will help you understand the text. Keep in mind that some of the texts you read may eventually be used as sources for writing. In these cases, it is especially important that you understand what you are reading and can formulate a thoughtful response to the writer's ideas. (For information on how to evaluate the sources you read, see Chapter 16.)

To get the most out of your reading, you should use **active reading** strategies. In practical terms, that means actively participating in the reading process: approaching an assigned reading with a clear understanding of your purpose and marking the text to help you understand what you are reading.

REMINDER **NAMING YOUR FILES**

As you take notes about your sources and save each new draft as a separate file, it's important to give each file an accurate and descriptive title so that you can find it when you need it. Your file name should identify the class for which you're writing and the date you updated the file.

Comp-Plagiarism essay_9-25-17

Once you develop a system that works for you, you should use it consistently — for example, always listing elements (class, assignment, date) in the same order for each project. You can also create a separate folder for each class and then use subfolders for each assignment, gathering together all your notes and drafts for an assignment. A folder system will be particularly useful if you regularly use a remote storage site such as Dropbox or Google Drive, where files can easily become confused or be overwritten.

CLOSE VIEW

Determining Your Purpose

Even before you start reading, you should consider some questions about your **purpose** – why you are reading. The answers to these questions will help you understand what kind of information you hope to get out of your reading and how you will use this information.

CHECKLIST **QUESTIONS ABOUT YOUR PURPOSE**

- ☐ Will you be expected to discuss what you are reading? If so, will you discuss it in class? In a conference with your instructor?
- ☐ Will you have to write about what you are reading? If so, will you be expected to write an informal response (for example, a journal entry) or a more formal one (for example, an essay)?
- ☐ Will you be tested on the material?

Previewing

When you **preview**, you try to get a sense of the writer's main idea, key supporting points, and general emphasis. At this stage, you don't read every word; instead, you **skim** the text. You can begin by focusing on the title, the first paragraph (which often contains a purpose statement or overview), and the last paragraph (which may contain a summary of the writer's main idea). You should also look for clues to the writer's message in the passage's other **visual signals**.

Recognizing Visual Signals

- Look at the title.
- Look at the opening and closing paragraphs.
- Look at each paragraph's first sentence.
- Look for headings.
- Look for *italicized* and **boldfaced** words.
- Look for numbered lists.
- Look for bulleted lists (like this one).
- Look at any visuals (graphs, charts, tables, photographs, and so on).
- Look at any information that is boxed.
- Look at any information that is in **color**.

When you have finished previewing the passage, you should have a general sense of what the writer wants to communicate.

As you read and reread, you will record your reactions in writing. These notes will help you understand the writer's ideas and your own thoughts about those ideas. Every reader develops a different system of recording responses, but many readers learn to use a combination of *highlighting* and *annotating*.

Highlighting

When you **highlight**, you mark the text. You might, for example, underline (or double underline) important concepts, box key terms, number a series of related points, circle an unfamiliar word (or place a question mark beside it), draw a vertical line in the margin beside a particularly interesting passage, draw arrows to connect related points, or star discussions of the central issues or main idea.

At this stage, you continue to look for visual signals, but now, as you read more closely, you also begin to pay attention to the text's **verbal signals**.

Recognizing Verbal Signals

- Look for phrases that signal emphasis ("The *primary* reason"; "The *most important* idea").
- Look for repeated words and phrases.
- Look for words that signal addition (*also, in addition, furthermore*).
- Look for words that signal time sequence (*first, after, then, next, finally*).

- Look for words that identify causes and effects (*because, as a result, for this reason*).
- Look for words that introduce examples (*for example, for instance*).
- Look for words that signal comparison (*likewise, similarly*).
- Look for words that signal contrast (*unlike, although, in contrast*).
- Look for words that signal contradiction (*however, on the contrary*).
- Look for words that signal a narrowing of the writer's focus (*in fact, specifically, in other words*).
- Look for words that signal summaries or conclusions (*to sum up, in conclusion*).

LaunchPad

For more practice on critical reading strategies, see the LearningCurve on Critical Reading in the LaunchPad for *Patterns*.

The following pages reprint a column by journalist Brent Staples that focuses on the issue of plagiarism among college students. The column, "Cutting and Pasting: A Senior Thesis by (Insert Name)," and the accompanying headnote and background material have been highlighted by a student.

BRENT STAPLES

Cutting and Pasting: A Senior Thesis by (Insert Name)

Born in 1951 in Chester, Pennsylvania, Brent Staples is a writer and member of the editorial board of the *New York Times.* He often writes about culture, politics, race, and education. Staples has a B.A. in behavioral science from Widener University and a Ph.D. in psychology from the University of Chicago. Before joining the *New York Times,* he wrote for the *Chicago Sun-Times, Chicago Reader, Chicago Magazine,* and the jazz magazine *Down Beat*. His work has also appeared in publications such as *Ms.* and *Harper's*. Staples is the author of a memoir, *Parallel Time: Growing Up in Black and White* (1994).

Background on prevalence of cheating and plagiarism in high school and college Studies suggest that high school and college students are increasingly likely to cheat or plagiarize. For example, one Duke University study conducted from 2002 to 2005 showed that 70 percent of the 50,000 undergraduate students surveyed admitted to cheating on occasion. A 2008 survey of high school students by the Center for Youth Ethics at the Josephson Institute showed that 82 percent had copied from another student's work, and 36 percent said that they had used the Internet to plagiarize an assignment. Moreover, students tend to view such academic dishonesty with indifference: according to surveys by the Center for Academic Integrity, only 29 percent of undergraduates believe that unattributed copying from the web rises to the level of "serious cheating."

Observers have proposed various reasons for the prevalence of plagiarism. Some point to new technologies that allow instant access to an apparently "com- (1)
mon" store of unlimited information as sites like *Wikipedia* challenge traditional notions of singular authorship, originality, and intellectual property. Others see the problem as the result of declining personal morality and of a culture that (2)
rewards shady behavior. And many view plagiarism as the unavoidable conse- (3)
quence of the pressures many students feel.

Academic institutions have responded to the problem in a number of ways. Most colleges now use the Internet-based detection service Turnitin.com, which scans students' essays for plagiarism. A recent study by the National Bureau of Economic Research concluded that simply showing a web tutorial on the issue could reduce instances of plagiarism by two-thirds. Schools such as Duke University and Bowdoin College now require incoming students to complete this online instruction before they enroll. Additionally, the research of Rutgers professor Ronald McCabe, who founded the Center for Academic Integrity, indicates that honor codes — already in place at many colleges and universities — help create a campus culture of academic integrity.

A friend who teaches at a well-known eastern university told me recently that plagiarism was turning him into a cop. He begins the semester collecting evidence, in the form of an in-class essay that gives him a sense of how well students think and write. He looks back at the samples later when students turn in papers that feature their own, less-than-perfect prose alongside expertly written passages lifted verbatim from the Web. 1

"I have to assume that in every class, someone will do it," he said. "It doesn't stop them if you say, 'This is plagiarism. I won't accept it.' I have to tell them that it is a failing offense and could lead me to file a complaint with the university, which could lead to them being put on probation or being asked to leave." 2

Not everyone who gets caught knows enough about what they did to be remorseful. Recently, for example, a student who plagiarized a sizable chunk of a paper essentially told my friend to keep his shirt on, that what he'd done was no big deal. Beyond that, the student said, he would be ashamed to go home to the family with an F. 3

* As my friend sees it: "This represents a shift away from the view of education as the process of intellectual engagement through which we learn to think critically and toward the view of education as mere training. In training, you are trying to find the right answer at any cost, not trying to improve your mind." 4

Like many other professors, he no longer sees traditional term papers as a valid index of student competence. To get an accurate, Internet-free reading of how much students have learned, he gives them written assignments in class — where they can be watched. 5

These kinds of precautions are no longer unusual in the college world. As Trip Gabriel pointed out in the *Times* recently, more than half the colleges in the country have retained services that check student papers for material lifted from the Internet and elsewhere. Many schools now require incoming students to take online tutorials that explain what plagiarism is and how to avoid it. 6

Nationally, discussions about plagiarism tend to focus on questions of ethics. But as David Pritchard, a physics professor at the Massachusetts Institute of Technology, * told me recently: "The big sleeping dog here is not the moral issue. The problem is that kids don't learn if they don't do the work." 7

Prof. Pritchard and his colleagues illustrated the point in a study of cheating behavior by M.I.T. students who used an online system to complete homework. The 8 students who were found to have copied the most answers from others started out with the same math and physics skills as their harder-working classmates. But by skipping the actual work in homework, they fell behind in understanding and became significantly more likely to fail.

* * The Pritchard axiom – that repetitive cheating under- 9
mines learning – has ominous implications for a world in which even junior high school students cut and paste from the Internet instead of producing their own writing.

If we look closely at plagiarism as practiced by young- 10
sters, we can see that they have a different relationship to the printed word than did the generations before them. When many young people think of writing, they don't think of fashioning original sentences into a sustained thought. They think of making something like a collage of found passages and ideas from the Internet.

They become like rap musicians who construct what 11
✓ they describe as new works by "sampling" (which is to say, cutting and pasting) beats and refrains from the works of others.

This habit of mind is already pervasive in the culture 12
and will be difficult to roll back. But parents, teachers, and policy makers need to understand that this is not just a matter of personal style or generational expression. It's a question of whether we can preserve the methods through which education at its best teaches people to think critically and originally.

• • •

The student who highlighted Staples's column and its headnote was preparing for a class discussion of a group of related articles on the problem of academic cheating. To prepare for class, she began by highlighting the essay to identify the writer's key ideas and mark points she might want to think further about. This highlighting laid the groundwork for the careful annotations she would make when she reread the article.

Exercise 1

Preview the following essay. Then, highlight it to identify the writer's main idea and key supporting points. (Previewing and highlighting the article's headnote, including the background material provided, will help you understand the article's ideas.) You might circle unfamiliar words, underline key terms or concepts, or draw lines or arrows to connect related ideas.

MOISÉS NAÍM

The YouTube Effect

A long-time journalist, professor, politician, and public intellectual, Moisés Naím is the author and editor of several books, including *Illicit: How Smugglers, Traffickers, and Copycats Are Hijacking the Global Economy* (2006) and *The End of Power: From Boardrooms to Battlefields and Churches to States, Why Being in Charge Isn't What It Used to Be* (2013). His writing has appeared in many magazines, journals, and newspapers. Educated at the Universidad Metropolitana in Venezuela and the Massachusetts Institute of Technology, he has served as the Venezuelan Minister of Trade and Industry, the editor of *Foreign Policy* magazine, and a columnist for the Spanish newspaper *El Pais*. Naím is now a distinguished fellow at the Carnegie Endowment for International Peace and is a member of international organizations such as the Council in Foreign Relations and the World Economic Forum.

Background on YouTube In the following column from 2006, Moisés Naím writes, "YouTube has 34 million monthly visitors, and 65,000 new videos are posted every day." Today, the video hosting and sharing site, founded in 2005, has a billion monthly visitors, and hundreds of thousands of new videos are posted daily. Even as other social media platforms such as Twitter and Tumblr have arisen, YouTube remains an Internet fixture. It is available in seventy-six different languages and has distinctive localized versions in eighty-eight different countries. Moreover, its influence during the past decade — over everything from global politics to popular music to criminal justice — has been transformative. Although much of its content is notoriously frivolous, YouTube has changed our relationship to media (and, perhaps, to reality itself) since we no longer need to rely entirely on large news organizations to document current events. Instead, as the culture and technology critic Clay Shirky has observed, "we are increasingly becoming part of one another's [media] infrastructure."

A video shows a line of people trudging up a snow-covered footpath. A shot is heard; the first person in line falls. A voice-over says, "They are killing them like dogs." Another shot, and another body drops to the ground. A Chinese soldier fires his rifle again. Then a group of soldiers examines the bodies. 1

These images were captured in the Himalayas by a member of a mountaineering expedition who claims to have stumbled on the killing. The video first aired on Romanian television, but it only gained worldwide attention when it was posted on YouTube, the video-sharing website. (To view it, go to YouTube.com and type "Tibet, ProTV, China".) Human rights groups say the slain Tibetan refugees included monks, women, and children. The Chinese government had claimed the soldiers shot in self-defense after they were attacked by 70 refugees, but the video seems to render that explanation absurd. The U.S. ambassador to China lodged a complaint. 2

3 Welcome to the "YouTube effect." It is the phenomenon whereby video clips, often produced by individuals acting on their own, are rapidly disseminated worldwide on websites such as YouTube and Google Video. YouTube has 34 million monthly visitors, and 65,000 new videos are posted every day. Most are frivolous, produced by and for the teenagers who make up the majority of the site's visitors. But some are serious. YouTube includes videos posted by terrorists, human rights groups, and U.S. soldiers in Iraq. Some are clips of incidents that have political consequences or document important trends, such as global warming, illegal immigration, and corruption. Some videos reveal truths. Others spread propaganda and outright lies.

4 Fifteen years ago, the world marveled at the "CNN effect" and believed that the unblinking eyes of TV cameras, beyond the reach of censors, would bring greater global accountability. These expectations were, to some degree, fulfilled. Since the early 1990s, electoral frauds have been exposed, democratic uprisings energized, famines contained, and wars started or stopped thanks to the CNN effect. But the YouTube effect will be even more powerful. Although international news operations employ thousands of professional journalists, they will never be as omnipresent as millions of people carrying cellphones that can record video. Thanks to the ubiquity of video technology, the world was able to witness a shooting in a 19,000-foot-high mountain pass in Tibet.

5 This phenomenon is amplified by a double-echo chamber: One echo is produced when content first posted on the Web is re-aired by mainstream TV networks. The second echo occurs when television clips – until now ephemeral – gain a permanent presence through websites such as YouTube. Bloggers and activists everywhere are recognizing the power of citizen-produced and Web-distributed videos as the ultimate testimony. Witness.org arms individuals in conflict zones with video cameras so they can record and expose human rights abuses. Electoral watchdogs are taping elections. Even Al Qaeda created a special media production unit called Al Sahab ("The Cloud").

6 YouTube is a mixed blessing: It is now harder to know what to believe. How do we know that what we see in a video clip posted by a "citizen journalist" is not a manipulated montage? How do we know, for example, that the YouTube video of terrorized American soldiers crying and praying while under fire was filmed in Iraq and not staged somewhere else to manipulate public opinion? The more than 86,000 people who viewed it in the first 10 days of its posting will never know.

7 Governments are already feeling the heat of the YouTube effect – and cracking down online. Almost a third of all reporters jailed this year were Internet journalists. The U.S. military recently ordered its soldiers to stop posting videos online. Iran's government restricts connection speeds to limit its people's access to video streaming.

8 But these measures have not stopped the proliferation of Web videos shot by U.S. soldiers in Iraq or kept savvy Iranians from viewing the images they want to see. And although Beijing has been effective in censoring the content its citizens can view, it has yet to figure out a way to prevent a growing number of videos of peasant rebellions from being posted online. In the long run,

Web video censorship will fail because the same anonymity that makes videos difficult to authenticate also makes it harder to enforce governmental *diktats*.

The good news is that the YouTube effect is already creating a strong 9
demand for reliable guides — individuals, institutions, and technologies — that we can trust to help us sort facts from lies online. The millions of bloggers who are constantly watching, fact-checking, and exposing mistakes are a powerful example of "the wisdom of crowds" being assisted by a technology that is as open and omnipresent as we are.

• • •

Annotating

When you **annotate**, you carry on a conversation with the text. In marginal notes, you can ask questions, suggest possible parallels with other reading selections or with your own ideas and experiences, argue with the writer's points, comment on the writer's style or word choice, or define unfamiliar terms and concepts.

The questions below can guide you as you read and help you make useful annotations.

REMINDER TAKING NOTES

If you use your computer when you take notes instead of writing annotations on the page, be sure to label each note so that you remember where it came from. (You will need this information for your essay's parenthetical references and works-cited page.) Include the author's name and the title of the reading selection, as well as the page on which the information you are citing appears. Also note the page and paragraph number where you found the information so that you will be able to find it again.

CLOSE VIEW

CHECKLIST QUESTIONS FOR CRITICAL READING

- ☐ What is the writer's general subject?
- ☐ What is the writer's main idea?
- ☐ What are the writer's key supporting points?
- ☐ Does the writer seem to have a particular purpose in mind?
- ☐ What kind of audience is the writer addressing?
- ☐ What are the writer's assumptions about the audience? About the subject?
- ☐ Are the writer's ideas consistent with your own?
- ☐ Does the writer reveal any **bias**?
- ☐ Do you have any knowledge that challenges the writer's ideas?
- ☐ Is any information missing?
- ☐ Are any sequential or logical links missing?
- ☐ Can you identify themes or ideas that also appear in other works you have read?
- ☐ Can you identify parallels with your own experience?

The following pages reproduce the student's highlighting of "Cutting and Pasting: A Senior Thesis by (Insert Name)" from pages 17–19 and also include her annotations. (She annotated the headnote and background material as well, but these annotations are not shown here.)

Teachers as cops

A friend who teaches at a well-known eastern university told me recently that plagiarism was turning him into a cop. He begins the semester collecting evidence, in the form of an in-class essay that gives him a sense of how well students think and write. He looks back at the samples later when students turn in papers that feature their own, less-than-perfect prose alongside expertly written passages lifted verbatim from the Web. 1

Teachers resigned to situation

"I have to assume that in every class, someone will do it," he said. "It doesn't stop them if you say, 'This is plagiarism. I won't accept it.' I have to tell them that it is a failing offense and could lead me to file a complaint with the university, which could lead to them being put on probation or being asked to leave." 2

Not everyone who gets caught knows enough about what they did to be remorseful. Recently, for example, a student who plagiarized a sizable chunk of a paper essentially told my friend to keep his shirt on, that what he'd done was no big deal. Beyond that, the student said, he would be ashamed to go home to the family with an F. 3 4

Key problem — Move from "intellectual engagement" and critical thinking to "mere training" *

As my friend sees it: "This represents a shift away from the view of education as the process of intellectual engagement through which we learn to think critically and toward the view of education as mere training. In training, you are trying to find the right answer at any cost, not trying to improve your mind."

Like many other professors, he no longer sees traditional term papers as a valid index of student competence. To get an accurate, Internet-free reading of how much students have learned, he gives them written assignments in class — where they can be watched. 5

Colleges as police states!

These kinds of precautions are no longer unusual in the college world. As Trip Gabriel pointed out in the *Times* recently, more than half the colleges in the country have retained services that check student papers for material lifted from the Internet and elsewhere. Many schools now require incoming students to take online tutorials that explain what plagiarism is and how to avoid it. 6

Nationally, discussions about plagiarism tend to focus on questions of ethics. But as David Pritchard, 7

Problem isn't just ethics

a physics professor at the Massachusetts Institute of * Technology, told me recently: "The big sleeping dog here is not the moral issue. The problem is that kids don't learn if they don't do the work."

Prof. Pritchard and his colleagues illustrated the point in a study of cheating behavior by M.I.T. students who used an online system to complete homework. The students who were found to have copied the most answers from others started out with the same math and physics skills as their harder-working classmates. But by skipping the actual work in homework, they fell behind in understanding and became significantly more likely to fail. 8

** The Pritchard axiom – that repetitive cheating undermines learning – has ominous implications for a world in which even junior high school students cut and paste from the Internet instead of producing their own writing. 9

True

If we look closely at plagiarism as practiced by youngsters, we can see that they have a different relationship to the printed word than did the generations before them. When many young people think of writing, they don't think of fashioning original sentences into a sustained thought. They think of making something like a collage of found passages and ideas from the Internet. 10

"Cutting and pasting" = "sampling"

They become like rap musicians who construct ✓ what they describe as new works by "sampling" (which is to say, cutting and pasting) beats and refrains from the works of others. 11

What's the answer to this question? (What can schools do? Who is responsible for solving the problem?)

This habit of mind is already pervasive in the culture and will be difficult to roll back. But parents, teachers, and policy makers need to understand that this is not just a matter of personal style or generational expression. It's a question of whether we can preserve the methods through which education at its best teaches people to think critically and originally. 12

• • •

As illustrated above, the student who annotated Staples's column on plagiarism supplemented her highlighting with brief marginal summaries to help her understand key points. She also wrote down questions that she thought would help her focus her comments during class discussion.

SUMMARIZING KEY IDEAS

One strategy that can help you understand what you are reading is **summarizing** a writer's key ideas, as the student writer does in her marginal annotations of the Staples column on pages 23–24. Putting a writer's ideas into your own words can make an unfamiliar or complex concept more accessible and useful to you. For more on summarizing, see page 728.

Exercise 2

Now, add annotations to the Naím essay and related material that you highlighted for Exercise 1. This time, focus on summarizing the writer's key points and on asking questions that will prepare you for discussing (and perhaps writing about) this essay.

Reading Visual Texts

The process you use when you react to a **visual text** – a photograph; an advertisement; a diagram, graph, or chart; an infographic; or a work of fine art, for example – is much the same as the one you use when you respond to a written text. Here, too, your goal is to understand the text, and highlighting and annotating a visual text can help you interpret it.

With visual texts, however, instead of identifying elements such as words and ideas, you identify visual elements. These elements might include the use of color; the arrangement of shapes; the contrast between large and small or light and dark; and, of course, the particular images the visual includes.

As you approach a visual, you might ask questions like those on the following checklist.

CHECKLIST READING VISUAL TEXTS

- ☐ For what purpose was the visual created?
- ☐ What kind of audience is it aimed at?
- ☐ How would you characterize the visual? For example, is it a work of fine art? An advertisement? A technical diagram? A chart or graph? An infographic?
- ☐ What is the visual's most important or most striking image? What makes this image dominate the page?
- ☐ How is blank space used to emphasize (or de-emphasize) individual images?
- ☐ How does contrast between light and dark (or use of color) emphasize (or de-emphasize) individual images?
- ☐ What objects are depicted in the visual?
- ☐ Does the visual include any images of people? If so, how do the people depicted interact with one another? What is their relationship to various objects depicted in the visual?
- ☐ Does the visual include any words? If so, what is their function? What is the relationship between the visual's words and its images?

The following photograph, one of four included in "Four Tattoos" (page 218), illustrates a student's highlighting and annotating of a visual text. (See page 219 for study questions about these images.)

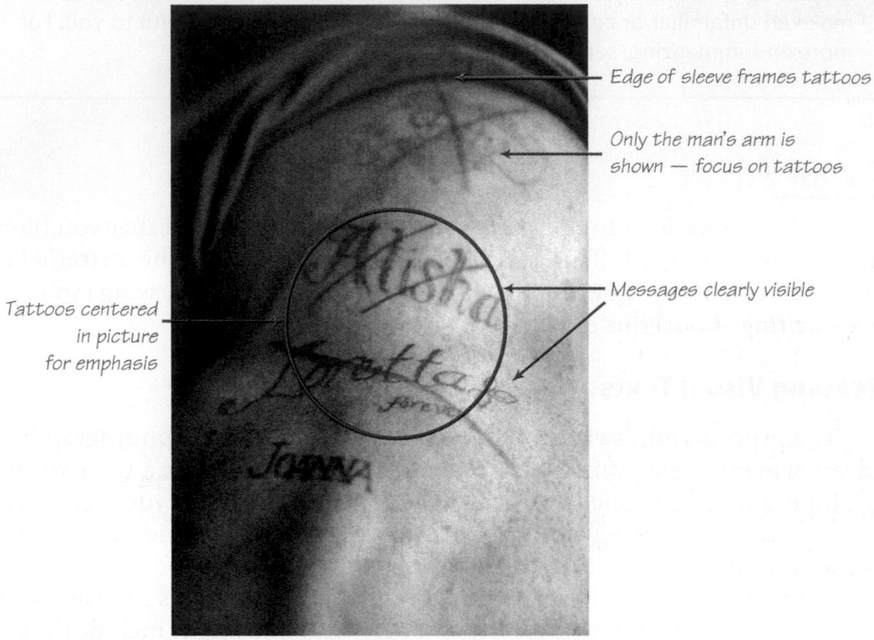

Charles Thatcher, "~~Alisha, Loretta~~" (© Charles Thatcher/Getty Images)

Exercise 3

In this book, visuals are included in Chapters 6 through 14, where they are the first reading selection in each chapter. Choose one of these visuals, and highlight and annotate it. When you have finished, write a sentence that sums up what you think the visual is trying to communicate and how successful it is at accomplishing its goals.

2

Invention

Invention, or **prewriting**, is an important (and, frequently, the most neglected) part of the writing process. During invention, you discover what interests you about your subject and consider what ideas to develop in your essay.

When you are given a writing assignment, you may be tempted to start writing a first draft immediately. Before writing, however, you should be sure you understand your assignment and its limits, and you should think about what you want to say. Time spent on these issues now will pay off later when you draft your essay.

Understanding Your Assignment

Almost everything you write in college begins as an **assignment**. Some assignments are direct and easy to understand, but others are difficult and complex.

Before beginning to write, you need to understand exactly what your assignment is asking you to do. If the assignment is a question, read it carefully several times, and underline its keywords. If the assignment is given orally by your instructor, be sure to copy it accurately. (A mistaken word – *analyze* for *compare,* for example – can make quite a difference.) If you are confused about anything, ask your instructor for clarification. Remember that no matter how well written an essay is, it will fall short if it does not address the assignment.

Setting Limits

Once you understand the assignment, you should consider its *length, purpose, audience,* and *occasion* and your own *knowledge* of the subject. Each of these factors helps you determine what you will say about your subject.

Length

Often, your instructor will specify the **length** of an assignment, and this word or page limit has a direct bearing on your essay's focus. For example, you would need a narrower topic for a two-page essay than for a ten-page one. Similarly, you could not discuss a question as thoroughly during an hour-long exam as you might in a paper written over several days.

If your instructor sets no page limit, consider how the nature of the assignment suggests a paper's length. A *summary* of a chapter or an article, for instance, should be much shorter than the original, whereas an *analysis* of a poem will most likely be longer than the poem itself. If you are uncertain about the appropriate length for your assignment, consult your instructor.

Purpose

Your **purpose** also limits what you say and how you say it. For example, if you were writing a job application letter, you would not emphasize the same elements of college life as you would in an email to a friend. In the first case, you would want to convince the reader to hire you, so you might include your grade point average, a list of the relevant courses you took, and perhaps the work you did for a service-learning course. In the second case, you would want to inform and perhaps entertain, so you might share anecdotes about dorm life or describe one of your favorite instructors. In each case, your purpose would help you determine what information to include to evoke a particular response in a specific audience.

In general, you can classify your purposes for writing according to your relationship to the audience.

- In **expressive writing**, you convey personal feelings or impressions to readers. Expressive writing is used in diaries, personal emails, and journals, and often in narrative and descriptive essays as well.
- In **informative writing**, you inform readers about something. Informative writing is used in essay exams, lab reports, and expository essays, as well as in some research papers and personal web pages.
- In **persuasive writing**, you try to convince readers to act or think in a certain way. Persuasive writing is used in editorials, argumentative essays, proposals, research papers, and many types of electronic documents.

In addition to these general purposes, you might have a more specific purpose: to analyze, entertain, hypothesize, assess, summarize, question, report, recommend, suggest, evaluate, describe, recount, request, instruct, and so on. For example, suppose you wrote a report on homelessness in your community. Your general purpose might be to *inform* readers of the situation, but you might also want to *assess* the problem and *instruct* readers how to help those in need.

Audience

To be effective, your essay should be written with a particular **audience** in mind. An audience can be an *individual* (your instructor, for example), or it can be a *group* (like your classmates or coworkers). Your essay can address a *specialized* audience (such as a group of medical doctors or economists) or a *general* or *universal* audience whose members have little in common (such as the readers of a newspaper or magazine).

In college, your audience is usually your instructor, and your purpose in most cases is to demonstrate your mastery of the subject matter, your reasoning ability, and your competence as a writer. Other audiences may include classmates, professional colleagues, or members of your community. Considering the age and gender of your audience, its political and religious values, its social and educational level, and its interest in your subject may help you define it.

Often, you will find that your audience is just too diverse to be categorized. In such cases, many writers imagine a general (or universal) audience and make points that they think will appeal to a variety of readers. At other times, writers identify a common denominator, a role that characterizes the entire audience. For instance, when a report on the environmental dangers of disposable plastic bags asserts, "Now is the time for conservation-minded individuals to demand that single-use plastic bags be banned," it automatically casts its audience in the role of "conservation-minded individuals."

After you define your audience, you have to determine how much (or how little) its members know about your subject. This consideration helps you decide how much information your readers will need in order to understand the discussion. Are they highly informed? If so, you can present your points without much explanation. Are they relatively uninformed? If that is the case, you will have to include definitions of key terms, background information, and summaries of basic research.

Keep in mind that experts in one field will need background information in other fields. If, for example, you were writing an analysis of Joseph Conrad's novella *Heart of Darkness*, you could assume that the literature instructor who assigned the work would not need a plot summary. If you wrote an essay for your history instructor that used *Heart of Darkness* to illustrate the evils of European colonialism in nineteenth-century Africa, however, you would probably include a short plot summary. (Even though your history instructor would know a lot about colonialism in Africa, she might not be familiar with Conrad's work.)

Occasion

Occasion refers to the situation (or situations) that leads someone to write about a topic. In an academic writing situation, the occasion is almost always a specific assignment. The occasion suggests a specific audience – for example, a history instructor – as well as a specific purpose – for example, to discuss the major causes of World War I. In fact, even the format of an essay – whether you use (or do not use) headings or whether you present your response to an assignment as an essay, as a technical report, or as a PowerPoint presentation – is determined by the occasion for your writing. For this reason, a paper suitable for a psychology or sociology class might not be suitable for a composition class.

Like college writing assignments, each writing task you do outside of school requires an approach that suits the occasion. An email to coworkers, for instance, will be less formal than a report to a manager. In addition, the occasion suggests how much (or how little) information the piece of writing includes. Finally, your occasion suggests your purpose. For example, a message to members of an online discussion group might be strictly informational, whereas an email to a state senator about preserving a local landmark would be persuasive as well as informative.

Knowledge

What you know (and do not know) about a subject determines what you can say about it. Before writing about any subject, ask yourself what you know about the subject and what you need to find out.

Different writing situations require different kinds of knowledge. A personal essay will draw on your own experiences and observations; an argumentative essay often requires you to do research. In many cases, your page limit and the amount of time you have to do the assignment will help you decide how much information you need to gather before you can begin.

CHECKLIST SETTING LIMITS

Length

- ☐ Has your instructor specified a length?
- ☐ Does the nature of your assignment suggest a length?

Purpose

- ☐ Is your general purpose to express personal feelings? To inform? To persuade?
- ☐ In addition to your general purpose, do you have any more specific purposes?
- ☐ Does your assignment provide any guidelines about purpose?

Audience

- ☐ Is your audience a group or an individual?
- ☐ Are you going to address a specialized or a general audience?
- ☐ Should you take into consideration the audience's age, gender, education, biases, or political or social values?
- ☐ Should you cast your audience in a particular role?
- ☐ How much can you assume your audience knows about your subject?

Occasion

- ☐ Are you writing in class or at home?
- ☐ Are you addressing a situation outside the academic setting?
- ☐ What special approaches does your occasion for writing require?

Knowledge

- ☐ What do you know about your subject?
- ☐ What do you need to find out?

Exercise 1

Decide whether or not each of the following topics is appropriate for the stated limits, and then write a few sentences to explain why each topic is or is not acceptable.

1. *A two-to-three-page paper* A history of animal testing in medical research labs
2. *A two-hour final exam* The effectiveness of online courses
3. *A one-hour in-class essay* An interpretation of one of Andy Warhol's paintings of Campbell's soup cans
4. *An email to your college newspaper* A discussion of your school's policy on plagiarism

Exercise 2

Make a list of the different audiences to whom you speak or write in your daily life. (Consider all the different people you see regularly, such as family members, your roommate, instructors, your boss, and your friends.) Then, record your answers to the following questions:

1. Do you speak or write to each person in your life in the same way and about the same things? If not, how do your approaches to these people differ?
2. List some subjects that would interest some of these people but not others. How do you account for these differences?
3. Choose one of the following subjects, and describe how you would speak or write to different audiences about it.
   - A change that improved your life
   - Censoring Internet content
   - Taking a year off before college
   - Reality TV shows

Moving from Subject to Topic

Although many essays begin as specific assignments, some begin as broad areas of interest or concern. These **general subjects** always need to be narrowed to **specific topics** that can be discussed within the limits of the assignment. For example, a subject like fracking could be interesting, but it is too broad to write about. You need to limit such a subject to a topic that can be covered within the time and space available.

GENERAL SUBJECT	SPECIFIC TOPIC
Tablets	The benefits of using touchscreen tablets in elementary school classrooms
Herman Melville's *Billy Budd*	Billy Budd as a Christ figure
Social media	One unforeseen result of Twitter
Fracking	Should fracking be banned?

Two strategies can help you narrow a general subject to a specific topic: *questions for probing* and *freewriting*.

Questions for Probing

One way to move from a general subject to a specific topic is to examine your subject by asking a series of questions about it. These **questions for probing** are useful because they reflect how your mind operates – for example, by finding similarities and differences or by dividing a whole into its parts. By asking the questions on the following checklist, you can explore your subject systematically. Not all questions will work for every subject, but any single question may elicit many different answers, and each answer is a possible topic for your essay.

CHECKLIST QUESTIONS FOR PROBING

What happened?
When did it happen?
Where did it happen?
Who did it?
What does it look like?
What are its characteristics?
What impressions does it make?
What are some typical cases or examples of it?
How did it happen?
What makes it work?
How is it made?
Why did it happen?
What caused it?
What are its effects?
How is it like other things?
How is it different from other things?
What are its parts or types?
How can its parts or types be separated or grouped?
Do its parts or types fit into a logical order?
Into what categories can its parts or types be arranged?
On what basis can it be categorized?
How can it be defined?
How does it resemble other members of its class?
How does it differ from other members of its class?

When applied to a subject, some of these questions can yield many workable topics, including some you might never have considered had you not asked the questions. For example, by applying this approach to the general subject "the Brooklyn Bridge," you can generate more ideas and topics than you need:

What happened? A short history of the Brooklyn Bridge

What does it look like? A description of the Brooklyn Bridge

How is it made? The construction of the Brooklyn Bridge

What are its effects? The impact of the Brooklyn Bridge on American writers

How does it differ from other members of its class? Innovations in the design of the Brooklyn Bridge

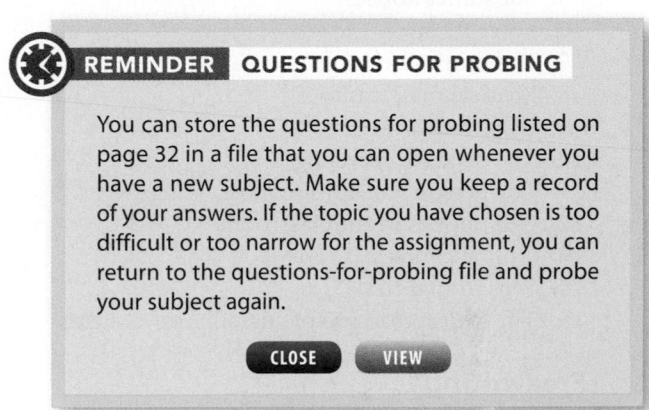

> **REMINDER QUESTIONS FOR PROBING**
>
> You can store the questions for probing listed on page 32 in a file that you can open whenever you have a new subject. Make sure you keep a record of your answers. If the topic you have chosen is too difficult or too narrow for the assignment, you can return to the questions-for-probing file and probe your subject again.
>
> CLOSE VIEW

At this point in the writing process, you want to come up with possible topics, and the more ideas you have, the wider your choice. Begin by jotting down all the topics you think of. (You can repeat the process of probing several times to limit topics further.) Once you have a list of topics, eliminate those that do not interest you, are too complex, or do not fit your assignment. When you have discarded these less promising topics, you should have several left. You can then select the topic that best suits your essay's length, purpose, audience, and occasion, as well as your interests and your knowledge of the subject.

Exercise 3

Indicate whether each of the following is a general subject or a specific topic that is narrow enough for a short essay.

1. An argument against fast-food ads that are aimed at young children
2. Home schooling
3. Texting and driving
4. Changes in U.S. immigration laws
5. Requiring college students to study a foreign language
6. The advantages of eTextbooks
7. A comparison of small-town and big-city living
8. Student loans
9. The advantages of service-learning courses
10. The drawbacks of self-driving cars

Exercise 4

In preparation for writing a 750-word essay, choose two of the following general subjects, and generate three or four specific topics from each by using as many of the questions for probing as you can.

1. The writing center
2. Job interviews
3. Identity theft
4. Genetically modified food
5. Substance abuse
6. Voter ID laws
7. The minimum wage
8. Medical marijuana
9. Cyberbullying
10. The need for recycling
11. The person you admire most
12. Cell phones in the classroom
13. Online courses
14. Sensational trials
15. The widespread use of surveillance cameras

Freewriting

Another strategy for moving from subject to topic is **freewriting**. You can use freewriting at any stage of the writing process – for example, to generate supporting information or to find a thesis. However, freewriting is a particularly useful way to narrow a general subject or assignment.

When you freewrite, you write for a fixed period, perhaps five or ten minutes, without stopping and without paying attention to spelling, grammar, or punctuation. Your goal is to get your ideas down on paper so that you can react to them and shape them. If you have nothing to say, write down anything until ideas begin to emerge – and in time they will. The secret is to *keep writing*. Try to focus on your subject, but don't worry if you wander off in other directions. The object of freewriting is to let your ideas flow. Often, your best ideas will come from the unexpected connections you make as you write.

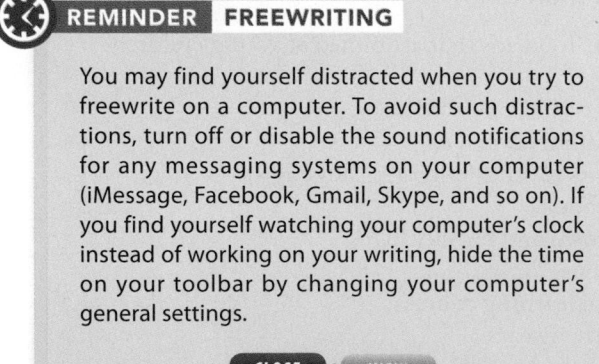

REMINDER FREEWRITING

You may find yourself distracted when you try to freewrite on a computer. To avoid such distractions, turn off or disable the sound notifications for any messaging systems on your computer (iMessage, Facebook, Gmail, Skype, and so on). If you find yourself watching your computer's clock instead of working on your writing, hide the time on your toolbar by changing your computer's general settings.

CLOSE VIEW

After completing your freewriting, read what you have written, and look for ideas you can write about. Some writers underline ideas they think they might explore in their essays. Any of these ideas could become essay topics, or they could become subjects for other freewriting exercises. You might want to freewrite again, using a new idea as your focus. This process of writing more and more specific freewriting exercises – called **focused freewriting** or **looping** – can often yield a great deal of useful information and help you decide on a workable topic.

A STUDENT WRITER: Freewriting

After reading, highlighting, and annotating Henry Louis Gates Jr.'s "'What's in a Name?'" (page 2), Laura Bobnak, a student in a composition class, decided to write an essay in response to this Writing Workshop question.

> Write about a time when you, like Gates's father, could have spoken out in protest but chose not to. Would you make the same decision today?

In an attempt to narrow this assignment to a workable topic, Laura did the following freewriting exercise.

> Write for ten minutes . . . ten minutes . . . at 9 o'clock in the morning — Just what I want to do in the morning — If you can't think of something to say, just write about anything. Right! Time to get this over with — An experience — should have talked — I can think of plenty of times I should have kept quiet! I should have brought a bottle of water to class. I wonder what the people next to me are writing about. That reminds me. Next to me. Jeff Servin in chemistry. The time I saw him cheating. I was mad but I didn't do anything. I studied so hard and all he did was cheat. I was so mad. Nobody else seemed to care. What's the difference between now and then? It's only a year and a half. . . . Honor code? Maturity? A lot of people cheated in high school. I bet I could write about this — Before and after, etc. My attitude then and now.

After some initial thought, Laura discovered an idea that could be the basis for her essay. Although her discussion of the incident still had to be developed, Laura's freewriting helped her come up with a possible topic for her essay: a time she saw someone cheating and did not speak out.

Exercise 5

Do a five-minute freewriting exercise on one of the topics you generated in Exercise 4 (page 34).

Exercise 6

Read what you have just written, underline the most interesting ideas, and choose one idea as a topic you could write about in a short essay. Freewrite about this topic for another five minutes to narrow it further and to generate ideas for your essay. Underline the ideas that seem most useful.

Finding Something to Say

Once you have narrowed your subject to a workable topic, you need to find something to say about it. *Brainstorming* and *journal writing* are useful tools for generating ideas, and both can be helpful at this stage of the writing process (and whenever you need to find additional material).

Brainstorming

Brainstorming is a way of discovering ideas about your topic. You can brainstorm in a group, exchanging ideas with several students in your composition class. You can also brainstorm on your own, recording every fact, idea, or detail you can think of that relates to your topic. Your brainstorming can take the form of an orderly list, or it can be random notes. Your notes might include words, phrases, statements, questions, or even drawings or diagrams. Some items may be inspired by your class notes; others may be from your reading or from talking with friends; and still others may be ideas you have begun to wonder about, points you thought of while moving from subject to topic, or thoughts that occurred to you as you brainstormed.

A STUDENT WRITER: Brainstorming

Laura Bobnak made the brainstorming notes shown on page 38. After reading these notes several times, Laura decided to compare her current and earlier attitudes toward cheating. She knew that she could write a lot about this topic and relate it to the assignment, and she felt confident that her topic would be interesting both to her instructor and to the other students in the class.

REMINDER BRAINSTORMING

When you brainstorm on a computer, turn off Spelling and Grammar check so that you do not get distracted by the correction prompts. (You can address these technical issues at a later stage of the writing process.)

CLOSE VIEW

Journal Writing

Journal writing can be a useful source of ideas at any stage of the writing process. Many writers routinely keep a journal, jotting down experiences and ideas they may want to use when they write. They write journal entries even when they have no particular writing project in mind. Often, these journal entries are the kernels from which longer pieces of writing develop. Your instructor may ask you to keep a writing journal, or you may decide to do so on your own. In either case, you will find your journal entries are likely to be more narrowly focused than freewriting or brainstorming, perhaps examining a small part of a reading selection or even one particular statement. Sometimes, you will write in your journal in response to specific questions, such as the Journal Entry assignments that appear throughout this book. Assignments like those can help you start thinking about a reading selection you may later discuss in class or write about.

A STUDENT WRITER: **Journal Writing**

In the following journal entry, Laura Bobnak explores one idea from her brainstorming notes: her thoughts about her college's honor code.

> At orientation, the dean of students talked about the college's honor code. She talked about how we were a community of scholars who were here for a common purpose — to take part in an intellectual conversation. According to her, the purpose of the honor code is to make sure this conversation continues uninterrupted. This idea sounded dumb at orientation, but now it makes sense. If I saw someone cheating, I'd tell the instructor. First, though, I'd ask the *student* to go to the instructor. I don't see this as "telling" or "snitching." We're all here to get an education, and we should be able to assume everyone is being honest and fair. Besides, why should I go to all the trouble of studying while someone else does nothing and gets the same grade?

Even though Laura eventually included only a small part of this entry in her essay, writing in her journal helped her focus her ideas about her topic.

Grouping Ideas

Once you have generated material for your essay, you need to group ideas that belong together. *Clustering* and *outlining* can help you do that.

REMINDER KEEPING A JOURNAL

Keeping your journal in a computer file has some obvious advantages. Not only can you maintain a neat record of your ideas, but you can also easily move entries from your journal into an essay without retyping them. Word-processing software like Word or Pages also enables you to bold, italicize, underline, and add color to your journal entries. With these tools, you can easily differentiate your ideas from those of your sources. This is important because if you paste material from your sources directly into your paper without documenting it, you are committing plagiarism. (For information on avoiding plagiarism, see Chapter 17.)

CLOSE VIEW

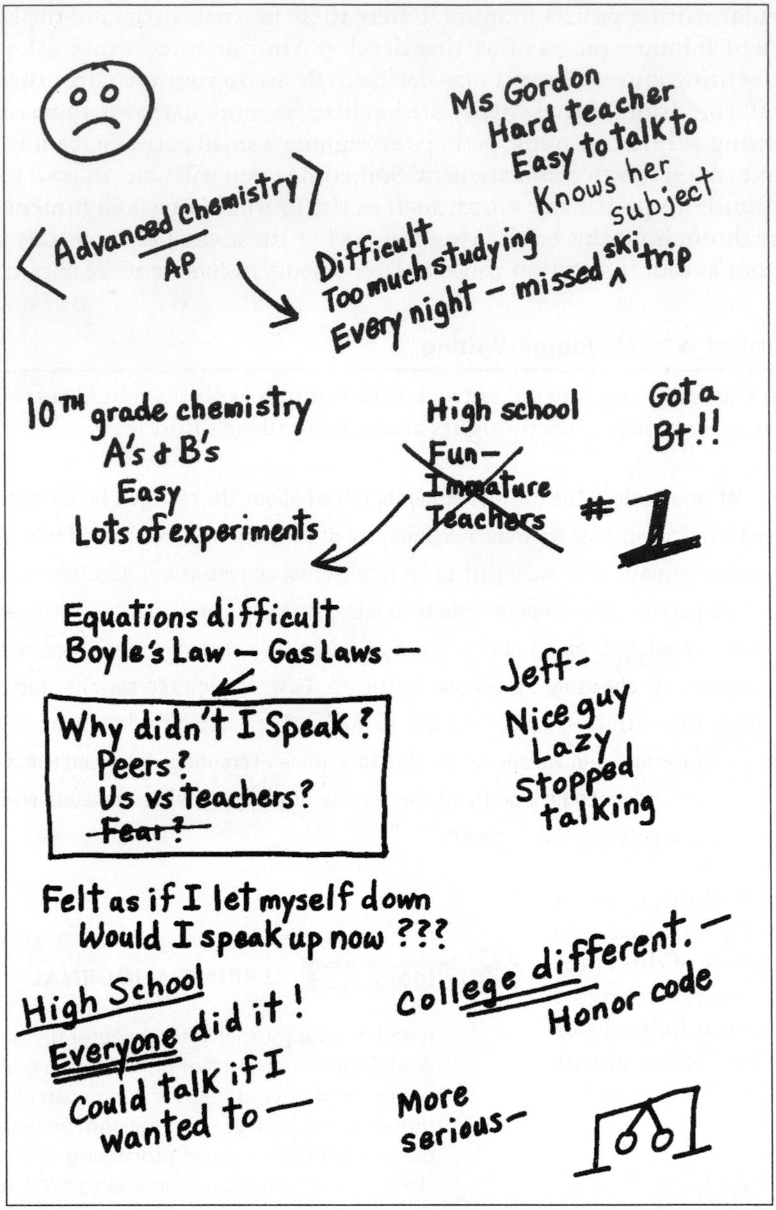

Laura's brainstorming notes

Clustering

Clustering or **mapping** is a way of visually arranging ideas so that you can tell at a glance where they belong and whether or not you need more information. Although you can use clustering at an earlier stage of the writing process, it is especially useful now for seeing how your ideas fit together. (Clustering can also help you narrow your essay's topic even further. If you find that your cluster diagram is too detailed, you can write about just one branch of the cluster.)

Begin clustering by writing your topic in the center of a sheet of paper. After circling the topic, surround it with the words and phrases that identify the major points you intend to discuss. (You can get ideas from your brainstorming notes, from your journal, and from your freewriting.) Circle these words and phrases, and connect them to the topic in the center. Next, construct other clusters of ideas relating to each major point, and draw lines connecting them to the appropriate point. By dividing and subdividing your points, you get more specific as you move outward from the center. In the process, you identify the facts, details, examples, and opinions that illustrate and expand your main points.

A STUDENT WRITER: Clustering

Because Laura Bobnak was not very visually oriented, she chose not to use this method of grouping her ideas. If she had, however, her cluster diagram would have looked like the one below.

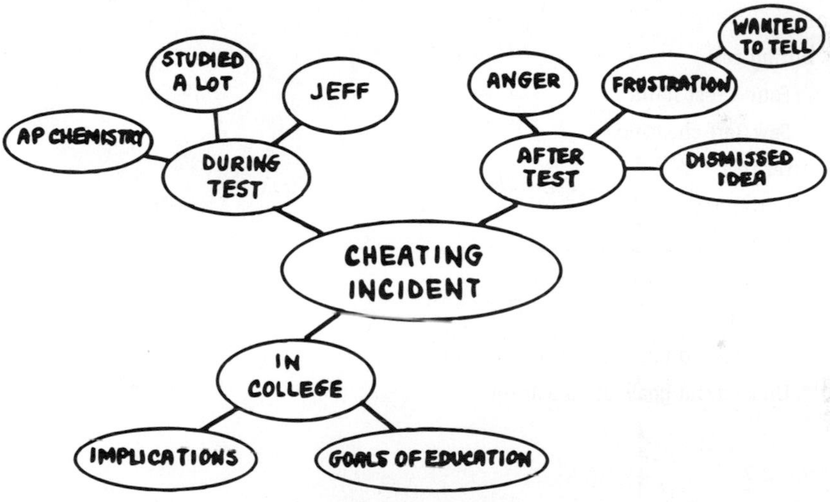

Making an Informal Outline

As an alternative or follow-up to clustering, you can organize your notes from brainstorming or other invention techniques into an **informal outline**. Informal outlines do not include

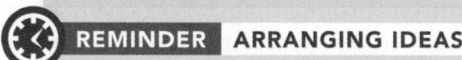

REMINDER ARRANGING IDEAS

Experimenting with different arrangements for your ideas is easy on a computer. Turn on "track changes" (or your word-processing program's equivalent) so that you can retain a record of how you rearranged your thoughts as your paper's structure evolved.

CLOSE VIEW

all the major divisions and subdivisions of your essay the way formal outlines do; they simply suggest the general shape of your emerging essay. Quite often, an informal outline is just a list of your major points presented in a tentative order. Sometimes, however, an informal outline will include supporting details or suggest a pattern of development.

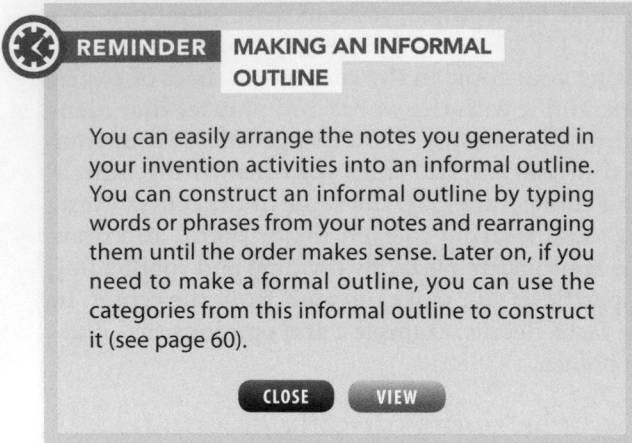

REMINDER **MAKING AN INFORMAL OUTLINE**

You can easily arrange the notes you generated in your invention activities into an informal outline. You can construct an informal outline by typing words or phrases from your notes and rearranging them until the order makes sense. Later on, if you need to make a formal outline, you can use the categories from this informal outline to construct it (see page 60).

CLOSE VIEW

A STUDENT WRITER: Making an Informal Outline

The following informal outline shows how Laura Bobnak grouped her ideas.

During test
  Found test hard
  Saw Jeff cheating
After test
  Got angry
  Wanted to tell
  Dismissed idea
In college
  Understand implications of cheating
  Understand goals of education

Exercise 7

Continue your work on the topic you selected in Exercise 6 (page 36). Brainstorm about your topic; then, select the ideas you plan to explore in your essay, and use either clustering or an informal outline to help you group related ideas together.

Understanding Thesis and Support

Once you have grouped your ideas, you need to consider your essay's thesis. A **thesis** is the main idea of your essay, its central point. The concept of **thesis and support** – stating your thesis and developing ideas that explain and expand it – is central to college writing.

Introductory paragraph

Thesis statement

Body paragraph

(support for thesis)

Body paragraph

(support for thesis)

Body paragraph

(support for thesis)

Body paragraph

(support for thesis)

Concluding paragraph

Restatement of thesis or review of key points

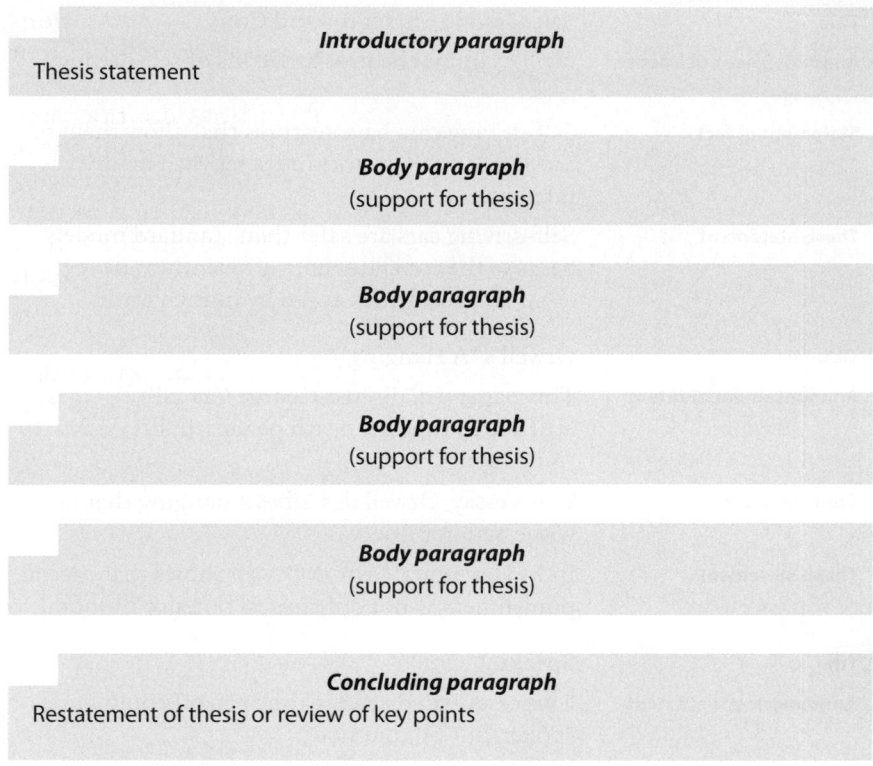

The essays you write will consist of several paragraphs: an **introduction** that presents your thesis statement, several **body paragraphs** that develop and support your thesis, and a **conclusion** that reinforces your thesis and provides closure. Your thesis holds this structure together; it is the center that the rest of your essay develops around.

Developing a Thesis

Defining the Thesis Statement

A **thesis statement** is more than a *title,* an *announcement of your intent,* or a *statement of fact.* Although a descriptive title orients your readers, it is not detailed enough to reveal your essay's purpose or direction. An announcement of your intent can reveal more, but it is stylistically distracting. Finally, a statement of fact – such as a historical fact or a statistic – is a dead end and therefore cannot be developed into an essay. For example, a statement like "Alaska became a state in 1959" or "Tuberculosis is highly contagious" or "The population of Greece is about eleven million" provides your essay with no direction. A judgment or opinion, however, *can* be an effective thesis – for instance, "The continuing threat of tuberculosis, particularly in the inner cities, suggests it is necessary to frequently test high-risk populations."

Title	Self-Driving Cars: Pros and Cons
Announcement of intent	I will examine the pros and cons of self-driving cars.
Statement of fact	Self-driving cars have features that allow them to accelerate, brake, park, and steer with no driver interaction.
Thesis statement	Self-driving cars are safer than standard models because they operate more efficiently and eliminate accidents caused by human error.
Title	Orwell's "A Hanging"
Announcement of intent	This paper will discuss George Orwell's attitude toward the death penalty in his essay "A Hanging."
Statement of fact	In his essay, Orwell describes a hanging that he witnessed in Burma.
Thesis statement	In "A Hanging," George Orwell shows that capital punishment is not only brutal but also immoral.
Title	Speaking Out
Announcement of intent	This essay will discuss a time when I could have spoken out but did not.
Statement of fact	Once I saw someone cheating and did not speak out.
Thesis statement	As I look back at the cheating I witnessed, I wonder why I kept silent and what would have happened if I had acted.

WHAT A GOOD THESIS DOES

For writers

It helps writers plan an essay.
It helps writers organize ideas in an essay.
It helps writers unify all the ideas in an essay.

For readers

It identifies the main idea of an essay.
It guides readers through an essay.
It clarifies the subject and the focus of an essay.

Deciding on a Thesis

No rules determine when you draft your thesis; the decision depends on the scope of your assignment, your knowledge of the subject, and your method of writing. When you know a lot about a subject, you may come up with a thesis before doing any invention activities (freewriting or brainstorming, for example). At other times, you may have to review your notes and then think of a single statement that communicates your position on the topic. Occasionally, your assignment may specify a thesis by telling you to take a particular position on a topic. In any case, you should decide on a thesis statement before you begin to write your first draft.

As you write, you will continue to discover new ideas, and you will probably move in directions that you did not anticipate. For this reason, the thesis statement you develop at this stage of the writing process is only **tentative**. Still, because a tentative thesis helps you focus your ideas, it is essential at the initial stages of writing. As you draft your essay, review your thesis statement in light of the points you make, and revise it accordingly.

Stating Your Thesis

It is a good idea to include a one-sentence statement of your thesis early in your essay. An effective thesis statement has the following three characteristics.

1. **An effective thesis statement clearly expresses your essay's main idea.** It does more than state your topic; it indicates what you will say about your topic, and it signals how you will approach your material. The following thesis statement, from the essay "Grant and Lee: A Study in Contrasts" by Bruce Catton (page 392), clearly communicates the writer's main idea.

> They [Grant and Lee] were two strong men, these oddly different generals, and they represented the strengths of two conflicting currents that, through them, had come into final collision.

This statement says that the essay will compare and contrast Grant and Lee. Specifically, it indicates that Catton will present the two Civil War generals as symbols of two opposing historical currents. If the statement had been less fully developed – for example, had Catton written, "Grant and Lee were quite different from each other" – it would have just echoed the essay's title.

2. **An effective thesis statement communicates your essay's purpose.** Whether your purpose is to evaluate or analyze or simply to describe or inform, your thesis statement should communicate that purpose to your readers. In general terms, your thesis can be **expressive**, conveying a mood or impression; it can be **informative**, perhaps listing the major points you will discuss or presenting an objective overview of the essay; or it can be **persuasive**, taking a strong stand or outlining the position you will argue.

Each of the following thesis statements communicates a different purpose.

To express feelings The city's homeless families live in heartbreaking surroundings.

To inform The plight of the homeless has become so serious that it is a major priority for many city governments.

To persuade The best way to address the problems of the homeless is to renovate abandoned city buildings to create suitable housing for homeless families.

3. **An effective thesis statement is clearly worded.** To communicate your essay's main idea, an effective thesis statement should be clearly worded. (It should also speak for itself. It is not necessary to write, "My thesis is that . . ." or "The thesis of this paper is. . . .") The thesis statement should

An Effective Thesis

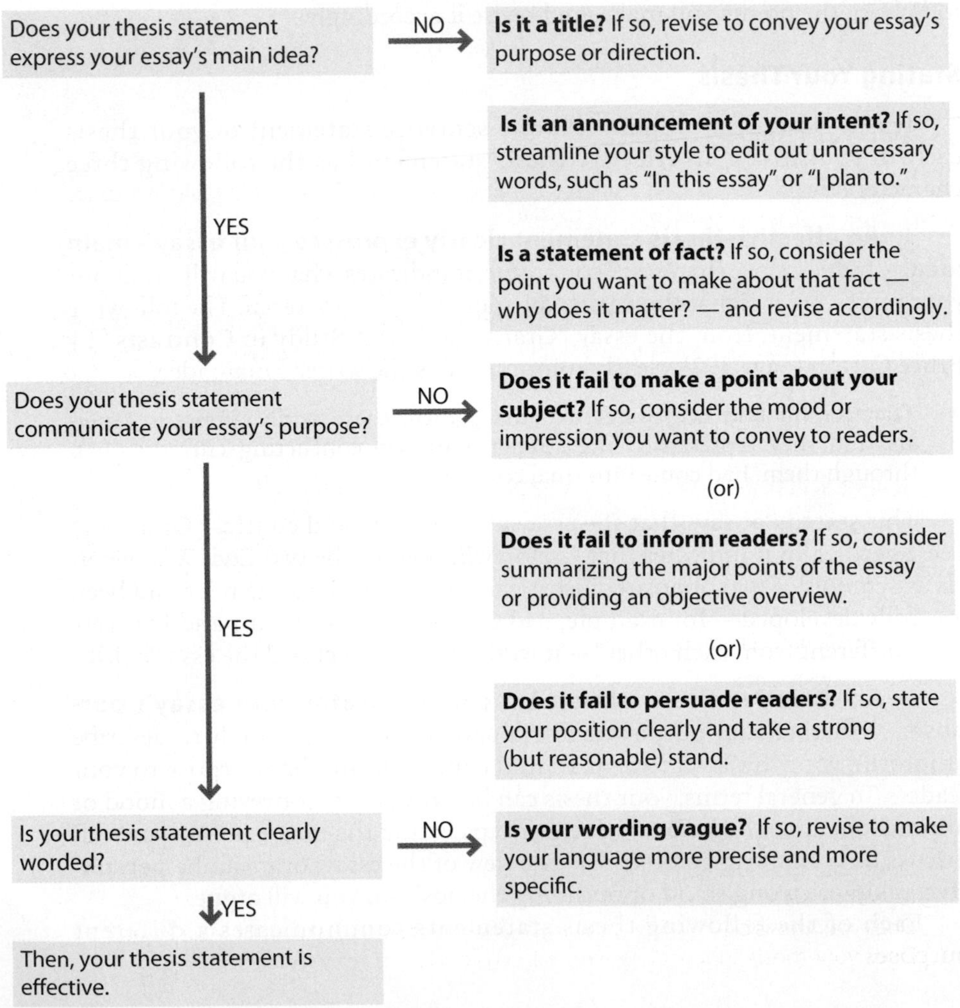

give a straightforward and accurate indication of what follows, and it should not mislead readers about the essay's direction, emphasis, scope, content, or viewpoint. Vague language, irrelevant details, and unnecessarily complex terminology have no place in a thesis statement. Keep in mind, too, that your thesis statement should not make promises that your essay is not going to keep. For example, if you are going to discuss just the *effects* of new immigration laws, your thesis statement should not emphasize the *causes* that led to their passage.

Your thesis statement should not include every point you will discuss in your essay. Still, it should be specific enough to indicate your direction and scope. The sentence "Immigration laws have not been effective" is not an effective thesis statement because it does not give your essay much focus. The following sentence, however, *is* an effective thesis statement. It clearly indicates what the writer is going to discuss, and it establishes a specific direction for the essay.

> Because they do not take into account the economic causes of immigration, current immigration laws do little to decrease the number of undocumented workers coming into the United States.

Implying a Thesis

Like an explicitly stated thesis, an **implied thesis** conveys an essay's main focus, but it does not do so explicitly. Instead, the selection and arrangement of the essay's ideas suggest the focus. Professional writers sometimes prefer this option because an implied thesis is subtler than a stated thesis. (An implied thesis is especially useful in narratives, descriptions, and some arguments, where an explicit thesis would seem heavy-handed or arbitrary.) In most college writing, however, you should state your thesis to avoid any risk of being misunderstood or of wandering away from your topic.

A STUDENT WRITER: Developing a Thesis

After experimenting with different ways of arranging her ideas for her essay, Laura Bobnak summed them up in a tentative thesis statement.

> As I look back at the cheating I witnessed, I wonder why I kept silent and what would have happened if I had acted.

CHECKLIST STATING YOUR THESIS

- ☐ Do you state your thesis in one complete, concise sentence?
- ☐ Does your thesis indicate your purpose?
- ☐ Is your thesis suited to the assignment?
- ☐ Does your thesis clearly convey the main idea you intend to support in your essay?
- ☐ Does your thesis suggest how you will organize your essay?

Exercise 8

Assess the strengths and weaknesses of the following as thesis statements.

1. My instructor has an attendance policy.
2. My instructor should change her attendance policy because it is bad.
3. My instructor should change her attendance policy because it is unreasonable, inflexible, and unfair.
4. For many students, a community college makes more sense than a four-year college or university.
5. Some children exhibit violent behavior.
6. Violence is a problem in our society.
7. Conflict-resolution courses should be taught to help prevent violence in America's schools.
8. Social networking sites such as Instagram can cause problems.
9. Instagram attracts many college students.
10. College students should be careful of what material they put on their Facebook pages because prospective employers routinely check them.

Exercise 9

Rewrite the following factual statements to make them effective thesis statements. Make sure each thesis statement is a clearly and specifically worded sentence.

1. Henry David Thoreau thought that we should get in touch with nature and lead more meaningful lives.
2. Several Supreme Court decisions have said that art containing explicit sexual images is not necessarily pornographic.
3. Many women earn less money than men do, in part because they drop out of the workforce during their child-rearing years.
4. People who watch more than five hours of television a day tend to think the world is more violent than do people who watch less than two hours of television daily.
5. In recent years, the suicide rate among teenagers – especially middle- and upper-middle-class teenagers – has risen dramatically.

Exercise 10

Read the following sentences from "The Argument Culture" by Deborah Tannen. Then, formulate a one-sentence thesis statement that summarizes the key points Tannen makes about the nature of argument in our culture.

- "More and more, our public interactions have become like arguing with a spouse."
- "Nearly everything is framed as a battle or game in which winning or losing is the main concern."
- "The argument culture pervades every aspect of our lives today."

- "Issues from global warming to abortion are depicted as two-sided arguments, when in fact most Americans' views lie somewhere in the middle."
- "What's wrong with the argument culture is the ubiquity, the knee-jerk nature of approaching any issue, problem, or public person in an adversarial way."
- "If you fight to win, the temptation is great to deny facts that support your opponent's views and say only what supports your side."
- "We must expand the notion of 'debate' to include more dialogue."
- "Perhaps it is time to re-examine the assumption that audiences always prefer a fight."
- "Instead of insisting on hearing 'both sides,' let's insist on hearing 'all sides.' "

Exercise 11

Going through as many steps as you need, draft an effective thesis statement for the essay you have been working on.

3

Arrangement

Each of the tasks discussed in Chapter 2 represents choices you have to make about your topic and your material. Now, before you begin to write, you have another choice to make: how to arrange your material into an essay.

Recognizing a Pattern

Deciding how to structure an essay is easy when your assignment specifies a particular pattern of development. That may be the case in a composition class, where the instructor may assign a descriptive or a narrative essay. Also, certain assignments or exam questions suggest how your material should be structured. For example, an instructor might ask you to tell about how something works, or an exam question might ask you to trace the circumstances leading up to an event. If you are perceptive, you will realize that your instructor is asking for a process essay and that the exam question is asking for either a narrative or a cause-and-effect response. The most important things are to recognize the clues that such assignments give (or those that you find in your topic or thesis statement) and to structure your essay accordingly.

One clue to structuring your essay can be found in the questions you asked when you probed your subject (see page 32). For example, if questions like "What happened?" and "When did it happen?" yielded the most useful information about your topic, you should consider structuring your essay as a narrative. The chart on the next page links various questions to the patterns of development that they suggest. Notice how the terms in the right-hand column – narration, description, and so on – identify patterns of development that can help order your ideas. Chapters 6 through 13 explain and illustrate each of these patterns.

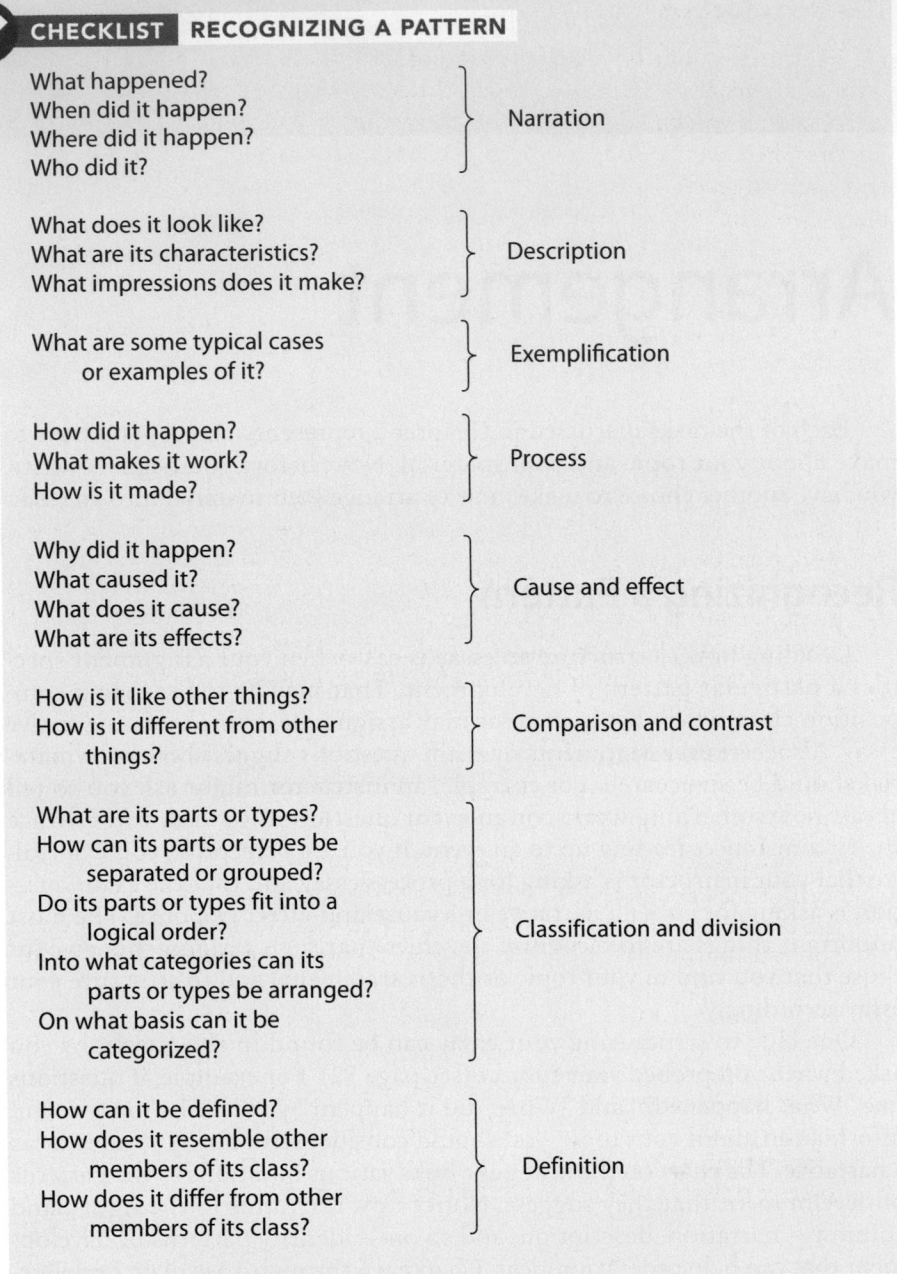

CHECKLIST RECOGNIZING A PATTERN

What happened? When did it happen? Where did it happen? Who did it?	Narration
What does it look like? What are its characteristics? What impressions does it make?	Description
What are some typical cases or examples of it?	Exemplification
How did it happen? What makes it work? How is it made?	Process
Why did it happen? What caused it? What does it cause? What are its effects?	Cause and effect
How is it like other things? How is it different from other things?	Comparison and contrast
What are its parts or types? How can its parts or types be separated or grouped? Do its parts or types fit into a logical order? Into what categories can its parts or types be arranged? On what basis can it be categorized?	Classification and division
How can it be defined? How does it resemble other members of its class? How does it differ from other members of its class?	Definition

Understanding the Parts of the Essay

No matter what pattern of development you use, your essay should have a beginning, a middle, and an end – that is, an *introduction,* a *body,* and a *conclusion.*

The Introduction

Your **introduction**, usually one paragraph and rarely more than two, transports readers from their world into the world of your essay. A weak introduction will cause readers to lose interest in your essay. A strong introduction, however, will make them care about the issues you are discussing and want to read further. For this reason, an effective introduction usually identifies your subject, creates interest, and states your thesis.

Here are several effective strategies you can use to introduce an essay. (Note that in each of these introductory paragraphs, the thesis is underlined.)

1. You can begin with *background information.* This approach works particularly well on exams, when there is no need (or time) for subtlety.

> The federal minimum wage was introduced by Franklin Delano Roosevelt in 1938. Since then, the minimum wage has been raised twenty-two times by twelve different presidents. (States can also set a minimum wage, as long as it does not fall below the federal level.) However, the Fair Labor Standards Act exempts certain categories of workers – for example, those who work for tips, some agricultural workers, home care aides, and employees of some small businesses – from the federal minimum wage requirements. As a result, many low-wage workers receive much less than the minimum wage. Given the current economic situation, both federal and state governments should immediately reevaluate wage exemptions so that all American workers are treated fairly. (economics exam)

2. You can introduce an essay with your own original *definition* of a relevant term or concept. This technique is especially useful for research papers or exams, when the meaning of a specific term is crucial.

> Democracy is a form of government in which people choose leaders by voting. For democracy to work, elected representatives must have reasoned debates about important issues and be willing to compromise. Recently, however, both Republicans and Democrats have become more and more divided along party lines. As a result, hostility between the two parties is worse than it has been in decades. Sadly, a recent study suggests that these divisions are greatest among those who are most involved in the political process. The result is that partisan animosity has increased, and many people in government believe that the opposing party's policies threaten the well-being of the country. Unless something is done to encourage bipartisan cooperation, we will soon become a nation divided, one that will be unable to agree on solutions to the nation's most pressing problems.
>
> (political science essay)

3. You can begin your essay with an *anecdote* or *story* that leads readers to your thesis.

> Three years ago, I went with my grandparents to my first auction. They live in a small town outside of Lancaster, Pennsylvania, where it is common for people to auction off the contents of a home when someone moves or dies. As I walked through the crowd, I smelled the funnel cakes frying in the food trucks, heard the hypnotic chanting of the auctioneer, and sensed the excitement of the crowd. Two hours later, I walked off with an old trunk

that I had bought for thirty dollars and a passion for auctions that I still have today. (composition essay)

4. You can begin with a *question.*

What was it like to live through the Holocaust? The late Elie Wiesel, in *One Generation After,* answers this question by presenting a series of accounts about ordinary people who found themselves imprisoned in Nazi death camps. As he does so, he challenges some of the assumptions we have about the Holocaust and those who survived. (sociology book report)

5. You can begin with a *quotation.* If it arouses interest, it can encourage your audience to read further.

"The rich are different," F. Scott Fitzgerald wrote more than ninety years ago. Apparently, they still are. As an examination of the tax code shows, the wealthy receive many more benefits than the middle class or the poor do. (accounting paper)

6. You can begin with a *surprising statement.* An unexpected statement catches readers' attention and makes them want to read more.

Believe it or not, many people who live in the suburbs are not white and rich. My family, for example, fits into neither of these categories. Ten years ago, my family and I came to the United States from Pakistan. My parents were poor then, and by some standards, they are still poor even though they both work two jobs. Still, they eventually saved enough to buy a small house in the suburbs of Chicago. Throughout the country, there are many suburban families like mine who are working hard to make ends meet so that their children can get a good education and go to college. (composition essay)

7. You can begin with a *contradiction.* You can open your essay with an idea that most people believe is true and then get readers' attention by showing that it is inaccurate or ill-advised.

Many people think that after the Declaration of Independence was signed in 1776, the colonists defeated the British army in battle after battle. This commonly held belief is incorrect. The truth is that the colonial army lost most of its battles. The British were defeated not because the colonial army was stronger, but because George Washington refused to be lured into a costly winner-take-all battle and because the British government lost interest in pursuing an expensive war three thousand miles from home. (history take-home exam)

8. You can begin with a *fact* or *statistic.*

Recently, the National Council on Teacher Quality released a report that said that of the 1,400 teacher-preparation programs in the United States, 1,100 are inadequate. According to this report, undergraduate teacher-preparation programs are not rigorous enough and do not include sufficient classroom-teaching experience. In addition, future educators are rarely required to major in the specific subject areas they are going to teach. Although many educators agree with this negative assessment, they do not agree on what should be done to remedy the situation. Instead of trying to modify existing programs, educators should look at new, more cost-effective ways of improving teacher training. (education essay)

No matter which strategy you select, your introduction should be consistent in tone with the rest of your essay. If it is not, it can misrepresent your intentions and even damage your credibility. (For this reason, it is a good idea not to write your introduction until after you have finished your rough draft.) A technical report, for instance, should have an introduction that reflects the formality and objectivity the occasion requires. The introduction to an autobiographical essay, however, could have a more informal, subjective tone.

CHECKLIST WHAT NOT TO DO IN AN INTRODUCTION

- ☐ **Don't apologize.** Never use phrases such as "in my opinion" or "I may not be an expert, but. . . ." By doing so, you suggest that you don't really know your subject.
- ☐ **Don't begin with a dictionary definition.** Avoid beginning an essay with phrases like "According to Webster's Dictionary. . . ." This type of introduction is overused and trite. If you want to use a definition, develop your own.
- ☐ **Don't announce what you intend to do.** Don't begin with phrases such as "In this paper I will . . ." or "The purpose of this essay is to. . . ." Use your introduction to create interest in your topic, and let readers discover your intention when they get to your thesis statement.
- ☐ **Don't wander.** Your introduction should draw readers into your essay as soon as possible. Avoid irrelevant comments or annoying digressions that will distract readers and make them want to stop reading.

Exercise 1

Look through magazine articles or the essays in this book, and find one example of each kind of introduction. Why do you think each introductory strategy was chosen? What other strategies might have worked?

The Body Paragraphs

The middle section, or **body**, of your essay develops your thesis. The body paragraphs present the **support** – examples, reasons, facts, and so on – that convinces your audience that your thesis is reasonable. To do so, each body paragraph should be *unified, coherent,* and *well developed.* It should also follow a particular pattern of development and should clearly support your thesis.

- *Each body paragraph should be unified.* A paragraph is **unified** when each sentence relates directly to the main idea of the paragraph. Frequently, the main idea of a paragraph is stated in a **topic sentence**. Like a thesis statement, a topic sentence acts as a guidepost, making it easy for readers to follow the paragraph's discussion. Although the placement of a topic sentence depends on a writer's purpose and subject, beginning writers often make it the first sentence of a paragraph.

Sometimes the main idea of a paragraph is not stated but **implied** by the sentences in the paragraph. Professional writers often use this technique because they believe that in some situations – especially narratives and descriptions – a topic sentence can seem forced or awkward. As a beginning writer, however, you will find it helpful to use topic sentences to keep your paragraphs focused.

Whether or not you include a topic sentence, remember that each sentence in a paragraph should develop the paragraph's main idea. If the sentences in a paragraph do not support the main idea, the paragraph will lack unity.

In the following excerpt from a student essay, notice how the topic sentence (underlined) unifies the paragraph by summarizing its main idea:

> <u>Another problem with fast food is that it contains additives.</u> Fast-food companies know that to keep their customers happy, they have to give them food that tastes good, and this is where the trouble starts. For example, to give fries flavor, McDonald's used to fry their potatoes in beef fat. Shockingly, their fries actually had more saturated fat than their hamburgers did. When the public found out how unhealthy their fries were, the company switched to vegetable oil. What most people don't know, however, is that McDonald's adds a chemical derived from animals to the vegetable oil to give it the taste of beef tallow.

The topic sentence, placed at the beginning of the paragraph, enables readers to grasp the writer's point immediately. The examples that follow all relate to that point, making the paragraph unified.

- *Each body paragraph should be coherent.* A paragraph is **coherent** if its sentences are smoothly and logically connected to one another. Coherence can be strengthened in three ways. First, you can repeat **keywords** to carry concepts from one sentence to another and to echo important terms. Second, you can use **pronouns** to refer to key nouns in previous sentences. Finally, you can use **transitions**, words or expressions that show chronological sequence, cause and effect, and so on (see the list of transitions on page 55). These three strategies for connecting sentences – which you can also use to connect paragraphs within an essay – indicate for your readers the exact relationships among your ideas.

The following paragraph, from George Orwell's "Shooting an Elephant" (page 131), uses repeated keywords, pronouns, and transitions to achieve coherence.

> I got up. The Burmans were already racing past me across the mud. It was obvious that the elephant would never rise again, but he was not dead. He was breathing very rhythmically with long rattling gasps, his great mound of a side painfully rising and falling. His mouth was wide open – I could see far down into caverns of pale pink throat. I waited a long time for him to die, but his breathing did not weaken. Finally I fired my two remaining shots into the spot where I thought his heart must be. The thick blood welled out of him like red velvet, but still he did not die. His body did not even jerk when the shots hit him, the tortured breathing continued without a pause. He was dying, very slowly and in great agony, but in some world remote from me where not even a bullet could damage him further. I felt that I had got to put an end to that dreadful noise. It seemed dreadful to see the great beast lying there, powerless to move and yet powerless to die, and not even to be able to finish him. I sent back for my small rifle and poured shot after shot into his heart and down his throat. They seemed to make no impression. The tortured gasps continued as steadily as the ticking of a clock.

TRANSITIONS

SEQUENCE OR ADDITION

again	first, . . . second, . . . third	next
also	furthermore	one . . . another
and	in addition	still
besides	last	too
finally	moreover	

TIME

afterward	finally	simultaneously
as soon as	immediately	since
at first	in the meantime	soon
at the same time	later	subsequently
before	meanwhile	then
earlier	next	until
eventually	now	

COMPARISON

also	likewise
in comparison	similarly
in the same way	

CONTRAST

although	in contrast	on the one hand . . .
but	instead	on the other hand . . .
conversely	nevertheless	still
despite	nonetheless	whereas
even though	on the contrary	yet
however		

EXAMPLES

for example	specifically
for instance	that is
in fact	thus
namely	

CONCLUSIONS OR SUMMARIES

as a result	in summary
in conclusion	therefore
in short	thus

CAUSES OR EFFECTS

as a result	so
because	then
consequently	therefore
since	

Orwell keeps his narrative coherent by using transitional expressions (*already*, *finally*, *when the shots hit him*) to signal the passing of time. He uses pronouns (*he*, *his*) in nearly every sentence to refer back to the elephant, the topic of his paragraph. Finally, he repeats keywords like *shots* and *die* (and its variants *dead* and *dying*) to link the whole paragraph's sentences together.

- *Each body paragraph should be well developed.* A paragraph is **well developed** if it contains the support that readers need to understand its main idea. If a paragraph is not adequately developed, readers will think they have been given only a partial explanation of the subject.

If you decide you need more information in a paragraph, you can look back at your brainstorming notes. If that doesn't help, you can freewrite or brainstorm again, talk with friends and instructors, read more about your topic, or (with your instructor's permission) do some research. Your assignment and your topic will determine the kind and amount of information you need.

TYPES OF SUPPORT

- **Examples** Specific illustrations of a general idea or concept
- **Reasons** Underlying causes or explanations
- **Facts** Pieces of information that can be verified or proved
- **Statistics** Numerical data (for example, results of studies by reputable authorities or organizations)
- **Details** Parts or portions of a whole (for example, steps in a process)
- **Expert opinions** Statements by recognized authorities in a particular field
- **Personal experiences** Events that you lived through
- **Visuals** Diagrams, charts, graphs, or photographs

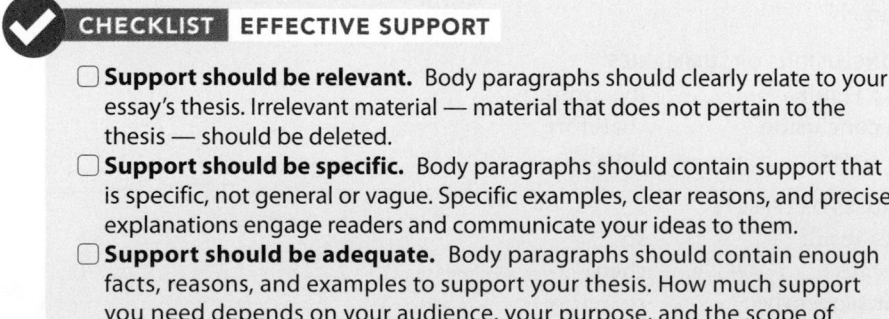

CHECKLIST EFFECTIVE SUPPORT

- ☐ **Support should be relevant.** Body paragraphs should clearly relate to your essay's thesis. Irrelevant material — material that does not pertain to the thesis — should be deleted.
- ☐ **Support should be specific.** Body paragraphs should contain support that is specific, not general or vague. Specific examples, clear reasons, and precise explanations engage readers and communicate your ideas to them.
- ☐ **Support should be adequate.** Body paragraphs should contain enough facts, reasons, and examples to support your thesis. How much support you need depends on your audience, your purpose, and the scope of your thesis.

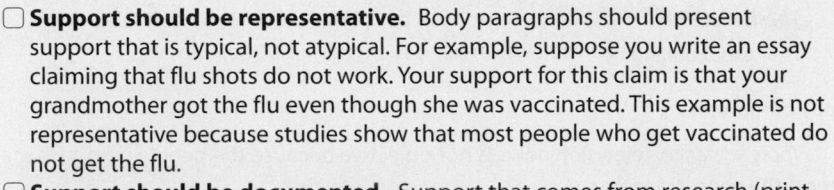

☐ **Support should be representative.** Body paragraphs should present support that is typical, not atypical. For example, suppose you write an essay claiming that flu shots do not work. Your support for this claim is that your grandmother got the flu even though she was vaccinated. This example is not representative because studies show that most people who get vaccinated do not get the flu.

☐ **Support should be documented.** Support that comes from research (print sources and the Internet, for example) should be documented. (For more information on using proper documentation, see Chapter 18 and the Appendix.) **Plagiarism** — failure to document the ideas and words of others — is not only unfair but is also dishonest. Always use proper documentation to acknowledge your debt to your sources, and keep in mind that words and ideas you borrow from the essays in this book must also be documented. (For more information on avoiding plagiarism, see Chapter 17.)

The following student paragraph uses two examples to support its topic sentence.

Example 1

Just look at how males have been taught that extravagance is a positive characteristic. Scrooge, the main character of Dickens's *A Christmas Carol,* is portrayed as an evil man until he gives up his miserly ways and freely distributes gifts and money on Christmas Day. This behavior, of course, is rewarded when people change their opinions about him and decide that he isn't such a bad person after all.

Example 2

Diamond Jim Brady is another interesting example. This individual was a nineteenth-century financier who was known for his extravagant taste in women and food. On any given night, he would eat enough food to feed at least ten of the numerous poor who roamed the streets of New York at that time. Yet, despite his selfishness and infantile self-gratification, Diamond Jim Brady's name has become associated with the good life.

• *Each body paragraph should follow a particular pattern of development.* In addition to making sure your body paragraphs are unified, coherent, and well developed, you need to organize each paragraph according to a specific pattern of development. (Chapters 6 through 13 each begin with a paragraph-length example of the pattern discussed in the chapter.)

• *Each body paragraph should clearly support the thesis statement.* No matter how many body paragraphs your essay has – three, four, five, or even more – each paragraph should introduce and develop an idea that supports the essay's thesis. Each paragraph's topic sentence should express one of these supporting points. The diagram on the next page illustrates this thesis-and-support structure.

Introductory paragraph

Thesis statement: Despite the emphasis by journalists on objective reporting, there are three reasons why television news is anything but objective.

Body paragraph

Topic sentence: Television news is not objective because the people who gather and report the news are biased.

Body paragraph

Topic sentence: In addition, television news is not objective because networks face pressure from sponsors.

Body paragraph

Topic sentence: Finally, television news is not objective because networks focus on ratings rather than content.

Concluding paragraph

Restatement of thesis: Even though television journalists claim they strive for objectivity, the truth is that this ideal has been impossible to achieve.

Exercise 2

Choose a body paragraph from one of the essays in this book. Using the criteria discussed on pages 53–57, decide whether the paragraph is unified, coherent, and well developed.

Exercise 3

Choose one essay in this book, and underline its thesis statement. Then, determine how its body paragraphs support that thesis statement. (Note that in a long essay, several body paragraphs may develop a single supporting point, and some paragraphs may serve as transitions from one point to another.)

REMINDER LABELING YOUR NOTES

You can use your word-processing program to insert comments into your notes and to label ideas that seem to suggest certain essay structures (narrative, cause and effect, process, and so on). This tip can be used along with the checklist on page 50 to get a sense of how to structure your essay.

CLOSE VIEW

The Conclusion

Because readers remember best what they read last, your **conclusion** is very important. It is your final word on your subject and your last chance to influence your readers, to demonstrate the importance of your ideas, and to suggest the broader implications of your thesis. For this reason, you should always end your essay in a way that reinforces your main point and gives a sense of closure.

Like your introduction, your conclusion is rarely longer than a paragraph. Regardless of its length, however, your conclusion should be consistent with the rest of your essay; that is, it should not introduce points you have not discussed earlier. Frequently, a conclusion will restate your essay's main idea or review your key points.

Here are several strategies you can use to conclude an essay:

1. You can conclude your essay by *reviewing your key points* or by *restating your thesis in different words.*

> Rotation of crops provided several benefits. It enriched soil by giving it a rest; it enabled farmers to vary their production; and it ended the cycle of "boom or bust" that had characterized the prewar South's economy when cotton was the primary crop. Of course, this innovation did not solve all the economic problems of the postwar South, but it did lay the groundwork for the healthy economy this region enjoys today. (history exam)

2. You can end a discussion of a problem with a *recommendation of a course of action.*

> Not surprisingly, the population of students with disabilities attending American colleges and universities is growing each year. Even so, many of these students find that some campuses are not equipped to address the diverse range of needs that these students have. This situation exists even though students with disabilities are protected by local, state, and federal laws that guarantee them an equal level of access. For this reason, colleges must do more to make their campuses, classrooms, and social situations accessible to all students, regardless of their individual needs. (public health essay)

3. You can conclude with a *prediction.* Be sure, however, that your prediction follows logically from the points you have made in the essay. Your conclusion is no place to make new points or to change direction.

> Despite recent advances in helmet technology, the number of head injuries in football remains unacceptably high. This is especially true for high school players, who face a higher risk of concussions than college players do. As current research has shown, there is limited evidence that current helmet design can eliminate, or even cut, the risk of concussions. As a result of repeated football-related head trauma, players experience a number of disturbing effects, including depression, suicide, and chronic traumatic encephalopathy. Unless this situation can be reversed, the future of football is in serious doubt. As they have done with boxing, fans will tune out and find other less dangerous sports to watch. (composition essay)

4. You can end with a relevant *quotation.*

> In *Walden,* Henry David Thoreau says, "The mass of men lead lives of quiet desperation." This sentiment is reinforced by a drive through the Hill

District of our city. Perhaps the work of the men and women who run the clinic on Jefferson Street cannot totally change this situation, but it can give us hope to know that some people, at least, are working for the betterment of us all. (social work essay)

CHECKLIST WHAT NOT TO DO IN A CONCLUSION

- ☐ **Don't end by repeating the exact words of your thesis and listing your main points.** Avoid boring endings that tell readers what they already know.
- ☐ **Don't end with an empty phrase.** Avoid ending with a cliché like "This just goes to prove that you can never be too careful."
- ☐ **Don't introduce new points or go off in new directions.** Your conclusion should not introduce new points for discussion. It should reinforce the points you have already made in your essay.
- ☐ **Don't end with an unnecessary announcement.** Don't end by saying that you are ending — for example, "In conclusion, let me say. . . ." The tone of your conclusion should signal that the essay is drawing to a close.

Exercise 4

Look through magazine articles or the essays in this book, and find one example of each kind of conclusion. Why do you think each concluding strategy was chosen? What other strategies might have worked?

Constructing a Formal Outline

Before you begin to write, you may decide to construct a **formal outline** to guide you. Whereas informal outlines are preliminary lists that remind you which points to discuss, formal outlines are detailed, multilevel constructions that indicate the exact order in which you will present your key points and supporting details. The complexity of your assignment determines which type of outline you need. For a short essay, an informal outline like the one on page 40 is probably sufficient. For a longer, more complex essay, however, you will need a formal outline.

One way to construct a formal outline is to copy down the main headings from your informal outline. Then, arrange ideas from your brainstorming notes or cluster diagram as subheadings under the appropriate headings. As you work on your outline, make sure each idea you include supports your thesis. Ideas that don't fit should be reworded or discarded. As you revise your essay, continue to refer to your outline to make sure your thesis and support are logically related. The guidelines that follow will help you prepare a formal outline.

CHECKLIST CONSTRUCTING A FORMAL OUTLINE

- ☐ Write your thesis statement at the top of the page.
- ☐ Group main headings under roman numerals (*I, II, III, IV,* and so on), and place them flush with the left-hand margin.
- ☐ Indent each subheading under the first word of the heading above it. Use capital letters (A, B, C, and so on) before major points, and use numbers before supporting details.
- ☐ Capitalize the first letter of the first word of each heading.
- ☐ Make your outline as simple as possible, avoiding overly complex divisions of ideas. (Try not to go beyond third-level headings — *1, 2, 3,* and so on.)
- ☐ Construct either a **topic outline**, with headings expressed as short phrases or single words ("Advantages and disadvantages"), or a **sentence outline**, with headings expressed as complete sentences ("The advantages of advanced placement chemistry outweigh the disadvantages"). *Never use both phrases and complete sentences in the same outline.*
- ☐ Express all headings at the same level in parallel terms. (If roman numeral *I* is a noun, *II, III,* and *IV* should also be nouns.)
- ☐ Make sure each heading contains at least two subdivisions. You cannot have a *1* without a *2* or an *A* without a *B.*
- ☐ Make sure your headings do not overlap.

A STUDENT WRITER: Constructing a Formal Outline

The topic outline Laura Bobnak constructed follows the guidelines discussed above. Notice that her outline focuses on the body of her paper and does not include the introduction or conclusion: these sections are usually developed after the body has been drafted. (Compare this formal outline with the informal outline on page 40, in which Laura simply grouped her brainstorming notes under three general headings.)

Thesis statement: As I look back at the cheating I witnessed, I wonder why I kept silent and what would have happened if I had acted.

I. The incident
    A. Test situation
    B. My observation
    C. My reactions
        1. Anger
        2. Silence
II. Reasons for keeping silent
    A. Other students' attitudes
    B. My fears
III. Current attitude toward cheating
    A. Effects of cheating on education
    B. Effects of cheating on students

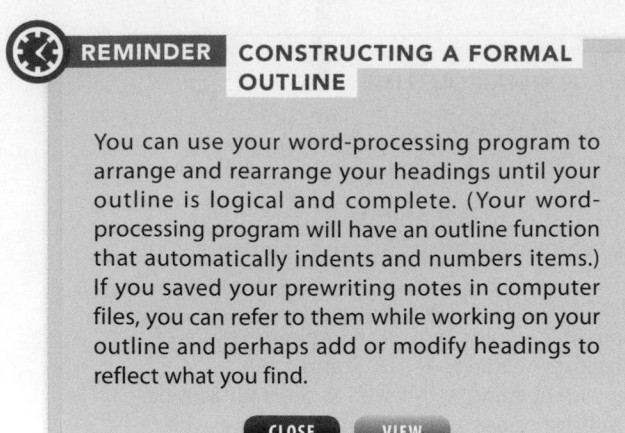

REMINDER **CONSTRUCTING A FORMAL OUTLINE**

You can use your word-processing program to arrange and rearrange your headings until your outline is logical and complete. (Your word-processing program will have an outline function that automatically indents and numbers items.) If you saved your prewriting notes in computer files, you can refer to them while working on your outline and perhaps add or modify headings to reflect what you find.

CLOSE VIEW

This outline enabled Laura to arrange her points so that they supported her thesis. As she went on to draft her essay, the outline reminded her to emphasize the contrast between her present and former attitudes toward cheating.

Exercise 5

Read the thesis statement you developed in Chapter 2, Exercise 11 (on page 47), as well as all the notes you made for the essay you are planning. Then, make a topic outline that lists the points you will discuss in your essay. When you are finished, check to make sure your outline conforms to the guidelines on the checklist on page 61.

4

Drafting and Revising

After you decide on a thesis and an arrangement for your ideas, you can begin to draft and revise your essay. Keep in mind that even as you carry out these activities, you may have to generate more material or revise your thesis statement.

Writing Your First Draft

The purpose of your **first draft** is to get your ideas down on paper so that you can react to them. Experienced writers know that the first draft is nothing more than a work in progress; it exists to be revised. With this in mind, you should expect to cross out and extensively rearrange material. In addition, don't be surprised if you think of new ideas as you write. If a new idea comes to you, go with it. Some of the best writing comes from unexpected turns or accidents. The following guidelines will help you prepare your first draft.

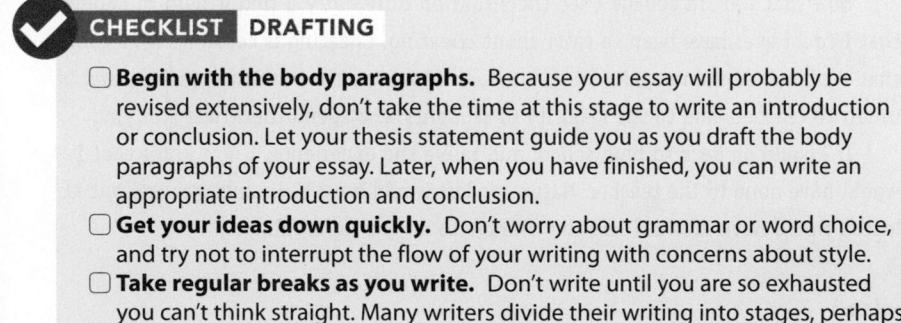

CHECKLIST DRAFTING

- ☐ **Begin with the body paragraphs.** Because your essay will probably be revised extensively, don't take the time at this stage to write an introduction or conclusion. Let your thesis statement guide you as you draft the body paragraphs of your essay. Later, when you have finished, you can write an appropriate introduction and conclusion.
- ☐ **Get your ideas down quickly.** Don't worry about grammar or word choice, and try not to interrupt the flow of your writing with concerns about style.
- ☐ **Take regular breaks as you write.** Don't write until you are so exhausted you can't think straight. Many writers divide their writing into stages, perhaps

completing one or two body paragraphs and then taking a short break. This strategy is more efficient than trying to write a complete first draft without stopping.

- ☐ **Leave yourself time to revise.** Remember, your first draft is a *rough draft*. All writing benefits from revision, so allow enough time to write two or more drafts.

A STUDENT WRITER: Writing a First Draft

Here is the first draft of Laura Bobnak's essay on the following topic: "Write about a time when you, like Henry Louis Gates Jr.'s father, could have spoken out but chose not to. Would you make the same decision today?"

1 When I was in high school, I had an experience like the one Henry Louis Gates Jr. talks about in his essay. It was then that I saw a close friend cheat in chemistry class. As I look back at the cheating I witnessed, I wonder why I kept silent and what would have happened if I had acted.

2 The incident I am going to describe took place during the final exam for my advanced placement chemistry class. I had studied hard for it, but even so, I found the test difficult. As I struggled to balance a particularly difficult equation, I noticed that my friend Jeff, who was sitting across from me, was acting strangely. I noticed that he was copying material from his cell phone. After watching him for a while, I dismissed the incident and got back to my test.

3 After the test was over, I began to think about what I had seen. The more I thought about it the angrier I got. It seemed unfair that I had studied for weeks to memorize formulas and equations while all Jeff had done was to copy them onto his cell phone. For a moment I considered going to the teacher, but I quickly rejected this idea. After all, cheating was something everybody did. Besides, I was afraid if I told on Jeff, my friends would stop talking to me.

4 Now that I am in college I see the situation differently. I find it hard to believe that I could ever have been so calm about cheating. Cheating is certainly something that students should not take for granted. It undercuts the education process and is unfair to teachers and to the majority of students who spend their time studying.

5 If I could go back to high school and relive the experience, I now know that I would have gone to the teacher. Naturally Jeff would have been angry at me, but at least I would have known I had the courage to do the right thing.

Exercise 1

Write a draft of the essay you have been working on in Chapters 2 and 3. Be sure to look back at all your notes as well as your outline.

Revising Your Essay

Revision is not something you do after your essay is finished. It is a continuing process during which you consider the logic and clarity of your ideas as well as how effectively they are presented.

Revision is not simply a matter of proofreading or editing, of crossing out one word and substituting another or correcting errors in spelling and punctuation; revision involves reseeing and rethinking what you have written. When you revise, you may find yourself adding and deleting extensively, reordering whole sentences or paragraphs as you reconsider what you want to communicate to your audience.

Revision can take a lot of time, so don't be discouraged if you have to go through three or four drafts before you think your essay is ready to submit. The following advice can help you when you revise your essay.

- ***Give yourself a cooling-off period.*** Put your first draft aside for several hours or even a day or two if you can. This cooling-off period lets you distance yourself from your essay so that you can read it more objectively when you return to it. When you read it again, you will see things you missed the first time.
- ***Revise on hard copy.*** Because a printed-out draft shows you all the pages of your paper and enables you to see your handwritten edits, revise on hard copy instead of directly on the computer screen.
- ***Read your draft aloud.*** Before you revise, read your draft aloud to help you spot choppy sentences, missing words, or phrases that do not sound right.
- ***Take advantage of opportunities to get feedback.*** Your instructor may organize peer-editing groups, distribute a revision checklist, refer students to a writing center, or schedule one-on-one conferences. Make use of as many of these opportunities for feedback as you can; each offers you a different way of gaining information about what you have written.
- ***Try not to get overwhelmed.*** It is easy to become overwhelmed by all the feedback you get about your draft. To avoid this, approach revision systematically. Don't automatically make all the changes people suggest; consider the validity of each change. Also ask yourself whether comments suggest larger issues. For example, does a comment about a series of choppy sentences suggest a need for you to add transitions, or does it mean you need to rethink your ideas?
- ***Don't let your ego get in the way.*** Everyone likes praise, and receiving negative criticism is never pleasant. Experienced writers know, however, that they must get honest feedback if they are going to improve their work. Learn to see criticism – whether from an instructor or from your peers – as a necessary part of the revision process.
- ***Revise in stages.*** Deal with the large elements (essay and paragraph structure) before moving on to the smaller elements (sentence structure and word choice).

How you revise — what specific strategies you decide to use — depends on your own preference, your instructor's instructions, and the time available. Like the rest of the writing process, revision varies from student to student and from assignment to assignment. Five useful revision strategies — *revising with an outline, revising with a checklist, revising with your instructor's written comments, revising in a conference,* and *revising in a peer-editing group* — are discussed in the pages that follow.

Revising with an Outline

When you begin the revision process, you can check your essay's structure by making a **review outline**. Either an informal outline or a formal one can show you whether you have left out any important points. An outline can also show you whether your essay follows a particular pattern of development. Finally, an outline can clarify the relationship between your thesis statement and your body paragraphs. (See pages 60–62 for guidelines for constructing an outline.)

Revising with a Checklist

If you have time, you can use a detailed **revision checklist**, like the one that follows, adapting it to your own writing needs.

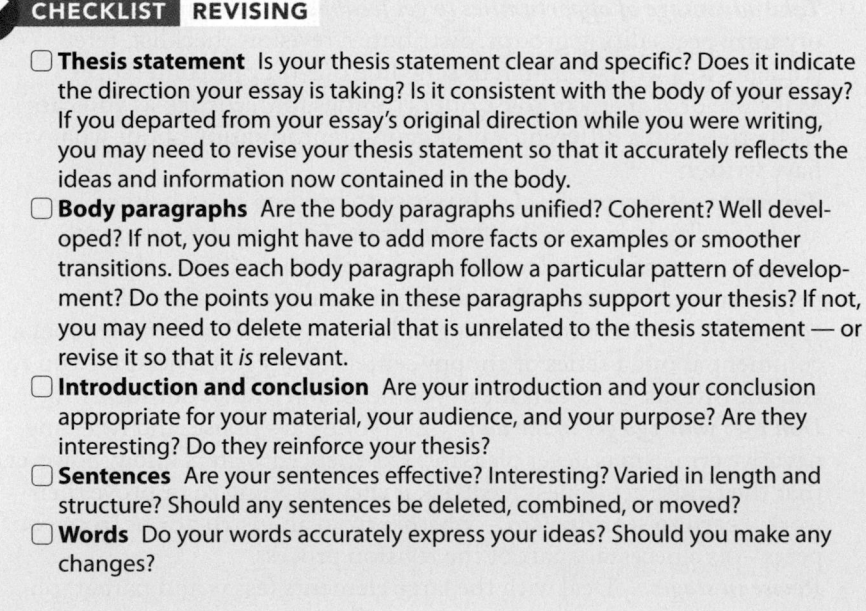

CHECKLIST REVISING

- ☐ **Thesis statement** Is your thesis statement clear and specific? Does it indicate the direction your essay is taking? Is it consistent with the body of your essay? If you departed from your essay's original direction while you were writing, you may need to revise your thesis statement so that it accurately reflects the ideas and information now contained in the body.
- ☐ **Body paragraphs** Are the body paragraphs unified? Coherent? Well developed? If not, you might have to add more facts or examples or smoother transitions. Does each body paragraph follow a particular pattern of development? Do the points you make in these paragraphs support your thesis? If not, you may need to delete material that is unrelated to the thesis statement — or revise it so that it *is* relevant.
- ☐ **Introduction and conclusion** Are your introduction and your conclusion appropriate for your material, your audience, and your purpose? Are they interesting? Do they reinforce your thesis?
- ☐ **Sentences** Are your sentences effective? Interesting? Varied in length and structure? Should any sentences be deleted, combined, or moved?
- ☐ **Words** Do your words accurately express your ideas? Should you make any changes?

Revising with Your Instructor's Written Comments

Your **instructor's written comments** on a draft of your essay can suggest changes in content, arrangement, or style. These comments may question your logic, suggest a clearer thesis statement, ask for more explicit transitions, recommend that a paragraph be relocated, or even propose a new direction for your essay. They may also recommend stylistic changes or ask you to provide more support in one or more of your body paragraphs. You may decide to incorporate these suggestions into the next draft of your essay, or you may decide not to. Whatever the case, you should take your instructor's comments seriously and make reading and responding to them a part of your revision process.

Here is a paragraph from the first draft of Laura Bobnak's essay, which she submitted by email. Her instructor used Microsoft Word's *Comment* tool to insert comments onto her draft.

> Your tentative thesis statement is good — as far as it goes. It doesn't address the second half of the assignment — namely, would you make the same decision today?

When I was in high school, I had an experience like the one Henry Louis Gates Jr. talks about in his essay. It was then that I saw a close friend cheat in chemistry class. As I look back at the cheating I witnessed, I wonder why I kept silent and what would have happened if I had acted.

REMINDER REVISING

It is usually not a good idea to revise directly on the computer screen. Reading on a screen tends to encourage skimming, whereas revision requires careful close reading. Additionally, many screens (particularly on a phone or tablet) show only a portion of a page. That makes it difficult to move back and forth easily between pages and paragraphs to make sure that all your content supports your thesis. For these reasons, it is a good idea to revise on a hard copy of your essay. Once you have written out your corrections, you can type them into your paper.

CLOSE VIEW

Revising in a Conference

A one-on-one **conference with your instructor** can also help you revise. If your instructor encourages (or requires) you to schedule a conference, make an appointment in advance, arrive on time, and be prepared. Before the conference, read all your drafts carefully, and bring a copy of your most recent draft as well as a list of any questions you have. During the conference, ask your instructor to clarify marginal comments or to help you revise a particular section of your essay that is giving you trouble. Make sure you take notes during the conference so that you will have a record of what you and your instructor discussed. Remember that the more prepared for the conference you are, the more you will get out of it. (Some instructors use email, video links, or a chat room to answer questions and to give students feedback.)

If your instructor is not available or if you want another opinion about your work, a **conference with a writing tutor** at your campus writing center can be helpful. In the writing center, tutors meet with you on a one-on-one basis to address your concerns. Because writing tutors are collaborators, they will engage you in discussion to help you develop your own ideas. In addition, writing tutors can help you diagnose your writing problems, offer you feedback on drafts of your papers, suggest strategies to make your writing clearer and more effective, and identify grammatical or mechanical problems. (Many writing centers also have tutors who specialize in helping students whose first language is not English.) Keep in mind, however, that the writing center is a not a proofreading or editing service. The goal of the writing center is to make you a better writer, not to do your writing for you. For this reason, writing center tutors will not rewrite any part of an essay for you or insert their own words into your text.

Revising in a Peer-Editing Group

Another revision strategy involves getting feedback from other students. Sometimes this process is formal: an instructor may require students to exchange papers and evaluate their classmates' work according to certain standards, perhaps by completing a **peer-editing worksheet**. (See page 71 for an example.) Often, however, getting feedback from others is an informal process. Even if a friend is unfamiliar with your topic, he or she can still tell you whether you are getting your point across and maybe even advise you about how to communicate more effectively. (Remember, though, that your critic should be only your reader, not your ghostwriter.)

Getting feedback from others mirrors how people in the real world actually write. For example, businesspeople circulate reports to get feedback from coworkers; academics routinely collaborate when they write. (And, as you may have realized, this book is also the result of a collaboration.)

Your classmates can be helpful as you write the early drafts of your essay, providing suggestions that can guide you through the revision process. In addition, they can respond to questions you may have about your essay, such as whether your introduction works or whether one of your supporting points needs more explanation. When you are asked to critique another student's work, the following guidelines should help you.

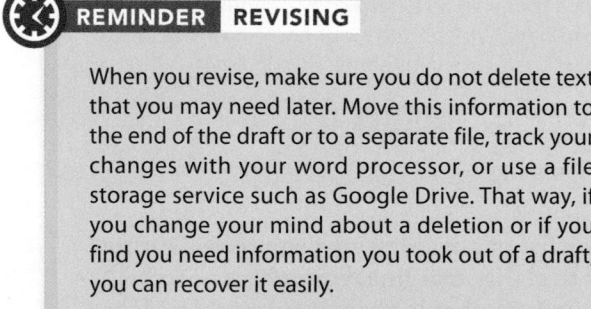

REMINDER REVISING

When you revise, make sure you do not delete text that you may need later. Move this information to the end of the draft or to a separate file, track your changes with your word processor, or use a file storage service such as Google Drive. That way, if you change your mind about a deletion or if you find you need information you took out of a draft, you can recover it easily.

CLOSE VIEW

CHECKLIST GUIDELINES FOR PEER EDITING

- ☐ **Be positive.** Remember that your purpose is to help other students improve their essays.
- ☐ **Be tactful.** Be sure to emphasize the good points about the essay. Mention one or two things the writer has done particularly well before you offer your suggestions.
- ☐ **Be specific.** Offer concrete suggestions about what the writer could do better. Vague words like *good* or *bad* provide little help.
- ☐ **Be involved.** If you are doing a critique orally, make sure you interact with the writer. Ask questions, listen to responses, and explain your comments.
- ☐ **Look at the big picture.** Don't focus exclusively on issues such as spelling and punctuation. At this stage, the clarity of the thesis statement, the effectiveness of the support, and the organization of the writer's ideas are much more important.
- ☐ **Be thorough.** When possible, write down and explain your comments, either on a form your instructor provides or in the margins of the draft you are reviewing.

Strategies for Revising

Strategy	Advantages
Outlining  Aaron Ontiveroz/Getty Images	• Enables you to see relationships between your ideas • Shows you whether your points support your thesis • Highlights topics and subtopics to show you whether you have covered everything • Shows you if you have put enough – but not too much – emphasis on each idea • Shows you whether any information is missing
Checklist  © Andrey_Popov/Shutterstock	• Enables you to revise in an orderly way • Enables you to learn to revise independently • Helps you focus on specific aspects of your writing

(continued)

Strategies for Revising (continued)

Strategy	Advantages
Instructor's Written Comments 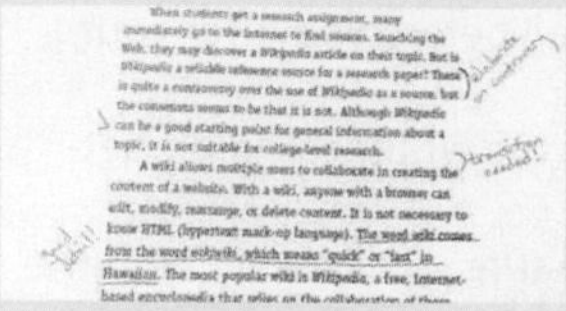	• Enables you to get specific feedback from your primary audience • Provides a road map for you to follow as you revise your essay • Helps you understand what your instructor is looking for and how to improve your writing throughout the course • Helps identify problem areas that you can continue to work on in the writing center
Instructor Conferences  © Monkey Business Images/Shutterstock	• Enables you to meet your instructors in a relaxed atmosphere outside the classroom • Provides one-on-one feedback that can't be obtained in the classroom • Builds a student–teacher relationship • Enables you to collaborate with your instructors • Allows you to ask questions that you might not ask in a classroom setting
Writing Center Conferences  © Amir Ridhwan/Shutterstock	• Offers you a less formal, less stressful environment than a conference with your instructor • Enables you to get help from trained tutors (both students and professionals) • Gives you a perspective other than your instructor's • Offers specialized help if your first language is not English
Peer Editing  © antoniodiaz/Shutterstock	• Enables you and others working on the same assignment to share insights • Gives you the experience of writing for a real audience • Offers you several different readers' reactions to your work • Enables you to benefit from the ideas of your classmates

A STUDENT WRITER: Revising a First Draft

When she revised the first draft of her essay (page 64), Laura Bobnak followed some of the revision strategies discussed above. After writing her rough draft, she put it aside for a few hours and then reread it. Later, her instructor divided the class into pairs and had them read each other's essays and fill out **peer-editing worksheets**. After reading and discussing the following worksheet (filled out by one of her classmates), Laura focused on a number of areas she thought needed revision.

PEER-EDITING WORKSHEET

1. What is the essay's thesis? Is it clearly worded? Does it provide a focus for the essay?

   "As I look back at the cheating I witnessed, I wonder why I kept silent and what would have happened if I had acted." The thesis is clear and gives a good idea of what the essay is about.

2. Do the body paragraphs clearly support the essay's thesis? Should any of the topic sentences be revised? Which, if any, could be more clearly worded?

   The topic sentences seem fine — each one seems to tell what the paragraph is about.

3. How do the body paragraphs develop the essay's main idea? Where could the writer have used more detail?

   Each of the body paragraphs tells a part of the narrative. In paragraph 2, you could add more detail about how the exam room was set up — I really can't picture the scene.

4. Can you follow the writer's ideas? Does the essay need transitions?

   I have no problem following your ideas. Maybe you could have added some more transitions, but I think the essay moves OK.

5. Which points are especially clear? What questions do you have that are not answered in the essay?

   I think you clearly explained what you didn't like about Jeff's cheating. I'm not sure what AP chemistry is like, though. Do people cheat because it's so hard?

6. If this were your essay, what would you change before you handed it in?

   I'd add more detail and explain more about AP chemistry. Also, what were the other students doing while the cheating was going on?

7. Overall, do you think the paper is effective? Explain.

   Good paper; cheating is a big issue, and I think your essay really gets this across.

A peer-editing worksheet for each pattern of development appears at the end of the introductions for Chapters 6 through 15.

Points for Special Attention: First Draft

The Introduction

When she wrote her first draft (page 64), Laura knew she would have to expand her introduction. At this stage, though, she was more concerned with her thesis statement, which, as her instructor's comments pointed out, didn't address the second half of the assignment: to explain whether she would act differently today.

Keeping in mind the feedback she received, Laura rewrote her introduction. First, she created a context for her discussion by specifically linking her story to Gates's essay. Next, she decided to postpone mentioning her subject – cheating – until later in the essay, hoping this strategy would stimulate the curiosity of her readers and make them want to read further. Finally, she revised her thesis statement to reflect the specific wording of the assignment.

The Body Paragraphs

The students in her peer-editing group said Laura needed to expand her body paragraphs. Although she had expected most of her readers to be familiar with courses like advanced placement chemistry, she discovered some were not. In addition, some students in her group thought she should expand the paragraph in which she described her reaction to the cheating. They wondered what the other students had thought about the incident. Did they know? Did they care? Laura's classmates were curious, and they thought other readers would be, too.

Before revising the body paragraphs, Laura did some brainstorming for additional ideas. She decided to describe the difficulty of advanced placement chemistry and the pressure the students in the class had felt. She also decided to summarize discussions she had had with several of her classmates after the test. In addition, she wanted to explain in more detail her present views on cheating; she felt that the paragraph presenting these ideas did not contrast enough with the paragraphs dealing with her high school experiences.

To make sure her sentences led smoothly into one another, Laura added transitions and rewrote entire sentences when necessary, signaling the progression of her thoughts by adding words and phrases such as *therefore, for this reason, for example,* and *as a result.* In addition, she repeated keywords so that important concepts would be reinforced.

The Conclusion

Laura's biggest concern as she revised was to make sure her readers would see the connection between her essay and the assignment. To make this connection clear, she decided to mention in her conclusion a specific effect the incident had on her: its impact on her friendship with Jeff. She also decided to link her reactions to those of Henry Louis Gates Jr. Like him, she had been upset by the actions of someone she knew. By employing this strategy, she was able to bring her essay full circle and develop an idea she had alluded to in her introduction. Thus, rewriting her conclusion helped Laura reinforce her thesis statement and provide closure to her essay.

A STUDENT WRITER: Revising a Second Draft

The following draft incorporates Laura's revisions as well as some preliminary editing of grammar and punctuation.

Speaking Out

1 In his essay "'What's in a Name?'" Henry Louis Gates Jr. recalls an incident from his past in which his father did not speak up. Perhaps he kept silent because he was afraid or because he knew that nothing he said or did would change the situation in Piedmont, West Virginia. Although I have never encountered the kind of prejudice Gates describes, I did have an experience in high school where, like Gates's father, I could have spoken up but did not. As I now look back at the cheating I witnessed, I know I would not make the same decision today.

2 The incident I am going to describe took place during the final examination in my advanced placement chemistry class. The course was very demanding and required hours of studying every night. Every day after school, I would meet with other students to outline chapters and answer homework questions. Sometimes we would even work on weekends. We would often ask ourselves whether we had gotten in over our heads. As the semester dragged on, it became clear to me, as well as to the other students in the class, that passing the course was not something we could take for granted. Test after test came back with grades that were well below the "As" and "Bs" I was used to getting in the regular chemistry course I took in tenth grade. By the time we were ready to take the final exam, most of us were worried that we would fail the course — despite the teacher's assurances that she would mark on a curve.

3 The final examination for advanced placement chemistry was given on a Friday morning from nine to twelve o'clock. As I struggled to balance a particularly complex equation, I noticed that the person sitting across from me was acting strangely. I thought I was imagining things, but as I stared I saw Jeff, my friend and study partner, fumbling with his test booklet. I realized that he was copying material from his cell phone he had hidden under his test booklet. After watching him for a while, I dismissed the incident and finished my test.

4 Surprisingly, when I mentioned the incident to others in the class, they all knew what Jeff had done. The more I thought about Jeff's actions, the angrier I got. It seemed unfair that I had studied for weeks to memorize formulas and equations while all Jeff had done was to copy them onto his cell phone. For a moment I considered going to the teacher, but I quickly rejected this idea. Cheating was nothing

new to me or to others in my school. Many of my classmates cheated at one time or another. Most of us saw school as a war between us and the teachers, and cheating was just another weapon in our arsenal. The worst crime I could commit would be to turn Jeff in. As far as I was concerned, I had no choice. I fell in line with the values of my high school classmates and dismissed the incident as "no big deal."

I find it hard to believe that I could ever have been so complacent about 5
cheating. The issues that were simple in high school now seem complex. I now ask questions that never would have occurred to me in high school. Interestingly, Jeff and I are no longer very close. Whenever I see him, I have the same reaction Henry Louis Gates Jr. had when he met Mr. Wilson after he had insulted his father.

Points for Special Attention: Second Draft

Laura could see that her second draft was stronger than her first, but she decided to schedule a conference with her instructor to help her improve her draft further.

The Introduction

Although Laura was satisfied with her introduction, her instructor identified a problem. Laura had assumed that everyone reading her essay would be familiar with Gates's essay, but her instructor pointed out that this might not be the case. To accommodate readers who didn't know about or remember Gates's comments, her instructor suggested that she add a brief explanation of the problems Gates's father had faced.

The Body Paragraphs

After rereading her first body paragraph, Laura thought she could sharpen its focus. Her instructor agreed, suggesting that she delete the first sentence of the paragraph, which seemed too conversational. She also decided she could delete the sentences that explained how difficult advanced placement chemistry was, even though she had added this material at the suggestion of a classmate. After all, cheating, not advanced placement chemistry, was the subject of her paper. She realized that if she included this kind of detail, she might distract readers from the real subject of her discussion.

Her instructor also pointed out that in the second body paragraph, the first and second sentences did not seem to be connected, so Laura decided to connect these ideas by adding a short discussion of her own reaction to the test. Her instructor also suggested that Laura add more transitional words and phrases to this paragraph to clarify the sequence of events she was describing. Phrases such as *at first* and *about a minute passed* would help readers follow her discussion.

Laura thought the third body paragraph was her best, but, even so, she thought she needed to add more material. She and her instructor decided that she should expand her discussion of the students' reactions to cheating. More information – perhaps some dialogue – would help Laura make the point that cheating was condoned by the students in her class.

The Conclusion

Laura's conclusion began by mentioning her present attitude toward cheating and then suddenly shifted to the effect that cheating had on her relationship with Jeff. Her instructor suggested that she take her discussion about her current view of cheating out of her conclusion and put it in a separate paragraph. By doing so, she could focus her conclusion on the effect that cheating had on both Jeff and her. This strategy enabled Laura to present her views about cheating in more detail and also helped her end her essay forcefully.

Working with Sources

Her instructor also suggested that Laura consider adding a quotation from Gates's essay to her conclusion to connect his experience to Laura's. He reminded her not to forget to document the quotation and to use correct MLA documentation format (as explained and illustrated in Chapter 18 of this text).

The Title

Laura's original title was only a working title, and now she wanted one that would create interest and draw readers into her essay. She knew, however, that a humorous, cute, or catchy title would undermine the seriousness of her essay. After she rejected a number of possibilities, she decided on "The Price of Silence." This title was thought-provoking and also descriptive, and it prepared readers for what was to follow in the essay.

CHOOSING A TITLE

Because it is the first thing in your essay that readers see, your title should create interest. Usually, single-word titles and cute ones do little to draw readers into your essay. To be effective, a title should reflect your purpose and your tone. The titles of some of the essays in this book illustrate the various kinds of titles you can use:

Statement of essay's focus: "Grant and Lee: A Study in Contrasts"

Question: "What Motivates Terrorists?"

Unusual angle: "Thirty-Eight Who Saw Murder Didn't Call the Police"

Controversy: "A Peaceful Woman Explains Why She Carries a Gun"

Provocative wording: "How to Build a Monster from Spare Parts"

Quotation: "What's Really Important about 'Trigger Warnings'"

Humor: "The Dog Ate My Tablet, and Other Tales of Woe"

A STUDENT WRITER: Preparing a Final Draft

Based on the decisions she made during and after her conference, Laura revised and edited her draft and handed in this final version of her essay.

The Price of Silence

Introduction (provides background)

In his essay "'What's in a Name?'" Henry Louis Gates Jr. recalls an incident from his past in which his father encountered prejudice and did not speak up. Perhaps he kept silent because he was afraid or because he knew that nothing he said or did would change the racial situation in Piedmont, West Virginia. Although I have never encountered the kind of prejudice Gates describes, I did have an experience in high school where, like Gates's father, I could have spoken out but did not. As I look back at the cheating incident that I witnessed, I realize that I have outgrown the immaturity and lack of confidence that made me keep silent. 1

Thesis statement

Narrative begins

In my senior year in high school I, along with fifteen other students, took advanced placement chemistry. The course was very demanding and required hours of studying every night. As the semester dragged on, it became clear to me, as well as to the other students in the class, that passing the course was not something we could take for granted. Test after test came back with grades that were well below the As and Bs I was used to getting in the regular chemistry course I had taken in tenth grade. By the time we were ready to take the final exam, most of us were worried that we would fail the course — despite the teacher's assurances that she would mark on a curve. 2

Key incident occurs

The final examination for advanced placement chemistry was given on a Friday morning between nine o'clock and noon. I had studied all that week, but, even so, I found the test difficult. I knew the material, but I had a hard time answering the long questions that were asked. As I struggled to balance a particularly complex equation, I noticed that the person sitting across from me was acting strangely. At first I thought I was imagining things, but as I stared I saw Jeff, my friend and study partner, fumbling with his test booklet. About a minute passed before I realized that he was copying material from a cell phone he had hidden under his test booklet. After a short time, I stopped watching him and finished my test. 3

Narrative continues: reactions to the incident

It was not until after the test that I began thinking about what I had seen. Surprisingly, when I mentioned the incident to others in the class, they all knew what Jeff had done. Some 4 even thought that Jeff's actions were justified. "After all," one student said, "the test was hard." But the more I thought about Jeff's actions, the angrier I got. It seemed unfair that I had studied for weeks to memorize formulas and equations while all Jeff had done was copy them onto his cell phone. For a moment I considered going to the teacher, but I quickly rejected this idea. Cheating was nothing new to me or to others in my school. Many of my classmates cheated at one time or another. Most of us saw school as a war between us and the teachers, and cheating was just another weapon in our arsenal. The worst crime I could commit would be to turn Jeff in. As far as I was concerned, I had no choice. I fell in line with the values of my high school classmates and dismissed the incident as "no big deal."

Narrative ends

Analysis of key incident

Now that I am in college, however, I see the situation differently. I find it hard to believe that I could ever have been so complacent about cheating. The issues that were simple in high school now seem complex — especially in light of the honor code that I follow in college. I now ask questions that never would have occurred to me in high school. What, for example, are the implications of cheating? What would happen to the educational system if cheating became the norm? What are my obligations to all those who are involved in education? Aren't teachers and students interested in achieving a common goal? The answers to these questions give me a sense of the far-reaching effects of my failure to act. If confronted with the same situation today, I know I would speak out regardless of the consequences. 5

Jeff is now a first-year student at the state university and, like me, he was given credit for AP chemistry. I feel certain that by not turning him in, I failed not only myself but also Jeff. I gave in to peer pressure instead of doing what I knew to be right. The worst that would have happened to Jeff had I spoken up is that he would have had to repeat chemistry in summer school. By doing so, he would have proven to himself that he could, like the rest of us in the class, pass on his own. In the long run, this knowledge would have served him better than the knowledge that he could cheat whenever he faced a difficult situation. 6

Conclusion (aftermath of incident)

Interestingly, Jeff and I are no longer very close. Whenever I see him, I have the same reaction Henry Louis Gates Jr. had when he met Mr. Wilson after he had insulted his father: "'I never again looked [him] in the eye'" (4). 7

Work Cited

Gates, Henry Louis, Jr. "'What's in a Name?'" *Patterns for College Writing,* 14th ed., edited by Laurie G. Kirszner and Stephen R. Mandell, Bedford/St. Martin's, 2018, pp. 2–4.

With each draft of her essay, Laura sharpened the focus of her discussion. In the process, she clarified her thoughts about her subject and reached some new and interesting conclusions. Although much of Laura's paper is a narrative, it also includes a contrast between her current ideas about cheating and the ideas she had in high school. Perhaps Laura could have explained the reasons behind her current ideas about cheating more fully. Even so, her paper gives a straightforward account of the incident and analyzes its significance without drifting off into clichés or simplistic moralizing. Especially effective is Laura's conclusion, in which she discusses the long-term effects of her experience and quotes Gates. By concluding in this way, she makes sure her readers will not lose sight of the implications of her experience. Finally, Laura documents the quotation she uses in her conclusion and includes a works-cited page at the end of her essay.

Exercise 2

Use the checklist on page 66 to help you revise your draft. If you prefer, outline your draft and use that outline to help you revise.

Exercise 3

Have another student read your second draft. Then, using the student's peer-critique checklist on page 69 as your guide, revise your draft.

Exercise 4

Using the essay on pages 76–78 as your guide, label the final draft of your own essay. In addition to identifying your introduction, conclusion, and thesis statement, you should also label the main points of your essay.

5

Editing and Proofreading

When you finish revising your essay, it is tempting to just submit it to your instructor and breathe a sigh of relief, but you should resist this temptation. You still have to *edit* and *proofread* your paper to fix any problems that may remain after you revise.

When you **edit**, you search for grammatical errors, check punctuation, and look over your sentence style and word choice one last time. When you **proofread**, you look for spelling errors, typos, incorrect spacing, or problems with your essay's format. The idea is to look carefully for any error, no matter how small, that might weaken your essay's message or undermine your credibility. Remember, this is your last chance to make sure your essay says exactly what you want it to say.

Editing for Grammar

As you edit, keep in mind that certain grammatical errors occur more frequently than others and even more frequently in particular kinds of writing. By focusing on these errors, as well as on those errors you yourself are most likely to make, you will learn to edit your essays quickly and efficiently.

Learning the few rules that follow will help you to identify the most common errors. Later on, when you practice writing essays shaped by various patterns of development, the **Grammar in Context** section in each chapter can help you to recognize and correct these common errors.

Be Sure Subjects and Verbs Agree

Subjects and verbs must agree in number. A singular subject takes a singular verb.

Stephanie Ericsson discusses ten kinds of liars.

A plural subject takes a plural verb.

Chronic liars are different from occasional liars.

Liars and plagiarists have a lot in common.

For information on editing for subject–verb agreement with indefinite pronoun subjects, see the **Grammar in Context** section of Chapter 15 (pages 669–70).

Be Sure Verb Tenses Are Accurate and Consistent

Unintentional shifts in verb tense can be confusing to readers. Verb tenses in the same passage should be the same unless you are referring to two different time periods.

Single time period: Lee surrendered (*past tense*) to Grant on April 9, 1865, and then he addressed (*past tense*) his men.

Two different time periods: In "Songs of the Summer of 1963 . . . and Today," Juan Williams compares (*present tense*) contemporary music with music that was (*past tense*) popular fifty years earlier.

For more information on editing for consistent verb tenses, as well as to eliminate unwarranted shifts in voice, person, and mood, see the **Grammar in Context** section of Chapter 9 (pages 264–265).

Be Sure Pronoun References Are Clear

A pronoun is a word that takes the place of a noun in a sentence. Every pronoun should clearly refer to a specific **antecedent**, the word (a noun or pronoun) it replaces. Pronouns and antecedents must agree in number.

- Singular pronouns refer to singular antecedents.

  When she was attacked, Kitty Genovese was on her way home from work.

- Plural pronouns refer to plural antecedents.

  The people who watched the attack gave different reasons for their reluctance to call for help.

For information on editing for pronoun–antecedent agreement with indefinite pronouns, see the **Grammar in Context** section of Chapter 15 (pages 669–70).

Be Sure Sentences Are Complete

A **sentence** is a group of words that includes a subject and a verb and expresses a complete thought. A **fragment** is an incomplete sentence, one that is missing a subject, a verb, or both a subject and a verb or that has a subject and a verb but does not express a complete thought.

Sentence:	Although it was written in 1963, Martin Luther King Jr.'s "Letter from Birmingham Jail" remains just as powerful today as it was then.
Fragment (no subject):	Remains just as powerful today.
Fragment (no verb):	Martin Luther King Jr.'s "Letter from Birmingham Jail."
Fragment (no subject or verb):	Written in 1963.
Fragment (includes subject and verb but does not express a complete thought):	Although it was written in 1963.

To correct a fragment, you need to supply the missing part of the sentence (a subject, a verb, or both – or an entire independent clause). Often, you will find that the missing words appear in an adjacent sentence.

Be Careful Not to Run Sentences Together without Proper Punctuation

There are two kinds of **run-ons**: *comma splices* and *fused sentences.*

A **comma splice** is an error that occurs when two independent clauses are connected by just a comma.

Comma splice:	As Linda Hasselstrom points out, women who live alone need to learn how to protect themselves~~,~~; sometimes that means carrying a gun.

A **fused sentence** is an error that occurs when two independent clauses are connected without any punctuation.

Fused sentence:	Residents of isolated rural areas may carry guns for protection^, but sometimes these guns may be used against them.

For more information on editing run-ons, including additional ways to correct them, see the **Grammar in Context** section of Chapter 6 (page 100).

Be Careful to Avoid Misplaced and Dangling Modifiers

Modifiers are words and phrases that describe other words in a sentence. To avoid confusion, place modifiers as close as possible to the words they modify.

Limited by her circumstances, the protagonist of Jamaica Kincaid's "'Girl'" has a difficult life.

Working hard at seemingly endless repetitive tasks, she feels trapped.

A **misplaced modifier** appears to modify the wrong word because it is placed incorrectly in the sentence.

Misplaced modifier:	Judith Ortiz Cofer wonders why Latin women are so often stereotyped as either "hot tamales" or low-level workers in her essay "The Myth of the Latin Woman: I Just Met a Girl Named Maria." *(Does Cofer's essay stereotype Latin women?)*
Correct:	In her essay "The Myth of the Latin Woman: I Just Met a Girl Named Maria," Judith Ortiz Cofer wonders why Latin women are so often stereotyped as either "hot tamales" or low-level workers.

A **dangling modifier** "dangles" because it cannot logically describe any word in the sentence.

Dangling modifier:	Visiting ground zero, the absence of the World Trade Center was strikingly obvious. (*Who was visiting ground zero?)*
Correct:	Visiting ground zero, Suzanne Berne found the absence of the World Trade Center strikingly obvious.

For more information on editing to correct misplaced and dangling modifiers, see the **Grammar in Context** section of Chapter 7 (pages 158–59).

Be Sure Sentence Elements Are Parallel

Parallelism is the use of matching grammatical elements (words, phrases, or clauses) to express similar ideas. Used effectively – for example, with paired items or items in a series – parallelism makes the links between related ideas clear and emphasizes connections.

Paired items:	As Deborah Tannen points out, men speak more than women in public but less than women at home.
Items in a series:	Amy Tan says, "I spend a great deal of my time thinking about the power of language – the way it can evoke an emotion, a visual image, a complex idea, or a simple truth" (458).

Faulty parallelism – using items that are not parallel in a context in which parallelism is expected – makes ideas difficult to follow and will likely confuse your readers.

Faulty parallelism: As Deborah Tannen points out, men speak more than women in public, but at home less talking is done by them.

Correct: As Deborah Tannen points out, men tend to speak more than women in public, but they tend to talk less at home.

Faulty parallelism: Amy Tan says she often thinks about "the power of language" – for example, how it suggests images or emotions or complicated ideas can also be suggested or language can communicate a "simple truth" (458).

Correct: Amy Tan says, "I spend a great deal of my time thinking about the power of language – the way it can evoke an emotion, a visual image, a complex idea, or a simple truth" (458).

For more information on using parallelism to strengthen your writing, see the **Grammar in Context** section of Chapter 11 (page 377).

CHECKLIST EDITING FOR GRAMMAR

- ☐ **Subject–verb agreement** Do all your verbs agree with their subjects? Remember that singular subjects take singular verbs and that plural subjects take plural verbs.
- ☐ **Verb tenses** Are all your verb tenses accurate and consistent? Have you avoided unnecessary shifts in tense?
- ☐ **Pronoun reference** Do pronouns clearly refer to their antecedents?
- ☐ **Fragments** Does each group of words punctuated as a sentence have both a subject and a verb and express a complete thought? If not, can you correct the fragment by adding the missing words or by attaching it to an adjacent sentence?
- ☐ **Run-ons** Have you been careful not to connect two independent clauses without the necessary punctuation? Have you avoided comma splices and fused sentences?
- ☐ **Modification** Does every modifier point clearly to the word it modifies? Have you avoided misplaced and dangling modifiers?
- ☐ **Parallelism** Have you used matching words, phrases, or clauses to express equivalent ideas? Have you avoided faulty parallelism?

Editing for Punctuation

Like grammatical errors, certain punctuation errors are more common than others, particularly in certain contexts. By understanding a few punctuation rules, you can learn to identify and correct these errors in your writing.

Learn When to Use Commas — and When Not to Use Them

Commas separate certain elements of a sentence. They are used most often in the following situations:

- To separate an introductory phrase or clause from the rest of the sentence

  In Janice Mirikitani's poem "Suicide Note," the speaker is a college student.

  According to the speaker, her parents have extremely high expectations for her.

  Although she has tried her best, she has disappointed them.

NOTE: Do not use a comma if a dependent clause *follows* an independent clause: She has disappointed them although she has tried her best.

- To separate two independent clauses that are joined by a coordinating conjunction

  The speaker in "Suicide Note" tried to please her parents, but they always expected more of her.

- To separate elements in a series

  Janice Mirikitani has studied creative writing, edited a literary magazine, and published several books of poetry.

For more information on using commas in a series, see the **Grammar in Context** section of Chapter 8 (pages 209–10).

- To separate a **nonrestrictive clause** (a clause that does not supply information that is essential to the sentence's meaning) from the rest of the sentence

  The poem's speaker, who is female, thinks her parents would like her to be a son.

NOTE: Do not use commas to set off a **restrictive clause** (a clause that supplies information that is vital to the sentence's meaning): The child who is overlooked is often the daughter.

Learn When to Use Semicolons

Semicolons, like commas, separate certain elements of a sentence. However, semicolons separate only grammatically equivalent elements – for example, two closely related independent clauses.

In Burma, George Orwell learned something about the nature of imperialism; it was not an easy lesson.

Shirley Jackson's "The Lottery" is fiction; however, many early readers thought it was a true story.

In most cases, commas separate items in a series. However, when one or more of the items in a series already include commas, separate the items with semicolons. This will make the series easier to follow.

Orwell set his works in Paris, France; London, England; and Moulmein, Burma.

Learn When to Use Apostrophes

Apostrophes have two uses: to indicate missing letters in contractions and to show possession or ownership.

- In contractions:

  Amy Chua notes, "I've thought long and hard about how Chinese parents can get away with what they do" (404).

- To show possession:

  Chua's essay lists a number of things her daughters were never allowed to do, including having a playdate, watching TV, and choosing their own extracurricular activities.

NOTE: Be careful not to confuse contractions with similar-sounding possessive pronouns.

CONTRACTION	POSSESSIVE
they're (= they are)	their
it's (= it is, it has)	its
who's (= who is, who has)	whose
you're (= you are)	your

Learn When to Use Quotation Marks

Quotation marks are used to set off quoted speech or writing.

At the end of his essay, E. B. White feels "the chill of death" (194).

Special rules govern the use of other punctuation marks with quotation marks:

- Commas and periods are always placed before quotation marks.
- Colons and semicolons are always placed after quotation marks.
- Question marks and exclamation points can go either before or after quotation marks, depending on whether or not they are part of the quoted material.

Quotation marks are also used to set off the titles of essays ("Once More to the Lake"), stories ("The Lottery"), and poems ("Shall I compare thee to a Summer's day?").

NOTE: Italics are used to set off titles of books, periodicals, and plays: *Life on the Mississippi, College English, Hamlet.*

For information on formatting quotations in research papers, see Chapter 17.

Learn When to Use Dashes and Colons

Dashes are occasionally used to set off and emphasize information within a sentence.

> Jessica Mitford wrote a scathing critique of the funeral industry — and touched off an uproar. Her book *The American Way of Death* was widely read around the world.

Because this usage is somewhat informal, dashes should be used in moderation in your college writing.

Colons are used to introduce lists, examples, and clarifications. A colon should always be preceded by a complete sentence.

> Bich Minh Nguyen feels a sense of nostalgia for the snack cakes of her childhood: "Ho Hos, Ding Dongs, Sno Balls, Zingers, Donettes, Suzy Q's" (170).

For more information on using colons, see the **Grammar in Context** section of Chapter 12 (pages 439–40).

CHECKLIST EDITING FOR PUNCTUATION

- ☐ **Commas** Have you used commas when necessary — and only when necessary?
- ☐ **Semicolons** Have you used semicolons between only grammatically equivalent elements?
- ☐ **Apostrophes** Have you used apostrophes in contractions and possessive nouns and (when necessary) in possessive pronoun forms?
- ☐ **Quotation marks** Have you used quotation marks to set off quoted speech or writing and to set off titles of essays, stories, and poems? Have you used other punctuation correctly with quotation marks?
- ☐ **Dashes and colons** Have you used dashes in moderation? Is every colon that introduces a list, an example, or a clarification preceded by a complete sentence?

Exercise 1

Reread the essay you wrote in Chapters 2 through 4, and edit it for grammar and punctuation.

Exercise 2

Run a grammar check, and then make any additional corrections you think are necessary.

Editing for Sentence Style and Word Choice

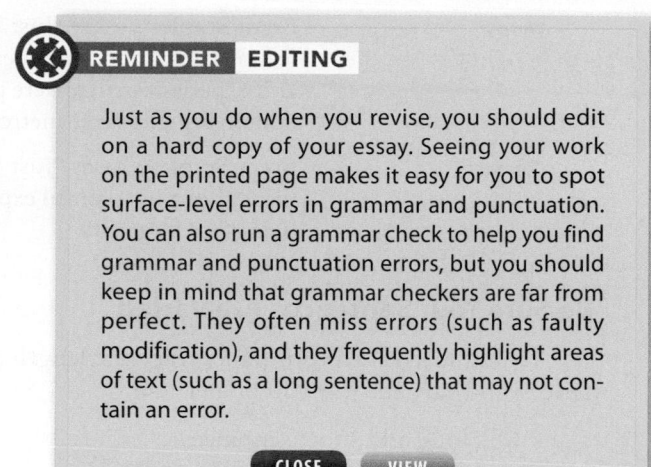

REMINDER EDITING

Just as you do when you revise, you should edit on a hard copy of your essay. Seeing your work on the printed page makes it easy for you to spot surface-level errors in grammar and punctuation. You can also run a grammar check to help you find grammar and punctuation errors, but you should keep in mind that grammar checkers are far from perfect. They often miss errors (such as faulty modification), and they frequently highlight areas of text (such as a long sentence) that may not contain an error.

CLOSE VIEW

As you edit your essay for grammar and punctuation, you should also be looking one last time at how you construct sentences and choose words. So that your essay is as clear, readable, and convincing as possible, your sentences should be not only correct but also concise and varied. In addition, every word should mean exactly what you want it to mean, and your language should be free of clichés.

Eliminate Awkward Phrasing

As you review your essay's sentences, check carefully for awkward phrasing, and do your best to smooth it out.

Awkward: The reason Thomas Jefferson drafted the Declaration of Independence was because he felt the king was a tyrant.

Correct: The reason Thomas Jefferson drafted the Declaration of Independence was that he felt the king was a tyrant.

For more information about this error, see the **Grammar in Context** section of Chapter 10 (page 327).

Awkward: *Patriotism* is when you feel love and support for your country.

Correct: *Patriotism* is a feeling of love and support for one's country.

For more information about this error, see the **Grammar in Context** section of Chapter 13 (pages 487–88).

Be Sure Your Sentences Are Concise

A **concise** sentence is efficient; it is not overloaded with extra words and complicated constructions. To make sentences concise, you need to eliminate repetition and redundancy, delete empty words and expressions, and cut everything that is not absolutely necessary.

Wordy: Brent Staples's essay "Just Walk On By" explores his feelings, thoughts, and ideas about various events and experiences that were painful to him as a black man living in a large metropolitan city.

Concise: Brent Staples's essay "Just Walk On By" explores his ideas about his painful experiences as a black man living in a large city.

Be Sure Your Sentences Are Varied

To add interest to your paper, vary the length and structure of your sentences, and vary the way you open them.

- Mix long and short sentences.

  As time went on, and as he saw people's hostile reactions to him, Brent Staples grew more and more uneasy. Then, he had an idea.

- Mix simple, compound, and complex sentences.

  Simple sentence (*one independent clause*): Staples grew more and more uneasy.

  Compound sentence (*two independent clauses*): Staples grew more and more uneasy, but he stood his ground.

  Complex sentence (*dependent clause, independent clause*): Although Staples grew more and more uneasy, he continued to walk in the neighborhood.

For more information on how to form compound and complex sentences, see the **Grammar in Context** section of Chapter 14 (pages 535–36).

- Vary your sentence openings. Instead of beginning every sentence with the subject (particularly with a pronoun like *he* or *this*), begin some sentences with an introductory word, phrase, or clause that ties it to the preceding sentence.

  Even though many of the details of the incident have been challenged, the 1964 murder of Kitty Genovese, discussed in Martin Gansberg's "Thirty-Eight Who Saw Murder Didn't Call the Police," remains relevant today. For one thing, urban crime remains a problem, particularly for women. Moreover, many people are still reluctant to intervene when they witness a crime. Although more than fifty years have gone by, the story of Kitty Genovese and the people who watched her die still stirs strong emotional responses.

Choose Your Words Carefully

- **Use specific descriptive language**

  Vague: The rain beat upon the roof with a loud noise.

  Specific: "The rain beat upon the low, shingled roof with a force and clatter that threatened to break an entrance and deluge them there" (Chopin 197).

- **Choose words that develop specific supporting examples and explanations**

  Vague: Melany Hunt was eager to change her appearance, but this decision turned out to be a bad thing.

  Specific: Melany Hunt was eager to change her appearance, but she eventually regretted this decision, concluding that the change was a mistake and that "some impulses should definitely be resisted" (271).

- Avoid **clichés**, overused expressions that rely on tired figures of speech.

  Clichés: We were as free as the birds.

  Revised: "We were free like comets in the heavens, and we did whatever our hearts wanted" (Truong 672).

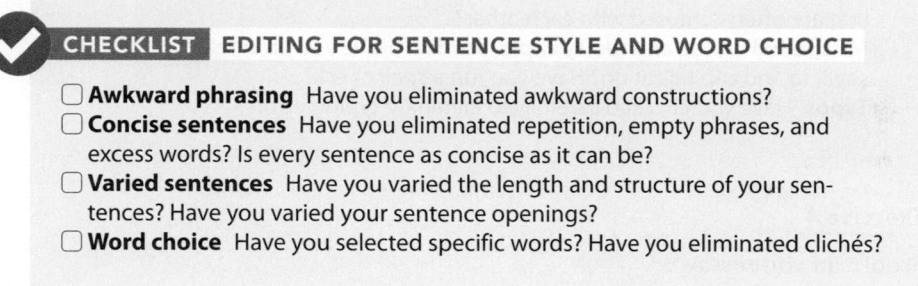

CHECKLIST EDITING FOR SENTENCE STYLE AND WORD CHOICE

- ☐ **Awkward phrasing** Have you eliminated awkward constructions?
- ☐ **Concise sentences** Have you eliminated repetition, empty phrases, and excess words? Is every sentence as concise as it can be?
- ☐ **Varied sentences** Have you varied the length and structure of your sentences? Have you varied your sentence openings?
- ☐ **Word choice** Have you selected specific words? Have you eliminated clichés?

Exercise 3

Check your essay's sentence style and word choice.

Proofreading Your Essay

When you proofread, you check your essay for surface errors, such as commonly confused words, misspellings, faulty capitalization, and incorrect italic use; then, you check for typographical errors.

Check for Commonly Confused Words

Even if you have carefully considered your choice of words during the editing stage, you may have missed some errors. As you proofread, look carefully to see if you can spot any **commonly confused words** – *its* for *it's*, *there* for *their*, or *affect* for *effect*, for example – that a spell check will not catch.

For more information on how to distinguish between *affect* and *effect*, see the **Grammar in Context** section of Chapter 10 (page 327).

Check for Misspellings and Faulty Capitalization

It makes no sense to work hard on an essay and then undermine your credibility with spelling and mechanical errors. If you have any doubt about how a word is spelled or whether or not to capitalize it, check a dictionary (in print or online).

Check for Typos

The last step in the proofreading process is to read carefully and look for typos. Make sure you have spaced correctly between words and have not accidentally typed an extra letter, omitted a letter, or transposed two letters. Reading your essay *backward* — one sentence at a time — will help you focus on individual sentences, which in turn can help you see errors more clearly.

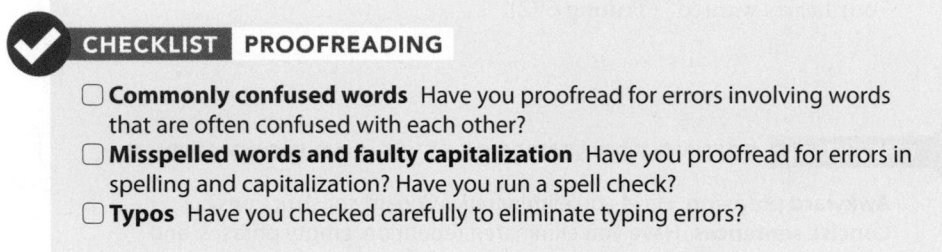

CHECKLIST PROOFREADING

- ☐ **Commonly confused words** Have you proofread for errors involving words that are often confused with each other?
- ☐ **Misspelled words and faulty capitalization** Have you proofread for errors in spelling and capitalization? Have you run a spell check?
- ☐ **Typos** Have you checked carefully to eliminate typing errors?

Exercise 4

Proofread your essay.

LaunchPad

For more practice with editing and proofreading, see the LearningCurve activities in the LaunchPad for *Patterns*.

REMINDER SPELL CHECKERS

You should certainly use the spell check to help you locate misspelled words and incorrect strings of letters caused by typos, but keep in mind that it will not discover every error. For example, it will not identify many misspelled proper nouns or foreign words, nor will it highlight words that are spelled correctly but used incorrectly — *work* for *word* or *form* for *from*, for example. For this reason, you must still proofread carefully — even after reviewing material highlighted by the spell check.

CLOSE VIEW

Checking Your Paper's Format

The final thing to consider is your paper's **format**, or how your paragraphs, sentences, and words look on the page. Your instructor will give you some general guidelines about format — telling you, for example, to type your last name and the page number at the top right of each page — and, of course, you should follow these guidelines. Students writing in the humanities usually follow the format illustrated on page 91. (For information on MLA documentation format, see Chapter 18.)

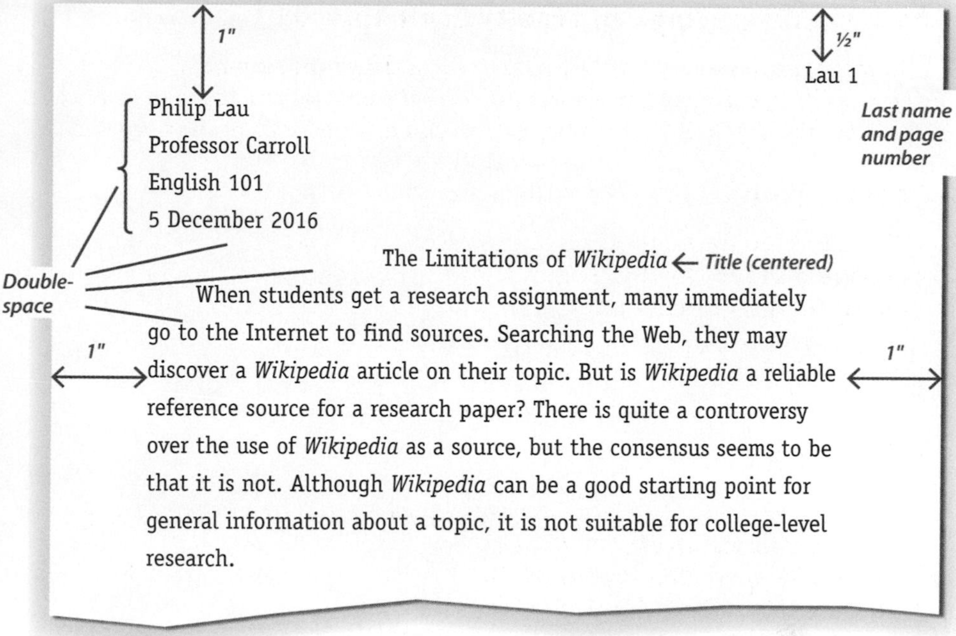
Lau 1

Philip Lau
Professor Carroll
English 101
5 December 2016

The Limitations of *Wikipedia*

When students get a research assignment, many immediately go to the Internet to find sources. Searching the Web, they may discover a *Wikipedia* article on their topic. But is *Wikipedia* a reliable reference source for a research paper? There is quite a controversy over the use of *Wikipedia* as a source, but the consensus seems to be that it is not. Although *Wikipedia* can be a good starting point for general information about a topic, it is not suitable for college-level research.

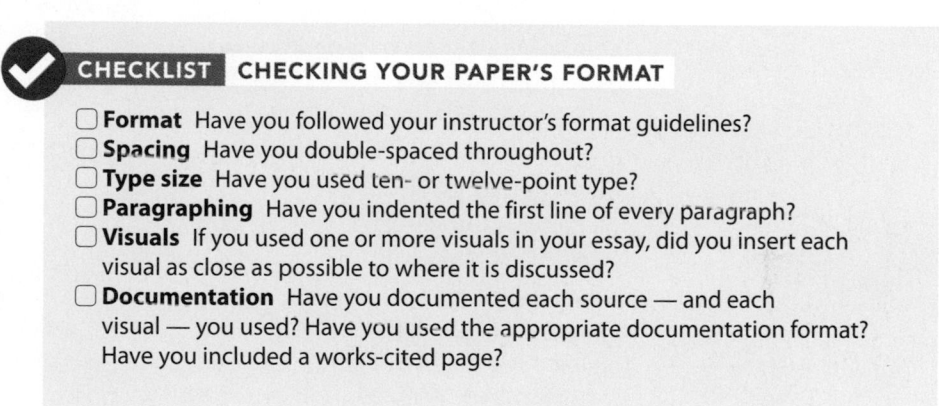

CHECKLIST CHECKING YOUR PAPER'S FORMAT

- ☐ **Format** Have you followed your instructor's format guidelines?
- ☐ **Spacing** Have you double-spaced throughout?
- ☐ **Type size** Have you used ten- or twelve-point type?
- ☐ **Paragraphing** Have you indented the first line of every paragraph?
- ☐ **Visuals** If you used one or more visuals in your essay, did you insert each visual as close as possible to where it is discussed?
- ☐ **Documentation** Have you documented each source — and each visual — you used? Have you used the appropriate documentation format? Have you included a works-cited page?

Exercise 5

Make any necessary corrections to your essay's format, and then submit your final draft.

PART TWO

Readings for Writers

The relationship between reading and writing is a complex one. Sometimes you will write an essay based on your own experience; more often than not, however, you will respond in writing to something you have read. The essays in this book give you a chance to do both.

As you are probably aware, the fact that information appears in print or online does not mean it should be taken at face value. Of course, many of the books and articles you read will be reliable, but some – especially material found on many websites and blogs – will include contradictions, biased ideas, or even inaccurate or misleading information. For this reason, your goal should not be simply to understand what you read but to assess the credibility of the writers and, eventually, to judge the soundness of their ideas.

When you read the essays and other texts in this book, you should approach them critically. In other words, you should question (and sometimes challenge) the writers' ideas and, in the process, try to create new interpretations that you can explore in your writing. Approaching a text in this way is not easy, for it requires you to develop your own analytical and critical skills and your own set of standards to help you judge and interpret what you read. Only after you have read and critically evaluated a text can you begin to draw your ideas together and write about them.

Every reading selection in Chapters 6 through 15 is accompanied by a series of questions intended to guide you through the reading process. In many ways, these questions are a warm-up for the intellectual workout of writing an essay. The more time you devote to them, the more you will be practicing your analytical skills. In a real sense, then, these questions will help you develop the critical thinking skills you will need when you write. In becoming a proficient reader, you will also gain confidence in yourself as a writer.

Each reading selection in Chapters 6 through 14 is organized around one dominant pattern of development. In your outside reading, however, you will often find more than one pattern used in a single piece of writing (as in Chapter 15, Combining the Patterns, page 667). When you write, then, do not think you must follow these patterns blindly; instead, think of them as tools for making your writing more effective, and adapt them to your subject, your audience, and your purpose for writing.

In addition to the reading selections, each chapter also includes a visual text such as a piece of fine art, an advertisement, or a photograph. By visually reinforcing the chapter's basic rhetorical concept, each visual text serves as a bridge to the chapter's essays. Following each visual is a set of questions designed to help you understand not just the image but also the rhetorical pattern that is the chapter's focus.

6

Narration

What Is Narration?

Narration tells a story by presenting events in an orderly, logical sequence. In the following paragraph from "The Stone Horse," essayist Barry Lopez recounts the history of the exploration of the California desert.

Topic sentence

Western man did not enter the California desert until the end of the eighteenth century, 250 years after Coronado brought his soldiers into the Zuni pueblos in a bewildered search for the cities of Cibola. The earliest appraisals of the land were cursory, hurried. People traveled *through* it, en route to Santa Fe or the California coastal settlements.

Narrative traces developments through the nineteenth century

Only miners tarried. In 1823 what had been Spain's became Mexico's, and in 1848 what had been Mexico's became America's; but the bare, jagged mountains and dry lake beds, the vast and uniform plains of creosote bush and yucca plants, remained as obscure as the northern Sudan until the end of the nineteenth century.

Narration can be the dominant pattern in many kinds of writing (as well as in speech). Histories, biographies, and autobiographies have a narrative structure, as do personal letters, diaries, and journals, as well as some personal web pages and posts on blogs and social networking sites. Narration is the dominant pattern in many works of fiction and poetry, and it is an essential part of casual conversation. Narration also underlies folk and fairy tales and many news reports. In fact, anytime you tell what happened, you are using narration.

Using Narration

Narration can provide the structure for an entire essay, but narrative passages may also appear in essays that are not primarily narrative. For example, in an argumentative essay supporting stricter gun-safety legislation, you might devote one or two paragraphs to the story of a child accidentally killed by a handgun. In this chapter, however, we focus on narration as the dominant pattern of a piece of writing.

Throughout your college career, many of your assignments will call for narration. In an English composition class, you may be asked to write about an experience that was important to your development as an adult; on a European history exam, you may need to relate the events that led to Napoleon's defeat at the Battle of Waterloo; and in a technical writing class, you may be asked to write a report tracing a company's negligent actions. In each of these situations (as well as in many additional assignments), your writing has a primarily narrative structure.

The skills you develop in narrative writing will also help you in other kinds of writing. A *process essay,* such as an explanation of a laboratory experiment, is like a narrative because it outlines a series of steps in chronological order; a *cause-and-effect essay,* such as your answer to an exam question that asks you to analyze the events that caused the Great Depression, also resembles a narrative in that it traces a sequence of events. Although a process essay explains how to do something and a cause-and-effect essay explains why events occur, writing both these kinds of essays will be easier after you master narration. (Process essays and cause-and-effect essays are discussed and illustrated in Chapters 9 and 10, respectively.)

Planning a Narrative Essay

Developing a Thesis Statement

Although the purpose of a narrative may be simply to recount events or to create a particular mood or impression, in college writing a narrative essay is more likely to present a sequence of events for the purpose of supporting a thesis. For instance, in a narrative about your problems with credit card debt, your purpose may be to show your readers that college students should not have easy access to credit cards. Accordingly, you do not simply tell the story of your unwise spending. Rather, you select and arrange details to show your readers why having a credit card encouraged you to spend money you didn't have. Although it is usually best to include an explicit **thesis statement** ("My negative experiences with credit have convinced me that college students should not have easy access to credit cards"), you may also imply your thesis through your selection and arrangement of events.

Including Enough Detail

Narratives, like other types of writing, need to include rich, specific details if they are to be convincing. Each detail should help to create a picture for the reader; even exact times, dates, and geographic locations can be helpful. Look, for example, at the following paragraph from the essay "My Mother Never Worked" by Bonnie Smith-Yackel, which appears later in this chapter:

> In the winter she sewed night after night, endlessly, begging cast-off clothing from relatives, ripping apart coats, dresses, blouses, and trousers to remake them to fit her four daughters and son. Every morning and every evening she milked cows, fed pigs and calves, cared for chickens, picked eggs, cooked meals, washed dishes, scrubbed floors, and tended and loved her children. In the

> spring she planted a garden once more, dragging pails of water to nourish and sustain the vegetables for the family. In 1936 she lost a baby in her sixth month.

This list of details adds interest and authenticity to the narrative. The central figure in the narrative is a busy, productive woman, and readers know this because they are given an exhaustive catalog of her activities.

Varying Sentence Structure

When narratives present a long series of events, all the sentences can begin to sound alike: "She sewed dresses. She milked cows. She fed pigs. She fed calves. She cared for chickens." Such a string of sentences may become monotonous for your readers. You can eliminate this monotony by varying your sentence structure – for instance, by using a variety of sentence openings or by combining simple sentences as Smith-Yackel does in "My Mother Never Worked": "In the winter she sewed night after night, endlessly. . . . Every morning and every evening she milked cows, fed pigs and calves, cared for chickens. . . ."

Maintaining Clear Narrative Order

Many narratives present events in the exact order in which they occurred, moving from first event to last. Whether or not you follow a strict **chronological order** depends on the purpose of your narrative. If you are writing a straightforward account of a historical event or summarizing a record of poor management practices, you will probably want to move directly from beginning to end. In a personal-experience essay or a fictional narrative, however, you may want to engage your readers' interest by beginning with an event from the middle of your story, or even from the end, and then presenting the events that led up to it. You may also decide to begin in the present and then use one or more **flashbacks** (shifts into the past) to tell your story. To help readers follow the order of events in your narrative, it is very important to use correct verb tenses and clear transitional words and phrases.

Using Correct Verb Tenses. Verb tense is extremely important in writing that recounts events in a fixed order because tenses indicate temporal (time) relationships. When you write a narrative, you should be careful to keep verb tenses consistent and accurate so that your readers can follow the sequence of events. Naturally, you need to shift tenses to reflect an actual time shift in your narrative. For instance, convention requires that you use present tense when discussing works of literature ("When Hamlet's mother *marries* his uncle . . ."), but a flashback to an earlier point in the story calls for a shift from present to past tense ("Before his mother's marriage, Hamlet *was* . . ."). Nevertheless, you should avoid unwarranted shifts in verb tense; they will make your narrative confusing.

Using Transitions. Transitions – connecting words or phrases – help link events in time, enabling narratives to flow smoothly. Without them, narratives would lack coherence, and readers would be unsure of the correct sequence of events. Transitions indicate the order of events, and they also signal shifts in time. In narrative writing, the transitions commonly used for these purposes include *first, second, next, then, later, at the same time, meanwhile, immediately, soon, before, earlier, after, afterward, now,* and *finally*. In addition to transitional words and phrases, specific time markers – such as *three years later, in 1927, after two hours,* and *on January 3* – indicate how much time has passed between events. (A more complete list of transitions appears on page 55.)

Structuring a Narrative Essay

Like other essays, a **narrative** essay has an introduction, a body, and a conclusion. If your essay's thesis is explicitly stated, it will, in most cases, appear in the **introduction**. The **body paragraphs** of your essay will recount the events that make up your narrative, following a clear and orderly plan. Finally, the **conclusion** will give your readers the sense that your narrative is complete, perhaps by restating your thesis in different words or by summarizing key points or events.

Suppose you are assigned to write a short history paper about the Battle of Waterloo. You plan to support the thesis that if Napoleon had kept more troops in reserve, he might have defeated the British troops serving under Wellington. Based on this thesis, you decide that the best way to organize your paper is to present the five major phases of the battle in chronological order. An informal outline of your essay might look like the one that follows.

SAMPLE OUTLINE: Narration

INTRODUCTION
(thesis statement)

If Napoleon had kept more troops in reserve, he might have broken Wellington's line with another infantry attack and thus won the Battle of Waterloo.

POINT 1
(support of thesis)

Phase 1 of the battle: Napoleon attacked the Château of Hougoumont.

POINT 2
(support for thesis)

Phase 2 of the battle: the French infantry attacked the British lines.

POINT 3
(support for thesis)

Phase 3 of the battle: the French cavalry staged a series of charges against the British lines that had not been attacked before; Napoleon committed his reserves.

POINT 4
(support for thesis)
Phase 4 of the battle: the French captured La Haye Sainte, their first success of the day but an advantage that Napoleon, having committed troops elsewhere, could not maintain without reserves.

POINT 5
(support for thesis)
Phase 5 of the battle: the French infantry was decisively defeated by the combined thrust of the British infantry and the remaining British cavalry.

CONCLUSION
Restatement of thesis (in different words) or review of key points or events

By discussing the five phases of the battle in chronological order, you clearly support your thesis. As you expand your informal outline into a historical narrative, exact details, dates, times, and geographic locations are extremely important. Without them, your statements are open to question. In addition, to keep your readers aware of the order of events, you must select appropriate transitional words and phrases and pay careful attention to verb tenses.

Revising a Narrative Essay

When you revise a narrative essay, consider the items on the revision checklist on page 66. In addition, pay special attention to the items on the following checklist, which apply specifically to narrative essays.

REVISION CHECKLIST NARRATION

- ☐ Does your assignment call for narration?
- ☐ Does your essay's thesis communicate the significance of the events you discuss?
- ☐ Have you included enough specific detail?
- ☐ Have you varied your sentence structure?
- ☐ Have you made the order of events clear to readers?
- ☐ Have you varied sentence openings and combined short sentences to avoid monotony?
- ☐ Do your transitions indicate the order of events and signal shifts in time?

Editing a Narrative Essay

When you edit your narrative essay, follow the guidelines on the editing checklists on pages 83, 86, and 89. In addition, focus on the grammar, mechanics, and punctuation issues that are particularly relevant to narrative essays. One of these issues — avoiding run-on sentences — is discussed next.

GRAMMAR IN CONTEXT AVOIDING RUN-ONS

When writing narrative essays, particularly personal narratives and essays that include dialogue, writers can easily lose sight of sentence boundaries and create **run-ons**. There are two kinds of run-ons: *fused sentences* and *comma splices,* and both should be avoided.

A **fused sentence** occurs when two sentences are incorrectly joined without punctuation.

CORRECT (TWO SENTENCES):	"The sun came out hot and bright, endlessly, day after day. The crops shriveled and died" (Smith-Yackel 124).
INCORRECT (FUSED SENTENCE):	The sun came out hot and bright, endlessly, day after day the crops shriveled and died.

A **comma splice** occurs when two sentences are incorrectly joined with just a comma.

INCORRECT (COMMA SPLICE):	The sun came out hot and bright, endlessly, day after day, the crops shriveled and died.

Five Ways to Correct These Errors

1. **Use a period to create two separate sentences.**

   The sun came out hot and bright, endlessly, day after day. The crops shriveled and died.

2. **Join the sentences with a comma and a coordinating conjunction (*and, or, nor, for, so, but, yet*).**

   The sun came out hot and bright, endlessly, day after day, and the crops shriveled and died.

3. **Join the sentences with a semicolon.**

   The sun came out hot and bright, endlessly, day after day; the crops shriveled and died.

4. **Join the sentences with a semicolon and a transitional word or phrase (followed by a comma), such as *however, therefore,* or *for example.* (See page 55 for a list of transitional words and phrases.)**

   The sun came out hot and bright, endlessly, day after day; eventually, the crops shriveled and died.

5. **Create a complex sentence by adding a subordinating conjunction (*although, because, if,* and so on) or a relative pronoun (*who, which, that,* and so on) to one of the sentences.**

   As the sun came out hot and bright, endlessly, day after day, the crops shriveled and died.

LaunchPad

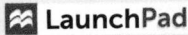

For more practice on avoiding run-ons, see the LearningCurve on Run-Ons and Comma Splices in the LaunchPad for *Patterns*.

EDITING CHECKLIST NARRATION

- ☐ Have you avoided run-ons?
- ☐ Do your verb tenses clearly indicate time relationships between events?
- ☐ Have you avoided unnecessary tense shifts?
- ☐ If you use dialogue, have you punctuated correctly and capitalized where necessary?

A STUDENT WRITER: Literacy Narrative

In the following essay, student Erica Sarno traces her development as a writer. Her assignment was to write a **literacy narrative**, a personal account focusing on her experiences with reading and writing.

Becoming a Writer

Introduction

1 I used to think that writing was just about filling pages. Composing an essay for school meant getting the job done and checking it off my to-do list. During my last two years of high school, however, my attitude started to change. Several experiences helped me understand that writing is not a skill that some people are born with and others are not. I learned that if I wanted to write, all I needed were a desire to express myself to others and a willing audience.

Thesis statement

Realizing that there was someone on the other side of the page, eager to listen, helped me develop into a more effective writer.

Narrative begins (junior year)

2 My first real lesson in my development as a writer took place in Mrs. Strickland's junior English class. Mrs. Strickland was hard to approach. She dressed as if she expected to be giving a press conference at the White House. She wore conservative suits and silk scarves, and she had a helmet of dyed blonde hair. We seemed to disappoint her just because we were high school students. Maybe I saw her lack of interest in us and our work as a challenge because, one day, I took a risk and wrote a very personal essay about losing my aunt to cancer. When I got the paper back, Mrs. Strickland had written only, "Did you read the instructions?" I could not believe it. For the first time, I had actually written about what was important to me rather than just filling the pages with words, and she had not even read past my introduction! Still, I knew that I had something to say. I just needed someone to listen.

Narrative continues (senior year)

3 The next year, I had Dr. Kelleher for senior English. My year with Dr. K profoundly changed the way I see myself as a writer (and as

a reader). Finally, a teacher was paying attention to what I had written. His only rule for writing was "Don't be boring!" I rewrote sentences, hoping for an exclamation point or one of Dr. K's other special marks in the margin. Dr. K had a whole list of codes and abbreviations, like "BTH" ("Better than Hemingway") or "the knife" (when the writer slayed the opponent in an argument). I also relied on Dr. K to tell me when I was falling into my old habit of just filling the page. He would write a funny comment like, "Come back! Log out of Facebook!" Then, he would give me a chance to try again. Trusting him to be a generous reader and an honest critic helped me develop my voice and my confidence as a writer.

Narrative shifts to focus on reading

Meanwhile, I started to become a better reader, too. I could tell when a writer was writing to me, wanting me to understand. I could also tell when a writer was writing just to get the job done. Instead of just skimming the assigned reading, I got in the habit of writing in the margins and making notes about what I thought. I underlined ideas that spoke to me, and I wrote "Really??" next to ideas that seemed silly. Instead of assuming that an assigned reading would be boring, I gave every assignment a chance. Whether I liked a book or not, I felt that I could explain my reasons. I was finally seeing for myself that writing is just another way for people to talk to each other. 4

Narrative moves outside the classroom

Eventually, in the spring of my senior year, I experienced what it feels like to connect with a broader audience. I suggested a series of columns about "senioritis" to the school paper, and even though I had never written for the public before, the editor loved my idea. I knew what I wanted to say, and I knew I could collect plenty of stories to help me illustrate my ideas. What I did not predict was how much I would learn from the experience of writing those six columns. Knowing that hundreds of people would be reading my pieces, I revised them over and over again. When Dr. K read one of my last columns aloud to our class, I got to see how my work affected people. Watching the expressions on my classmates' faces and hearing them laugh at the funny parts helped me understand the power of good writing. In that moment, I truly connected with my audience. 5

Conclusion

Although I still have a lot to learn, I now understand how important the relationship between the writer and the reader is. When I write, I am writing to be heard. When I read, I am reading to understand. The communication may not be perfect, but I know I am not alone in my task. And even though I am not in Dr. K's class 6 anymore, I still sometimes imagine that he will be reading what I have written. Thinking about him reminds me that someone cares about what I have to say.

Points for Special Attention

Assignment. Erica's assignment was to write a literacy narrative. At first, she considered writing about her favorite childhood books or about how she learned to read, but in the end she decided to focus on more recent experiences because she could remember them more clearly (and therefore could include more specific detail).

Thesis Statement. Because her focus was on her development as a writer, Erica was careful to include the words *develop* and *writer* in her thesis statement. Her thesis statement also clearly explains the key factor that encouraged her development – the presence of an interested reader.

Structure. In her essay's first two body paragraphs, Erica discusses her junior and senior English classes. Instead of just contrasting the two teachers, however, she explains how she herself changed as a result of their different approaches. In paragraph 4, she explains the connection between her reading and her writing, and in paragraph 5, she recounts her development into someone writing for a wider audience.

Topic Sentences. To move her narrative along, Erica was careful to include transitional words and phrases – *The next year, Meanwhile, Eventually* – in her topic sentences to show the movement from one stage of her development to the next.

Working with Sources. Erica's assignment made it clear that although other assignments in the course would be source-based, this narrative essay was to be based solely on her own memories and reflections.

Focus on Revision

When she reread an early draft of her essay, Erica immediately saw a problem: she had written a comparison-and-contrast essay instead of a narrative. Instead of focusing on her development as a writer, she had simply compared her junior- and senior-year English classes. This problem was revealed by her draft's thesis statement – "The difference between junior and senior year of high school was the difference between being ignored and being heard" – as well as by the topic sentences of her first two body paragraphs:

First body paragraph: Mrs. Strickland was an uninspiring teacher.

Second body paragraph: Unlike Mrs. Strickland, Dr. Kelleher encouraged me as a writer.

Erica also noticed that her entire essay dealt with classroom style, further highlighting the contrast between her two teachers. Realizing that her development as a writer had also taken place outside the classroom, she condensed her discussion of the two English classes and added material about reading (paragraph 4) and about writing for her school paper (paragraph 5).

When she wrote her next draft, Erica was careful to include transitions and topic sentences that signaled her focus on her development over time, not on the differences between two classes or two teachers. Finally, as she reviewed her draft, she realized that her original summary statement – "Knowing that there was someone on the other side of the page made me a better writer" – could be expanded into an appropriate and effective thesis statement.

A STUDENT WRITER: Narration

The following essay is typical of the informal narrative writing many students are asked to do in English composition classes. It was written by Tiffany Forte in response to the assignment "Write an informal essay about a goal or dream you had when you were a child."

My Field of Dreams

Introduction

When I was young, I was told that when I grew up I could be anything I wanted to be, and I always took for granted that this was true. I knew exactly what I was going to be, and I would spend hours dreaming about how wonderful my life would be when I grew up. One day, though, when I did grow up, I realized that things had not turned out the way I had always expected they would. 1

Thesis statement

Narrative begins

When I was little, I never played with baby dolls or Barbies. I was the only girl in the neighborhood where I lived, so I always played with boys. We would play army or football or (my favorite) baseball. 2

Almost every summer afternoon, all the boys in my neighborhood and I would meet by the big oak tree to get a baseball game going. Surprisingly, I was always one of the first to be picked for a team. I was very fast, and (for my size) I could hit the ball far. I loved baseball more than anything, and I wouldn't miss a game for the world. 3

My dad played baseball too, and every Friday night I would go to the field with my mother to watch him play. It was just like the big leagues, with lots of people, a snack bar, and lights that shone so high and bright you could see them a mile away. I loved my dad's games. When all the other kids would wander off and play, I would sit and cheer on my dad and his team. My attention was focused on the field, and my heart would jump with every pitch. 4

Even more exciting than my dad's games were the major league games. The Phillies were my favorite team, and I always looked forward to watching them on television. My dad would make popcorn, and we would sit and watch in anticipation of a Phillies victory. We would go wild, yelling and screaming at all the big plays. When the Phillies would win, I would be so excited I couldn't sleep; when they would lose, I would go to bed angry, just like my dad. 5

Key experience introduced (pars. 6–7)

It was when my dad took me to my first Phillies game that I decided I wanted to be a major league baseball player. The excitement began when we pulled into the parking lot of the old Veterans Stadium. There were thousands of cars. As we walked from the car to the stadium, my dad told me to hold on to his hand and not to let go no matter what. When we gave the man our tickets and entered the stadium, I understood why. There were mobs of people everywhere. They were walking around the stadium and standing in long lines for hot dogs, beer, and souvenirs. It was the most wonderful thing I had ever seen. When we got to our seats, I looked down at the tiny baseball diamond below and felt as if I were on top of the world. 6

The cheering of the crowd, the singing, and the chants were almost more than I could stand. I was bursting with excitement. Then, in the bottom of the eighth inning, with the score tied and two outs, Mike Schmidt came up to bat and hit the game-winning home run. The crowd went crazy. Everyone in the whole stadium was standing, and I found myself yelling and screaming along with everyone else. When Mike Schmidt came out of the dugout to receive his standing ovation, I felt a lump in my throat and butterflies in my stomach. He was everyone's hero that night, and I could only imagine the pride he must have felt. I slept the whole way home and dreamed of what it would be like to be the hero of the game. 7

Narrative continues

The next day, when I met with the boys at the oak tree, I told them that when I grew up, I was going to be a major league baseball player. They all laughed at me and said I could never be a baseball player because I was a girl. I told them that they were all wrong and that I would show them. 8

Analysis of childhood experiences

In the years to follow, I played girls' softball in a competitive fast-pitch league, and I was very good. I always wanted to play baseball with the boys, but there were no mixed leagues. After a few years, I realized that the boys from the oak tree were right: I was never going to be a major league baseball player. I realized that what I had been told when I was younger wasn't the whole truth. What no 9 one had bothered to tell me was that I could be anything I wanted to be — as long as it was something that was appropriate for a girl to do.

Conclusion

In time, I would get over the loss of my dream. I found new dreams, acceptable for a young woman, and I moved on to other things. Still, every time I watch a baseball game and someone hits a home run, I get those same butterflies in my stomach and think, for just a minute, about what might have been. 10

Points for Special Attention

Assignment. Tiffany's assignment was to write about a goal or dream she had when she was a child. As a nontraditional student, a good deal older than most of her classmates, Tiffany found this assignment challenging at first. She wondered if her childhood dreams would be different from those of her classmates, and she was somewhat hesitant to share her drafts with her peer-editing group. As it turned out, though, her childhood dreams were not very different from those of the other students in her class.

Introduction. Tiffany's introduction is straightforward, yet it arouses reader interest by setting up a contrast between what she expected and what actually happened. Her optimistic expectation – that she could be anything she wanted to be – is contradicted by her thesis statement, encouraging readers to read on to learn how things turned out and why.

Thesis Statement. Although the assignment called for a personal narrative, the instructor made it clear that the essay should have an explicitly stated thesis that made a point about a childhood goal or dream. Tiffany knew she wanted to write about her passion for baseball, but she also knew that just listing a series of events would not fulfill the assignment. Her thesis statement – "One day, though, when I did grow up, I realized that things had not turned out the way I had always expected they would" – puts her memories in context, suggesting that she will use them to support a general conclusion about the gap between dreams and reality.

Structure. The body of Tiffany's essay traces the chronology of her involvement with baseball – playing with the neighborhood boys, watching her father's games, watching baseball on television, and, finally, attending her first major league game. Each body paragraph introduces a different aspect of her experience with baseball, culminating in the vividly described Phillies game. The balance of the essay (paragraphs 8–10) summarizes the aftermath of that game, gives a brief overview of Tiffany's later years in baseball, and presents her conclusion.

Detail. Personal narratives like Tiffany's need a lot of detail because the writers want readers to see, hear, and feel what they did. To present an accurate picture, Tiffany includes all the significant sights and sounds she can remember: the big oak tree, the lights on the field, the popcorn, the excited cheers, the food and souvenir stands, the crowds, and so on. She also names Mike Schmidt ("everyone's hero"), his team, and the stadium where she saw him play. Despite all these details, though, she omits some important information – for example, how old she was at each stage of her essay.

Working with Sources. Tiffany's essay is very personal, and she supports her thesis with experiences and observations from her own childhood. Although she could have consulted sources to find specific information about team standings or players' stats – or even quoted her hero, Mike Schmidt – she decided that her own memories would provide convincing support for her thesis.

Verb Tense. Maintaining clear chronological order is very important in narrative writing, where unwarranted shifts in verb tenses can confuse readers. Knowing this, Tiffany was careful to avoid unnecessary tense shifts. In her conclusion, she shifts from past to present tense, but this shift is both necessary and clear. Elsewhere she uses *would* to identify events that recurred regularly. For example, in paragraph 5 she says, "My dad *would* make popcorn" rather than "My dad *made* popcorn," which would have suggested that he did so only once.

Transitions. Tiffany's skillful use of transitional words and expressions links her sentences and moves her readers smoothly through her essay. In addition to transitional words such as *when* and *then,* she uses specific time markers – "When I was little," "Almost every summer afternoon," "every Friday night," "As we walked," "The next day," "In the years to follow," and "After a few years" – to advance the narrative and carry her readers along.

Focus on Revision

In their responses to an earlier draft of Tiffany's essay, several students in her peer-editing group recommended that she revise one particularly monotonous paragraph. (As one student pointed out, all its sentences began with the subject, making the paragraph seem choppy and its ideas disconnected.) Here is the paragraph from her draft:

> My dad played baseball too. I went to the field with my mother every Friday night to watch him play. It was just like the big leagues. There were lots of people and a snack bar. The lights shone so high and bright you could see them a mile away. I loved my dad's games. All the other kids would wander off and play. I would sit and cheer on my dad and his team. My attention was focused on the field. My heart would jump with every pitch.

In the revised version of the paragraph (now paragraph 4 of her essay), Tiffany varies sentence length and opening strategies:

> My dad played baseball too, and every Friday night I would go to the field with my mother to watch him play. It was just like the big leagues, with

> lots of people, a snack bar, and lights that shone so high and bright you could see them a mile away. I loved my dad's games. When all the other kids would wander off and play, I would sit and cheer on my dad and his team. My attention was focused on the field, and my heart would jump with every pitch.

After reading Tiffany's revised draft, another student suggested that she might still polish her essay a bit. For instance, she could add some dialogue, quoting the boys' taunts and her own reply in paragraph 8. She could also revise to eliminate **clichés** (overused expressions), substituting fresher, more original language for phrases such as "I felt a lump in my throat and butterflies in my stomach" and "felt as if I were on top of the world." In the next draft of her essay, Tiffany followed up on these suggestions.

PEER-EDITING WORKSHEET NARRATION

1. What point is the writer making about the essay's subject? Is this point explicitly stated in a thesis statement? If so, where? If not, can you state the essay's thesis in one sentence?
2. List some details that enrich the narrative. Where could more detail be added? What kind of detail? Be specific.
3. Does the writer vary sentence structure and avoid monotonous strings of similar sentences? Should any sentences be combined? If so, which ones? Can you suggest different openings for any sentences?
4. Should any transitions be added to clarify the order in which events occurred? If so, where?
5. Do verb tenses establish a clear chronological order? Identify any verb tenses you believe need to be changed.
6. Does the writer avoid run-on sentences? Point out any fused sentences or comma splices.
7. What could the writer *add* to this essay?
8. What could the writer *delete* from this essay?
9. What is the essay's greatest strength? Why?
10. What is the essay's greatest weakness? What steps should the writer take to correct this problem?

The selections that follow illustrate some of the many possibilities open to writers of narrative essays. The first selection, a visual text, is followed by questions designed to illustrate how narration can operate in visual form.

MARJANE SATRAPI

from *Persepolis II* (Graphic Fiction)*

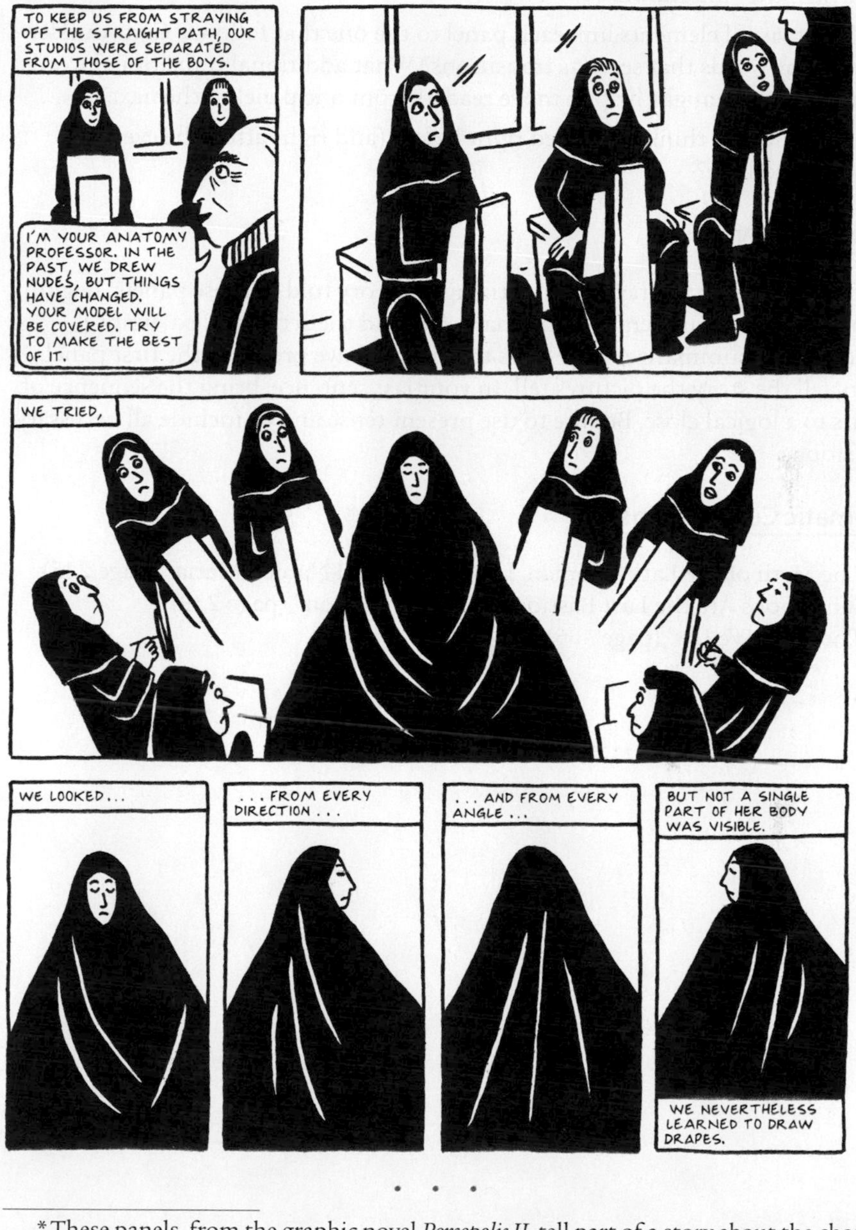

• • •

*These panels, from the graphic novel *Persepolis II,* tell part of a story about the changes in the life of a young girl during Iran's Islamic revolution. In 1979, the secular monarch was overthrown, and a government run by Islamic religious leaders instituted new rules, including extreme regulations on how women could dress.

continued

Reading Images

1. Look carefully at the panels on page 109, and read the footnote that appears below them. Then, list the events depicted in the panels in the order in which they are shown.
2. What visual elements link each panel to the one that follows? Can you identify any words that serve as transitions? What additional transitional words and phrases might help to move readers from one panel to the next?
3. What do you think happened right before (and right after) the events depicted here?

Journal Entry

Write a narrative paragraph summarizing the story told in these panels. Begin with a sentence that identifies the characters and the setting. Next, write a sentence that summarizes the events that might have preceded the first panel. Then, tell the story the pictures tell. In your last sentence, bring the sequence of events to a logical close. Be sure to use present tense and to include all necessary transitions.

Thematic Connections

- "The Myth of the Latin Woman: I Just Met a Girl Named Maria" (page 225)
- "Why Looks Are the Last Bastion of Discrimination" (page 239)
- "The Ways We Lie" (page 466)

JUNOT DÍAZ

The Money

Born in the Dominican Republic in 1968 and raised in New Jersey, Junot Díaz earned his bachelor's degree from Rutgers University and an M.F.A. in creative writing from Cornell University. He is the author of several works of fiction, including *Drown* (1996), *The Brief Wondrous Life of Oscar Wao* (2007), and *This Is How You Lose Her* (2012). The winner of many awards, including a Pulitzer Prize and MacArthur and Guggenheim Fellowships, Díaz is the fiction editor at *Boston Review* and the Rudge and Nancy Allen Professor of Writing at the Massachusetts Institute of Technology.

Background on Dominicans in the United States Dominicans living in the United States account for 3 percent of the U.S. Hispanic population; they numbered about 1.5 million when the Census Bureau made its American Community Survey in 2011. For many years, the Northeast has been home to the majority of Dominicans in the United States. Although historically almost half settled in New York City, in recent years they have established sizable populations in several other northeastern states, such as New Jersey, Massachusetts, and Pennsylvania. Dominicans living in the United States are significantly more likely to have been born outside the United States, as Díaz was, than the general Hispanic population (56 percent versus 36 percent). The Dominican population also has a slightly higher poverty rate compared to all Hispanics; however, it can also claim a higher level of education. Dominicans have had an impact on American food, music, and culture, and they are an integral part of social and commercial life in the United States, where they are teachers, bankers, lawyers, small business owners, entrepreneurs, and workers. With a long history of activism, Dominicans have also begun to wield political influence as elected officials in U.S. state, city, and local governments.

All the Dominicans I knew in those days sent money home. My mother didn't have a regular job besides caring for us five kids, so she scrimped the loot together from whatever came her way. My father was always losing his forklift jobs, so it wasn't like she ever had a steady flow. But my grandparents were alone in Santo Domingo, and those remittances, beyond material support, were a way, I suspect, for Mami to negotiate the absence, the distance, caused by our diaspora. She chipped dollars off the cash Papi gave her for our daily expenses, forced our already broke family to live even broker. That was how she built the nut — two, maybe three hundred dollars — that she sent home every six months or so. 1

We kids knew where the money was hidden, but we also knew that to touch it would have meant a violent punishment approaching death. I, who 2 could take the change out of my mother's purse without thinking, couldn't have brought myself even to look at that forbidden stash.

So what happened? Exactly what you'd think. The summer I was twelve, 3
my family went away on a "vacation" – one of my father's half-baked get-to-know-our-country-better-by-sleeping-in-the-van extravaganzas – and when we returned to Jersey, exhausted, battered, we found our front door unlocked. My parents' room, which was where the thieves had concentrated their search, looked as if it had been tornado-tossed. The thieves had kept it simple; they'd snatched a portable radio, some of my Dungeons & Dragons hardcovers, and, of course, Mami's remittances.

It's not as if the robbery came as a huge 4
surprise. In our neighborhood, cars and apartments were always getting jacked, and the kid stupid enough to leave a bike unattended for more than a tenth of a second was the kid who was never going to see that bike again. Everybody got hit; no matter who you were, eventually it would be your turn.

"Everybody got hit; no matter who you were, eventually it would be your turn."

And that summer it was ours. 5

Still, we took the burglary pretty hard. When you're a recent immigrant, 6
it's easy to feel targeted. Like it wasn't just a couple of assholes that had it in for you but the whole neighborhood – hell, maybe the whole country.

No one took the robbery as hard as my mom, though. She cursed the 7
neighborhood, she cursed the country, she cursed my father, and of course she cursed us kids, swore that we had run our gums to our idiot friends and they had done it.

And this is where the tale should end, right? Wasn't as if there was going 8
to be any "C.S.I."-style investigation or anything. Except that a couple of days later I was moaning about the robbery to these guys I was hanging with at that time and they were cursing sympathetically, and out of nowhere it struck me. You know when you get one of those moments of mental clarity? When the nictitating membrane* obscuring the world suddenly lifts? That's what happened. I realized that these two dopes I called my friends had done it. They were shaking their heads, mouthing all the right words, but I could see the way they looked at each other, the Raskolnikov glances. I *knew*.

Now, it wasn't like I could publicly denounce these dolts or go to the 9
police. That would have been about as useless as crying. Here's what I did: I asked the main dope to let me use his bathroom (we were in front of his apartment) and while I pretended to piss I unlatched the window. Then we all headed to the park as usual, but I pretended that I'd forgotten something back home. Ran to the dope's apartment, slid open the bathroom window, and in broad daylight wriggled my skinny ass in.

Where the hell did I get these ideas? I have not a clue. I guess I was reading 10
way too much Encyclopedia Brown and the Three Investigators in those days.

---

* Eds. note – Transparent inner eyelid found in birds, reptiles, and some mammals.

And if mine had been a normal neighborhood this is when the cops would have been called and my ass would have been caught *burglarizing*.

The dolt and his family had been in the U.S. all their lives and they had a ton of stuff, a TV in every room, but I didn't have to do much searching. I popped up the dolt's mattress and underneath I found my D.&D. books and most of my mother's money. He had thoughtfully kept it in the same envelope. 11

And that was how I solved the Case of the Stupid Morons. My one and only case. 12

The next day at the park, the dolt announced that someone had broken into *his* apartment and stolen all his savings. This place is full of thieves, he complained bitterly, and I was, like, No kidding. 13

It took me two days to return the money to my mother. The truth was I was seriously considering keeping it. But in the end the guilt got to me. I guess I was expecting my mother to run around with joy, to crown me her favorite son, to cook me my favorite meal. Nada. I'd wanted a party or at least to see her happy, but there was nothing. Just two hundred and some dollars and fifteen hundred or so miles – that's all there was. 14

• • •

Comprehension

1. Díaz grew up poor. How does he communicate this fact to readers?
2. According to Díaz, why is the money in his mother's "forbidden stash" (2) different from the money in her purse? Do you think this distinction makes sense?
3. How did Díaz solve "the Case of the Stupid Morons" (12)?
4. What does Díaz mean when he says, "Just two hundred and some dollars and fifteen hundred or so miles – that's all there was" (14)?
5. In paragraph 6, Díaz says, "When you're a recent immigrant, it's easy to feel targeted"; in paragraph 9, he states matter-of-factly that going to the police was not an option for him. What relationship, if any, do you see between these two statements?

Purpose and Audience

1. Even though Díaz uses a very informal style, full of slang expressions, he also uses words like *diaspora* (1) and expressions like "Raskolnikov glances" (8). What does the use of such language tell you about him – and about how he sees his audience?
2. This essay does not have a stated thesis. What is Díaz's main idea? Write a sentence that could serve as a thesis statement. Where in the essay could this sentence be added? *Should* such a sentence be added? Why or why not?
3. Does this essay have a persuasive purpose, or is Díaz just trying to share his memories with readers? Explain.

Style and Structure

1. Identify the one- and two-sentence paragraphs in this essay. Are these very brief paragraphs effective as they are, or should they be expanded or combined with other paragraphs? Explain.
2. This is a personal, informal essay, and it uses first person and contractions. It also includes a number of fragments. Identify a few fragments, and try to turn each one into a complete sentence. Then, explain why you think Díaz used each fragment.
3. In paragraphs 3, 8, and 10, Díaz asks **rhetorical questions**. How would you answer these questions?
4. **Vocabulary Project.** What words, besides *morons,* does Díaz use to describe the thieves? Which word seems most appropriate to you? Why?
5. Like a crime story, Díaz's narrative moves readers through events from the crime itself to its effect to its final outcome. Identify each of these sections of the narrative.

Journal Entry

Do you think Díaz feels more angry at the "morons" or at himself? Does he also feel frustration? Disappointment? If so, with whom (or what)?

Writing Workshop

1. Díaz mentions Encyclopedia Brown and the Three Investigators, fictional young detectives whose adventures he followed. When you were young, what was as important to you as these fictional characters were to Díaz? In a narrative essay, trace the development of your fascination with a particular fictional character, pastime, or hobby.
2. When he returns the money to his mother, Díaz expects "a party or at least to see her happy" (14), but that isn't the reaction he gets. Write a narrative essay about a time when you expected a particular reaction or outcome but were disappointed or surprised.
3. **Working with Sources.** Consult several dictionaries to find out what the term *diaspora* has meant throughout history. Then, write a narrative essay tracing your own family's diaspora, focusing on your family's movement from one country, region, or neighborhood to another. Include a definition from one of the dictionaries you consult, and be sure to include parenthetical documentation and a works-cited page. (See Chapter 18 for information on MLA documentation.)

Combining the Patterns

Díaz discusses both his family's life in a Dominican neighborhood in New Jersey and his relatives' lives back in Santo Domingo. If he wanted to write a **comparison-and-contrast** paragraph comparing his life to his relatives', what details might he include? Do you think he should add such a paragraph? If so, why – and where?

Thematic Connections

- "Indian Education" (page 140)
- "The Ways We Lie" (page 466)
- "Tortillas" (page 500)

OCEAN VUONG

Surrendering

Poet, fiction writer, and essayist Ocean Vuong was born in Ho Chi Minh City (Saigon), Vietnam, in 1988 and immigrated with his family to the United States in 1990. He received his B.A. in English from Brooklyn College. Vuong's writing has appeared in many publications, including the *New Yorker, New Republic, Kenyon Review,* and the *American Poetry Review*. His 2016 book of poems *Night Sky with Exit Wounds* won the 2016 Whiting Award. Among Vuong's many other awards and honors are a Pushcart Prize and the Stanley Kunitz Prize for Younger Poets.

Background on National Poetry Month In this narrative, Vuong writes about a specific assignment that affected his relationship with the English language and spurred his development as a writer: "One early-spring afternoon, when I was in fourth grade, we got an assignment in language-arts class: we had two weeks to write a poem in honor of National Poetry Month." In 1996, following the model of Black History Month in February and Women's History Month in March, the Academy of American Poets (AAP) established April as National Poetry Month. President Bill Clinton proclaimed, "National Poetry Month offers us a welcome opportunity to celebrate not only the unsurpassed body of literature produced by our poets in the past, but also the vitality and diversity of voices reflected in the works of today's American poetry." From the beginning, the AAP sought to bring poetry into classrooms through lesson plans, curricular material, and assignments such as the one Vuong describes. While many have lauded the annual celebration, it also has its detractors. For example, the poet and critic Charles Bernstein has written: "National Poetry Month is about making poetry safe for readers by promoting examples of the art form at its most bland and its most morally 'positive.' The message is: Poetry is good for you. But, unfortunately, promoting poetry as if it were an 'easy listening' station just reinforces the idea that poetry is culturally irrelevant."

1 Reading and writing, like any other crafts, come to the mind slowly, in pieces. But for me, as an E.S.L. student from a family of illiterate rice farmers, who saw reading as snobby, or worse, the experience of working through a book, even one as simple as "Where the Wild Things Are," was akin to standing in quicksand, your loved ones corralled at its safe edges, their arms folded in suspicion and doubt as you sink.

> "I was, in a sense, immigrating all over again, except this time into English."

2 My family immigrated to the U.S. from Vietnam in 1990, when I was two. We lived, all seven of us, in a one-bedroom apartment in Hartford, Connecticut, and I spent my first five years in America surrounded, inundated, by the Vietnamese language. When I entered kindergarten, I was, in a sense,

immigrating all over again, except this time into English. Like any American child, I quickly learned my ABCs, thanks to the age-old melody (one I still sing rapidly to myself when I forget whether "M" comes before "N"). Within a few years, I had become fluent – but only in speech, not in the written word.

One early-spring afternoon, when I was in fourth grade, we got an assignment in language-arts class: we had two weeks to write a poem in honor of National Poetry Month. Normally, my poor writing abilities would excuse me from such assignments, and I would instead spend the class mindlessly copying out passages from books I'd retrieved from a blue plastic bin at the back of the room. The task allowed me to camouflage myself; as long as I looked as though I were doing something smart, my shame and failure were hidden. The trouble began when I decided to be dangerously ambitious. Which is to say, I decided to write a poem. 3

"Where is it?" the teacher asked. He held my poem up to the fluorescent classroom lights and squinted, the way one might examine counterfeit money. I could tell, by the slowly brightening room, that it had started to snow. I pointed to my work dangling from his fingers. "No, where is the poem you plagiarized? How did you even write something like this?" Then he tipped my desk toward me. The desk had a cubby attached to its underside, and I watched as the contents spilled from the cubby's mouth: rectangular pink erasers, crayons, yellow pencils, wrinkled work sheets where dotted letters were filled in, a lime Dum Dum lollipop. But no poem. I stood before the rubble at my feet. Little moments of ice hurled themselves against the window as the boys and girls, my peers, stared, their faces as unconvinced as blank sheets of paper. 4

Weeks earlier, I'd been in the library. It was where I would hide during recess. Otherwise, because of my slight frame and soft voice, the boys would call me "pansy" and "fairy" and pull my shorts around my ankles in the middle of the schoolyard. I sat on the floor beside a tape player. From a box of cassettes, I chose one labelled "Great American Speeches." I picked it because of the illustration, a microphone against a backdrop of the American flag. I picked it because the American flag was one of the few symbols I recognized. 5

Through the headset, a robust male voice surged forth, emptying into my body. The man's inflections made me think of waves on a sea. Between his sentences, a crowd – I imagined thousands – roared and applauded. I imagined their heads shifting in an endless flow. His voice must possess the power of a moon, I thought, something beyond my grasp, my little life. Then a narrator named the man as a Dr. Martin Luther King, Jr. I nodded, not knowing why a doctor was speaking like this. But maybe these people were ill, and he was trying to cure them. There must have been medicine in his words – can there be medicine in words? "I have a dream," I mouthed to myself as the doctor spoke. It occurred to me that I had been mouthing my grandmother's stories as well, the ones she had been telling me ever since I was born. Of course, not being able to read does not mean that one is empty of stories. 6

My poem was called "If a Boy Could Dream." The phrases "promised land" and "mountaintop" sounded golden to me, and I saw an ochre-lit field, 7 a lushness akin to a spring dusk. I imagined that the doctor was dreaming of springtime. So my poem was a sort of ode to spring. From the gardening shows my grandmother watched, I'd learned the words for flowers I had never seen in person: foxglove, lilac, lily, buttercup. "If a boy could dream of golden fields, full of lilacs, tulips, marigolds . . ."

I knew words like "if" and "boy," but others I had to look up. I sounded out the words in my head, a dictionary in my lap, and searched the letters. After a few days, the poem appeared as gray graphite words. The paper a white flag. I had surrendered, had written. 8

Looking back, I can see my teacher's problem. I was, after all, a poor student. "Where is it?" he said again. 9

"It's right here," I said, pointing to my poem pinched between his fingers. 10

I had read books that weren't books, and I had read them using everything but my eyes. From that invisible "reading," I had pressed my world onto paper. As such, I was a fraud in a field of language, which is to say, I was a writer. I have plagiarized my life to give you the best of me. 11

• • •

Comprehension

1. The title of this essay is "Surrendering." Who is surrendering – and to what? Is this an effective title? Why or why not?
2. In paragraph 3, Vuong calls his decision to write a poem "dangerously ambitious." Why is this decision "ambitious"? In what sense is it dangerous?
3. How does his teacher view Vuong as a student? Why? How do you think Vuong viewed his teacher? How do you suppose he views his teacher now?
4. How do Vuong's classmates treat him? Why? How does he respond?
5. From what sources does Vuong learn English words? Do you think his use of any of these sources constitutes plagiarism? Why or why not?

Purpose and Audience

1. In his introduction, Vuong identifies himself as "an E.S.L. student from a family of illiterate rice farmers" (1). Why does he begin his essay with this information?
2. Does this essay state a thesis? If so, where? If not, supply an appropriate one-sentence thesis statement.
3. Beyond conveying his experiences to readers, what other purpose does Vuong have?
4. Do you think Vuong considers his primary audience to be immigrants like himself or assimilated Americans? How can you tell?
5. Vuong ends his essay with the sentence, "I have plagiarized my life to give you the best of me" (11). What does he mean? Who is the "you" he refers to here? What do these words tell you about his purpose for writing this essay?

Style and Structure

1. Where does Vuong include dialogue? What do the quoted words add to the essay? Should Vuong have included more examples of his own speech? If so, where?
2. List some of the transitional words and phrases Vuong uses to move readers from sentence to sentence and from paragraph to paragraph. Do you think he supplies enough transitions to move his narrative smoothly along? Does he need to add any chronological links?
3. In paragraph 5, his words "Weeks earlier" introduce a flashback. Where does this flashback end?
4. In paragraphs 5 through 7, when Vuong describes the experience of listening to a speech by Martin Luther King Jr. and the poem he wrote in response to the speech, he refers several times to King as "a doctor." He also refers to medicine and to ill people. What do these references reveal about Vuong?
5. **Vocabulary Project.** What wider meaning does Vuong give to the word *immigrating* in paragraph 2? How does this usage support the themes of his essay?
6. Vuong uses **figures of speech** (such as **metaphor** and **simile**) very effectively in this essay. In paragraph 4, for example, he describes his classmates' faces as "as unconvinced as blank sheets of paper." Identify as many metaphors and similes as you can, and explain how each helps to convey Vuong's impressions of his experiences.

Journal Entry

The poem Vuong wrote was called "If a Boy Could Dream." What dreams do you think he wrote about in this poem?

Writing Workshop

1. Write a **literacy narrative** tracing your development as a writer. You may focus on your preschool years or on your experiences during your years in elementary school, middle school, high school, or college. (Before you begin to write, read the student essay "Becoming a Writer," page 101.)
2. **Working with Sources.** Look online for King's famous "I Have a Dream" speech; then, read the speech and listen to a recording of it. Now, write a narrative essay that traces the development of your own (or your family's) dreams. If you quote from King's speech, be sure to cite this source and to include a works-cited page. (See Chapter 18 for information on MLA documentation.)
3. Write a narrative essay from the point of view of Vuong's fourth-grade teacher (or one of Vuong's classmates). In your essay, tell the same story Vuong tells, but give your narrator's interpretation of events instead of Vuong's. If you like, you may invent additional events and dialogue.

Combining the Patterns

"Surrendering" is a narrative essay, but it also incorporates a good deal of **description**. Given Vuong's primary purpose for writing, do you think description is the most effective way to enrich his narrative? Why or why not? Should he also have devoted some of his essay to exploring **causes and effects** or developing a **comparison** or **contrast**?

Thematic Connections

- "Cutting and Pasting: A Senior Thesis by (Insert Name)" (page 17)
- "The Price of Silence" (page 76)
- "On Plagiarism" (page 509)
- "Letter from Birmingham Jail" (page 558)
- "The Park" (page 671)

BONNIE SMITH-YACKEL

My Mother Never Worked

Bonnie Smith-Yackel was born into a farm family in Willmar, Minnesota, in 1937. She began writing as a young homemaker in the early 1960s and for the next fourteen years published short stories, essays, and book reviews in such publications as *Catholic Digest, Minnesota Monthly,* and *Ms.* magazine, as well as in several local newspapers. As Smith-Yackel explains it, "The catalyst for writing the [following] essay shortly after my mother's death was recounting my telephone conversation with Social Security to the lawyer who was helping me settle my mother's estate. When I told him what the SS woman had said, he responded: 'Well, that's right. Your mother didn't work, you know.' At which point I stood and said, 'She worked harder throughout her life than you or a hundred men like you!' and stomped out of his office, drove home, sat down and wrote the essay in one sitting." Although this narrative essay, first published in *Women: A Journal of Liberation* in 1975, is based on personal experience, it also makes a broader statement about how society values "women's work."

Background on Social Security benefits Social Security is a federal insurance program that requires workers to contribute a percentage of their wages to a fund from which they may draw benefits if they become unemployed due to disability. After retirement, workers can receive a monthly income from this fund, which also provides a modest death benefit to survivors. The contribution is generally deducted directly from a worker's paycheck, and employers must contribute a matching amount. According to federal law, a woman who is a homemaker, who has never been a wage earner, is eligible for Social Security benefits only through the earnings of her deceased husband. (The same would be true for a man if the roles were reversed.) Therefore, a homemaker's survivors would not be eligible for the death benefit. Although the law has been challenged in the courts, the survivors of a homemaker who has never been a wage earner are still not entitled to a Social Security death benefit.

"Social Security Office." (The voice answering the telephone sounds very self-assured.) 1

"I'm calling about . . . my mother just died . . . I was told to call you and see about a . . . death-benefit check, I think they call it. . . ." 2

"I see. Was your mother on Social Security? How old was she?" 3

"Yes . . . she was seventy-eight. . . ." 4

"Do you know her number?" 5

"No . . . I, ah . . . don't you have a record?" 6

"Certainly. I'll look it up. Her name?" 7

"Smith. Martha Smith. Or maybe she used Martha Ruth Smith? . . . Sometimes she used her maiden name . . . Martha Jerabek Smith?" 8

"If you'd care to hold on, I'll check our records – it'll be a few minutes." 9

"Yes. . . ." 10

Her love letters – to and from Daddy – were in an old box, tied with ribbons and stiff, rigid-with-age leather thongs: 1918 through 1920; hers written on stationery from the general store she had worked in full-time and managed, single-handed, after her graduation from high school in 1913; and his, at first, on YMCA or Soldiers and Sailors Club stationery dispensed to the fighting men of World War I. He wooed her thoroughly and persistently by mail, and though she reciprocated all his feelings for her, she dreaded marriage. . . . 11

"It's so hard for me to decide when to have my wedding day – that's all I've thought about these last two days. I have told you dozens of times that I won't be afraid of married life, but when it comes down to setting the date and then picturing myself a married woman with half a dozen or more kids to look after, it just makes me sick. . . . I am weeping right now – I hope that some day I can look back and say how foolish I was to dread it all." 12

They married in February, 1921, and began farming. Their first baby, a daughter, was born in January, 1922, when my mother was twenty-six years old. The second baby, a son, was born in March, 1923. They were renting farms; my father, besides working his own fields, also was a hired man for two other farmers. They had no capital initially, and had to gain it slowly, working from dawn until midnight every day. My town-bred mother learned to set hens and raise chickens, feed pigs, milk cows, plant and harvest a garden, and can every fruit and vegetable she could scrounge. She carried water nearly a quarter of a mile from the well to fill her wash boilers in order to do her laundry on a scrub board. She learned to shuck grain, feed threshers, shock and husk corn, feed corn pickers. In September, 1925, the third baby came, and in June, 1927, the fourth child – both daughters. In 1930, my parents had enough money to buy their own farm, and that March they moved all their livestock and belongings themselves, fifty-five miles over rutted, muddy roads. 13

In the summer of 1930 my mother and her two eldest children reclaimed a forty-acre field from Canadian thistles, by chopping them all out with a hoe. In the other fields, when the oats and flax began to head out, the green and blue of the crops were hidden by the bright yellow of wild mustard. My mother walked the fields day after day, pulling each mustard plant. She raised a new flock of baby chicks – five hundred – and she spaded up, planted, hoed, and harvested a half-acre garden. 14

During the next spring their hogs caught cholera and died. No cash that fall. 15

And in the next year the drought hit. My mother and father trudged from the well to the chickens, the well to the calf pasture, the well to the barn, and from the well to the garden. The sun came out hot and bright, endlessly, day after day. The crops shriveled and died. They harvested half the corn, and ground the other half, stalks and all, and fed it to the cattle as fodder. With the price at four cents a bushel for the harvested crop, they couldn't afford to haul it into town. They burned it in the furnace for fuel that winter. 16

In 1934, in February, when the dust was still so thick in the Minnesota 17
air that my parents couldn't always see from the house to the barn, their fifth child – a fourth daughter – was born. My father hunted rabbits daily, and my mother stewed them, fried them, canned them, and wished out loud that she could taste hamburger once more. In the fall the shotgun brought prairie chickens, ducks, pheasant, and grouse. My mother plucked each bird, carefully reserving the breast feathers for pillows.

In the winter she sewed night after night, endlessly, begging cast-off 18
clothing from relatives, ripping apart coats, dresses, blouses, and trousers to remake them to fit her four daughters and son. Every morning and every evening she milked cows, fed pigs and calves, cared for chickens, picked eggs, cooked meals, washed dishes, scrubbed floors, and tended and loved her children. In the spring she planted a garden once more, dragging pails of water to nourish and sustain the vegetables for the family. In 1936 she lost a baby in her sixth month.

In 1937 her fifth daughter was born. She was forty-two years old. In 1939 19
a second son, and in 1941 her eighth child – and third son.

But the war had come, and prosperity of a sort. The herd of cattle had 20
grown to thirty head; she still milked morning and evening. Her garden was more than a half acre – the rains had come, and by now the Rural Electricity Administration and indoor plumbing. Still she sewed – dresses and jackets for the children, housedresses and aprons for herself, weekly patching of jeans, overalls, and denim shirts. She still made pillows, using feathers she had plucked, and quilts every year – intricate patterns as well as patchwork, stitched as well as tied – all necessary bedding for her family. Every scrap of cloth too small to be used in quilts was carefully saved and painstakingly sewed together in strips to make rugs. She still went out in the fields to help with the haying whenever there was a threat of rain.

In 1959 my mother's last child graduated from high school. A year later 21
the cows were sold. She still raised chickens and ducks, plucked feathers, made pillows, baked her own bread, and every year made a new quilt – now for a married child or for a grandchild. And her garden, that huge, undying symbol of sustenance, was as large and cared for as in all the years before. The canning, and now freezing, continued.

In 1969, on a June afternoon, mother and father started out for town 22
so that she could buy sugar to make rhubarb jam for a daughter who lived in Texas. The car crashed into a ditch. She was paralyzed from the waist down.

In 1970 her husband, my father, died. My mother struggled to regain 23
some competence and dignity and order in her life. At the rehabilitation institute, where they gave her physical therapy and trained her to live usefully in a wheelchair, the therapist told me: "She did fifteen pushups today – fifteen! She's almost seventy-five years old! I've never known a woman so strong!"

> "Well, you see — your mother never worked."

From her wheelchair she canned pickles, baked bread, ironed clothes, wrote dozens of letters weekly to her friends and her "half dozen or more kids," and made three patchwork housecoats and one quilt. She made balls and balls of carpet rags — enough for five rugs. And kept all her love letters. 24

"I think I've found your mother's records — Martha Ruth Smith; married to Ben F. Smith?" 25

"Yes, that's right." 26

"Well, I see that she was getting a widow's pension. . . ." 27

"Yes, that's right." 28

"Well, your mother isn't entitled to our $255 death benefit." 29

"Not entitled! But why?" 30

The voice on the telephone explains patiently: 31

"Well, you see — your mother never worked." 32

• • •

Comprehension

1. What kind of work did Martha Smith do while her children were growing up? List some of the chores she performed.
2. Why aren't Martha Smith's survivors entitled to a death benefit when their mother dies?
3. How does the federal government define *work*?

Purpose and Audience

1. What point is the writer trying to make? Why do you suppose her thesis is never explicitly stated?
2. This essay appeared in *Ms.* magazine and other publications whose audiences are sympathetic to feminist goals. Could it have appeared in a magazine whose audience had a more traditional view of gender roles? Explain.
3. Smith-Yackel says very little about her father in this essay. Why do you think she does not tell readers more about him? Should she have added material about him?
4. This essay was first published in 1975. Do you think it is dated, or do you think the issues it raises are still relevant today?

Style and Structure

1. Is the essay's title effective? If so, why? If not, what alternate title can you suggest?
2. Smith-Yackel could have outlined her mother's life without framing it with the telephone conversation. Why do you think she includes this frame?
3. What strategies does Smith-Yackel use to indicate the passing of time in her narrative?

4. This narrative piles details one on top of another. Why does the writer include so many details?
5. In paragraphs 20 and 21, what is accomplished by the repetition of the word *still*?
6. **Vocabulary Project.** Try substituting equivalent words for those italicized in this sentence:

   He *wooed* her *thoroughly* and *persistently* by mail, and though she *reciprocated* all his feelings for her, she *dreaded* marriage . . . (11).

   How do your substitutions change the sentence's meaning?

Journal Entry

Do you believe that a homemaker who has never been a wage earner should be entitled to a Social Security death benefit for her survivors? Explain your reasoning.

Writing Workshop

1. **Working with Sources.** Interview one of your parents or grandparents (or another person you know who reminds you of Smith-Yackel's mother) about his or her work history, and write a chronological narrative based on what you learn. Include a thesis statement that your narrative can support, and quote your subject's responses when possible. Be sure to include parenthetical documentation for these quotations, and also include a works-cited page. (See Chapter 18 for information on MLA documentation.)
2. Write Martha Smith's obituary as it might have appeared in her hometown newspaper. (If you are not familiar with the form of an obituary, read a few in your local paper or online at Legacy.com or Obituaries.com.)
3. Write a narrative account of a typical day at the worst job you ever had. Include a thesis statement that expresses your negative feelings.

Combining the Patterns

Because of the repetitive nature of the farm chores Smith-Yackel describes in her narrative, some passages come very close to explaining a **process**, a series of repeated steps that always occur in a predictable order. Identify several such passages. If Smith-Yackel's essay were written entirely as a process explanation, what, if anything, would have to be added? What material would have to be left out? How would these omissions change the essay?

Thematic Connections

- "Midnight" (page 213)
- "'Girl'" (page 254)
- "I Want a Wife" (page 496)

MARTIN GANSBERG

Thirty-Eight Who Saw Murder Didn't Call the Police

Martin Gansberg (1920–1995), a native of Brooklyn, New York, was a reporter and editor for the *New York Times* for forty-three years. The following article, written for the *Times* two weeks after the 1964 murder it recounts, earned Gansberg an award for excellence from the Newspaper Reporters Association of New York. Gansberg's thesis, although not explicitly stated, still retains its power.

Background on the Kitty Genovese murder case The events reported here took place on March 14, 1964, as contemporary American culture was undergoing a complex transition. The relatively placid years of the 1950s were giving way to more troubling times: the civil rights movement was leading to social unrest in the South and in northern inner cities, the escalating war in Vietnam was creating angry political divisions, President John F. Kennedy had been assassinated just four months earlier, violent imagery was increasing in television and film, crime rates were rising, and a growing drug culture was becoming apparent. The brutal, senseless murder of Kitty Genovese — and, more important, her neighbors' failure to respond immediately to her cries for help — became a nationwide, and even worldwide, symbol for what was perceived as an evolving culture of violence and indifference.

In recent years, some of the details Gansberg mentions have been challenged. For example, as the *New York Times* now acknowledges, there were only two attacks on Ms. Genovese, not three; the first attack may have been shorter than first reported; the second attack may have occurred in the apartment house foyer, where neighbors would not have been able to see Genovese; and some witnesses may, in fact, actually *have* called the police. In April 2016, the murderer of Kitty Genovese died in prison, bringing the case back to national attention, and in June of that same year, Kitty Genovese's brother Bill Genovese and director James Solomon released *The Witness,* a documentary tracing Bill's search for the truth about his sister's murder. The film comes to the conclusion that the incident did not occur just as Gansberg had reported it. At the time, however, the world was shocked by the incident, and even today social scientists around the world debate the causes of "the Genovese syndrome."

For more than half an hour thirty-eight respectable, law-abiding citizens in Queens watched a killer stalk and stab a woman in three separate attacks in Kew Gardens. 1

Twice their chatter and the sudden glow of their bedroom lights interrupted him and frightened him off. Each time he returned, sought her out, and stabbed her again. Not one person telephoned the police during the assault; one witness called after the woman was dead. 2

3 That was two weeks ago today.

4 Still shocked is Assistant Chief Inspector Frederick M. Lussen, in charge of the borough's detectives and a veteran of twenty-five years of homicide investigations. He can give a matter-of-fact recitation on many murders. But the Kew Gardens slaying baffles him – not because it is a murder, but because the "good people" failed to call the police.

> "Not one person telephoned the police during the assault; one witness called after the woman was dead."

5 "As we have reconstructed the crime," he said, "the assailant had three chances to kill this woman during a thirty-five-minute period. He returned twice to complete the job. If we had been called when he first attacked, the woman might not be dead now."

6 This is what the police say happened beginning at 3:20 A.M. in the staid, middle-class, tree-lined Austin Street area:

7 Twenty-eight-year-old Catherine Genovese, who was called Kitty by almost everyone in the neighborhood, was returning home from her job as manager of a bar in Hollis. She parked her red Fiat in a lot adjacent to the Kew Gardens Long Island Rail Road Station, facing Mowbray Place. Like many residents of the neighborhood, she had parked there day after day since her arrival from Connecticut a year ago, although the railroad frowns on the practice.

8 She turned off the lights of her car, locked the door, and started to walk the one hundred feet to the entrance of her apartment at 82-70 Austin Street, which is in a Tudor building, with stores in the first floor and apartments on the second.

9 The entrance to the apartment is in the rear of the building because the front is rented to retail stores. At night the quiet neighborhood is shrouded in the slumbering darkness that marks most residential areas.

10 Miss Genovese noticed a man at the far end of the lot, near a seven-story apartment house at 82-40 Austin Street. She halted. Then, nervously, she headed up Austin Street toward Lefferts Boulevard, where there is a call box to the 102nd Police Precinct in nearby Richmond Hill.

11 She got as far as a street light in front of a bookstore before the man grabbed her. She screamed. Lights went on in the ten-story apartment house at 82-67 Austin Street, which faces the bookstore. Windows slid open and voices punctuated the early-morning stillness.

12 Miss Genovese screamed: "Oh, my God, he stabbed me! Please help me! Please help me!"

13 From one of the upper windows in the apartment house, a man called down: "Let that girl alone!"

14 The assailant looked up at him, shrugged, and walked down Austin Street toward a white sedan parked a short distance away. Miss Genovese struggled to her feet.

15 Lights went out. The killer returned to Miss Genovese, now trying to make her way around the side of the building by the parking lot to get to her apartment. The assailant stabbed her again.

"I'm dying!" she shrieked. "I'm dying!" 16

Windows were opened again, and lights went on in many apartments. The assailant got into his car and drove away. Miss Genovese staggered to her feet. A city bus, 0–10, the Lefferts Boulevard line to Kennedy International Airport, passed. It was 3:35 A.M. 17

The assailant returned. By then, Miss Genovese had crawled to the back of the building, where the freshly painted brown doors to the apartment house held out hope for safety. The killer tried the first door; she wasn't there. At the second door, 82-62 Austin Street, he saw her slumped on the floor at the foot of the stairs. He stabbed her a third time – fatally. 18

It was 3:50 by the time the police received their first call, from a man who was a neighbor of Miss Genovese. In two minutes they were at the scene. The neighbor, a seventy-year-old woman, and another woman were the only persons on the street. Nobody else came forward. 19

The man explained that he had called the police after much deliberation. He had phoned a friend in Nassau County for advice, and then he had crossed the roof of the building to the apartment of the elderly woman to get her to make the call. 20

"I didn't want to get involved," he sheepishly told police. 21

Six days later, the police arrested Winston Moseley, a twenty-nine-year-old business machine operator, and charged him with homicide. Moseley had no previous record. He is married, has two children, and owns a home at 133-19 Sutter Avenue, South Ozone Park, Queens. On Wednesday, a court committed him to Kings County Hospital for psychiatric observation. 22

When questioned by the police, Moseley also said that he had slain Mrs. Annie May Johnson, twenty-four, of 146-12 133d Avenue, Jamaica, on Feb. 29 and Barbara Kralik, fifteen, of 174-17 140th Avenue, Springfield Gardens, last July. In the Kralik case, the police are holding Alvin L. Mitchell, who is said to have confessed to that slaying. 23

The police stressed how simple it would have been to have gotten in touch with them. "A phone call," said one of the detectives, "would have done it." The police may be reached by dialing "0" for operator or SPring 7-3100. 24

Today witnesses from the neighborhood, which is made up of one-family homes in the $35,000 to $60,000 range with the exception of the two apartment houses near the railroad station, find it difficult to explain why they didn't call the police. 25

A housewife, knowingly if quite casually, said, "We thought it was a lovers' quarrel." A husband and wife both said, "Frankly, we were afraid." They seemed aware of the fact that events might have been different. A distraught woman, wiping her hands in her apron, said, "I didn't want my husband to get involved." 26

One couple, now willing to talk about that night, said they heard the first screams. The husband looked thoughtfully at the bookstore where the killer first grabbed Miss Genovese. 27

"We went to the window to see what was happening," he said, "but the light from our bedroom made it difficult to see the street." The wife, still apprehensive, added: "I put out the light and we were able to see better." 28

Asked why they hadn't called the police, she shrugged and replied: "I don't know." 29

A man peeked out from a slight opening in the doorway to his apartment and rattled off an account of the killer's second attack. Why hadn't he called the police at the time? "I was tired," he said without emotion. "I went back to bed." 30

It was 4:25 A.M. when the ambulance arrived to take the body of Miss Genovese. It drove off. "Then," a solemn police detective said, "the people came out." 31

• • •

Comprehension

1. According to Gansberg, how much time elapsed between the first stabbing of Kitty Genovese and the time when the people finally came out?
2. What excuses do the neighbors make for not coming to Kitty Genovese's aid?

Purpose and Audience

1. This article appeared in 1964, just two weeks after the incident. What effect was it intended to have on its audience? Do you think it has the same impact today, or has its impact changed or diminished?
2. What is the article's main point? Why does Gansberg imply his thesis rather than state it explicitly?
3. What is Gansberg's purpose in describing the Austin Street area as "staid, middle-class, tree-lined" (6)?
4. Why do you suppose Gansberg provides the police department's phone number in his article? (Note that New York City did not have 911 emergency service in 1964.)

Style and Structure

1. Gansberg is very precise in this article, especially in his references to time, addresses, and ages. Why?
2. The objective newspaper style is dominant in this article, but the writer's anger shows through. Point to words and phrases that reveal his attitude toward his material.
3. Because this article was originally set in the narrow columns of a newspaper, it has many short paragraphs. Would the narrative be more effective if some of these brief paragraphs were combined? If so, why? If not, why not? Give examples to support your answer.
4. **Vocabulary Project.** The word *assailant* appears frequently in this article. Why is it used so often? What effect is this repetition likely to have on readers? What other words could have been used?

5. Review the dialogue quoted in this article. Does it strengthen Gansberg's narrative? Would the article be more compelling with additional dialogue? Without dialogue? Explain.
6. This article does not have a formal conclusion; nevertheless, the last paragraph sums up the writer's attitude. How?

Journal Entry

Because they provide easy access to 911 service – and because many also have the ability to record video – cell phones have dramatically changed the way people respond to crimes they witness or are victim to. How might the availability of cell phones have changed Kitty Genovese's story?

Writing Workshop

1. In your own words, write a ten-sentence **summary** (see page 728) of this newspaper article. Try to reflect Gansberg's order and emphasis, as well as his ideas, and be sure to include all necessary transitions.
2. Rewrite the article as if it were a blog post by one of the thirty-eight people who watched the murder. Summarize what you saw, and explain why you decided not to call for help. (You may invent details that Gansberg does not include.)
3. **Working with Sources.** If you have ever been involved in or witnessed a situation in which someone was in trouble, write a narrative essay about the incident. If people failed to help the person in trouble, explain why you think no one acted. If people did act, tell how. Be sure to account for your own actions. In your essay's introduction, refer to Gansberg's account of Kitty Genovese's murder. If you quote Gansberg, be sure to include documentation and a works-cited page. (See Chapter 18 for information on MLA documentation.)

Combining the Patterns

Because the purpose of this newspaper article is to give basic factual information, it has no extended descriptions of the victim, the witnesses, or the crime scene. It also does not explain *why* those who watched did not act. Where might passages of **description** or **cause and effect** be added? How might such additions change the article's effect on readers? Do you think they would strengthen the article?

Thematic Connections

- "Shooting an Elephant" (page 131)
- "The Lottery" (page 304)
- "Photos That Change History" (page 356)

GEORGE ORWELL

Shooting an Elephant

George Orwell (1903–1950) was born Eric Blair in Bengal, India, where his father was a British civil servant. Rather than attend university, Orwell joined the Imperial Police in neighboring Burma (now renamed Myanmar), where he served from 1922 to 1927. Finding himself increasingly opposed to British colonial rule, Orwell left Burma to live and write in Paris and London. A political liberal and a fierce moralist, Orwell is best known today for his novels *Animal Farm* (1945) and *1984* (1949), which portray the dangers of totalitarianism. In "Shooting an Elephant," written in 1936, he recalls an incident from his days in Burma that clarified his thinking about British colonial rule.

Background on British imperialism The British had gradually taken over Burma through a succession of wars beginning in 1824; by 1885, the domination was complete. Like a number of other European countries, Britain had forcibly established colonial rule in countries throughout the world during the eighteenth and nineteenth centuries, primarily to exploit their natural resources. This empire building, known as *imperialism,* was justified by the belief that European culture was superior to the cultures of the indigenous peoples, particularly in Asia and Africa. Therefore, imperialist nations claimed, it was "the white man's burden" to bring civilization to these "heathen" lands. In most cases, such control could be achieved only through force. Anti-imperialist sentiment began to grow in the early twentieth century, but colonial rule continued until the mid-twentieth century in much of the less-developed world. Not until the late 1940s did many European colonies begin to gain independence. The British ceded home rule to Burma in 1947.

In Moulmein, in Lower Burma, I was hated by large numbers of people — the only time in my life that I have been important enough for this to happen to me. I was sub-divisional police officer of the town, and in an aimless, petty kind of way anti-European feeling was very bitter. No one had the guts to raise a riot, but if a European woman went through the bazaars alone somebody would probably spit betel juice over her dress. As a police officer I was an obvious target and was baited whenever it seemed safe to do so. When a nimble Burman tripped me up on the football field and the referee (another Burman) looked the other way, the crowd yelled with hideous laughter. This happened more than once. In the end the sneering yellow faces of young men that met me everywhere, the insults hooted after me when I was at a safe distance, got badly on my nerves. The young Buddhist priests were the worst of all. There were several thousands of them in the town and none of them seemed to have anything to do except stand on street corners and jeer at Europeans. 1

2 All this was perplexing and upsetting. For at that time I had already made up my mind that imperialism was an evil thing and the sooner I chucked up my job and got out of it the better. Theoretically – and secretly, of course – I was all for the Burmese and all against their oppressors, the British. As for the job I was doing, I hated it more bitterly than I can perhaps make clear. In a job like that you see the dirty work of Empire at close quarters. The wretched prisoners huddling in the stinking cages of the lockups, the grey, cowed faces of the long-term convicts, the scarred buttocks of the men who had been flogged with bamboos – all these oppressed me with an intolerable sense of guilt. But I could get nothing into perspective. I was young and ill-educated and I had had to think out my problems in the utter silence that is imposed on every Englishman in the East. I did not even know that the British Empire is dying, still less did I know that it is a great deal better than the younger empires that are going to supplant it.* All I knew was that I was stuck between my hatred of the empire I served and my rage against the evil-spirited little beasts who tried to make my job impossible. With one part of my mind I thought of the British Raj** as an unbreakable tyranny, as something clamped down, in *saecula saeculorum,**** upon the will of prostrate peoples; with another part I thought that the greatest joy in the world would be to drive a bayonet into a Buddhist priest's guts. Feelings like these are the normal by-products of imperialism; ask any Anglo-Indian official, if you can catch him off duty.

"It was a tiny incident in itself, but it gave me a better glimpse than I had had before of the real nature of imperialism. . . ."

3 One day something happened which in a roundabout way was enlightening. It was a tiny incident in itself, but it gave me a better glimpse than I had had before of the real nature of imperialism – the real motives for which despotic governments act. Early one morning the sub-inspector at a police station the other end of the town rang me up on the phone and said that an elephant was ravaging the bazaar. Would I please come and do something about it? I did not know what I could do, but I wanted to see what was happening and I got on to a pony and started out. I took my rifle, an old .44 Winchester and much too small to kill an elephant, but I thought the noise might be useful *in terrorem.*† Various Burmans stopped me on the way and told me about the elephant's doings. It was not, of course, a wild elephant, but a tame one which had gone "must."‡ It had been chained up, as tame

* Eds. note – Orwell was writing in 1936, when Hitler and Stalin were in power and World War II was only three years away.

** Eds. note – The former British rule of the Indian subcontinent.

*** Eds. note – From time immemorial.

† Eds. note – For the purpose of frightening.

‡ Eds. note – Was in heat, a condition likely to wear off.

elephants always are when their attack of "must" is due, but on the previous night it had broken its chain and escaped. Its mahout,* the only person who could manage it when it was in that state, had set out in pursuit, but had taken the wrong direction and was now twelve hours' journey away, and in the morning the elephant had suddenly reappeared in the town. The Burmese population had no weapons and were quite helpless against it. It had already destroyed somebody's bamboo hut, killed a cow, and raided some fruit-stalls and devoured the stock; also it had met the municipal rubbish van and, when the driver jumped out and took to his heels, had turned the van over and inflicted violences upon it.

The Burmese sub-inspector and some Indian constables were waiting 4 for me in the quarter where the elephant had been seen. It was a very poor quarter, a labyrinth of squalid bamboo huts, thatched with palm-leaf, winding all over a steep hillside. I remember that it was a cloudy, stuffy morning at the beginning of the rains. We began questioning people as to where the elephant had gone, and, as usual, failed to get any definite information. That is invariably the case in the East; a story always sounds clear enough at a distance, but the nearer you get to the scene of events the vaguer it becomes. Some of the people said that the elephant had gone in one direction, some said that he had gone in another, some professed not even to have heard of an elephant. I had almost made up my mind that the whole story was a pack of lies, when we heard yells a little distance away. There was a loud, scandalized cry of "Go away, child! Go away this instant!" and an old woman with a switch in her hand came round the corner of a hut, violently shooing away a crowd of naked children. Some more women followed, clicking their tongues and exclaiming; evidently there was something that the children ought not to have seen. I rounded the hut and saw a man's dead body sprawling in the mud. He was an Indian, a black Dravidian coolie,** almost naked, and he could not have been dead many minutes. The people said that the elephant had come suddenly upon him round the corner of the hut, caught him with its trunk, put its foot on his back, and ground him into the earth. This was the rainy season and the ground was soft, and his face had scored a trench a foot deep and a couple of yards long. He was lying on his belly with arms crucified and head sharply twisted to one side. His face was coated with mud, the eyes wide open, the teeth bared and grinning with an expression of unendurable agony. (Never tell me, by the way, that the dead look peaceful. Most of the corpses I have seen looked devilish.) The friction of the great beast's foot had stripped the skin from his back as neatly as one skins a rabbit. As soon as I saw the dead man I sent an orderly to a friend's house nearby to borrow an elephant rifle. I had already sent back the pony, not wanting it to go mad with fright and throw me if it smelled the elephant.

The orderly came back in a few minutes with a rifle and five cartridges, 5 and meanwhile some Burmans had arrived and told us that the elephant was

* Eds. note — A keeper and driver of an elephant.

** Eds. note — An unskilled laborer.

in the paddy* fields below, only a few hundred yards away. As I started forward practically the whole population of the quarter flocked out of the houses and followed me. They had seen the rifle and were all shouting excitedly that I was going to shoot the elephant. They had not shown much interest in the elephant when he was merely ravaging their homes, but it was different now that he was going to be shot. It was a bit of fun to them, as it would be to an English crowd; besides they wanted the meat. It made me vaguely uneasy. I had no intention of shooting the elephant – I had merely sent for the rifle to defend myself if necessary – and it is always unnerving to have a crowd following you. I marched down the hill, looking and feeling a fool, with the rifle over my shoulder and an ever-growing army of people jostling at my heels. At the bottom, when you got away from the huts, there was a metalled road and beyond that a miry waste of paddy fields a thousand yards across, not yet ploughed but soggy from the first rains and dotted with coarse grass. The elephant was standing eight yards from the road, his left side towards us. He took not the slightest notice of the crowd's approach. He was tearing up bunches of grass, beating them against his knees to clean them and stuffing them into his mouth.

I had halted on the road. As soon as I saw the elephant I knew with perfect certainty that I ought not to shoot him. It is a serious matter to shoot a working elephant – it is comparable to destroying a huge and costly piece of machinery – and obviously one ought not to do it if it can possibly be avoided. And at that distance, peacefully eating, the elephant looked no more dangerous than a cow. I thought then and I think now that his attack of "must" was already passing off; in which case he would merely wander harmlessly about until the mahout came back and caught him. Moreover, I did not in the least want to shoot him. I decided that I would watch him for a little while to make sure that he did not turn savage again, and then go home. 6

But at that moment I glanced round at the crowd that had followed me. It was an immense crowd, two thousand at the least and growing every minute. It blocked the road for a long distance on either side. I looked at the sea of yellow faces above the garish clothes – faces all happy and excited over this bit of fun, all certain that the elephant was going to be shot. They were watching me as they would watch a conjurer about to perform a trick. They did not like me, but with the magical rifle in my hands I was momentarily worth watching. And suddenly I realized that I should have to shoot the elephant after all. The people expected it of me and I had got to do it; I could feel their two thousand wills pressing me forward, irresistibly. And it was at this moment, as I stood there with the rifle in my hands, that I first grasped the hollowness, the futility of the white man's dominion in the East. Here was I, the white man with his gun, standing in front of the unarmed native crowd – seemingly the leading actor of the piece; but in reality I was only an absurd puppet pushed to and fro by the will of those yellow faces behind. I perceived in this moment that when the white man turns 7

* Eds. note – Wet land for growing rice.

tyrant it is his own freedom that he destroys. He becomes a sort of hollow, posing dummy, the conventionalized figure of a sahib.* For it is the condition of his rule that he shall spend his life in trying to impress the "natives," and so in every crisis he has got to do what the "natives" expect of him. He wears a mask, and his face grows to fit it. I had got to shoot the elephant. I had committed myself to doing it when I sent for the rifle. A sahib has got to act like a sahib; he has got to appear resolute, to know his own mind and do definite things. To come all that way, rifle in hand, with two thousand people marching at my heels, and then to trail feebly away, having done nothing – no, that was impossible. The crowd would laugh at me. And my whole life, every white man's life in the East, was one long struggle not to be laughed at.

But I did not want to shoot the elephant. I watched him beating his 8 bunch of grass against his knees, with the preoccupied grandmotherly air that elephants have. It seemed to me that it would be murder to shoot him. At that age I was not squeamish about killing animals, but I had never shot an elephant and never wanted to. (Somehow it always seems worse to kill a *large* animal.) Besides, there was the beast's owner to be considered. Alive, the elephant was worth at least a hundred pounds; dead, he would only be worth the value of his tusks, five pounds, possibly. But I had got to act quickly. I turned to some experienced-looking Burmans who had been there when we arrived, and asked them how the elephant had been behaving. They all said the same thing: he took no notice of you if you left him alone, but he might charge if you went too close to him.

It was perfectly clear to me what I ought to do. I ought to walk up to 9 within, say, twenty-five yards of the elephant and test his behavior. If he charged I could shoot, if he took no notice of me it would be safe to leave him until the mahout came back. But also I knew that I was going to do no such thing. I was a poor shot with a rifle and the ground was soft mud into which one would sink at every step. If the elephant charged and I missed him, I should have about as much chance as a toad under a steamroller. But even then I was not thinking particularly of my own skin, only of the watchful yellow faces behind. For at that moment, with the crowd watching me, I was not afraid in the ordinary sense, as I would have been if I had been alone. A white man mustn't be frightened in front of "natives"; and so, in general, he isn't frightened. The sole thought in my mind was that if anything went wrong those two thousand Burmans would see me pursued, caught, trampled on, and reduced to a grinning corpse like that Indian up the hill. And if that happened it was quite probable that some of them would laugh. That would never do. There was only one alternative. I shoved the cartridges into the magazine and lay down on the road to get a better aim.

The crowd grew very still, and a deep, low, happy sigh, as of people who 10 see the theatre curtain go up at last, breathed from innumerable throats. They were going to have their bit of fun after all. The rifle was a beautiful German

* Eds. note – An official. The term was used among Hindus and Muslims in colonial India.

thing with cross-hair sights. I did not then know that in shooting an elephant one would shoot to cut an imaginary bar running from ear-hole to ear-hole. I ought, therefore, as the elephant was sideways on, to have aimed straight at his ear-hole; actually I aimed several inches in front of this, thinking the brain would be further forward.

When I pulled the trigger I did not hear the bang or feel the kick – one never does when a shot goes home – but I heard the devilish roar of glee that went up from the crowd. In that instant, in too short a time, one would have thought, even for the bullet to get there, a mysterious, terrible change had come over the elephant. He neither stirred nor fell, but every line on his body had altered. He looked suddenly stricken, shrunken, immensely old, as though the frightful impact of the bullet had paralyzed him without knocking him down. At last, after what seemed a long time – it might have been five seconds, I dare say – he sagged flabbily to his knees. His mouth slobbered. An enormous senility seemed to have settled upon him. One could have imagined him thousands of years old. I fired again into the same spot. At the second shot he did not collapse but climbed with desperate slowness to his feet and stood weakly upright, with legs sagging and head drooping. I fired a third time. That was the shot that did for him. You could see the agony of it jolt his whole body and knock the last remnant of strength from his legs. But in falling he seemed for a moment to rise, for as his hind legs collapsed beneath him he seemed to tower upwards like a huge rock toppling, his trunk reaching skywards like a tree. He trumpeted, for the first and only time. And then down he came, his belly towards me, with a crash that seemed to shake the ground even where I lay. 11

I got up. The Burmans were already racing past me across the mud. It was obvious that the elephant would never rise again, but he was not dead. He was breathing very rhythmically with long rattling gasps, his great mound of a side painfully rising and falling. His mouth was wide open – I could see far down into caverns of pale pink throat. I waited a long time for him to die, but his breathing did not weaken. Finally I fired my two remaining shots into the spot where I thought his heart must be. The thick blood welled out of him like red velvet, but still he did not die. His body did not even jerk when the shots hit him, the tortured breathing continued without a pause. He was dying, very slowly and in great agony, but in some world remote from me where not even a bullet could damage him further. I felt that I had got to put an end to that dreadful noise. It seemed dreadful to see the great beast lying there, powerless to move and yet powerless to die, and not even to be able to finish him. I sent back for my small rifle and poured shot after shot into his heart and down his throat. They seemed to make no impression. The tortured gasps continued as steadily as the ticking of a clock. 12

In the end I could not stand it any longer and went away. I heard later that it took him half an hour to die. Burmans were bringing dahs* and baskets even before I left, and I was told they had stripped his body almost to the bones by the afternoon. 13

* Eds. note – Heavy knives.

Afterwards, of course, there were endless discussions about the shooting of the elephant. The owner was furious, but he was only an Indian and could do nothing. Besides, legally I had done the right thing, for a mad elephant has to be killed, like a mad dog, if its owner fails to control it. Among the Europeans opinion was divided. The older men said I was right, the younger men said it was a damn shame to shoot an elephant for killing a coolie, because an elephant was worth more than any damn Coringhee coolie. And afterwards I was very glad that the coolie had been killed; it put me legally in the right and it gave me a sufficient pretext for shooting the elephant. I often wondered whether any of the others grasped that I had done it solely to avoid looking a fool. 14

• • •

Comprehension

1. Why is Orwell "hated by large numbers of people" (1) in Burma? Why does he have mixed feelings toward the Burmese people?
2. Why do the local officials want something done about the elephant? Why does the crowd want Orwell to shoot the elephant?
3. Why does Orwell finally decide to kill the elephant? What makes him hesitate at first?
4. Why does Orwell say at the end that he was glad the coolie had been killed?

Purpose and Audience

1. One of Orwell's purposes in telling his story is to show how it gave him a glimpse of "the real nature of imperialism" (3). What does he mean? How does his essay illustrate this purpose?
2. Do you think Orwell wrote this essay to inform or to persuade his audience? How did Orwell expect his audience to react to his ideas? How can you tell?
3. What is the essay's thesis?

Style and Structure

1. What does Orwell's first paragraph accomplish? Where does the introduction end and the narrative itself begin?
2. The essay includes almost no dialogue. Why do you think Orwell's voice as narrator is the only one readers hear? Is the absence of dialogue a strength or a weakness? Explain.
3. Why do you think Orwell devotes so much attention to the elephant's misery (11–12)? Do you think this passage should come with a "trigger warning"? (See pages 607–08 for information on trigger warnings.)
4. Orwell's essay includes a number of editorial comments, which appear within parentheses or dashes. How would you characterize these comments? Why are they set off from the text?

5. **Vocabulary Project.** Because Orwell is British, he frequently uses words or expressions that an American writer would not likely use. Substitute a contemporary American word or phrase for each of the following, making sure it is appropriate in Orwell's context.

raise a riot (1)	rubbish van (3)	a bit of fun (5)
rang me up (3)	inflicted violences (3)	I dare say (11)

What other expressions in Orwell's essay might need to be "translated" for a contemporary American audience?

6. Consider the following statements: "Some of the people said that the elephant had gone in one direction, some said that he had gone in another" (4); "Among the Europeans opinion was divided. The older men said I was right, the younger men said it was a damn shame to shoot an elephant" (14). How do these comments reinforce the idea expressed in paragraph 2 ("All I knew was that I was stuck between my hatred of the empire I served and my rage against the evil-spirited little beasts")? What other comments reinforce this idea?

Journal Entry

Do you think Orwell is a coward? Do you think he is a racist? Explain your conclusions.

Writing Workshop

1. **Working with Sources.** Orwell says that even though he hated British imperialism and sympathized with the Burmese people, he found himself a puppet of the system. Write a narrative essay about a time when you had to do something that went against your beliefs or convictions. Begin by summarizing Orwell's situation in Burma, and go on to show how your situation was similar to his. If you quote Orwell, be sure to include documentation and a works-cited page. (See Chapter 18 for information on MLA documentation.)
2. Orwell's experience taught him something not only about himself but also about something beyond himself – the way British imperialism worked. Write a narrative essay that reveals how an incident in your life taught you something about some larger social or political force as well as about yourself.
3. Write an objective, factual newspaper article recounting the events Orwell describes.

Combining the Patterns

Implicit in this narrative essay is an extended **comparison and contrast** that highlights the differences between Orwell and the Burmese people. Review the essay, and list the most obvious differences Orwell perceives between himself and them. Do you think his perceptions are accurate? If all the differences were set forth in a single paragraph, how might such a paragraph change your perception of Orwell's dilemma? Of his character?

Thematic Connections

- "Thirty-Eight Who Saw Murder Didn't Call the Police" (page 126)
- "Just Walk On By: A Black Man Ponders His Power to Alter Public Space" (page 233)
- "The Untouchable" (page 489)
- Debate: "Do College Students Need Trigger Warnings?" (page 607)

SHERMAN ALEXIE

Indian Education (Fiction)

Sherman Alexie, the son of a Coeur d'Alene Indian father and a Spokane Indian mother, was born in 1966 and grew up on the Spokane Reservation in Wellpinit, Washington, home to some eleven hundred Spokane tribal members. Realizing as a teenager that his educational opportunities there were extremely limited, Alexie made the unusual decision to attend high school off the reservation in nearby Reardan. Later a scholarship student at Gonzaga University, he received a bachelor's degree in American studies from Washington State University at Pullman. While in college, he began publishing poetry; within a year of graduation, his first collection, *The Business of Fancydancing* (1992), appeared. It was followed by *The Lone Ranger and Tonto Fistfight in Heaven* (1993), a short-story collection, and the novels *Reservation Blues* (1995) and *Indian Killer* (1996), all of which garnered numerous awards and honors. Alexie also wrote the screenplay for the film *Smoke Signals* (1998) and wrote and directed *The Business of Fancydancing* (2002). His young adult novel, *The Absolutely True Diary of a Part-Time Indian,* won the 2007 National Book Award for Young People's Literature. *War Dances,* a collection of his stories and poems, was published in 2009 and received the PEN/Faulkner Award for Fiction in 2010.

Background on the U.S. government's "Indian schools" By the mid-1800s, most Native American tribes had been overwhelmed by the superior weapons of the U.S. military and confined to reservations. Beginning in the late 1800s and continuing into the 1950s, government policymakers established boarding schools for Native American youth to help them assimilate into the dominant culture and thus become "civilized." To this end, children were forcibly removed from their homes for long periods to separate them from native traditions. At the boarding schools, they were given a cursory academic education and spent most of their time studying Christian teachings and working to offset the cost of their schooling. Students were punished for speaking their own language or practicing their own religion. Responding to protests from the American Indian movement in the 1970s, the U.S. government began to send fewer Native Americans to boarding schools and retreated from its goal of assimilation at boarding schools and at newly established reservation schools. Such schools still exist, however. Today, government funding for Native American schools remains considerably lower than for other public schools, and students often make do with inadequate and antiquated facilities, equipment, and textbooks. In part because of such educational failures, few Native American students go on to college, and the incidence of alcohol and drug abuse among Native Americans is higher than in any other U.S. population.

First Grade

My hair was too short and my U.S. Government glasses were horn-rimmed, ugly, and all that first winter in school, the other Indian boys chased me from one corner of the playground to the other. They pushed me down, buried me in the snow until I couldn't breathe, thought I'd never breathe again. 1

They stole my glasses and threw them over my head, around my outstretched hands, just beyond my reach, until someone tripped me and sent me falling again, facedown in the snow. 2

I was always falling down; my Indian name was Junior Falls Down. Sometimes it was Bloody Nose or Steal-His-Lunch. Once, it was Cries-Like-a-White-Boy, even though none of us had seen a white boy cry. 3

Then it was a Friday morning recess and Frenchy SiJohn threw snowballs at me while the rest of the Indian boys tortured some other *top-yogh-yaught* kid, another weakling. But Frenchy was confident enough to torment me all by himself, and most days I would have let him. 4

But the little warrior in me roared to life that day and knocked Frenchy to the ground, held his head against the snow, and punched him so hard that my knuckles and the snow made symmetrical bruises on his face. He almost looked like he was wearing war paint. 5

But he wasn't the warrior. I was. And I chanted *It's a good day to die, it's a good day to die,* all the way down to the principal's office. 6

Second Grade

Betty Towle, missionary teacher, redheaded and so ugly that no one ever had a puppy crush on her, made me stay in for recess fourteen days straight. 7

"Tell me you're sorry," she said. 8

"Sorry for what?" I asked. 9

"Everything," she said and made me stand straight for fifteen minutes, eagle-armed with books in each hand. One was a math book; the other was English. But all I learned was that gravity can be painful. 10

For Halloween I drew a picture of her riding a broom with a scrawny cat on the back. She said that her God would never forgive me for that. 11

Once, she gave the class a spelling test but set me aside and gave me a test designed for junior high students. When I spelled all the words right, she crumpled up the paper and made me eat it. 12

"You'll learn respect," she said. 13

She sent a letter home with me that told my parents to either cut my braids or keep me home from class. My parents came in the next day and dragged their braids across Betty Towle's desk. 14

"Indians, indians, indians." She said it without capitalization. She called me "indian, indian, indian." 15

And I said, *Yes, I am. I am Indian. Indian, I am.* 16

Third Grade

17 My traditional Native American art career began and ended with my very first portrait: *Stick Indian Taking a Piss in My Backyard.*

18 As I circulated the original print around the classroom, Mrs. Schluter intercepted and confiscated my art.

19 *Censorship,* I might cry now. *Freedom of expression,* I would write in editorials to the tribal newspaper.

20 In third grade, though, I stood alone in the corner, faced the wall, and waited for the punishment to end.

21 I'm still waiting.

Fourth Grade

22 "You should be a doctor when you grow up," Mr. Schluter told me, even though his wife, the third grade teacher, thought I was crazy beyond my years. My eyes always looked like I had just hit-and-run someone.

23 "Guilty," she said. "You always look guilty."

24 "Why should I be a doctor?" I asked Mr. Schluter.

25 "So you can come back and help the tribe. So you can heal people."

26 That was the year my father drank a gallon of vodka a day and the same year that my mother started two hundred different quilts but never finished any. They sat in separate, dark places in our HUD house and wept savagely.

27 I ran home after school, heard their Indian tears, and looked in the mirror. *Doctor Victor,* I called myself, invented an education, talked to my reflection. *Doctor Victor to the emergency room.*

Fifth Grade

28 I picked up a basketball for the first time and made my first shot. No. I missed my first shot, missed the basket completely, and the ball landed in the dirt and sawdust, sat there just like I had sat there only minutes before.

29 But it felt good, that ball in my hands, all those possibilities and angles. It was mathematics, geometry. It was beautiful.

30 At that same moment, my cousin Steven Ford sniffed rubber cement from a paper bag and leaned back on the merry-go-round. His ears rang, his mouth was dry, and everyone seemed so far away.

31 But it felt good, that buzz in his head, all those colors and noises. It was chemistry, biology. It was beautiful.

32 Oh, do you remember those sweet, almost innocent choices that the Indian boys were forced to make?

Sixth Grade

33 Randy, the new Indian kid from the white town of Springdale, got into a fight an hour after he first walked into the reservation school.

Stevie Flett called him out, called him a squawman, called him a pussy, and called him a punk. 34

Randy and Stevie, and the rest of the Indian boys, walked out into the playground. 35

"Throw the first punch," Stevie said as they squared off. 36

"No," Randy said. 37

"Throw the first punch," Stevie said again. 38

"No," Randy said again. 39

"Throw the first punch!" Stevie said for the third time, and Randy reared back and pitched a knuckle fastball that broke Stevie's nose. 40

We all stood there in silence, in awe. 41

That was Randy, my soon-to-be first and best friend, who taught me the most valuable lesson about living in the white world: *Always throw the first punch.* 42

Seventh Grade

I leaned through the basement window of the HUD house and kissed the white girl who would later be raped by her foster-parent father, who was also white. They both lived on the reservation, though, and when the headlines and stories filled the papers later, not one word was made of their color. 43

Just Indians being Indians, someone must have said somewhere and they were wrong. 44

But on the day I leaned through the basement window of the HUD house and kissed the white girl, I felt the good-byes I was saying to my entire tribe. I held my lips tight against her lips, a dry, clumsy, and ultimately stupid kiss. 45

But I was saying good-bye to my tribe, to all the Indian girls and women I might have loved, to all the Indian men who might have called me cousin, even brother. 46

I kissed that white girl and when I opened my eyes, she was gone from the reservation, and when I opened my eyes, I was gone from the reservation, living in a farm town where a beautiful white girl asked my name. 47

"Junior Polatkin," I said, and she laughed. 48

After that, no one spoke to me for another five hundred years. 49

Eighth Grade

At the farm town junior high, in the boys' bathroom, I could hear voices from the girls' bathroom, nervous whispers of anorexia and bulimia. I could hear the white girls' forced vomiting, a sound so familiar and natural to me after years of listening to my father's hangovers. 50

"Give me your lunch if you're just going to throw it up," I said to one of those girls once. 51

I sat back and watched them grow skinny from self-pity. 52

• • •

53 Back on the reservation, my mother stood in line to get us commodities. We carried them home, happy to have food, and opened the canned beef that even the dogs wouldn't eat.

54 But we ate it day after day and grew skinny from self-pity.

55 There is more than one way to starve.

Ninth Grade

56 At the farm town high school dance, after a basketball game in an overheated gym where I had scored twenty-seven points and pulled down thirteen rebounds, I passed out during a slow song.

57 As my white friends revived me and prepared to take me to the emergency room where doctors would later diagnose my diabetes, the Chicano teacher ran up to us.

58 "Hey," he said. "What's that boy been drinking? I know all about these Indian kids. They start drinking real young."

59 Sharing dark skin doesn't necessarily make two men brothers.

Tenth Grade

60 I passed the written test easily and nearly flunked the driving, but still received my Washington State driver's license on the same day that Wally Jim killed himself by driving his car into a pine tree.

61 No traces of alcohol in his blood, good job, wife and two kids.

62 "Why'd he do it?" asked a white Washington State trooper.

63 All the Indians shrugged their shoulders, looked down at the ground.

64 "Don't know," we all said, but when we look in the mirror, see the history of our tribe in our eyes, taste failure in the tap water, and shake with old tears, we understand completely.

65 Believe me, everything looks like a noose if you stare at it long enough.

Eleventh Grade

> "This morning I pick up the sports page and read the headline: INDIANS LOSE AGAIN."

66 Last night I missed two free throws which would have won the game against the best team in the state. The farm town high school I play for is nicknamed the "Indians," and I'm probably the only actual Indian ever to play for a team with such a mascot.

67 This morning I pick up the sports page and read the headline: INDIANS LOSE AGAIN.

68 Go ahead and tell me none of this is supposed to hurt me very much.

Twelfth Grade

69 I walk down the aisle, valedictorian of this farm town high school, and my cap doesn't fit because I've grown my hair longer than it's ever been. Later, I

stand as the school-board chairman recites my awards, accomplishments, and scholarships.

I try to remain stoic for the photographers as I look toward the future. 70

Back home on the reservation, my former classmates graduate: a few can't 71
read, one or two are just given attendance diplomas, most look forward to the parties. The bright students are shaken, frightened, because they don't know what comes next.

They smile for the photographer as they look back toward tradition. 72

The tribal newspaper runs my photograph and the photograph of my former 73
classmates side by side.

Postscript: Class Reunion

Victor said, "Why should we organize a reservation high school reunion? 74
My graduating class has a reunion every weekend at the Powwow Tavern."

• • •

Reading Literature

1. Instead of linking events with transitional phrases that establish chronology, Alexie uses headings to move readers through his story. How do these headings indicate the passage of time? Are the headings enough, or do you think Alexie should have opened each section of the story with a transitional phrase? (Try to suggest some possibilities.)
2. The narrator's experiences in each grade in school are illustrated by specific incidents. What do these incidents have in common? What do they reveal about the narrator? About his schools?
3. Explain the meaning of each of these statements in the context of the story:
   - "There is more than one way to starve" (55).
   - "Sharing dark skin doesn't necessarily make two men brothers" (59).
   - "Believe me, everything looks like a noose if you stare at it long enough" (65).

Journal Entry

What does the "Postscript: Class Reunion" section (74) tell readers about Indian education? Is this information consistent with what we have learned in the rest of the story, or does it come as a surprise? Explain.

Thematic Connections

- "The Money" (page 111)
- "The Dog Ate My Tablet, and Other Tales of Woe" (page 452)
- The Declaration of Independence (page 550)

Writing Assignments for Narration

1. Trace the path you expect to follow to establish yourself in your chosen profession, considering possible obstacles you may face and how you expect to deal with them. Include a thesis statement that conveys the importance of your goals. If you like, you may refer to an essay in this book that focuses on work, such as "My Mother Never Worked" (page 121).
2. Write a personal narrative looking back from some point in the far future on your own life as you hope others will see it. Use third person if you like, and write your own obituary; or, use first person, assessing your life in a letter to your great-grandchildren.
3. Write a news article recounting in objective terms the events described in an essay that appears anywhere in this text, such as "Grant and Lee: A Study in Contrasts" (page 392) or "Emmett Till and Tamir Rice, Sons of the Great Migration" (page 422). Include a descriptive headline.
4. Write the introductory narrative for the home page of your family's (or community's) website. In this historical narrative, trace the roots of your family or your hometown or community. Be sure to include specific detail, dialogue, and descriptions of people and places. (You may also include visuals if you like.)
5. Write an account of one of these "firsts": your first serious argument with your parents, your first experience with physical violence or danger, your first extended stay away from home, your first encounter with someone whose culture was very different from your own, or your first experience with the serious illness or death of a close friend or relative. Make sure your essay includes a thesis statement your narrative can support.
6. **Working with Sources.** Both George Orwell and Martin Gansberg deal with the consequences of failing to act. Write an essay or story recounting what would have happened if Orwell had *not* shot the elephant or if one of the eyewitnesses *had* called the police right away. Be sure to document references to Orwell or Gansberg and to include a works-cited page. (See Chapter 18 for information on MLA documentation.)
7. **Working with Sources.** Write a narrative about a time when you were an outsider, isolated because of social, intellectual, or ethnic differences between you and others. Did you resolve the problems your isolation created? Explain. If you like, you may refer to the Orwell essay in this chapter or to "Just Walk On By" (page 233), taking care to include parenthetical documentation and a works-cited page. (See Chapter 18 for information on MLA documentation.)
8. Imagine a meeting between any two people who appear in this chapter's reading selections. Using dialogue and narrative, write an account of this meeting.
9. Using Sherman Alexie's story as a model, write the story of your own education.

10. List the five books you have read that most influenced you at important stages of your life. Then, write your literary autobiography, tracing your personal development through these books. (Or, write your wardrobe autobiography – discussing what you wore at different times of your life – or your film or music autobiography.)

Collaborative Activity for Narration

Working with a group of students of about your own age, write a history of your television-viewing habits. Start by working individually to list all your most-watched television shows in chronological order, beginning as far back as you can remember. Then, compile a single list that reflects a consensus of the group's preferences, perhaps choosing one or two representative programs for each stage of your life (preschool, elementary school, and so on). Have a different student write a paragraph on each stage, describing the chosen programs in as much detail as possible and using "we" as the subject. Finally, combine the individual paragraphs to create a narrative essay that traces the group's changing tastes in television shows. Be sure to discuss changes in how you accessed programs as well as the content of the shows you watched. The essay's thesis statement should express what your group's television preferences reveal about your generation's development.

7

Description

What Is Description?

You use **description** to tell readers about the physical characteristics of a person, place, or thing. Description relies on the five senses: sight, hearing, taste, touch, and smell. In the following paragraph from "Knoxville: Summer 1915," James Agee uses sight, touch, and sound to recreate a summer's evening for his audience.

Topic sentence	It is not of games children play in the evening that I want to speak now, it is of a contemporaneous atmosphere that has little to do with them; that of fathers and families, each in his space of lawn, his shirt fish-
Description using sight	like pale in the unnatural light and his face nearly anonymous, hosing their lawns. The hoses were attached to spigots that stood out of the brick foundations of the houses. The nozzles were variously set
Description using touch	but usually so there was a long sweet stream of spray, the nozzle wet in the hand, the water trickling the right forearm and the peeled-back cuff, and the water whishing out a long loose and low-curved cone, and so gentle a sound. First an insane noise of violence in
Description using sound	the nozzle, then the still irregular sound of adjustment, then the smoothing into steadiness and a pitch as accurately tuned to the size and style of stream as any violin. So many qualities of sound out of one hose: so many choral differences out of those several hoses that were in earshot. Out of any one hose, the almost dead silence of the release, and the short still arch of the separate big drops, silent as a held breath, and the only noise the flattering noise on leaves and the slapped grass at the fall of each big drop. That, and the intense hiss with the intense stream; that, and the same intensity not growing less but growing more quiet and delicate with the turn of the nozzle, up to that extreme tender whisper when the water was just a wide bell of film.

A descriptive essay tells what something looks like or what it feels like, sounds like, smells like, or tastes like. However, description often goes beyond personal sense impressions: novelists can create imaginary landscapes, historians can paint word pictures of historical figures or events, and scientists can describe physical phenomena they have never actually seen. When you write description, you use language to create a vivid impression for your readers.

Using Description

In your college writing, you use description in many different kinds of assignments. In a comparison-and-contrast essay, for example, you may describe the designs of two proposed buildings to show that one is more energy efficient than the other. In an argumentative essay, you may describe a fish kill in a local river to make the point that industrial waste dumping is a problem. Through description, you communicate your view of the world to your readers. If your readers come to understand or share your view, they are likely to accept your observations, your judgments, and, eventually, your conclusions. Therefore, in almost every essay you write, knowing how to write effective description is important.

Understanding Objective Description

Description can be *objective* or *subjective*. In an **objective description**, you focus on the object itself rather than on your personal reactions to it. Your purpose is to present a precise, literal picture of your subject. Many writing situations require exact descriptions of apparatus or conditions, and in these cases, your goal is to construct an accurate picture for your audience. A biologist describing what he sees through an electron microscope and a historian describing a Civil War battlefield would both write objectively. The biologist would not, for instance, say how exciting his observations were, nor would the historian say how disappointed she was at the outcome of the battle. Many newspaper reporters also try to achieve this level of objectivity, as do writers of technical reports, scientific papers, and certain types of business correspondence. Still, objectivity is an ideal that writers strive for but never fully achieve. In fact, by selecting some details and leaving out others, writers are making subjective decisions.

In the following descriptive passage, Shakespearean scholar Thomas Marc Parrott aims for objectivity by giving his readers the factual information they need to visualize Shakespeare's theater:

> The main or outer stage [of Shakespeare's theater] was a large platform, which projected out into the audience. Sections of the floor could be removed to make such things as the grave in the grave digger's scene in *Hamlet,* or they could be transformed into trapdoors through which characters could disappear, as in *The Tempest.* The players referred to the space

beneath the platform as the Hell. At the rear of the platform and at the same level was the smaller, inner stage, or alcove. . . . Above the alcove at the level of the second story, there was another curtained stage, the chamber. . . . The action of the play would move from one scene to another, using one, two, or all of them. Above the chamber was the music gallery; . . . and above this were the windows, "The Huts," where characters and lookouts could appear.

Artist's rendering of the Globe Theatre, London.

Note that Parrott is not interested in responding to or evaluating the theater he describes. Instead, he chooses words that convey sizes and directions, such as *large* and *above.*

Objective descriptions are sometimes accompanied by **visuals**, such as diagrams, drawings, or photographs. A well-chosen visual can enhance a description by enabling writers to avoid tedious passages of description that might confuse readers. For example, the illustration on page 151, which accompanies Parrott's description of Shakespeare's theater, makes the passage much easier to understand, helping readers visualize the multiple stages where Shakespeare's plays were performed.

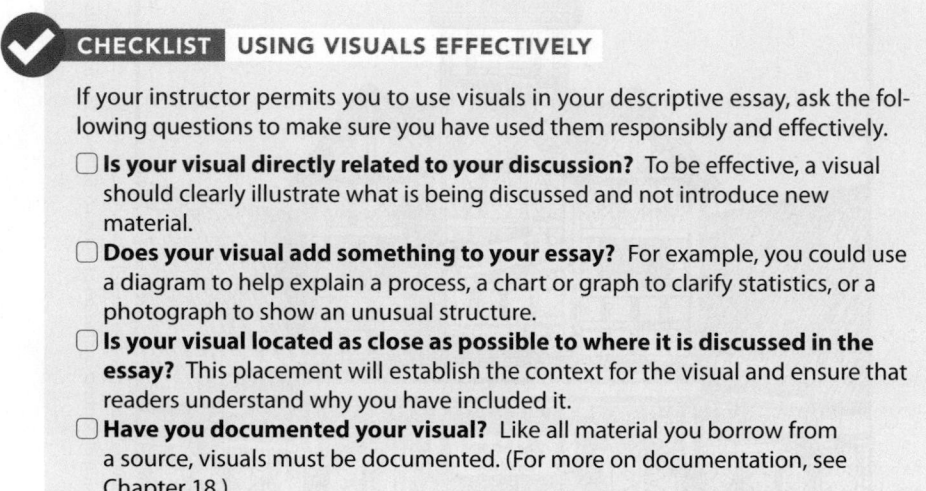

CHECKLIST USING VISUALS EFFECTIVELY

If your instructor permits you to use visuals in your descriptive essay, ask the following questions to make sure you have used them responsibly and effectively.

- ☐ **Is your visual directly related to your discussion?** To be effective, a visual should clearly illustrate what is being discussed and not introduce new material.
- ☐ **Does your visual add something to your essay?** For example, you could use a diagram to help explain a process, a chart or graph to clarify statistics, or a photograph to show an unusual structure.
- ☐ **Is your visual located as close as possible to where it is discussed in the essay?** This placement will establish the context for the visual and ensure that readers understand why you have included it.
- ☐ **Have you documented your visual?** Like all material you borrow from a source, visuals must be documented. (For more on documentation, see Chapter 18.)

REMINDER FINDING VISUALS

You can find visuals on the Internet, on DVDs, in clip-art compilations, or from Google Images. You can also scan pictures you find in print sources or download pictures you take with your phone or with a digital camera. Once the visual is downloaded onto your computer as a file, you can cut and paste it into your essay. Remember, however, that all visual material you get from a source — whether print or Internet — must be documented.

CLOSE VIEW

Understanding Subjective Description

In contrast to objective description, **subjective description** conveys your personal response to your subject. Here your perspective is not necessarily stated explicitly; often it is revealed indirectly, through your choice of words and phrasing. If a first-year composition assignment asks you to describe a place that has special meaning to you, you could give a subjective reaction to your topic by selecting and emphasizing details that show your feelings about the place. For example, you could write a subjective description of your room by focusing on particular objects – your desk, your window, and your bookshelves – and explaining the meanings these things have for you. Thus, your desk could be a "warm brown rectangle of wood whose surface reveals the scratched impressions of a thousand school assignments."

A subjective description should convey not just a literal record of sights and sounds but also their significance. For example, if you objectively described a fire that destroyed a house in your neighborhood, you might include the fire's temperature, duration, and scope. In addition, you might describe, as accurately as possible, the fire's movement and intensity. If you subjectively described the fire, however, you would try to re-create for your audience a sense of how the fire made you feel – your reactions to the noise, to the dense smoke, to the destruction.

In the following passage, notice how Mark Twain subjectively describes a sunset on the Mississippi River:

> I still kept in mind a certain wonderful sunset which I witnessed when steamboating was new to me. A broad expanse of the river was turned to blood; in the middle distance the red hue brightened into gold, through which a solitary log came floating, black and conspicuous; in one place a long, slanting mark lay sparkling upon the water; in another the surface was broken by boiling, tumbling rings, that were as many-tinted as an opal.

In this passage, Twain conveys his strong emotional reaction to the sunset by using vivid, powerful images, such as the river "turned to blood," the "solitary log . . . black and conspicuous," and the "boiling, tumbling rings." He also chooses words that suggest great value, such as *gold* and *opal.*

Neither objective nor subjective description exists independently. Objective descriptions usually include some subjective elements, and subjective descriptions need some objective elements to convey a sense of reality. The skillful writer adjusts the balance between objectivity and subjectivity to suit the topic, thesis, audience, and purpose as well as occasion for writing.

Using Objective and Subjective Language

As the passages by Parrott and Twain illustrate, both objective and subjective descriptions rely on language that appeals to readers' senses. But these two types of description use language differently. Objective descriptions rely on precise, factual language that presents a writer's observations without conveying his or her attitude toward the subject. Subjective descriptions, however, often use richer and more suggestive language than objective descriptions do. They are more likely to rely on the **connotations** of words, their emotional associations, than on their **denotations**, or more literal meanings (such as those found in a dictionary). In addition, they may deliberately provoke the reader's imagination with striking phrases or vivid language, including **figures of speech** (also called **figurative language**) such as *simile, metaphor, personification,* and *allusion.*

- A **simile** uses *like* or *as* to compare two dissimilar things. These comparisons occur frequently in everyday speech – for example, when someone claims to be "happy as a clam," "free as a bird," or "hungry as a bear." As a rule, however, you should avoid overused expressions like these in your writing. Effective writers constantly strive to create original similes. In his essay "Once More to the Lake" (page 189), for instance, E. B. White uses a striking simile to describe the annoying sound of boats on a lake when he says that in the evening, "they whined about one's ears *like mosquitoes.*" Later in the same essay, he describes a thunderstorm as being "*like the revival of an old melodrama* that I had seen long ago with childish awe."
- A **metaphor** compares two dissimilar things without using *like* or *as*. Instead of saying that something is *like* something else, a metaphor says it *is* something else. Mark Twain uses a metaphor when he says, "A broad expanse of the river was turned to blood."
- **Personification** speaks of concepts or objects as if they had life or human characteristics. If you say that the wind whispered or that an engine died, you are using personification.
- An **allusion** is a reference to a person, place, event, or quotation that the writer assumes readers will recognize. In "Letter from Birmingham Jail" (page 558), for example, Martin Luther King Jr. enriches his argument by alluding to biblical passages and proverbs that he expects his audience of clergy to be familiar with.

Your purpose and audience determine whether you should use objective or subjective description. An assignment that specifically asks for reactions calls for a subjective description. Legal, medical, technical, business, and scientific writing assignments, however, require objective descriptions because their primary purpose is to give the audience factual information. Even in these areas, though, figures of speech are often used to describe an unfamiliar object or concept. For example, in their pioneering article on the structure of DNA, scientists James Watson and Francis Crick use a simile when they describe a molecule of DNA as looking like two spiral staircases winding around each other.

Selecting Details

Sometimes inexperienced writers pack their descriptions with general words such as *nice, great, terrific,* or *awful,* substituting their own reactions to an object for the qualities of the object itself. To produce an effective description, however, you must do more than just *say* something is wonderful; you must also use details that evoke this response in your readers, as Twain does with the sunset. (Twain does use the word *wonderful* at the beginning of his description, but he then goes on to supply many specific details that make the scene he describes vivid and specific.)

All good descriptive writing, whether objective or subjective, relies on **specific details**. Your aim is not simply to *tell* readers what something looks like but to *show* them. Every person, place, or thing has its special characteristics, and you should use your powers of observation to detect them. Then, you need to select the specific words that will enable your readers to imagine what you describe. Don't be satisfied with "He looked angry" when you can say, "His face flushed, and one corner of his mouth twitched as he tried to control his anger." What's the difference? In the first case, you simply identify the man's emotional state. In the second, you provide enough detail so that readers can tell not only that he was angry but also how he revealed the intensity of his anger.

Of course, you could have provided even more detail by describing the man's beard, his wrinkles, or any number of other features. Keep in mind, however, that not all details are equally useful or desirable. You should include only those that contribute to the **dominant impression** – the mood or quality emphasized in the piece of writing – you wish to create. Thus, in describing a man's face to show how angry he was, you would probably not include the shape of his nose or the color of his hair. (After all, a person's hair color does not change when he or she gets angry.) In fact, the number of particulars you use is less important than their quality and appropriateness. You should select and use only those details relevant to your purpose.

Factors such as the level, background, and knowledge of your audience also influence the kinds of details you include. For example, a description of a DNA molecule written for high school students would contain more basic descriptive details than a description written for college biology majors. In addition, the more advanced description would contain details – the sequence of amino acid groups, for instance – that might be inappropriate for high school students.

Planning a Descriptive Essay

Developing a Thesis Statement

Writers of descriptive essays often use an **implied thesis** when they describe a person, place, or thing. This technique allows them to suggest the essay's main idea through the selection and arrangement of details. When they use description to support a particular point, however, many writers prefer to use an **explicitly stated thesis**. This strategy lets readers see immediately what point the writer is making; an example is, "The sculptures that adorn Philadelphia's City Hall are a catalog of nineteenth-century artistic styles."

Whether you state or imply your thesis, the details of your descriptive essay must work together to create a single dominant impression. In many cases, your thesis may be just a statement of the dominant impression; sometimes, however, your thesis may go further and make a point about that dominant impression.

Organizing Details

When you plan a descriptive essay, you usually begin by writing down descriptive details in no particular order. You then arrange these details in a way that supports your thesis and communicates your dominant impression. As you consider how to arrange your details, keep in mind that you have a number of options. For example, you can move from a specific description of an object to a general description of other things around it. Or you can reverse this order, beginning with the general and proceeding to the specific. You can also progress from the least important feature to the most important one, from the smallest to the largest item, from the least unusual to the most unusual detail, or from left to right, right to left, top to bottom, or bottom to top. Another option is to combine approaches, using different organizing schemes in different parts of the essay. The strategy you choose depends on the dominant impression you want to convey, your thesis, and your purpose and audience.

Using Transitions

Be sure to include all the transitional words and phrases readers need to follow your description. Without them, readers will have difficulty understanding the relationship of one detail to another. Throughout your description, especially in the topic sentences of your body paragraphs, use words or phrases indicating the spatial arrangement of details. In descriptive essays, the transitions commonly used include *above, adjacent to, at the bottom, at the top, behind, below, beyond, in front of, in the middle, next to, over, under, through,* and *within.* (A more complete list of transitions appears on page 55.)

Structuring a Descriptive Essay

Descriptive essays begin with an **introduction** that presents the **thesis** or establishes the dominant impression that the rest of the essay will develop. Each **body paragraph** includes details that support the thesis or convey the dominant impression. The **conclusion** reinforces the thesis or dominant impression, perhaps echoing an idea stated in the introduction or using a particularly effective simile or metaphor.

Suppose your first-year composition instructor has asked you to write a short essay describing a person, place, or thing. After thinking about the assignment for a day or two, you decide to write an objective description of the National Air and Space Museum in Washington, DC, because you have visited it recently and many details are fresh in your mind. The museum is large and has many different exhibits, so you know you cannot describe them all. Therefore, you decide to concentrate on one, the heavier-than-air flight exhibit, and you choose as your topic the display you remember most vividly: *The Spirit of St. Louis*, the airplane Charles Lindbergh flew solo across the Atlantic in 1927. You begin by brainstorming to recall all the details you can. When you read over your notes, you realize you could present the details of the airplane in the order in which your eye took them in, from front to rear. The dominant impression you wish to create is how small and fragile *The Spirit of St. Louis* appears, and your thesis statement communicates this impression. An informal outline for your essay might look like the one that follows.

SAMPLE OUTLINE: Descriptive Essay

INTRODUCTION
(thesis statement)
It is startling that a plane as small as *The Spirit of St. Louis* could fly across the Atlantic.

POINT 1
(support of thesis)
Front of plane: Single engine, tiny cockpit

POINT 2
(support for thesis)
Middle of plane: Short wingspan, extra gas tanks

POINT 3
(support for thesis)
Rear of plane: Limited cargo space filled with more gas tanks

CONCLUSION
Restatement of thesis (in different words) or review of key points or details

Revising a Descriptive Essay

When you revise a descriptive essay, consider the items on the revision checklist on page 66. In addition, pay special attention to the items on the following checklist, which apply specifically to descriptive essays.

REVISION CHECKLIST DESCRIPTION

- ☐ Does your assignment call for description?
- ☐ Does your descriptive essay clearly communicate its thesis or dominant impression?
- ☐ Is your description primarily objective or subjective?
- ☐ If your description is primarily objective, have you used precise, factual language? Would your essay be enriched by a visual?
- ☐ If your description is primarily subjective, have you used figures of speech as well as words that convey your feelings and emotions?
- ☐ Have you included enough specific details?
- ☐ Have you arranged your details in a way that supports your thesis and communicates your dominant impression?
- ☐ Have you used the transitional words and phrases that readers need to follow your description?

Editing a Descriptive Essay

When you edit your descriptive essay, follow the guidelines in the editing checklists on pages 83, 86, and 89. In addition, focus on the grammar, mechanics, and punctuation issues that are particularly relevant to descriptive essays. One of these issues – avoiding misplaced and dangling modifiers – is discussed below.

GRAMMAR IN CONTEXT AVOIDING MISPLACED AND DANGLING MODIFIERS

When writing descriptive essays, you use **modifying words** and **phrases** to describe people, places, and objects. Because these modifiers are important in descriptive essays, you need to place them correctly to ensure they clearly refer to the words they describe.

Avoiding Misplaced Modifiers A **misplaced modifier** appears to modify the wrong word because it is placed incorrectly in the sentence. Sentences that contain misplaced modifiers are always illogical and frequently humorous.

MISPLACED: E. B. White's son swam in the lake wearing an old bathing suit. (*Was the lake wearing a bathing suit?*)

MISPLACED: From the cabin, the sounds of the woods were heard by E. B. White and his son. (*Were the sounds of the woods inside the cabin?*)

In these sentences, the phrases *wearing an old bathing suit* and *from the cabin* appear to modify words that they cannot logically modify. You can correct these errors and avoid confusion by moving each modifier as close as possible to the word it is supposed to modify.

CORRECT: Wearing an old bathing suit, E. B. White's son swam in the lake.

CORRECT: From the cabin, E. B. White and his son heard the sounds of the woods.

Avoiding Dangling Modifiers A modifier "dangles" when it cannot logically modify any word that appears in the sentence. Often, these **dangling modifiers** come at the beginning of sentences (as present or past participle phrases), where they illogically seem to modify the words that come immediately after them.

DANGLING: Determined to get a better look, the viewing platform next to St. Paul's Chapel was crowded. (*Who was determined to get a better look?*)

DANGLING: Standing on the corner, the cranes, jackhammers, and bulldozers worked feverishly at ground zero. (*Who was standing on the corner?*)

In the preceding sentences, the phrases *determined to get a better look* and *standing on the corner* seem to modify *the viewing platform* and *cranes, jackhammers, and bulldozers,* respectively. However, these sentences make no sense. How can a viewing platform get a better look? How can cranes, jackhammers, and bulldozers stand on a corner? In addition, the two sentences do not contain the words that the modifying phrases are supposed to describe. In each case, you can correct the problem by supplying the missing word and rewriting the sentence accordingly.

CORRECT: Determined to get a better look, people crowded the viewing platform next to St. Paul's Chapel.

CORRECT: Standing on the corner, people watched the cranes, jackhammers, and bulldozers work feverishly at ground zero.

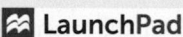

LaunchPad

For more practice on misplaced and dangling modifiers, see the LearningCurve on Modifier Placement in the LaunchPad for *Patterns*.

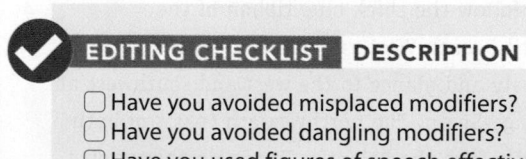

EDITING CHECKLIST DESCRIPTION

- ☐ Have you avoided misplaced modifiers?
- ☐ Have you avoided dangling modifiers?
- ☐ Have you used figures of speech effectively?
- ☐ Have you avoided general words such as *nice, great,* and *terrific*?

A STUDENT WRITER: Objective Description

The following essay, an objective description of a globe from 1939, was written by Mallory Cogan for a composition class. The assignment was to write a description of an object that has special meaning for her.

My Grandfather's Globe

Introduction

1 Each afternoon, sunlight slants through the windows of my grandfather's bedroom. Slowly, slowly, it sweeps over the bookshelves. Late in the day, just before the light disappears altogether, it rests sleepily on a globe in the corner. My grandfather bought this globe in 1939, just before World War II. The world has changed since then, and the globe is a record of what it looked like at that time.

Thesis statement

Description of Western Hemisphere

2 Turning the globe left, I begin my world tour with the Western Hemisphere. The blue of the Pacific Ocean gives way to the faded pinks, browns, and oranges of North and South America. In the north is a large area dotted with lakes and bays. This is the Dominion of Canada, now simply Canada. In the far north, the Canadian mainland breaks into islands that extend into the Arctic Ocean. Below it is the multicolored United States. To the north, Canada sprawls and breaks apart; to the south, Mexico narrows, then curves east, extended by the uneven strip of land that is Central America. This strip of land is connected to the northernmost part of South America. South America, in the same colors as the United States, looks like a face in profile looking east, with a nose extending into the Atlantic Ocean and a long neck that narrows as it reaches toward Antarctica at the South Pole.

Description of Africa

3 As I trace the equator east across the Atlantic Ocean, I come to French Equatorial Africa. The huge African continent, like a fat boomerang, is labeled with names of European countries. A large, kidney-shaped purple area to the northwest is called French West Africa. To the east, about halfway down the continent, is the Belgian Congo, a substantial orange splotch that straddles the equator. On the eastern coast just above the equator is a somewhat smaller, almost heart-shaped yellow area called Italian East Africa. These regions, once European colonies, are now divided into dozens of independent countries.

Description of Europe

4 Moving north, I follow the thick blue ribbon of the Mediterranean Sea until I reach Western Europe. I pause on yellow, boot-shaped Italy and glance to the west and southwest at purple France and orange Spain. The northwestern coasts of both countries extend slightly into the Atlantic. To the northwest of France, the pink clusters of the British Isles droop like bunches of grapes.

Description of Europe and changes since 1939

5 Looking eastward, I see a water stain on Germany. It extends down through Italy and across the Mediterranean, ending in the Sahara Desert on the African continent. Following the stain back into Europe, I look north, where Norway, Sweden, and Finland reach toward the rest of Europe. Returning to Germany, I move east, through Poland. On a modern globe, I would find Belarus and Ukraine on Poland's eastern border. On this globe, however, my finger passes directly into a vast area called the Union of Soviet Socialist Republics. The U.S.S.R. (today called the Russian Federation) cuts a wide swath across the northern part of the Asian continent; there is plenty of room for its long name to be displayed horizontally across the country's light-brown surface. Still in the southern half of the country, I travel east, crossing the landlocked Caspian Sea into a region of the U.S.S.R. called Turkistan, now the country of Turkmenistan. To the southeast, green Afghanistan sits between light-purple Iran to the west and pink India to the east. India is cone shaped, but with a pointed top, and green rectangular Nepal sits atop its western border.

Description of China and additional changes

6 Looking north again, I continue moving east. In Tibet, there is a small tear in the globe. I continue into China's vast interior. Just as the U.S.S.R. blankets the northern part of the Asian continent, China spreads over much of the southeast. I notice that China's borders on this globe are different from what they are today. On my grandfather's globe, China includes Mongolia but not a purple region to the northwest labeled Manchoukuo, also known as Manchuria. Following Manchoukuo to its southern border, I see a strip of land that extends into the sea, surrounded by water on three sides. The area is small, so its name — Chosen — has been printed in the Sea of Japan to the east. Today, it is called Korea.

Description of Southeast Asia

7 Backtracking west and dropping south, past China's southern border, I see Siam, now called Thailand. Siam is a three-leaf clover with a stem that hangs down. Wrapped along its eastern border, bordering two of its "leaves," is a purple country called French Indo-China. Today, this region is divided into the countries of Cambodia, Laos, and Vietnam. Bordering Siam on the west is the larger country of Burma, in pink. Like Siam, Burma is top-heavy, like a flower or a clover with a thin stem.

Description of Indonesia and Australia

8 Tracing that stem south, I come to the numerous islands of Indonesia, splashes of yellow spreading east-west along, above, and below the equator. I do not need to travel much farther before I arrive at a large landmass: Australia. This

country is pink and shaped like half of a very thick doughnut. On Australia's eastern coast is the Pacific; on its western coast is the Indian Ocean.

Conclusion Of course, it is not surprising that I would end where I started, with the ocean, since water covers seventy percent of the Earth. Still, countries — not oceans — are what interest me most about this globe. The shifting names and borders of countries that no longer exist remind me that although the world seems fixed, just as it did to the people of 1939, it is always changing. The change happens slowly, like the sun crossing my grandfather's room. Caught at any single moment, the world, like the afternoon light, appears still and mysterious. 9

Points for Special Attention

Objective Description. Because her essay is primarily an objective description, Mallory uses concrete language and concentrates on the shapes, colors, and surroundings of the countries she describes.

This objective description does include a few subjective elements. For example, in her introduction, Mallory says that the sunlight rests "sleepily" on her grandfather's globe. In her conclusion, she observes that the world represented by her grandfather's globe is "still and mysterious." (Her instructor had told the class that they could include a few subjective comments to convey the special meaning that the items they describe have for them.)

Figurative Language. To give readers a clear sense of what the countries on the globe look like, Mallory uses figurative language. For example, she uses similes when she describes South America as "like a face in profile" and Africa as looking "like a fat boomerang." She also uses metaphor when she says that the Mediterranean Sea is a "thick blue ribbon" and Siam is "a three-leaf clover with a stem that hangs down." Finally, Mallory uses personification when she says that the Belgian Congo "straddles the equator." By using these figures of speech, Mallory creates a vivid and striking picture of her grandfather's globe.

Structure. Mallory structures her description by moving from north to south as she moves east around the globe. She begins by describing the colors of North America, and then she describes South America. She directs her readers' attention to specific areas – for example, Central America. She then moves east, to Africa, and repeats the process of describing the regions in the north (Western Europe) and then in the south (Africa). As she does so, she notes that some countries, such as the U.S.S.R., have changed names since the globe was made in 1939. She repeats the pattern of moving east, north, and south and ends by describing Australia. Mallory frames her description of the globe with a description of her grandfather's bedroom. In her conclusion, she connects the sunlight in her grandfather's room to the world pictured on the globe by observing that both seem "still and mysterious."

Selection of Detail. Mallory's instructor defined her audience as people who know about the world today but have never seen her grandfather's globe and do not know much about the world in 1939. For this reason, Mallory includes details such as the tear in Tibet and the water stain that runs through Germany and Italy. In addition, she explains how some countries' names and borders differ from those that exist today.

Working with Sources. Before she wrote her essay, Mallory thought about looking at old atlases or history books. She decided that because her assignment called for a description of an object – not an analysis of how the world changed due to war or to the decline of colonialism – she did not have to consult these sources. She did, however, look up a few facts, such as the current name of Manchoukuo, but since facts are considered common knowledge, she did not have to document her sources for this information.

Focus on Revision

During a conference, Mallory's instructor suggested three possible changes. First, he thought that Mallory should consider including descriptions of additional countries, such as Japan in Asia and Chile, Argentina, and Brazil in South America. He thought that without these descriptions, readers might not fully appreciate how much information the globe contained. Next, he suggested that Mallory add more detail about the globe itself, such as its size, whether it was on a table or on a floor stand, and the materials from which it was constructed. Finally, he suggested that Mallory include a picture of the globe in her essay. He thought that this picture would give students a clearer idea of what the globe looked like and would eliminate the need to add more description.

Mallory decided to write a short paragraph (to be inserted between paragraphs 1 and 2) that provided a general description of the globe. She also decided to add a picture because even with all the vivid description she included, she thought the globe might be hard to picture. However, she decided she had mentioned enough countries in her essay and that adding more would be repetitious and might cause readers to lose interest.

A STUDENT WRITER: Subjective Description

The essay that follows, a subjective description of an area in Burma (also known as Myanmar since a military coup in 1989), was written by Mary Lim for her composition class. Her assignment was to write an essay about a place that had a profound effect on her. Mary's essay uses **subjective description** so that readers can share, as well as understand, her experience.

The Valley of Windmills

Introduction

In my native country of Burma, strange happenings and exotic scenery are not unusual, for Burma is a mysterious land that in some areas seems to have been ignored by time. Mountains stand jutting their rocky peaks into the clouds as they have for thousands of years. Jungles are so dense with exotic vegetation that human beings or large animals cannot even enter. But one of the most fascinating areas in Burma is the Valley of Windmills, nestled between the tall mountains near the beautiful city of Taungaleik. In this fertile valley there is beautiful and breathtaking scenery, but there are also old, massive, and gloomy structures that can disturb a person deeply. 1

Description (identifying the scene)

Description (moving toward the valley)

The road to Taungaleik twists out of the coastal flatlands into those heaps of slag, shale, and limestone that are the Tenasserim Mountains in the southern part of Burma. The air grows rarer and cooler, and stones become grayer, the highway a little more precarious at its edges, until, ahead, standing in ghostly sentinel across the lip of a pass, is a line of squat forms. They straddle the road and stand at intervals up hillsides on either side. Are they boulders? Are they fortifications? Are they broken wooden crosses on graves in an abandoned cemetery? 2

Description (immediate view)

These dark figures are windmills standing in the misty atmosphere. They are immensely old and distinctly evil, some merely turrets, some with remnants of arms hanging derelict from their snouts, and most of them covered with dark green moss. Their decayed but still massive forms seem to turn and sneer at visitors. Down the pass on the other side is a circular green plateau that lies like an arena below, where there are still more windmills. Massed in the plain behind them, as far as the eye can see, in every field, above every hut, stand ten thousand iron windmills, silent and sailless. They seem to await only a call from a watchman to clank, whirr, flap, and groan into action. Visitors suddenly feel cold. Perhaps it is a sense of loneliness, the cool air, the desolation, or the weirdness of the arcane windmills — but something chills them. 3

Description (more distant view)

Conclusion

As you stand at the lip of the valley, contrasts rush in to overwhelm you. Beyond, glittering on the mountainside like a solitary jewel, is Taungaleik in the territory once occupied by the Portuguese. Below, on rolling hillsides, are the dark windmills, still enveloped in morning mist. These ancient windmills can remind a person of the impermanence of life and the mystery that still surrounds these hills. In a strange way, the scene in the valley can be disturbing, but it also can offer insight into the contradictions that define life here in Burma. 4

Description (windmills contrasted with city)

Thesis statement

Points for Special Attention

Subjective Description. One of the first things her classmates noticed when they read Mary's essay was her use of vivid details. The road to Taungaleik is described in specific terms: it twists "out of the coastal flatlands" into the mountains, which are "heaps of slag, shale, and limestone." The iron windmills are decayed and stand "silent and sailless" on a green plateau that "lies like an arena." Through her use of detail, Mary creates her dominant impression of the Valley of Windmills as dark, mysterious, and disquieting. The point of her essay — the thesis — is stated in the last paragraph: the Valley of Windmills embodies the contrasts that characterize life in Burma.

Subjective Language. By describing the windmills, Mary conveys her sense of foreboding. When she first introduces them, she questions whether these "squat forms" are "boulders," "fortifications," or "broken wooden crosses," each of which has a menacing connotation. After telling readers what they are, she uses personification, describing the windmills as dark, evil, sneering figures with "arms hanging derelict." She sees them as ghostly sentinels awaiting "a call from a watchman" to spring into action. With this figure of speech, Mary skillfully re-creates the unearthly quality of the scene.

Structure. Mary's purpose in this essay was to give her readers the experience of being in the Valley of Windmills. She uses an organizing scheme that takes readers along the road to Taungaleik, up into the Tenasserim Mountains, and finally to the pass where the windmills wait. From her perspective on the lip of the valley, she describes the details closest to her and then those farther away, as if following the movement of her eyes. She ends by bringing her readers back to the lip of the valley, contrasting Taungaleik "glittering on the mountainside" with the windmills "enveloped in morning mist." With her description, Mary builds up to her thesis about the nature of life in her country. She withholds the explicit statement of her main point until her last paragraph, when readers are fully prepared for it.

Focus on Revision

Mary's peer-editing group suggested that she make two changes. One student thought that Mary's thesis about life in Burma needed additional support. The student pointed out that although Mary's description is quite powerful, it does not fully convey the contrasts she alludes to in her conclusion.

Mary decided that adding another paragraph discussing something about her life (perhaps her reasons for visiting the windmills) could help supply this missing information. She could, for example, tell her readers that right after her return from the valley, she found out that a friend had been accidentally shot by border guards and that it was this event that had caused her to characterize the windmills as she did. Such information would help explain the passage's somber mood and underscore the ideas presented in the conclusion.

Working with Sources. Another student suggested that Mary add some information about the political situation in Burma. He pointed out that few, if any, students in the class knew much about that country, not knowing, for example, that after a coup in 1989, the military threw out the civilian government and changed the name of Burma to Myanmar. In addition, he said that he had no idea how repressive the current government of Burma was. For this reason, the student thought readers would benefit from a paragraph that gave a short history of the country. Mary considered this option but decided that such information would distract readers from the main point of her description. (A sample peer-editing worksheet for description appears below.)

PEER-EDITING WORKSHEET: DESCRIPTION

1. What is the essay's dominant impression or thesis?
2. What points does the writer emphasize in the introduction? Should any other points be included? If so, which ones?
3. Would you characterize the essay as primarily an objective or subjective description? What leads you to your conclusion?
4. Point out some examples of figures of speech. Could the writer use figures of speech in other places? If so, where?
5. What specific details does the writer use to help readers visualize what is being described? Where could the writer have used more details? Would a visual have helped readers understand what is being described?
6. Are all the details necessary? Can you identify any that seem excessive or redundant? Where could the writer have provided more details to support the thesis or convey the dominant impression?
7. How are the details in the essay arranged? What other arrangement could the writer have used?
8. List some transitional words and phrases the writer uses to help readers follow the discussion. Which sentences need transitional words or phrases to link them to other sentences?
9. Do any sentences contain misplaced or dangling modifiers? If so, which ones?
10. How effective is the essay's conclusion? Does the conclusion reinforce the dominant impression?

The following selections illustrate various ways description can shape an essay. As you read them, pay particular attention to the differences between objective and subjective description. The first selection, a visual text, is followed by questions designed to illustrate how description can operate in visual form.

ANSEL ADAMS

Jackson Lake (Photo)

National Archives Catalog, Ansel Adams

• • •

Reading Images

1. This photograph, "Jackson Lake," was taken by the well-known photographer and environmentalist Ansel Adams. Describe what you see in the picture, starting with the image of the driftwood and then moving away toward the mountains.
2. Think of a few similes or metaphors that might be used to describe the lake. How would these figures of speech help someone who has not seen the picture visualize the lake and its surroundings?
3. What dominant impression do you think the photographer wanted to create? How do the details in the picture communicate this dominant impression?

Journal Entry

Go to Google Images and find other photographs by Ansel Adams. Choose one, and decide what dominant impression you think Adams was trying to create. Is it different from or similar to the dominant impression created by Adams in the photograph reproduced here?

Thematic Connections

- “Once More to the Lake” (page 189)
- “Photos That Change History” (page 356)
- *The Kiss* (page 389)
- “Naming of Parts” (page 476)
- “Tortillas” (page 500)

BICH MINH NGUYEN

Goodbye to My Twinkie Days

Writer Bich Minh Nguyen was born in 1974 in the Vietnamese city of Saigon, now known as Ho Chi Minh City. In 1975, her family fled to the United States, where they settled in Grand Rapids, Michigan. Nguyen holds an M.F.A. in creative writing from the University of Michigan and teaches writing and literature at Purdue University. Her books include a memoir, *Stealing Buddha's Dinner* (2007), which won a PEN/Jerard Award from the PEN American Center, and the novels *Short Girls* (2009) and *Pioneer Girl* (2014).

Background on the snack cake Individually wrapped, inexpensive, accessible, and unpretentious — the American snack cake is a democratic and egalitarian representation of mass-produced efficiency. Moreover, these processed products are also a guilty pleasure, even in today's health-conscious era. Although the Twinkie is perhaps the most iconic American snack cake, it is part of a larger history of mass-produced baked goods stretching back to the late nineteenth and early twentieth centuries. Although the Twinkie remains one of the best-selling snack cakes in history, it was not the first one produced. In 1888, Norman Drake established Drake Brothers, a commercial bakery in Brooklyn, New York, that sold individual slices of "Drake's Cakes" pound cake. Eventually, the company became better known for treats such as Yodels and Ring Dings. In the South, the first Moon Pie was sold by the Chattanooga Baking Company in 1917. Exactly who sold the first mass-produced snack cake remains a subject of dispute, however. For example, the Philadelphia company Tastykake claims that its individually packaged Junior layer cakes and chocolate cupcakes appeared in 1914 and 1915, predating Hostess products and the Moon Pie by several years. Regardless, no one disagrees that the first Twinkie appeared in 1930, created by baker James Dewar. The Hostess brand filed for bankruptcy in 2011, fueling fears that the Twinkie would disappear forever, yet the snack cake returned to store shelves — with the help of a new parent corporation — in 2013.

When I heard this week that the Hostess cake company was going out of business, I decided to pay my respects: I went out and bought a ten-pack box of Twinkies. 1

Though the more immediate cause of the company's trouble is a labor dispute with members of the Bakery, Confectionery, Tobacco Workers and Grain Millers International Union, its demise has been a long time coming. After all, we're not supposed to eat like this anymore. The partially hydrogenated oils, artificial flavors, high fructose corn syrup – Michael Pollan would not approve. Mr. Pollan, I swear that I have not tasted a Twinkie in years. I would not feed them to my kids. 2

But I can't stop the nostalgia, rising even now in the recitation of names: Ho Hos, Ding Dongs, Sno Balls, Zingers, Donettes, Suzy Q's. Generations of us carried these Hostess treats in our lunchboxes, traded them, saved bites of frosting and cream for last. Soon, unless another company buys the brands, they'll be nothing but liquidated assets. 3

"Junk food" is a phrase at once grotesque and appealing. We know it's bad, and that's why we want it. The Twinkie, introduced in 1930, was a best-selling treat of the Depression and is still one of the company's top items. The inventor got the idea after seeing baking equipment for strawberry cakes go unused when the fruit was out of season. (It seems incredible now that mass-production of food once shifted with the seasons.) We have Hostess largely to thank for the very concept of the "snack cake," lifting sweets from dessert time to anytime. Of the company's many products – the chocolate CupCakes with the white squiggle across the top, Fruit Pies, Dolly Madison cakes, even Wonder Bread – the Twinkie, fresh from the package or deep-fried at a county fair, has been its most enduring icon. 4

> "'Junk food' is a phrase at once grotesque and appealing."

For me, a child of Vietnamese immigrants growing up in Michigan in the 1980s, Twinkies were a ticket to assimilation: the golden cake, more golden than the hair I wished I had, filled with sweet white cream. Back then, junk foods seemed to represent an ideal of American indulgence. 5

They've since become a joke, a stereotype of shallow suburbia. For Asian-Americans, to be a twinkie is to be a sellout: yellow on the outside, white on the inside. Even the name "Hostess" seems quaintly outdated, like "stewardess" or "butler." On the box of Twinkies I bought there's a cartoon of a Twinkie as a cowboy; his sidekick is a short, swarthy chocolate cupcake. Whether Hostess meant to evoke the Lone Ranger and Tonto or was simply trying to recapture a glory-days notion of sweet-toothed kids playing dress-up, the company seems determined to be retro. 6

Yet maybe that's exactly why the Twinkie has continued to fascinate: it is already a relic. When I opened one, the smell of sugary, fake, buttery-ish vanilla took me back to my elementary school and the basketball lines on the floor of the gym that doubled as our lunchroom. The underside of the cake had the same three white dots where the cream filling had been punched in, and it tasted like what it was, a blend of shortening and corn syrup, coating the tongue. I didn't think the Twinkie would thrill the way it used to, and it didn't. But it tasted like memory. 7

We might bake our own cakes now, eat whole grain bread, and try to follow those grocery store Food Rules, but who among us can forget being sugar-shocked by processed goods? What will it mean if Twinkies and Zingers become footnotes, gone the way of Uneeda Biscuit and Magic Middles? There's nothing like junk foods, emblems of our shared pop culture, to create a conversation and establish common ground. Losing the Twinkie will mean 8 losing a connection to our shared past; it will be another part of the long goodbye to our youth. As Hostess goes under, we become older.

According to popular myth, Twinkies are so stuffed with chemicals and preservatives that they will last for decades. Hostess insists that the shelf life is more like twenty-five days. I decided to store the rest of mine in the cupboard above my refrigerator, out of reach but available, just in case. I may never eat them, but I like knowing that they exist, that I can still taste my way back to the childhood living room where I watched episodes of *Silver Spoons* and dreamed of all the possibilities yet to be consumed. 9

• • •

Comprehension

1. Despite saying that she has not eaten a Twinkie in years and that she would not give one to her children, Nguyen buys a ten-pack. Why?
2. According to Nguyen, what is the significance of a "snack cake"?
3. In paragraph 5, Nguyen says, "Twinkies were a ticket to assimilation." What does she mean? In what sense is junk food particularly American?
4. What special meaning do Hostess Twinkies have for Asian Americans?
5. What significance would losing Twinkies have for Nguyen? For all Americans?

Purpose and Audience

1. How much does Nguyen assume her readers know about Twinkies? How can you tell?
2. What is Nguyen's purpose? Is she writing about how much she will miss Twinkies, or is she writing about something else? Explain.
3. Does this essay have an explicitly stated thesis, or is the thesis implied? What dominant impression does Nguyen want to convey?

Style and Structure

1. Nguyen begins her essay with a one-sentence paragraph. How effective is this opening strategy? How else could she have begun her essay?
2. In paragraph 2, Nguyen refers to Michael Pollan, who writes about culture and food – especially about how industrial food production has lost touch with nature. Why does Nguyen mention Pollan? What point is she trying to make?
3. In paragraph 6, Nguyen includes one sentence that contains a colon and another that contains a semicolon. Instead of the colon, why doesn't Nguyen use a comma? Instead of the semicolon, why doesn't she use a period?

4. **Vocabulary Project.** In paragraph 4, Nguyen discusses junk food. What do you think she means by this term? Is your definition of junk food different from Nguyen's? If so, how?
5. In paragraph 6, Nguyen describes the box that contains the Twinkies. In paragraph 7, she describes a Twinkie itself. Are these descriptions primarily objective or subjective? What specific words lead you to your conclusion?

Journal Entry

What snack food do you most associate with your childhood? Is this association positive or negative? Why?

Writing Workshop

1. **Working with Sources.** Write an essay in which you describe a food that is as meaningful to you as Twinkies are to Nguyen. Make sure your essay has a clear thesis and includes at least one reference to Nguyen's essay. Be sure to document all material that you borrow from Nguyen's essay and to include a works-cited page. (See Chapter 18 for information on MLA documentation.)
2. Write an email to someone in another country in which you describe the foods that you traditionally eat on a particular holiday. Assume the person is not familiar with the foods you describe. Be sure your description conveys a clear dominant impression.
3. Write an essay in which you describe a parent or grandparent (or any other older person) who has had a great influence on you. Make sure you include basic biographical information as well as a detailed physical description.

Combining the Patterns

In addition to describing Nguyen's fascination for Twinkies, this essay examines **causes and effects** (in paragraph 2). What purpose does this cause-and-effect paragraph serve?

Thematic Connections

- "My Field of Dreams" (page 104)
- "Surrendering" (page 116)
- "Why the Post Office Makes America Great" (page 220)
- "Tortillas" (page 500)

SUZANNE BERNE

Ground Zero

Suzanne Berne was born in Washington, DC, in 1961. She has worked as a journalist and has also published book reviews, personal essays, and four well-received novels, including *The Ghost at the Table* (2006) and *The Dogs of Littlefield* (2016). Her writing has also appeared in *Ploughshares, Agni,* the *New York Times Magazine*, and other publications. She currently teaches English at Boston College. In the following essay, which appeared on the *New York Times* op-ed page in April 2002, Berne describes a personal pilgrimage to the former site of the World Trade Center in New York City.

Background on the terrorist attacks of 9/11 The September 11, 2001, terrorist attacks that destroyed the twin towers of New York's World Trade Center and severely damaged the Pentagon stunned the nation and the world. People watched in horror as camera crews recorded the collapse of the towers while victims jumped to their deaths. The three hijacked aircraft that crashed into these targets, and a fourth that crashed into a field in rural Pennsylvania, caused the deaths of nearly three thousand people. An outpouring of grief, outrage, fear, and patriotism consumed the nation in the ensuing months. Although many, like Berne, are drawn to visit ground zero, some family members of the victims — particularly of those whose unidentified remains are still at the site — expressed concern that it not become a tourist attraction. A memorial at the site, which opened in May 2014, includes two huge reflecting pools where the original twin towers stood. The names of the nearly three thousand people who were killed in the September 11 attacks in New York City, in Pennsylvania, and at the Pentagon in Arlington, Virginia (as well as those killed in the 1993 World Trade Center bombings), are inscribed around the edges of the pools. An underground museum houses exhibits that convey the experiences of responders, victims, and witnesses.

On a cold, damp March morning, I visited Manhattan's financial district, 1
a place I'd never been, to pay my respects at what used to be the World Trade Center. Many other people had chosen to do the same that day, despite the raw wind and spits of rain, and so the first thing I noticed when I arrived on the corner of Vesey and Church Streets was a crowd.

Standing on the sidewalk, pressed against aluminum police barricades, 2
wearing scarves that flapped into their faces and woolen hats pulled over their ears, were people apparently from everywhere. Germans, Italians, Japanese. An elegant-looking Norwegian family in matching shearling coats. People from Ohio and California and Maine. Children, middle-aged couples, older people. Many of them were clutching cameras and video recorders, and they were all craning to see across the street, where there was nothing to see.

At least, nothing is what it first looked like, the space that is now ground 3
zero. But once your eyes adjust to what you are looking at, "nothing" becomes something much more potent, which is absence.

But to the out-of-towner, ground zero looks at first simply like a con- 4
struction site. All the familiar details are there: the wooden scaffolding; the cranes, the bulldozers, and forklifts; the trailers and construction workers in hard hats; even the dust. There is the pound of jackhammers, the steady beep-beep-beep of trucks backing up, the roar of heavy machinery.

So much busyness is reassuring, and it is possible to stand looking at 5
the cranes and trucks and feel that mild curiosity and hopefulness so often inspired by construction sites.

Then gradually your eyes do adjust, exactly as if you have stepped from a 6
dark theater into a bright afternoon, because what becomes most striking about this scene is the light itself.

Ground zero is a great bowl of light, 7
an emptiness that seems weirdly spacious and grand, like a vast plaza amid the dense tangle of streets in lower Manhattan. Light reflecting off the Hudson River vaults into the site, soaking everything – especially on an overcast morning – with a watery glow. This is the moment when absence begins to assume a material form, when what is not there becomes visible.

"Ground zero is a great bowl of light, an emptiness that seems weirdly spacious and grand. . ."

Suddenly you notice the periphery, the skyscraper shrouded in black plas- 8
tic, the boarded windows, the steel skeleton of the shattered Winter Garden. Suddenly there are the broken steps and cracked masonry in front of Brooks Brothers. Suddenly there are the firefighters, the waiting ambulance on the other side of the pit, the police on every corner. Suddenly there is the enormous cross made of two rusted girders.

And suddenly, very suddenly, there is the little cemetery attached to St. 9
Paul's Chapel, with tulips coming up, the chapel and grounds miraculously undamaged except for a few plastic-sheathed gravestones. The iron fence is almost invisible beneath a welter of dried pine wreaths, banners, ribbons, laminated poems and prayers and photographs, swags of paper cranes, withered flowers, baseball hats, rosary beads, teddy bears. And flags, flags everywhere, little American flags fluttering in the breeze, flags on posters drawn by Brownie troops, flags on T-shirts, flags on hats, flags streaming by, tied to the handles of baby strollers.

It takes quite a while to see all of this; it takes even longer to come up with 10
something to say about it.

An elderly man standing next to me had been staring fixedly across the 11
street for some time. Finally he touched his son's elbow and said: "I watched those towers being built. I saw this place when they weren't there." Then he stopped, clearly struggling with, what for him, was a double negative, recalling an absence before there was an absence. His son, waiting patiently, took a few photographs. "Let's get out of here," the man said at last.

Again and again I heard people say, "It's unbelievable." And then they 12
would turn to each other, dissatisfied. They wanted to say something more expressive, more meaningful. But it *is* unbelievable, to stare at so much

devastation, and know it for devastation, and yet recognize that it does not look like the devastation one has imagined.

Like me, perhaps, the people around me had in mind images from television and newspaper pictures: the collapsing buildings, the running office workers, the black plume of smoke against a bright blue sky. Like me, they were probably trying to superimpose those terrible images onto the industrious emptiness right in front of them. The difficulty of this kind of mental revision is measured, I believe, by the brisk trade in World Trade Center photograph booklets at tables set up on street corners. 13

Determined to understand better what I was looking at, I decided to get a ticket for the viewing platform beside St. Paul's. This proved no easy task, as no one seemed to be able to direct me to South Street Seaport, where the tickets are distributed. Various police officers whom I asked for directions waved me vaguely toward the East River, differing degrees of boredom and resignation on their faces. Or perhaps it was a kind of incredulousness. Somewhere around the American Stock Exchange, I asked a security guard for help and he frowned at me, saying, "You want tickets to the disaster?" 14

Finally I found myself in line at a cheerfully painted kiosk, watching a young juggler try to entertain the crowd. He kept dropping the four red balls he was attempting to juggle, and having to chase after them. It was noon; the next available viewing was at 4 P.M. 15

Back I walked, up Fulton Street, the smell of fish in the air, to wander again around St. Paul's. A deli on Vesey Street advertised a view of the World Trade Center from its second-floor dining area. I went in and ordered a pastrami sandwich, uncomfortably aware that many people before me had come to that same deli for pastrami sandwiches who would never come there again. But I was here to see what I could, so I carried my sandwich upstairs and sat down beside one of the big plate-glass windows. 16

And there, at last, I got my ticket to the disaster. 17

I could see not just into the pit now, but also its access ramp, which trucks had been traveling up and down since I had arrived that morning. Gathered along the ramp were firefighters in their black helmets and black coats. Slowly they lined up, and it became clear that this was an honor guard, and that someone's remains were being carried up the ramp toward the open door of an ambulance. 18

Everyone in the dining room stopped eating. Several people stood up, whether out of respect or to see better, I don't know. For a moment, everything paused. 19

Then the day flowed back into itself. Soon I was outside once more, joining the tide of people washing around the site. Later, as I huddled with a little crowd on the viewing platform, watching people scrawl their names or write "God Bless America" on the plywood walls, it occurred to me that a form of repopulation was taking effect, with so many visitors to this place, thousands of visitors, all of us coming to see the wide emptiness where so many were 20 lost. And by the act of our visiting – whether we are motivated by curiosity or horror or reverence or grief, or by something confusing that combines them all – that space fills up again.

• • •

Comprehension

1. What does Berne mean when she says that as her eyes adjust to what she is seeing, "'nothing' becomes something much more potent, which is absence" (3)?
2. Why does it take "quite a while" (10) to see all the details at ground zero? Why does it take "even longer" (10) to think of something to say about it?
3. According to Berne, how were the television pictures of ground zero different from the actual experience of seeing it?
4. How does the area around ground zero contrast with the site itself? How does Berne react to this contrast?
5. What does Berne mean in her conclusion when she says that with so many visitors coming to see ground zero, a form of "repopulation" (20) is taking place? Do you think she is being **sarcastic**?

Purpose and Audience

1. Does Berne state or imply her thesis? Why do you think she makes the decision she does? State Berne's thesis in your own words.
2. What is Berne's purpose in writing her essay?
3. What assumptions does Berne make about her readers' ideas about ground zero? How can you tell?

Style and Structure

1. Why does Berne begin her essay by saying she had never before visited Manhattan's financial district?
2. What organizational scheme does Berne use? What are the advantages and disadvantages of this scheme?
3. In paragraph 3, Berne says that ground zero at first looks like "nothing"; in paragraph 4, she says that it looks like a construction site. Then, in paragraph 7, she describes ground zero as "a great bowl of light." And finally, in her conclusion, she refers to it as a "pit" (18). Why do you think Berne describes ground zero in so many different ways?
4. Berne leaves a space between paragraphs 17 and 18. In what way does the space (as well as paragraph 17) reinforce a shift in her essay's focus?
5. Why does Berne end her essay with a description of the crowd standing on the viewing platform? Why do you suppose she feels the need to include these observations?

6. In paragraphs 8 and 9, Berne repeats the word *suddenly*. What is the effect of this repetition? Could she have achieved this effect some other way?
7. **Vocabulary Project.** Look up the meaning of the term *ground zero*. What connotations does this term have? Why is it an appropriate title for Berne's essay?

Journal Entry

Go to the website wtc.vjs.org and look at film clips of ground zero just after the twin towers collapsed. Are your reactions to these images similar to or different from Berne's?

Writing Workshop

1. **Working with Sources.** Write an essay describing what you saw in the film clips you watched for your journal entry. Be sure to include an explicitly stated thesis and to use descriptive details to convey your reactions to the event. Try to include a quotation from Berne's essay in your paper. Be sure to document the quotation and to include a works-cited page. (See Chapter 18 for information on MLA documentation.)
2. Write a description of a place from several different vantage points, as Berne does. Make sure each of your perspectives provides different information about the place you are describing.
3. Write a subjective description of a scene you remember from your childhood. In your thesis statement and in your conclusion, explain how your adult impressions of the scene differ from those of your childhood.

Combining the Patterns

In addition to containing a great deal of description, this essay also uses **comparison and contrast**. In paragraphs 1 through 10, what two ways of seeing ground zero does Berne compare? What points about each view of ground zero does she contrast?

Thematic Connections

- From *Persepolis II* (page 109)
- "Shooting an Elephant" (page 131)
- "What Motivates Terrorists?" (page 344)
- "Photos That Change History" (page 356)

MARINA KEEGAN

Stability in Motion

Author and playwright Marina Keegan (1989–2012) was raised in Wayland, Massachusetts, and attended Yale University, where she majored in English. While at Yale, she was an intern at the *New Yorker* magazine and the *Paris Review*. Her work was read on National Public Radio and was published in the *New York Times* as well as the *New Yorker*. She also organized a campus protest, Occupy Morgan Stanley, which opposed on-campus corporate recruiting by the financial industry. That issue informed her writing as well: in 2012, she wrote "Even Artichokes Have Doubts" for the *Yale Daily News,* a widely discussed article that explored why so many Yale graduates chose to work in consulting or finance. Ironically, given the subject of "Stability in Motion," Keegan was killed at the age of twenty-two in a car crash on Cape Cod.

Background on the automobile in the twentieth century Although he did not invent the automobile, Henry Ford built the first mass-produced car that was both reliable and affordable. Consequently, the automobile moved from being a toy of the rich to a necessity of everyday life and profoundly changed people's employment patterns, social interactions, and living conditions. In the post–World War II boom of the 1950s and 1960s, cars came to represent freedom and individuality for America's teenagers. Drive-in movie theaters and fast-food restaurants became staples of everyday life, and hit songs like "409" by the Beach Boys and "Mustang Sally" by Wilson Pickett romanticized the joys of driving a fast car. By the time Marina Keegan got her first car in the 1990s, concerns about pollution, safety, and urban congestion had begun to dampen American's romance with the car. Today, because of rising tuition and student-loan debt, many millennials cannot afford cars and as a result are turning to other less expensive means of transportation.

My 1990 Camry's DNA was designed inside the metallic walls of the Toyota Multinational Corporation's headquarters in Tokyo, Japan; transported via blueprint to the North American Manufacturing nerve center in Hebron, Kentucky; grown organ by organ in four major assembly plants in Alabama, New Jersey, Texas, and New York; trucked to 149 Arsenal Street in Watertown, Massachusetts; and steered home by my grandmother on September 4, 1990. It featured a 200 hp, 3.0 L V6 engine, a four-speed automatic, and an adaptive Variable Suspension System. She deemed the car too "high tech." In 1990 this meant a cassette player, a cup holder, and a manually operated moon roof. 1

During its youth, the car traveled little. In fifteen years my grandmother accumulated a meager twenty-five thousand miles, mostly to and from the market, my family's house, and the Greek jewelry store downtown. The black exterior remained glossy and spotless, the beige interior crisp and pristine. 2

Tissues were disposed of, seats vacuumed, and food prohibited. My grandmother's old-fashioned cleanliness was an endearing virtue – one that I evidently did not inherit.

I acquired the old Camry through an awkward transaction. Ten days before my sixteenth birthday, my grandfather died. He was eighty-six and it had been long expected, yet I still felt a guilty unease when I heard the now surplus car would soon belong to me. For my grandmother, it was a symbolic goodbye. She needed to see only *one* car in her garage – needed to comprehend her loss more tangibly. Grandpa's car was the "nicer" of the two, so that one she would keep. Three weeks after the funeral, my grandmother and I went to the bank, I signed a check for exactly one dollar, and the car was legally mine. That was that. When I drove her home that evening, I manually opened the moon roof and put on a tape of Frank Sinatra. My grandma smiled for the first time in weeks. 3

Throughout the next three years, the car evolved. When I first parked the Toyota in my driveway, it was spotless, full of gas, and equipped with my grandmother's version of survival necessities. The glove compartment had a magnifying glass, three pens, and the registration in a little Ziploc bag. The trunk had two matching black umbrellas, a first aid kit, and a miniature sewing box for emergency repairs. Like my grandmother's wrists, everything smelled of Opium perfume. 4

For a while, I maintained this immaculate condition. Yet one Wrigley's wrapper led to two and soon enough my car underwent a radical transformation – the vehicular equivalent of a midlife crisis. Born and raised in proper formality, the car saw me as *that* friend from school, the bad example who washes away naïveté and corrupts the clean and innocent. We were the same age, after all – both eighteen. The Toyota was born again, crammed with clutter, and exposed to decibel levels it had never fathomed. I filled it with giggling friends and emotional phone calls, borrowed skirts and bottled drinks. 5

The messiness crept up on me. Parts of my life began falling off, forming an eclectic debris that dribbled gradually into every corner. Empty sushi containers, Diet Coke cans, half-full packs of gum, sweaters, sweatshirts, socks, my running shoes. My clutter was nondiscriminatory. I had every variety of newspaper, scratched-up English paper, biology review sheet, and Spanish flash card discarded on the seats after I'd sufficiently studied on my way to school. The left door pocket was filled with tiny tinfoil balls, crumpled after consuming my morning English muffin. By Friday, I had the entire house's supply of portable coffee mugs. By Sunday, someone always complained about their absence and I would rush out, grab them all, and surreptitiously place them in the dishwasher. 6

My car was not gross; it was occupied, cluttered, cramped. It became an extension of my bedroom, and thus an extension of myself. I had two bumper stickers on the back: REPUBLICANS FOR VOLDEMORT and the symbol for the Equal Rights Campaign. On the back side windows were OBAMA '08 signs that my parents made me take down because they "dangerously blocked my sight lines." The trunk housed my guitar but was also the library, filled with textbooks and novels, the giant tattered copy of *The Complete Works of William* 7

Shakespeare and all one hundred chapters of *Harry Potter* on tape. A few stray cassettes littered the corners, their little brown insides ripped out, tangled and mutilated. They were the casualties of the trunk trenches, sprawled out forgotten next to the headband I never gave back to Meghan.

On average, I spent two hours a day driving. It was nearly an hour each way 8
to school, and the old-fashioned Toyota – regarded with lighthearted amusement by my classmates – came to be a place of comfort and solitude amid the chaos of my daily routine. My mind was free to wander, my muscles to relax. No one was watching or keeping score. Sometimes I let the deep baritone of NPR's Tom Ashbrook lecture me on oil shortages. Other times I played repetitive mix tapes with titles like *Pancake Breakfast, Tie-Dye and Granola,* and *Songs for the Highway When It's Snowing.*

Ravaging my car, I often found more than just physical relics. For two 9
months I could hardly open the side door without reliving the first time he kissed me. His dimpled smile was barely visible in the darkness, but it nevertheless made me stumble backward when I found my way blushingly back into the car. On the backseat there was the June 3 issue of the *New York Times* that I couldn't bear to throw out. When we drove home together from the camping trip, he read it cover to cover while I played Simon and Garfunkel – hoping he'd realize all the songs were about us. We didn't talk much during that ride. We didn't need to. He slid his hand into mine for the first time when we got off the highway; it was only after I made my exit that I realized I should have missed it. Above this newspaper are the fingernail marks I dug into the leather of my steering wheel on the night we decided to *just be friends*. My car listened to me cry for all twenty-two-and-a-half miles home.

The physical manifestations of my memories soon crowded the car. My 10
right back speaker was broken from the time my older brother and I pulled an all-nighter singing shamelessly during our rainy drive home from the wedding. I remember the sheer energy of the storm, the lights, the music – moving through us, transcending the car's steel shell, and tracing the city. There was the folder left behind from the day I drove my dad to an interview the month after he lost his job. It was coincidental that *his* car was in the shop, but I knew he felt more pathetic that it was he, not his daughter, in the passenger seat. I kept my eyes on the road, feeling the confused sadness of a child who catches a parent crying.

I talked a lot in my car. Thousands of 11
words and songs and swears are absorbed in its fabric, just like the orange juice I spilled on my way to the dentist. It knows what happened when Allie went to Puerto Rico, understands the difference between the way I look at Nick and the way I look at Adam, and remembers the first time I experimented with talking to myself. I've practiced for auditions, college interviews, Spanish oral presentations, and debates. There's something novel about swearing alone in the car. Yet with the

"Thousands of words and songs and swears are absorbed in its fabric, just like the orange juice I spilled on my way to the dentist."

pressures of APs and SATs and the other acronyms that haunt high school, the act became more frequent and less refreshing.

My car has seen three drive-in movies. During *The Dark Knight*, its battery died and, giggling ferociously, we had to ask the overweight family in the next row to jump it. The smell of popcorn permeated every crevice of the sedan, and all rides for the next week were like a trip to the movies. There was a variety of smells in the Camry. At first it smelled like my grandmother – perfume, mint, and mothballs. I went through a chai-tea phase during which my car smelled incessantly of Indian herbs. Some mornings it would smell slightly of tobacco and I would know immediately that my older brother had kidnapped it the night before. For exactly three days it reeked of marijuana. Dan had removed the shabbily rolled joint from behind his ear and our fingers had trembled as the five of us apprehensively inhaled. Nothing happened. Only the seats seemed to absorb the plant and get high. Mostly, however, it smelled like nothing to me. Yet when I drove my friends, they always said it had a distinct aroma. I believe this functioned in the same way as not being able to taste your own saliva or smell your own odor – the car and I were pleasantly immune to each other. 12

In the Buckingham Browne & Nichols High School yearbook I was voted worst driver, but on most days I will refute this superlative. My car's love for parking tickets made me an easy target, but I rarely received other violations. My mistakes mostly harmed me, not others – locking my keys in the car or parking on the wrong side of the road. Once, last winter, I needed to refill my windshield wiper fluid and in a rushed frenzy poured an entire bottle of similarly blue antifreeze inside. Antifreeze, as it turns out, burns out engines if used in excess. I spent the next two hours driving circles around my block in a snowstorm, urgently expelling the antifreeze squirt by thick blue squirt. I played no music during this vigil. I couldn't find a playlist called *Poisoning Your Car.* 13

It may have been awkward-looking and muddled, but I was attached to my car. It was a portable home that heated my seat in winter and carried me home at night. I had no diary and rarely took pictures. That old Toyota Camry was an odd documentation of my adolescence. When I was seventeen, the car was seventeen. My younger brother entered high school last September and I passed my ownership on to him. In the weeks before I left for college, my parents made me clean it out for his sake. I spread six trash bags over the driveway, filling them with my car's contents as the August sun heated their black plastic. The task was strange, like deconstructing a scrapbook, unpeeling all the pictures and whiting out the captions. 14

Just like for my grandmother, it was a symbolic good-bye. Standing outside my newly vacuumed car, I wondered, if I tried hard enough, whether I could smell the Opium perfume again, or if I searched long enough, whether I'd find the matching umbrellas and the tiny sewing kit. My brother laughed at my nostalgia, reminding me that I could still drive the car when I came home. He didn't understand that it wasn't just the driving I'd miss. That it was the tinfoil balls, the *New York Times,* and the broken speaker; the fingernail marks, the stray cassettes, and the smell of chai. Alone that night and parked in my driveway, I listened to Frank Sinatra with the moon roof slid back. 15

Comprehension

1. How does Keegan acquire her grandmother's car? Why does she call this transaction "awkward" (3)?
2. In paragraph 4, Keegan says that her car "evolved," and in paragraph 5, she says that her car was "born again." What does she mean?
3. Keegan observes that her car was not "gross." Instead, she says, "it was occupied, cluttered, cramped" (7). Why do you think she makes this distinction? Does it make sense?
4. How are Keegan and her grandmother different? How are they alike?
5. What are the "physical manifestations of her memories" that Keegan refers to in paragraph 10? How do they "crowd" her car?

Purpose and Audience

1. Does "Stability in Motion" have an explicitly stated thesis? If so, where? If not, suggest a one-sentence thesis statement for this essay.
2. What dominant impression is Keegan trying to create? Is she successful? Why or why not?
3. Is "Stability in Motion" primarily an objective or subjective description? What words and phrases lead you to your conclusion?

Style and Structure

1. What is the significance of the essay's title? In what sense is it a **paradox**?
2. Why does Keegan begin her essay with the details of her car's manufacture? How does this information help set up the rest of her discussion?
3. An **elegy** is a poem that is written to express praise and sorrow for someone who is dead. In what sense is this essay an elegy?
4. To which of the five senses does Keegan appeal as she describes her car? Find examples of each type.
5. Keegan concludes by repeating an image that she uses at the beginning of her essay. What is this image? Do you think this concluding strategy is effective? Why or why not?
6. **Vocabulary Project.** Throughout her essay, Keegan uses similes, metaphors, personification, and allusion. Find examples of this **figurative language**. What does Keegan accomplish by using this kind of language?

Journal Entry

Based on the things Keegan kept in her car, how would you describe her? What was important to her?

Writing Workshop

1. Go through your own car (or room), and list ten things you find there. Then, write an essay in which you describe some of these items, and, like Keegan, tell why they are important.
2. What possession – like Keegan's Toyota – has a special meaning to you? Write an essay in which you describe the item, and be sure to discuss the qualities that give the item you describe significance.
3. **Writing with Sources.** Go online, and find a picture of a 1990 Toyota Camry. Then, write an objective description of the car, pointing out any differences you see between the car in the picture and the car Keegan describes. In your essay, make specific references to "Stability in Motion." Be sure to document all references to Keegan's essay and to include a works-cited page. (See Chapter 18 for information on MLA documentation.)

Combining the Patterns

At several points in her essay, Keegan uses **comparison** – for example, when she compares her treatment of the car to her grandmother's treatment of it. What do these comparisons add to Keegan's essay?

Thematic Connections

- "Goodbye to My Twinkie Days" (page 169)
- "Once More to the Lake" (page 189)
- "Photos That Change History" (page 356)
- "Songs of the Summer of 1963 . . . and Today" (page 397)

HEATHER ROGERS

The Hidden Life of Garbage

Journalist Heather Rogers (b. 1970) has written articles on the environmental effects of mass production and consumption for the *New York Times Magazine*, the *Utne Reader*, *Architecture*, and a variety of other publications. Her 2002 documentary film *Gone Tomorrow: The Hidden Life of Garbage* has been screened at festivals around the world and served as the basis for a book of the same title. Named an Editor's Choice by the *New York Times* and the *Guardian*, the book, published in 2005, traces the history and politics of household garbage in the United States, drawing connections between modern industrial production, consumer culture, and our contemporary throwaway lifestyle. In the following excerpt from that book, Rogers provides a detailed description of a giant landfill in central Pennsylvania and asks readers to think about the ramifications of accumulating so much trash. Her most recent book is *Green Gone Wrong: How Our Economy Is Undermining the Environmental Revolution* (2010).

Background on waste disposal Human beings have always faced the question of how to dispose of garbage. The first city dump was established in ancient Athens, and the government of Rome had begun the collection of municipal trash by 200 C.E. Even as late as the 1800s, garbage was, at worst, simply thrown out into the streets of U.S. cities or dumped into rivers and ditches; in more enlightened communities, it might have been carted to foul-smelling open dumps or burned in incinerators, creating clouds of dense smoke. Experiments with systematically covering the garbage in dumps began as early as the 1920s, and the first true "sanitary landfill," as it was called, was created in Fresno, California, in 1937. Today, more than 60 percent of the solid waste in the United States ends up in landfills, and the amount of waste seems to keep growing. According to the Energy Information Administration, the amount of waste produced in the United States has more than doubled in the past thirty years, and it is estimated that the average American generates an astounding 4.5 pounds of trash every day.

In the dark chill of early morning, heavy steel garbage trucks chug and creep along neighborhood collection routes. A worker empties the contents of each household's waste bin into the truck's rear compaction unit. Hydraulic compressors scoop up and crush the dross, cramming it into the enclosed hull. When the rig is full, the collector heads to a garbage depot called a "transfer station" to unload. From there the rejectamenta is taken to a recycling center, an incinerator, or, most often, to what's called a "sanitary landfill." 1

Land dumping has long been the favored disposal method in the U.S. thanks to the relative low cost of burial and North America's abundant supply of unused acreage. Although the great majority of our castoffs go to landfills, they are places the public is not meant to see. Today's garbage graveyards 2 are sequestered, guarded, veiled. They are also high-tech, and, increasingly, located in rural areas that receive much of their rubbish from urban centers that no longer bury their own wastes.

There's a reason landfills are tucked away, on the edge of town, in otherwise untraveled terrain, camouflaged by hydroseeded, neatly tiered slopes. If people saw what happened to their waste, lived with the stench, witnessed the scale of destruction, they might start asking difficult questions. Waste Management Inc., the largest rubbish handling corporation in the world, operates its Geological Reclamation Operations and Waste Systems (GROWS) landfill just outside Morrisville, Pennsylvania – in the docile river valley near where Washington momentously crossed the Delaware leading his troops into Trenton in 1776. Sitting atop the landfill's 300-foot-high butte composed entirely of garbage, the logic of our society's unrestrained consuming and wasting quickly unravels. 3

Up here is where the dumping takes place; it is referred to as the fill's "working face." Clusters of trailer trucks, yellow earthmovers, compacting machines, steamrollers, and water tankers populate this bizarre, thirty-acre nightmare. Churning in slow motion through the surreal landscape, these machines are remaking the earth in the image of garbage. Scores of seagulls hover overhead then suddenly drop into the rotting piles. The ground underfoot is torn from the metal treads of the equipment. Potato chip wrappers, tattered plastic bags, and old shoes poke through the dirt as if floating to the surface. The smell is sickly and sour. 4

The aptly named GROWS landfill is part of Waste Management Inc.'s (WMI) 6,000-acre garbage treatment complex, which includes a second landfill, an incinerator, and a state-mandated leaf composting lot. GROWS is one of a new breed of waste burial sites referred to as "mega-fills." These high-tech, high-capacity dumps are comprised of a series of earth-covered "cells" that can be ten to one hundred acres across and up to hundreds of feet deep – or tall, as is the case at GROWS. (One Virginia whopper has disposal capacity equivalent to the length of one thousand football fields and the height of the Washington Monument.) As of 2002, GROWS was the single largest recipient of New York City's garbage in Pennsylvania, a state that is the country's biggest depository for exported waste. 5

WMI's Delaware-side operation sits on land that has long served the interests of industry. Overlooking a rambling, mostly decommissioned US Steel factory, WMI now occupies the former grounds of the Warner Company. In the previous century, Warner surface mined the area for gravel and sand, much of which was shipped to its cement factory in Philadelphia. The area has since been converted into a reverse mine of sorts; instead of extraction, workers dump, pack, and fill the earth with almost forty million pounds of municipal wastes daily. 6

Back on top of the GROWS landfill, twenty-ton dump trucks gather at the low end of the working face, where they discharge their fetid cargo. Several feet up a dirt bank, a string of large trailers are being detached from semi trucks. In rapid succession each container is tipped almost vertical by a giant hydraulic lift and, within seconds, twenty-four tons of putrescence cascades 7 down into the day's menacing valley of trash. In the middle of the dumping is a "landfill compactor" – which looks like a bulldozer on steroids with mammoth metal spiked wheels – that pitches back and forth, its fifty tons crushing the detritus into the earth. A smaller vehicle called a "track loader" maneuvers on tank treads, channeling the castoffs from kitchens and offices into the compactor's path. The place runs like a well-oiled machine, with only a handful of workers orchestrating the burial.

Get a few hundred yards from the landfill's working face and it's hard 8
to smell the rot or see the debris. The place is kept tidy with the help of thirty-five-foot-tall fencing made of "litter netting" that surrounds the perimeter of the site's two landfills. As a backup measure, teams of "paper pickers" constantly patrol the area retrieving discards carried off by the wind. Small misting machines dot fence tops, roads, and hillsides, spraying a fine, invisible chemical-water mixture into the air, which binds with odor molecules and pulls them to the ground.

In new state-of-the-art landfills, the cells that contain the trash are 9
built on top of what is called a " liner." The liner is a giant underground bladder intended to prevent contamination of groundwater by collecting leachate – liquid wastes and the rainwater that seeps through buried trash – and channeling it to nearby water treatment facilities. WMI's two Morrisville landfills leach on average 100,000 gallons daily. If this toxic stew contaminated the site's groundwater it would be devastating.

Once a cell is filled, which might take years, it is closed off or "capped." 10
The capping process entails covering the garbage with several feet of dirt, which gets graded, then packed by steamrollers. After that, layers of clay-embedded fabric, synthetic mesh, and plastic sheeting are draped across the top of the cell and joined with the bottom liner (which is made of the same materials) to encapsulate all those outmoded appliances, dirty diapers, and discarded wrappers.

Today's landfill regulations, ranging from liner construction to postcap- 11
ping oversight, mean that disposal areas like WMI's GROWS are potentially less dangerous than the dumps of previous generations. But the fact remains that these systems are short-term solutions to the garbage problem. While they may not seem toxic now, all those underground cells packed with plastics, solvents, paints, batteries, and other hazardous materials will someday have to be treated since the liners won't last forever. Most liners are expected to last somewhere between thirty and fifty years. That time frame just happens to coincide with the postclosure liability private landfill operators are subject to: thirty years after a site is shuttered, its owner is no longer responsible for contamination, the public is.

There is a palpable tension at waste 12
treatment facilities, as though at any minute the visitor will uncover some illegal activity. But what's most striking at these places isn't what they might be hiding; it's what's in plain view. The lavish resources

"But what's most striking at these places isn't what they might be hiding; it's what's in plain view."

dedicated to destroying used commodities and making that obliteration acceptable, even "green," is what's so astounding. Each landfill (not to mention garbage collection systems, transfer stations, recycling centers, and incinerators) is an expensive, complex operation that uses the latest methods developed and perfected at laboratories, universities, and corporate campuses across the globe.

The more state-of-the-art, the more "environmentally responsible" the operation, the more the repressed question pushes to the surface: what if we didn't have so much trash to get rid of? 13

• • •

Comprehension

1. According to Rogers, why are landfills "tucked away, on the edge of town, in otherwise untraveled terrain" (3)?
2. What is the landfill's "working face" (4)? How does it compare with other parts of the landfill?
3. Why does Rogers think the GROWS landfill is "aptly named" (5)? What **connotations** do you think Waste Management Inc. intended the name GROWS to have? What connotations does Rogers think the name has?
4. What are the dangers of the "new state-of-the-art landfills" (9)? What point does Rogers make about liners being "expected to last somewhere between thirty and fifty years" (11)?
5. According to Rogers, what is the "repressed question" (13) that is not being asked?

Purpose and Audience

1. At what point in the essay does Rogers state her thesis? Why do you think she places the thesis where she does?
2. What dominant impression does Rogers try to create in her description? Is she successful?
3. What is Rogers's attitude toward waste disposal in general and toward disposal companies like Waste Management Inc. in particular? Do you share her feelings?

Style and Structure

1. Rogers begins her essay with a description of garbage trucks collecting trash. What specific things does she describe? How does this description establish the context for the rest of the essay?
2. What determines the order in which details are arranged in Rogers's essay?
3. Is this essay a subjective or objective description of the landfill? Explain.
4. In paragraph 13, why does Rogers put the phrase *environmentally responsible* in quotation marks? What impression is she trying to convey?

5. Rogers never offers a solution to the problems she writes about. Should she have done so? Is her failure to offer a solution a shortcoming of the essay?
6. **Vocabulary Project.** Some critics of waste disposal methods accuse both municipalities and waste disposal companies of "environmental racism." Research this term on the web. Do you think the methods described by Rogers are examples of environmental racism? Explain.

Journal Entry

What do you think you and your family could do to reduce the amount of garbage you produce? How realistic are your suggestions?

Writing Workshop

1. Write an essay in which you describe the waste that you see generated at your school, home, or job. Like Rogers, write your description in a way that will motivate people to do something about the problem.
2. **Working with Sources.** In 1986, the city of Philadelphia hired a company to dispose of waste from a city incinerator. More than thirteen thousand tons of waste – some of which was hazardous – was loaded onto a ship called the *Khian Sea,* which unsuccessfully tried to dispose of it. After two years, the cargo mysteriously disappeared. Go to Google Images, and find several pictures of the *Khian Sea.* Then, write a description of the ship and its cargo. Make sure the thesis statement of your description clearly conveys your dominant impression. If you wish, you may insert one of the images you found into your essay. Be sure to document the image and to include a works-cited page. (See Chapter 18 for information on MLA documentation.)
3. Describe a place that has played an important role in your life. Include a narrative passage that conveys the place's significance to you.

Combining the Patterns

In paragraphs 9 and 10, Rogers includes a **definition** as well as a **process** description. Explain how these paragraphs help Rogers develop her description.

Thematic Connections

- "The Embalming of Mr. Jones (page 297)
- "The Irish Famine, 1845–1849" (page 328)
- "On Dumpster Diving" (page 676)

E. B. WHITE

Once More to the Lake

Elwyn Brooks White was born in 1899 in Mount Vernon, New York. He joined the newly founded *New Yorker* in 1925 and was associated with the magazine until his death in 1985. In 1937, White moved his family to a farm in Maine and began writing a monthly column for *Harper's* magazine titled "One Man's Meat." A collection of some of these essays appeared under the same title in 1942. In addition to this and other essay collections, White published two popular children's books, *Stuart Little* (1945) and *Charlotte's Web* (1952). He also wrote a classic writer's handbook, *The Elements of Style* (1959), a revision of a text by one of his Cornell professors, William Strunk.

Background on continuity and change In a sense, White's essay is a reflection on continuity and change. While much had remained the same at the Maine lake since 1904, the year White first began coming with his parents, the world outside had undergone a significant transformation by the time he returned years later with his son. Auto and air travel had become commonplace; the invention of innumerable electrical appliances and machines had revolutionized the home and the workplace; movies had gone from primitive, silent, black-and-white shorts to sophisticated productions with sound and sometimes color; and the rise of national advertising had spurred a new and greatly expanded generation of consumer products. Moreover, the country had suffered through World War I, enjoyed a great economic expansion, experienced a period of social revolution, and been devastated by a great economic depression. Within this context, White relives his childhood through his son's eyes.

One summer, along about 1904, my father rented a camp on a lake in 1
Maine and took us all there for the month of August. We all got ringworm from some kittens and had to rub Pond's Extract on our arms and legs night and morning, and my father rolled over in a canoe with all his clothes on; but outside of that the vacation was a success and from then on none of us ever thought there was any place in the world like that lake in Maine. We returned summer after summer — always on August 1st for one month. I have since become a salt-water man, but sometimes in summer there are days when the restlessness of the tides and the fearful cold of the sea water and the incessant wind which blows across the afternoon and into the evening make me wish for the placidity of a lake in the woods. A few weeks ago this feeling got so strong I bought myself a couple of bass hooks and a spinner and returned to the lake where we used to go, for a week's fishing and to revisit old haunts.

I took along my son, who had never had any fresh water up his nose and 2
who had seen lily pads only from train windows. On the journey over to the lake I began to wonder what it would be like. I wondered how time would have marred this unique, this holy spot — the coves and streams, the hills that the

sun set behind, the camps and the paths behind the camps. I was sure that the tarred road would have found it out and I wondered in what other ways it would be desolated. It is strange how much you can remember about places like that once you allow your mind to return into the grooves which lead back. You remember one thing, and that suddenly reminds you of another thing. I guess I remembered clearest of all the early mornings, when the lake was cool and motionless, remembered how the bedroom smelled of the lumber it was made of and the wet woods whose scent entered through the screen. The partitions in the camp were thin and did not extend clear to the top of the rooms, and as I was always the first up I would dress softly so as not to wake the others, and sneak out into the sweet outdoors and start out in the canoe, keeping close along the shore in the long shadows of the pines. I remembered being very careful never to rub my paddle against the gunwale for fear of disturbing the stillness of the cathedral.

"You remember one thing, and that suddenly reminds you of another thing."

The lake had never been what you would call a wild lake. There were cot- 3
tages sprinkled around the shores, and it was in farming country although the shores of the lake were quite heavily wooded. Some of the cottages were owned by nearby farmers, and you would live at the shore and eat your meals at the farmhouse. That's what our family did. But although it wasn't wild, it was a fairly large and undisturbed lake and there were places in it which, to a child at least, seemed infinitely remote and primeval.

I was right about the tar: it led to within half a mile of the shore. But 4
when I got back there, with my boy, and we settled into a camp near a farmhouse and into the kind of summertime I had known, I could tell that it was going to be pretty much the same as it had been before — I knew it, lying in bed the first morning, smelling the bedroom, and hearing the boy sneak quietly out and go off along the shore in a boat. I began to sustain the illusion that he was I, and therefore, by simple transposition, that I was my father. This sensation persisted, kept cropping up all the time we were there. It was not an entirely new feeling, but in this setting it grew much stronger. I seemed to be living a dual existence. I would be in the middle of some simple act, I would be picking up a bait box or laying down a table fork, or I would be saying something, and suddenly it would be not I but my father who was saying the words or making the gesture. It gave me a creepy sensation.

We went fishing the first morning. I felt the same damp moss covering 5
the worms in the bait can, and saw the dragonfly alight on the tip of my rod as it hovered a few inches from the surface of the water. It was the arrival of this fly that convinced me beyond any doubt that everything was as it always had been, that the years were a mirage and there had been no years. The small waves were the same, chucking the rowboat under the chin as we fished at anchor, and the boat was the same boat, the same color green and the ribs broken in the same places, and under the floor-boards the same freshwater

leavings and débris – the dead helgramite,* the wisps of moss, the rusty discarded fishhook, the dried blood from yesterday's catch. We stared silently at the tips of our rods, at the dragonflies that came and went. I lowered the tip of mine into the water, tentatively, pensively dislodging the fly, which darted two feet away, poised, darted two feet back, and came to rest again a little farther up the rod. There had been no years between the ducking of this dragonfly and the other one – the one that was part of memory. I looked at the boy, who was silently watching his fly, and it was my hands that held his rod, my eyes watching. I felt dizzy and didn't know which rod I was at the end of.

We caught two bass, hauling them in briskly as though they were mackerel, pulling them over the side of the boat in a businesslike manner without any landing net, and stunning them with a blow on the back of the head. When we got back for a swim before lunch, the lake was exactly where we had left it, the same number of inches from the dock, and there was only the merest suggestion of a breeze. This seemed an utterly enchanted sea, this lake you could leave to its own devices for a few hours and come back to, and find that it had not stirred, this constant and trustworthy body of water. In the shallows, the dark, water-soaked sticks and twigs, smooth and old, were undulating in clusters on the bottom against the clean ribbed sand, and the track of the mussel was plain. A school of minnows swam by, each minnow with its small individual shadow, doubling the attendance, so clear and sharp in the sunlight. Some of the other campers were in swimming, along the shore, one of them with a cake of soap, and the water felt thin and clear and unsubstantial. Over the years there had been this person with the cake of soap, this cultist, and here he was. There had been no years. 6

Up to the farmhouse to dinner through the teeming, dusty field, the road under our sneakers was only a two-track road. The middle track was missing, the one with the marks of the hooves and the splotches of dried, flaky manure. There had always been three tracks to choose from in choosing which track to walk in; now the choice was narrowed down to two. For a moment I missed terribly the middle alternative. But the way led past the tennis court, and something about the way it lay there in the sun reassured me; the tape had loosened along the backline, the alleys were green with plantains and other weeds, and the net (installed in June and removed in September) sagged in the dry noon, and the whole place steamed with midday heat and hunger and emptiness. There was a choice of pie for dessert, and one was blueberry and one was apple, and the waitresses were the same country girls, there having been no passage of time, only the illusion of it as in a dropped curtain – the waitresses were still fifteen; their hair had been washed, that was the only difference – they had been to the movies and seen the pretty girls with the clean hair. 7

Summertime, oh summertime, pattern of life indelible, the fade-proof lake, the woods unshatterable, the pasture with the sweetfern and the juniper forever and ever, summer without end; this was the background, and the 8

* Eds. note – An insect larva often used as bait.

life along the shore was the design, the cottages with their innocent and tranquil design, their tiny docks with the flagpole and the American flag floating against the white clouds in the blue sky, the little paths over the roots of the trees leading from camp to camp and the paths leading back to the outhouses and the can of lime for sprinkling, and at the souvenir counters at the store the miniature birch-bark canoes and the post cards that showed things looking a little better than they looked. This was the American family at play, escaping the city heat, wondering whether the newcomers in the camp at the head of the cove were "common" or "nice," wondering whether it was true that the people who drove up for Sunday dinner at the farmhouse were turned away because there wasn't enough chicken.

It seemed to me, as I kept remembering all this, that those times and those summers had been infinitely precious and worth saving. There had been jollity and peace and goodness. The arriving (at the beginning of August) had been so big a business in itself, at the railway station the farm wagon drawn up, the first smell of the pine-laden air, the first glimpse of the smiling farmer, and the great importance of the trunks and your father's enormous authority in such matters, and the feel of the wagon under you for the long ten-mile haul, and at the top of the last long hill catching the first view of the lake after eleven months of not seeing this cherished body of water. The shouts and cries of the other campers when they saw you, and the trunks to be unpacked, to give up their rich burden. (Arriving was less exciting nowadays, when you sneaked up in your car and parked it under a tree near the camp and took out the bags and in five minutes it was all over, no fuss, no loud wonderful fuss about trunks.) 9

Peace and goodness and jollity. The only thing that was wrong now, really, was the sound of the place, an unfamiliar nervous sound of the outboard motors. This was the note that jarred, the one thing that would sometimes break the illusion and set the years moving. In those other summertimes all motors were inboard; and when they were at a little distance, the noise they made was a sedative, an ingredient of summer sleep. They were one-cylinder and two-cylinder engines, and some were make-and-break and some were jump-spark, but they all made a sleepy sound across the lake. The one-lungers throbbed and fluttered, and the twin-cylinder ones purred and purred, and that was a quiet sound too. But now the campers all had outboards. In the daytime, in the hot mornings, these motors made a petulant, irritable sound; at night, in the still evening when the afterglow lit the water, they whined about one's ears like mosquitoes. My boy loved our rented outboard, and his great desire was to achieve singlehanded mastery over it, and authority, and he soon learned the trick of choking it a little (but not too much), and the adjustment of the needle valve. Watching him I would remember the things you could do with the old one-cylinder engine with the heavy flywheel, how you could have it eating out of your hand if you got really close to it spiritually. Motor boats in those days didn't have clutches, and you would make a landing by shutting off the motor at the proper time and coasting in with a dead rudder. But there was a way of reversing them, if you learned the trick, by cutting the switch and putting it on again exactly on the final dying revolution of the flywheel, so 10 that it would kick back against compression and begin reversing. Approaching a dock in a strong following breeze, it was difficult to slow up sufficiently by the ordinary coasting method, and if a boy felt he had complete mastery over his motor, he was tempted to keep it running beyond its time and then reverse it a few feet from the dock. It took a cool nerve, because if you threw the switch a twentieth of a second too soon you could catch the flywheel when it still had speed enough to go up past center, and the boat would leap ahead, charging bull-fashion at the dock.

We had a good week at the camp. The bass were biting well and the sun shone endlessly, day after day. We would be tired at night and lie down in the accumulated heat of the little bedrooms after the long hot day and the breeze would stir almost imperceptibly outside and the smell of the swamp drift in through the rusty screens. Sleep would come easily and in the morning the red squirrel would be on the roof, tapping out his gay routine. I kept remembering everything, lying in bed in the mornings – the small steamboat that had a long rounded stern like the lip of a Ubangi,* how quietly she ran on the moonlight sails, when the older boys played their mandolins and the girls sang and we ate doughnuts dipped in sugar, and how sweet the music was on the water in the shining night, and what it had felt like to think about girls then. After breakfast we would go up to the store and the things were in the same place – the minnows in a bottle, the plugs and spinners disarranged and pawed over by the youngsters from the boys' camp, the fig newtons and the Beeman's gum. Outside, the road was tarred and cars stood in front of the store. Inside, all was just as it had always been, except there was more Coca-Cola and not so much Moxie** and root beer and birch beer and sarsaparilla.*** We would walk out with a bottle of pop apiece and sometimes the pop would backfire up our noses and hurt. We explored the streams, quietly, where the turtles slid off the sunny logs and dug their way into the soft bottom; and we lay on the town wharf and fed worms to the tame bass. Everywhere we went I had trouble making out which was I, the one walking at my side, the one walking in my pants. 11

One afternoon while we were there at that lake a thunderstorm came up. It was like the revival of an old melodrama that I had seen long ago with childish awe. The second-act climax of the drama of the electrical disturbance over a lake in America had not changed in any important respect. This was the big scene, still the big scene. The whole thing was so familiar, the first feeling of oppression and heat and a general air around camp of not wanting to go very far away. In midafternoon (it was all the same) a curious darkening of the sky, and a lull in everything that had made life tick; and then the way the boats suddenly swung the other way at their moorings with the coming of a breeze out of the new quarter, and the premonitory rumble. Then the kettle drum, then the snare, then the bass drum and cymbals, then crackling light against 12

* Eds. note – A member of an African tribe known for wearing mouth ornaments that stretch the lips into a saucerlike shape.

**Eds. note – A soft drink that was popular in the early twentieth century.

***Eds. note – A sweetened carbonated beverage flavored with birch oil and sassafras.

the dark, and the gods grinning and licking their chops in the hills. Afterward the calm, the rain steadily rustling in the calm lake, the return of light and hope and spirits, and the campers running out in joy and relief to go swimming in the rain, their bright cries perpetuating the deathless joke about how they were getting simply drenched, and the children screaming with delight at the new sensation of bathing in the rain, and the joke about getting drenched linking the generations in a strong indestructible chain. And the comedian who waded in carrying an umbrella.

When the others went swimming my son said he was going in too. He pulled his dripping trunks from the line where they had hung all through the shower, and wrung them out. Languidly, and with no thought of going in, I watched him, his hard little body, skinny and bare, saw him wince slightly as he pulled up around his vitals the small, soggy, icy garment. As he buckled the swollen belt suddenly my groin felt the chill of death. 13

• • •

Comprehension

1. How are the writer and his son alike? How are they different? What does White mean when he says, "I seemed to be living a dual existence" (4)?
2. In paragraph 5, White says that "no years" seemed to have gone by between past and present; elsewhere, he senses that things are different. How do you account for these conflicting feelings?
3. Why does White feel disconcerted when he discovers that the road to the farmhouse has two tracks, not three? What do you make of his comment that "now the choice was narrowed down to two" (7)?
4. How does sound "break the illusion and set the years moving" (10)?
5. What is White referring to in the essay's last sentence?

Purpose and Audience

1. What is the thesis of this essay? Is it stated or implied?
2. Do you think White expects the ending of his essay to surprise his audience? Explain.
3. What age group do you think this essay would appeal to most? Why?

Style and Structure

1. List the specific changes that have taken place on the lake. Does White emphasize these changes or play them down? Explain.
2. What ideas and images does White repeat throughout his essay? What is the purpose of this repetition?
3. White goes to great lengths to describe how things look, feel, smell, taste, and sound. How does that help him achieve his purpose in this essay?
4. How does White's conclusion echo the first paragraph of the essay?

5. **Vocabulary Project.** Underline ten words in the essay that refer to one of the five senses, and make a list of synonyms you could use for these words. How close do your substitutions come to capturing White's meaning?

Journal Entry

Do you identify more with the father or with the son in this essay? Why?

Writing Workshop

1. Write a description of a scene you remember from your childhood. In your essay, discuss how your current view of the scene differs from the view you had when you were a child.
2. **Working with Sources.** Assume you are a travel agent. Stressing the benefits White describes, write a descriptive brochure designed to bring tourists to the lake. Remember to include parenthetical documentation for references to White's essay and to include a works-cited page. (See Chapter 18 for information on MLA documentation.)
3. Write an essay describing yourself from the perspective of one of your parents (or another close relative). Make sure your description conveys both the qualities your parent likes and the qualities he or she would want to change.

Combining the Patterns

White opens his essay with a short narrative about his first trip to the lake in 1904. How does this use of **narration** provide a context for the entire essay?

Thematic Connections

- "My Field of Dreams" (page 104)
- "Surrendering" (page 116)
- "Goodbye to My Twinkie Days" (page 169)
- "The Park" (page 671)

KATE CHOPIN

The Storm (Fiction)

Kate Chopin (1851–1904) was born Catherine O'Flaherty in St. Louis, Missouri. In 1870, she married Oscar Chopin and moved with him to New Orleans. After suffering business reversals, Chopin relocated to Cloutierville, Louisiana, to be closer to his extended Creole family. Oscar Chopin died suddenly in 1882, and Kate Chopin, left with six children to raise, returned to St. Louis. There she began writing short stories, many set in the colorful Creole country of central Louisiana. Her first collection, *Bayou Folk,* was published in 1894, followed by *A Night in Arcadie* in 1897. Her literary success was cut short, however, with the publication of her first novel, *The Awakening* (1899), a story of adultery that outraged many of her critics and readers because it was told sympathetically from a woman's perspective. Her work languished until the middle of the twentieth century, when it was rediscovered, largely by feminist literary scholars.

Background on Creole culture The following story was probably written about the same time as *The Awakening,* but Chopin never attempted to publish it. Its frank sexuality — franker than that depicted in her controversial novel — and its focus on an adulterous liaison between two lovers (Calixta and Alcée) would have been too scandalous for middle-class readers of the day. Even within the more liberal Creole culture in which the story is set, Calixta's actions would have been outrageous. While Creole men were expected to have mistresses, Creole wives were expected to remain true to their wedding vows. The Creoles themselves were descendants of the early Spanish and French settlers in Louisiana, and they lived lives quite separate from — and, they believed, superior to — those whose ancestors were British. Their language became a mix of French and English, as did their mode of dress and cuisine. A strong Creole influence can still be found in New Orleans and the surrounding Louisiana countryside; Mardi Gras, for example, is a Creole tradition.

I

The leaves were so still that even Bibi thought it was going to rain. Bobinôt, who was accustomed to converse on terms of perfect equality with his little son, called the child's attention to certain sombre clouds that were rolling with sinister intention from the west, accompanied by a sullen, threatening roar. They were at Friedheimer's store and decided to remain there till the storm had passed. They sat within the door on two empty kegs. Bibi was four years old and looked very wise. 1

"Mama'll be 'fraid, yes," he suggested with blinking eyes. 2

"She'll shut the house. Maybe she got Sylvie helpin' her this evenin'," Bobinôt responded reassuringly. 3

"No; she ent got Sylvie. Sylvie was helpin' her yistiday," piped Bibi. 4

5 Bobinôt arose and going across to the counter purchased a can of shrimps, of which Calixta was very fond. Then he returned to his perch on the keg and sat stolidly holding the can of shrimps while the storm burst. It shook the wooden store and seemed to be ripping great furrows in the distant field. Bibi laid his little hand on his father's knee and was not afraid.

II

6 Calixta, at home, felt no uneasiness for their safety. She sat at a side window sewing furiously on a sewing machine. She was greatly occupied and did not notice the approaching storm. But she felt very warm and often stopped to mop her face on which the perspiration gathered in beads. She unfastened her white sacque at the throat. It began to grow dark, and suddenly realizing the situation she got up hurriedly and went about closing windows and doors.

7 Out on the small front gallery she had hung Bobinôt's Sunday clothes to air and she hastened out to gather them before the rain fell. As she stepped outside, Alcée Laballière rode in at the gate. She had not seen him very often since her marriage, and never alone. She stood there with Bobinôt's coat in her hands, and the big rain drops began to fall. Alcée rode his horse under the shelter of a side projection where the chickens had huddled and there were plows and a harrow piled up in the corner.

8 "May I come and wait on your gallery till the storm is over, Calixta?" he asked.

9 "Come 'long in, M'sieur Alcée."

10 His voice and her own startled her as if from a trance, and she seized Bobinôt's vest. Alcée, mounting to the porch, grabbed the trousers and snatched Bibi's braided jacket that was about to be carried away by a sudden gust of wind. He expressed an intention to remain outside, but it was soon apparent that he might as well have been out in the open: the water beat in upon the boards in driving sheets, and he went inside, closing the door after him. It was even necessary to put something beneath the door to keep the water out.

11 "My! what a rain! It's good two years sence it rain' like that," exclaimed Calixta as she rolled up a piece of bagging and Alcée helped her to thrust it beneath the crack.

12 She was a little fuller of figure than five years before when she married; but she had lost nothing of her vivacity. Her blue eyes still retained their melting quality; and her yellow hair, dishevelled by the wind and rain, kinked more stubbornly than ever about her ears and temples.

13 The rain beat upon the low, shingled roof with a force and clatter that threatened to break an entrance and deluge them there. They were in the dining room — the sitting room — the general utility room. Adjoining was her bed room, with Bibi's couch along side her own. The door stood open, and the room with its white, monumental bed, its closed shutters, looked dim and mysterious.

14 Alcée flung himself into a rocker and Calixta nervously began to gather up from the floor the lengths of a cotton sheet which she had been sewing.

"If this keeps up, *Dieu sait** if the levees goin' to stan' it!" she exclaimed. 15

"What have you got to do with the levees?" 16

"I got enough to do! An' there's Bobinôt with Bibi out in that storm – if 17
he only didn't left Friedheimer's!"

"Let us hope, Calixta, that Bobinôt's got sense enough to come in out of 18
a cyclone."

She went and stood at the window with a greatly disturbed look on her 19
face. She wiped the frame that was clouded with moisture. It was stiflingly hot. Alcée got up and joined her at the window, looking over her shoulder. The rain was coming down in sheets obscuring the view of far-off cabins and enveloping the distant wood in a gray mist. The playing of the lightning was incessant. A bolt struck a tall chinaberry tree at the edge of the field. It filled all visible space with a blinding glare and the crash seemed to invade the very boards they stood upon.

Calixta put her hands to her eyes, and 20
with a cry, staggered backward. Alcée's arm encircled her, and for an instant he drew her close and spasmodically to him.

> "Calixta put her hands to her eyes, and with a cry, staggered backward."

*"Bonté!"*** she cried, releasing her- 21
self from his encircling arm and retreating from the window, "the house'll go next! If I only knew w'ere Bibi was!" She would not compose herself; she would not be seated. Alcée clasped her shoulders and looked into her face. The contact of her warm, palpitating body when he had unthinkingly drawn her into his arms, had aroused all the old-time infatuation and desire for her flesh.

"Calixta," he said, "don't be frightened. Nothing can happen. The house is 22
too low to be struck, with so many tall trees standing about. There! aren't you going to be quiet? say, aren't you?" He pushed her hair back from her face that was warm and steaming. Her lips were as red and moist as pomegranate seed. Her white neck and a glimpse of her full, firm bosom disturbed him powerfully. As she glanced up at him the fear in her liquid blue eyes had given place to a drowsy gleam that unconsciously betrayed a sensuous desire. He looked down into her eyes and there was nothing for him to do but to gather her lips in a kiss. It reminded him of Assumption.***

"Do you remember – in Assumption, Calixta?" he asked in a low voice 23
broken by passion. Oh! she remembered; for in Assumption he had kissed her and kissed and kissed her; until his senses would well nigh fail, and to save her he would resort to a desperate flight. If she was not an immaculate dove in those days, she was still inviolate; a passionate creature whose very defenselessness had made her defense, against which his honor forbade him to prevail. Now – well, now – her lips seemed in a manner free to be tasted, as well as her round, white throat and her whiter breasts.

---

* Eds. note – God knows.

** Eds. note – Goodness!

*** Eds. note – A parish near New Orleans.

They did not heed the crashing torrents, and the roar of the elements made her laugh as she lay in his arms. She was a revelation in that dim, mysterious chamber; as white as the couch she lay upon. Her firm, elastic flesh that was knowing for the first time its birthright, was like a creamy lily that the sun invites to contribute its breath and perfume to the undying life of the world. 24

The generous abundance of her passion, without guile or trickery, was like a white flame which penetrated and found response in depths of his own sensuous nature that had never yet been reached. 25

When he touched her breasts they gave themselves up in quivering ecstasy, inviting his lips. Her mouth was a fountain of delight. And when he possessed her, they seemed to swoon together at the very borderland of life's mystery. 26

He stayed cushioned upon her, breathless, dazed, enervated, with his heart beating like a hammer upon her. With one hand she clasped his head, her lips lightly touching his forehead. The other hand stroked with a soothing rhythm his muscular shoulders. 27

The growl of the thunder was distant and passing away. The rain beat softly upon the shingles, inviting them to drowsiness and sleep. But they dared not yield. 28

The rain was over; and the sun was turning the glistening green world into a palace of gems. Calixta, on the gallery, watched Alcée ride away. He turned and smiled at her with a beaming face; and she lifted her pretty chin in the air and laughed aloud. 29

III

Bobinôt and Bibi, trudging home, stopped without at the cistern to make themselves presentable. 30

"My! Bibi, w'at will yo' mama say! You ought to be asham'. You oughtn' put on those good pants. Look at 'em! An' that mud on yo' collar! How you got that mud on yo' collar, Bibi? I never saw such a boy!" Bibi was the picture of pathetic resignation. Bobinôt was the embodiment of serious solicitude as he strove to remove from his own person and his son's the signs of their tramp over heavy roads and through wet fields. He scraped the mud off Bibi's bare legs and feet with a stick and carefully removed all traces from his heavy brogans. Then, prepared for the worst – the meeting with an over-scrupulous housewife, they entered cautiously at the back door. 31

Calixta was preparing supper. She had set the table and was dripping coffee at the hearth. She sprang up as they came in. 32

"Oh, Bobinôt! You back! My! but I was uneasy. W'ere you been during the rain? An' Bibi? he ain't wet? he ain't hurt?" She had clasped Bibi and was kissing him effusively. Bobinôt's explanations and apologies which he had been composing all along the way, died on his lips as Calixta felt him to see if he were dry, and seemed to express nothing but satisfaction at their safe return. 33

"I brought you some shrimps, Calixta," offered Bobinôt, hauling the can from his ample side pocket and laying it on the table. 34

"Shrimps! Oh, Bobinôt! you too good fo' anything!" and she gave him a smacking kiss on the cheek that resounded. "*J'vous réponds,** we'll have a feas' tonight! umph-umph!" 35

Bobinôt and Bibi began to relax and enjoy themselves, and when the three sated themselves at table they laughed much and so loud that anyone might have heard them as far away as Laballière's. 36

IV

Alcée Laballière wrote to his wife, Clarisse, that night. It was a loving letter, full of tender solicitude. He told her not to hurry back, but if she and the babies liked it at Biloxi, to stay a month longer. He was getting on nicely; and though he missed them, he was willing to bear the separation a while longer – realizing that their health and pleasure were the first things to be considered. 37

V

As for Clarisse, she was charmed upon receiving her husband's letter. She and the babies were doing well. The society was agreeable; many of her old friends and acquaintances were at the bay. And the first free breath since her marriage seemed to restore the pleasant liberty of her maiden days. Devoted as she was to her husband, their intimate conjugal life was something which she was more than willing to forego for a while. 38

So the storm passed and everyone was happy. 39

• • •

Reading Literature

1. How does the storm help set in motion the action of the story? List the events caused by the storm.
2. Is the last line of the story to be taken literally, or is it meant to be **ironic** (that is, does it actually suggest the opposite meaning)? Explain.
3. What do the story's specific descriptive details tell us about Calixta?

Journal Entry

On one level, the story's title refers to the storm that takes place through much of the story. To what else could the story's title refer?

Thematic Connections

- "'Girl'" (page 254)
- *The Kiss* and *LOVE* (pages 389–90)
- "Sex, Lies, and Conversation" (page 415)
- "The Ways We Lie" (page 466)

* Eds. note – I tell you.

Writing Assignments for Description

1. Choose a character from a book, movie, or video game who you think is interesting. Write a descriptive essay conveying what makes this character so special.
2. Several of the essays in this chapter deal with the way journeys change how the writers see themselves. For example, in "Once More to the Lake," a visit to a campground forces E. B. White to confront his own mortality, and in "The Hidden Life of Garbage," a visit to a landfill outside Morrisville, Pennsylvania, enables Heather Rogers to grasp the enormity of the task of disposing of garbage in the United States. Write an essay describing a place you have traveled to. Make sure that, in addition to describing the place, you explain how it has taught you something about yourself.
3. Locate some photographs of your relatives. Describe three of these pictures, including details that provide insight into the lives of the people you discuss. Use your descriptive passages to support a thesis about your family.
4. **Working with Sources.** Visit an art museum (or go to a museum site on the web), and select a painting that interests you. Study it carefully, and then write an essay-length description of it. Before you write, decide how you will organize your details and whether you will write a subjective or objective description. If possible, include a photograph of the painting in your essay. Be sure to document the photograph and to include a works-cited page. (See Chapter 18 for information on MLA documentation.)
5. Select an object you are familiar with, and write an objective description of it. Include a diagram.
6. Assume you are writing an email to someone in another country who knows little about life in the United States. Describe to this person something you consider typically American – for example, a state fair or a food court in a shopping mall.
7. Visit your college library, and write a brochure in which you describe the reference area. Be specific, and select an organizing scheme before you begin your description. Your purpose is to acquaint students with some of the reference materials they will use. If possible, include a diagram that will help orient students to this section of the library.
8. Describe your neighborhood to a visitor who knows nothing about it. Include as much specific detail as you can.
9. After reading "Ground Zero," write a description of a sight or scene that fascinated, surprised, or shocked you. Your description should explain why you were so deeply affected by what you saw.
10. Write an essay describing an especially frightening horror film. What specific sights and sounds make this film so horrifying? Include a thesis statement assessing the film's success as a horror film. (Be careful not to simply summarize the plot of the film.)

Collaborative Activity for Description

Working in groups of three or four students, go to Google Maps, Street View, and select a city you would like to visit. Then, as a group, write a description of a street, a building, or even a block in that city, making sure to include as much physical detail as possible.

8

Exemplification

What Is Exemplification?

Exemplification uses one or more particular cases, or **examples**, to illustrate or explain a general point or an abstract concept. In the following paragraph from *Sexism and Language,* Alleen Pace Nilsen uses a series of well-chosen examples to illustrate her statement that the armed forces use words that have positive masculine connotations to encourage recruitment.

Topic sentence

Series of related examples

The armed forces, particularly the Marines, use the positive masculine connotation as part of their recruitment psychology. They promote the idea that to join the Marines (or the Army, Navy, or Air Force) guarantees that you will become a man. But this brings up a problem, because much of the work that is necessary to keep a large organization running is what is traditionally thought of as *woman's work.* Now, how can the Marines ask someone who has signed up for a *man-sized job* to do *woman's work*? Since they can't, they euphemize and give the jobs titles that are more prestigious or, at least, don't make people think of females. Waitresses are called *orderlies,* secretaries are called *clerk-typists,* nurses are called *medics,* assistants are called *adjutants,* and cleaning up an area is called *policing* the area. The same kind of word glorification is used in civilian life to bolster a man's ego when he is doing such tasks as cooking and sewing. For example, a *chef* has higher prestige than a *cook* and a *tailor* has higher prestige than a *seamstress.*

Using Exemplification

When watching interviews on television (or on YouTube or other online sites) or listening to classroom discussions, you have probably noticed that the most effective exchanges occur when participants support their points with specific examples. Sweeping generalizations and vague statements are not nearly as effective as specific observations, anecdotes, details, and opinions. It is one thing to say, "The mayor is corrupt and should not be reelected" and another to illustrate your point by saying, "The mayor should not be reelected because he has fired two city workers who refused to contribute to his campaign fund, has put his family and friends on the city payroll, and has used public employees to make improvements to his home." The same principle applies to writing: many of the most effective essays use examples extensively. Exemplification is used in every kind of writing situation to *explain and clarify*, to *add interest*, and to *persuade*.

Using Examples to Explain and Clarify

Writers often use examples to explain and clarify their ideas. For instance, on a midterm exam in a film course, you might write, "Even though horror movies seem modern, they really aren't." You may think your statement is perfectly clear, but if that is all you say about horror movies, you should not be surprised if your exam comes back with a question mark in the margin next to this sentence. After all, you have only made a general statement about your subject. It is not specific, nor does it anticipate readers' questions about how horror movies are not modern. To be certain your audience knows exactly what you mean, state your point precisely: "Even though horror movies seem modern, two of the most memorable ones are adaptations of nineteenth-century Gothic novels." Then, use examples to ensure clarity and avoid ambiguity. For example, you could illustrate your point by discussing two films – *Frankenstein,* directed by James Whale, and *Dracula,* directed by Todd Browning – and linking them to the nineteenth-century novels on which they are based. With the benefit of these specific examples, readers would know what you mean: that the literary roots of such movies are in the past, not that their cinematic techniques or production methods are dated. Moreover, readers would know exactly which horror movies you are discussing.

Using Examples to Add Interest

Writers also use well-chosen examples to add interest. Brent Staples does this in his essay "Just Walk On By," which appears later in this chapter. In itself, the claim that during his time away from home Staples became "thoroughly familiar with the language of fear" is not very interesting. This statement becomes compelling, however, when Staples illustrates it with specific examples – experiences he had while walking the streets at night. For example, his presence apparently inspired so much fear in people that they locked their car doors as he walked past or crossed to the other side of the street when they saw him approaching.

When you use exemplification, choose examples that are interesting as well as pertinent. Test the effectiveness of your examples by putting yourself in your readers' place. If you don't find your essay lively and absorbing, chances are your readers won't either. If this is the case, try to add more thought-provoking and spirited examples. After all, your goal is to communicate ideas to your readers, and imaginative examples can make the difference between an engrossing essay and one that is a chore to read.

Using Examples to Persuade

Although you can use examples to explain or to add interest, examples are also an effective way of persuading people that what you are saying is reasonable and worth considering. A few well-chosen examples can provide effective support for otherwise unconvincing general statements. For instance, a broad statement that school districts across the country cannot cope with the numerous students with limited English skills is one that needs support. If you make such a statement in an essay, you need to back it up with appropriate examples – such as that in Massachusetts alone, the number of students who speak English as a second language increased by more than 20 percent over the past ten years. In other words, as of 2013, more than 70,000 Massachusetts students lacked proficiency in English. Similarly, a statement in a biology essay that DDT should continue to be banned is unconvincing without persuasive examples such as these to support it:

- Although DDT has been banned since December 31, 1972, scientists are finding traces of it in the eggs of various fish and waterfowl.
- Certain lakes and streams cannot be used for sport and recreation because DDT levels are dangerously high, presumably because of farmland runoff.
- Because of its stability as a compound, DDT does not degrade quickly; therefore, existing residues will threaten the environment well into the twenty-first century.

Planning an Exemplification Essay

Developing a Thesis Statement

The **thesis statement** of an exemplification essay makes a point that the rest of the essay will support with examples. This statement usually identifies your topic as well as the main point you want to make about it.

The examples you gather during the invention stage of the writing process can help you develop your thesis. By doing so, they can help you test your ideas as well as the ideas of others. For instance, suppose you plan to write an essay for a composition class about students' writing skills. Your tentative thesis is that writing well is an inborn talent and that teachers can do little to help people write better. But is that really true? Has it been true in your own life? To test your point, you brainstorm about the various teachers you have had who tried to help you improve your writing.

As you assemble your list, you remember a teacher you had in high school. She was strict, required lots of writing, and seemed to accept nothing less than perfection. At the time, neither you nor your classmates liked her, but looking back, you recall her one-on-one conferences, her organized lessons, her helpful comments on your essays, and her timely replies to your emails. You realize that after completing her class, you felt much more comfortable writing. When examining some essays you saved, you are surprised to see how much your writing actually improved during that year. These examples lead you to reevaluate your ideas and to revise your thesis:

> Even though some people seem to have a natural flair for writing, a good teacher can make a difference.

Providing Enough Examples

Unfortunately, no general rule exists to tell you when you have enough examples. The number you need depends on your thesis statement. If, for instance, your thesis is that an educational institution, like a business, needs careful financial management, a single detailed examination of one college or university could provide all the examples you need to support your point.

If, however, your thesis is that conflict between sons and fathers is a major theme in Franz Kafka's writing, more than one example would be necessary. A single example would show only that the theme is present in *one* of Kafka's works. In this case, the more examples you include, the more effectively you support your point.

For some thesis statements, however, even several examples would not be enough. Examples alone, for instance, could not demonstrate convincingly that children from small families have more successful careers than children from large families. This thesis would have to be supported with a **statistical study** – that is, by collecting and interpreting numerical data representing a great many examples.

Choosing a Fair Range of Examples

Selecting a sufficient **range of examples** is just as important as choosing an appropriate number. If you want to persuade readers that Colin Powell was an able general, you should choose examples from several stages of his military career. Likewise, if you want to convince readers that outdoor advertising ruins the scenic views from major highways, you should discuss an area larger than your immediate neighborhood. Your objective in each case is to choose a cross section of examples to represent the full range of your topic.

Similarly, if you want to argue for a ban on smoking in all public spaces, you should not limit your examples to restaurants. To be convincing, you should include examples involving many public places, such as parks, beaches, and sports stadiums. For the same reason, one person's experience is not enough to support a general conclusion involving many people unless you can clearly establish that the experience is typical.

If you decide you cannot cite a fair range of examples that support your thesis, reexamine it. Rather than switching to a new topic, try to narrow your thesis. After all, the only way your essay will be convincing is if your readers believe that your thesis is supported by your examples and that your examples fairly represent the scope of your topic.

Of course, to be convincing you must not only *choose* examples effectively but also *use* them effectively. You should keep your thesis statement in mind as you write, taking care not to get so involved with one example that you digress from your main point. No matter how carefully developed, no matter how specific and lively, your examples accomplish nothing if they do not support your essay's main idea.

Using Transitions

Be sure to use transitional words and phrases to introduce your examples. Without them, readers will have difficulty seeing the connection between an example and the general statement it is illustrating. In some cases, transitions will help you connect examples to your thesis statement ("*Another* successful program for the homeless provides telephone answering services for job seekers"). In other cases, transitions will link examples to topic sentences ("*For instance,* I have written articles for my college newspaper"). In exemplification essays, the most frequently used transitions include *for example, for instance, in fact, namely, specifically, that is,* and *thus.* (A more complete list of transitions appears on page 55.)

Structuring an Exemplification Essay

Exemplification essays usually begin with an **introduction** that includes the *thesis statement*, which is supported by examples in the body of the essay. Each **body paragraph** may develop a separate example, present a point illustrated by several brief examples, or explore one part of a single extended example that is developed throughout the essay. The **conclusion** reinforces the essay's main idea, perhaps restating the thesis. At times, however, variations of this basic pattern are advisable and even necessary. For instance, beginning your essay with a striking example might stimulate your reader's interest and curiosity; ending with one might vividly reinforce your thesis.

Exemplification presents one special organizational problem. If you do not select your examples carefully and arrange them effectively, your essay can become a thesis statement followed by a list or by ten or fifteen brief, choppy paragraphs. One way to avoid this problem is to develop your best examples fully in separate paragraphs and then discard the others. Another effective strategy is to group related examples together in one paragraph.

Within each paragraph, you can arrange examples **chronologically**, beginning with those that occurred first and moving to those that occurred later. You can also arrange examples **in order of increasing complexity**, beginning with the simplest and moving to the most difficult or complex.

Finally, you can arrange examples **in order of importance**, beginning with those that are less significant and moving to those that are most significant or persuasive.

The following informal outline for an essay evaluating the nursing care at a hospital illustrates one way to arrange examples. Notice how the writer presents examples in order of increasing importance under three general headings: *patient rooms*, *emergency room*, and *clinics*.

SAMPLE OUTLINE: Exemplification

INTRODUCTION

Thesis statement — Because of its focus on the patient, the nursing care at Montgomery Hospital can serve as a model for other medical facilities.

PARAGRAPH 1: IN PATIENT ROOMS

Example 1: Being responsive

Example 2: Establishing rapport

Example 3: Delivering bedside care

PARAGRAPH 2: IN EMERGENCY ROOM

Example 4: Staffing treatment rooms

Example 5: Circulating among patients in the waiting room

Example 6: Maintaining good working relationships with physicians

PARAGRAPH 3: IN CLINICS

Example 7: Preparing patients

Example 8: Assisting during treatment

Example 9: Instructing patients after treatment

CONCLUSION

Restatement of thesis (in different words) or review of key points or examples

Revising an Exemplification Essay

When you revise an exemplification essay, consider the items on the revision checklist on page 66. In addition, pay special attention to the items on the following checklist, which apply specifically to exemplification essays.

REVISION CHECKLIST EXEMPLIFICATION

- ☐ Does your assignment call for exemplification?
- ☐ Does your essay have a clear thesis statement that identifies the point you will illustrate?
- ☐ Do your examples explain and clarify your thesis statement?
- ☐ Have you provided enough examples?
- ☐ Have you used a range of examples?
- ☐ Are your examples persuasive?
- ☐ Do your examples add interest?
- ☐ Have you used transitional words and phrases that reinforce the connection between your examples and your thesis statement?

Editing an Exemplification Essay

When you edit your exemplification essay, follow the guidelines on the editing checklists on pages 83, 86, and 89. In addition, focus on the grammar, mechanics, and punctuation issues that are most relevant to exemplification essays. One of these issues – using commas in a series – is discussed here.

GRAMMAR IN CONTEXT USING COMMAS IN A SERIES

When you write an exemplification essay, you often use a **series of examples** to support a statement or to illustrate a point. When you use a series of three or more examples in a sentence, you should separate them with commas.

- Always use commas to separate three or more items – words, phrases, or clauses – in a series.

  In "Just Walk On By," Brent Staples says, "I was surprised, embarrassed, and dismayed all at once" (234).

  In "Just Walk On By," Staples observes that the woman thought she was being stalked by a mugger, by a rapist, or by something worse (234).

  "Waitresses are called *orderlies*, secretaries are called *clerk-typists*, nurses are called *medics*, assistants are called *adjutants*, and cleaning up an area is called *policing* the area" (Nilsen 203).

NOTE: Although newspaper and magazine writers routinely leave out the comma before the last item in a series of three or more items, you should always include this comma in your college writing.

- Do not use a comma after the final element in a series of three or more items.

INCORRECT: Staples was shocked, horrified, and disillusioned, to be taken for a mugger.

CORRECT: Staples was shocked, horrified, and disillusioned to be taken for a mugger.

- Do not use commas if all the elements in a series of three or more items are separated by coordinating conjunctions (*and, or, but,* and so on).

  According to Deborah L. Rhode, society discriminates against unattractive people in three ways: they are less likely to be hired and less likely to get raises and less likely to get promoted. (*no commas*)

LaunchPad

For more practice on using commas in a series, see the LearningCurve on Commas in the LaunchPad for *Patterns*.

EDITING CHECKLIST EXEMPLIFICATION

- ☐ Have you used commas to separate three or more items in a series?
- ☐ Have you made sure not to use a comma after the last element in a series?
- ☐ Have you made sure not to use a comma in a series with items separated by coordinating conjunctions?
- ☐ Are all the elements in a series stated in **parallel** terms (see page 376)?

A STUDENT WRITER: Exemplification

Exemplification is frequently used in nonacademic writing situations, such as business reports, memos, and proposals. One of the most important situations for using exemplification is in a letter you write to apply for a job.* Kristy Bredin's letter of application to a prospective employer follows.

* Eds. note—In business letters, paragraphs are not indented and extra space is added between paragraphs.

1028 Geissinger Street
Bethlehem, PA 18018
September 7, 2017

Kim Goldstein, Internship Coordinator
Rolling Stone
1290 Avenue of the Americas
New York, NY 10104-0298

Dear Ms. Goldstein:

Introduction

Thesis statement

I am writing to apply for the paid online internship that you posted on RollingStone.com. I believe that my education and my experience in publishing qualify me for the position you advertised. 1

Examples

I am currently a senior at Moravian College, where I am majoring in English (with a concentration in creative writing) and music. Throughout my college career, I have maintained a 3.4 average. After I graduate in May, I would like to find a full-time job in publishing. For this reason, I am very interested in your internship. It would not only give me additional editorial and administrative experience, but it would also give me insight into a large-scale publishing operation. An internship at RollingStone.com would also enable to me to read, edit, and possibly write articles about popular music — a subject I know a lot about. 2

Examples

Throughout college, I have been involved in writing and editing. I have served as both secretary and president of the Literary Society and have written, edited, and published its annual newsletter. I have also worked as a tutor in Moravian's Writing Center; as a literature editor for the *Manuscript*, Moravian's literary magazine; and as a features editor for the *Comeneian*, the student newspaper. In these jobs I have gained a good deal of practical experience in publishing as well as insight into dealing with people. In addition, I acquired professional editing experience as well as experience posting across platforms this past semester, when I worked as an intern for Taylor and Francis (Routledge) Publishing in New York. 3

Conclusion

I believe that my education and my publishing experience make me a good candidate for your position. As your ad requested, I 4 have enclosed my résumé, information on Moravian's internship program, and several writing samples for your consideration. You can contact me by phone at (484) 625-6731 or by email at stkab@ moravian.edu. I will be available for an interview anytime after September 23. I look forward to meeting with you to discuss my qualifications.

Sincerely,

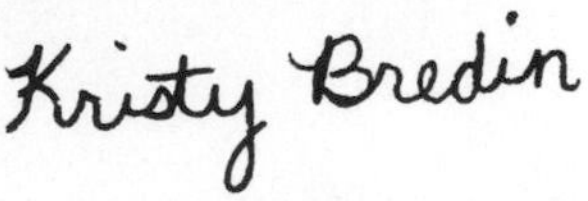

Kristy Bredin

Points for Special Attention

Organization. Exemplification is ideally suited for letters of application. The best way Kristy Bredin can support her claims about her qualifications for the internship at RollingStone.com is to give examples of her educational and professional qualifications. For this reason, the body of her letter is divided into two categories – her educational record and her editorial experience.

Each of the body paragraphs has a clear purpose and function. The second paragraph contains two examples pertaining to Kristy's educational record. The third paragraph contains examples of her editorial experience. These examples tell the prospective employer what qualifies Kristy for the internship. Within these two body paragraphs, she arranges her examples in order of increasing importance. Because her practical experience as an editor relates directly to the position she is applying for, Kristy considers this her strongest point and presents it last.

Kristy ends her letter on a strong note, expressing her willingness to be interviewed and giving the first date she will be available for an interview. Because people remember best what they read last, a strong conclusion is essential here, just as it is in other writing situations.

Persuasive Examples. To support a thesis convincingly, examples should convey specific information, not generalizations. Saying "I am a good student who is not afraid of responsibility" means very little. It is far better to say, as Kristy does, "Throughout my college career, I have maintained a 3.4 average" and "I have served as both secretary and president of the Literary Society." A letter of application should specifically show a prospective employer how your strengths and background correspond to the employer's needs; well-chosen examples can help you accomplish this goal.

Focus on Revision

After reading her letter, the students in Kristy's peer-editing group identified several areas they thought needed work.

One student thought Kristy should have mentioned that she had taken a desktop publishing course as an elective and worked with publishing and graphics software when she was the features editor of the student newspaper. Kristy agreed that this expertise would make her a more attractive candidate for the job and thought she could work these examples into her third paragraph.

Another student asked Kristy to explain how her experience as secretary and president of the Literary Society relates to the job she is applying for. If her purpose is to show that she can assume responsibility, she should say so; if it is to illustrate that she can supervise others, she should make that point clear.

A third student suggested that Kristy expand the discussion of her internship with Taylor and Francis Publishing in New York. Specific examples of her duties there would be persuasive because they would give her prospective employer a clear idea of her experience. (A peer-editing worksheet for exemplification can be found on pages 216–17.)

Working with Sources. Kristy's instructor recommended that Kristy refer to the ad to which she was responding. He said that this strategy would help Kristy's readers – potential employers – see that she was tailoring her letter to the specific job at RollingStone.com. Kristy considered this suggestion and decided to quote the language of the ad in her letter.

A STUDENT WRITER: Exemplification

The following essay, by Grace Ku, was written for a composition class in response to the following assignment: "Write an essay about the worst job you (or someone you know) ever had. If you can, include a quotation from one of the essays in your textbook. Make sure you include documentation as well as a works-cited page."

Midnight

Introduction

1 It was eight o'clock, and I was staring at the television set wondering what new political challenge would President Bartlet face on a rerun of *The West Wing*. I was glued to the set like an average thirteen-year-old while leisurely eating cold Chef Boyardee spaghetti out of the can. As I watched the show, I fell asleep on the floor fully clothed in a pair of jeans and a T-shirt, wondering when my parents would come home. Around midnight I woke up to a rustling noise: my parents had finally arrived from a long day at work. I could see in their tired faces the grief and hardship of working at a dry-cleaning plant.

Thesis statement

Transitional paragraph provides background

2 Although my parents lived in the most technologically advanced country in the world, their working conditions were like those of nineteenth-century factory workers. Because they were immigrants with little formal education and spoke broken English, they could get jobs only as laborers. Therefore, they worked at a dry-cleaning plant that was as big as a factory, a place where hundreds of small neighborhood cleaners sent their clothes to be processed. Like Bonnie Smith-Yackel's mother in the essay "My Mother Never Worked," my parents constantly "struggled to regain some competence and dignity and order" in their lives (123).

Quotation from essay in textbook

Series of brief examples: physical demands

3 At work, my parents had to meet certain quotas. Each day they had to clean and press several hundred garments — shirts, pants, and other clothing. By themselves, every day, they did the work of four laborers. The muscles of my mother's shoulders and arms grew hard as iron from working with the press, a difficult job even for a man. In addition to pressing, my father serviced the washing machines. As a result, his work clothes always smelled of oil.

Example: long hours

4 Not only were my parents' jobs physically demanding, but they also required long hours. My parents went to work at five o'clock in the morning and came home between nine o'clock at night and midnight. Each day they worked over twelve hours at the dry-cleaning plant, where eight-hour workdays and labor unions did not exist. They were allowed to take only two ten- to twenty-minute breaks — one for lunch and one for dinner. They did not stop even when they were burned by a hot iron or by steam from a press. The scars on their arms made it obvious that they worked at a dry-cleaning plant. My parents' burned skin would blister and later peel off, exposing raw flesh. In time, these injuries would heal, but other burns would soon follow.

Example: frequent burns

Example: low pay

5 In addition to having to work long hours and suffering painful injuries, my parents were paid below minimum wage. Together their paychecks were equal to that of a single unionized worker (even though they did the work of four). They used this money to feed and care for a household of five people.

Conclusion

6 As my parents silently entered our home around midnight, they did not have to complain about their jobs. I could see their anguish in their faces and their fatigue in the slow movements of their bodies. Even though they did not speak, their eyes said, "We

Restatement of thesis

hate our jobs, but we work so that our children will have better lives than we do."

Work Cited

Works-cited list (begins new page)

Smith-Yackel, Bonnie. "My Mother Never Worked." *Patterns for College Writing*, 14th ed., edited by Laurie G. Kirszner and Stephen R. Mandell, Bedford/St. Martin's, 2017, 121–24.

Points for Special Attention

Organization. Grace Ku begins her introduction by describing herself as a thirteen-year-old sitting on the floor watching television. At first, her behavior seems typical of many American children, but two things suggest problems: first, she is eating her cold dinner out of a can, and second, even though it is late in the evening, she is still waiting for her parents to return from work. This opening prepares readers for her thesis that her parents' jobs produce only grief and hardship.

In the body of her essay, Grace presents the examples that support her thesis statement. In paragraph 2, she sets the stage for the discussion to follow, explaining that her parents' working conditions were similar to those of nineteenth-century factory workers. In paragraph 3, she presents a series of examples that illustrate how physically demanding her parents' jobs were. In the remaining body paragraphs, she gives three other examples to show how unpleasant the jobs were: how long her parents worked, how often they were injured, and how little they were paid.

Grace concludes her essay by returning to the scene in her introduction, using a quotation that she wants to stay with her readers after they have finished the essay.

Working with Sources. Because her assignment asked students to include a quotation from an essay in their textbook, Grace looked for essays that had to do with work. After reading three of them, she decided that the sentiments expressed by Bonnie Smith-Yackel in "My Mother Never Worked" most closely mirrored her own. For this reason, at the end of paragraph 2, she included a quotation from Smith-Yackel's essay that helped her put her parents' struggles into perspective. Grace was careful to include quotation marks as well as MLA documentation. She also included bibliographic information for the essay in a works-cited page at the end of her essay. (See Chapter 18 for information on MLA documentation.)

Enough Examples. Certainly no single example, no matter how graphic, could adequately support the thesis of this essay. To establish the pain and difficulty of her parents' jobs, Grace uses several examples. Although additional examples would have added even more depth to the essay, the ones she uses are vivid and compelling enough to support her thesis that her parents had to endure great hardship to make a living.

Range of Examples. Grace selects examples that illustrate the full range of her subject. She draws from her parents' daily experience and does not include atypical examples. She also includes enough detail so that her readers, who she assumes do not know much about working in a dry-cleaning plant, will understand her points. She does not, however, provide so much detail that her readers get bogged down and lose interest.

Effective Examples. All of Grace's examples support her thesis statement. While developing these examples, she never loses sight of her main idea; consequently, she does not get sidetracked in irrelevant discussions. She also avoids the temptation to preach to her readers about the injustice of her parents' situation. By allowing her examples to speak for themselves, Grace paints a powerful portrait of her parents and their hardships.

Focus on Revision

After reading this draft, a classmate thought Grace could go into more detail about her parents' situation and could explain her examples in more depth – possibly writing about the quotas her parents had to meet or the other physical dangers of their jobs.

Grace thought she should expand the discussion in paragraph 5 about her parents' low wages, perhaps anticipating questions some of her readers might have about working conditions. For example, was it legal for her parents' employer to require them to work overtime without compensation or to pay them less than the minimum wage? If not, how was the employer able to get away with such practices?

Grace also thought she should move the information about her parents' work-related injuries from paragraph 4 to paragraph 3, where she discusses the physical demands of their jobs.

Finally, she decided to follow the advice of another student and include comments by her parents to make their experiences more immediate to readers.

PEER-EDITING WORKSHEET EXEMPLIFICATION

1. What strategy does the writer use in the essay's introduction? Would another strategy be more effective?
2. What is the essay's thesis? Does it make a point that the rest of the essay will support with examples?
3. What specific points do the body paragraphs make?
4. Does the writer use one example or several to illustrate each point? Should the writer use more examples? Fewer? Explain.
5. Does the writer use a sufficient range of examples? Are they explained in enough depth?

6. Do the examples add interest? How persuasive are they? List a few other examples that might be more persuasive.
7. What transitional words and phrases does the writer use to introduce examples? What other transitional words and phrases should be added? Where?
8. In what order are the examples presented? Would another order be more effective? Explain.
9. Has the writer used a series of three or more examples in a single sentence? If so, are these examples separated by commas?
10. What strategy does the writer use in the conclusion? What other strategy could be used?

The selections in this chapter all depend on exemplification to explain and clarify, to add interest, or to persuade. The first selection, a visual text, is followed by questions designed to illustrate how exemplification can operate in visual form.

CHARLES THATCHER, CARRIE VILLINES, GUIDO KOPPES, AND ANTHONY BRADSHAW*

Four Tattoos (Photos)

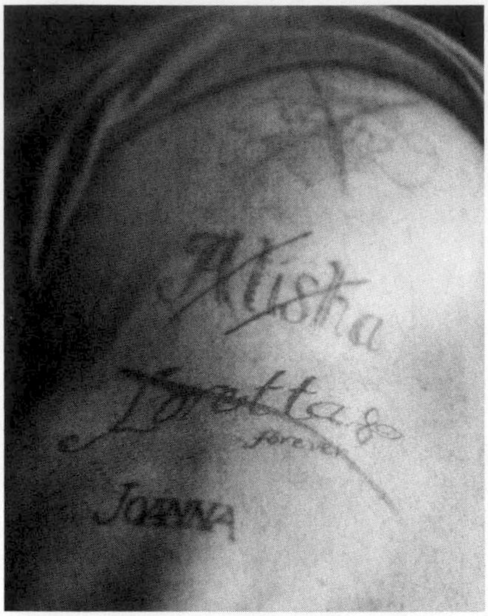

Charles Thatcher, "~~Alisha~~, ~~Loretta~~"

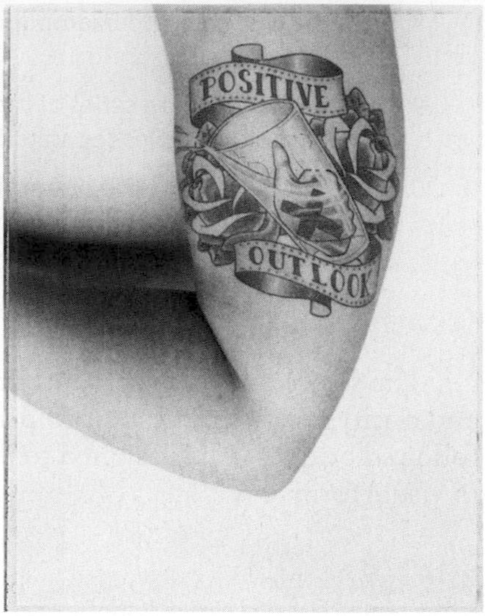

Carrie Villines, "Positive Outlook"

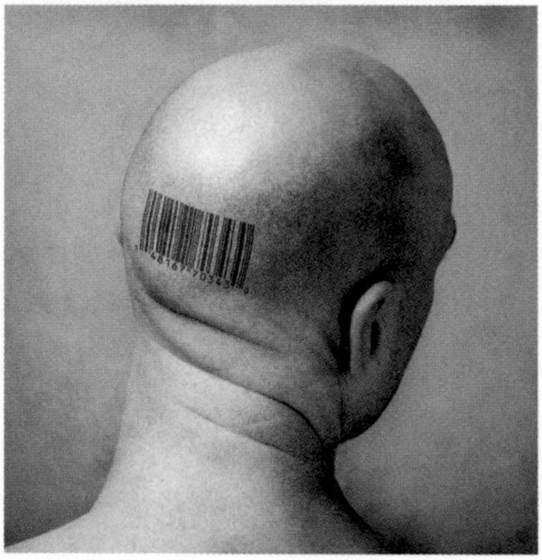

Anthony Bradshaw, "Bar Code"

Guido Koppes, "Owl"

* Photos shown clockwise from top left.
(Charles Thatcher/Getty Images; Carrie Villines/Getty Images; Guido Koppes/AGE Fotostock; Anthony Bradshaw/Getty Images)

• • •

Reading Images

1. How would you describe each of the four tattoos pictured on the previous page? List the prominent features of each, and then write two or three sentences that describe each of them.
2. After studying the four pictures (and reviewing your answer to question 1), write a one-sentence general statement that sums up your ideas about tattoos. For example, why do you think people get tattoos? Do you see them as a way for people to express themselves? As a way of demonstrating individuality? As a form of rebellion? As an impulsive act? As something else?
3. List several examples that support the general statement you made in question 2. What examples could you use to support this general statement?

Journal Entry

Would you ever get a tattoo? Write a paragraph answering this question. Use your answers to the questions above to support the main idea in your topic sentence. (If you have a tattoo, give several reasons you decided to get it.)

Thematic Connections

- "Why Looks Are the Last Bastion of Discrimination" (page 239)
- "Medium Ash Brown" (page 270)
- "Inked Well" (page 691)

ZEYNEP TUFEKCI

Why the Post Office Makes America Great

Zeynep Tufekci was born in 1951 in Istanbul, Turkey, and is an associate professor at the University of North Carolina's School of Information and Library Science. She is also a faculty associate at Harvard University's Berkman Center for Internet and Society and a former fellow at the Center for Information Technology Policy at Princeton University. She earned a B.A. in sociology from Istanbul University in Turkey and an M.S. and Ph.D. from the University of Texas at Austin. She is the author of *Twitter and Tear Gas: The Power and Fragility of Networked Protest* (2017). Her writing appears regularly on the blog *Technosociology* as well as in the *Atlantic* and the *New York Times.*

Background on the U.S. Postal Service Article I, Section 8, of the United States Constitution specifies that "The Congress shall have Power . . . To establish Post Offices and post Roads." In the years since its founding, the U.S. Postal Service (U.S.P.S.) has grown into the largest mail service in the world: it delivers hundreds of billions of pieces of mail annually. With more than 600,000 workers, it is also the third largest civilian employer in the United States, and it has an operating revenue of $68.8 billion. Most Americans take for granted that for less than fifty cents, they can send a piece of mail across the country and that it will show up within a few days. Recently, however, some critics have charged that in the digital age, a government-run post office makes no sense. They point out that in 2015, the post office recorded a net loss of $5.1 billion, mostly because of competition from private companies like Federal Express and newer communication technologies. Recent proposals have included privatizing the U.S.P.S., shrinking its workforce, and eliminating Saturday delivery, but maybe those seeking to change or reform the service should take a moment to reflect on the "magic" of the U.S. mail. Tufekci provides a provocative perspective not only on the postal service, but on the importance of high-quality, publicly accessible infrastructure.

I was transported recently to a place that is as enchanting to me as any 1
winter wonderland: my local post office.

In line, I thought fondly of the year I came to this country from Turkey as 2
an adult and discovered the magic of reliable mail service. Dependable infrastructure is magical not simply because it works, but also because it allows innovation to thrive, including much of the Internet-based economy that has grown in the past decade. You can't have Amazon or eBay without a reliable way to get things to people's homes.

Of course, infrastructure is also boring, so we get used to it and forget 3
what a gift it truly is. I never do, maybe because I discovered it so late.

4 My first year in the United States was full of surprises. I remember trying to figure out if the 24-ounce glass of ice water the waitress placed in front of me was a pitcher, to be shared by the whole table. But where was the spout? I had expected some of what I encountered—I had seen enough movies, and came to this country expecting big cars and big houses and wide open spaces. I got used to gigantic glasses.

> "My first year in the United States was full of surprises."

5 But I didn't expect the post office.

6 The first time I needed to mail something, I trekked over to my campus's post office, looking for the line to get my envelope weighed. The staff was used to befuddled international students like me, I suppose, and one clerk took my envelope without fuss, said "first class letter," and took my change.

7 Then I discovered some vending machines outside the office. People came and bought stamps. "So many people must be into stamp collecting," I thought to myself. Was that another weird American quirk? Otherwise, why would people waste money buying stamps in advance, without having their letters weighed?

8 Something I take for granted now just didn't occur to me: There were standardized rates, and you could just slap a stamp on your letter, drop it in a mailbox, and it would go to its destination.

9 I then encountered a visa service that asked me to mail in my passport. My precious, precious passport. With a self-addressed, stamped envelope for its return. I laughed at the audacity of the request. Despite being a broke student, I booked a plane trip. I couldn't envision putting my passport in the mail. I've since learned that this is a common practice, and I've even done it once or twice myself. But it still does not come easy to me.

10 I noticed that Americans were a particularly patriotic bunch: So many of them had red flags on their mailboxes. Sometimes they would put those flags up. I presumed it was to celebrate national holidays I did not yet know about. But why did some people have their flags up while others did not? And why weren't they American flags anyway? As in Istanbul, where I grew up, I assumed patriotism had different interpretations and expressions.

11 The mystery was solved when I noticed a letter carrier *emptying* a mailbox. I was slightly unnerved: Was the mail being stolen? He then went over to another mailbox with the flag up, and emptied that box, too. I got my hint when he skipped the mailbox with the flag down.

12 Yes, I was told, in the United States, mail gets picked up from your house, six days a week, free of charge.

13 I told my friends in Turkey about all this. They shook their heads in disbelief, wondering how easily I had been recruited as a C.I.A. agent, saying implausibly flattering things about my new country. The United States in the world's imagination is a place of risk taking and ruthless competition, not one of reliable public services.

14 I bit my tongue and did not tell my already suspicious friends that the country was also dotted with libraries that provided books to all patrons free

of charge. They wouldn't believe me anyway since I hadn't believed it myself. My first time in a library in the United States was very brief: I walked in, looked around, and ran right back out in a panic, certain that I had accidentally used the wrong entrance. Surely, these open stacks full of books were reserved for staff only. I was used to libraries being rare, and their few books inaccessible. To this day, my heart races a bit in a library.

Over the years, I've come to appreciate the link between infrastructure, innovation – and even ruthless competition. Much of our modern economy thrives here because you can order things online and expect them to be delivered. There are major private delivery services, too, but the United States Postal Service is often better equipped to make it to certain destinations. In fact, Internet sellers, and even private carriers, often use the U.S.P.S. as their delivery mechanism to addresses outside densely populated cities. 15

Almost every aspect of the most innovative parts of the United States, from cutting-edge medical research to its technology scene, thrives on publicly funded infrastructure. The post office is struggling these days, in some ways because of how much people rely on the web to do much of what they used to turn to the post office for. But the Internet is a testament to infrastructure, too: It exists partly because the National Science Foundation funded much of the research that makes it possible. Even some of the Internet's biggest companies, like Google, got a start from N.S.F.-funded research. 16

Infrastructure is often the least-appreciated part of what makes a country strong, and what makes innovation take flight. From my spot in line at the post office, I see a country that does both well; not a country that emphasizes one at the expense of the other. 17

• • •

Comprehension

1. Why does Tufekci call the post office "magical" (2)?
2. What surprises did Tufekci encounter during her first year in the United States? Why was the post office her biggest surprise?
3. Tufekci says she was surprised by some things that most Americans take for granted. What were those things?
4. How did Tufekci's friends in Turkey react when she told them about what life was like in the United States?
5. What does Tufekci mean when she says, "Infrastructure is often the least-appreciated part of what makes a country strong" (17)?

Purpose and Audience

1. How does Tufekci expect her readers to react to her essay? How do you know?
2. Is this essay primarily about the post office or about something else? Explain.
3. Does Tufekci state her thesis? If so, where? If not, what do you think her thesis is?

4. What does Tufekci hope to accomplish with her essay? Does she want to change people's minds? Inform them? Move them to action? Something else?

Style and Structure

1. This essay begins with a one-sentence introduction. Why do you think Tufekci begins this way?
2. Paragraphs 5 and 12 are single sentences. What function do these paragraphs serve?
3. Does Tufekci include enough examples? Does she provide a sufficient range of examples?
4. What determines how Tufekci groups her examples? Are they arranged chronologically? In order of importance? Of increasing complexity? According to some other organizing principle? Explain.
5. **Vocabulary Project.** In paragraph 15, Tufekci discusses *infrastructure, innovation,* and *competition*. What do these three terms mean? According to Tufekci, how are they linked?
6. What ideas does Tufekci emphasize in her conclusion? Do you agree with this strategy? How else could she have ended her essay?

Journal Entry

Does your experience support Tufekci's main idea? Do you think the post office is as important as she says it is?

Writing Workshop

1. Write an essay in which you, like Tufekci, discuss a place that is "as enchanting to [you] as any winter wonderland" (1). Be sure to include specific examples to support your thesis.
2. Assume you are writing to a Facebook friend in another country who is not familiar with American culture. Explain some things you take for granted that would be alien to this person – for example, all-you-can-eat buffets, drive-in pharmacies, and Uber. Make sure you include specific examples to illustrate your points.
3. **Working with Sources.** In a letter to the editor about Tufekci's essay, Robert Hunter writes, "Unfortunately, the post office is under attack, overpriced and underfunded by Congress – under pressure from its commercial competitors that want it to go away." Hunter goes on to say, "Congress should fund the postal system like any other nation-unifying service and enable it to do its essential job." Do some research about the financial status of the post office. Then, write an essay in which you agree or disagree with Hunter's comments. Be sure to document all references to Tufekci's essay and to Hunter's response and to include a works-cited page. (See Chapter 18 for information on MLA documentation.)

Combining the Patterns

Tufekci includes several **narrative** paragraphs in her essay. For example, in paragraph 4, she tells about a time she thought a twenty-four-ounce glass was a pitcher. What purpose do these narrative paragraphs serve?

Thematic Connections

- "Goodbye to My Twinkie Days" (page 169)
- "Mother Tongue" (page 458)
- "Tortillas" (page 500)
- "On Patriotism" (page 697)

JUDITH ORTIZ COFER

The Myth of the Latin Woman: I Just Met a Girl Named Maria

Born in Puerto Rico in 1952, Judith Ortiz Cofer moved to New Jersey with her family when she was four. She is the Regents' and Franklin Professor of English and Creative Writing, Emerita, at the University of Georgia. Widely anthologized, Cofer has published essays, poetry, novels, and the short-story collection *An Island Like You: Stories of the Barrio* (1995). In a recent interview, she commented on her early writing: "Poetry allowed me to become intimate with English. And it allowed me to master the one skill that I try to teach my students — and if that's the only thing I accomplish, I consider it a success — and that is succinctness: economy and concentration of language. Why use fifteen words when one clear, elegant sentence will do it?"

Background on images of Hispanic women in film During the era of silent film, Hispanic performers found a niche with the popularity of the stereotypical "Latin lover." Although Hispanic actors enjoyed success, only a handful of Hispanic actresses, such as Myrtle Gonzalez and Beatriz Michelena, played in leading roles that did not always cast them as Latina. For example, Mexican-born Dolores del Rio, the only Hispanic actress to achieve international stardom during the period, played characters named Evelyn Iffield and Jeanne Lamont as well as Carlotta de Silva and Carmelita de Granados. In the late 1920s, however, the advent of sound brought many fewer movie roles for Hispanic actresses. Some who found success during the 1930s and 1940s conformed to broad stereotypes — for example, "Mexican Spitfire" Lupe Vélez, Carmen "the Lady in the Tutti-Frutti Hat" Miranda, and Maria Montez's hot-blooded seductresses. Others concealed their Hispanic identities on-screen (as was the case for Margarita Carmen Cansino, whose hair was dyed, eyebrows heavily plucked, and skin lightened to make her into the movie star Rita Hayworth). In the 1950s and 1960s, actresses such as Katy Jurado and Rita Moreno (who won a supporting actress Academy Award for her performance in *West Side Story*) rarely played leads. The 1960s saw the stardom of Raquel Welch (born Jo Raquel Tejada), who, like Hayworth, played down her Hispanic roots, but it was not until the 1990s that young performers such as Jessica Alba, Jennifer Lopez, Penelope Cruz, and Salma Hayek came into their own, playing Latinas who are more than stereotypes or characters whose ethnicity completely defines them.

On a bus trip to London from Oxford University where I was earning some graduate credits one summer, a young man, obviously fresh from a pub, spotted me and as if struck by inspiration went down on his knees in the aisle. With both hands over his heart he broke into an Irish tenor's rendition of 1

"Maria" from *West Side Story*.* My politely amused fellow passengers gave his lovely voice the round of gentle applause it deserved. Though I was not quite as amused, I managed my version of an English smile: no show of teeth, no extreme contortions of the facial muscles – I was at this time of my life practicing reserve and cool. Oh, that British control, how I coveted it. But "Maria" had followed me to London, reminding me of a prime fact of my life: you can leave the island, master the English language, and travel as far as you can, but if you are a Latina, especially one like me who so obviously belongs to Rita Moreno's** gene pool, the island travels with you.

2 This is sometimes a very good thing – it may win you that extra minute of someone's attention. But with some people, the same things can make *you* an island – not a tropical paradise but an Alcatraz, a place nobody wants to visit. As a Puerto Rican girl living in the United States*** and wanting like most children to "belong," I resented the stereotype that my Hispanic appearance called forth from many people I met.

3 Growing up in a large urban center in New Jersey during the 1960s, I suffered from what I think of as "cultural schizophrenia." Our life was designed by my parents as a microcosm of their *casas*† on the island. We spoke in Spanish, ate Puerto Rican food bought at the *bodega*,‡ and practiced strict Catholicism at a church that allotted us a one-hour slot each week for mass, performed in Spanish by a Chinese priest trained as a missionary for Latin America.

4 As a girl I was kept under strict surveillance by my parents, since my virtue and modesty were, by their cultural equation, the same as their honor. As a teenager I was lectured constantly on how to behave as a proper *senorita*. But it was a conflicting message I received, since the Puerto Rican mothers also encouraged their daughters to look and act like women and to dress in clothes our Anglo friends and their mothers found too "mature" and flashy. The difference was, and is, cultural; yet I often felt humiliated when I appeared at an American friend's party wearing a dress more suitable to a semi-formal than to a playroom birthday celebration. At Puerto Rican festivities, neither the music nor the colors we wore could be too loud.

5 I remember Career Day in our high school, when teachers told us to come dressed as if for a job interview. It quickly became obvious that to the Puerto Rican girls "dressing up" meant wearing their mother's ornate jewelry and clothing, more appropriate (by mainstream standards) for the company Christmas party than as daily office attire. That morning I had agonized in front of my closet, trying to figure out what a "career girl" would wear. I knew how to dress for school (at the Catholic school I attended, we all wore

---

* Eds. note – A Broadway musical, based on *Romeo and Juliet*, about two rival New York street gangs, one Anglo and one Puerto Rican.

** Eds. note – Puerto Rico-born actress who won an Oscar for her role in the 1961 movie version of *West Side Story*.

*** Eds. note – Although it is an island, Puerto Rico is part of the United States.

† Eds. note – Homes.

‡ Eds. note – Small grocery store.

uniforms), I knew how to dress for Sunday mass, and I knew what dresses to wear for parties at my relatives' homes. Though I do not recall the precise details of my Career Day outfit, it must have been a composite of these choices. But I remember a comment my friend (an Italian American) made in later years that coalesced my impressions of that day. She said that at the business school she was attending, the Puerto Rican girls always stood out for wearing "everything at once." She meant, of course, too much jewelry, too many accessories. On that day at school we were simply made the negative models by the nuns, who were themselves not credible fashion experts to any of us. But it was painfully obvious to me that to the others, in their tailored skirts and silk blouses, we must have seemed "hopeless" and "vulgar." Though I now know that most adolescents feel out of step much of the time, I also know that for the Puerto Rican girls of my generation that sense was intensified. The way our teachers and classmates looked at us that day in school was just a taste of the cultural clash that awaited us in the real world, where prospective employers and men on the street would often misinterpret our tight skirts and jingling bracelets as a "come-on."

Mixed cultural signals have perpetuated certain stereotypes – for example, that of the Hispanic woman as the "hot tamale" or sexual firebrand. It is a one-dimensional view that the media have found easy to promote. In their special vocabulary, advertisers have designated "sizzling" and "smoldering" as the adjectives of choice for describing not only the foods but also the women of Latin America. From conversations in my house I recall hearing about the harassment that Puerto Rican women endured in factories where the "boss-men" talked to them as if sexual innuendo was all they understood, and worse, often gave them the choice of submitting to their advances or being fired. 6

> "Mixed cultural signals have perpetuated certain stereotypes—for example, that of the Hispanic woman as the 'hot tamale' or sexual firebrand."

It is custom, however, not chromosomes, that leads us to choose scarlet over pale pink. As young girls, it was our mothers who influenced our decisions about clothes and colors – mothers who had grown up on a tropical island where the natural environment was a riot of primary colors, where showing your skin was one way to keep cool as well as to look sexy. Most important of all, on the island, women perhaps felt freer to dress and move more provocatively since, in most cases, they were protected by the traditions, mores, and laws of a Spanish/Catholic system of morality and machismo whose main rule was: *You may look at my sister, but if you touch her I will kill you.* The extended family and church structure could provide a young woman with a circle of safety in her small pueblo on the island; if a man "wronged" a girl, everyone would close in to save her family honor. 7

My mother has told me about dressing in her best party clothes on Saturday nights and going to the town's plaza to promenade with her girlfriends in front of the boys they liked. The males were thus given an 8 opportunity to admire the women and to express their admiration in the form of *piropos:* erotically charged street poems they composed on the spot. (I have myself been subjected to a few *piropos* while visiting the island, and they can be outrageous, although custom dictates that they must never cross into obscenity.) This ritual, as I understand it, also entails a show of studied indifference on the woman's part; if she is "decent," she must not acknowledge the man's impassioned words. So I do understand how things can be lost in translation. When a Puerto Rican girl dressed in her idea of what is attractive meets a man from the mainstream culture who has been trained to react to certain types of clothing as a sexual signal, a clash is likely to take place. I remember the boy who took me to my first formal dance leaning over to plant a sloppy, over-eager kiss painfully on my mouth; when I didn't respond with sufficient passion, he remarked resentfully: "I thought you Latin girls were supposed to mature early," as if I were expected to *ripen* like a fruit or vegetable, not just grow into womanhood like other girls.

It is surprising to my professional friends that even today some people, 9 including those who should know better, still put others "in their place." It happened to me most recently during a stay at a classy metropolitan hotel favored by young professional couples for weddings. Late one evening after the theater, as I walked toward my room with a colleague (a woman with whom I was coordinating an arts program), a middle-aged man in a tuxedo, with a young girl in satin and lace on his arm, stepped directly into our path. With his champagne glass extended toward me, he exclaimed "Evita!"*

Our way blocked, my companion and I listened as the man half-recited, 10 half-bellowed "Don't Cry for Me, Argentina." When he finished, the young girl said: "How about a round of applause for my daddy?" We complied, hoping this would bring the silly spectacle to a close. I was becoming aware that our little group was attracting the attention of the other guests. "Daddy" must have perceived this too, and he once more barred the way as we tried to walk past him. He began to shout-sing a ditty to the tune of "La Bamba"—except the lyrics were about a girl named Maria whose exploits rhymed with her name and gonorrhea. The girl kept saying "Oh, Daddy" and looking at me with pleading eyes. She wanted me to laugh along with the others. My companion and I stood silently waiting for the man to end his offensive song. When he finished, I looked not at him but at his daughter. I advised her calmly never to ask her father what he had done in the army. Then I walked between them and to my room. My friend complimented me on my cool handling of the situation, but I confessed that I had really wanted to push the jerk into the swimming pool. This same man—probably a corporate executive, well-educated, even worldly by most standards—would not have been likely to regale an Anglo woman with a dirty song in public. He might have checked his impulse by assuming that she could be somebody's wife or mother, or at least *somebody* who might take offense. But, to him, I was just an Evita or a Maria: merely a character in his cartoon-populated universe.

---

* Eds. note—A Broadway musical about Eva Duarte de Perón, the former first lady of Argentina.

Another facet of the myth of the Latin woman in the United States is the menial, the domestic – Maria the housemaid or countergirl. It's true that work as domestics, as waitresses, and in factories is all that's available to women with little English and few skills. But the myth of the Hispanic menial – the funny maid, mispronouncing words and cooking up a spicy storm in a shiny California kitchen – has been perpetuated by the media in the same way that "Mammy" from *Gone with the Wind* became America's idea of the black woman for generations. Since I do not wear my diplomas around my neck for all to see, I have on occasion been sent to that "kitchen" where some think I obviously belong. 11

One incident has stayed with me, though I recognize it as a minor offense. 12 My first public poetry reading took place in Miami, at a restaurant where a luncheon was being held before the event. I was nervous and excited as I walked in with notebook in hand. An older woman motioned me to her table, and thinking (foolish me) that she wanted me to autograph a copy of my newly published slender volume of verse, I went over. She ordered a cup of coffee from me, assuming that I was the waitress. (Easy enough to mistake my poems for menus, I suppose.) I know it wasn't an intentional act of cruelty. Yet of all the good things that happened later, I remember that scene most clearly, because it reminded me of what I had to overcome before anyone would take me seriously. In retrospect I understand that my anger gave my reading fire. In fact, I have almost always taken any doubt in my abilities as a challenge, the result most often being the satisfaction of winning a convert, of seeing the cold, appraising eyes warm to my words, the body language change, the smile that indicates I have opened some avenue for communication. So that day as I read, I looked directly at that woman. Her lowered eyes told me she was embarrassed at her faux pas, and when I willed her to look up at me, she graciously allowed me to punish her with my full attention. We shook hands at the end of the reading and I never saw her again. She has probably forgotten the entire incident, but maybe not.

Yet I am one of the lucky ones. There are thousands of Latinas without the 13 privilege of an education or the entrees into society that I have. For them life is a constant struggle against the misconceptions perpetuated by the myth of the Latina. My goal is to try to replace the old stereotypes with a much more interesting set of realities. Every time I give a reading, I hope the stories I tell, the dreams and fears I examine in my work, can achieve some universal truth that will get my audience past the particulars of my skin color, my accent, or my clothes.

I once wrote a poem in which I called all Latinas "God's brown daughters." 14 This poem is really a prayer of sorts, offered upward, but also, through the human-to-human channel of art, outward. It is a prayer for communication and for respect. In it, Latin women pray "in Spanish to an Anglo God/with a Jewish heritage," and they are "fervently hoping/that if not omnipotent,/at least He be bilingual."

• • •

Comprehension

1. What does Cofer mean by "cultural schizophrenia" (3)?
2. What "conflicting message" (4) did Cofer receive from her family?
3. What points does Cofer make by including each of the following in her essay?
   - The story about the young man in Oxford (1)
   - The story about Career Day (5)
   - The story about the poetry reading (12)
4. According to Cofer, what stereotypes are commonly applied to Latinas?
5. How does Cofer explain why she and other Puerto Rican women like to dress as they do? Why do outsiders think they dress this way?
6. What exactly is "the myth of the Latin woman" (11)?
7. How does Cofer hope to help people see beyond the stereotypes she describes? Is she successful?

Purpose and Audience

1. Which of the following do you think is Cofer's thesis? Why?
   - "[I]f you are a Latina, especially one like me who so obviously belongs to Rita Moreno's gene pool, the island travels with you" (1).
   - "As a Puerto Rican girl living in the United States . . . I resented the stereotype that my Hispanic appearance called forth from many people I met" (2).
   - "My goal is to try to replace the old stereotypes with a much more interesting set of realities" (13).
2. Why does Cofer begin paragraph 13 with "Yet I am one of the lucky ones"? How do you think she expects her audience to react to this statement?
3. Despite its use of Spanish words, this essay is directed at an Anglo audience. How can you tell?

Style and Structure

1. Cofer opens her essay with a story about an incident in her life. Considering her subject matter and her audience, is this an effective opening strategy? Why or why not?
2. What do you think Cofer means to suggest with these expressions in paragraph 8?
   - "erotically charged"
   - "studied indifference"
   - "lost in translation"
   - "mainstream culture"
3. Cofer does not introduce the stereotype of the Latina as "the menial, the domestic" until paragraph 11, when she devotes two paragraphs to this part of the

stereotype. Why does she wait so long? Should this discussion have appeared earlier? Should it have been deleted altogether? Explain your reasoning.

4. Cofer uses exemplification to support her thesis. Does she provide enough examples? Are they the right kinds of examples?
5. How do you interpret the lines of poetry that Cofer quotes in her conclusion? Is this an effective concluding strategy? Why or why not?
6. **Vocabulary Project.** Cofer uses Spanish words throughout this essay, and she does not define them. Find definitions of these words in a Spanish/English dictionary, such as SpanishDict.com, or at Google Translate. Would the English equivalents be just as effective as – or even more effective than – the Spanish words?

Journal Entry

On the basis of what she writes here, it seems as if Cofer does not confront the people who stereotype her and does not show anger, even in the incident described in paragraphs 9 and 10. Do you think she should have acted differently, or do you admire her restraint?

Writing Workshop

1. What stereotypes are applied by outsiders to your racial or ethnic group (or to people of your gender, intended profession, or geographic region)? Write an exemplification essay in which you argue that these stereotypes are untrue and potentially harmful. Support your thesis with passages of narration, comparison and contrast, and cause and effect.
2. Think of some books, films, advertisements, or TV shows that feature characters of your own racial or ethnic group. Write a classification essay in which you discuss the different ways in which these characters are portrayed. Use exemplification and description to explain your categories. In your thesis, evaluate the accuracy of these characterizations.
3. **Working with Sources.** In paragraph 1 of her essay, Cofer says that "you can leave the island, master the English language, and travel as far as you can, but if you are a Latina, especially one like me who so obviously belongs to Rita Moreno's gene pool, the island travels with you." Editing this statement to suit your own "gene pool," use it as the thesis of an essay about the problems you have fitting in to some larger segment of society. Be sure to acknowledge Cofer as your source, including parenthetical documentation for references to her essay, and to include a works-cited page. (See Chapter 18 for information on MLA documentation.)

Combining the Patterns

The examples Cofer uses are personal narratives – stories of her own experience. What are the advantages and disadvantages of using **narration** here? Would other kinds of examples be more effective? Explain.

Thematic Connections

- "'What's in a Name?'" (page 2)
- "Surrendering" (page 116)
- "Indian Education" (page 140)
- "Just Walk On By: A Black Man Ponders His Power to Alter Public Space" (page 233)

BRENT STAPLES

Just Walk On By: A Black Man Ponders His Power to Alter Public Space

Born in Chester, Pennsylvania, in 1951, Brent Staples joined the staff of the *New York Times* in 1985, writing on culture and politics, and he became a member of its editorial board in 1990. His columns appear regularly on the paper's op-ed pages. Staples has also written a memoir, *Parallel Time: Growing Up in Black and White* (1994), about his escape from the poverty and violence of his childhood.

Background on racial profiling "Just Walk On By" can be read in the light of controversies surrounding racial profiling of criminal suspects, which occurs, according to the American Civil Liberties Union, "when the police target someone for investigation on the basis of that person's race, national origin, or ethnicity. Examples of profiling are the use of race to determine which drivers to stop for minor traffic violations ('driving while black') and the use of race to determine which motorists or pedestrians to search for contraband." Although law enforcement officials have often denied that they profile criminals solely on the basis of race, studies have shown a high prevalence of police profiling directed primarily at African and Hispanic Americans. A number of states have enacted laws barring racial profiling, and some people have won court settlements when they objected to being interrogated by police solely because of their race. Since the terrorist attacks of September 11, 2001, however, people of Arab descent have been targets of heightened interest at airports and elsewhere. In addition, the passage of a strict anti-illegal immigration law in Arizona in 2010 caused many Hispanics to fear that they would be singled out for scrutiny solely on the basis of race. (Just before the bill was scheduled to take effect, a federal judge blocked sections that required police to check immigration status during traffic violations, detentions, and arrests. The United States Supreme Court subsequently upheld that portion of the law.) Clearly, these events, as well as incidents that sparked the current Black Lives Matter movement, have added to the continuing controversy surrounding the association of criminal behavior with particular ethnic groups.

My first victim was a woman — white, well dressed, probably in her early twenties. I came upon her late one evening on a deserted street in Hyde Park, a relatively affluent neighborhood in an otherwise mean, impoverished section of Chicago. As I swung onto the avenue behind her, there seemed to be a discreet, uninflammatory distance between us. Not so. She cast back a worried glance. To her, the youngish black man — a broad six feet two inches with a beard and billowing hair, both hands shoved into the pockets of a bulky military jacket — seemed menacingly close. After a few more quick glimpses, she picked up her pace and was soon running in earnest. Within seconds she disappeared into a cross street. 1

> "It was in the echo of that terrified woman's footfalls that I first began to know the unwieldy inheritance I'd come into—the ability to alter public space in ugly ways."

That was more than a decade ago. I was twenty-two years old, a graduate student newly arrived at the University of Chicago. It was in the echo of that terrified woman's footfalls that I first began to know the unwieldy inheritance I'd come into – the ability to alter public space in ugly ways. It was clear that she thought herself the quarry of a mugger, rapist, or worse. Suffering a bout of insomnia, however, I was stalking sleep, not defenseless wayfarers. As a softy who is scarcely able to take a knife to a raw chicken – let alone hold it to a person's throat – I was surprised, embarrassed, and dismayed all at once. Her flight made me feel like an accomplice in tyranny. It also made it clear that I was indistinguishable from the muggers who occasionally seeped into the area from the surrounding ghetto. That first encounter, and those that followed, signified that a vast, unnerving gulf lay between nighttime pedestrians – particularly women – and me. And I soon gathered that being perceived as dangerous is a hazard in itself. I only needed to turn a corner into a dicey situation, or crowd some frightened, armed person in a foyer somewhere, or make an errant move after being pulled over by a policeman. Where fear and weapons meet – and they often do in urban America – there is always the possibility of death. 2

In that first year, my first away from my hometown, I was to become thoroughly familiar with the language of fear. At dark, shadowy intersections in Chicago, I could cross in front of a car stopped at a traffic light and elicit the *thunk, thunk, thunk, thunk* of the driver – black, white, male, or female – hammering down the door locks. On less traveled streets after dark, I grew accustomed to but never comfortable with people who crossed to the other side of the street rather than pass me. Then there were the standard unpleasantries with police, doormen, bouncers, cab drivers, and others whose business it is to screen out troublesome individuals *before* there is any nastiness. 3

I moved to New York nearly two years ago and I have remained an avid night walker. In central Manhattan, the near-constant crowd cover minimizes tense one-on-one street encounters. Elsewhere – visiting friends in SoHo, where sidewalks are narrow and tightly spaced buildings shut out the sky – things can get very taut indeed. 4

Black men have a firm place in New York mugging literature. Norman Podhoretz in his famed (or infamous) 1963 essay, "My Negro Problem – and Ours," recalls growing up in terror of black males; they "were tougher than we were, more ruthless," he writes – and as an adult on the Upper West Side of Manhattan, he continues, he cannot constrain his nervousness when he meets black men on certain streets. Similarly, a decade later, the essayist and novelist Edward Hoagland extols a New York where once "Negro bitterness bore down mainly on other Negroes." Where some see mere panhandlers, Hoagland sees "a mugger who is clearly screwing up his nerve to do more than just 5 *ask* for money." But Hoagland has "the New Yorker's quick-hunch posture for broken-field maneuvering," and the bad guy swerves away.

I often witness that "hunch posture," from women after dark on the warrenlike streets of Brooklyn where I live. They seem to set their faces on neutral and, with their purse straps strung across their chests bandolier style, they forge ahead as though bracing themselves against being tackled. I understand, of course, that the danger they perceive is not a hallucination. Women are particularly vulnerable to street violence, and young black males are drastically overrepresented among the perpetrators of that violence. Yet these truths are no solace against the kind of alienation that comes of being ever the suspect, against being set apart, a fearsome entity with whom pedestrians avoid making eye contact. 6

It is not altogether clear to me how I reached the ripe old age of twenty-two without being conscious of the lethality nighttime pedestrians attributed to me. Perhaps it was because in Chester, Pennsylvania, the small, angry industrial town where I came of age in the 1960s, I was scarcely noticeable against a backdrop of gang warfare, street knifings, and murders. I grew up one of the good boys, had perhaps a half-dozen fist fights. In retrospect, my shyness of combat has clear sources. 7

Many things go into the making of a young thug. One of those things is the consummation of the male romance with the power to intimidate. An infant discovers that random flailings send the baby bottle flying out of the crib and crashing to the floor. Delighted, the joyful babe repeats those motions again and again, seeking to duplicate the feat. Just so, I recall the points at which some of my boyhood friends were finally seduced by the perception of themselves as tough guys. When a mark cowered and surrendered his money without resistance, myth and reality merged – and paid off. It is, after all, only manly to embrace the power to frighten and intimidate. We, as men, are not supposed to give an inch of our lane on the highway; we are to seize the fighter's edge in work and in play and even in love; we are to be valiant in the face of hostile forces. 8

Unfortunately, poor and powerless young men seem to take all this nonsense literally. As a boy, I saw countless tough guys locked away; I have since buried several, too. They were babies, really – a teenage cousin, a brother of twenty-two, a childhood friend in his mid-twenties – all gone down in episodes of bravado played out in the streets. I came to doubt the virtues of intimidation early on. I chose, perhaps even unconsciously, to remain a shadow – timid, but a survivor. 9

The fearsomeness mistakenly attributed to me in public places often has a perilous flavor. The most frightening of these confusions occurred in the late 1970s and early 1980s when I worked as a journalist in Chicago. One day, rushing into the office of a magazine I was writing for with a deadline story in hand, I was mistaken for a burglar. The office manager called security and, with an ad hoc posse, pursued me through the labyrinthine halls, nearly to my editor's door. I had no way of proving who I was. I could only move briskly toward the company of someone who knew me. 10

Another time I was on assignment for a local paper and killing time before an interview. I entered a jewelry store on the city's affluent Near North Side. 11

The proprietor excused herself and returned with an enormous red Doberman pinscher straining at the end of a leash. She stood, the dog extended toward me, silent to my questions, her eyes bulging nearly out of her head. I took a cursory look around, nodded, and bade her good night. Relatively speaking, however, I never fared as badly as another black male journalist. He went to nearby Waukegan, Illinois, a couple of summers ago to work on a story about a murderer who was born there. Mistaking the reporter for the killer, police hauled him from his car at gunpoint and but for his press credentials would probably have tried to book him. Such episodes are not uncommon. Black men trade tales like this all the time.

In "My Negro Problem – and Ours," Podhoretz writes that the hatred he feels for blacks makes itself known to him through a variety of avenues – one being his discomfort with that "special brand of paranoid touchiness" to which he says blacks are prone. No doubt he is speaking here of black men. In time, I learned to smother the rage I felt at so often being taken for a criminal. Not to do so would surely have led to madness – via that special "paranoid touchiness" that so annoyed Podhoretz at the time he wrote the essay. 12

I began to take precautions to make myself less threatening. I move about with care, particularly late in the evening. I give a wide berth to nervous people on subway platforms during the wee hours, particularly when I have exchanged business clothes for jeans. If I happen to be entering a building behind some people who appear skittish, I may walk by, letting them clear the lobby before I return, so as not to seem to be following them. I have been calm and extremely congenial on those rare occasions when I've been pulled over by the police. 13

And on late-evening constitutionals along streets less traveled by, I employ what has proved to be an excellent tension-reducing measure: I whistle melodies from Beethoven and Vivaldi and the more popular classical composers. Even steely New Yorkers hunching toward nighttime destinations seem to relax, and occasionally they even join in the tune. Virtually everybody seems to sense that a mugger wouldn't be warbling bright, sunny selections from Vivaldi's *Four Seasons.* It is my equivalent of the cowbell that hikers wear when they know they are in bear country. 14

• • •

Comprehension

1. Why does Staples characterize the woman he encounters in paragraph 1 as a "victim"?
2. What does Staples mean when he says he has the power to "alter public space" (2)?
3. Why does Staples walk the streets at night?
4. What things, in Staples's opinion, contribute to "the making of a young thug" (8)? According to Staples, why are young, poor, and powerless men especially likely to become thugs?
5. How does Staples attempt to make himself less threatening?

Purpose and Audience

1. What is Staples's thesis? Does he state it or imply it?
2. Does Staples use logic, emotion, or a combination of the two to appeal to his readers? How appropriate is his strategy?
3. What preconceptions does Staples assume his audience has? How does he challenge these preconceptions?
4. What is Staples trying to accomplish with his first sentence? Do you think he succeeds? Why or why not?

Style and Structure

1. Why does Staples mention Norman Podhoretz? Could he make the same points without referring to Podhoretz's essay?
2. Staples begins his essay with an anecdote. How effective is this strategy? Do you think another opening strategy would be more effective? Explain.
3. Does Staples present enough examples to support his thesis? Are they representative? Would other types of examples be more convincing? Explain.
4. In what order does Staples present his examples? Would another order be more effective? Explain.
5. **Vocabulary Project.** In paragraph 8, Staples uses the word *thug.* List as many synonyms as you can for this word. Do all these words convey the same idea, or do they differ in their connotations? Explain. (If you like, consult an online thesaurus at thesaurus.com.)

Journal Entry

Have you ever been in a situation such as the ones Staples describes, where you perceived someone (or someone perceived you) as threatening? How did you react? After reading Staples's essay, do you think you would react the same way now?

Writing Workshop

1. Use your journal entry to help you write an essay using a single long example to support this statement: "When walking alone at night, you can (or cannot) be too careful."
2. **Working with Sources.** Relying on examples from your own experience and from Staples's essay, write an essay discussing what part you think race plays in people's reactions to Staples. Do you think his perceptions are accurate? Be sure to include parenthetical documentation for Staples's words and ideas and a works-cited page. (See Chapter 18 for information on MLA documentation.)
3. How accurate is Staples's observation concerning the "male romance with the power to intimidate" (8)? What does he mean by this statement? What

examples from your own experience support (or do not support) the idea that this "romance" is an element of male upbringing in our society?

Combining the Patterns

In paragraph 8, Staples uses **cause and effect** to demonstrate what goes "into the making of a young thug." Would several **examples** have better explained how a youth becomes a thug?

Thematic Connections

- "A Peaceful Woman Explains Why She Carries a Gun" (page 350)
- "Emmett Till and Tamir Rice, Sons of the Great Migration" (page 422)
- "The Ways We Lie" (page 466)
- "Letter from Birmingham Jail" (page 558)

DEBORAH L. RHODE

Why Looks Are the Last Bastion of Discrimination

Deborah L. Rhode (b. 1952) is the Ernest McFarland Professor of Law and the director of the Center on the Legal Profession at Stanford University. She earned her undergraduate and law degrees at Yale University, and she served as a law clerk for former Supreme Court Justice Thurgood Marshall. She has published many books on gender, legal ethics, and professional responsibility, including *The Difference "Difference" Makes: Women and Leadership* (2003), *The Beauty Bias: The Injustice of Appearance in Life and Law* (2010), and *The Trouble with Lawyers* (2015). A columnist for the *National Law Journal,* Rhode has also written for the *New York Times, Slate,* the *Boston Globe,* and other publications. The following essay originally appeared in the *Washington Post* in 2010.

Background on appearance-based discrimination The United States Supreme Court has ruled that the Constitution bars discrimination on the basis of race, sex, religion, national origin, and ethnicity. Although some see "lookism" as a civil rights issue similar to racism and sexism, others worry that addressing the issue with legislation encroaches on individual freedom and unnecessarily creates another legally protected group. As Rhode notes, however, the state of Michigan and six local jurisdictions throughout the United States have enacted legal prohibitions on appearance discrimination. In Michigan, for example, a Hooters waitress sued the chain after she was told to lose weight and improve her looks. Lawyers for Hooters argued that employees at the restaurant — who wear tank tops and tight shorts — are entertainers as much as servers. In 2011, the suit was settled out of court.

In the nineteenth century, many American cities banned public appearances by "unsightly" individuals. A Chicago ordinance was typical: "Any person who is diseased, maimed, mutilated, or in any way deformed, so as to be an unsightly or disgusting subject . . . shall not . . . expose himself to public view, under the penalty of a fine of $1 for each offense." 1

Although the government is no longer in the business of enforcing such discrimination, it still allows businesses, schools, and other organizations to indulge their own prejudices. Over the past half-century, the United States has expanded protections against discrimination to include race, religion, sex, age, disability, and, in a growing number of jurisdictions, sexual orientation. Yet bias based on appearance remains perfectly permissible in all but one state and six cities and counties. Across the rest of the country, looks are the last bastion of acceptable bigotry. 2

We all know that appearance matters, but the price of prejudice can be steeper than we often assume. In Texas in 1994, an obese woman was rejected for a job as a bus driver when a company doctor assumed she was not up to the task after watching her, in his words, "waddling down the hall." He did 3 not perform any agility tests to determine whether she was, as the company would later claim, unfit to evacuate the bus in the event of an accident.

In New Jersey in 2005, one of the Borgata Hotel Casino's "Borgata babe" cocktail waitresses went from a Size 4 to a Size 6 because of a thyroid condition. When the waitress, whose contract required her to keep "an hourglass figure" that was "height and weight appropriate," requested a larger uniform, she was turned down. "Borgata babes don't go up in size," she was told. (Unless, the waitress noted, they have breast implants, which the casino happily accommodated with paid medical leave and a bigger bustier.) 4

And in California in 2001, Jennifer Portnick, a 240-pound aerobics instructor, was denied a franchise by Jazzercise, a national fitness chain. Jazzercise explained that its image demanded instructors who are "fit" and "toned." But Portnick was both: She worked out six days a week, taught back-to-back classes, and had no shortage of willing students. 5

Such cases are common. In a survey by the National Association to Advance Fat Acceptance, 62 percent of its overweight female members and 42 percent of its overweight male members said they had been turned down for a job because of their weight. 6

And it isn't just weight that's at issue; it's appearance overall. According to a national poll by the Employment Law Alliance in 2005, 16 percent of workers reported being victims of appearance discrimination more generally—a figure comparable to the percentage who in other surveys say they have experienced sex or race discrimination. 7

> "Conventional wisdom holds that beauty is in the eye of the beholder, but most beholders tend to agree on what is beautiful."

Conventional wisdom holds that beauty is in the eye of the beholder, but most beholders tend to agree on what is beautiful. A number of researchers have independently found that, when people are asked to rate an individual's attractiveness, their responses are quite consistent, even across race, sex, age, class, and cultural background. Facial symmetry and unblemished skin are universally admired. Men get a bump for height, women are favored if they have hourglass figures, and racial minorities get points for light skin color, European facial characteristics, and conventionally "white" hairstyles. 8

Yale's Kelly Brownell and Rebecca Puhl and Harvard's Nancy Etcoff have each reviewed hundreds of studies on the impact of appearance. Etcoff finds that unattractive people are less likely than their attractive peers to be viewed as intelligent, likable, and good. Brownell and Puhl have documented that overweight individuals consistently suffer disadvantages at school, at work, and beyond. 9

Among the key findings of a quarter-century's worth of research: Unattractive people are less likely to be hired and promoted, and they earn lower salaries, even in fields in which looks have no obvious relationship to professional duties. (In one study, economists Jeff Biddle and Daniel Hamermesh estimated that for lawyers, such prejudice can translate to a pay cut of as 10 much as 12 percent.) When researchers ask people to evaluate written essays, the same material receives lower ratings for ideas, style, and creativity when an accompanying photograph shows a less attractive author. Good-looking professors get better course evaluations from students; teachers in turn rate good-looking students as more intelligent.

Not even justice is blind. In studies that simulate legal proceedings, unattractive plaintiffs receive lower damage awards. And in a study released this month, Stephen Ceci and Justin Gunnell, two researchers at Cornell University, gave students case studies involving real criminal defendants and asked them to come to a verdict and a punishment for each. The students gave unattractive defendants prison sentences that were, on average, twenty-two months longer than those they gave to attractive defendants. 11

Just like racial or gender discrimination, discrimination based on irrelevant physical characteristics reinforces invidious stereotypes and undermines equal-opportunity principles based on merit and performance. And when grooming choices come into play, such bias can also restrict personal freedom. 12

Consider Nikki Youngblood, a lesbian who in 2001 was denied a photo in her Tampa high school yearbook because she would not pose in a scoop-necked dress. Youngblood was "not a rebellious kid," her lawyer explained. "She simply wanted to appear in her yearbook as herself, not as a fluffed-up stereotype of what school administrators thought she should look like." Furthermore, many grooming codes sexualize the workplace and jeopardize employees' health. The weight restrictions at the Borgata, for example, reportedly contributed to eating disorders among its waitresses. 13

Appearance-related bias also exacerbates disadvantages based on gender, race, ethnicity, age, sexual orientation, and class. Prevailing beauty standards penalize people who lack the time and money to invest in their appearance. And weight discrimination, in particular, imposes special costs on people who live in communities with shortages of healthy food options and exercise facilities. 14

So why not simply ban discrimination based on appearance? 15

Employers often argue that attractiveness is job-related; their workers' appearance, they say, can affect the company's image and its profitability. In this way, the Borgata blamed its weight limits on market demands. Customers, according to a spokesperson, like being served by an attractive waitress. The same assumption presumably motivated the L'Oreal executive who was sued for sex discrimination in 2003 after allegedly ordering a store manager to fire a salesperson who was not "hot" enough. 16

Such practices can violate the law if they disproportionately exclude groups protected by civil rights statutes – hence the sex discrimination suit. Abercrombie & Fitch's notorious efforts to project what it called a "classic American" look led to a race discrimination settlement on behalf of minority job-seekers who said they were turned down for positions on the sales floor. But unless the victims of appearance bias belong to groups already protected by civil rights laws, they have no legal remedy. 17

As the history of civil rights legislation suggests, customer preferences should not be a defense for prejudice. During the early civil rights era, employers 18 in the South often argued that hiring African Americans would be financially ruinous; white customers, they said, would take their business elsewhere. In rejecting this logic, Congress and the courts recognized that customer preferences often reflect and reinforce precisely the attitudes that society is seeking to eliminate. Over the decades, we've seen that the most effective way of combating prejudice is to deprive people of the option to indulge it.

Similarly, during the 1960s and 1970s, major airlines argued that the male business travelers who dominated their customer ranks preferred attractive female flight attendants. According to the airlines, that made sex a bona fide occupational qualification and exempted them from antidiscrimination requirements. But the courts reasoned that only if sexual allure were the "essence" of a job should employers be allowed to select workers on that basis. Since airplanes were not flying bordellos, it was time to start hiring men. 19

Opponents of a ban on appearance-based discrimination also warn that it would trivialize other, more serious forms of bias. After all, if the goal is a level playing field, why draw the line at looks? "By the time you've finished preventing discrimination against the ugly, the short, the skinny, the bald, the knobbly-kneed, the flat-chested, and the stupid," Andrew Sullivan wrote in the London *Sunday Times* in 1999, "you're living in a totalitarian state." Yet intelligence and civility are generally related to job performance in a way that appearance isn't. 20

We also have enough experience with prohibitions on appearance discrimination to challenge opponents' arguments. Already, one state (Michigan) and six local jurisdictions (the District of Columbia; Howard County, Md.; San Francisco; Santa Cruz, Calif.; Madison, Wis.; and Urbana, Ill.) have banned such discrimination. Some of these laws date back to the 1970s and 1980s, while some are more recent; some cover height and weight only, while others cover looks broadly; but all make exceptions for reasonable business needs. 21

Such bans have not produced a barrage of loony litigation or an erosion of support for civil rights remedies generally. These cities and counties each receive between zero and nine complaints a year, while the entire state of Michigan totals about 30, with fewer than one a year ending up in court. 22

Although the laws are unevenly enforced, they have had a positive effect by publicizing and remedying the worst abuses. Because Portnick, the aerobics instructor turned away by Jazzercise, lived in San Francisco, she was able to bring a claim against the company. After a wave of sympathetic media coverage, Jazzercise changed its policy. 23

This is not to overstate the power of legal remedies. Given the stigma attached to unattractiveness, few will want to claim that status in public litigation. And in the vast majority of cases, the cost of filing suit and the difficulty of proving discrimination are likely to be prohibitive. But stricter anti-discrimination laws could play a modest role in advancing healthier and more inclusive ideals of attractiveness. At the very least, such laws could reflect our principles of equal opportunity and raise our collective consciousness when we fall short. 24

• • •

Comprehension

1. Why, according to Rhode, are looks "the last bastion of acceptable bigotry" (2)?
2. Why does the government allow organizations to engage in appearance discrimination?
3. What forms of discrimination do unattractive people face?
4. Why do some people object to banning discrimination based on appearance? How does Rhode address these objections?
5. According to Rhode, how effective are laws that prohibit appearance discrimination? What positive effects might they have?

Purpose and Audience

1. Does Rhode assume that her readers are aware of the problem she discusses? How can you tell?
2. What preconceived attitudes about appearance does Rhode assume her readers have?
3. Where does Rhode state her thesis? Why does she state it where she does instead of earlier in her essay?
4. Is Rhode's purpose simply to inform her readers or to persuade them? Explain.

Style and Structure

1. The first half of Rhode's essay contains a series of short examples. What do these examples illustrate? Do you think Rhode should have made her point with fewer examples developed in more depth?
2. Paragraph 15 is a **rhetorical question**. What is the purpose of this rhetorical question? How effective is it?
3. The second half of Rhode's essay addresses objections to laws banning appearance discrimination. How effectively does Rhode respond to these objections?
4. At several points in her essay, Rhode cites statistics. Is this kind of evidence convincing? Is it more convincing than additional examples would be?
5. **Vocabulary Project.** What words or phrases convey Rhode's feelings toward her subject? Do you think these emotional words and phrases undercut her essay in any way? What other language could she have used instead of these words and phrases?

Journal Entry

Do you believe, as Rhode does, that "stricter anti-discrimination laws could play a modest role in advancing healthier and more inclusive ideals of attractiveness" (24)?

Writing Workshop

1. Do you think Rhode makes a convincing case? Write an email to her in which you agree or disagree with her position.
2. Write an essay that shows how Rhode's ideas apply (or do not apply) to a school, a business, or an organization that you know well.
3. **Working with Sources.** According to the article "Appearance-Based Discrimination" on the HRM Guide website, unattractive people are not the only ones who face discrimination. "Regardless of who the real person may be," says the article, "stereotypes associated with piercings and tattoos can and do affect others. In general, individuals with tattoos and body piercings are often viewed as 'rougher' or 'less educated.'" Write an essay in which you use examples from your own experience to support or to challenge this statement. Be sure your essay includes at least one reference to Rhode's essay. Document all references to Rhode, and include a works-cited page. (See Chapter 18 for information on MLA documentation.)

Combining the Patterns

In paragraphs 1 and 2, Rhode uses **comparison and contrast**. In these paragraphs, she compares nineteenth-century laws that penalized "'unsightly' individuals" to the actions of government today. How does this comparison help Rhode prepare her readers for her thesis?

Thematic Connections

- "Indian Education" (page 140)
- "Four Tattoos" (page 218)
- "The Myth of the Latin Woman: I Just Met a Girl Named Maria" (page 225)
- "Inked Well" (page 691)

MAIA SZALAVITZ

Ten Ways We Get the Odds Wrong

Maia Szalavitz (b. 1965), a journalist who writes about science, health, addiction, and public policy, has published articles in the *New York Times*, the *Washington Post*, *New Scientist*, *Time* magazine, and many other publications. She is the author of *Help at Any Cost: How the Troubled-Teen Industry Cons Parents and Hurts Kids* (2006) as well as the coauthor of *The Boy Who Was Raised as a Dog* (2007) and *Born for Love: Why Empathy Is Essential — and Endangered* (2010), with Bruce D. Perry. Her most recent book, *Unbroken Brain: A Revolutionary New Way of Understanding Addiction* (2016), explores the possibility that addictions are actually a form of learning disorder.

Background on odds and risks Odds making is most often associated with sports and casino gambling, although people can place bets on nearly everything from presidential races to celebrity deaths and the weather. For sporting events (such as NFL games), professional oddsmakers are generally less interested in predicting the winner than in setting an appropriate line for "spread-betting," creating a situation that will attract an equal number of bettors on both sides. The result is that the oddsmakers reduce their risks and make money regardless of the outcome. Odds making and risk assessment are not just confined to sports betting, however. The first stirrings of the modern insurance industry in the seventeenth and eighteenth centuries coincided with advancements in mathematics and probability theory. As a result of advances in both statistics and technology, the actuarial sciences — the use of mathematics and statistics to assess risk — now flourish not only in the insurance sector, but also in finance, global economics, medicine, and public policy. The management of risk has become so central to our social and economic lives that the German sociologist Ulrich Beck famously coined the term *risk society* to define the modern world.

1 Is your gym locker room crawling with drug-resistant bacteria? Is the guy with the bulging backpack a suicide bomber? And what about that innocent-looking arugula: Will pesticide residue cause cancer, or do the leaves themselves harbor *E. coli*? But wait! Not eating enough vegetables is also potentially deadly.

2 These days, it seems like everything is risky, and worry itself is bad for your health. The more we learn, the less we seem to know — and if anything makes us anxious, it's uncertainty. At the same time, we're living longer, healthier lives. So why does it feel like even the lettuce is out to get us?

3 The human brain is exquisitely adapted to respond to risk — uncertainty about the outcome of actions. Faced with a precipice or a predator, the brain is biased to make certain decisions. Our biases reflect the choices that kept our ancestors alive. But we have yet to evolve similarly effective responses to statistics, media coverage, and fear-mongering politicians. For most of human

existence twenty-four-hour news channels didn't exist, so we don't have cognitive shortcuts to deal with novel uncertainties.

Still, uncertainty unbalances us, pitching us into anxiety and producing an array of cognitive distortions. Even minor dilemmas like deciding whether to get a cell phone (brain cancer vs. dying on the road because you can't call for help?) can be intolerable for some people. And though emotions are themselves critical to making rational decisions, they were designed for a world in which dangers took the form of predators, not pollutants. Our emotions push us to make snap judgments that once were sensible – but may not be anymore. 4

"Our emotions push us to make snap judgments that once were sensible—but may not be anymore."

I. We Fear Snakes, Not Cars

Risk and emotion are inseparable.

Fear feels like anything but a cool and detached computation of the odds. But that's precisely what it is, a lightning-fast risk assessment performed by your reptilian brain, which is ever on the lookout for danger. The amygdala flags perceptions, sends out an alarm message, and – before you have a chance to think – your system gets flooded with adrenaline. "This is the way our ancestors evaluated risk before we had statistics," says Paul Slovic, president of Decision Research. Emotions are decision-making shortcuts. 5

As a result of these evolved emotional algorithms, ancient threats like spiders and snakes cause fear out of proportion to the real danger they pose, while experiences that should frighten us – like fast driving – don't. Dangers like speedy motorized vehicles are newcomers on the landscape of life. The instinctive response to being approached rapidly is to freeze. In the ancestral environment, this reduced a predator's ability to see you – but that doesn't help when what's speeding toward you is a car. 6

II. We Fear Spectacular, Unlikely Events

Fear skews risk analysis in predictable ways.

Fear hits primitive brain areas to produce reflexive reactions before the situation is even consciously perceived. Because fear strengthens memory, catastrophes such as earthquakes, plane crashes, and terrorist incidents completely capture our attention. As a result, we overestimate the odds of dreadful but infrequent events and underestimate how risky ordinary events are. The drama and excitement of improbable events make them appear to be more common. The effect is amplified by the fact that media tend to cover what's dramatic and exciting, Slovic notes. The more we see something, the more common we think it is, even if we are watching the same footage over and over. 7

After 9/11, 1.4 million people changed their holiday travel plans to avoid flying. The vast majority chose to drive instead. But driving is far more 8 dangerous than flying, and the decision to switch caused roughly 1,000 additional auto fatalities, according to two separate analyses comparing traffic patterns in late 2001 to those the year before. In other words, 1,000 people who chose to drive wouldn't have died had they flown instead.

III. We Fear Cancer but Not Heart Disease

We underestimate threats that creep up on us.

Humans are ill-prepared to deal with risks that don't produce immediate negative consequences, like eating a cupcake or smoking cigarettes. As a result, we are less frightened of heart disease than we should be. Heart disease is the end result of actions that one at a time (one cigarette or one french fry) aren't especially dangerous. But repeated over the years, those actions have deadly consequences. "Things that build up slowly are very hard for us to see," says Kimberly Thompson, a professor of risk analysis at the Harvard School of Public Health. Obesity and global warming are in that category. "We focus on the short-term even if we know the long-term risk." 9

Our difficulty in understanding how small risks add up accounts for many unplanned pregnancies. At most points during the menstrual cycle, the odds of pregnancy are low, but after a year of unprotected sex, 85 percent of couples experience it. 10

IV. No Pesticide in My Backyard — Unless I Put It There

We prefer that which (we think) we can control.

If we feel we can control an outcome, or if we choose to take a risk voluntarily, it seems less dangerous, says David Ropeik, a risk consultant. "Many people report that when they move from the driver's seat to the passenger's seat, the car in front of them looks closer and their foot goes to the imaginary brake. You're likely to be less scared with the steering wheel in your hand, because you can do something about your circumstances, and that's reassuring." Could explain why your mother always criticizes your driving. 11

The false calm a sense of control confers, and the tendency to worry about dangers we can't control, explains why when we see other drivers talking on cell phones we get nervous but we feel perfectly fine chatting away ourselves. Similarly, because homeowners themselves benefit if they kill off bugs that are destroying their lawns, people fear insecticide less if they are using it in their own backyard than if a neighbor uses the same chemical in the same concentration, equally close to them. The benefits to us reduce the level of fear. "Equity is very important," says Slovic, and research shows that if people who bear the risk also get the benefit, they tend to be less concerned about it. 12

V. We Speed Up When We Put Our Seat Belts On

We substitute one risk for another.

Insurers in the United Kingdom used to offer discounts to drivers who purchased cars with safer brakes. "They don't anymore," says John Adams, a 13 risk analyst and emeritus professor of geography at University College. "There weren't fewer accidents, just different accidents."

Why? For the same reason that the vehicles most likely to go out of control in snowy conditions are those with four-wheel drive. Buoyed by a false sense of safety that comes with the increased control, drivers of four-wheel-drive vehicles take more risks. "These vehicles are bigger and heavier, which should keep them on the road," says Ropeik. "But police report that these drivers go faster, even when roads are slippery." 14

Both are cases of risk compensation: People have a preferred level of risk, and they modulate their behavior to keep risk at that constant level. Features designed to increase safety—four-wheel drive, seat belts, or air bags—wind up making people drive faster. The safety features may reduce risks associated with weather, but they don't cut overall risk. "If I drink a diet soda with dinner," quips Slovic, "I have ice cream for dessert." 15

VI. Teens May Think Too Much about Risk—and Not Feel Enough

Why using your cortex isn't always smart.

Parents worry endlessly that their teens will drive, get pregnant, or overdose on drugs; they think youth feel immortal and don't consider negative consequences. Curiously, however, teens are actually less likely than adults to fall into the trap of thinking, "It won't happen to me." In fact, teens massively overestimate the odds of things like contracting HIV or syphilis if they have sex. One study found that teens thought a sexually active girl had a 60 percent chance of getting AIDS. So why do they do it anyway? 16

Teens may not be irrational about risk but too rational, argues Valerie Reyna, a psychologist at Cornell University. Adults asked to consider absurd propositions like "Is it a good idea to drink Drano?" immediately and intuitively say no. Adolescents, however, take more than twice as long to think about it. Brain-scan research shows that when teens contemplate things like playing Russian roulette or drinking and driving, they primarily use rational regions of the brain—certain regions of cortex—while adults use emotional regions like the insula. 17

When risky decisions are weighed in a rational calculus, benefits like fitting in and feeling good now can outweigh real risks. As a result, teaching reasoned decision-making to teens backfires, argues Reyna. Instead, she says, we should teach kids to rule out risks based on emotional responses—for example, by considering the worst-case scenario, as adults do. But research suggests there may be no way to speed up the development of mature decision-making. Repetition and practice are critical to emotional judgment—which means that it takes time to learn this skill. 18

VII. Why Young Men Will Never Get Good Rates on Car Insurance

The "risk thermostat" varies widely.

People tend to maintain a steady level of risk, sensing what range of odds is comfortable for them and staying within it. "We all have some propensity 19 to take risk," says Adams. "That's the setting on the 'risk thermostat.'" Some people have a very high tolerance for risk, while others are more cautious.

Forget the idea of a risk-taking personality. If there's a daredevil gene that globally affects risk-taking, researchers haven't found it. Genes do influence impulsivity, which certainly affects the risks people take. And testosterone inclines males to take more risks than females. But age and situation matter as much as gender. Men fifteen to twenty-five are very risk-prone compared to same-age women and older people. 20

More importantly, one person's risk thermostat may have different settings for different types of risk. "Somebody who has their whole portfolio in junk bonds is not necessarily also a mountain climber," explains Baruch Fischhoff, a professor of psychology at Carnegie Mellon University. 21

VIII. We Worry about Teen Marijuana Use, but Not about Teen Sports

Risk arguments cannot be divorced from values.

If the risks of smoking marijuana are coldly compared to those of playing high-school football, parents should be less concerned about pot smoking. Death by marijuana overdose has never been reported, while thirteen teen players died of football-related injuries in 2006 alone. And marijuana impairs driving far less than the number one drug used by teens: alcohol. Alcohol and tobacco are also more likely to beget addiction, give rise to cancer, and lead to harder drug use. 22

If the comparison feels absurd, it's because judgments of risk are inseparable from value judgments. We value physical fitness and the lessons teens learn from sports, but disapprove of unearned pleasure from recreational drugs. So we're willing to accept the higher level of risk of socially preferred activities — and we mentally magnify risks associated with activities society rejects, which leads us to do things like arresting marijuana smokers. 23

"Risk decisions are not about risks alone," says Slovic. "People usually take risks to get a benefit." The value placed on that benefit is inherently subjective, so decisions about them cannot be made purely "on the science." 24

IX. We Love Sunlight but Fear Nuclear Power

Why "natural" risks are easier to accept.

The word radiation stirs thoughts of nuclear power, X-rays, and danger, so we shudder at the thought of erecting nuclear power plants in our neighborhoods. But every day we're bathed in radiation that has killed many more people than nuclear reactors: sunlight. It's hard for us to grasp the danger because sunlight feels so familiar and natural. 25

Our built-in bias for the natural led a California town to choose a toxic poison made from chrysanthemums over a milder artificial chemical to fight mosquitoes: People felt more comfortable with a plant-based product. We see what's "natural" as safe — and regard the new and "unnatural" as frightening. 26

Any sort of novelty — including new and unpronounceable chemicals — evokes a low-level stress response, says Bruce Perry, a child psychiatrist at 27

Child Trauma Academy. When a case report suggested that lavender and tea-tree oil products caused abnormal breast development in boys, the media shrugged and activists were silent. If these had been artificial chemicals, there likely would have been calls for a ban, but because they are natural plant products, no outrage resulted. "Nature has a good reputation," says Slovic. "We think of natural as benign and safe. But malaria's natural and so are deadly mushrooms."

X. We Should Fear Fear Itself

Why worrying about risk is itself risky.

Though the odds of dying in a terror attack like 9/11 or contracting Ebola are infinitesimal, the effects of chronic stress caused by constant fear are significant. Studies have found that the more people were exposed to media portrayals of the 2001 attacks, the more anxious and depressed they were. Chronically elevated stress harms our physiology, says Ropeik. "It interferes with the formation of bone, lowers immune response, increases the likelihood of clinical depression and diabetes, impairs our memory and our fertility, and contributes to long-term cardiovascular damage and high blood pressure." 28

The physiological consequences of overestimating the dangers in the world—and revving our anxiety into overdrive—are another reason risk perception matters. It's impossible to live a risk-free life: Everything we do increases some risks while lowering others. But if we understand our innate biases in the way we manage risks, we can adjust for them and genuinely stay safer—without freaking out over every leaf of lettuce. 29

• • •

Comprehension

1. What does Szalavitz mean in paragraph 3 when she says, "The human brain is exquisitely adapted to respond to risk . . ."?
2. Why, according to Szalavitz, have human beings been unable to develop effective responses to risks posed by "statistics, media coverage, and fear-mongering politicians" (3)?
3. How does Szalavitz explain the following in her essay?
   - We fear snakes but not cars.
   - We fear spectacular, unlikely events.
   - We fear cancer but not heart disease.
   - We fear pesticides in our neighbor's yard but not in our own yard.
   - We speed up when we put on seat belts.
   - We fear nuclear power but not sunlight.
4. What is a "risk thermostat"? What does Szalavitz mean when she says that "one person's risk thermostat may have different settings for different types of risk" (21)?

5. According to Szalavitz, what are the consequences of overestimating the dangers of the world? How does understanding our "innate biases" (29) help us manage the way we respond to risk?

Purpose and Audience

1. Szalavitz states her thesis at the end of paragraph 4. What information does she present in her first four paragraphs? Would readers be able to understand her thesis without this information? Explain.
2. What preconceived ideas does Szalavitz assume her readers have about risk? How can you tell?
3. What is Szalavitz's purpose in writing this essay? To inform readers? To persuade them? Or does she have some other purpose in mind?
4. Szalavitz's essay appeared in *Psychology Today,* a publication aimed at readers who are interested in psychology. How would Szalavitz have to revise this essay to make it appeal to readers with more general interests?

Style and Structure

1. Szalavitz uses headings and subheadings to introduce the sections of her essay. Why? Would her essay be as effective without these headings and subheadings?
2. Szalavitz presents ten examples to support her thesis. Does she present enough examples? Does she include a fair range of examples? Are all her examples necessary? Are they equally appropriate and convincing?
3. Szalavitz draws some of her examples from research sources. Would the essay have been more or less convincing if all Szalavitz's examples were drawn from her own experience? Explain.
4. Does Szalavitz arrange her examples in any particular order – for example, from least important to most important? Explain.
5. **Vocabulary Project.** At several points in her essay, Szalavitz defines some basic terms – for example, *risk* (3), *fear* (5), and *emotions* (5). Why does she think she has to define these terms for readers?

Journal Entry

Do you agree with Szalavitz when she says our emotions cause us to make snap decisions? Could she be accused of overstating her case?

Writing Workshop

1. Choose one of the ten types of risks Szalavitz discusses. Then, write an essay in which you use several examples from your own experience to illustrate Szalavitz's point about this risk.
2. Do you consider yourself to be risk averse or risk inclined? Write an essay in which you use at least four examples to support your thesis.

3. **Working with Sources.** The following quiz appeared along with Szalavitz's essay. Take the quiz, and then, on the basis of your score, write an essay in which you agree or disagree with Szalavitz's thesis. In your essay, use examples from the quiz as well as from Szalavitz's essay. Be sure to include parenthetical documentation and a works-cited page. (See Chapter 18 for information on MLA documentation.)

How good is your grasp of risk?

1. What's more common in the United States, (a) suicide or (b) homicide?
2. What's the more frequent cause of death in the United States, (a) pool drowning or (b) falling out of bed?
3. What are the top five causes of accidental death in America, following motor-vehicle accidents, and which is the biggest one?
4. Of the top two causes of nonaccidental death in America, (a) cancer and (b) heart disease, which kills more women?
5. What are the next three causes of nonaccidental death in the United States?
6. Which has killed more Americans, (a) bird flu or (b) mad cow disease?
7. How many Americans die from AIDS every year, (a) 12,995, (b) 129,950, or (c) 1,299,500?
8. How many Americans die from diabetes every year, (a) 72,820, (b) 728,200, or (c) 7,282,000?
9. Which kills more Americans, (a) appendicitis or (b) salmonella?
10. Which kills more Americans, (a) pregnancy and childbirth or (b) malnutrition?

ANSWERS (all refer to number of Americans per year, on average):

1. a
2. a
3. In order: drug overdose, fire, choking, falling down stairs, bicycle accidents
4. b
5. In order: stroke, respiratory disease, diabetes
6. No American has died from either one
7. a
8. a
9. a
10. b

Sources:

- Centers for Disease Control and Prevention (Division of Vital Statistics)
- National Transportation Safety Board

Combining the Patterns

Although this essay is primarily an exemplification, it contains several **cause-and-effect** paragraphs – for example, paragraphs 6 and 10. Read these two paragraphs, and determine what they contribute to the essay.

Thematic Connections

- "Ground Zero" (page 173)
- "Why Rational People Buy into Conspiracy Theories" (page 338)
- "The Ways We Lie" (page 466)

JAMAICA KINCAID

"Girl" (Fiction)

Jamaica Kincaid's novels, short stories, and nonfiction frequently reflect on race, colonialism, adolescence, gender, and the weight of family relationships and personal history. Born Elaine Potter Richardson in St. John's, Antigua, in 1949, she changed her name to Jamaica Kincaid in 1973 partly to avoid a negative response from her family, who disapproved of her writing. She moved to New York City at 17 and worked as a nanny. She began college but dropped out to write for *Ingenue,* a teen magazine, as well as the *Village Voice.* In 1985, she became a staff writer for the *New Yorker,* where she worked until 1996. Her first published work of fiction, "Girl," appeared in the magazine in 1978. Kincaid credits *New Yorker* editor William Shawn for "show[ing] me what my voice was. . . . He made me feel that what I thought, my inner life, my thoughts as I organized them, were important." The author of *Annie John* (1985), *My Brother* (1997), *Among Flowers: A Walk in the Himalaya* (2005), and many other books, Kincaid is a professor of African and African American Studies in Residence at Harvard University.

Background on slavery and colonialism in the West Indies Europeans brought Africans to the Caribbean islands in the sixteenth and seventeenth centuries to work as slaves, primarily on sugar plantations. In her nonfiction book *A Small Place,* Kincaid writes searingly of her native island's dark colonial history, the "large ships filled up with human cargo." The human beings, she says, were "forced to work under conditions that were cruel and inhuman, they were beaten, they were murdered, they were sold, their children were taken from them and these separations lasted forever." Although the British outlawed slavery in the 1830s, blacks remained the largest percentage of the population in the British Caribbean colonies. Antigua remained a British colony until 1981. After independence, economic conditions on the island declined, with many of the descendants of the original slaves living in poverty, some in abject poverty. Currently, the economy of Antigua is weak, relying mostly on tourism and government-service industries.

1 Wash the white clothes on Monday and put them on the stone heap; wash the color clothes on Tuesday and put them on the clothesline to dry; don't walk barehead in the hot sun; cook pumpkin fritters in very hot sweet oil; soak your little cloths right after you take them off; when buying cotton to make yourself a nice blouse, be sure that it doesn't have gum on it, because that way it won't hold up well after a wash; soak salt fish overnight before you cook it; is it true that you sing benna* in Sunday school?; always eat your food in such a way that it won't turn someone else's stomach; on Sundays try to walk like a lady and not like the slut you are so bent on becoming; don't sing benna in Sunday school; you mustn't speak to wharf-rat boys, not even to give

* Eds. note—Form of popular music.

directions; don't eat fruits on the street—flies will follow you; *but I don't sing benna on Sundays at all and never in Sunday school;* this is how to sew on a button; this is how to make a button-hole for the button you have just sewed on; this is how to hem a dress when you see the hem coming down and so to prevent yourself from looking like the slut I know you are so bent on becoming; this is how you iron your father's khaki shirt so that it doesn't have a crease; this is how you iron your father's khaki pants so that they don't have a crease; this is how you grow okra—far from the house, because okra tree harbors red ants; when you are growing dasheen, make sure it gets plenty of water or else it makes your throat itch when you are eating it; this is how you sweep a corner; this is how you sweep a whole house; this is how you sweep a yard; this is how you smile to someone you don't like too much; this is how you smile to someone you don't like at all; this is how you smile to someone you like completely; this is how you set a table for tea; this is how you set a table for dinner; this is how you set a table for dinner with an important guest; this is how you set a table for lunch; this is how you set a table for breakfast; this is how to behave in the presence of men who don't know you very well, and this way they won't recognize immediately the slut I have warned you against becoming; be sure to wash every day, even if it is with your own spit; don't squat down to play marbles—you are not a boy, you know; don't pick people's flowers—you might catch something; don't throw stones at blackbirds, because it might not be a blackbird at all; this is how to make a bread pudding; this is how to make doukona;* this is how to make pepper pot; this is how to make a good medicine for a cold; this is how to make a good medicine to throw away a child before it even becomes a child; this is how to catch a fish; this is how to throw back a fish you don't like, and that way something bad won't fall on you; this is how to bully a man; this is how a man bullies you; this is how to love a man, and if this doesn't work there are other ways, and if they don't work don't feel too bad about giving up; this is how to spit up in the air if you feel like it, and this is how to move quick so that it doesn't fall on you; this is how to make ends meet; always squeeze bread to make sure it's fresh; *but what if the baker won't let me feel the bread?*; you mean to say that after all you are really going to be the kind of woman who the baker won't let near the bread?

> "[T]his is how you set a table for lunch; this is how you set a table for breakfast. . . ."

• • •

Reading Literature

1. Who is the speaker in the story? To whom is she speaking?
2. What do the speaker's remarks suggest about being female? Do the speaker's ideas correspond to your own ideas about being female? Explain.

* Eds. note—A spiced pudding.

3. Do you think this story has political or social implications? For example, what does the speaker's list suggest about the status of working-class women who live in poverty in the West Indies?

Journal Entry

Write a journal entry in which you record the duties of a woman (or a man) in your family.

Thematic Connections

- "'What's in a Name?'" (page 2)
- "My Mother Never Worked" (page 121)
- "I Want a Wife" (page 496)
- "A Zombie Is a Slave Forever" (page 504)

Writing Assignments for Exemplification

1. Write a humorous essay about a ritual, ceremony, or celebration you experienced and the types of people who participated in it. Make a point about the event, and use the participants as examples to support your point.
2. Write an essay establishing that you are an optimistic (or pessimistic) person. Use examples to support your case.
3. If you could change three or four things at your school, what would they be? Use examples from your own experience to support your recommendations, and tie your recommendations together in your thesis statement.
4. **Working with Sources.** Write an essay discussing two or three of the greatest challenges facing the United States today. Refer to essays in this chapter, such as "Just Walk On By" (page 233), or to essays elsewhere in this book, such as "What Motivates Terrorists?" (page 344), "On Dumpster Diving" (page 676), or "On Patriotism" (page 697). Make sure you document any references to your sources and that you include a works-cited page. (See Chapter 18 for information on MLA documentation.)
5. Using your family and friends as examples, write an essay suggesting some of the positive or negative characteristics of Americans.
6. Write an essay presenting your formula for achieving success in college. You may, if you wish, talk about things such as scheduling time, maintaining a high energy level, and learning how to relax. Use examples from your own experience to make your point.
7. Write an exemplification essay discussing how cooperation has helped you achieve some important goal. Support your thesis with a single well-developed example.
8. Choose an event you believe illustrates a less-than-admirable moment in your life. Then, write an essay explaining your feelings about it.
9. Americans have always had a long-standing infatuation with music icons. Choose several pop groups or stars, old and new – such as Elvis Presley, the Beatles, Michael Jackson, Alicia Keys, Adele, Beyoncé Knowles, Drake, and Taylor Swift, to name only a few – and use them to illustrate the characteristics that you think make pop stars so appealing.

Collaborative Activity for Exemplification

The following passage appeared in a handbook given to parents of entering students at a midwestern university:

> The freshman experience is like no other – at once challenging, exhilarating, and fun. Students face academic challenges as they are exposed to many new ideas. They also face personal challenges as they meet many new people from diverse backgrounds. It is a time to mature and grow. It

is an opportunity to explore new subjects and familiar ones. There may be no more challenging and exciting time of personal growth than the first year of university study.

Working in groups of four, brainstorm to identify examples that support or refute the idea that there "may be no more challenging and exciting time of personal growth" than the first year of college. Then, choose one person from each group to tell the class the position the group took and explain the examples you collected. Finally, work together to write an essay that presents your group's position. Have one student write the first draft, two others revise this draft, and the last student edit and proofread the revised draft.

9

Process

What Is Process?

A **process** essay explains how to do something or how something occurs. It presents a sequence of steps and shows how those steps lead to a particular result. In the following paragraph from the college biology textbook *What Is Life? A Guide to Biology,* writer Jay Phelan explains a scientific process.

> **Process presents series of steps in chronological order**
>
> Researchers have developed a way to make the bacteria of interest identify themselves. First, a chemical is added to the entire population of bacterial cells, separating the double-stranded DNA into single strands. Next, a short sequence of single-stranded DNA is washed over the bacteria. Called a DNA probe, this DNA contains part of the sequence of the gene of interest and has also been modified so that it is radioactive. Bacteria with the gene of interest bind to this probe and glow with radioactivity. These cells can then be separated out and grown in large numbers—for example, vats of *E. coli* that produce human growth hormone.
>
> **Topic sentence**

Process, like narration, presents events in chronological order. Unlike a narrative, however, a process essay presents a particular series of events that produce the same outcome whenever it is duplicated. Because these events form a sequence with a fixed order, clarity is extremely important. Whether your readers will actually perform the process or are simply trying to understand how it occurs, your essay must make clear not only the order of the individual steps but also their relationships to one another and to the process as a whole. This means that you need to provide logical transitions between the steps in a process and that you need to present the steps in *strict* chronological order—that is, in the exact order in which they occur or are to be performed.

Depending on its purpose, a process essay can be either a set of *instructions* or a *process explanation.*

Understanding Instructions

The purpose of **instructions** is to enable readers to perform a process – for example, how to use a library's online databases or how to register for classes on a school's website. Recipes are structured as instructions, as are GPS directions and guidelines for assembling furniture or setting up a new computer. Instructions use the present tense and, like commands, they use the imperative mood, speaking directly to readers: "*Disconnect* the system, and *check* the electrical source."

Understanding Process Explanations

The purpose of a **process explanation** is not to enable readers to perform a process but rather to help them understand how it is carried out. Such essays may examine anything from how silkworms spin their cocoons to how Michelangelo and Leonardo da Vinci painted their masterpieces on plaster walls and ceilings.

A process explanation may use the first person (*I, we*) or the third (*he, she, it, they*, and so on), the past tense or the present. Because its readers need to understand the process, not perform it, a process explanation does not use the second person (*you*) or the imperative mood (commands). The style of a process explanation varies, depending on whether a writer is explaining a process that takes place regularly or one that occurred in the past and also depending on whether the writer or someone else carries out the steps. The following chart suggests the stylistic options available to writers of process explanations.

	First Person	***Third Person***
Present tense	"Before I begin writing my draft, I take some time to plan." *(habitual process performed by the writer)*	"Before he begins writing his draft, he takes some time to plan." *(habitual process performed by someone other than the writer)*
Past tense	"Before I began writing my draft, I took some time to plan." *(process performed in the past by the writer)*	"Before he began writing his draft, he took some time to plan." *(process performed in the past by someone other than the writer)*

Using Process

College writing frequently calls for instructions or process explanations. In a biology essay on genetic testing, you might devote a paragraph to an explanation of the process of amniocentesis; in an editorial about the negative side of fraternity life, you might include a brief account of the process of pledging. You can also organize an entire essay around a process pattern. In a literature essay, you might trace the steps in a fictional character's progress toward some new insight; on a finance midterm, you might explain the procedure for approving a commercial loan.

Planning a Process Essay

As you plan a process essay, remember that your primary goal is to explain the process accurately. This means that you need to distinguish between what usually or always happens and what occasionally or rarely happens as well as between necessary steps and optional ones. You should also mentally test all the steps in sequence to make sure the process really works as you say it does, checking carefully for omitted steps or incorrect information. If you are writing about a process you observed, try to test the accuracy of your explanation by observing the process again.

Accommodating Your Audience

As you write, remember to keep your readers' needs in mind. When necessary, explain the reasons for performing each step, describe unfamiliar materials or equipment, define terms, and warn readers about possible problems that may occur during the process. (Sometimes you may want to include illustrations to clarify one or more steps.) Besides complete information, your readers need a clear and consistent discussion, without ambiguities or digressions. For this reason, you should avoid unnecessary shifts in tense, person, voice, and mood. You should also be careful not to omit articles (*a, an,* and *the*); if you want your discussion to flow smoothly, you need to avoid the kind of choppy sentences often found in cookbooks.

Developing a Thesis Statement

Both instructions and process explanations can be written either to persuade or simply to present information. If its purpose is persuasive, a process essay may take a strong stand in a **thesis statement**, such as "Applying for food stamps is a needlessly complex process that discourages many qualified recipients" or "The process of slaughtering baby seals is inhumane and sadistic." Many process essays, however, communicate nothing more debatable than the procedure for blood typing. Even in such a case, though, the essay should have a clear thesis statement that identifies the process and perhaps tells why it is performed: "Typing their own blood can familiarize students with some basic laboratory procedures."

Using Transitions

Throughout your essay, use transitional words and phrases to make sure each step, each stage, and each paragraph lead logically to the next. Transitions such as *first, second, meanwhile, after this, next, then, at the same time, when you have finished,* and *finally* help establish sequential and chronological relationships so that readers can follow the process. (A more complete list of transitions appears on page 55.)

Structuring a Process Essay

Like other essays, a process essay generally consists of three sections. The **introduction** identifies the process and indicates why and under what circumstances it is performed. This section may include information about necessary materials or preliminary preparations, or it may present an overview of the process, perhaps even listing its major stages. The essay's thesis is also usually stated in the introduction.

Each paragraph in the **body** of the essay typically treats one major stage of the process. Each stage may group several steps, depending on the nature and complexity of the process. These steps are presented in chronological order, interrupted only for essential definitions, explanations, or cautions. Every step must be included and must appear in its proper place.

A short process essay may not need a formal **conclusion**. If an essay does have a conclusion, however, it will often briefly review the procedure's major stages. Such an ending is especially useful if the essay has outlined a technical procedure that may seem complicated to general readers. The conclusion may also reinforce the thesis by summarizing the results of the process or explaining its significance.

Suppose you are taking a midterm exam in a course in childhood and adolescent behavior. One essay question calls for a process explanation: "Trace the stages that children go through in acquiring language." After thinking about the question, you draft the following thesis statement: "Although individual cases may differ, most children acquire language in a predictable series of stages." You then plan your essay and develop an informal outline, which might look like the one below.

SAMPLE OUTLINE: Process

INTRODUCTION

Thesis statement: Although individual cases may differ, most children acquire language in a predictable series of stages.

FIRST STAGE
(two to twelve months)

Prelinguistic behavior, including "babbling" and appropriate responses to nonverbal cues.

SECOND STAGE
(end of first year)

Single words as commands or requests; infant catalogs his or her environment.

THIRD STAGE
(beginning of second year)

Expressive jargon (flow of sounds that imitates adult speech); real words along with jargon.

FOURTH AND FINAL STAGE
(middle of second year to beginning of third year)
Two-word phrases; longer strings; missing parts of speech.

CONCLUSION
Restatement of thesis (in different words) or review of major stages of process.

Your essay, when completed, will show not only what the stages of the process are but also how they relate to one another. In addition, it will support the thesis that children learn language through a well-defined process.

Revising a Process Essay

When you revise a set of instructions or a process explanation, consider the items on the revision checklist on page 66. In addition, pay special attention to the items on the following checklist, which apply specifically to revising process essays.

REVISION CHECKLIST PROCESS

- ☐ Does your assignment call for a set of instructions or a process explanation?
- ☐ Is your essay's style appropriate for the kind of process essay (instructions or process explanation) you are writing?
- ☐ Does your essay have a clearly stated thesis that identifies the process and perhaps tells why it is (or was) performed?
- ☐ Have you included all necessary steps?
- ☐ Are the steps presented in strict chronological order?
- ☐ Do transitions clearly indicate where one step ends and the next begins?
- ☐ Have you included all necessary reminders and cautions?

Editing a Process Essay

When you edit your process essay, follow the guidelines on the editing checklists on pages 83, 86, and 89. In addition, focus on the grammar, mechanics, and punctuation issues that are particularly relevant to process essays. One of these issues – avoiding unnecessary shifts in tense, person, voice, and mood – is discussed on pages 264–65.

GRAMMAR IN CONTEXT AVOIDING UNNECESSARY SHIFTS

To explain a process to readers, you need to use consistent verb **tense** (past or present), **person** (first, second, or third), **voice** (active or passive), and **mood** (statements or commands). Unnecessary shifts in tense, person, voice, or mood can confuse readers and make it difficult for them to follow your process.

Avoiding Shifts in Tense Use present tense for a process that is performed regularly.

> "The body is first laid out in the undertaker's morgue – or rather, Mr. Jones is reposing in the preparation room – to be readied to bid the world farewell" (Mitford 298).

Use past tense for a process that was performed in the past.

> "Soon the men began to gather, surveying their own children, speaking of planting and rain, tractors and taxes" (Jackson 305).

Shift from present to past tense only when you need to indicate a change in time: *Usually, I study several days before a test, but this time I studied the night before.*

Avoiding Shifts in Person In process explanations, use first or third person.

FIRST PERSON (*I*): "I reached for the box of Medium Ash Brown hair color just as my friend Veronica grabbed the box labeled Sparkling Sherry" (Hunt 270).

FIRST PERSON (*WE*): "We decided to use my bathroom to color our hair" (Hunt 271).

THIRD PERSON (*HE*): "The embalmer, having allowed an appropriate interval to elapse, returns to the attack, but now he brings into play the skill and equipment of sculptor and cosmetician" (Mitford 300).

In instructions, use second person.

SECOND PERSON (*YOU*): "If you sometimes forget to pay bills, or if you have large student loans, you may have a problem" (McGlade 266).

When you give instructions, be careful not to shift from third to second person.

INCORRECT: If a person sometimes forgets to pay bills, or if someone has large student loans, you may have a problem. (shift from third to second person)

CORRECT: If you sometimes forget to pay bills, or if you have large student loans, you may have a problem. (second person used consistently)

Avoiding Shifts in Voice Use active voice when you want to emphasize the person performing the action.

"In the last four years, I have moved eight times, living in three dorm rooms, two summer sublets, and three apartments in three different cities" (McGlade 266).

Use passive voice to emphasize the action itself rather than the person performing it.

"The patching and filling completed, Mr. Jones is now shaved, washed, and dressed" (Mitford 301).

Do not shift between the active and the passive voice, especially within a sentence, unless your intent is to change your emphasis.

INCORRECT: The first draft of my essay was completed, and then I started the second draft. (shift from passive to active voice)

CORRECT: I completed the first draft of my essay, and then I started the second draft. (active voice used consistently)

Avoiding Shifts in Mood Use the indicative mood (statements) for process explanations.

"The children assembled first, of course" (Jackson 304).

Use the imperative mood (commands) only in instructions.

"Measure twice; cut once" (Piven and Borgenicht 289).

Be careful not to shift from the imperative mood to the indicative mood.

INCORRECT: First, check your credit report for errors, and you should report any errors you find. (shift from imperative to indicative mood)

CORRECT: First, check your credit report for errors, and report any errors you find. (imperative mood used consistently)

CORRECT: First, you should check your credit report for errors, and you should report any errors you find. (indicative mood used consistently)

LaunchPad

For more practice on avoiding unnecessary shifts, see the LearningCurve on Verb Tenses and Shifts in the LaunchPad for *Patterns*.

EDITING CHECKLIST PROCESS

- ☐ Have you used commas correctly in a series of three or more steps, including a comma before the *and?*
- ☐ Have you used parallel structure for items in a series?
- ☐ Have you avoided unnecessary shifts in tense?
- ☐ Have you avoided unnecessary shifts in person?
- ☐ Have you avoided unnecessary shifts in voice?
- ☐ Have you avoided unnecessary shifts in mood?

A STUDENT WRITER: Instructions

The following student essay, "The Search," by Eric McGlade, gives readers instructions on how to find an apartment. It was written for a composition class in response to the assignment "Write an essay giving practical instructions for doing something many people you know will need to do at one time or another."

The Search

Introduction

1 In the last four years, I have moved eight times, living in three dorm rooms, two summer sublets, and three apartments in three different cities. I would not recommend this experience to anyone. Finding an apartment is time consuming, stressful, and expensive, so the best advice is to stay where you are. However, if you must move, here are a few tips to help you survive the search.

Thesis statement

First major stage of process: before the search

First step: review your finances

2 Before you begin your search, take some time to plan. First, figure out what you can afford. (Here's a hint — you can afford less than you think.) Most experts say you should spend no more than one-third of your net income on rent. Find a budgeting worksheet online, and see for yourself how car insurance, electricity, and other expenses can add up. Remember, your new landlord may charge a security deposit and the first month's rent, and there may also be pet, parking, cleaning, or moving-in fees.

Second step: check your credit history

3 Next, consider your credit history. If you sometimes forget to pay bills, or if you have large student loans, you may have a problem. Landlords usually run a credit check on potential renters. If you are particularly concerned about your credit rating, order a credit report from one of the three main credit bureaus: TransUnion, Equifax, or Experian. If you find that your credit isn't perfect, don't panic. First, check your credit report for errors, and report any errors you find to the credit bureau. Second, adopt good financial habits immediately.

Start paying bills on time, and try to consolidate any debts at a lower interest rate. If a landlord does question your credit, be prepared to explain any extenuating circumstances in the past and to point out your current good behavior.

Third step: consider where to live

After you know what you can afford, you need to figure out where you want to (and can afford to) live. Keep in mind important factors such as how close the apartment is to your school or workplace and how convenient the neighborhood is. Is public transportation located nearby? Is on-street parking available? Can you easily get to a supermarket, coffee shop, convenience store, and laundromat? If possible, visit each potential neighborhood both during the day and at night. A business district may be bustling during the day but deserted (and even dangerous) at night. If you visit both early and late, you will get a more accurate impression of how safe the neighborhood feels. 4

Fourth step: consider a roommate

During this stage, consider whether or not you are willing to live with a roommate. You will sacrifice privacy, but you will be able to afford a better apartment. If you do decide to live with a roommate, the easiest way to proceed is to find a friend who also needs an apartment. If this isn't possible, try to find an apartment that comes with a roommate — one with one roommate moving out but the other roommate remaining. The third option is to find another apartment seeker and go apartment hunting together. Some websites, such as www.roommates.com, cater to this type of search, but, unfortunately, most require a fee. However, your school housing office might have a list of students looking for roommates. 5

Transitional paragraph

Now, you are ready to start looking. You can find the perfect apartment through a real estate agent, by checking your local newspaper or school's housing listings, by asking your friends and family, or by visiting websites such as Craigslist. 6

Second major stage of process: during the search

First step: do research

Each of these methods has pros and cons. A real estate agent might help you find your dream apartment quickly, but you will usually have to pay a fee. As for newspaper listings, stick to your local paper's online listings; unless you are looking for a second vacation home in Maui, national listings are not your best bet. An even better idea is to check your school's housing listings, where you are likely to find fellow students in search of apartments in your price range. 7

Second step: spread the word

Meanwhile, spread the word. Tell everyone you know that you are apartment hunting. After all, your stepsister's uncle's 8 mother-in-law may live in a building with a vacant apartment. This method isn't the most efficient, but the results can be amazing. As a bonus, you will receive practical advice about your neighborhood, such as what to watch out for and what problems other renters have had.

Third step: try Craigslist

Finally, if you are hunting in a major city, I have but one word: Craigslist. Craigslist.org has free apartment listings arranged by city and neighborhood. You can hunt for an apartment by price, by number of bedrooms, or by length of lease. If you are on a tight moving schedule and need a place immediately, this website is especially helpful because of the sheer volume of its listings. Craigslist also has the added benefit of providing a general price range for your ideal neighborhood. 9

Fourth step: visit apartments

Once you have identified some possibilities, it's time to visit apartments. Get a good look at each one, and ask yourself some questions. Is it furnished or unfurnished? Are all the appliances in good working order? Will your bed fit in the bedroom? How much closet space will you have? Are there phone, cable, and Internet hookups? Is it a sunny apartment (south facing), or is it dark (north facing)? In the bathroom, turn on the faucets in the sink and shower; check for rust and poor water pressure. As you walk through the apartment, check the cell-phone reception (leaning out the window of your bathroom to talk on the phone is not fun). Most important, do not forget to take notes. After seeing fourteen apartments, you may confuse Apartment A, with the six pets and funny smell, with Apartment G, with the balcony and renovated kitchen. 10

Third major stage of process: after the search

First step: check your lease

And now, at last, the search is over: you have found your apartment. Congratulations! Unfortunately, your work is not yet over. Now, it is time to read your lease. It will be long and boring, but it is a very important document. Among other things, your lease should specify the length of the rental period, a rent due date, fees for late rent payments, the amount of the security deposit, and the conditions required for the return of the security deposit. If you have decided to live with a roommate, you might ask the landlord to divide the rent on your lease. This way, if your roommate moves to Brazil, you will not have to pay his or her share of the rent. Be sure to read your lease thoroughly and bring up any concerns with your landlord. 11

Second step: get insurance and activate utilities

Before you move in, you have a few more things to do: get renter's insurance to protect you from theft or damage to your possessions; arrange to get your utilities hooked up; submit a postal 12 change-of-address form; and inform your bank or credit-card company about your upcoming move. Finally, start packing!

Conclusion If you plan ahead and shop smart, you can find your perfect apartment. Remember to figure out what you can afford, check out the neighborhoods, consider a roommate, use multiple search methods, and take careful notes when you visit potential apartments. Yes, happy endings do occur. I am now in the third month of a two-year lease, and I have no plans to move anytime soon. 13

Points for Special Attention

Introduction. Eric McGlade's essay begins by giving readers some background on his own experience as an apartment hunter. This strategy gives him some credibility, establishing him as an "expert" who can explain the process. Eric then narrows his focus to the difficulties of apartment hunting and ends his introduction with a thesis statement telling readers that the process can be made easier.

Structure. Eric divides his essay into the three major stages of apartment hunting: what to do before, during, and after the search. After his introduction, Eric includes four paragraphs that explain what to do before the search gets under way. In paragraphs 6 through 10, he explains how to go about the actual hunt for an apartment. Then, in paragraphs 11 and 12, he tells readers what they should do after they locate an apartment (but before they move in). In his conclusion, he restates his thesis, summarizes the steps in the process, and returns to his own experience to reassure readers that a positive outcome is possible.

Purpose and Style. Because Eric's assignment asked him to give practical advice for a process readers could expect to perform, he decided that he should write the essay as a set of instructions. Therefore, he uses the second person ("If *you* find that *your* credit isn't perfect, don't panic") and the present tense, with many of his verbs in the form of commands ("First, *figure* out what you can afford").

Transitions. To make his essay clear and easy to follow, Eric includes transitions that indicate the order in which each step is to be performed ("First," "Next," "Now," "Meanwhile," "Finally," and so on), as well as expressions such as "During this stage." He also includes transitional sentences to move his essay from one stage of the process to the next:

- "Before you begin your search, take some time to plan" (2).
- "Now, you are ready to start looking" (6).
- "Once you have identified some possibilities, it's time to visit apartments" (10).
- "And now, at last, the search is over: you have found your apartment" (11).

Finally, paragraph 6 serves as a transitional paragraph, moving readers from the preliminary steps to the start of the actual search for an apartment.

Focus on Revision

When he met with the students in his peer-editing group, Eric learned they had all gone through the apartment-hunting process and therefore had some practical suggestions to make. In the draft they reviewed, Eric included a number of anecdotes about his own experiences, but his readers thought that those narratives, although amusing, were distracting and got in the way of the process. Eric agreed, and he deleted this material. His classmates also thought that mentioning his experiences briefly in his introduction would be sufficient, but Eric decided to return briefly to his own story in his conclusion, adding the two "happy ending" sentences that now conclude his essay. In addition, he followed his classmates' suggestion to expand his conclusion by adding a review of the steps of the process to help readers remember what they had read. These additions gave him a fully developed conclusion.

In terms of his essay's content, his fellow students were most concerned with paragraph 10, which seemed to them to rush through a very important part of the process: visiting the apartments. They also observed that the information in this paragraph was not arranged in any logical order and that Eric had failed to mention other considerations (for example, whether the apartment needed repairs or painting, whether it was noisy, whether it included air conditioning). One student suggested that Eric expand his discussion and divide the information into two separate paragraphs: one on the apartment's mechanical systems (plumbing, electricity, and so on) and another on its physical appearance (size of rooms, light, and so on). In the final draft of his essay, Eric did just that. (A sample peer-editing worksheet for process appears on pages 273–74.)

Working with Sources. Although the students in Eric's peer-editing group did not suggest any specific revisions to his introductory paragraph, he thought his essay needed a more interesting opening. So, in his final draft, he planned to quote key phrases from some of the Craigslist ads he rejected. He thought they might add some humor to an otherwise straightforward essay.

A STUDENT WRITER: Process Explanation

The essay that follows, "Medium Ash Brown," by Melany Hunt, is a **process explanation**. It was written for a composition class in response to the assignment "Write an essay explaining a process that changed your appearance in some way."

Medium Ash Brown

Introduction

1 The beautiful chestnut-haired woman pictured on the box seemed to beckon to me. I reached for the box of Medium Ash Brown hair color just as my friend Veronica grabbed the box labeled Sparkling

Sherry. I can't remember our reasons for wanting to change our hair color, but they seemed to make sense at the time. Maybe we were just bored. I do remember that the idea of transforming our appearance came up unexpectedly. Impulsively, we decided to change our hair color—and, we hoped, ourselves—that very evening. The process that followed taught me that some impulses should definitely be resisted.

Thesis statement

Materials assembled

2 We decided to use my bathroom to color our hair. Inside each box of hair color, we found two little bottles and a small tube wrapped in a page of instructions. Attached to the instruction page itself were two very large, one-size-fits-all plastic gloves, which looked and felt like plastic sandwich bags. The directions recommended having some old towels around to soak up any spills or drips that might occur. Under the sink we found some old, frayed towels that I figured my mom had forgotten about, and we spread them around the bathtub. After we put our gloves on, we began the actual coloring process. First we poured the first bottle into the second, which was half-full of some odd-smelling liquid. The smell was not much better after we combined the two bottles. The directions advised us to cut off a small section of hair to use as a sample. For some reason, we decided to skip this step.

First stage of process: preparing the color

Second stage of process: applying the color

3 At this point, Veronica and I took turns leaning over the tub to wet our hair for the color. The directions said to leave the color on the hair for fifteen to twenty minutes, so we found a little timer and set it for fifteen minutes. Next, we applied the color to our hair. Again, we took turns, squeezing the bottle in order to cover all our hair. We then wrapped the old towels around our sour-smelling hair and went outside to get some fresh air.

Third stage of process: rinsing

4 After the fifteen minutes were up, we rinsed our hair. According to the directions, we were to add a little water and scrub as if we were shampooing our hair. The color lathered up, and we rinsed our hair until the water ran clear. So far, so good.

Last stage of process: applying conditioner

5 The last part of the process involved applying the small tube of conditioner to our hair (because colored hair becomes brittle and easily damaged). We used the conditioner as directed, and then we dried our hair so that we could see the actual color. Even before I looked in the mirror, I heard Veronica's gasp.

Outcome of process

6 "Nice try," I said, assuming she was just trying to make me nervous, "but you're not funny."

7 "Mel," she said, "look in the mirror." Slowly, I turned around. My stomach turned into a lead ball when I saw my reflection. My

hair was the putrid greenish-brown color of a winter lawn, dying in patches yet still a nice green in the shade.

The next day in school, I wore my hair tied back under a baseball cap. I told only my close friends what I had done. After they were finished laughing, they offered their deepest, most heartfelt condolences. They also offered many suggestions — none very helpful — on what to do to get my old hair color back. 8

Conclusion It is now three months later, and I still have no idea what prompted me to color my hair. My only consolation is that I resisted my first impulse: to use a wild color, like blue or fuchsia. Still, as I wait for my hair to grow out, and as I assemble a larger and larger collection of baseball caps, it is small consolation indeed. 9

Points for Special Attention

Structure. In Melany's opening paragraph, her thesis statement makes it very clear that the experience she describes is not one she would recommend to others. The temptation she describes in her introduction's first few sentences lures readers into her essay, just as the picture on the box lured her. Her second paragraph lists the contents of the box and explains how she and her friend assembled the other necessary materials. Then, she explains the first stage in the process: preparing the color. Paragraphs 3 through 5 describe the other stages in the process in chronological order, and paragraphs 6 through 8 record Melany's and her friend Veronica's reactions to their experiment. In paragraph 9, Melany sums up the impact of her experience and once again expresses her annoyance with herself for her impulsive act.

Purpose and Style. Melany's purpose is not to enable others to duplicate the process she explains; on the contrary, she wants to discourage readers from doing what she did. Consequently, she presents her process not as a set of instructions but as a process explanation, using first person and past tense to explain her and her friend's experiences. She also largely eliminates cautions and reminders that her readers, who are not likely to undertake the process, will not need to know.

Detail. Melany's essay includes vivid descriptive detail that gives readers a clear sense of the process and its outcome. Throughout, her emphasis is on the negative aspects of the process – the "odd-smelling liquid" and the "putrid greenish-brown color" of her hair, for instance – and this emphasis is consistent with her essay's purpose.

Transitions. To move readers smoothly through the process, Melany includes clear transitions ("First," "At this point," "Next," "then") and clearly identifies the beginning of the process ("After we put our gloves on, we began the actual coloring process") as well as the end ("The last part of the process").

Focus on Revision

The writing center tutor who read Melany's draft thought it was clearly written and structured and that its ironic, self-mocking tone was well suited to her audience and purpose. He thought, however, that some minor revisions would make her essay even more effective. Specifically, he thought that paragraph 2 began too abruptly: paragraph 1 recorded the purchase of the hair color, and paragraph 2 opened with the sentence "We decided to use my bathroom to color our hair," leaving readers wondering how much time had passed between purchase and application. Because the thesis rests on the idea of the foolishness of an impulsive gesture, it is important for readers to understand that the girls presumably went immediately from the store to Melany's house.

After thinking about this criticism, Melany decided to write a clearer opening for paragraph 2: "As soon as we paid for the color, we returned to my house, where, eager to begin our transformation, we locked ourselves in my bathroom. Inside each box. . . ." She also decided to divide paragraph 2 into two paragraphs, one describing the materials and another beginning with "After we put our gloves on," which introduces the first step in the process.

Another possible revision Melany considered was developing Veronica's character further. Although both girls purchase and apply hair color, readers never learn what happens to Veronica. Melany knew she could easily add a brief paragraph after paragraph 7, describing Veronica's "Sparkling Sherry" hair in humorous terms. Her writing center tutor agreed that it would be a good addition, and Melany planned to add this material in her essay's final draft.

Working with Sources. Melany's tutor suggested that she might refer in her essay to Judith Ortiz Cofer's "The Myth of the Latin Woman: I Just Met a Girl Named Maria" (p. 225), which also examines the idea of changing one's outward appearance. (In fact, the class's assignment – "Write an essay explaining a process that changed your appearance in some way" – was inspired by their discussion of Cofer's essay.) Melany considered this suggestion but decided not to add a reference to Cofer. After all, Cofer is critical of outside pressure to change the way she looks (in her case, to bury her ethnic identity and blend into the dominant culture). Melany, on the other hand, gives in to social pressure, hoping to look more glamorous – more like the woman on the hair dye box. More important, Melany thought Cofer's serious discussion of her self-image would not be a good fit for her own lighthearted essay. In fact, she was concerned that adding such a reference might seem to trivialize the important issues Cofer discusses.

PEER-EDITING WORKSHEET PROCESS

1. What process does this essay describe?
2. Does the writer include all the information the audience needs? Is any vital step or piece of information missing? Is any step or piece of information

irrelevant? Is any necessary definition, explanation, or caution missing or incomplete?

3. Is the essay a set of instructions or a process explanation? How can you tell? Why do you think the writer chose this strategy rather than the alternative? Do you think it was the right choice?
4. Does the writer consistently follow the stylistic conventions for the strategy—instructions or process explanation—he or she has chosen?
5. Are the steps presented in a clear, logical order? Are they grouped logically into paragraphs? Should any steps be combined or relocated? If so, which ones?
6. Does the writer use enough transitions to move readers through the process? Should any transitions be added? If so, where?
7. Does the writer need to revise to correct confusing shifts in tense, person, voice, or mood? If so, where?
8. Is the essay interesting? What descriptive details would add interest to the essay? Would a visual be helpful?
9. How would you characterize the writer's opening strategy? Is it appropriate for the essay's purpose and audience? What alternative strategy might be more effective?
10. How would you characterize the writer's closing strategy? Would a different conclusion be more effective? Explain.

The reading selections that follow illustrate how varied the uses of process writing can be. The first selection, a visual text, is followed by questions designed to illustrate how process can operate in visual form.

NATIONAL GEOGRAPHIC

Yellowstone Fires, Past and Future

Serotinous cone
Lodgepole pine
Mountain bluebird
Elk
Lupine
Aspen seedling
Heartleaf arnica
Ross's sedge
Fireweed
Lodgepole pine
SOON AFTER A FIRE
Roots of perennial flowers and grasses can survive large fires. Heat triggers lodgepole pines' serotinous cones to release seeds; those that survive take hold in newly mineral-rich soil that's open to sunlight.
1 YEAR AFTER
Aspen and lodgepole pine seedlings start small but establish quickly. Studies of the 1988 fires show that most pine seedlings germinated from seeds released from cones on fire-killed trees.
2 YEARS AFTER
Flowering plants and wildflowers take hold. Elk and foraging mammals return to burned areas, as some of their food sources, such as aspen seedlings, grow larger.
25 YEARS AFTER
Most burned trunks have fallen, and new lodgepole pines have grown to be 10 to 15 feet tall. The ecosystem has shown it can adapt well to severe fires—when they happen only every few centuries.

Twombly, Matthew/National Geographic Creative

• • •

Reading Images

1. What process do these four images illustrate? Would the images be able to communicate this process on their own, without the text?
2. Study the four illustrations closely. What specific changes do you observe from one illustration to the next?
3. What message do these illustrations convey? Is this message positive or negative? Explain.

Journal Entry

Write a short paragraph that explains the process illustrated in these illustrations.

Thematic Connections

- "Once More to the Lake" (page 189)
- "Photos That Change History" (page 356)
- "The Obligation to Endure" (page 550)

NAOMI ROSENBERG

How to Tell a Mother Her Child Is Dead

Naomi Rosenberg attended medical school at the University of Pennsylvania, graduating in 2013. In 2010, while working toward her degree, Rosenberg took a year off to help provide medical care to victims of the Haitian earthquake. As part of this work, she helped to start a group home where these refugees could continue their treatment and receive support for getting back on their feet. After graduation, Rosenberg accepted a residency at Temple University Hospital in Philadelphia, where she is also an assistant professor of emergency medicine. She participated in a nonfiction writing workshop through the Narrative Medicine program at Temple University and wrote the following essay in response to the prompt, "Tell someone how to do something that you know how to do."

Background on emergency rooms Although early hospitals in the United States had dedicated "accident rooms" or "accident wards" for those suffering from sudden injuries, they were typically staffed by teams of registered nurses and hospital interns, most of whom had no specific training in handling trauma. Doctors saw their patients in offices and spent little or no time serving in the unglamorous accident rooms. Injured patients were usually brought in by police patrol wagons or by family or friends because ambulances were rare and typically found only in major urban centers such as New York or Chicago. Even when an ambulance was available to transport a patient, there were no emergency medical technicians (EMTs) trained to begin medical care en route to the hospital. Instead, ambulance services were often managed by the directors of funeral homes, who had vehicles already designed for transporting people who were lying down.

Things changed rapidly in the 1960s, however, when an increasing number of medical professionals were choosing to specialize in emergency medicine. This created an opportunity for doctors to acquire the sort of expertise that was lacking in the accident rooms that currently existed. The first formal emergency departments appeared in the United States in 1961, when independent groups of physicians in Virginia and Michigan recognized the need for urgent care that would be available around the clock and opened dedicated emergency medicine practices. Around the same time, a standardized curriculm was created for EMTs, who were — and are — able to serve as important first responders. In the years that followed, emergency medicine became a formal field of academic study and the number of emergency rooms rapidly expanded. Today there are well over five thousand emergency rooms across the United States, with over 130 million visits per year.

First you get your coat. I don't care if you don't remember where you left it, you find it. If there was a lot of blood you ask someone to go quickly to the basement to get you a new set of scrubs. You put on your coat and you go into the bathroom. You look in the mirror and you say it. You use the mother's name and you use her child's name. You may not adjust this part in any way. 1

I will show you: If it were my mother you would say, "Mrs. Rosenberg. I have terrible, terrible news. Naomi died today." You say it out loud until you can say it clearly and loudly. How loudly? Loudly enough. If it takes you fewer than five tries you are rushing it and you will not do it right. You take your time. 2

> "You never make her wait. She is his mother."

After the bathroom you do nothing before you go to her. You don't make a phone call, you do not talk to the medical student, you do not put in an order. You never make her wait. She is his mother. 3

When you get inside the room you will know who the mother is. Yes, I'm very sure. Shake her hand and tell her who you are. If there is time you shake everyone's hand. Yes, you will know if there is time. You never stand. If there are no seats left, the couches have arms on them. 4

You will have to make a decision about whether you will ask what she already knows. If you were the one to call her and tell her that her son had been shot then you have already done part of it, but you have not done it yet. You are about to do it now. You never make her wait. She is his mother. Now you explode the world. Yes, you have to. You say something like: "Mrs. Booker. I have terrible, terrible news. Ernest died today." 5

Then you wait. 6

You will not stand up. You may leave yourself in the heaviness of your breath or the racing of your pulse or the sight of your shoelaces on your shoe, but you will not stand up. You are here for her. She is his mother. 7

If the mother has another son with her and he has punched the wall or broken the chair, do not be worried. The one that punched the wall or broke the chair will be better than the one who looks down and refuses to cry. The one who punched the wall or broke the chair will be much easier than the sister who looks up and closes her eyes as they fill. 8

Security is already outside the room and when they hear the first loud noise they will know to come in. No, you will not have to tell them. They know about the family room in the emergency department in summer in North Philadelphia. It is all right. They will be kind. If the chair cannot be sat in again that is all right. We have money for new chairs every summer. If he does not break your chair you stay in your chair. If he does you find a new place to sit. You are here for the mother and you have more to do. 9

If she asks you, you will tell her what you know. You do not lie. But do not say he was murdered or he was killed. Yes, I know that he was, but that is not what you say. You say that he died; that is the part that you saw and that you 10 know. When she asks if he felt any pain, you must be very careful. If he did not, you assure her quickly. If he did, you do not lie. But his pain is over now. Do not ever say he was lucky that he did not feel pain. He was not lucky. She is not lucky. Don't make that face. The depth of the stupidity of the things you will say sometimes is unimaginable.

Before you leave you break her heart one more time. "No, I'm so sorry, but you cannot see him. There are strict rules when a person dies this way and the police have to take him first. We cannot let you in. I'm so sorry." You do not ever say "the body." It is not a body. It is her son. You want to tell her that you know that he was hers. But she knows that and she does not need for you to tell her. Instead you tell her you will give her time and come back in case she has questions. More questions, or questions for the first time. If she has no questions you do not give her the answers to the questions she has not asked. 11

When you leave the room, do not yell at the medical student who has a question. When you get home, do not yell at your husband. If he left his socks on the floor again today, it is all right. 12

• • •

Comprehension

1. Why is it Rosenberg's responsibility to tell the mother about the death of her child? Why does Rosenberg not ask someone else to break the difficult news?
2. Why does Rosenberg recommend practicing in front of a mirror before breaking the news to the mother? Why is this better than practicing in front of her fellow doctors?
3. Why does Rosenberg warn readers to "never stand" (4)?
4. Why does Rosenberg say not to worry if members of the family begin breaking the furniture? Why does she seem to think this is a healthy response?
5. Why does Rosenberg say that readers must break the mother's heart "one more time" (11)?
6. In paragraph 11, Rosenberg cautions readers not to give the mother "the answers to the questions she has not asked." What does she mean? Why is such a caution necessary?

Purpose and Audience

1. Rosenberg is a resident at a large urban hospital. How does this position qualify her to write this essay?
2. Where in the process does Rosenberg begin her essay? Why might she have chosen this moment as her starting point?

3. In paragraph 9, Rosenberg explains that security knows about "the family room in the emergency department in summer in North Philadelphia." What does security know? What does this comment tell you about Rosenberg?
4. What is this essay's thesis? Is it stated or implied? Explain.
5. What does Rosenberg hope to achieve in this essay? For example, does she simply intend to present information about her experiences, or does she hope to change her readers' attitudes? What evidence in the essay supports your stance?
6. Rosenberg spends a great deal of time explaining what *not* to do. Why do you think she does this?
7. Why does Rosenberg include paragraph 11? How would the essay be different without this paragraph?

Style and Structure

1. How is the style of this essay different from that of this chapter's other process essays?
2. What stylistic clues indicate that this essay is a set of instructions rather than a process explanation?
3. List the steps in the process Rosenberg describes. Would you include any other steps? If so, where would you add them? Are there any steps that you would take out?
4. Do you think the steps in this process will always occur in the same order? Why or why not?
5. Rosenberg does not expect most of her readers to carry out the process she describes. Why, then, does she write a series of instructions rather than just explaining the process?
6. Identify some of the transitional words Rosenberg uses to move readers from one step to the next. Does she need to include additional transitions? If so, where?
7. Note the frequent use of "you" in this essay. To whom does it refer? Is "you" the same person as the audience for the essay?
8. Rosenberg repeats the phrase "She is his mother" numerous times throughout the first half of the essay. What point is she trying to make?
9. In paragraph 2, Rosenberg says, "You take your time." In paragraph 5, however, she says you should "never make her wait." Is this advice contradictory? Explain.

10. **Vocabulary Project.** In paragraph 11, Rosenberg says, "It is not a body. It is her son." Why does she make this distinction? Identify other places in the essay where she makes suggestions about the words a doctor should and should not use. What other words would you suggest that a doctor use or avoid in this situation?
11. Throughout her essay, Rosenberg addresses the responses she thinks her readers might have (for instance, "Don't make that face. The depth of the stupidity of the things you will say sometimes is unimaginable" in paragraph 10). Why does she include these responses? Do you think readers will respond in the ways she imagines they will?
12. Why does Rosenberg conclude her essay with instructions for how to behave after leaving the hospital? What do these instructions tell you about the impact of completing the process she describes?

Journal Entry

Do you think this essay's headnote should warn readers that the subject matter may be upsetting, or do you believe such a warning is unnecessary – or even insulting?

Writing Workshop

1. Write a set of instructions for how to complete a task that is emotionally difficult, such as breaking up with a longtime partner or consoling someone who is grieving. Be specific, including advice about the best setting for the conversation, the importance of word choice, and cautions against taking certain actions.
2. **Working with Sources.** Write a set of guidelines for the security team at a hospital like the one in which Rosenberg works. Advise them on how to "know to come in," how to "be kind" while making sure that everyone is safe, and how to make allowances for the grief of families (10). Consider doing some additional research into the psychology of grief to help support your guidelines, and be sure to include parenthetical documentation and a works-cited page for any material you incorporate. (See Chapter 18 for information on MLA documentation.)
3. Assume that you are one of the family members whom Rosenberg addressed in the family room. Write an essay in which you give Rosenberg instructions for how to address grieving families. Make sure you tell her which of her assumptions were correct and which were misguided. You may also want to address aspects of the situation that Rosenberg did not cover.

Combining the Patterns

What does Rosenberg gain by structuring her essay as instructions rather than as a **narrative**? What, if anything, does she lose?

Thematic Connections

- "My Mother Never Worked" (page 121)
- "Ground Zero" (page 173)
- "Emmett Till and Tamir Rice, Sons of the Great Migration" (page 422)
- "Naming of Parts" (page 476)
- "'Hope' is the thing with feathers" (page 513)

STANLEY FISH

Getting Coffee Is Hard to Do

Literary critic and legal scholar Stanley Fish (b. 1938) has had a long and distinguished academic career. An authority on the seventeenth-century poet John Milton, Fish is widely recognized for his revolutionary approach to literary criticism, as summarized in his groundbreaking book *Is There a Text in This Class? The Authority of Interpretive Communities* (1980). A regular contributor to popular journals and op-ed pages in newspapers nationwide, Fish has also been a guest columnist for the *New York Times*, where the following essay originally appeared. He is currently the Floersheimer Distinguished Visiting Professor of Law at the Benjamin N. Cardozo School of Law at Yeshiva University. His most recent books are *Think Again* (2015) and *Winning Arguments: What Works and Doesn't Work in Politics, the Bedroom, the Courtroom, and the Classroom* (2016).

Background on U.S. coffee-drinking trends Coffee consumption in the United States goes back to the earliest English settlers. In fact, the British tax imposed on tea that led to the rebellious Boston Tea Party resulted in coffee becoming the most popular American drink. However, the popularity of gourmet coffees can be traced back to 1966, when Dutch immigrant Alfred Peet, a coffee importer who was unhappy with the general quality of coffee in the United States, opened a shop in Berkeley, California, where he sold his own special roast. Trained in coffee roasting by Peet, the founders of Starbucks opened their first outlet in Seattle in 1971, selling quality coffee beans and coffee-making equipment. Returning from a buying trip to Italy in 1985, then-marketing director Howard Schultz suggested that Starbucks become a true coffeehouse in the Italian tradition, a gathering spot where people could enjoy freshly roasted and brewed coffee. Despite being met with skepticism, Schultz would eventually take over the business and turn it into a worldwide phenomenon.

A coordination problem (a term of art in economics and management) occurs when you have a task to perform, the task has multiple and shifting components, the time for completion is limited, and your performance is affected by the order and sequence of the actions you take. The trick is to manage it so that the components don't bump into each other in ways that produce confusion, frustration, and inefficiency. 1

You will face a coordination problem if you are a general deploying troops, tanks, helicopters, food, tents, and medical supplies, or if you are the CEO of a large company juggling the demands of design, personnel, inventory, and production. 2

And these days, you will face a coordination problem if you want to get a cup of coffee. 3

> "As you walk in, everything is saying, 'This is very sophisticated, and you'd better be up to it.'"

It used to be that when you wanted a 4
cup of coffee you went into a nondescript place fitted out largely in linoleum, Formica, and neon, sat down at a counter, and, in response to a brisk "What'll you have, dear?" said, "Coffee and a cheese Danish." Twenty seconds later, tops, they arrived, just as you were settling into the sports page.

Now it's all wood or concrete floors, 5
lots of earth tones, soft, high-style lighting, open barrels of coffee beans, folk-rock and indie music, photographs of urban landscapes, and copies of *The Onion*. As you walk in, everything is saying, "This is very sophisticated, and you'd better be up to it."

It turns out to be hard. First you have to get in line, and you may have one 6
or two people in front of you who are ordering a drink with more parts than an internal combustion engine, something about "double shot," "skinny," "breve," "grande," "au lait," and a lot of other words that never pass my lips. If you are patient and stay in line (no bathroom breaks), you get to put in your order, but then you have to find a place to stand while you wait for it. There is no such place. So you shift your body, first here and then there, trying not to get in the way of those you can't help get in the way of.

Finally, the coffee arrives. 7

But then your real problems begin when you turn, holding your prize, and 8
make your way to where the accessories – things you put in, on, and around your coffee – are to be found. There is a staggering array of them, and the order of their placement seems random in relation to the order of your needs. There is no "right" place to start, so you lunge after one thing and then after another with awkward reaches.

Unfortunately, two or three other people are doing the same thing, and 9
each is doing it in a different sequence. So there is an endless round of "excuse me," "no, excuse me," as if you were in an old Steve Martin routine.

But no amount of politeness and care is enough. After all, there are so 10
many items to reach for – lids, cup jackets, straws, napkins, stirrers, milk, half and half, water, sugar, Splenda, the wastepaper basket, spoons. You and your companions may strive for a ballet of courtesy, but what you end up performing is more like bumper cars. It's just a question of what will happen first – getting what you want or spilling the coffee you are trying to balance in one hand on the guy reaching over you.

I won't even talk about the problem of finding a seat. 11

And two things add to your pain and trouble. First, it costs a lot, $3 12
and up. And worst of all, what you're paying for is the privilege of doing the work that should be done by those who take your money. The coffee shop experience is just one instance of the growing practice of shifting the burden of labor to the consumer – gas stations, grocery and drug stores, bagel shops (why should I put on my own cream cheese?), airline check-ins, parking lots. It's insert this, swipe that, choose credit or debit, enter

your PIN, push the red button, error, start again. At least when you go on a "vacation" that involves working on a ranch, the work is something you've chosen. But none of us has chosen to take over the jobs of those we pay to serve us.

Well, it's Sunday morning, and you're probably reading this with a cup of coffee. I hope it was easy to get. 13

• • •

Comprehension

1. How does Fish describe the traditional process of getting a cup of coffee (4)? What does he see as the main difference between getting a cup of coffee in a diner or coffee shop and getting coffee in today's coffee bars?
2. According to Fish, how do the two kinds of coffee shops differ in terms of their physical setting?
3. List some of the obstacles Fish says customers face in a modern-day coffee bar.
4. Whom, or what, does Fish blame for the situation he describes?
5. Note that Fish does not mention paying for the coffee. Do you think the omission of this step is significant in any way? Explain.

Purpose and Audience

1. What purpose do the first two paragraphs of this essay serve? Are they necessary, or could the essay begin with paragraph 3?
2. What is actually the point of this essay? Is Fish simply trying to explain how difficult it has become to get a cup of coffee (as his title suggests), or does he have a more specific – and perhaps more serious – purpose in mind? (Read paragraph 12 carefully before you answer this question.)
3. In one sentence, state this essay's thesis. Does this thesis statement appear in the essay? If so, where?
4. Do you think Fish is exaggerating the difficulty of getting a cup of coffee? If so, what might be his purpose for doing so?
5. Who is the "you" Fish addresses in this essay? What does this use of *you* tell you about how he sees his audience?

Style and Structure

1. This essay includes several one-sentence paragraphs. Locate each one, and explain why you think it is so short. Should any of these one-sentence paragraphs be developed further? If so, how? Should any be combined with an adjacent paragraph?
2. List the steps in the process Fish describes. Then, group the steps into general stages in the process. Give each stage a name.

3. Where does Fish include cautions and reminders? Give some examples. Given his audience's likely familiarity with the process he describes, are these tips necessary? If not, why do you think he includes them?
4. This essay is a process explanation. Do you think it would have been more effective if Fish had written it in the form of instructions? Explain.
5. **Vocabulary Project.** As Fish illustrates, the world of the coffee bar has its own vocabulary. List and define five words that are part of this specialized vocabulary. (You can define words Fish includes here, or you can create your own list.)
6. Would you characterize Fish's tone as amused? Annoyed? Puzzled? What is his attitude toward the process he describes?

Journal Entry

Do you agree with Fish that the process he describes is a problem? Why or why not?

Writing Workshop

1. **Working with Sources.** Write an essay describing another process that is "hard to do" – specifically, something that is more complicated today than it used to be. For possible topics, see paragraph 12 of Fish's essay. Begin by summarizing Fish's position, and be sure to include parenthetical documentation and a works-cited page. (See Chapter 18 for information on MLA documentation.)
2. Write a set of instructions for ordering, eating, and cleaning up after a meal in a fast-food restaurant. Assume your audience has never eaten in a fast-food restaurant before. Use "Getting Fast Food Is Easy to Do" as your essay's title.

Combining the Patterns

Fish includes several other patterns of development in his process essay. Locate examples of **definition**, **comparison and contrast**, **description**, **exemplification**, and **narration**. How do these passages support the process explanation?

Thematic Connections

- "Goodbye to My Twinkie Days" (page 169)
- "Tortillas" (page 500)
- The Declaration of Independence (page 550)

JOSHUA PIVEN AND DAVID BORGENICHT

How to Build a Monster from Spare Parts

Joshua Piven and David Borgenicht are the authors of the best-seller *The Worst-Case Scenario Survival Handbook* (1999), which provides tongue-in-cheek "expert" advice on such dilemmas as "How to Break into a Parked Car" and "How to Escape from a Mountain Lion." The book's success sparked a series that now includes *The Worst-Case Scenario: Weddings* (2004) and *The Complete Worst-Case Scenario Survival Handbook: Man Skills* (2010).

Background on Frankenstein Although Piven and Borgenicht do not explicitly refer to Mary Shelley's 1818 novel *Frankenstein* in the following instructions, they are clearly playing on the archetypal "mad scientist" character and storyline from this work, as well as to its many film versions and parodies. Through a series of letters, Shelley's book tells the story of the ambitious Dr. Victor Frankenstein, who builds a creature and animates it with the "principle of life" but then, horrified by his "monster," abandons it. Shelley's novel received its most iconic film treatment in the 1931 film *Frankenstein*, with Boris Karloff in the role of the monster. Over the years, however, many popular culture versions of the story have flattened the book's complex themes and effaced the sophistication of the hyperarticulate monster, who educates himself by reading the works of Plutarch, Goethe, and John Milton. Indeed, the book's full title suggests one of the story's main preoccupations: *Frankenstein; or, The Modern Prometheus*. In Greek mythology, the titan Prometheus transgressed by stealing fire from the gods and giving it to humans. He is punished by Zeus, king of the gods, for this act. Like other mythic tales, such as the story of Icarus and Daedalus, the story of Prometheus is about — among other things — the limits placed on human beings and the dangers of exceeding those limits. *Frankenstein* fits in the same tradition.

1. Locate a mountain castle.

Find a castle where you can work undisturbed, away from nosy villagers 1
but with close access to graveyards.

2. Hire an assistant.

Digging up graves is hard physical labor. An assistant with a strong back, 2
even if hunched, will be invaluable in excavating the necessary body parts.

3. Gather your materials.

What's true in many craft and construction activities is also true here: The 3
quality of your materials drives the quality of your results. Find the freshest by seeking out newly dug graves, which are indicated by large quantities of

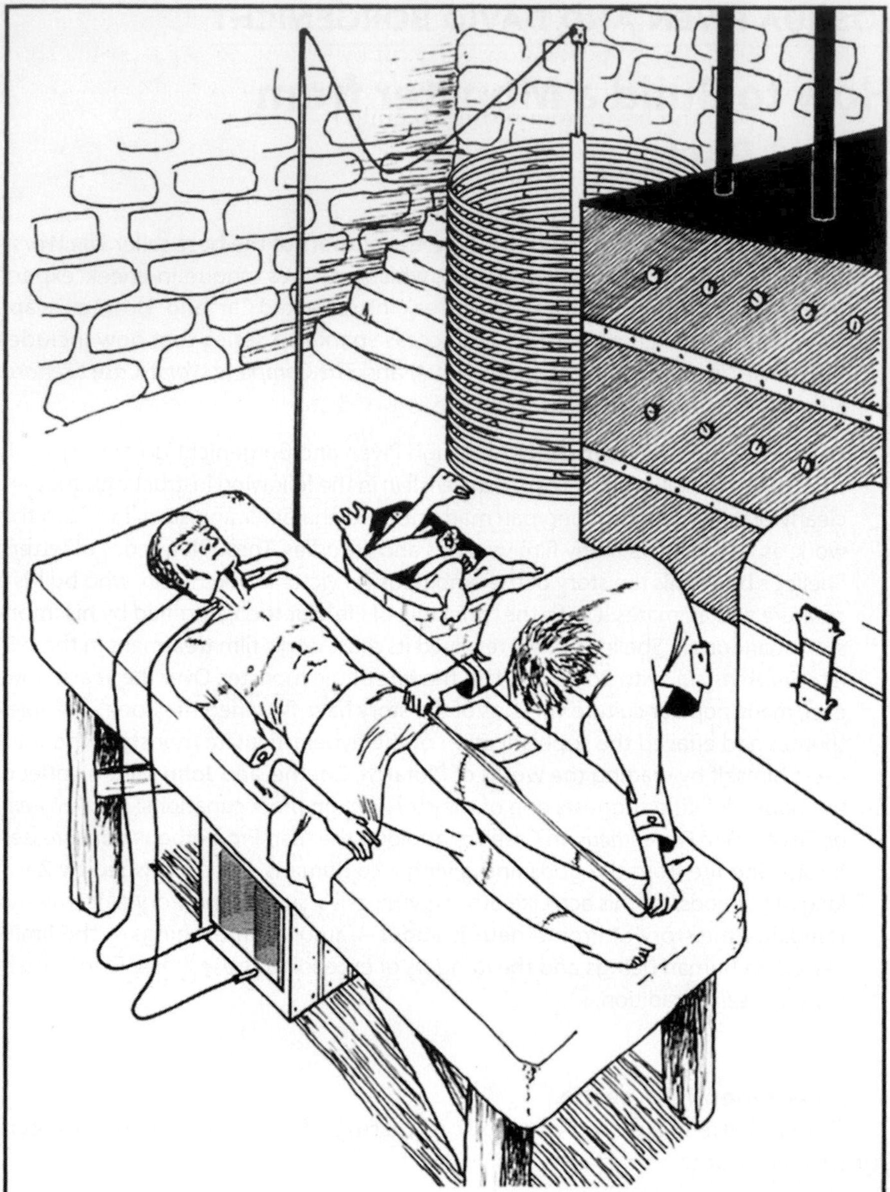
Use the carpenter's rule of thumb: measure twice; cut once.

flowers or groups of weeping mourners. Dig at night by the light of the moon. Take the whole corpse (you never know how you might need to kit it out for parts later on) and restore the gravesite to resemble the state in which you found it to avoid suspicion.

4. Keep parts preserved until you're ready to stitch them together.

Avoid the danger of postexhumation rot by storing body parts on a snow 4
bank or in a freezing underground dungeon until you have secured all the necessary pieces and have enough time to build the body properly.

5. Measure twice; cut once.

Measure your incisions and dismemberments twice before using your 5
saw. The effort spent in ensuring that each cut is made exactly as you want it will save time by avoiding having to acquire replacement parts.

6. Stitch and rivet carefully.

The human body is an unimaginably intricate and delicate network of 6
interlocking systems. Unless you are a trained surgeon, in which case your success rate at this task is at least 50 percent higher, you will be aligning these systems on a rough macroscopic level and then trusting the sheer power of violent electricity to fuse the messy bits together. Make your sutures tight and close together with a well-rated surgical thread, and solder the neck-bolted electrodes firmly into place, extending an inch into muscle tissue beneath the cauterized skin.

7. Watch the weather reports.

Wait for a raging thunderstorm. Pay attention to forecasts a few hours in 7
advance—better to be doing your prep work before the rain starts.

8. Activate the body.

Strap your undead creation to a table with leather shackles. Position the 8
table to face an open window. Using extra-long jumper cables, attach the monster's electrode bolts to the lightning rod affixed to the roof, wrapping them securely to the rod with heavy electrical tape. Wait for a lightning bolt to strike the rod, sending electricity surging through the wires and galvanizing the creature's nervous system into first reflexive and then sustainable activity. That is: life. *Life!*

9. Laugh maniacally.

Lean back, clutch at the sky, and cackle. 9

10. Relax and enjoy your success.

Nothing can possibly go wrong now. 10

• • •

Comprehension

1. This set of instructions begins very abruptly. What happens before the first step ("Locate a mountain castle.")?
2. How much time do you think this process takes? What makes you think so?

3. What materials are required for this process? Are all these items listed in paragraph 3?
4. This essay includes many allusions to the story of Frankenstein. Identify as many of these references as you can. (If you are not familiar with the story, read a summary online.)

Purpose and Audience

1. What main idea is implied in this set of instructions? Write a sentence that could serve as the essay's thesis statement.
2. What kinds of readers might find this essay entertaining? What kinds might react negatively to these instructions? Why?
3. Does the visual on page 288 help to explain the process? If so, how? What other purpose might it serve?
4. What information do the last two steps give you about the writers' purpose?

Style and Structure

1. This selection is neither structured nor formatted like most of the other readings in this book. What does it include that most other readings do not? What elements are missing that most other readings include? Should any of these missing elements be added? Why or why not?
2. What stylistic features tell you that this is a set of instructions rather than a process explanation?
3. Instructions are directed at people who may actually have to perform a process. Obviously, that is not the case here, so why do the writers choose to write instructions rather than simply explaining the process?
4. Where do the writers include the cautions and reminders that are usually present in instructions? Do you think readers need any additional warnings or reminders?
5. How do the writers move readers from one step of the process to the next? Would the addition of transitional words and expressions be helpful? Suggest some transitions that could be added.
6. **Vocabulary Project.** What connotations do the terms *spare parts* (title) and *replacement parts* (5) have? In what contexts are these expressions generally used? Given their common usage, why are these expressions used here?

Journal Entry

Generally speaking, what is your reaction to these instructions? Do you find the essay humorous or distasteful?

Writing Workshop

1. **Working with Sources.** This essay is from one of a series of books by Piven et al. that provides instructions for coping with "worst-case scenarios," such as escaping from a stadium riot or putting out a microwave fire. Find the tables of contents for several of these books on Amazon.com, and choose a scenario to use as the topic for a set of instructions of your own. In your introduction, use some of the listed chapter titles to illustrate the concept of a "worst-case scenario" and to give your essay some context. Be sure to cite Amazon.com as your source and to include a work-cited page. (See Chapter 18 for information on documenting sources.)
2. This selection is more a list of steps than a fully developed essay. Expand these instructions, including introductory and concluding paragraphs and any additional steps or advice (including warnings) you think are necessary. Be sure to add transitions between sentences and paragraphs to make the process flow smoothly. If you like, you can include illustrations.

Combining the Patterns

How might more **description** strengthen this essay? What, specifically, might the writers want to describe?

Thematic Connections

- "The Embalming of Mr. Jones" (page 297)
- "Rube Goldberg Machine" (page 332)
- "Naming of Parts" (page 476)
- "A Zombie Is a Slave Forever" (page 504)

ARTHUR MILLER

Get It Right: Privatize Executions

One of the leading playwrights of the twentieth century, Arthur Miller (1915–2005) had his first play produced on Broadway in 1944. Although it was not a success, his next Broadway production, *All My Sons* (1947), received positive reviews and the New York Drama Critics' Circle Award. However, it was his 1949 play *Death of a Salesman* that established Miller as a major voice in the American theater: opening to ecstatic reviews, it went on to win the Pulitzer Prize for Drama that year. Another important play, *The Crucible* (1953), was set during the Salem witch trials of the late seventeenth century but was written as an allegory for the persecution of suspected Communists in the 1950s. (Miller himself was called before the House Un-American Activities Committee and convicted of contempt of Congress because he refused to testify; his conviction was overturned on appeal in 1958.) Although his plays from the 1960s on did not achieve the success of his earlier works, Miller's artistic legacy is assured; his moral vision, as evidenced in the following 1992 essay, continues to move readers and playgoers around the world.

Background on public executions Public executions of convicted felons can be traced back at least as far as the ancient civilizations of Greece and Rome and were common in European countries until well into the nineteenth century (public executions were conducted in England, for example, until 1868). Over time, they have been carried out by crucifixion, stoning, burning at the stake, and beheading, among other methods. By the 1600s in England and in the American colonies, however, public executions were most often accomplished by hanging, usually in a public square. These hangings, which were meant to teach spectators a moral lesson, ironically took on a festive, carnival-like air and were considered a form of free entertainment. By the early 1800s, authorities in a number of states began to require that hangings be performed in the privacy of prisons, in part because the crowds witnessing them had become so rowdy and in part because it was believed that public executions could stir sentiments against capital punishment. Still, public executions persisted in some areas of the United States until the twentieth century; the last was performed in 1936 in Owensboro, Kentucky. Today, public executions continue in countries operating under Muslim law and under repressive regimes, such as that of North Korea. In this essay, Miller makes the somewhat radical suggestion that execution be both "privatized"—that is, run not by the government but by private companies—and public.

The time has come to consider the privatization of executions. 1

There can no longer be any doubt that government—society itself—is 2 incapable of doing anything right, and this certainly applies to the executions of convicted criminals.

At present, the thing is a total loss, to the convicted person, to his family, 3
and to society. It need not be so.

People can be executed in places like Shea Stadium* before immense 4
paying audiences. The income from the spectacle could be distributed to the prison that fed and housed him or to a trust fund for prisoner rehabilitation and his own family and/or girlfriend, as he himself chose.

The condemned would of course get a percentage of the gate, to be nego- 5
tiated by his agent or a promoter, if he so desired.

The take would, without question, be sizable, considering the immense 6
number of Americans in favor of capital punishment. A $200 to $300 ringside seat would not be excessive, with bleachers going for, say, $25.

As with all sports events, a certain ritual would seem inevitable and would 7
quickly become an expected part of the occasion. The electric chair would be set on a platform, like a boxing ring without the rope, around second base.

Once the audience was seated, a soprano would come forward and sing 8
"The Star-Spangled Banner." When she stepped down, the governor, holding a microphone, would appear and describe the condemned man's crimes in detail, plus his many failed appeals.

Then the governor would step aside 9
and a phalanx of police officers or possibly National Guard or Army troops would mount the platform and surround the condemned. This climactic entrance might be accompanied by a trumpet fanfare or other musical number by the police or Army band, unless it was thought to offend good taste.

"Next, a minister or priest would appear and offer a benediction, asking God's blessing on the execution."

Next, a minister or priest would appear 10
and offer a benediction, asking God's blessing on the execution.

The condemned, should he desire, could make a short statement and 11
even a plea of innocence. This would only add to the pathos of the occasion and would of course not be legally binding. He would then be strapped into the chair.

Finally, the executioner, hooded to protect himself from retaliation, 12
would proceed to the platform. He would walk to a console where, on a solemn signal from the governor, he would pull the switch.

The condemned man would instantly surge upward against his bindings, 13
with smoke emitting from his flesh. This by itself would provide a most powerful lesson for anyone contemplating murder. For those not contemplating murder, it would be a reminder of how lucky they are to have been straight and honest in America.

For the state, this would mean additional income; for the audience, an 14
intense and educational experience – people might, for example, wish to bring their children.

* Eds. note – Demolished in 2009 and replaced by Citi Field, where the New York Mets now play.

And for the condemned, it would have its achievement aspect, because he would know that he had not lived his life for nothing. 15

Some might object that such proceedings are so fundamentally attractive that it is not too much to imagine certain individuals contemplating murder in order to star in the program. But no solution to any profound social problem is perfect. 16

Finally, and perhaps most important, it is entirely possible that after witnessing a few dozen privatized executions, the public might grow tired of the spectacle – just as it seizes on all kinds of entertainment only to lose interest once their repetitiousness becomes too tiresomely apparent. 17

Then perhaps we might be willing to consider the fact that in executing prisoners we merely add to the number of untimely dead without diminishing the number of murders committed. 18

At that point, the point of boredom, we might begin asking why it is that Americans commit murder more often than any other people. At the moment, we are not bored enough with executions to ask this question; instead, we are apparently going to demand more and more of them, most probably because we never get to witness any in person. 19

My proposal would lead us more quickly to boredom and away from our current gratifying excitement – and ultimately perhaps to a wiser use of alternating current. 20

• • •

Comprehension

1. What process does Miller describe? List the individual steps in this process.
2. Which of Miller's recommendations are most outrageous? Is any part of his scheme actually plausible? Explain.
3. In paragraph 6, Miller notes that many Americans support capital punishment. Do you think Miller was one of these people? Why or why not?
4. Why, according to Miller, do executions need to be privatized rather than performed by the government?
5. What specific benefits does Miller say will result from his plan?
6. In paragraph 20, Miller suggests that his proposal might ultimately lead to "a wiser use of alternating current." What does he mean by "alternating current"?

Purpose and Audience

1. This essay begins with an abrupt statement of a very controversial thesis. Why does Miller choose this approach? Is it effective?
2. What kind of reaction do you think Miller hoped to get from his audience? For instance, does he want them to be amused? Shocked? Guilty? Angry? Explain your conclusion.
3. How would you characterize Miller's primary purpose in writing this essay? What do you think he hoped to accomplish?

Style and Structure

1. Because this essay was first published in a newspaper and set in columns, it has relatively short paragraphs. Which paragraphs, if any, could be combined? Which would you leave as they are? Are there any advantages to using one- or two-sentence paragraphs in this essay?
2. Where does the actual process begin? Where does it end?
3. What words and phrases link the steps in the process? Do you think any additional transitions are needed? If so, where?
4. **Vocabulary Project.** Miller repeats the word *execution* many times. What alternatives does he have? What different connotations does each of these possible alternatives suggest?
5. Much of this essay's tone is ironic, and Miller clearly intended that many of his statements not be taken literally. How do you suppose he expected readers to react to each of the following?
   - "unless it was thought to offend good taste" (9)
   - "he would know that he had not lived his life for nothing" (15)
   - "no solution to any profound social problem is perfect" (16)
6. Miller seems to suggest that executions are not unlike sporting events. How, according to Miller, are they alike? Is this a valid **analogy**?

Journal Entry

Many people who support capital punishment see it as a deterrent to crime. Do you think Miller's proposal, if enacted, could serve as a deterrent? Why or why not?

Writing Workshop

1. Using past tense, rewrite the process section of Miller's essay from the point of view of someone who has just witnessed a public execution. Give the condemned person an identity, a history, and a family, and explain the crime for which he or she is being punished. In your thesis, take a stand on whether or not this person deserves to be executed.
2. **Working with Sources.** Write a process essay expressing your strong disapproval of the idea of public executions. Quoting Miller where necessary, use the steps in the process he describes to support your position. To convince readers this practice is inhumane, add descriptive details – for example, information about the observers' reactions and the sensationalist news coverage. Be sure to include parenthetical documentation that cites Miller as the source of your quoted material and to include a works-cited page. (See Chapter 18 for information on MLA documentation.)

Combining the Patterns

Although the body of this essay is structured as a process, the essay as a whole makes a powerful **argument**. Does Miller have a debatable thesis? Do you think he needs more evidence to support his thesis, or is the process itself enough? Does he consider the possible objections of his audience? Does he refute these objections?

Thematic Connections

- "Shooting an Elephant" (page 131)
- "The Lottery" (page 304)
- "Photos That Change History" (page 356)
- "A Modest Proposal" (page 706)

JESSICA MITFORD

The Embalming of Mr. Jones

Jessica Mitford (1917–1996) was born in Batsford Mansion, England, to a wealthy, aristocratic family. Rebelling against her sheltered upbringing, she became involved in left-wing politics and eventually immigrated to the United States. Mitford wrote two volumes of autobiography: *Daughters and Rebels* (1960), about her eccentric family, and *A Fine Old Conflict* (1977). In the 1950s, she began a career in investigative journalism, which produced the books *The American Way of Death* (1963), about abuses in the funeral business; *Kind and Usual Punishment* (1973), about the U.S. prison system; and *The American Way of Birth* (1992), about the crisis in American obstetrical care.

Background on the funeral industry "The Embalming of Mr. Jones" is excerpted from *The American Way of Death,* a scathing critique of the funeral industry in the United States. The book prompted angry responses from morticians but also led to increased governmental regulation, culminating in a 1984 Federal Trade Commission ruling requiring funeral homes to disclose in writing the prices for all goods and services, as well as certain consumer rights; barring funeral homes from forcing consumers to purchase more than they really want; and forbidding funeral directors from misleading consumers regarding state laws governing the disposal of bodies. Still, industry critics charge that many abuses continue. Although funeral services can be purchased for less than a thousand dollars, the standard rate is between two and four thousand dollars — and it can go much higher. The difference in cost is based largely on the price of a casket, and grieving family members are often strongly pressured into buying the most expensive caskets, which may be marked up as much as 500 percent. Advocates for reform suggest consumers choose cremation over burial (in 2015, nearly half of all Americans who died were cremated rather than buried) and that they hold memorial services in churches or other settings, where costs are much lower than in funeral homes.

Embalming is indeed a most extraordinary procedure, and one must wonder at the docility of Americans who each year pay hundreds of millions of dollars for its perpetuation, blissfully ignorant of what it is all about, what is done, how it is done. Not one in ten thousand has any idea of what actually takes place. Books on the subject are extremely hard to come by. They are not to be found in most libraries or bookshops. 1

In an era when huge television audiences watch surgical operations in the comfort of their living rooms, when, thanks to the animated cartoon, the geography of the digestive system has become familiar territory even to the nursery school set, in a land where the satisfaction of curiosity about almost all matters is a national pastime, the secrecy surrounding embalming can, surely, hardly be attributed to the inherent gruesomeness of the subject. Custom in this regard has within this century suffered a complete reversal. In the 2 early days of American embalming, when it was performed in the home of the deceased, it was almost mandatory for some relative to stay by the embalmer's side and witness the procedure. Today, family members who might wish to be in attendance would certainly be dissuaded by the funeral director. All others, except apprentices, are excluded by law from the preparation room.

"For those who have the stomach for it, let us part the formaldehyde curtain."

3 A close look at what does actually take place may explain in large measure the undertaker's intractable reticence concerning a procedure that has become his major *raison d'être*.* Is it possible he fears that public information about embalming might lead patrons to wonder if they really want this service? If the funeral men are loath to discuss the subject outside the trade, the reader may, understandably, be equally loath to go on reading at this point. For those who have the stomach for it, let us part the formaldehyde curtain. . . .

4 The body is first laid out in the undertaker's morgue – or rather, Mr. Jones is reposing in the preparation room – to be readied to bid the world farewell.

5 The preparation room in any of the better funeral establishments has the tiled and sterile look of a surgery, and indeed the embalmer-restorative artist who does his chores there is beginning to adopt the term "dermasurgeon" (appropriately corrupted by some mortician-writers as "demisurgeon") to describe his calling. His equipment, consisting of scalpels, scissors, augers, forceps, clamps, needles, pumps, tubes, bowls, and basin, is crudely imitative of the surgeon's, as is his technique, acquired in a nine- or twelve-month post-high-school course in an embalming school. He is supplied by an advanced chemical industry with a bewildering array of fluids, sprays, pastes, oils, powders, creams, to fix or soften tissue, shrink or distend it as needed, dry it here, restore the moisture there. There are cosmetics, waxes, and paints to fill and cover features, even plaster of Paris to replace entire limbs. There are ingenious aids to prop and stabilize the cadaver: a Vari-Pose Head Rest, the Edwards Arm and Hand Positioner, the Repose Block (to support the shoulders during the embalming), and the Throop Foot Positioner, which resembles an old-fashioned stocks.

6 Mr. John H. Eckels, president of the Eckels College of Mortuary Science, thus describes the first part of the embalming procedure: "In the hands of a skilled practitioner, this work may be done in a comparatively short time and without mutilating the body other than by slight incision – so slight that it scarcely would cause serious inconvenience if made upon a living person. It is necessary to remove all the blood, and doing this not only helps in the disinfecting, but removes the principal cause of disfigurements due to discoloration."

7 Another textbook discusses the all-important time element: "The earlier this is done, the better, for every hour that elapses between death and

* Eds. note – Reason for being (French).

embalming will add to the problems and complications encountered. . . ." Just how soon should one get going on the embalming? The author tells us, "On the basis of such scanty information made available to this profession through its rudimentary and haphazard system of technical research, we must conclude that the best results are to be obtained if the subject is embalmed before life is completely extinct – that is, before cellular death has occurred. In the average case, this would mean within an hour after somatic death." For those who feel that there is something a little rudimentary, not to say haphazard, about this advice, a comforting thought is offered by another writer. Speaking of fears entertained in early days of premature burial, he points out, "One of the effects of embalming by chemical injection, however, has been to dispel fears of live burial." How true; once the blood is removed, chances of live burial are indeed remote.

To return to Mr. Jones, the blood is drained out through the veins and 8 replaced by embalming fluid pumped in through the arteries. As noted in *The Principles and Practices of Embalming*, "every operator has a favorite injection and drainage point – a fact which becomes a handicap only if he fails or refuses to forsake his favorites when conditions demand it." Typical favorites are the carotid artery, femoral artery, jugular vein, subclavian vein. There are various choices of embalming fluid. If Flextone is used, it will produce a "mild, flexible rigidity. The skin retains a velvety softness, the tissues are rubbery and pliable. Ideal for women and children." It may be blended with B. and G. Products Company's Lyf-Lyk tint, which is guaranteed to reproduce "nature's own skin texture . . . the velvety appearance of living tissue." Suntone comes in three separate tints: Suntan; Special Cosmetic Tint, a pink shade "especially indicated for young female subjects"; and Regular Cosmetic Tint, moderately pink.

About three to six gallons of a dyed and perfumed solution of formalde- 9 hyde, glycerin, borax, phenol, alcohol, and water is soon circulating through Mr. Jones, whose mouth has been sewn together with a "needle directed upward between the upper lip and gum and brought out through the left nostril," with the corners raised slightly "for a more pleasant expression." If he should be buck-toothed, his teeth are cleaned with Bon Ami and coated with colorless nail polish. His eyes, meanwhile, are closed with flesh-tinted eye caps and eye cement.

The next step is to have at Mr. Jones with a thing called a trocar. This is a 10 long, hollow needle attached to a tube. It is jabbed into the abdomen, poked around the entrails and chest cavity, the contents of which are pumped out and replaced with "cavity fluid." This done, and the hole in the abdomen sewed up, Mr. Jones's face is heavily creamed (to protect the skin from burns which may be caused by leakage of the chemicals), and he is covered with a sheet and left unmolested for a while. But not for long – there is more, much more, in store for him. He has been embalmed, but not yet restored, and the best time to start restorative work is eight to ten hours after embalming, when the tissues have become firm and dry.

The object of all this attention to the corpse, it must be remembered, is to 11 make it presentable for viewing in an attitude of healthy repose. "Our customs require the presentation of our dead in the semblance of normality . . .

unmarred by the ravages of illness, disease, or mutilation," says Mr. J. Sheridan Mayer in his *Restorative Art.* This is rather a large order since few people die in the full bloom of health, unravaged by illness and unmarked by some disfigurement. The funeral industry is equal to the challenge: "In some cases the gruesome appearance of a mutilated or disease-ridden subject may be quite discouraging. The task of restoration may seem impossible and shake the confidence of the embalmer. This is the time for intestinal fortitude and determination. Once the formative work is begun and affected tissues are cleaned or removed, all doubts of success vanish. It is surprising and gratifying to discover the results which may be obtained."

The embalmer, having allowed an appropriate interval to elapse, returns to 12
the attack, but now he brings into play the skill and equipment of sculptor and cosmetician. Is a hand missing? Casting one in plaster of Paris is a simple matter. "For replacement purposes, only a cast of the back of the hand is necessary; this is within the ability of the average operator and is quite adequate." If a lip or two, a nose, or an ear should be missing, the embalmer has at hand a variety of restorative waxes with which to model replacements. Pores and skin texture are simulated by stippling with a little brush, and over this cosmetics are laid on. Head off? Decapitation cases are rather routinely handled. Ragged edges are trimmed, and head joined to torso with a series of splints, wires, and sutures. It is a good idea to have a little something at the neck—a scarf or high collar—when time for viewing comes. Swollen mouth? Cut out tissue as needed from inside the lips. If too much is removed, the surface contour can easily be restored by padding with cotton. Swollen necks and cheeks are reduced by removing tissue through vertical incisions made down each side of the neck. "When the deceased is casketed, the pillow will hide the suture incisions. . . . as an extra precaution against leakage, the suture may be painted with liquid sealer."

The opposite condition is more likely to present itself—that of emacia- 13
tion. His hypodermic syringe now loaded with massage cream, the embalmer seeks out and fills the hollowed and sunken areas by injection. In this procedure the backs of the hands and fingers and the underchin area should not be neglected.

Positioning the lips is a problem that recurrently challenges the ingenu- 14
ity of the embalmer. Closed too tightly, they tend to give a stern, even disapproving expression. Ideally, embalmers feel, the lips should give the impression of being ever so slightly parted, the upper lip protruding slightly for a more youthful appearance. This takes some engineering, however, as the lips tend to drift apart. Lip drift can sometimes be remedied by pushing one or two straight pins through the inner margin of the lower lip and then inserting them between the two front upper teeth. If Mr. Jones happens to have no teeth, the pins can just as easily be anchored in his Armstrong Face Former and Denture Replacer. Another method to maintain lip closure is to dislocate the lower jaw, which is then held in its new position by a wire run through holes which have been drilled through the upper jaws at the midline. As the French are fond of saying, *il faut souffrir pour être belle.**

* Eds. note—It is necessary to suffer in order to be beautiful.

If Mr. Jones has died of jaundice, the embalming fluid will very likely turn him green. Does this deter the embalmer? Not if he has intestinal fortitude. Masking pastes and cosmetics are heavily laid on, burial garments and casket interiors are color-correlated with particular care, and Jones is displayed beneath rose-colored lights. Friends will say, "How *well* he looks." Death by carbon monoxide, on the other hand, can be rather a good thing from an embalmer's viewpoint: "One advantage is the fact that this type of discoloration is an exaggerated form of a natural pink coloration." This is nice because the healthy glow is already present and needs but little attention. 15

The patching and filling completed, Mr. Jones is now shaved, washed, and dressed. Cream-based cosmetic, available in pink, flesh, suntan, brunette, and blonde, is applied to his hands and face, his hair is shampooed and combed (and, in the case of Mrs. Jones, set), his hands manicured. For the horny-handed son of toil special care must be taken; cream should be applied to remove ingrained grime, and the nails cleaned. "If he were not in the habit of having them manicured in life, trimming and shaping is advised for better appearance – never questioned by kin." 16

Jones is now ready for casketing (this is the present participle of the verb "to casket"). In this operation his right shoulder should be depressed slightly "to turn the body a bit to the right and soften the appearance of lying flat on the back." Positioning the hands is a matter of importance, and special rubber positioning blocks may be used. The hands should be cupped slightly for a more lifelike, relaxed appearance. Proper placement of the body requires a delicate sense of balance. It should lie as high as possible in the casket, yet not so high that the lid, when lowered, will hit the nose. On the other hand, we are cautioned, placing the body too low "creates the impression that the body is in a box." 17

Jones is next wheeled into the appointed slumber room where a few last touches may be added – his favorite pipe placed in his hand or, if he was a great reader, a book propped into position. (In the case of little Master Jones a Teddy bear may be clutched.) Here he will hold open house for a few days, visiting hours 10 A.M. to 9 P.M. 18

• • •

Comprehension

1. How, according to Mitford, has the public's knowledge of embalming changed? How does she explain this change?
2. To what other professionals does Mitford compare the embalmer? Are these analogies flattering or critical? Explain.
3. List the major stages in the process of embalming and restoration.

Purpose and Audience

1. Mitford's purpose in this essay is to convince her audience of something. What is her thesis?

2. Do you think Mitford expects her audience to agree with her thesis? How can you tell?
3. In one of her books, Mitford refers to herself as a *muckraker,* one who informs the public of misconduct. Does she achieve this status here? Cite specific examples.
4. Mitford's tone in this essay is subjective, even judgmental. What effect does her tone have on you? Does it encourage you to trust her? Should she have presented her facts in a more objective way? Explain.

Style and Structure

1. Identify the stylistic features that distinguish this process explanation from a set of instructions.
2. In this selection, as in many process essays, a list of necessary materials is provided before the start of the procedure. What additional details does Mitford include along with the list in paragraph 5? What effect do these details have on you?
3. Locate Mitford's remarks about the language of embalming. How do her comments about euphemisms, newly coined words, and other aspects of language help to support her thesis?
4. **Vocabulary Project.** Reread paragraphs 5 through 9 carefully. Then, list all the words in this section of the essay that suggest surgical techniques and all the words that suggest cosmetic artistry. What do your lists tell you about Mitford's intent in these paragraphs?
5. Throughout the essay, Mitford quotes various experts. How does she use their remarks to support her thesis?
6. Give examples of transitional phrases that link the various stages of Mitford's process.
7. Mitford uses a good deal of **sarcasm** and biased language in this essay. Identify some examples. Do you think her use of this kind of language strengthens or weakens her essay? Why?

Journal Entry

What are your thoughts about how your religion or culture deals with death and dying? What practices, if any, make you uncomfortable? Why?

Writing Workshop

1. Use the information in this process explanation to help you prepare a two-page set of instructions for undertakers. Unlike Mitford, keep your essay objective.
2. **Working with Sources.** In the role of a funeral director, write a blog post taking issue with Mitford's essay. As you explain the process of embalming, paraphrase or quote two or three of Mitford's statements and argue against

them, making sure to identify the source of these quotations. Your objective is to defend the practice of embalming as necessary and practical. Be sure to include parenthetical documentation citing Mitford as your source, and include a works-cited page. (See Chapter 18 for information on MLA documentation.)

3. Write an explanation of a process you personally find disgusting – or delightful. Make your attitude clear in your thesis statement and in your choice of words.

Combining the Patterns

Although Mitford structures this essay as a process, many passages rely heavily on subjective **description**. Where is her focus on descriptive details most obvious? What is her purpose in describing particular individuals and objects as she does? How do these descriptive passages help support her essay's thesis?

Thematic Connections

- "How to Build a Monster from Spare Parts" (page 287)
- "Shall I compare thee to a summer's day?" (page 428)
- "The Ways We Lie" (page 466)

SHIRLEY JACKSON

The Lottery (Fiction)

Shirley Jackson (1916–1965) is best known for her subtly macabre stories of horror and suspense, most notably her best-selling novel *The Haunting of Hill House* (1959), which Stephen King has called "one of the greatest horror stories of all time." She also published wryly humorous reflections on her experiences as a wife and mother of four children. Many of her finest stories and novels were not anthologized until after her death.

Background on the initial reaction to "The Lottery" "The Lottery" first appeared in the *New Yorker* in 1948, three years after the end of World War II. Jackson was living somewhat uneasily in the New England college town of Bennington, Vermont, a village very similar to the setting of "The Lottery." She felt herself an outsider there, a sophisticated intellectual in an isolated, closely knit community that was suspicious of strangers. Here, Jackson (whose husband was Jewish) experienced frequent encounters with anti-Semitism. At the time, the full atrocity of Germany's wartime program to exterminate Jews, now called the Holocaust, had led many social critics to contemplate humanity's terrible capacity for evil. Most Americans, however, wished to put the horrors of the war behind them, and many readers reacted with outrage to Jackson's tale of an annual small-town ritual, calling it "nasty," "nauseating," and even "perverted." Others, however, immediately recognized its genius, its power, and its many layers of meaning. This classic tale is now one of the most widely anthologized of all twentieth-century short stories.

The morning of June 27th was clear and sunny, with the fresh warmth of a full-summer day; the flowers were blossoming profusely and the grass was richly green. The people of the village began to gather in the square, between the post office and the bank, around ten o'clock; in some towns there were so many people that the lottery took two days and had to be started on June 26th, but in this village, where there were only about three hundred people, the whole lottery took less than two hours, so it could begin at ten o'clock in the morning and still be through in time to allow the villagers to get home for noon dinner. 1

The children assembled first, of course. School was recently over for the summer, and the feeling of liberty sat uneasily on most of them; they tended to gather together quietly for a while before they broke into boisterous play, and their talk was still of the classroom and the teacher, of books and reprimands. Bobby Martin had already stuffed his pockets full of stones, and the other boys soon followed his example, selecting the smoothest and roundest stones; Bobby and Harry Jones and Dickie Delacroix—the villagers pronounced his name "Dellacroy"—eventually made a great pile of stones in one corner of the square and guarded it against the raids of the other boys. The 2 girls stood aside, talking among themselves, looking over their shoulders at the boys, and the very small children rolled in the dust or clung to the hands of their older brothers or sisters.

Soon the men began to gather, surveying their own children, speaking of planting and rain, tractors and taxes. They stood together, away from the pile of stones in the corner, and their jokes were quiet and they smiled rather than laughed. The women, wearing faded house dresses and sweaters, came shortly after their menfolk. They greeted one another and exchanged bits of gossip as they went to join their husbands. Soon the women, standing by their husbands, began to call to their children, and the children came reluctantly, having to be called four or five times. Bobby Martin ducked under his mother's grasping hand and ran, laughing, back to the pile of stones. His father spoke up sharply, and Bobby came quickly and took his place between his father and his oldest brother. 3

The lottery was conducted – as were the square dances, the teenage club, the Halloween program – by Mr. Summers, who had time and energy to devote to civic activities. He was a round-faced, jovial man and he ran the coal business, and people were sorry for him, because he had no children and his wife was a scold. When he arrived in the square, carrying the black wooden box, there was a murmur of conversation among the villagers, and he waved and called "Little late today, folks." The postmaster, Mr. Graves, followed him, carrying a three-legged stool, and the stool was put in the center of the square and Mr. Summers set the black box down on it. The villagers kept their distance, leaving a space between themselves and the stool, and when Mr. Summers said, "Some of you fellows want to give me a hand?" there was a hesitation before two men, Mr. Martin and his oldest son, Baxter, came forward to hold the box steady on the stool while Mr. Summers stirred up the papers inside it. 4

The original paraphernalia for the lottery had been lost long ago, and the black box now resting on the stool had been put into use even before Old Man Warner, the oldest man in town, was born. Mr. Summers spoke frequently to the villagers about making a new box, but no one liked to upset even as much tradition as was represented by the black box. There was a story that the present box had been made with some pieces of the box that had preceded it, the one that had been constructed when the first people settled down to make a village here. Every year, after the lottery, Mr. Summers began talking about a new box, but every year the subject was allowed to fade off without anything's being done. The black box grew shabbier each year; by now it was no longer completely black but splintered badly along one side to show the original wood color, and in some places faded and stained. 5

Mr. Martin and his oldest son, Baxter, held the black box securely on the stool until Mr. Summers had stirred the papers thoroughly with his hand. Because so much of the ritual had been forgotten or discarded, Mr. Summers had been successful in having slips of paper substituted for the chips of wood that had been used for generations. Chips of wood, Mr. Summers had argued, had been all very well when the village was tiny, but now that the population 6 was more than three hundred and likely to keep on growing, it was necessary to use something that would fit more easily into the black box. The night before the lottery, Mr. Summers and Mr. Graves made up the slips of paper and put them in the box, and it was then taken to the safe of Mr. Summers' coal company and locked up until Mr. Summers was ready to take it to the square the next morning. The rest of the year, the box was put away, sometimes one place, sometimes another; it had spent one year in Mr. Graves' barn and another year underfoot in the post office, and sometimes it was set on a shelf in the Martin grocery and left there.

There was a great deal of fussing to be done before Mr. Summers declared the lottery open. There were the lists to make up – of heads of families, heads of households in each family, members of each household in each family. There was the proper swearing-in of Mr. Summers by the postmaster, as the official of the lottery; at one time, some people remembered, there had been a recital of some sort, performed by the official of the lottery, a perfunctory, tuneless chant that had been rattled off duly each year; some people believed that the official of the lottery used to stand just so when he said or sang it, others believed that he was supposed to walk among the people, but years and years ago this part of the ritual had been allowed to lapse. There had been, also, a ritual salute, which the official of the lottery had had to use in addressing each person who came up to draw from the box, but this also had changed with time, until now it was felt necessary only for the official to speak to each person approaching. Mr. Summers was very good at all this; in his clean white shirt and blue jeans, with one hand resting carelessly on the black box, he seemed very proper and important as he talked interminably to Mr. Graves and the Martins. 7

Just as Mr. Summers finally left off talking and turned to the assembled villagers, Mrs. Hutchinson came hurriedly along the path to the square, her sweater thrown over her shoulders, and slid into place in the back of the crowd. "Clean forgot what day it was," she said to Mrs. Delacroix, who stood next to her, and they both laughed softly. "Thought my old man was out back stacking wood," Mrs. Hutchinson went on, "and then I looked out the window and the kids were gone, and then I remembered it was the twenty-seventh and came a-running." She dried her hands on her apron, and Mrs. Delacroix said, "You're in time, though. They're still talking away up there." 8

Mrs. Hutchinson craned her neck to see through the crowd and found her husband and children standing near the front. She tapped Mrs. Delacroix on the arm as a farewell and began to make her way through the crowd. The people separated good-humoredly to let her through; two or three people said, in voices just loud enough to be heard across the crowd, "Here comes your Missus, Hutchinson," and "Bill, she made it after all." Mrs. Hutchinson reached her husband, and Mr. Summers, who had been waiting, said cheerfully, "Thought we were going to have to get on without you, Tessie." Mrs. Hutchinson said, grinning, "Wouldn't have me leave m'dishes in the sink, now, would you, Joe?" and soft laughter ran through the crowd as the people stirred back into position after Mrs. Hutchinson's arrival. 9

"Well, now," Mr. Summers said soberly, "guess we better get started, get 10
this over with, so's we can go back to work. Anybody ain't here?"

"Dunbar," several people said. "Dunbar, Dunbar." 11

Mr. Summers consulted his list. "Clyde Dunbar," he said. "That's right. 12
He's broke his leg, hasn't he? Who's drawing for him?"

"Me, I guess," a woman said, and Mr. Summers turned to look at her. 13
"Wife draws for her husband," Mr. Summers said. "Don't you have a grown boy to do it for you, Janey?" Although Mr. Summers and everyone else in the village knew the answer perfectly well, it was the business of the official of the lottery to ask such questions formally. Mr. Summers waited with an expression of polite interest while Mrs. Dunbar answered.

"Horace's not but sixteen yet," Mrs. Dunbar said regretfully. "Guess I 14
gotta fill in for the old man this year."

"Right," Mr. Summers said. He made a note on the list he was holding. 15
Then he asked, "Watson boy drawing this year?"

A tall boy in the crowd raised his hand. "Here," he said. "I'm drawing for 16
m'mother and me." He blinked his eyes nervously and ducked his head as several voices in the crowd said things like "Good fellow, Jack," and "Glad to see your mother's got a man to do it."

"Well," Mr. Summers said, "guess that's everyone. Old Man Warner 17
make it?"

"Here," a voice said, and Mr. Summers nodded. 18

A sudden hush fell on the crowd as Mr. Summers cleared his throat and 19
looked at the list. "All ready?" he called. "Now, I'll read the names—heads of families first—and the men come up and take a paper out of the box. Keep the paper folded in your hand without looking at it until everyone has had a turn. Everything clear?"

The people had done it so many times that they only half listened to the 20
directions; most of them were quiet, wetting their lips, not looking around. Then Mr. Summers raised one hand high and said, "Adams." A man disengaged himself from the crowd and came forward. "Hi, Steve," Mr. Summers said, and Mr. Adams said, "Hi, Joe." They grinned at one another humorlessly and nervously. Then Mr. Adams reached into the black box and took out a folded paper. He held it firmly by one corner as he turned and went hastily back to his place in the crowd, where he stood a little apart from his family, not looking down at his hand.

"Allen," Mr. Summers said. "Anderson. . . . Betham." 21

"Seems like there's no time at all between lotteries any more," 22
Mrs. Delacroix said to Mrs. Graves in the back row. "Seems like we got through the last one only last week."

"Time sure goes fast," Mrs. Graves said. 23

"Clark. . . . Delacroix." 24

"There goes my old man," Mrs. Delacroix said. She held her breath while 25
her husband went forward.

"Dunbar," Mr. Summers said, and Mrs. Dunbar went steadily to the box 26
while one of the women said, "Go on, Janey," and another said, "There she goes."

"We're next," Mrs. Graves said. She watched while Mr. Graves came around from the side of the box, greeted Mr. Summers gravely, and selected a slip of paper from the box. By now, all through the crowd there were men holding the small folded papers in their large hands, turning them over and over nervously. Mrs. Dunbar and her two sons stood together, Mrs. Dunbar holding the slip of paper. 27

"Harburt. . . . Hutchinson." 28

"Get up there, Bill," Mrs. Hutchinson said, and the people near her laughed. 29

"Jones." 30

"They do say," Mr. Adams said to Old Man Warner, who stood next to him, "that over in the north village they're talking of giving up the lottery." 31

Old Man Warner snorted. "Pack of crazy fools," he said. "Listening to the young folks, nothing's good enough for *them.* Next thing you know, they'll be wanting to go back to living in caves, nobody work any more, live *that* way for a while. Used to be a saying about 'Lottery in June, corn be heavy soon.' First thing you know, we'd all be eating stewed chickweed and acorns. There's *always* been a lottery," he added petulantly. "Bad enough to see young Joe Summers up there joking with everybody." 32

"Some places have already quit lotteries," Mrs. Adams said. 33

"Nothing but trouble in *that,*" Old Man Warner said stoutly. "Pack of young fools." 34

"Martin." And Bobby Martin watched his father go forward. "Overdyke. . . . Percy." 35

"I wish they'd hurry," Mrs. Dunbar said to her older son. "I wish they'd hurry." 36

"They're almost through," her son said. 37

"You get ready to run tell Dad," Mrs. Dunbar said. 38

Mr. Summers called his own name and then stepped forward precisely and selected a slip from the box. Then he called, "Warner." 39

"Seventy-seventh year I been in the lottery," Old Man Warner said as he went through the crowd. "Seventy-seventh time." 40

"Watson." The tall boy came awkwardly through the crowd. Someone said, "Don't be nervous, Jack," and Mr. Summers said, "Take your time, son." 41

"Zanini." 42

After that, there was a long pause, a breathless pause, until Mr. Summers, holding his slip of paper in the air, said, "All right fellows." For a minute, no one moved, and then all the slips of paper were opened. Suddenly, all the women began to speak at once, saying, "Who is it?," "Who's got it?," "Is it the Dunbars?," "Is it the Watsons?" Then the voices began to say, "It's Hutchinson. It's Bill," "Bill Hutchinson's got it." 43

"Go tell your father," Mrs. Dunbar said to her older son. 44

People began to look around to see the Hutchinsons. Bill Hutchinson was standing quiet, staring down at the paper in his hand. Suddenly, Tessie Hutchinson shouted to Mr. Summers, "You didn't give him time enough to take any paper he wanted. I saw you. It wasn't fair!" 45

"Be a good sport, Tessie," Mrs. Delac- 46
roix called, and Mrs. Graves said, "All of us took the same chance."

> "'Be a good sport, Tessie,' Mrs. Delacroix called, and Mrs. Graves said, 'All of us took the same chance.'"

"Shut up, Tessie," Bill Hutchinson said. 47

"Well, everyone," Mr. Summers said, 48
"that was done pretty fast, and now we've got to be hurrying a little more to get it done in time." He consulted his next list. "Bill," he said, "you draw for the Hutchinson family. You got any other households in the Hutchinsons?"

"There's Don and Eva," Mrs. Hutchinson yelled. "Make *them* take their 49
chance!"

"Daughters draw with their husbands' families, Tessie," Mr. Summers 50
said gently. "You know that as well as anyone else."

"It wasn't *fair*," Tessie said. 51

"I guess not, Joe," Bill Hutchinson said regretfully. "My daughter draws 52
with her husband's family, that's only fair. And I've got no other family except the kids."

"Then, as far as drawing for families is concerned, it's you," Mr. Summers 53
said in explanation, "and as far as drawing for households is concerned, that's you, too. Right?"

"Right," Bill Hutchinson said. 54

"How many kids, Bill?" Mr. Summers asked formally. 55

"Three," Bill Hutchinson said. "There's Bill, Jr., and Nancy, and little Dave. 56
And Tessie and me."

"All right, then," Mr. Summers said. "Harry, you got their tickets back?" 57

Mr. Graves nodded and held up the slips of paper. "Put them in the box, 58
then," Mr. Summers directed. "Take Bill's and put it in."

"I think we ought to start over," Mrs. Hutchinson said, as quietly as she 59
could. "I tell you it wasn't *fair*. You didn't give him time enough to choose. *Every*body saw that."

Mr. Graves had selected the five slips and put them in the box, and he 60
dropped all the papers but those onto the ground, where the breeze caught them and lifted them off.

"Listen, everybody," Mrs. Hutchinson was saying to the people around her. 61

"Ready, Bill?" Mr. Summers asked, and Bill Hutchinson, with one quick 62
glance around at his wife and children, nodded.

"Remember," Mr. Summers said, "take the slips and keep them folded 63
until each person has taken one. Harry, you help little Dave." Mr. Graves took the hand of the little boy, who came willingly with him up to the box. "Take a paper out of the box, Davy," Mr. Summers said. Davy put his hand into the box and laughed. "Take just *one* paper," Mr. Summers said. "Harry, you hold it for him." Mr. Graves took the child's hand and removed the folded paper from the tight fist and held it while little Dave stood next to him and looked up at him wonderingly.

"Nancy next," Mr. Summers said. Nancy was twelve, and her school 64
friends breathed heavily as she went forward, switching her skirt, and took a slip daintily from the box. "Bill, Jr.," Mr. Summers said, and Billy, his face red and his feet over-large, nearly knocked the box over as he got a paper out. "Tessie," Mr. Summers said. She hesitated for a minute, looking around defiantly, and then set her lips and went up to the box. She snatched a paper out and held it behind her.

"Bill," Mr. Summers said, and Bill Hutchinson reached into the box and 65
felt around, bringing his hand out at last with the slip of paper in it.

The crowd was quiet. A girl whispered, "I hope it's not Nancy," and the 66
sound of the whisper reached the edges of the crowd.

"It's not the way it used to be," Old Man Warner said clearly. "People ain't 67
the way they used to be."

"All right," Mr. Summers said. "Open the papers. Harry, you open little 68
Dave's."

Mr. Graves opened the slip of paper and there was a general sigh through 69
the crowd as he held it up and everyone could see that it was blank. Nancy and Bill, Jr., opened theirs at the same time, and both beamed and laughed, turning around to the crowd and holding their slips of paper above their heads.

"Tessie," Mr. Summers said. There was a pause, and then Mr. Summers 70
looked at Bill Hutchinson, and Bill unfolded his paper and showed it. It was blank.

"It's Tessie," Mr. Summers said, and his voice was hushed. "Show us her 71
paper, Bill."

Bill Hutchinson went over to his wife and forced the slip of paper out of 72
her hand. It had a black spot on it, the black spot Mr. Summers had made the night before with the heavy pencil in the coal-company office. Bill Hutchinson held it up, and there was a stir in the crowd.

"All right, folks," Mr. Summers said. "Let's finish quickly." 73

Although the villagers had forgotten the ritual and lost the original black 74
box, they still remembered to use stones. The pile of stones the boys had made earlier was ready; there were stones on the ground with the blowing scraps of paper that had come out of the box. Mrs. Delacroix selected a stone so large she had to pick it up with both hands and turned to Mrs. Dunbar. "Come on," she said. "Hurry up."

Mrs. Dunbar had small stones in both hands, and she said, gasping for 75
breath, "I can't run at all. You'll have to go ahead and I'll catch up with you."

The children had stones already, and someone gave little Davy Hutchin- 76
son a few pebbles.

Tessie Hutchinson was in the center of a cleared space by now, and she 77
held her hands out desperately as the villagers moved in on her. "It isn't fair," she said. A stone hit her on the side of the head.

Old Man Warner was saying, "Come on, come on, everyone." Steve Adams 78
was in the front of the crowd of villagers, with Mrs. Graves beside him.

"It isn't fair, it isn't right," Mrs. Hutchinson screamed, and then they were 79
upon her.

• • •

Reading Literature

1. List the stages in the process of the lottery. Then, identify passages that explain the reasoning behind each step. How logical are these explanations?
2. Why is it significant that the process has continued essentially unchanged for so many years? What does this fact suggest about the townspeople?
3. Do you see this story as an explanation of a brutal process carried out in one town, or do you see it as a universal statement about dangerous tendencies in modern society – or in human nature? Explain your reasoning.

Journal Entry

What do you think it would take to stop a process like this lottery? What would have to be done – and who would have to do it?

Thematic Connections

- "Thirty-Eight Who Saw Murder Didn't Call the Police" (page 126)
- "Shooting an Elephant" (page 131)
- "Get It Right: Privatize Executions" (page 292)

Writing Assignments for Process

1. Jessica Mitford describes the process of doing a job. Write an essay summarizing the steps you took in applying for, performing, or quitting a job.
2. Write a set of instructions explaining in objective terms how the lottery Shirley Jackson describes should be conducted. Imagine you are setting these steps down in writing for generations of your fellow townspeople to follow.
3. Write a consumer-oriented article for your school newspaper explaining how to apply for financial aid, a work-study job, or an internship.
4. List the steps in the process you follow when you study for an important exam. Then, interview two friends about how they study, and take notes about their usual routine. Finally, combine the most helpful strategies into a set of instructions aimed at students entering your school.
5. **Working with Sources.** Think of a series of steps in a bureaucratic process that you had to go through to accomplish something – getting a driver's license or becoming a U.S. citizen, for instance. Write an essay explaining that process, and include a thesis statement that evaluates the process's efficiency. Before you begin writing, consult a website that outlines the process, and refer to this explanation when necessary in your essay. Be sure to document any references to the site and to include a works-cited page. (See Chapter 18 for information on MLA documentation.)
6. Imagine you have encountered a visitor from another country (or another planet) who is not familiar with a social ritual you take for granted. Try to outline the steps involved in the ritual you are familiar with, such as choosing sides for a game or pledging a fraternity or sorority.
7. Write a process essay explaining how you went about putting together a collection, a scrapbook, a writing portfolio, a website, or an album of some kind. Be sure your essay makes clear why you collected or compiled your materials.
8. Explain how a certain ritual or ceremony is conducted in your religion. Make sure your explanation makes it possible for someone of another faith to understand the process, and include a thesis statement that explains why the ritual is important.
9. Think of a process you believe should be modified or discontinued. Formulate a thesis that presents your negative feelings, and then explain the process so that you make your objections clear to your readers.
10. Give readers instructions for the process of participating in a potentially dangerous but worthwhile physical activity such as skydiving, rock climbing, or white-water rafting. Be sure to include all necessary cautions.

Collaborative Activity for Process

Working with three other students, create an illustrated instructional pamphlet to help new students survive four of your college's first "ordeals," such as registering for classes, purchasing textbooks, eating in the cafeteria, and moving into a dorm. Before beginning, decide as a group which processes to write about, whether you want your pamphlet to be practical and serious or humorous and irreverent, and what kinds of illustrations it should include. Then, decide who will write about which process – each student should do one – and who will provide the illustrations. When all of you are ready, assemble your individual efforts into a single unified piece of writing.

10

Cause and Effect

What Is Cause and Effect?

Process describes *how* something happens; **cause and effect** analyzes *why* something happens. Cause-and-effect essays examine causes, describe effects, or do both. In the following paragraph, journalist Tom Wicker considers the effects of a technological advance on a village in India.

Cause

Effects

Topic sentence

When a solar-powered water pump was provided for a well in India, the village headman took it over and sold the water, until stopped. The new liquid abundance attracted hordes of unwanted nomads. Village boys who had drawn water in buckets had nothing to do, and some became criminals. The gap between rich and poor widened, since the poor had no land to benefit from irrigation. Finally, village women broke the pump, so they could gather again around the well that had been the center of their social lives. Moral: technological advances have social, cultural, and economic consequences, often unanticipated.

Cause and effect, like narration, links situations and events together in time, with causes preceding effects. But causality involves more than sequence: cause-and-effect analysis explains why something happened – or is happening – and predicts what probably will happen. Thus, an essay that examines causes and effects can focus on questions as varied as the following:

- What might have caused climate change, and what effects of climate change have been observed?
- What changes might occur if the United States becomes a "majority minority" nation?

- What impact will the Black Lives Matter movement have on future local and national elections?
- How did the deregulation of the airline industry change air travel?
- Why have SAT scores been steadily declining?

Sometimes many different causes can be responsible for one effect. For example, as the following diagram illustrates, many elements may contribute to an individual's decision to leave his or her country of origin and immigrate to the United States.

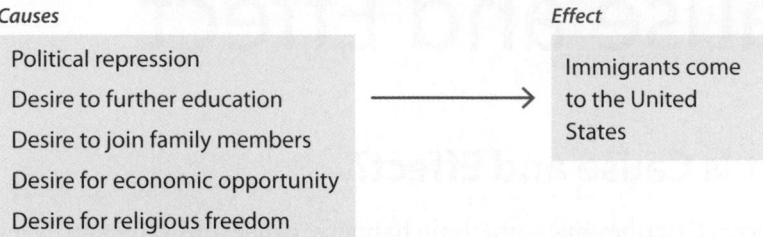

Causes		*Effect*
Political repression Desire to further education Desire to join family members Desire for economic opportunity Desire for religious freedom	⟶	Immigrants come to the United States

Similarly, a single cause can produce many different effects. Immigration, for instance, has had a variety of effects on the United States.

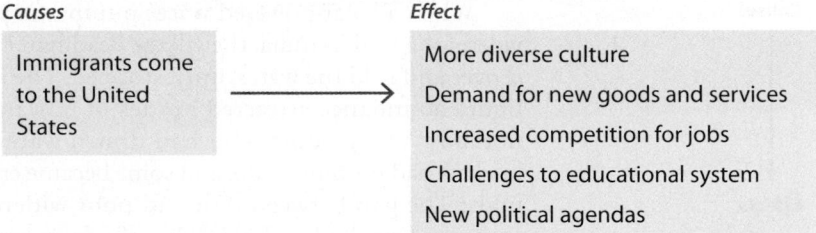

Causes		*Effect*
Immigrants come to the United States	⟶	More diverse culture Demand for new goods and services Increased competition for jobs Challenges to educational system New political agendas

Using Cause and Effect

Of course, causal relationships are rarely as neat as the preceding boxes suggest; in fact, such relationships are often subtle and complex. As you examine situations that seem suited to cause-and-effect analysis, you will discover that most complex situations involve numerous causes and many different effects.

Consider the following two examples.

The Case of the Losing Team. A professional basketball team, recently stocked with the best players money can buy, has had a mediocre season. Because the individual players are talented and were successful under other coaches, fans blame the current coach for the team's losing streak and want him fired, but is the coach alone responsible? Maybe the inability of the players to function well as a team contributed to their poor performance. Perhaps some of the players are suffering from injuries, personal problems, or drug dependency. Maybe the lack of support from fans has affected the team's morale. Clearly, other elements besides the new coach could have caused the losing streak. (And, of course, the team's losing streak might also have any number of consequences, from declining attendance at games to the city's refusal to build a new arena.)

Timothy A. Clary/Getty Images

The Case of the Car-Free Millennials. In recent years, all Americans—but particularly the generation known as millennials—have been driving less. Today, more than a fourth of people between age sixteen and thirty-four do not own cars. What has caused this situation? One possible explanation is that it is expensive to buy and maintain a car, and as it has become harder for young people to find good jobs, many are unable to afford cars. Another possible explanation is that more young people are moving to big cities and close-in suburbs and therefore rely on public transportation, bicycles, and walking. Moreover, innovations such as car-sharing, bike-sharing, and ride-sharing programs and high-speed rail—as well as jobs that allow workers to telecommute—have made it possible for many to get along without owning a car. Even if they can afford cars, millennials might also be motivated to make an effort to avoid the negative effect that vehicles have on the environment. All in all, many young people seem to be managing without cars. What effects might this decline in automobile ownership have? Could it hurt the auto industry, thereby causing autoworkers to lose their jobs? Would it have a negative effect on other jobs, such as those in car dealerships or parts manufacturers? Could it encourage cities to fund more public transportation projects? Or, will the loss of revenue from gas taxes have the opposite effect, making cities and states unable to fund such projects? Could this decline in car ownership help contribute to saving the planet?

Remember that when you write about situations such as the two described above you need to give a balanced analysis. This means that you should try to consider all possible causes and effects, not just the most obvious ones or the first ones you think of.

Understanding Main and Contributory Causes

Even when you have identified several causes of a particular effect, one—the *main cause*—is always more important than the others, the *contributory causes.* Understanding the distinction between the **main** (most important) **cause** and the **contributory** (less important) **causes** is vital for planning a cause-and-effect essay because once you identify the main cause, you can emphasize it in your essay and downplay the other causes. How, then, can you tell which cause is most important? Sometimes the main cause is obvious, but often it is not, as the following example shows.

Civic Center Roof Cleanup, Hartford, Connecticut, by Richard Welling, 1978, color Polaroid instant print on paper, gift of the Richard Welling Family, courtesy of the Connecticut Historical Society.

The Case of the Hartford Roof Collapse. During one winter a number of years ago, an unusually large amount of snow accumulated on the roof of the Civic Center in Hartford, Connecticut, and the roof fell in. Newspapers reported that the weight of the snow had caused the collapse, and they were partly right. Other buildings, however, had not been flattened by the snow, so the main cause seemed to lie elsewhere. Insurance investigators eventually determined that the roof design, not the weight of the snow (which was a contributory cause), was the main cause of the collapse.

These cause-and-effect relationships are shown in this diagram:

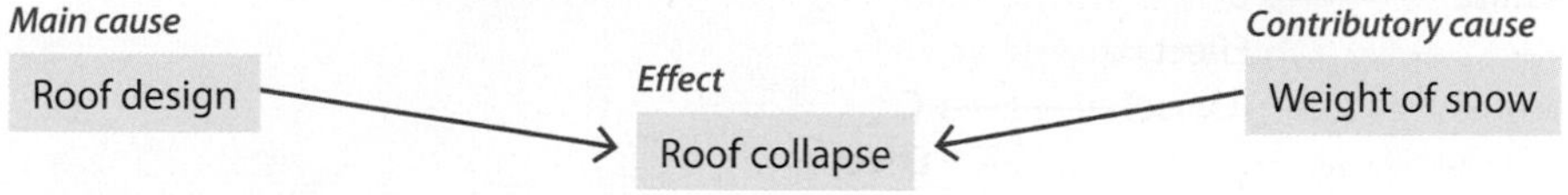

Because the main cause is not always the most obvious one, you should consider the significance of each cause very carefully as you plan your essay—and you should continue to evaluate the importance of each cause as you write and revise.

Understanding Immediate and Remote Causes

Another important distinction is the difference between an immediate cause and a remote cause. An **immediate cause** closely precedes an effect and is therefore relatively easy to recognize. A **remote cause** is less obvious, perhaps because it occurred in the past or far away. Assuming that the most obvious cause is always the most important one can be dangerous as well as shortsighted.

Reconsidering the Hartford Roof Collapse. Most people agreed that the snow was the immediate cause of the roof collapse, but further study by insurance investigators suggested remote causes that were not as apparent. The design of the roof was the most important remote cause of the collapse, but other remote causes were also examined. Perhaps the materials used in the roof's construction were partly to blame. Maybe maintenance crews had not done their jobs properly or necessary repairs had not been made. If you were the insurance investigator analyzing the causes of this event, you would want to assess all possible contributing factors. If you did not consider the remote as well as the immediate causes, you would reach an oversimplified and perhaps incorrect conclusion.

This diagram summarizes the cause-and-effect relationships discussed above.

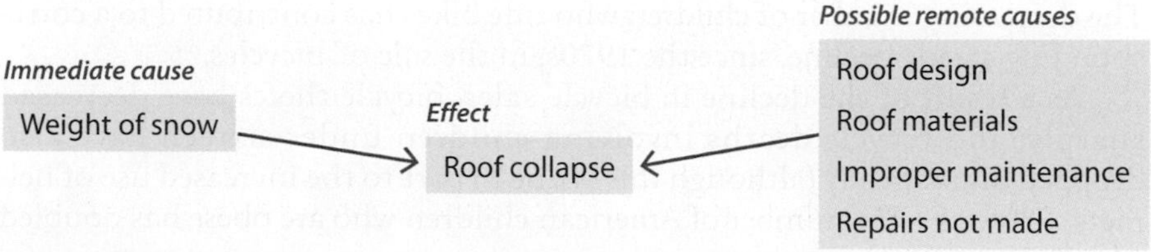

Remember that remote causes can be extremely important. In the Hartford roof collapse, as we have seen, a remote cause—the roof design—was actually the main cause of the accident.

Understanding Causal Chains

Sometimes an effect can also be a cause. This is true in a **causal chain**, where A causes B, B causes C, C causes D, and so on, as shown below.

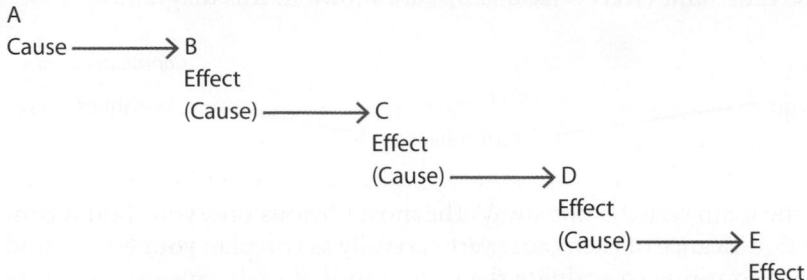

A
Cause ⟶ B
Effect
(Cause) ⟶ C
Effect
(Cause) ⟶ D
Effect
(Cause) ⟶ E
Effect

In causal chains, the result of one action is the cause of another. Leaving out any link in the chain, or failing to place any link in its proper order, destroys the logic and continuity of the chain.

A simple example of a causal chain is the recent suggestion by a group of retired generals that global warming might be a threat to U.S. national security. According to these generals, global warming could cause worldwide climate changes, such as droughts, which in turn might create a refugee crisis as people leave their homelands in search of clean water. The resulting refugee camps, the generals claim, become a breeding ground for terrorists, and it is these terrorists who threaten U.S. security.

Here is another example of a causal chain.

The Case of the Disappearing Bicycle. Today, the bicycle as a form of transportation for children is increasingly rare, with fewer than one percent of children now riding bicycles to school. In addition, fewer children ride bicycles for recreation than in the past. Causes cited for this decline include the absence of sidewalks in many newer suburban communities, parents' rising fears about crime and traffic accidents, the rise in the number of students who schedule back-to-back after-school activities (perhaps due in part to the increased number of households with no stay-at-home parent), the popularity of social media and video games, and the increased reliance on after-school jobs by teenagers (who often need cars, not bikes, to get to work). The decreasing number of children who ride bikes has contributed to a corresponding steady decline, since the 1970s, in the sale of bicycles.

As a result of the decline in bicycle sales, bicycle thefts have decreased sharply, and bicycle deaths involving children under sixteen have also dropped dramatically (although this is due in part to the increased use of helmets). However, the number of American children who are obese has doubled since the mid-1980s, in part because children get less and less exercise. So, factors such as fewer sidewalks and more working teenagers may have led to a decline in bicycle sales, which in turn could have had a far-reaching impact on children's health.

If your analysis of a situation reveals a causal chain, this discovery can be useful as you plan your essay. The identification of a causal chain suggests an organizational pattern, and following the chain helps you to discuss items in their logical order. Be careful, however, to keep your emphasis on the causal connections and not to lapse into narration.

Avoiding *Post Hoc* Reasoning

When developing a cause-and-effect essay, you should not assume that just because event A *precedes* event B, event A has *caused* event B. This illogical assumption, called ***post hoc* reasoning**, equates a chronological sequence with causality. When you fall into this trap – assuming, for instance, that you failed an exam because a black cat crossed your path the day before – you are mistaking coincidence for causality.

Consider the two following examples of *post hoc* reasoning.

The Case of the Magical Maggots. Until the late nineteenth century, many scientists accepted the notion of spontaneous generation; that is, they believed living things could arise directly from nonliving matter. To support their beliefs, they pointed to specific situations. For instance, they observed that maggots, the larvae of the housefly, seemed to arise directly from the decaying flesh of dead animals.

These scientists were confusing sequence with causality, assuming that because the presence of decaying meat preceded the appearance of maggots, the two were connected in a causal relationship. In fact, because the dead animals were exposed to the air, flies were free to lay eggs in the animals' bodies, and these eggs hatched into maggots. Therefore, the living maggots were not a direct result of the presence of nonliving matter. Although these scientists were applying the best technology and scientific theory of their time, hindsight reveals that their conclusions were not valid.

The Case of the Female Centenarians. Several years ago, medical researchers published findings reporting that female centenarians – women who had reached the age of one hundred – were four times as likely to have given birth when they were past forty as were women in a control group who had died at the age of seventy-three. Researchers saw no causal connection between childbirth after forty and long life, suggesting only that the centenarians might have been predisposed to live longer because they had reached menopause later than the other women. Local television newscasts and tabloid newspapers, however, misinterpreted the study's implications, presenting the relationship between late childbearing and long life as a causal one. In a vivid example of *post hoc* reasoning, one promotional spot for a local television newscast proclaimed, "Having kids late in life can help you live longer."

In your writing, as well as in your observations, it is neither logical nor fair to assume that a causal relationship exists unless clear, strong evidence supports that connection. When you revise a cause-and-effect essay, make sure you have not confused words such as *because, therefore,* and *consequently* (words that indicate a causal relationship) with words such as *then, next, subsequently, later,* and *afterward* (words that indicate a chronological relationship). When you use a word like *because,* you are signaling to readers that you are telling *why* something happened; when you use a word like *then,* you are only showing *when* it happened.

The ability to identify and analyze cause-and-effect relationships; to distinguish causes from effects and recognize causal chains; and to distinguish immediate from remote, main from contributory, and logical from illogical causes are all skills that will strengthen your writing.

Planning a Cause-and-Effect Essay

After you have sorted out the cause-and-effect relationships you will write about, you are ready to plan your essay. You have three basic options: to discuss causes, to discuss effects, or to discuss both causes and effects. Often, your assignment will suggest which of these options to use. Here are a few likely topics for cause-and-effect essays.

Focus on finding causes

- Discuss the factors that contributed to the declining population of state mental hospitals in the 1960s. (social work)
- Identify some possible causes of collective obsessional behavior. (psychology)

Focus on describing or predicting effects

- Evaluate the probable effects of moving elementary school children from a highly structured classroom to a relatively open classroom. (education)
- Discuss the impact of World War I on two of Ernest Hemingway's characters. (literature)

Focus on both causes and effects

- The 1840s were volatile years in Europe. Choose one social, political, or economic event that occurred during those years; analyze its causes; and briefly note how the event influenced later developments in European history. (history)

Developing a Thesis Statement

Of course, a cause-and-effect essay usually does more than just enumerate causes or effects; more often, it presents and supports a particular thesis. For example, an economics essay treating the major effects of the Vietnam War on the U.S. economy could be just a straightforward presentation of factual information – an attempt to inform readers of the war's economic impact. It is more likely, however, that the essay would not just list the war's effects but also indicate their significance. In fact, cause-and-effect analysis often requires you to weigh various factors so that you can assess their relative significance.

When you draft your **thesis statement**, be sure it identifies the relationships among the specific causes or effects you will discuss. This thesis statement should ideally tell your readers three things: the issues you plan to consider; the position you will take; and whether your emphasis will be on causes, effects, or both. Your thesis statement may also indicate explicitly or implicitly the cause or effect you consider most important and the order in which you will present your points.

Arranging Causes and Effects

When deciding on the sequence in which you will present causes or effects, you have several options. One option, of course, is chronological order: you can present causes or effects in the order in which they occurred. Another option is to introduce the main cause first and then the contributory causes – or, you can do just the opposite. If you want to stress positive consequences, begin by briefly discussing the negative ones; if you plan to emphasize negative results, summarize the less important positive effects first. Still another possibility is to begin by dismissing any events that were not causes and then explain what the real causes were. (This method is especially effective if you think your readers are likely to jump to *post hoc* conclusions.) Finally, you can begin with the most obvious causes or effects and move on to more subtle factors – and then to your analysis and conclusion.

Using Transitions

Cause-and-effect essays rely on clear transitions – *the first cause, the second cause; one result, another result* – to distinguish causes from effects and to help move readers from one cause or effect to the next. In essays that analyze complex causal relationships, transitions are even more important because they can help readers distinguish main from contributory causes (*the most important cause, another cause*) and immediate from remote causes (*the most obvious cause, a less apparent cause*). Transitions are also essential in a causal chain, where they can help readers sort out the sequence (*then, next*) as well as the causal relationships (*because, as a result, for this reason*). A more complete list of transitions appears on page 55.

Structuring a Cause-and-Effect Essay

Finding Causes

Suppose you are planning the social work essay mentioned earlier: "Discuss the factors that contributed to the declining population of state mental hospitals in the 1960s." Your assignment specifies an effect – the declining population of state mental hospitals – and asks you to discuss possible causes, which might include the following:

- An increasing acceptance of mental illness in our society
- Prohibitive costs of in-patient care
- Increasing numbers of mental health professionals, which made it possible to treat patients outside of hospitals

Many health professionals, however, believe that the most important cause was the development and use of psychotropic drugs, such as chlorpromazine (Thorazine), which can alter behavior. To emphasize this cause in your essay, you could draft the following thesis statement.

Less important causes **Effect** **Most important cause**	Although society's increasing acceptance of mental illness, the high cost of in-patient care, and the rise in the number of mental health professionals were all influential in reducing the population of state mental hospitals in the 1960s, the most important cause of this decline was the development and use of psychotropic drugs.

This thesis statement fully prepares your readers for your essay. It identifies the points you will consider, and it reveals your position: your assessment of the relative significance of the causes you identify. It states the less important causes first and indicates their secondary importance with *although*. In the body of your essay, the less important causes would be discussed first so that the essay could gradually build up to the most convincing material. An informal outline for your essay might look like the one that follows.

SAMPLE OUTLINE: Finding Causes

INTRODUCTION
(thesis statement)

Although society's increasing acceptance of mental illness, the high cost of in-patient care, and the rise in the number of mental health professionals were all influential in reducing the population of state mental hospitals in the 1960s, the most important cause of this decline was the development and use of psychotropic drugs.

POINT 1

First cause: Increasing acceptance of mental illness

POINT 2
Second cause: High cost of in-patient care

POINT 3
Third cause: Rise in the number of mental health professionals

POINT 4
Fourth (and most important) cause: Development and use of psychotropic drugs

CONCLUSION
Restatement of thesis (in different words) or summary of key points

Describing or Predicting Effects

Suppose you were planning an education essay on the topic mentioned earlier: "Evaluate the probable effects of moving elementary school children from a highly structured classroom to a relatively open classroom." For this assignment, you would focus on effects rather than on causes. After brainstorming to help you decide which specific points to discuss, you might draft this thesis statement.

Cause Moving children from a highly structured classroom to a relatively open one is desirable because it is likely to encourage **Effects** more independent play, more flexibility in forming friendship groups, and, ultimately, more creativity.

This thesis statement clearly tells readers the stand you will take and the main points you will consider in your essay. The thesis also clearly indicates that these points are *effects* of the open classroom. After introducing the cause, your essay would treat these three effects in the order in which they are presented in the thesis statement, building up to the most important effect. An informal outline of your essay might look like the one below.

SAMPLE OUTLINE: Describing or Predicting Effects

INTRODUCTION
(thesis statement)
Moving children from a highly structured classroom to a relatively open one is desirable because it is likely to encourage more independent play, more flexibility in forming friendship groups, and, ultimately, more creativity.

POINT 1
First effect: More independent play

POINT 2
Second effect: More flexibility in forming friendship groups

POINT 3
Third (and most important) effect: More creativity

CONCLUSION
Restatement of thesis (in different words) or summary of key points

Revising a Cause-and-Effect Essay

When you revise a cause-and-effect essay, consider the items on the revision checklist on page 66. In addition, pay special attention to the items on the following checklist, which apply specifically to cause-and-effect essays.

REVISION CHECKLIST CAUSE AND EFFECT

- ☐ Does your assignment call for a discussion of causes, effects, or both causes and effects?
- ☐ Does your essay have a clearly stated thesis that indicates whether you will focus on causes, effects, or both?
- ☐ Have you considered all possible causes and all possible effects?
- ☐ Have you distinguished between the main (most important) cause and the contributory (less important) causes?
- ☐ Have you distinguished between immediate and remote causes?
- ☐ Have you identified a causal chain in your reasoning?
- ☐ Have you avoided *post hoc* reasoning?
- ☐ Have you used transitional words and phrases to show how the causes and effects you discuss are related?

Editing a Cause-and-Effect Essay

When you edit your cause-and-effect essay, follow the guidelines on the editing checklists on pages 83, 86, and 89. In addition, focus on the grammar, mechanics, and punctuation issues that are particularly relevant to cause-and-effect essays. Two of these issues – avoiding faulty "the reason is because" constructions and using *affect* and *effect* correctly – are discussed here.

GRAMMAR IN CONTEXT AVOIDING "THE REASON IS BECAUSE"; USING *AFFECT* AND *EFFECT* CORRECTLY

Avoiding "the reason is because" When you discuss causes and effects, you may find yourself using the phrase "the reason is." If you follow this phrase with *because* ("the reason is *because*"), you will create an error.

The word *because* means "for the reason that." Therefore, it is redundant to say "the reason is because" (which literally means "the reason is for the reason that"). You can correct this error by substituting *that* for *because* ("the reason is *that*").

INCORRECT: One reason for the famine in nineteenth-century Ireland was because the potato crop failed.

CORRECT: One reason for the famine in nineteenth-century Ireland was that the potato crop failed.

Using Affect and Effect Correctly When you write a cause-and-effect essay, you will probably use the words *affect* and *effect* quite often. For this reason, it is important that you know the difference between *affect* and *effect*.

- *Affect*, usually a verb, means "to influence."

  Linda M. Hasselstrom believes that carrying a gun has affected her life in a positive way.

- *Effect*, usually a noun, means "a result."

  Linda M. Hasselstrom believes that carrying a gun has had a positive effect on her life.

NOTE: *Effect* can also be a verb meaning "to bring about" ("She worked hard to effect change in the community").

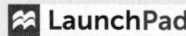

LaunchPad

For more practice on structuring your sentences, see the LearningCurve on Sentence Structure in the LaunchPad for *Patterns*.

EDITING CHECKLIST CAUSE AND EFFECT

- ☐ Have you used verb tenses correctly to distinguish among events that happened earlier, at the same time, and later?
- ☐ In a complex sentence that includes a dependent clause introduced by *because,* have you placed a comma after the dependent clause when it comes *before* the independent clause ("Because the party was so crowded, we left early")? Have you been careful *not* to use a comma when the dependent clause *follows* the independent clause ("We left early because the party was so crowded")?
- ☐ Have you used "the reason is that" (not "the reason is because")?
- ☐ Have you used *affect* and *effect* correctly?

A STUDENT WRITER: Cause and Effect

The following midterm exam, written for a history class, analyzes both the causes and the effects of the famine that occurred in Ireland during the 1840s. Notice how the writer, Evelyn Pellicane, concentrates on causes but also discusses briefly the effects of this tragedy, just as the exam question directs.

Question: The 1840s were volatile years in Europe. Choose one social, political, or economic event that occurred during those years, analyze its causes, and briefly note how the event influenced later developments in European history.

The Irish Famine, 1845–1849

Thesis statement

1 The Irish famine, which brought hardship and tragedy to Ireland during the 1840s, was caused and prolonged by four basic factors: the failure of the potato crop, the landlord-tenant system, errors in government policy, and the long-standing prejudice of the British toward Ireland.

First cause

2 The immediate cause of the famine was the failure of the potato crop. In 1845, potato disease struck the crop, and potatoes rotted in the ground. The 1846 crop also failed, and before long people were eating weeds. The 1847 crop was healthy, but there were not enough potatoes to go around, and in 1848 the blight struck again, leading to more and more evictions of tenants by landlords.

Second cause

3 The tenants' position on the land had never been very secure. Most had no leases and could be turned out by their landlords at any time. If a tenant owed rent, he was evicted — or, worse, put in prison, leaving his family to starve. The threat of prison caused many tenants to leave their land; those who could leave Ireland did so, sometimes with money provided by their landlords. Some landlords did try to take care of their tenants, but most did not. Many were absentee landlords who spent their rent money abroad.

Third cause

4 Government policy errors, although not an immediate cause of the famine, played an important role in creating an unstable economy and perpetuating starvation. In 1846, the government decided not to continue selling corn, as it had during the first year of the famine, claiming that low-cost purchases of corn by Ireland had paralyzed British trade by interfering with free enterprise. Therefore, 1846 saw a starving population, angry demonstrations, and panic; even those with money were unable to buy food. Still, the government insisted that if it sent food to Ireland, prices would rise in the rest of the United Kingdom and that this would be unfair to hardworking English and Scots. As a result, no food was sent. Throughout the years of the famine, the British government aggravated an already grave situation:

they did nothing to improve agricultural operations, to help people adjust to another crop, to distribute seeds, or to reform the landlord-tenant system that made the tenants' position so insecure.

Fourth cause

At the root of this poor government policy was the long-standing 5
British prejudice against the Irish. Hostility between the two countries went back some six hundred years, and the British were simply not about to inconvenience themselves to save the Irish. When the Irish so desperately needed grain to replace the damaged potatoes, it was clear that grain had to be imported from England. This meant, however, that the Corn Laws, which had been enacted to keep the price of British corn high by taxing imported grain, had to be repealed. The British were unwilling to repeal the Corn Laws. Even when they did supply cornmeal, they made no attempt to explain to the Irish how to cook this unfamiliar food. Moreover, the British government was determined to make Ireland pay for its own poor, so it forced the collection of taxes. Since many landlords could not collect the tax money, they were forced to evict their tenants. The British government's callous and indifferent treatment of the Irish has been called genocide.

Effects

As a result of this devastating famine, the population of 6
Ireland was reduced from about nine million to about six and one-half million. During the famine years, men roamed the streets looking for work, begging when they found none. Epidemics of "famine fever" and dysentery reduced the population drastically. The most important historical result of the famine, however, was the massive immigration to the United States, Canada, and Great Britain of poor, unskilled people who had to struggle to fit into a skilled economy and who brought with them a deep-seated hatred of the British. (This same hatred remained strong in Ireland itself — so strong that during World War II, Ireland, then independent, remained neutral rather than coming to England's aid.) Irish immigrants faced slums, fever epidemics, joblessness, and hostility — even anti-Catholic and anti-Irish riots — in Boston, New York, London, Glasgow, and Quebec. In Ireland itself, poverty and discontent continued, and by 1848 those emigrating from Ireland included a more highly skilled class of farmers, the ones Ireland needed to recover and to survive.

Conclusion (includes restatement of thesis)

The Irish famine, one of the great tragedies of the nineteenth 7
century, was a natural disaster compounded by the insensitivity of the British government and the archaic agricultural system of Ireland. Although the deaths that resulted depleted Ireland's resources even more, the men and women who immigrated to other countries permanently enriched those nations.

Points for Special Attention

Structure. This essay is relatively long; if it were not so clearly organized, it would be difficult to follow. Because the essay was to focus primarily on causes, Evelyn first introduces the effect—the famine itself—and then considers its causes. After she examines each cause in turn, she moves on to the results of the famine, treating the most important result last. In this essay, then, the famine is first treated as an effect and later, as a cause. In fact, the famine itself is the central link in a causal chain.

Evelyn devotes one paragraph to her introduction and one to each cause; she sums up the famine's results in a separate paragraph and devotes the final paragraph to her conclusion. (Depending on a particular essay's length and complexity, more—or less—than one paragraph may be devoted to each cause or effect.) An informal outline for her essay might look like this.

The Irish Famine

Introduction (including thesis statement)
First cause: Failure of the potato crop
Second cause: The landlord-tenant system
Third cause: Errors in government policy
Fourth cause: British prejudice
Results of the famine
Conclusion

Because Evelyn saw all the causes as important and interrelated, she decided not to present them in order of increasing importance. Instead, she begins with the immediate cause of the famine—the failure of the potato crop—and then digs more deeply until she arrives at the most remote cause, British prejudice.

Transitions. Because Evelyn considers a series of relationships as well as an intricate causal chain, the cause-and-effect relationships in this essay are both subtle and complex. Throughout the essay, many words suggest cause-and-effect connections: *brought, caused, leading to, therefore, as a result, so, since,* and the like. These words help readers to identify and understand the causal connections.

Answering an Exam Question. Before planning her answer, Evelyn read the exam question carefully. She saw that it asked for both causes and effects but that its wording directed her to spend more time on causes ("analyze") than on effects ("briefly note"), and this wording helped her to organize her discussion. In addition, she saw that she would need to indicate *explicitly* which were the causes ("government policy . . . played an important role") and which were the effects ("The most important historical result").

Evelyn's purpose was to convey factual information and thus to demonstrate her understanding of the course material. Rather than waste her limited time choosing a clever opening strategy or making elaborate attempts to engage her audience, she decided to begin her essay with a direct statement of her thesis.

Working with Sources. Evelyn was obviously influenced by outside sources; the ideas in the essay are not completely her own. Because this was an exam, however, and because the instructor expected students to base their essays on class notes and assigned readings, Evelyn was not required to document her sources.

Focus on Revision

Because this essay was written for an exam, Evelyn had no time—and no need—to revise it further. If she had been preparing this assignment outside of class, however, she might have done more. For example, she could have added a more arresting opening, such as a brief eyewitness account of the famine's effects. Her conclusion—appropriately brief and straightforward for an exam answer—could also have been developed further, perhaps with the addition of information about the nation's eventual recovery. Finally, adding statistics, quotations by historians, or a brief summary of life in Ireland before the famine could have further enriched the essay.

PEER-EDITING WORKSHEET CAUSE AND EFFECT

1. Paraphrase the essay's thesis. Is it explicitly stated? Should it be?
2. Does the essay focus on causes, effects, or both? Does the thesis statement clearly identify this focus? If not, how should the thesis statement be revised?
3. Does the writer consider *all* relevant causes or effects? Are any key causes or effects omitted? Are any irrelevant causes or effects included?
4. Make an informal outline of the essay. What determines the order of the causes or effects? Is this the most effective order? If not, what revisions do you suggest?
5. List the transitional words and phrases used to indicate causal connections. Are any additional transitions needed? If so, where?
6. Does the writer use *post hoc* reasoning? Point out any examples of illogical reasoning.
7. Are more examples or details needed to help readers understand causal connections? If so, where?
8. Do you find the writer's conclusions convincing? Why or why not?
9. Has the writer used any "the reason is because" constructions? If so, suggest revisions.
10. Are *affect* and *effect* used correctly? Point out any errors.

All the selections that follow focus on cause-and-effect relationships. Some readings focus on causes, others on effects. The first selection, a visual text, is followed by questions designed to illustrate how cause and effect can operate in visual form.

JEFFREY COOLIDGE

Rube Goldberg Machine

Jeffrey Coolidge/Getty Images

• • •

Reading Images

1. This image shows a device inspired by Rube Goldberg, a cartoonist and inventor known for devising complex machines that carry out simple tasks in roundabout, overly complex ways. What task is depicted here? In what straightforward way could it be completed?
2. Study the image carefully. Does every event have a cause? Does every cause have a result? Does this diagram illustrate a causal chain? Why or why not?
3. What is the end result depicted here? Which event do you see as the main cause? Which events are remote causes?

Journal Entry

Write a paragraph summarizing the cause-and-effect relationships depicted in this image.

Thematic Connections

- “Getting Coffee Is Hard to Do” (page 283)
- “How to Build a Monster from Spare Parts” (page 287)
- “Naming of Parts” (page 476)

JOSH BARRO

Why Stealing Cars Went Out of Fashion

Josh Barro, a journalist and political commentator, is currently a senior editor at *Business Insider*. Previously, he was a senior fellow at the Manhattan Institute for Policy Research. Barro appears regularly on MSNBC and Bloomberg Television. He is also the host of KCRW radio's political talk show "Left, Right, & Center."

Background on anti-car theft measures According to the National Highway Traffic Safety Administration, motor vehicle theft in the United States became a growing problem in the 1980s and peaked in the late 1980s and early 1990s. In 1990, for example, there were 1,270,000 car thefts; in 2014, there were 689,527. Although stolen cars may suggest images of joyriding teenagers engaged in a low-level property crime, law enforcement officials point out that these thefts can be connected to far more serious problems, such as terrorism and organized crime. Over the years, the federal government has passed major legislation to address the problem, including the Motor Vehicle Theft Law Enforcement Act of 1984 and the Anti Car Theft Act of 1992. Among other measures, these initiatives required vehicle identification numbers (VINs) on multiple parts of cars; increased federal penalties for car theft; and made the titling, registration, and car-salvaging process stricter and more highly regulated than it had been. Anti-theft devices on automobiles have also evolved, from car- and steering-wheel locks to car alarms and the improvements that Barro discusses in the following essay, which was written in 2014.

1 Auto theft isn't much of a problem anymore in New York City. In 1990, the city had 147,000 reported auto thefts, one for every 50 residents; last year, there were just 7,400, or one per 1,100. That's a 96 percent drop in the rate of car theft.

2 So, why did this happen? All crime has fallen, nationally and especially in New York. But there has also been a big shift in the economics of auto theft: Stealing cars is harder than it used to be, less lucrative, and more likely to land you in jail. As such, people have found other things to do.

"Stealing cars is harder than it used to be, less lucrative, and more likely to land you in jail."

3 The most important factor is a technological advance: engine immobilizer systems, adopted by manufacturers in the late 1990s and early 2000s. These make it essentially impossible to start a car without the ignition key, which contains a microchip uniquely programmed by the dealer to match the car.

Criminals generally have not been able to circumvent the technology or make counterfeit keys. "It's very difficult; not just your average perpetrator on the street is going to be able to steal those cars," said Capt. Don Boller, who leads the New York Police Department's auto crime division. Instead, criminals have stuck to stealing older cars. 4

You can see this in the pattern of thefts of America's most stolen car, the Honda Accord. About 54,000 Accords were stolen in 2013, 84 percent of them from model years 1997 or earlier, according to data from the National Insurance Crime Bureau, a trade group for auto insurers and lenders. Not coincidentally, Accords started to be sold with immobilizers in the 1998 model year. The Honda Civic, America's second-most stolen car, shows a similar pattern before and after it got immobilizer technology for model year 2001. 5

Old cars are easier to steal, and there are plenty of them still on the road. But there's an obvious problem with stealing them: They're not worth very much. Cars are typically stolen for parts, and as a car gets older, its parts become less valuable. 6

In New York, thieves often take old stolen cars to salvage yards, selling them for scrap for just hundreds of dollars. As *The Times* reported in April, they're helped by a New York State law that allows a car to be scrapped without its title if it is more than eight years old and worth less than $1,250. But in addition to not being very lucrative, that approach has gotten harder to get away with. According to Captain Boller, faster tracking through the National Motor Vehicle Title Information System has helped the city quickly identify stolen cars sold to salvage yards. Because you must present a photo I.D. to scrap a car without a title, the city has had success tracking down and arresting the sellers. 7

With fewer valuable stolen cars coming in, it has become less appealing to operate an illegal chop shop. And the decline in thefts has freed up the 85 detectives and supervisors of New York's auto crime division to focus on stopping organized car theft rings, the sorts of operations that actually have the ability to make coded keys for newer cars. "Our main goal is to get criminal enterprise charges on these groups," Captain Boller said of sending the groups' members to prison with longer sentences than apply to auto theft alone. 8

Similar efforts by law enforcement in other jurisdictions have cut into auto theft nationally, according to Roger Morris, the vice president of the National Insurance Crime Bureau. "You saw a dramatic impact on the professional car theft rings, the chop shops, and all that," he said. But while auto theft has been greatly reduced in New York, the national decline (62 percent) has not been as drastic. 9

Car theft remains a particular problem in California, which has the country's highest auto theft rate, nearly double the national average and five times New York State's. According to data compiled by the N.I.C.B., nine of the 10 metropolitan areas with the highest auto theft rates are in California, mostly up and down the inland Interstate 5 corridor. According to Mr. Morris, California's car thefts are often linked to Mexican organized crime, and N.I.C.B. helps auto insurers recover thousands of stolen cars from Mexico annually. 10

Some cars go even farther away. "A lot of them are getting shipped out of the country," said Carol Kaplan, the N.I.C.B.'s director of public affairs. Every year, Customs and Border Protection recovers dozens of cars that thieves try to smuggle out of the Ports of Los Angeles and Long Beach in shipping containers. 11

But while the port busts tend to recover high-end cars (one 2012 recovery included a 2010 Ferrari 458 Italia), California's thefts are heavily weighted toward older cars that can be slim-jimmed and hot-wired, and that are much more likely to end up in Mexico than in Asia. In time, those old cars will come off the road, leading to a further decline in auto thefts. 12

One of the factors that keeps car theft going in the United States is the reliability of old Hondas. Eventually, mid-1990s sedans should become too old to be worth stealing at all, but that hasn't happened yet. "They keep running," said Mr. Morris, and therefore they keep being stolen. 13

• • •

Comprehension

1. Why, according to Barro, has stealing cars gone "out of fashion"? List as many of his reasons as you can. Which one do you see as the main (most important) cause of this decline?
2. Barro's essay focuses on New York City, where auto thefts declined 96 percent between 1990 and 2013, but "the national decline (62 percent) has not been as drastic" (9). How does Barro explain this disparity?
3. Why does Barro focus on the Honda Accord? Does this focus support or undercut his conclusions?
4. Why are older cars easier to steal than newer cars? If older cars are "not worth very much" (6), why do thieves continue to steal them?
5. In paragraph 2, Barro notes that "people have found other things to do" instead of stealing cars. What "other things" might he have in mind?

Purpose and Audience

1. Do you think Barro's thesis is "Stealing cars is no longer as popular as it once was," or do you think he has a different point in mind? Explain.
2. Is Barro's sole purpose here to inform his audience, or does he have a persuasive purpose as well?
3. What expert opinion does Barro provide to support his points? Do these comments provide enough support? What other kinds of sources could he cite?

Style and Structure

1. Does this essay focus primarily on causes or on effects? How can you tell?
2. **Vocabulary Project.** What is a *chop shop* (9)? Do you think this informal usage – as well as the use of *port busts* (12) and *slim-jimmed and hot-wired* (12) – is appropriate? Why or why not?

3. Identify a **causal chain** in this essay, and use arrows to diagram it (as on page 320).
4. Do you think the expression "out of fashion" in Barro's title is effective, or do you think it trivializes his subject? Can you suggest another title?

Journal Entry

Barro's focus in this essay is on professional car thieves. Do you suppose stealing cars has also gone "out of fashion" among joyriding teenagers? Why or why not?

Writing Workshop

1. Imagine you are a police officer speaking at a local high school. Your purpose is to discourage students from "borrowing" cars for joyriding. Write out your speech, structuring it as a cause-and-effect essay that focuses on the likely negative consequences of such actions as well as on the reasons auto theft is not as easy as your audience might think.
2. **Working with Sources.** In paragraph 2, Barro notes that in recent years in New York City and across the nation, "all crime has fallen." Research crime statistics for your city or town, and identify a category of crime that has shown a decline. Then, write a cause-and-effect essay with the title "Why ________________ Has Gone Out of Fashion." Be sure to provide parenthetical documentation for any statistics you cite as well as for any other information you use (for example, analyses found in newspaper articles) and to include a works-cited page. (See Chapter 18 for information on MLA documentation.)

Combining the Patterns

Barro relies heavily on **exemplification** in this essay. Identify several of the examples he provides, and explain how each supports his essay's main idea.

Thematic Connections

- "The Money" (page 111)
- "Stability in Motion" (page 178)
- "Ten Ways We Get the Odds Wrong" (page 245)

MAGGIE KOERTH-BAKER

Why Rational People Buy into Conspiracy Theories

Maggie Koerth-Baker (b. 1981) is a senior science writer at *FiveThirtyEight*, a statistics-focused website that analyzes polling, economics, and sports. Previously, she was a science writer and editor at *Boing Boing*, a blog that covers technology and culture, as well as a columnist for the *New York Times*. Her work has also appeared in *Discover*, *Popular Science*, and other publications. Koerth-Baker is also the author of *Before the Lights Go Out: Conquering the Energy Crisis Before It Conquers Us* (2012).

Background on famous conspiracy theories In her essay, Koerth-Baker refers to historian Richard Hofstadter's famous 1965 work, *The Paranoid Style in American Politics*. For Hofstadter, American politics — and implicitly, American life — was often marked by a sense of "heated exaggeration, suspiciousness, and conspiratorial fantasy." However, the belief in such fantasies knows no geographical or temporal boundaries. For example, anti-Semitic conspiracy theories stretch back to at least the Middle Ages and, later, were infamously promoted in *The Protocols of the Elders of Zion* (1903), a fraudulent text that claimed to reveal a scheme for Jewish world domination. Despite being a hoax, *The Protocols* appealed to prominent figures like Adolf Hitler and Henry Ford. As Hofstadter suggested, however, the United States has long been fertile ground for conspiracy theories, as in the case of nineteenth-century American fears of Catholics and Freemasons. In the twentieth century, many such theories flourished — often related to communism and the dangerous presence of internal enemies. For example, some Americans viewed the widespread fluoridation of the U.S. water supply in the 1950s and early 1960s as a subversive plot. Other conspiracies have focused on extraterrestrials and the government cover-up of alien activity, as in the case of Area 51, a military installation in Nevada that has long been a topic of conspiracy theorists. As Hofstadter noted, American politics (and political figures) has often attracted conspiratorial thinking. This is evident in such recent theories as "The Clinton Body Count" (a list of people supposedly killed directly or indirectly by President Bill Clinton); the belief that President George W. Bush was actively complicit in the September 11, 2001, terrorist attacks; and the claim that President Barack Obama is not a U.S. citizen.

In the days following the bombings at the Boston Marathon, speculation online regarding the identity and motive of the unknown perpetrator or perpetrators was rampant. And once the Tsarnaev brothers were identified and the manhunt came to a close, the speculation didn't cease. It took a new form. A sampling: Maybe the brothers Tsarnaev were just patsies, fall guys set up to take the heat for a mysterious Saudi with high-level connections; or maybe 1 they were innocent, but instead of the Saudis, the actual bomber had acted on behalf of a rogue branch of our own government; or what if the Tsarnaevs were behind the attacks, but were secretly working for a larger organization?

Crazy as these theories are, those propagating them are not—they're quite normal, in fact. But recent scientific research tells us this much: if you think one of the theories above is plausible, you probably feel the same way about the others, even though they contradict one another. And it's very likely that this isn't the only news story that makes you feel as if shadowy forces are behind major world events. 2

"The best predictor of belief in a conspiracy theory is belief in other conspiracy theories," says Viren Swami, a psychology professor who studies conspiracy belief at the University of Westminster in England. Psychologists say that's because a conspiracy theory isn't so much a response to a single event as it is an expression of an overarching worldview. 3

As Richard Hofstadter wrote in his seminal 1965 book, *The Paranoid Style in American Politics*, conspiracy theories, especially those involving meddlesome foreigners, are a favorite pastime in this nation. Americans have always had the sneaking suspicion that somebody was out to get us—be it Freemasons, Catholics, or communists. But in recent years, it seems as if every tragedy comes with a round of yarn-spinning, as the Web fills with stories about "false flag" attacks and "crisis actors"—not mere theorizing but arguments for the existence of a completely alternate version of reality. 4

Since Hofstadter's book was published, our access to information has vastly improved, which you would think would have helped minimize such wild speculation. But according to recent scientific research on the matter, it most likely only serves to make theories more convincing to the public. What's even more surprising is that this sort of theorizing isn't limited to those on the margins. Perfectly sane minds possess an incredible capacity for developing narratives, and even some of the wildest conspiracy theories can be grounded in rational thinking, which makes them that much more pernicious. Consider this: 63 percent of registered American voters believe in at least one political conspiracy theory, according to a recent poll conducted by Fairleigh Dickinson University. 5

While psychologists can't know exactly what goes on inside our heads, they have, through surveys and laboratory studies, come up with a set of traits that correlate well with conspiracy belief. In 2010, Swami and a co-author summarized this research in *The Psychologist*, a scientific journal. They found, perhaps surprisingly, that believers are more likely to be cynical about the world in general and politics in particular. Conspiracy theories also seem to be more compelling to those with low self-worth, especially with regard to their sense of agency in the world at large. Conspiracy theories appear to be a way of reacting to uncertainty and powerlessness. 6

"Conspiracy theories appear to be a way of reacting to uncertainty and powerlessness."

Economic recessions, terrorist attacks, and natural disasters are massive, looming threats, but we have little power over when they occur or how or what happens afterward. In these moments of powerlessness and uncertainty, a part of the brain called the amygdala kicks into action. Paul Whalen, a scientist at Dartmouth College who studies the amygdala, says it doesn't exactly do anything on its own. Instead, the amygdala jump-starts the rest of the brain into analytical overdrive – prompting repeated reassessments of information in an attempt to create a coherent and understandable narrative, to understand what just happened, what threats still exist, and what should be done now. This may be a useful way to understand how, writ large, the brain's capacity for generating new narratives after shocking events can contribute to so much paranoia in this country. 7

"If you know the truth and others don't, that's one way you can reassert feelings of having agency," Swami says. It can be comforting to do your own research even if that research is flawed. It feels good to be the wise old goat in a flock of sheep. 8

Surprisingly, Swami's work has also turned up a correlation between conspiracy theorizing and strong support of democratic principles. But this isn't quite so strange if you consider the context. Kathryn Olmsted, a historian at the University of California, Davis, says that conspiracy theories wouldn't exist in a world in which real conspiracies don't exist. And those conspiracies – Watergate or the Iran-Contra Affair – often involve manipulating and circumventing the democratic process. Even people who believe that the Sandy Hook shooting was actually a drama staged by actors couch their arguments in concern for the preservation of the Second Amendment. 9

Our access to high-quality information has not, unfortunately, ushered in an age in which disagreements of this sort can easily be solved with a quick Google search. In fact, the Internet has made things worse. Confirmation bias – the tendency to pay more attention to evidence that supports what you already believe – is a well-documented and common human failing. People have been writing about it for centuries. In recent years, though, researchers have found that confirmation bias is not easy to overcome. You can't just drown it in facts. 10

In 2006, the political scientists Brendan Nyhan and Jason Reifler identified a phenomenon called the "backfire effect." They showed that efforts to debunk inaccurate political information can leave people more convinced that false information is true than they would have been otherwise. Nyhan isn't sure why this happens, but it appears to be more prevalent when the bad information helps bolster a favored worldview or ideology. 11

In that way, Swami says, the Internet and other media have helped perpetuate paranoia. Not only does more exposure to these alternative narratives help engender belief in conspiracies, he says, but the Internet's tendency toward tribalism helps reinforce misguided beliefs. 12

And that's a problem. Because while believing George W. Bush helped plan the September 11 attacks might make you *feel* in control, it doesn't 13 actually make you so. Earlier this year, Karen Douglas, a University of Kent psychologist, along with a student, published research in which they exposed people to conspiracy theories about climate change and the death of Princess Diana. Those who got information supporting the theories but not information debunking them were more likely to withdraw from participation in politics and were less likely to take action to reduce their carbon footprints.

Alex Jones, a syndicated radio host, can build fame as a conspiracy peddler; 14 politicians can hint at conspiracies for votes and leverage; but if conspiracy theories are a tool the average person uses to reclaim his sense of agency and access to democracy, it's an ineffective tool. It can even have dangerous health implications. For example, research has shown that African Americans who believe AIDS is a weapon loosed on them by the government (remembering the abuses of the Tuskegee experiment) are less likely to practice protected sex. And if you believe that governments or corporations are hiding evidence that vaccines harm children, you're less likely to have your children vaccinated. The result: pockets of measles and whooping-cough infections and a few deaths in places with low child-vaccination rates.

Psychologists aren't sure whether powerlessness causes conspiracy the- 15 ories or vice versa. Either way, the current scientific thinking suggests these beliefs are nothing more than an extreme form of cynicism, a turning away from politics and traditional media—which only perpetuates the problem.

• • •

Comprehension

1. What is a conspiracy theory? List some of the examples Koerth-Baker gives to illustrate this concept.
2. In paragraph 3, Koerth-Baker cites psychologists who say that "a conspiracy theory isn't so much a response to a single event as it is an expression of an overarching worldview." What do these psychologists mean?
3. What is "confirmation bias" (10)? What is the "backfire effect" (11)?
4. What traits "correlate well with conspiracy belief" (6)? How is belief in conspiracy theories related to "strong support of democratic principles" (9)?
5. How do the Internet and other media help "perpetuate paranoia" (12)?
6. According to Koerth-Baker, exactly why do "rational people buy into conspiracy theories"?
7. What effects of the belief in conspiracy theories does Koerth-Baker identify? Does she see these effects as generally positive or negative?

Purpose and Audience

1. This essay addresses a serious issue and relies for support on expert testimony, yet its style and tone are quite informal. What does this tell you about the writer's purpose and intended audience?

2. Koerth-Baker quotes psychology professor Viren Swami and political scientist Richard Hofstadter and also cites historians and scientists. How do the words of these experts support the point she is making?
3. Why do you think Koerth-Baker uses the phrase "rational people" (instead of just "people") in her title? How is her audience likely to respond to this phrase? How does she appeal to her audience in a similar way elsewhere in the essay – for example, with the statistic in paragraph 5?
4. Could any of the following sentences serve as the thesis of this essay?
   - "Crazy as these theories are, those propagating them are not – they're quite normal, in fact." (2)
   - "'The best predictor of belief in a conspiracy theory is belief in other conspiracy theories.'" (3)
   - "Psychologists aren't sure whether powerlessness causes conspiracy theories or vice versa." (15)

   If not, can you suggest a more appropriate thesis statement for this essay?

Style and Structure

1. As the title suggests, this essay's primary focus is on the causes of conspiracy theories. Where does Koerth-Baker discuss the effects?
2. Could this essay be diagrammed as a causal chain? Try to create a diagram to illustrate such a chain.
3. **Vocabulary Project.** What is paranoia? Look up this word in a few different dictionaries – including a medical or psychological dictionary – and explain how it might be related to belief in conspiracy theories.

Journal Entry

Reread this essay's first paragraph. Do any of the rumors Koerth-Baker cites seem plausible to you? Why or why not?

Writing Workshop

1. Visit one of the many conspiracy theory sites on the web, and skim some of the theories described there. Identify one theory that you think makes sense. Then, write a cause-and-effect essay in which you explain what led you to accept this theory.
2. **Working with Sources.** Conspiracy theories have been popular throughout history. Consult a few websites to get an overview of some popular conspiracy theories – for example, those surrounding the moon landing, 9/11, the assassination of JFK, or another historical event – and ask some of your friends which of these theories they find believable. Then, write an essay in which you try to account for what might have led to these theories and some possible effects of such beliefs. Be sure to provide parenthetical documentation for any references to Koerth-Baker's essay, and include a works-cited page. (See Chapter 18 for information on MLA documentation.)

Combining the Patterns

Koerth-Baker's essay uses **exemplification** to illustrate the causes and effects of conspiracy theories. Does she include enough examples? Could she have included more, or better, examples?

Thematic Connections

- "Ground Zero" (page 173)
- "Just Walk On By: A Black Man Ponders His Power to Alter Public Space" (page 233)
- "The Lottery" (page 304)
- "The Ways We Lie" (page 466)

SIMON COTTEE

What Motivates Terrorists?

Simon Cottee is a senior lecturer in criminology at the University of Kent in Canterbury, England, as well as a contributing writer to the *Atlantic* magazine. Previously, he worked at Bangor University in Wales and at the University of the West Indies in Trinidad. Cottee attended Cambridge University, the London School of Economics, and Keele University, where he earned a Ph.D. in criminology. He is the author of *Apostates: When Muslims Leave Islam* (2015) and coeditor of *Christopher Hitchens and His Critics: Terror, Iraq, and the Left* (2008).

Background on *American Pastoral* In discussing the motivations of contemporary international terrorists, criminologist and sociologist Simon Cottee takes what might appear to be a curious turn: a detour into the 1997 Philip Roth novel *American Pastoral*. In this novel, Seymour Levov, a father and successful businessman — one who created a seemingly idyllic life for his family — tries to discover what led his daughter to engage in terrorist bombings in the 1960s. Roth's novel details the lead character's desperate preoccupation with the motivation behind his daughter's radical violence, thus presenting a parallel between the protagonist and Cottee's own readers, who are presumably seeking the same answers about modern-day terrorist action. The action in the novel, however, is narrated from the perspective of a former classmate of Seymour Levov's brother, creating distance between the reader and a sense of the unreal in the recounting of Levov's tragic experiences. Roth concludes *American Pastoral*, which won the Pulitzer Prize for Fiction in 1998, with reflections on the false peace of society and the question of whether one person might ever truly understand another. *American Pastoral* was adapted into a movie directed by Ewan McGregor, which premiered at the 2016 Toronto International Film Festival.

One of the most frequently asked questions about terrorism is also the most intractable. Why? Why do they do it? Why do people join terrorist groups and participate in acts of terrorism? 1

There are as many answers to this question as there are terrorist groups, and everyone from clerics to caustic cab drivers seems to have a confident opinion on the subject, as though the interior world of terrorists can be easily mined and mapped. But this confidence is often misplaced, given how little scholars actually know about terrorism and the people who are involved in it. It also betrays an epic obliviousness about just how difficult it is to access the internal, subjective desires and emotions that shape the outer world. Instead of asking why people join terrorist groups and commit terrorist atrocities, a more worthwhile starting point for explanation is to ask how. 2

One culturally prevalent answer to the why question is that terrorists are "driven" or "pushed" to do it, and that the decisive driving or pushing agent 3 is pathology. This answer has evolved in recent years in line with advances in knowledge and moral sensibilities. In terrorism studies in the late 1960s, it was not uncommon for scholars to conceive of pathology as a psychological abnormality or affliction rooted inside the individual. Since the 1980s, this idea has fallen into disrepute, and the scholarly consensus now holds that the roots of terrorism lie not in the individual, but in the wider circumstances in which terrorists live and act.

This reflects a broader consensus in the social sciences about violence: 4 namely, that it is "socially determined," a product of deeper historical, economic, or cultural forces over and above the individual. It is perhaps best summarized by the renowned social psychologist Albert Bandura.* Drawing on studies of violence from across the human sciences, Bandura concluded that "it requires conducive social conditions rather than monstrous people to produce atrocious deeds. Given appropriate social conditions, decent, ordinary people can be led to do extraordinarily cruel things." Social scientists argue about the nature and impact of the "social conditions" in question, but few would question the essential point that violence, however personalized or idiosyncratic its expression, is primarily rooted in historical structures or social relationships, not individuals, still less their "pathological" mindsets.

This consensus is also reflected in much liberal-left commentary about 5 terrorism, especially of the jihadist variant. For example, in some quarters of the "radical" left it is asserted that the roots of jihadist terrorism lie not in Islam but in the myriad historical crimes and injustices of Western, and specifically U.S.-driven, imperialism – most notably, in the post-9/11 era, the 2003 invasion of Iraq. Jihadist violence, from this perspective, is an inevitable reaction fueled by Muslim anger and vengeance; and Westernized jihadists, far from rejecting the civilized norms and ideals proclaimed by the West, are in fact alienated from a West that excludes, demeans, and harasses Muslims.

The scholarly consensus on violence has a lot going for it. It humanizes 6 the perpetrators of violence by insisting on their ordinariness and contextualizing their actions. It obliges people to reflect on their own possible shortcomings and vulnerabilities, and how, in different circumstances, they too could do monstrous deeds. And it compels people to recognize that they do not act in a social vacuum, and that what they think, feel, and do is powerfully shaped by the broader historical circumstances in which they are compelled to live and act. Moreover, Westernized jihadists, as a recent report cogently suggested, assuredly *are* alienated and feel that they do not belong in a secular world that often mocks and challenges their religion and identity as Muslims.

But the consensus can't divest itself of the idea of pathology. Rather, it 7 simply relocates the notion, tracing the causes of violence to pathological "background factors" operating on the violent. No doubt this is a more illuminating and edifying narrative than that sketched out in earlier psychological accounts. But its explanatory power is limited, because, as the eminent sociologist Jack Katz has convincingly argued, "whatever the validity of the

* Eds. note – Albert Bandura (b. 1925): Influential Canadian-American social, cognitive, and educational psychologist.

hereditary, psychological, and social-ecological conditions of crime, many of those in the supposedly causal categories do not commit the crime at issue, . . . many who do commit the crime do not fit the causal categories, and . . . many who do fit the background categories and later commit the predicted crime go for long stretches without committing the crimes to which theory directs them." Or as the British writer David Aaronovitch once joked, "Why don't black lesbians blow up buses? Aren't they alienated enough?"

One of the most sensitive and profound explorations of terrorism in 8
recent years comes not from a scholar, but from a novelist. Philip Roth's *American Pastoral* is a murder mystery in which the focal point is not the who, but the why. The protagonist, Seymour Levov, is a successful businessman whose 16-year-old daughter Meredith ("Merry") blows up a post office to protest the Vietnam War, killing a bystander. All Seymour can think about is why Merry did it. She was an adored only child who grew up in a privileged and decent family in the idyllic hamlet of Old Rimrock, New Jersey. Seymour is desperate to locate "the wound" that caused Merry's violence. Was it her stutter? Was it that anomalous kiss on the mouth he gave her one summer when she was 11 and he 36? Or was it the mysterious firebrand Rita Cohen who radicalized her?

As the novel progresses, Seymour's disbelief gives way to clarity. But it is a 9
negative clarity. "He had learned the worst lesson that life can teach – that it makes no sense," Roth writes. He had learned that his daughter "was unknowable," and that "there are no reasons," that "reasons are in books." In capturing Seymour's efforts to understand the disaster that befalls his family, Roth holds up to scrutiny conventional efforts to explain terrorism – and exposes just how imaginatively cramped and simplifying they can be.

"Do terrorists have their reasons for committing atrocities?"

Do terrorists have their reasons for 10
committing atrocities? They certainly reel off any number of reasons in their pronouncements, but, as law professor Stephen Holmes has observed, "private motivations cannot always be gleaned from public justifications." Sometimes people do what they do for the reasons they profess. Sometimes not, because what they do is motivated by reasons that are too dark, shameful, or bizarre to be openly acknowledged. Sometimes people do things that are so morally contentious that when called to account they are liable to excuse or justify, rather than to explain, their actions. Terrorists unquestionably fall into this category.

And sometimes people do what they do without the slightest sense of 11
knowing why. I once met someone who robbed a liquor store in his teens. He was caught and did jail time for it. This person is now an accomplished writer. Doing that stick-up was a hinge moment in his life and today, some 30 years later, he still cannot make sense of it. The motive simply eludes him.

Terrorism scholar John Horgan has made a similar point. "The most 12
valuable interviews I've conducted [with former terrorists] have been ones in which the interviewees conceded, 'To be honest, I don't really know,'" he writes. "Motivation is a very complicated issue. To explain why any of us does

anything is a challenge." It's a challenge further compounded by the fact that some actions are informed by multiple motives, and even if these can be reliably identified it is often difficult to disentangle them and calculate their respective causal weight.

As Horgan suggests, a more manageable and useful question to ask about terrorism is not why, but how—and when and where? How did this specific person come to join this specific organization? What networks helped facilitate the act of joining, and where and how were these networks accessed or sought out? 13

Because these questions are about the circumstances of terrorism, and not the interior world of terrorists, they are not only more intellectually tractable for scholars, but also more directly relevant to efforts to prevent or stop terrorist recruitment. Law-enforcement agents can't disrupt a motive, but with the right intelligence and skills they may be able to disrupt a network of terrorist recruiters. Marc Sageman's work on Western "leaderless" jihadists demonstrates the promise of this kind of approach. Although Sageman has some interesting things to say about the why question, the strength of his research lies in showing just how decisive social and kinship networks are in the radicalization process. 14

This isn't to suggest that the why question should be abandoned, but rather that those who ask it better appreciate the magnitude of the question and acknowledge the possibility that some momentous life decisions will remain forever opaque and mysterious—not only to outside observers, but also to the people who take them and must live with the consequences. 15

• • •

Comprehension

1. After introducing the question of why people join terrorist groups, Cottee suggests a "more worthwhile" (2) question. What is this question?
2. According to Cottee, how has the concept of "pathology" (3) changed in recent years? How has this change altered the way experts see the roots of terrorism?
3. Where do modern scholars think the "roots of terrorism" (3) lie?
4. Summarize the "scholarly consensus on violence" (6). What are its strengths? What are its weaknesses? How does it humanize terrorists?
5. Does Cottee ever actually answer the question his title asks? If so, paraphrase his answer. If not, why not?

Purpose and Audience

1. Summarize the positions of sociologists Albert Bandura and Jack Katz, law professor Stephen Holmes, and terrorism expert John Horgan. How does Cottee use each of these experts to support his thesis?
2. Paragraph 7 closes with a comment by a British writer. For what purpose does Cottee include this comment? Do you find it helpful? Do you see it as a joke, or do you find it offensive? Explain.

3. In paragraphs 8 and 9, Cottee gives a detailed summary of Philip Roth's novel *American Pastoral*. How does this discussion help readers understand Cottee's conclusion about what motivates terrorists?
4. What point does the anecdote Cottee presents in paragraph 11 make? How does it answer the question of what motivates terrorists?
5. How does Cottee expect his readers to respond to his essay? Does he see them as receptive? Skeptical? Hostile? Something else?

Style and Structure

1. This essay focuses on examining causes. Does it also consider effects? If not, should it?
2. In paragraph 7, Cottee refers to Jack Katz as an "eminent sociologist." Why does he use the word *eminent*?
3. **Vocabulary Project.** Do you think Cottee should have defined any of the terms he uses – for example, *terrorism* (1), *jihadists* (5), or *pathology* (7)? Why or why not? What does the fact that he does not provide definitions tell you about how he sees his audience?

Journal Entry

Do you think the main cause of terrorism is individual "pathology" – for example, mental illness or disability – or feelings of alienation and anger caused by "background factors" (7) in society? Why?

Writing Workshop

1. **Working with Sources.** Research some recent acts of domestic terrorism, and use these incidents as support for your own "What Motivates Terrorists?" essay. Consider all possible motives each terrorist might have had. How are their motives alike? What conclusions can you draw from these similarities? Be sure to document your sources and to include a works-cited list. (See Chapter 18 for information on MLA documentation.)
2. Cottee's essay focuses on finding causes. Write a cause-and-effect essay in which you consider the emotional and practical *effects* of terrorism, or the threat of terrorism, on you and your family and your community. For example, what changes in behavior have you observed?
3. Choose a fictional character from a book, film, or video game, and write a cause-and-effect essay outlining what might motivate this individual to commit an act of terrorist violence. If you like, you may write your essay in the form of an obituary for the character you select.

Combining the Patterns

Do you think Cottee should have included a **definition** of terrorism in his essay? If so, where? Would a passage of **classification and division** (categorizing various kinds of terrorists or their different motives) have strengthened his essay?

Thematic Connections

- "The YouTube Effect" (page 20)
- "Ground Zero" (page 173)
- "The Ways We Lie" (page 466)
- "On Patriotism" (page 697)

LINDA M. HASSELSTROM

A Peaceful Woman Explains Why She Carries a Gun

Linda M. Hasselstrom (b. 1943) grew up in rural South Dakota in a cattle ranching family. After receiving a master's degree in American literature from the University of Missouri, she returned to South Dakota to run her own ranch. A highly respected poet, essayist, and writing teacher, she often focuses on everyday life in the American West in her work. Her publications include the poetry collections *Caught by One Wing* (1984), *Roadkill* (1987), and *Dakota Bones* (1991); the essay collection *Land Circle* (1991); and several books about ranching, including *Between Grass and Sky: Where I Live and Work* (2002). Her most recent book is *The Wheel of the Year: A Writer's Workbook* (2015).

Background on incidences of sexual assault Hasselstrom's gun ownership can certainly be considered in the context of the ongoing debate over how (and even whether) stricter gun safety measures should be enacted in the United States. In 2008, the Supreme Court overturned a thirty-two-year ban on handguns in Washington, DC, concluding that the ban violated individuals' right to keep and bear arms. In a ruling in 2010, it extended Second Amendment protection to every jurisdiction in the nation. Equally important, however, is that Hasselstrom's reason for carrying a gun is to protect herself from sexual assault. According to a recent National Crime Victimization survey, more than 200,000 women reported being sexually assaulted in the United States in that year. It is estimated that only one in six instances of sexual assault is actually reported to the police, so the number of such attacks is, in reality, much higher. A 2009 study conducted by the National Shooting Sports Foundation found that gun purchases by women were increasing and that 80 percent of the female gun buyers who responded to the survey had purchased a gun for self-defense.

I am a peace-loving woman. But several events in the past ten years* have convinced me I'm safer when I carry a pistol. This was a personal decision, but because handgun possession is a controversial subject, perhaps my reasoning will interest others. 1

I live in western South Dakota on a ranch twenty-five miles from the nearest town: for several years I spent winters alone here. As a freelance writer, I travel alone a lot—more than 100,000 miles by car in the last four years. With women freer than ever before to travel alone, the odds of our encountering trouble seem to have risen. Distances are great, roads are deserted, and the terrain is often too exposed to offer hiding places. 2

* Eds. note – This essay was written in 2014.

A woman who travels alone is advised, usually by men, to protect herself by avoiding bars and other "dangerous situations," by approaching her car like an Indian scout, by locking doors and windows. But these precautions aren't always enough. I spent years following them and still found myself in dangerous situations. I began to resent the idea that just because I am female, I have to be extra careful. 3

A few years ago, with another woman, I camped for several weeks in the West. We discussed self-defense, but neither of us had taken a course in it. She was against firearms, and local police told us Mace was illegal. So we armed ourselves with spray cans of deodorant tucked into our sleeping bags. We never used our improvised Mace because we were lucky enough to camp beside people who came to our aid when men harassed us. But on one occasion we visited a national park where our assigned space was less than fifteen feet from other campers. When we returned from a walk, we found our closest neighbors were two young men. As we gathered our cooking gear, they drank beer and loudly discussed what they would do to us after dark. Nearby campers, even families, ignored them: rangers strolled past, unconcerned. When we asked the rangers point-blank if they would protect us, one of them patted my shoulder and said, "Don't worry, girls. They're just kidding." At dusk we drove out of the park and hid our camp in the woods a few miles away. The illegal spot was lovely, but our enjoyment of that park was ruined. I returned from the trip determined to reconsider the options available for protecting myself. 4

At that time, I lived alone on the ranch and taught night classes in town. Along a city street I often traveled, a woman had a flat tire, called for help on her CB radio, and got a rapist who left her beaten. She was afraid to call for help again and stayed in her car until morning. For that reason, as well as because CBs work best along line-of-sight, which wouldn't help much in the rolling hills where I live, I ruled out a CB. 5

As I drove home one night, a car followed me. It passed me on a narrow bridge while a passenger flashed a blinding spotlight in my face. I braked sharply. The car stopped, angled across the bridge, and four men jumped out. I realized the locked doors were useless if they broke the windows of my pickup. I started forward, hoping to knock their car aside so I could pass. Just then another car appeared, and the men hastily got back in their car. They continued to follow me, passing and repassing. I dared not go home because no one else was there. I passed no lighted houses. Finally they pulled over to the roadside, and I decided to use their tactic: fear. Speeding, the pickup horn blaring, I swerved as close to them as I dared as I roared past. It worked: they turned off the highway. But I was frightened and angry. Even in my vehicle I was too vulnerable. 6

Other incidents occurred over the years. One day I glanced out at a field below my house and saw a man with a shotgun walking toward a pond full of ducks. I drove down and explained that the land was posted. I politely asked him to leave. He stared at me, and the muzzle of the shotgun began to rise. In a moment of utter clarity I realized that I was alone on the ranch, and that he could shoot me and simply drive away. The moment passed: the man left. 7

One night, I returned home from teaching a class to find deep tire ruts in the wet ground of my yard, garbage in the driveway, and a large gas tank empty. A light shone in the house: I couldn't remember leaving it on. I was too embarrassed to drive to a neighboring ranch and wake someone up. An hour of cautious exploration convinced me the house was safe, but once inside, with the doors locked, I was still afraid. I kept thinking of how vulnerable I felt, prowling around my own house in the dark. 8

My first positive step was to take a kung fu class, which teaches evasive or protective action when someone enters your space without permission. I learned to move confidently, scanning for possible attackers. I learned how to assess danger and techniques for avoiding it without combat. 9

I also learned that one must practice several hours every day to be good at kung fu. By that time I had married George: when I practiced with him, I learned how *close* you must be to your attacker to use martial arts, and decided a 120-pound woman dare not let a six-foot, 220-pound attacker get that close unless she is very, very good at self-defense. I have since read articles by several women who were extremely well trained in the martial arts, but were raped and beaten anyway. 10

I thought back over the times in my life when I had been attacked or threatened and tried to be realistic about my own behavior, searching for anything that had allowed me to become a victim. Overall, I was convinced that I had not been at fault. I don't believe myself to be either paranoid or a risk-taker, but I wanted more protection. 11

With some reluctance I decided to try carrying a pistol. George had always carried one, despite his size and his training in martial arts. I practiced shooting until I was sure I could hit an attacker who moved close enough to endanger me. Then I bought a license from the county sheriff, making it legal for me to carry the gun concealed. 12

But I was not yet ready to defend myself. George taught me that the most important preparation was mental: convincing myself I could actually *shoot a person.* Few of us wish to hurt or kill another human being. But there is no point in having a gun – in fact, gun possession might increase your danger – unless you know you can use it. I got in the habit of rehearsing, as I drove or walked, the precise conditions that would be required before I would shoot someone. 13

People who have not grown up with the idea that they are capable of protecting themselves – in other words, most women – might have to work hard to convince themselves of their ability, and of the necessity. Handgun ownership need not turn us into gunslingers, but it can be part of believing in, and relying on, *ourselves* for protection. 14

To be useful, a pistol has to be available. In my car, it's within instant reach. When I enter a deserted rest stop at night, it's in my purse, with my hand on the grip. When I walk from a dark parking lot into a motel, it's in my hand, under a coat. At home, it's on the headboard. In short, I take it with me almost everywhere I go alone. 15

Just carrying a pistol is not protection; avoidance is still the best approach to trouble. Subconsciously watching for signs of danger, I believe I've become 16 more alert. Handgun use, not unlike driving, becomes instinctive. Each time I've drawn my gun—I have never fired it at another human being—I've simply found it in my hand.

17 I was driving the half-mile to the highway mailbox one day when I saw a vehicle parked about midway down the road. Several men were standing in the ditch, relieving themselves. I have no objection to emergency urination, but I noticed they'd dumped several dozen beer cans in the road. Besides being ugly, cans can slash a cow's feet or stomach.

18 The men noticed me before they finished and made quite a performance out of zipping their trousers while walking toward me. All four of them gathered around my small foreign car, and one of them demanded what the hell I wanted.

19 "This is private land. I'd appreciate it if you'd pick up the beer cans."

20 "What beer cans?" said the belligerent one, putting both hands on the car door and leaning in my window. His face was inches from mine, and the beer fumes were strong. The others laughed. One tried the passenger door, locked; another put his foot on the hood and rocked the car. They circled, lightly thumping the roof, discussing my good fortune in meeting them and the benefits they were likely to bestow upon me. I felt very small and very trapped and they knew it.

21 "The ones you just threw out," I said politely.

22 "I don't see no beer cans. Why don't you get out here and show them to me, honey?" said the belligerent one, reaching for the handle inside my door.

23 "Right over there," I said, still being polite. "—there, and over there." I pointed with the pistol, which I'd slipped under my thigh. Within one minute the cans and the men were back in the car and headed down the road.

24 I believe this incident illustrates several important principles. The men were trespassing and knew it: their judgment may have been impaired by alcohol. Their response to the polite request of a woman alone was to use their size, numbers, and sex to inspire fear. The pistol was a response in the same language. Politeness didn't work: I couldn't match them in size or number. Out of the car, I'd have been more vulnerable. The pistol just changed the balance of power. It worked again recently when I was driving in a desolate part of Wyoming. A man played cat-and-mouse with me for thirty miles, ultimately trying to run me off the road. When his car passed mine with only two inches to spare, I showed him my pistol, and he disappeared.

25 When I got my pistol, I told my husband, revising the old Colt slogan, "God made men *and women,* but Sam Colt made them equal." Recently I have seen a gunmaker's ad with a similar sentiment. Perhaps this is an idea whose time has come, though the pacifist inside me will be saddened if the only way women can achieve equality is by carrying weapons.

> "The pistol just changed the balance of power."

26 We must treat a firearm's power with caution. "Power tends to corrupt, and absolute power corrupts absolutely," as a man (Lord Acton) once said. A

pistol is not the only way to avoid being raped or murdered in today's world, but, intelligently wielded, it can shift the balance of power and provide a measure of safety.

• • •

Comprehension

1. According to Hasselstrom, why does she carry a gun? In one sentence, summarize her rationale.
2. List the specific events that led Hasselstrom to her decision to carry a gun.
3. Other than carrying a gun, what means of protecting herself did Hasselstrom try? Why did she find these strategies unsatisfactory? Can you think of other strategies she could have adopted instead of carrying a gun?
4. Where in the essay does Hasselstrom express her reluctance to carry a gun?
5. In paragraph 13, Hasselstrom says that possessing a gun "might increase your danger – unless you know you can use it." Where else does she touch on the possible pitfalls of carrying a gun?
6. What does Hasselstrom mean when she says, "The pistol just changed the balance of power" (24)?

Purpose and Audience

1. How does paragraph 1 establish Hasselstrom's purpose for writing this essay? What other purpose might she have?
2. What purpose does paragraph 5 serve? Is it necessary?
3. Do you think this essay is aimed primarily at men or at women? Explain.
4. Do you think Hasselstrom expects her readers to agree with her position? Where does she indicate that she expects them to challenge her? How does she address this challenge?

Style and Structure

1. This essay is written in the first person, and it relies heavily on personal experience. Do you see this as a strength or a weakness? Explain your conclusion.
2. What is the main cause in this cause-and-effect essay – that is, what is the most important reason Hasselstrom gives for carrying a gun? Can you identify any contributory causes?
3. Could you argue that simply being a woman is justification enough for carrying a gun? Do you think this is Hasselstrom's position? Why or why not?
4. Think of Hasselstrom's essay as the first step in a possible causal chain. What situations might result from her decision to carry a gun?
5. In paragraph 25, Hasselstrom says that "the pacifist inside me will be saddened if the only way women can achieve equality is by carrying weapons."

In her title and elsewhere in the essay, Hasselstrom characterizes herself as a "peaceful woman." Do you think she is successful in portraying herself as a peace-loving woman who only reluctantly carries a gun?

6. **Vocabulary Project.** Some of the words and phrases Hasselstrom uses in this essay suggest that she sees her pistol as an equalizer, something that helps to compensate for her vulnerability. Identify the words and phrases she uses to characterize her gun in this way.

Journal Entry

Do you agree that carrying a gun is Hasselstrom's only choice, or do you think she could take other steps to ensure her safety? Explain.

Writing Workshop

1. Hasselstrom lives in a rural area, and the scenarios she describes apply to rural life. Rewrite this essay as "A Peaceful Urban (or Suburban) Woman Explains Why She Carries a Gun."
2. **Working with Sources.** What reasons might a "peace-loving" *man* have for carrying a gun? Write a cause-and-effect essay outlining such a man's motives, using any of Hasselstrom's reasons that might apply to him as well. Be sure to include parenthetical documentation for any references to Hasselstrom's essay, and also include a works-cited page. (See Chapter 18 for information on MLA documentation.)
3. Write a cause-and-effect essay presenting reasons to support a position that opposes Hasselstrom's: "A Peaceful Woman (or Man) Explains Why She (or He) Refuses to Carry a Gun."

Combining the Patterns

Several times in her essay, Hasselstrom uses **narration** to support her position. Identify these narrative passages. Are they absolutely essential to the essay? Could they be briefer? Could some be deleted? Explain.

Thematic Connections

- "Thirty-Eight Who Saw Murder Didn't Call the Police" (page 126)
- "Just Walk On By: A Black Man Ponders His Power to Alter Public Space" (page 233)
- Casebook: "Do Guns Have a Place on College Campuses?" (page 632)

KAREN MILLER PENSIERO

Photos That Change History

Karen Miller Pensiero is the editor for Newsroom Standards at the *Wall Street Journal*. She has held several different positions at that publication since 1985, including serving as money and markets editor of the *Wall Street Journal Europe* and director of corporate communications. She is a graduate of the University of Missouri School of Journalism.

Background on the Syrian refugee crisis Although antigovernment protests in Syria began as a peaceful part of the 2011 Arab Spring, these uprisings against the regime of Bashar al-Assad ultimately degenerated into a complex and deadly civil war. Various factions, including the so-called Islamic State, the Free Syrian Army, government forces, and various other subfactions and ethnic groups, continue to battle throughout the country and in neighboring Iraq. As a result, close to half a million people have been killed, many of them civilians. According to the United Nations, more than 6.5 million Syrians are internally displaced. Many have fled to Lebanon, Jordan, and Turkey; many others have tried crossing the Mediterranean Sea to Greece, as in the case of Aylan Kurdi and his family. This crisis has led to social and political repercussions throughout Europe as well as in the United States, ranging from dilemmas about military intervention to ethical and practical questions about the obligation to accept refugees. For example, Germany has committed to accepting nearly one million Syrian asylum seekers as part of a policy supported by Chancellor Angela Merkel. Concerns about immigration, assimilation, and terrorism, however, have led to contentious debates about the merits of such initiatives in Germany, France, the United States, and other countries.

For years, the news media have published photos of Syrian refugees: images of the dead, wounded, and displaced. But few of them seem to have made much of an impression — until last week,* when people around the world saw photos of a 3-year-old boy named Aylan Kurdi, whose lifeless body had washed up on a Turkish beach. 1

"Once in a while, an image breaks through the noisy, cluttered global culture and hits people in the heart and not the head," says Douglas Brinkley, a professor of history at Rice University. 2

The boy had drowned, along with his brother and mother, while trying to get from Turkey to the Greek island of Kos. The *Wall Street Journal* published an image of a Turkish officer carrying Aylan's dead body, with the boy's face not quite visible and the man looking away, as if not able to bring himself to look at the child. Other news organizations published an even more stark photo of the dead little boy, face down in the surf. 3

* Eds. note — This essay was written in 2015.

AP Photo/DHA/Nilufer Demir

A paramilitary police officer stands above the lifeless body of Aylan Kurdi, 3, who died after boats carrying desperate Syrian migrants to the Greek island of Kos capsized, near Bodrum, Turkey, Sept. 2.

Asked last week about this sudden shift in the migration debate, the documentary filmmaker and historian Ken Burns admitted that he once worried that the still image had been devalued, "that a picture was no longer worth a thousand words because there were so many of them." The photos of Aylan Kurdi are a reminder, he says, that "the power of the single image to convey complex information is still there. It has that power to shock and arrest us. To make us stop for just a second and interrupt the flow." 4

Though the issues have varied greatly over the decades, historians point to other eras when photographs have resonated in the same transformative way, creating new social awareness and spurring changes in policy. 5

One iconic instance is "Migrant Mother," shot by Dorothea Lange in 1936 as part of her work for the federal government's Resettlement Administration. The picture of a woman and her children in a camp in the Central Valley of California vividly captured the plight of American migrants affected by the Great Depression, widespread drought, and the Dust Bowl. 6

"The photos were part of a government effort to shape and support" the New Deal policies of President Franklin D. Roosevelt, says Joshua Brown, a professor of history at the Graduate Center of the City University of New York. "They were very carefully chosen for publication" to support those programs. 7

Martha A. Sandweiss, a professor of history at Princeton University, recalls a conversation she once had with Willard Van Dyke, a distinguished 8

"Migrant Mother": Florence Owens Thompson and her family during the Great Depression, photographed by Dorothea Lange in 1936, Nipomo, Calif. The photo was "part of a government effort to shape and support" the New Deal policies of President Franklin D. Roosevelt, says Prof. Brown.

documentary filmmaker who, late in life, returned to his roots in photography. She asked him why, and he said, " 'Migrant Mother.' No film ever changed as many minds or touched as many people as that photograph did."

As World War II drew to a close, Dwight D. Eisenhower, then the commanding general of Allied forces in Western Europe, sent film crews to Nazi concentration camps. He believed, according to Prof. Brinkley, that "people will deny what's happening if you don't have photographic evidence of everything." 9

Before the release of the photos to the public, "people heard about the tragedy of the Holocaust, and they heard statistics about it," Prof. Brinkley says, "but suddenly to see the degradation of human life to such a degree just sort of turned the whole world's head around. In many ways, it led to the creation of Israel." 10

Photography was also crucial in highlighting the injustice of Jim Crow in the South and publicizing the efforts of the civil-rights movement. 11

AP Photo

Gen. Dwight D. Eisenhower (center) views the dead in the courtyard of Ohrdruf, a sub-camp of the Buchenwald concentration camp, after its liberation by U.S. forces, Germany, April 12, 1945. When Eisenhower, then commanding general of Allied forces in Western Europe, learned of the concentration camps, he sent in film crews. "He made them take the Holocaust photos that shocked the world," says Douglas Brinkley, a professor of history at Rice University.

Prof. Brinkley sees similarities between those photos and last week's image of the dead Syrian boy.

12 "It all comes together with that photograph" of Aylan Kurdi, he says, "and that happens sometimes. It's still a rare moment, but it's something like the barking mad dogs of Bull Connor's Birmingham," referring to the white-supremacist public-safety commissioner who encouraged violence against peaceful protesters.

13 "The fire hoses had the same galvanizing effect," Prof. Brinkley says. "Once people saw those photos, they were repulsed by the Southern Jim Crow bigot system." Seeing such pictures "shifts people in the heart."

14 Prof. Brown says that the Student Nonviolent Coordinating Committee, a key group in the civil-rights movement, so valued the effect of photos that it had its own photographer. "There is no doubt," he says, "that the photographs of attacks on demonstrators played an important role in changing opinions."

15 Though many of history's most influential photos show the harsh reality of suffering or conflict, that's not the only way for images to make an impact. "Earthrise," the color photograph of our planet taken by astronaut Bill Anders

AP Photo

A 17-year-old civil-rights demonstrator is attacked by a police dog, May 3, 1963, Birmingham, Ala. President John F. Kennedy discussed this widely seen photo at a White House meeting the next afternoon. "Once people saw those photos," says Prof. Brinkley, "they were repulsed by the Southern Jim Crow bigot system."

on the *Apollo 8* mission in 1968, helped spark the global environmental movement, according to Prof. Brinkley.

Up to that point, "everybody thought going to the moon was about space 16
exploration," he says. But many of the astronauts began speaking in terms of our "fragile planet." He believes that the image played a critical role in winning support for the creation of the Environmental Protection Agency in 1970.

As for last week's photos of Aylan Kurdi, why were they such an effec- 17
tive call to action? For Prof. Brown, the familiarity of the child, in his little Velcro-strap shoes and red shirt, is what made the photo resonate. "The child looks so much like children you know," he says. "That contrast with our former beliefs of refugees makes a big difference."

Mr. Burns describes such photographs as "symbols of a moment." They 18
have "the power to transform the agonizingly slow conversation of politics and diplomacy to a kind of urgency that actually permits us as human beings to transcend the limitation" imposed by our own institutions.

"Still photographs are 'the DNA of our visual experience.'"

Still photographs are "the DNA of our 19
visual experience," says Mr. Burns. "We are brought together by them."

"Earthrise," taken by astronaut Bill Anders in 1968.

• • •

Comprehension

1. Why did the photo of Aylan Kurdi have such a great impact on people around the world while other similar photos did not?
2. In paragraph 4, historian Ken Burns expresses concerns that still photos may have been "devalued." Do you think a photo can have as great an impact as a video? Do you think it can have a greater impact? Explain.
3. List the individual images Pensiero cites as having created "new social awareness" and led to "changes in policy" (5). Why did these particular images have such a great impact?
4. Why did General Dwight D. Eisenhower send film crews to Nazi concentration camps? How did these photos "change history"?
5. In paragraph 13, historian Douglas Brinkley says that when people saw photos of violence in Birmingham, Alabama, in 1963, "they were repulsed," and opinions of the "Southern Jim Crow bigot system" changed. Do you think Brinkley is exaggerating the impact of these photos? What other factors might have led to this change?
6. In paragraph 15, Pensiero shifts her discussion from one kind of photo to another. How does her emphasis change?

Purpose and Audience

1. What experts does Pensiero quote? What qualifies each of them as an "expert" on this subject?
2. Where does Pensiero discuss photos that had a *positive* impact? Why does she include this discussion? Do you think she should have spent more time on such photos? Why or why not?
3. What do you think Pensiero wants readers to take away from reading her essay? Do you think her primary purpose is to make a point about history or a point about photos?
4. In one sentence, summarize Pensiero's thesis.

Style and Structure

1. **Vocabulary Project.** What stronger words might be substituted for the word *change* in this essay's title? Given the possible alternatives, do you think *change* is the best choice? Explain.
2. Pensiero begins and ends her essay with a discussion of Aylan Kurdi. Why does she emphasize his story and not another?
3. Would this essay have had as great an impact if the photos it discusses were not included? Could detailed descriptions of the photos have had a similar impact?
4. Why does Pensiero focus on photos from various time periods? Would a group of contemporary photos work just as well? Why or why not?
5. Why does Pensiero place the photo *Earthrise* last?

Journal Entry

What one specific image might have the power to change Americans' views of immigration, animal testing, school shootings, capital punishment, or climate change? Why?

Writing Workshop

1. What photo published during your lifetime do you think has the power to "change history"? Why, and how? Write a cause-and-effect essay that begins with a description of the photo and provides its social and historical context. If possible, include the photo in your essay.
2. Write a cause-and-effect essay called "Videos That Change History." In your essay, explain the possible impact on history of two or three recent viral cellphone videos. Do you expect the impact of these videos to last as long as some of the photos Pensiero discusses? Why or why not?
3. **Working with Sources.** Locate several iconic images, both positive and negative, of World War II, the Vietnam War, or the Iraq War. Which images – the positive ones or the negative ones – do you think are likely to

have the greatest impact on history? Why? Be sure to cite the source of the images you find and to include a works-cited list. (See Chapter 18 for information on MLA documentation.)

Combining the Patterns

Pensiero includes a good deal of **description** in this essay. Do you think she would have had to add more description if no pictures accompanied her essay? If so, where?

Thematic Connections

- "The YouTube Effect" (page 20)
- "Thirty-Eight Who Saw Murder Didn't Call the Police" (page 126)
- "How to Tell a Mother Her Child Is Dead" (page 277)
- "Emmett Till and Tamir Rice, Sons of the Great Migration" (page 422)
- "The Obligation to Endure" (page 550)
- "Letter from Birmingham Jail" (page 558)

JANICE MIRIKITANI

Suicide Note (Poetry)

Janice Mirikitani, a third-generation Japanese American, was born in Stockton, California, in 1941 and graduated from the University of California, Los Angeles, in 1962. In her poetry, Mirikitani often considers how racism in the United States affects Asian Americans, particularly the thousands of Japanese Americans held in internment camps during World War II. Her collections include *Shedding Silence* (1987), *We, the Dangerous: New and Selected Poems* (1995), and *Love Works* (2002). She has also edited anthologies of Japanese-American and developing-nation literature, as well as several volumes giving voice to children living in poverty. For many years, she has been president of the Glide Foundation, which sponsors outreach programs for the poor and homeless of San Francisco. Her most recent book, *Beyond the Possible: 50 Years of Creating Radical Change in a Community Called Glide* (2013), was coauthored with Reverend Cecil Williams.

Background on teenage suicide The following poem, which appears in *Shedding Silence,* takes the form of a suicide note written by a young Asian-American college student to her family and reveals the extreme pressure to excel placed on her by her parents and her culture. The theme, however, has considerable relevance beyond the Asian-American community. Tragically, some five thousand teenagers and young adults commit suicide annually in the United States (there are ten times as many attempts), and suicide is the third leading cause of death among fifteen- to twenty-four-year-olds. Among college students, suicide is the second leading cause of death; approximately one thousand college students take their own lives every year. The number of suicides by college students has tripled since the 1950s. Nationally, there are 7.29 suicides per year for every 100,000 students. Recent extensive media coverage of a number of youth suicides caused by bullying has increased awareness of this problem and has led to proposals for stronger antiharassment legislation.

How many notes written . . .
ink smeared like birdprints in snow.

not good enough   not pretty enough   not smart enough

dear mother and father.
I apologize
for disappointing you.
I've worked very hard,

not good enough

harder, perhaps to please you.
If only I were a son, shoulders broad
as the sunset threading through pine,

I would see the light in my mother's
eyes, or the golden pride reflected
in my father's dream
of my wide, male hands worthy of work
and comfort.
I would swagger through life
muscled and bold and assured,
drawing praises to me
like currents in the bed of wind, virile
with confidence.

not good enough   not pretty enough   not smart enough

I apologize.
Tasks do not come easily.
Each failure, a glacier.
Each disapproval, a bootprint.
Each disappointment,
ice above my river.
So I have worked hard.

not good enough

My sacrifice I will drop
bone by bone, perched
on the ledge of my womanhood,
fragile as wings.

not strong enough

It is snowing steadily
surely not good weather
for flying—this sparrow
sillied and dizzied by the wind
on the edge.

not smart enough

I make this ledge my altar
to offer penance.
This air will not hold me,
the snow burdens my crippled wings,
my tears drop like bitter cloth
softly into the gutter below.

not good enough   not pretty enough   not smart enough

Choices thin as shaved
ice. Notes shredded
drift like snow

on my broken body,
cover me like whispers

of sorries
sorries.
Perhaps when they find me
they will bury
my bird bones beneath
a sturdy pine
and scatter my feathers like
unspoken song
over this white and cold and silent
breast of earth.

• • •

Reading Literature

1. An author's note that originally introduced this poem explained the main cause of the student's death.

   An Asian-American college student was reported to have jumped to her death from her dormitory window. Her body was found two days later under a deep cover of snow. Her suicide note contained an apology to her parents for having received less than a perfect four-point grade average.

   What other causes might have contributed to her suicide?
2. Why does the speaker believe her life would be happier if she were male? Do you think she is correct?
3. What words, phrases, and images are repeated in this poem? What effect do these repetitions have on you?

Journal Entry

Whom (or what) do you blame for teenage suicides such as the one the poem describes? How might such deaths be eliminated?

Thematic Connections

- "Surrendering" (page 116)
- "Midnight" (page 213)
- "Why Chinese Mothers Are Superior" (page 402)
- "'Hope' is the thing with feathers" (page 513)

Writing Assignments for Cause and Effect

1. **Working with Sources.** Both "Thirty-Eight Who Saw Murder Didn't Call the Police" (page 126) and "On Dumpster Diving" (page 676) encourage readers, either directly or indirectly, to take action rather than remain uninvolved. Using information gleaned from these essays (or from others in the text) as support for your thesis, write an essay exploring the possible consequences of apathy, the possible causes of apathy, or both. Be sure to provide parenthetical documentation for any words or ideas that are not your own, and include a works-cited page. (See Chapter 18 for more information on MLA documentation.)
2. Identify a recent news report from a print or online newspaper that you believe will have the power to "change history." In a cause-and-effect essay, explain why the news report you chose is so powerful.
3. What effects do student suicides such as the one described in "Suicide Note" have on college students, faculty, and administrators? Interview some people on your campus to see how they believe campus life would change (or has changed) in response to a student suicide.
4. How do you account for the popularity of one of the following: Twitter, Facebook, hip-hop, video games, home schooling, reality TV, fast food, flash mobs, or sensationalist tabloids such as the *Star*? Write an essay considering remote as well as immediate causes for the success of the phenomenon you choose.
5. Between 1946 and 1964, the U.S. birthrate increased considerably. Some of the effects attributed to this "baby boom" include the 1960s antiwar movement, an increase in the crime rate, and the development of the women's movement. Write an essay exploring some possible effects on the nation's economy and politics of the aging baby-boom generation. What trends would you expect to find now that the first baby boomers have passed age seventy?
6. Write an essay tracing a series of events in your life that constitutes a causal chain. Indicate clearly both the sequence of events and the causal connections among them, and be careful not to confuse coincidence with causality.
7. In recent years, almost half of American marriages ended in divorce. However, among married couples of generation X, born between 1965 and 1980, the divorce rate is considerably lower. To what do you attribute this decline in divorce rate? Be as specific as possible, citing "case studies" of couples you are familiar with.
8. What do you see as the major cause of any one of these problems: binge drinking among college students, voter apathy, school shootings, childhood obesity, or academic cheating? Based on your identification of its cause, formulate some specific solutions for the problem you select.
9. Write an essay considering the likely effects of a severe, protracted shortage of one of the following commodities: clean water, rental housing, cell

phones, flu vaccine, or books. You may consider a community-, city-, or statewide shortage or a nation- or worldwide crisis.

10. Write an essay exploring the causes, effects, or both of increased violence by and against children in the United States.

Collaborative Activity for Cause and Effect

Working in groups of four, discuss your thoughts about the homeless population, and then list four effects the presence of homeless people is having on you, your community, and the nation. Assign each member of your group to write a paragraph explaining one of the effects the group identifies. Then, arrange the paragraphs in order of increasing importance, moving from the least to the most significant consequence. Finally, work together to turn your individual paragraphs into an essay: write an introduction, a conclusion, and transitions between paragraphs, and include a thesis statement in paragraph 1.

11

Comparison and Contrast

What Is Comparison and Contrast?

In the narrowest sense, *comparison* shows how two or more things are similar, and *contrast* shows how they are different. In most writing situations, however, the two related processes of **comparison and contrast** are used together. In the following paragraph from *Disturbing the Universe,* scientist Freeman Dyson compares and contrasts two different styles of human endeavor, which he calls "the gray and the green."

Topic sentence (outlines elements of comparison)

Point-by-point comparison

In everything we undertake, either on earth or in the sky, we have a choice of two styles, which I call the gray and the green. The distinction between the gray and green is not sharp. Only at the extremes of the spectrum can we say without qualification, this is green and that is gray. The difference between green and gray is better explained by examples than by definitions. Factories are gray, gardens are green. Physics is gray, biology is green. Plutonium is gray, horse manure is green. Bureaucracy is gray, pioneer communities are green. Self-reproducing machines are gray, trees and children are green. Human technology is gray, God's technology is green. Clones are gray, clades* are green. Army field manuals are gray, poems are green.

A special form of comparison, called **analogy**, explains an idea or thing by comparing it to a second, more familiar thing. In the following paragraph from *The Shopping Mall High School,* Arthur G. Powell, Eleanor Farrar, and David K. Cohen use analogy to shed light on the nature of contemporary American high schools.

* Eds. note—A group of organisms that evolved from a common ancestor.

Topic sentence (identifies elements of analogy)

Points of similarity

If Americans want to understand their high schools at work, they should imagine them as shopping malls. Secondary education is another consumption experience in an abundant society. Shopping malls attract a broad range of customers with different tastes and purposes. Some shop at Target, others at Bloomingdale's. In high schools a broad range of students also shop. They too can select from an astonishing variety of products and services conveniently assembled in one place with ample parking. Furthermore, in malls and schools many different kinds of transactions are possible. Both institutions bring hopeful purveyors and potential purchasers together. The former hope to maximize sales but can take nothing for granted. Shoppers have a wide discretion not only about what to buy but also about whether to buy.

Using Comparison and Contrast

Throughout our lives, we are bombarded with information from newspapers, television, radio, the Internet, and personal experience: the police strike in Memphis; city workers walk out in Philadelphia; the Senate debates government spending; taxes are raised in New Jersey. Somehow we must make sense of the jumbled facts and figures that surround us. One way we have of understanding such information is to put it side by side with other information and then to compare and contrast. Do the police in Memphis have the same complaints as the city workers in Philadelphia? What are the differences between the two situations? Is the national debate on spending analogous to the New Jersey debate on taxes? How do they differ?

We apply comparison and contrast every day to matters that directly affect us. When we make personal decisions, we consider alternatives, asking ourselves whether one option seems better than another. Should I major in history or business? What job opportunities will each major offer me? Should I register to vote as a Democrat, a Republican, or an Independent? What are the positions of each political party on government spending, health care, and taxes? To answer questions like these, we use comparison and contrast.

Planning a Comparison-and-Contrast Essay

Because comparison and contrast is central to our understanding of the world, this way of thinking is often called for in essays and on essay exams.

> Compare and contrast the attitudes toward science and technology expressed in Fritz Lang's *Metropolis* and George Lucas's *Star Wars.* (film)
>
> What are the similarities and differences between mitosis and meiosis? (biology)

Discuss the relative merits of establishing a partnership or setting up a corporation. (business law)

Discuss both the advantages and disadvantages of distance learning. (education)

Recognizing Comparison-and-Contrast Assignments

You are not likely to sit down and say to yourself, "I think I'll write a comparison-and-contrast essay today. Now what can I write about?" Instead, your assignment will suggest comparison and contrast, or you will decide comparison and contrast suits your purpose. In the preceding examples, for instance, the instructors phrased their questions to tell students how to treat the material. When you read these questions, certain keywords and phrases – *compare and contrast, similarities and differences, relative merits, advantages and disadvantages* – indicate that you should use a comparison-and-contrast pattern to organize your essay. Sometimes you may not even need a key phrase. Consider the question "Which of the two Adamses, John or Samuel, had the greater influence on the timing and course of the American Revolution?" Here the word *greater* is enough to suggest a contrast.

Even when your assignment is not worded to suggest comparison and contrast, your purpose may indicate this pattern of development. For instance, when you **evaluate**, you frequently use comparison and contrast. If, as a student in a management course, you are asked to evaluate two health-care systems, you can begin by researching the standards experts use in their evaluations. You can then compare each system's performance with those standards and contrast the systems with each other, concluding perhaps that both systems meet minimum standards but that one is more cost-efficient than the other. Or, if you are evaluating two of this year's new cars for a consumer newsletter, you can establish some criteria – fuel economy, safety features, reliability, handling, style – and compare and contrast the cars on each criterion. If each of the cars is better in different categories, your readers will have to decide which features matter most to them.

Establishing a Basis for Comparison

Before you can compare and contrast two things, you must be sure a **basis for comparison** exists – that the two things have enough in common to justify the comparison. For example, although cats and dogs are very different, they share several significant elements: they are mammals, they make good pets, and they are intelligent. Without these shared elements, there would be no basis for comparison and nothing of importance to discuss.

A comparison should lead you beyond the obvious. For instance, at first the idea of a comparison-and-contrast essay based on an analogy between bees and people might seem absurd: after all, these two creatures differ in species, physical structure, and intelligence. In fact, their differences are so obvious that an essay based on them might seem pointless. After further analysis, however, you might decide that bees and people have quite a few things in common. Both are social animals that live in complex social structures, and both have tasks to perform and roles to fulfill in their respective societies. Therefore, you *could* write about them, but you would focus on the common elements that seem most similar – social structures and roles – rather than on dissimilar elements. If you tried to draw an analogy between bees and SUVs or humans and golf tees, however, you would run into trouble. Although some points of comparison could be found, they would be trivial. Why bother to point out that both bees and SUVs can travel great distances or that both people and tees are needed to play golf? Neither statement establishes a significant basis for comparison.

When two subjects are very similar, the differences may be worth writing about. On the other hand, when two subjects are not very much alike, you may find that the similarities are worth considering.

Selecting Points for Discussion

After you decide which subjects to compare and contrast, you need to select the points you want to discuss. You do this by determining your emphasis – on similarities, differences, or both – and the major focus of your essay. If your purpose in comparing two types of houseplants is to explain that one is easier to grow than the other, you would select points having to do with plant care, not those having to do with plant biology.

When you compare and contrast, make sure you treat the same (or at least similar) points for each subject you discuss. For instance, if you were going to compare and contrast two novels, you might consider the following points in both works.

NOVEL A	NOVEL B
Minor characters	Minor characters
Major characters	Major characters
Themes	Themes

Try to avoid the common error of discussing entirely different points for each subject. Such an approach obscures any basis for comparison that might exist. The two novels, for example, could not be meaningfully compared or contrasted if you discussed dissimilar points.

NOVEL A	NOVEL B
Minor characters	Author's life
Major characters	Plot
Themes	Symbolism

Developing a Thesis Statement

After selecting the points you want to discuss, you are ready to develop your thesis statement. This **thesis statement** should tell readers what to expect in your essay, identifying not only the subjects to be compared and contrasted but also the point you will make about them. Your thesis statement should also indicate whether you will concentrate on similarities, differences, or both. In addition, it may list the points of comparison and contrast in the order in which they will be discussed in the essay.

The structure of your thesis statement can indicate the emphasis of your essay. As the following sentences illustrate, a thesis statement can highlight the essay's central concern by presenting it in the independent, rather than the dependent, clause of the sentence. Notice that the structure of the first thesis statement emphasizes similarities, whereas the structure of the second highlights differences.

> Even though television and radio are distinctly different media, they use similar strategies to appeal to their audiences.
>
> Although Melville's *Moby-Dick* and London's *The Sea Wolf* are both about the sea, the minor characters, major characters, and themes of *Moby-Dick* establish its greater complexity.

Structuring a Comparison-and-Contrast Essay

Like every other type of essay in this book, a comparison-and-contrast essay has an **introduction**, several **body paragraphs**, and a **conclusion**. Within the body of your essay, you can use either of two basic comparison-and-contrast strategies – **subject by subject** or **point by point**.

As you might expect, each organizational strategy has advantages and disadvantages. In general, you should use subject-by-subject comparison when your purpose is to emphasize overall similarities or differences, and you should use point-by-point comparison when your purpose is to emphasize individual points of similarity or difference.

Using Subject-by-Subject Comparison

In a **subject-by-subject comparison**, you essentially write a separate section about each subject, and you discuss the same points for both subjects. Use your basis for comparison to guide your selection of points, and arrange these points in some logical order, usually in order of their increasing significance. The following informal outline illustrates a subject-by-subject comparison.

INTRODUCTION
(thesis statement)

Even though television and radio are distinctly different media, they use similar strategies to appeal to their audiences.

SUBJECT 1: TELEVISION AUDIENCES

Point 1: Men

Point 2: Women

Point 3: Children

SUBJECT 2: RADIO AUDIENCES
Point 1: Men
Point 2: Women
Point 3: Children

CONCLUSION
Restatement of thesis (in different words) or review of key points

Subject-by-subject comparisons are most appropriate for short, uncomplicated essays. In longer essays, in which you might make many points about each subject, this organizational strategy demands too much of your readers, requiring them to keep track of all your points throughout your essay. In addition, because of the length of each section, your essay may seem like two completely separate essays. For longer or more complex essays, then, it is often best to use point-by-point comparison.

Using Point-by-Point Comparison

In a **point-by-point comparison**, you make a point about one subject and then follow it with a comparable point about the other. This alternating pattern continues throughout the body of your essay until all your points have been made. The following informal outline illustrates a point-by-point comparison.

INTRODUCTION
(thesis statement)
Although Melville's *Moby-Dick* and London's *The Sea Wolf* are both about the sea, the minor characters, major characters, and themes of *Moby-Dick* establish its greater complexity.

POINT 1: MINOR CHARACTERS
Book 1: *The Sea Wolf*
Book 2: *Moby-Dick*

POINT 2: MAJOR CHARACTERS
Book 1: *The Sea Wolf*
Book 2: *Moby-Dick*

POINT 3: THEMES
Book 1: *The Sea Wolf*
Book 2: *Moby-Dick*

CONCLUSION
Restatement of thesis (in different words) or review of key points

Point-by-point comparisons are useful for longer, more complicated essays in which you discuss many different points. (If you treat only one or two points of comparison, you should consider a subject-by-subject organization.) In a point-by-point essay, readers can follow comparisons or contrasts more easily and do not have to wait several paragraphs to find out, for example, the differences between minor characters in *Moby-Dick* and *The Sea Wolf* or to remember on page five what was said on page three. Nevertheless, it is easy to fall into a monotonous, back-and-forth movement between points when you write a point-by-point comparison. To avoid this problem, vary your sentence structure as you move from point to point—and be sure to use clear transitions.

Using Transitions

Transitions are especially important in comparison-and-contrast essays because readers need clear signals that identify individual similarities and differences. Without these cues, readers will have trouble following your discussion and may lose track of the significance of the points you are making. Some transitions indicating comparison and contrast are listed in the following box. (A more complete list of transitions appears on page 55.)

USEFUL TRANSITIONS FOR COMPARISON AND CONTRAST

COMPARISON

in comparison	like
in the same way	likewise
just as . . . so	similarly

CONTRAST

although	nevertheless
but	nonetheless
conversely	on the contrary
despite	on the one hand . . . on the other hand
even though	still
however	unlike
in contrast	whereas
instead	yet

Longer essays frequently include **transitional paragraphs** that connect one part of an essay to another. A transitional paragraph can be a single sentence that signals a shift in focus or a longer paragraph that provides a summary of what was said before. In either case, transitional paragraphs enable readers to pause and consider what has already been said before moving on to a new subject.

Revising a Comparison-and-Contrast Essay

When you revise your comparison-and-contrast essay, consider the items on the revision checklist on page 66. In addition, pay special attention to the items on the following checklist, which apply specifically to comparison-and-contrast essays.

REVISION CHECKLIST COMPARISON AND CONTRAST

- ☐ Does your assignment call for comparison and contrast?
- ☐ What basis for comparison exists between the two subjects you are comparing?
- ☐ Does your essay have a clear thesis statement that identifies both the subjects you are comparing and the points you are making about them?
- ☐ Do you discuss the same or similar points for both subjects?
- ☐ If you have written a subject-by-subject comparison, have you included a transition paragraph that connects the two sections of the essay?
- ☐ If you have written a point-by-point comparison, have you included appropriate transitions and varied your sentence structure to indicate your shift from one point to another?
- ☐ Have you included transitional words and phrases that indicate whether you are discussing similarities or differences?

Editing a Comparison-and-Contrast Essay

When you edit your comparison-and-contrast essay, follow the guidelines on the editing checklists on pages 83, 86, and 89. In addition, focus on the grammar, mechanics, and punctuation issues that are particularly relevant to comparison-and-contrast essays. One of these issues – using parallel structure – is discussed on next page.

GRAMMAR IN CONTEXT USING PARALLELISM

Parallelism – the use of matching nouns, verbs, phrases, or clauses to express the same or similar ideas – is frequently used in comparison-and-contrast essays to emphasize the similarities or differences between one point or subject and another.

- Use parallel structure with paired items or with items in a series.

  "For women, as for girls, intimacy is the fabric of relationships, and talk is the thread from which it is woven" (Tannen 416).

  "Lee was tidewater Virginia, and in his background were family, culture, and tradition . . . the age of chivalry transplanted to a New World which was making its own legends and its own myths" (Catton 392).

  According to Bruce Catton, Lee was strong, aristocratic, and dedicated to the Confederacy.

- Use parallel structure with paired items linked by correlative conjunctions (*not only/but also, both/and, neither/nor, either/or,* and so on).

  "In everything we undertake, **either** on earth **or** in the sky, we have a choice of two styles, which I call the gray and the green" (Dyson 369).

  Catton **not only** admires Grant **but also** respects him.

- Use parallel structure to emphasize the contrast between paired items linked by *as* or *than.*

  According to Deborah Tannen, conversation between men and women is **as** much a problem for men **as** a problem for women.

  As Deborah Tannen observes, most men are socialized to communicate through actions **rather than** to communicate through conversation.

LaunchPad

For more practice on parallelism, see the LearningCurve on Parallelism in the LaunchPad for *Patterns.*

EDITING CHECKLIST COMPARISON AND CONTRAST

- ☐ Have you used parallel structure with parallel elements in a series?
- ☐ Have you used commas to separate three or more parallel elements in a series?
- ☐ Have you used parallel structure with paired items linked by correlative conjunctions?
- ☐ Have you used parallel structure with paired items linked by *as* or *than*?

A STUDENT WRITER: Subject-by-Subject Comparison

The following essay, by Mark Cotharn, is a subject-by-subject comparison. It was written for a composition class whose instructor asked students to write an essay comparing two educational experiences.

Brains versus Brawn

Introduction

1 When people think about discrimination, they usually associate it with race or gender. But discrimination can take other forms. For example, a person can gain an unfair advantage at a job interview by being attractive, by knowing someone who works at the company, or by being able to talk about something (like sports) that has nothing to do with the job. Certainly, the people who do not get the job would claim that they were discriminated against, and to some extent they would be right. As a high school athlete, I experienced both sides of discrimination. When I was a sophomore, I benefited from discrimination. When I was a junior, however, I was penalized by it, treated as if there were no place for me in a classroom. As a result, I learned that discrimination, whether it helps you or hurts you, is wrong.

Thesis statement (emphasizing differences)

First subject: Mark helped by discrimination

Status of football

2 At my high school, football was everything, and the entire town supported the local team. In the summer, merchants would run special football promotions. Adults would wear shirts with the team's logo, students would collect money to buy equipment, and everyone would go to the games and cheer the team on. Coming out of junior high school, I was considered an exceptional athlete who was eventually going to start as varsity quarterback. Because of my status, I was enthusiastically welcomed by the high school. Before I entered the school, the varsity coach visited my home, and the principal called my parents and told them how well I was going to do.

Treatment by teachers

3 I knew that high school would be different from junior high, but I wasn't prepared for the treatment I received from my teachers. Many of them talked to me as if I were their friend, not their student. My math teacher used to keep me after class just to talk football; he would give me a note so I could be late for my next class. My biology teacher told me I could skip the afternoon labs so that I would have some time for myself before practice. Several of my teachers told me that during football season, I didn't have to hand in homework because it might distract me during practice. My Spanish teacher even told me that if I didn't do well on a test, I could take it over after the season. Everything I did seemed to be perfect.

Mark's reaction to treatment

Despite this favorable treatment, I continued to study hard. I knew that if I wanted to go to a good college, I would have to get good grades, and I resented the implication that the only way I could get good grades was by getting special treatment. I had always been a good student, and I had no intention of changing my study habits now that I was in high school. Each night after practice, I stayed up late outlining my notes and completing my class assignments. Any studying I couldn't do during the week, I would complete on the weekends. Of course my social life suffered, but I didn't care. I was proud that I never took advantage of the special treatment my teachers were offering me. 4

Transitional paragraph: signals shift from one subject to another

Then, one day, the unthinkable happened. The township redrew the school-district lines, and I suddenly found myself assigned to a new high school — one that was academically more demanding than the one I attended and, worse, one that had a weak football team. When my parents appealed to the school board to let me stay at my current school, they were told that if the board made an exception for me, it would have to make exceptions for others, and that would lead to chaos. My principal and my coach also tried to get the board to change its decision, but they got the same response. So, in my junior year, at the height of my career, I changed schools. 5

Second subject: Mark hurt by discrimination

Status of football

Unlike the people at my old school, no one at my new school seemed to care much about high school football. Many of the students attended the games, but their primary focus was on getting into college. If they talked about football at all, they usually discussed the regional college teams. As a result, I didn't have the status I had when I attended my former school. When I met with the coach before school started, he told me the football team was weak. He also told me that his main goal was to make sure everyone on the team had a chance to play. So, even though I would start, I would have to share the quarterback position with two seniors. Later that day, I saw the principal, who told me that although sports were an important part of school, academic achievement was more important. He made it clear that I would play football only as long as my grades did not suffer. 6

Treatment by teachers

Unlike the teachers at my old school, the teachers at my new school did not give any special treatment to athletes. When I entered my new school, I was ready for the challenge. What I was not ready for was the hostility of most of my new teachers. From the first day, in just about every class, my teachers made 7 it obvious that they had already made up their minds about what kind of student I was going to be. Some teachers told me I shouldn't expect any special consideration just because I was the team's quarterback. One even said in front of the class that I would have to study as hard as the other students if I expected to pass. I was hurt and embarrassed by these comments. I didn't expect anyone to give me anything, and I was ready to get the grades I deserved. After all, I had gotten good grades up to this point, and I had no reason to think that the situation would change. Even so, my teachers' preconceived ideas upset me.

Mark's reaction to treatment

Just as I had in my old school, I studied hard, but I didn't know how to deal with the prejudice I faced. At first, it really bothered me and even affected my performance on the football field. However, after a while, I decided that the best way to show my teachers that I was not the stereotypical jock was to prove to them what kind of student I really was. In the long run, far from discouraging me, their treatment motivated me, and I decided to work as hard in the classroom as I did on the football field. By the end of high school, not only had the team won half of its games (a record season), but I had also proved to my teachers that I was a good student. (I still remember the surprised look on the face of my chemistry teacher when she handed my first exam back to me and told me that I had received the second-highest grade in the class.) 8

Conclusion

Before I graduated, I talked to the teachers about how they had treated me during my junior year. Some admitted they had been harder on me than on the rest of the students, but others denied they had ever discriminated against me. Eventually, I realized that some of them would never understand what they had done. Even so, my experience did have some positive effects. I learned that you should judge people on their merits, not by your own set of assumptions. In addition, I learned that although some people are talented intellectually, others have special skills that should also be valued. And, as I found out, discriminatory treatment, whether it helps you or hurts you, is no substitute for fairness. 9

Restatement of thesis

Points for Special Attention

Basis for Comparison. Mark knew he could easily compare his two experiences. Both involved high school, and both focused on the treatment he had received as an athlete. In one case, Mark was treated better than other students because he was the team's quarterback; in the other, he was stereotyped as a "dumb jock" because he was a football player. Mark also knew that his comparison would make an interesting (and perhaps unexpected) point – that discrimination is unfair even when it gives a person an advantage.

Selecting Points for Comparison. Mark wanted to make certain that he would discuss the same (or at least similar) points for the two experiences he was going to compare. As he planned his essay, he consulted his brainstorming notes and made the following informal outline.

EXPERIENCE 1 (gained an advantage)	EXPERIENCE 2 (was put at a disadvantage)
Status of football	Status of football
Treatment by teachers	Treatment by teachers
My reaction	My reaction

Structure. Mark's essay makes three points about each of the two experiences he compares. Because his purpose was to convey the differences between the two experiences, he decided to use a subject-by-subject strategy. In addition, Mark thought he could make his case more convincingly if he discussed the first experience fully before moving on to the next one, and he believed readers would have no trouble keeping his individual points in mind as they read. Of course, Mark could have decided to do a point-by-point comparison. He rejected this strategy, though, because he thought that shifting back and forth between subjects would distract readers from his main point.

Transitions. Without adequate transitions, a subject-by-subject comparison can read like two separate essays. Notice that in Mark's essay, paragraph 5 is a **transitional paragraph** that connects the two sections of the essay. In it, Mark sets up the comparison by telling how he suddenly found himself assigned to another high school.

In addition to connecting the sections of an essay, transitional words and phrases can identify individual similarities or differences. Notice, for example, how the transitional word *however* emphasizes the contrast between the following sentences from paragraph 1.

WITHOUT TRANSITION

When I was a sophomore, I benefited from discrimination. When I was a junior, I was penalized by it.

WITH TRANSITION

When I was a sophomore, I benefited from discrimination. When I was a junior, *however,* I was penalized by it.

Topic Sentences. Like transitional phrases, topic sentences help guide readers through an essay. When reading a comparison-and-contrast essay, readers can easily forget the points being compared, especially if the essay is long. Direct, clearly stated topic sentences act as guideposts, alerting readers to the comparisons and contrasts you are making. For example, Mark's straightforward topic sentence at the beginning of paragraph 5 dramatically signals the movement from one experience to the other ("Then, one day, the unthinkable happened"). In addition, as in any effective comparison-and-contrast essay, each point discussed in connection with one subject is also discussed in connection with the other. Mark's topic sentences reinforce this balance.

FIRST SUBJECT

At my high school, football was everything, and the entire town supported the local team.

SECOND SUBJECT

Unlike the people at my old school, no one at my new school seemed to care much about high school football.

Focus on Revision

In general, Mark's classmates thought he could have spent more time talking about what he did to counter the preconceptions about athletes that teachers in *both* his schools had.

One student in his peer-editing group pointed out that the teachers at both schools seemed to think athletes were weak students. The only difference was that the teachers at Mark's first school were willing to make allowances for athletes, while the teachers at his second school were not. The student thought that although Mark alluded to this fact, he should have made his point more explicitly.

Another classmate thought Mark should acknowledge that some student athletes *do* fit the teachers' stereotypes (although many do not). This information would reinforce his thesis and help him demonstrate how unfair his treatment was.

After rereading his essay, along with his classmates' comments, Mark decided to add information about how demanding football practice was. Without this information, readers would have a hard time understanding how difficult it was for him to keep up with his studies. He also decided to briefly acknowledge that although he did not fit the negative stereotype of student athletes, some other student athletes do. This fact, however, did not justify the treatment he received at the two high schools he attended. (A sample peer-editing worksheet for comparison and contrast appears on page 388.)

Working with Sources. One of Mark's classmates suggested that he add a quotation from Judith Ortiz Cofer's essay "The Myth of the Latin Woman: I Just Met a Girl Named Maria" (page 225) to his essay. The student pointed out that Cofer, like Mark, was a victim of discrimination on the basis of stereotyping. By referring to Cofer's essay, Mark could widen the scope of his remarks and show how his experience was similar to that of someone who was stereotyped on the basis of ethnicity. Mark thought this was a good idea, and he decided to refer to Cofer's essay in the next draft of his essay. (Adding this reference would require him to include MLA parenthetical documentation as well as a works-cited page.)

A STUDENT WRITER: Point-by-Point Comparison

The following essay, by Maria Tecson, is a point-by-point comparison. It was written for a composition class whose instructor asked students to compare two websites about a health issue and to determine which is the more reliable information source.

A Comparison of Two Websites on Attention Deficit Disorder

Introduction

1 At first glance, the National Institute of Mental Health (NIMH) website and ADD.About.com — two sites on Attention Deficit Disorder — look a lot alike. Both have attractive designs, headings, and links to other websites. Because anyone can publish on the Internet, however, websites cannot be judged just on how they look. Colorful graphics and an appealing layout can often hide shortcomings that make sites unsuitable research sources. As a comparison of the NIMH and ADD.About.com websites shows, the first site is definitely a more useful source of information than the second.

Thesis statement (emphasizing differences)

First point: comparing home pages

NIMH home page

2 The first difference between the two websites is the design of their home pages. The NIMH page looks clear and professional. For example, the logos, tabs, links, search boxes, and text columns are placed carefully on the page (see fig. 1). Words are spelled correctly; tabs help users to navigate; and content is arranged topically, with headings such as "Definition" and "Signs and Symptoms." The page includes links to detailed reference lists and footnotes as well as to resources for further study. Finally, many of the pages associated with the NIMH site offer accessibility options, such as text in Spanish.

ADD home page

3 The ADD.About.com home page is more crowded than NIMH's ADHD/ADD home page; although it has less text, it contains more design elements, including a number of images and sidebars (see fig. 2). The arrangement of these elements on the page, the focus of the information presented, and the lack of misspellings indicate that it has been carefully designed. This page is engaging and visually stimulating, and it contains headings and links to research studies. However, it is not always clear how the design elements and sidebars are related to the information on the page. The home page

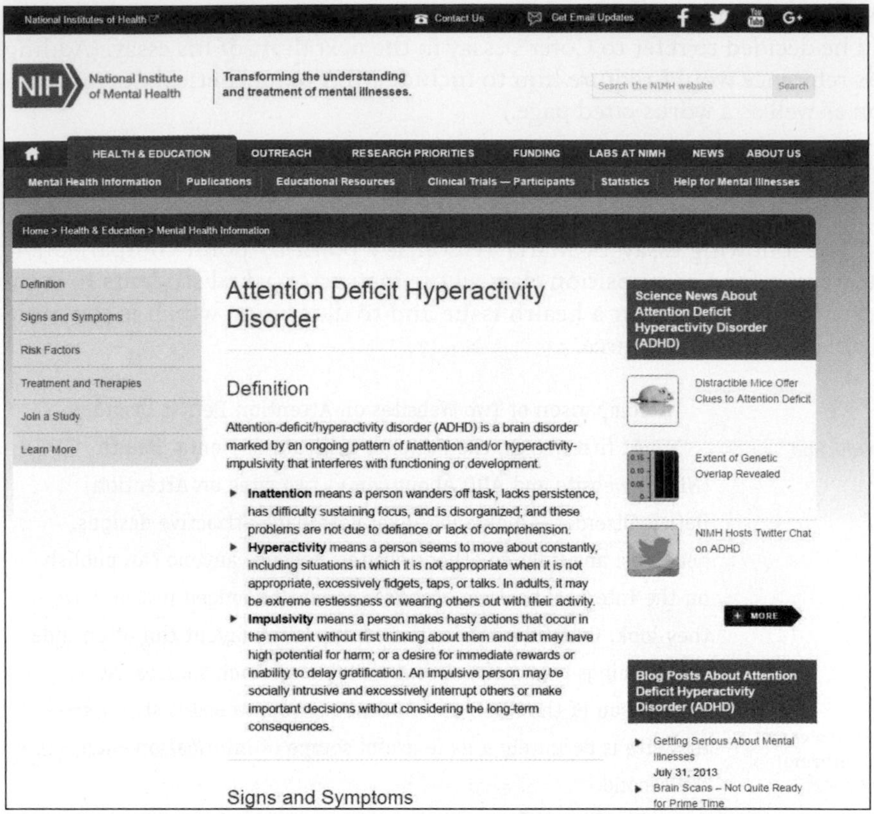

Fig. 1. National Institute of Mental Health. *Attention Deficit Hyperactivity Disorder,* www.nimh.nih.gov/health/topics/attention-deficit-hyperactivity-disorder-adhd/index.shtml. Accessed 28 Oct. 2016.

also lacks any clear accessibility options, which limits the site's use by a wide audience.

Second point: comparing sponsors

NIMH site sponsor

Another difference between the two websites is their purposes. The URL for the NIMH website indicates that it is a *.gov*—a website created by a branch of the United States government. The logo at the top left of the home page identifies the National Institute of Mental Health (NIMH) as the sponsor of the site. The "About Us" tab on the upper right-hand side of the page links to a description of NIMH as well as to contact information for this organization. A notice at the bottom of the page informs visitors that NIMH is part of the National Institutes of Health, which is, in turn, a part of the U.S. Department of Health and Human Services. Furthermore, the "About Us" tab includes the NIMH Strategic Plan, which informs readers that NIMH is the "lead federal agency for research on mental and behavioral disorders." 4

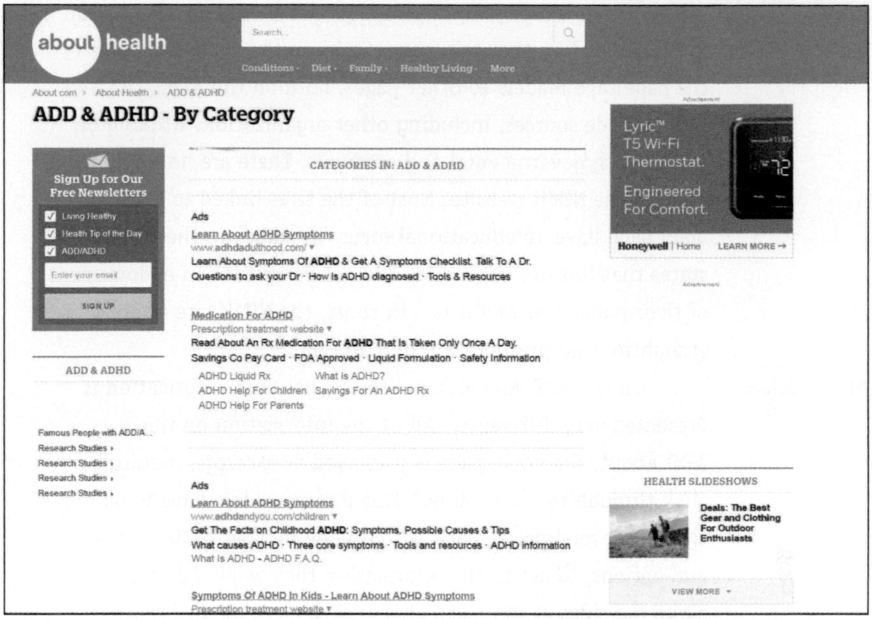

Fig. 2. Keath Low. "ADD/ADHD." *About*, add.about.com/od/. Accessed 28 Oct. 2016.

This description clearly indicates that the site's purpose is to give the American public the latest information about ADHD. For this reason, the website lists treatments and therapies used to treat ADHD and objectively evaluates the various treatment options available to patients.

The URL for ADD.About.com ends with *.com*, indicating that 5

ADD site sponsor

it is a commercial site. The sponsor of this website is About.com. At the very bottom of the page, a link called "Our Story" explains that the goal of About.com is to make "finding accessible, quality information — on almost every topic — as easy as a simple search." A careful examination of the site, however, indicates that About .com's purpose is not just to deliver information about mental health and behavioral disorders. Although ADD.About.com treats some of the same topics as the NIMH site, it also includes paid advertisements. These ads present a limited number of the treatments and products available for ADHD, which means that the About.com site highlights certain options over others for commercial reasons.

Third point: how sites present information

A final difference between the two websites is how they 6

present the information. The ADHD information on the NIMH site is largely concentrated on a single page. The page is long, listing one topic after another. The links on the sidebar take

NIMH information readers down the page to different sections, but the information is all included on the main page. Links on the right-hand side of the page take readers to other pages, both on the NIMH site and from outside sources, including other organizations working on ADHD, both governmental and academic. There are no ads of any kind on the NIMH website. Most of the sites linked to from the main page have an educational focus. In addition, the site clearly states that links to other sites "do not constitute an endorsement of their policies or products." In short, the NIMH site offers a straightforward presentation of material.

ADD information On the ADD.About.com website, however, information is presented very differently. All of the information on the ADD.About.com home page is displayed as excerpts, requiring a click-through to "Read More." This means readers have to go through several pages, each with a large number of links, ads, and options, to get to the information they want. Ads are listed along the sides of the page. This arrangement implies that the paid advertisements are equivalent to the other information on the site. Although the words "Ads" and "Advertisement" appear on the page, these labels do not stand out. In addition, the ads include everything from pharmaceuticals and for-profit schools, to outdoor clothing. As a result, they disrupt the clarity, focus, and usefulness of the About.com site. 7

Conclusion A comparison of the NIMH website and ADD.About.com website shows some clear differences between the two. The biggest difference is found in the reliability of information they present. The NIMH website makes it easy for users to understand where the information on the site comes from and why it is included. The About.com site, however, downplays its commercial associations and this possibly misleads readers about the reliability of the information they access. For this reason, the NIMH website is a much more useful source of information than the ADD.About.com website. 8

Restatement of thesis

Points for Special Attention

Structure. Maria's purpose in writing this essay was to compare two websites that deal with Attention Deficit Hyperactivity Disorder and to determine which is the more useful, more reliable source of information. She structured her essay as a point-by-point comparison, carefully discussing the same point for each subject. With this method of organization, she can be sure her readers will understand the specific differences between the NIMH website and the ADD.About.com website. Had Maria used a subject-by-subject comparison, her readers would have had to keep turning back to compare the points she made about one website with those she made about the other.

Topic Sentences. Without clear topic sentences, Maria's readers would have had difficulty determining where each discussion of the NIMH website ended and each discussion about the ADD.About.com website began. Maria uses topic sentences to distinguish the two subjects of her comparison and to make the contrast between them clear.

Point 1

The NIMH page looks clear and professional.

The ADD.About.com home page is more crowded than NIMH's ADHD/ADD home page; although it has less text, it contains more design elements, including a number of images and sidebars.

Point 2

The URL for the NIMH website indicates that it is a *.gov*—a website created by a branch of the United States government.

The URL for ADD.About.com ends with *.com,* indicating that it is a commercial site.

Point 3

The ADHD information on the NIMH site is largely concentrated on a single page.

On the ADD.About.com website, however, information is presented very differently.

Transitions. In addition to clear and straightforward topic sentences, Maria included **transitional sentences** to help readers move through the essay. These sentences identify the three points of contrast in the essay, and by establishing a parallel structure, they form a pattern that reinforces the essay's thesis.

The first difference between the two websites is the design of their home pages.

Another difference between the two websites is their purposes.

A final difference between the two websites is how they present the information.

Working with Sources. Maria knew it would be easier for her to compare the NIMH and ADD.About.com websites if she included visuals in her essay. Because readers would be able to see the pages of the sites she was comparing, she would not have to include long passages of description. She could then concentrate on making specific points and not get sidetracked describing physical features. Her instructor pointed out that if she added these two visuals, she would have to include a label (*Fig. 1, Fig. 2,* and so on) along with a caption under each one. He also told her that if the caption included complete source information, there was no need to list the source on her works-cited page. (See Chapter 18 for a discussion of MLA documentation.)

Focus on Revision

Maria's classmates thought the greatest strength of her essay was its use of supporting examples, which made the contrast between the two websites clear, but they also thought that more detail would improve her essay. For example, in paragraph 6, Maria could include a list of the other kinds of sites linked to on the NIMH website. In paragraph 7, she could also list some of the specific information presented on the ADD.About.com website and explain why it is problematic.

Maria thought these suggestions made sense. She also thought she could improve her conclusion: although it summed up the main points of her essay, it included little that would stay with readers after they finished. A sentence or two to caution readers about the need to carefully evaluate the information they find on websites would be a good addition.

PEER-EDITING WORKSHEET: COMPARISON AND CONTRAST

1. Does the essay have a clearly stated thesis? What is it?
2. What two things are being compared? What basis for comparison exists between the two?
3. Does the essay treat the same or similar points for each of its two subjects? List the points discussed.

FIRST SUBJECT	**SECOND SUBJECT**
a.	**a.**
b.	**b.**
c.	**c.**
d.	**d.**

   Are these points discussed in the same order for both subjects? Are the points presented in parallel terms?
4. Does the essay use a point-by-point or subject-by-subject strategy? Is this strategy the best choice? Why?
5. Are transitional words and phrases used appropriately to identify points of comparison and contrast? List some of the transitions used.
6. Are additional transitions needed? If so, where?
7. How could the introductory paragraph be improved?
8. How could the concluding paragraph be improved?

The selections that follow illustrate both subject-by-subject and point-by-point comparisons. The first selection, a pair of visual texts, is followed by questions designed to illustrate how comparison and contrast can operate in visual form.

AUGUSTE RODIN

The Kiss (Sculpture)

The Kiss, 1888–98 (marble)/Rodin, Auguste (1840–1917)/PHILIPPE GALARD/Musee Rodin, Paris, France/Bridgeman Images

continued

ROBERT INDIANA

LOVE (Sculpture)

Amanda Hall/robertharding/Getty Images

• • •

Reading Images

1. What characteristics do the two sculptures pictured on the preceding pages share? Do they share enough characteristics to establish a basis for comparison? Explain.
2. Make a list of points you could discuss if you were comparing the two sculptures.
3. What general statement could you make about these two sculptures? Do the points you listed in response to question 2 provide enough support for this general statement?

Journal Entry

How does each sculpture convey the idea of love? Which one do you believe conveys this idea more effectively? Why?

Thematic Connections

- "The Storm" (page 196)
- "Sex, Lies, and Conversation" (page 415)
- "Shall I compare thee to a summer's day?" (page 428)

BRUCE CATTON

Grant and Lee: A Study in Contrasts

Bruce Catton (1899–1978) was a respected journalist and an authority on the American Civil War. His studies were interrupted by his service during World War I, after which he worked as a journalist and then for various government agencies. Catton edited *American Heritage* magazine from 1954 until his death. Among his many books are *Mr. Lincoln's Army* (1951); *A Stillness at Appomattox* (1953), which won both a Pulitzer Prize for History and a National Book Award; and *Gettysburg: The Final Fury* (1974). Catton also wrote a memoir, *Waiting for the Morning Train* (1972), in which he recalls listening as a young boy to the reminiscences of Union Army veterans.

Background on Grant and Lee "Grant and Lee: A Study in Contrasts," which first appeared in a collection of historical essays titled *The American Story,* focuses on the two generals who headed the opposing armies during the Civil War (1861–1865). Robert E. Lee led the Army of Northern Virginia, the backbone of the Confederate forces, throughout much of the war. Ulysses S. Grant was named general-in-chief of the Union troops in March 1864. By the spring of 1865, although it seemed almost inevitable that the Southern forces would be defeated, Lee made an attempt to lead his troops to join another Confederate army in North Carolina. Finding himself virtually surrounded by Grant's forces near the small town of Appomattox, Virginia, Lee chose to surrender to Grant. The following essay considers these two great generals in terms of both their differences and their important similarities.

When Ulysses S. Grant and Robert E. Lee met in the parlor of a modest house at Appomattox Court House, Virginia, on April 9, 1865, to work out the terms for the surrender of Lee's Army of Northern Virginia, a great chapter in American life came to a close, and a great new chapter began. 1

These men were bringing the Civil War to its virtual finish. To be sure, other armies had yet to surrender, and for a few days the fugitive Confederate government would struggle desperately and vainly, trying to find some way to go on living now that its chief support was gone. But in effect it was all over when Grant and Lee signed the papers. And the little room where they wrote out the terms was the scene of one of the poignant, dramatic contrasts in American history. 2

They were two strong men, these oddly different generals, and they represented the strengths of two conflicting currents that, through them, had come into final collision. 3

Back of Robert E. Lee was the notion that the old aristocratic concept might somehow survive and be dominant in American life. 4

Lee was tidewater Virginia, and in his background were family, culture, and tradition . . . the age of chivalry transplanted to a New World which was making its own legends and its own myths. He embodied a way of life that had 5 come down through the age of knighthood and the English country squire. America was a land that was beginning all over again, dedicated to nothing much more complicated than the rather hazy belief that all men had equal rights and should have an equal chance in the world. In such a land Lee stood for the feeling that it was somehow of advantage to human society to have pronounced inequality in the social structure. There should be a leisure class, backed by ownership of land; in turn, society itself should be keyed to the land as the chief source of wealth and influence. It would bring forth (according to this ideal) a class of men with a strong sense of obligation to the community; men who lived not to gain advantage for themselves, but to meet the solemn obligations which had been laid on them by the very fact that they were privileged. From them the country would get its leadership; to them it could look for the higher values – of thought, of conduct, of personal deportment – to give it strength and virtue.

Lee embodied the noblest elements of this aristocratic ideal. Through 6 him, the landed nobility justified itself. For four years, the Southern states had fought a desperate war to uphold the ideals for which Lee stood. In the end, it almost seemed as if the Confederacy fought for Lee; as if he himself was the Confederacy . . . the best thing that the way of life for which the Confederacy stood could ever have to offer. He had passed into legend before Appomattox. Thousands of tired, underfed, poorly clothed Confederate soldiers, long since past the simple enthusiasm of the early days of the struggle, somehow considered Lee the symbol of everything for which they had been willing to die. But they could not quite put this feeling into words. If the Lost Cause, sanctified by so much heroism and so many deaths, had a living justification, its justification was General Lee.

Grant, the son of a tanner on the Western frontier, was everything Lee was 7 not. He had come up the hard way and embodied nothing in particular except the eternal toughness and sinewy fiber of the men who grew up beyond the mountains. He was one of a body of men who owed reverence and obeisance to no one, who were self-reliant to a fault, who cared hardly anything for the past but who had a sharp eye for the future.

These frontier men were the precise opposites of the tidewater aristocrats. 8 Back of them, in the great surge that had taken people over the Alleghenies and into the opening Western country, there was a deep, implicit dissatisfaction with a past that had settled into grooves. They stood for democracy, not from any reasoned conclusion about the proper ordering of human society, but simply because they had grown up in the middle of democracy and knew how it worked. Their society might have privileges, but they would be privileges each man had won for himself. Forms and patterns meant nothing. No man was born to anything, except perhaps to a chance to show how far he could rise. Life was competition.

Yet along with this feeling had come a deep sense of belonging to a 9 national community. The Westerner who developed a farm, opened a shop, or set up in business as a trader could hope to prosper only as his own community prospered – and his community ran from the Atlantic to the Pacific and from Canada down to Mexico. If the land was settled, with towns and highways and accessible markets, he could better himself. He saw his fate in terms of the nation's own destiny. As its horizons expanded, so did his. He had, in other words, an acute dollars-and-cents stake in the continued growth and development of his country.

And that, perhaps, is where the contrast between Grant and Lee becomes 10
most striking. The Virginia aristocrat, inevitably, saw himself in relation to his own region. He lived in a static society which could endure almost anything except change. Instinctively, his first loyalty would go to the locality in which that society existed. He would fight to the limit of endurance to defend it, because in defending it he was defending everything that gave his own life its deepest meaning.

The Westerner, on the other hand, would fight with an equal tenacity 11
for the broader concept of society. He fought so because everything he lived by was tied to growth, expansion, and a constantly widening horizon. What he lived by would survive or fall with the nation itself. He could not possibly stand by unmoved in the face of an attempt to destroy the Union. He would combat it with everything he had, because he could only see it as an effort to cut the ground out from under his feet.

"So Grant and Lee were in complete contrast, representing two diametrically opposed elements in American life."

So Grant and Lee were in complete 12
contrast, representing two diametrically opposed elements in American life. Grant was the modern man emerging; beyond him, ready to come on the stage, was the great age of steel and machinery, of crowded cities and a restless burgeoning vitality. Lee might have ridden down from the old age of chivalry, lance in hand, silken banner fluttering over his head. Each man was the perfect champion of his cause, drawing both his strengths and his weaknesses from the people he led.

Yet it was not all contrast, after all. Different as they were—in background, 13
in personality, in underlying aspiration—these two great soldiers had much in common. Under everything else, they were marvelous fighters. Furthermore, their fighting qualities were really very much alike.

Each man had, to begin with, the great virtue of utter tenacity and fidel- 14
ity. Grant fought his way down the Mississippi Valley in spite of acute personal discouragement and profound military handicaps. Lee hung on in the trenches at Petersburg after hope itself had died. In each man there was an indomitable quality . . . the born fighter's refusal to give up as long as he can still remain on his feet and lift his two fists.

Daring and resourcefulness they had, too; the ability to think faster 15
and move faster than the enemy. These were the qualities which gave Lee the dazzling campaigns of Second Manassas and Chancellorsville and won Vicksburg for Grant.

Lastly, and perhaps greatest of all, there was the ability, at the end, to 16
turn quickly from war to peace once the fighting was over. Out of the way these two men behaved at Appomattox came the possibility of a peace of

reconciliation. It was a possibility not wholly realized, in the years to come, but which did, in the end, help the two sections to become one nation again . . . after a war whose bitterness might have seemed to make such a reunion wholly impossible. No part of either man's life became him more than the part he played in this brief meeting in the McLean house at Appomattox. Their behavior there put all succeeding generations of Americans in their debt. Two great Americans, Grant and Lee—very different, yet under everything very much alike. Their encounter at Appomattox was one of the great moments of American history.

• • •

Comprehension

1. What took place at Appomattox Court House on April 9, 1865? Why did the meeting at Appomattox signal the closing of "a great chapter in American life" (1)?
2. How does Robert E. Lee represent aristocracy? How does Ulysses S. Grant represent Lee's opposite?
3. According to Catton, where is it that "the contrast between Grant and Lee becomes most striking" (10)?
4. What similarities does Catton see between the two men?
5. Why, according to Catton, are "succeeding generations of Americans" (16) in debt to Grant and Lee?

Purpose and Audience

1. Catton's purpose in contrasting Grant and Lee is to make a statement about the differences between two currents in U.S. history. Summarize these differences. Do you think the differences still exist today? Explain.
2. Is Catton's purpose in comparing Grant and Lee the same as his purpose in contrasting them? That is, do their similarities also make a statement about U.S. history? Explain.
3. State the essay's thesis in your own words.

Style and Structure

1. Does Catton use subject-by-subject or point-by-point comparison? Why do you think he chooses the strategy he does?
2. In this essay, topic sentences are extremely helpful to the reader. Explain the functions of the following sentences: "Grant . . . was everything Lee was not" (7); "So Grant and Lee were in complete contrast" (12); "Yet it was not all contrast, after all" (13); and "Lastly, and perhaps greatest of all . . ." (16).
3. Catton uses transitions skillfully in his essay. Identify the transitional words or expressions that link each paragraph to the preceding one.

4. Why do you suppose Catton provides the background for the meeting at Appomattox but presents no information about the dramatic meeting itself?
5. **Vocabulary Project.** Go to an online thesaurus, and look up **synonyms** for each of the following words. Then, determine whether each synonym would be as effective as the word used in this essay.

   deportment (5) obeisance (7) indomitable (14)
   sanctified (6) diametrically (12)

Journal Entry

Compare your attitudes about the United States with those held by Grant and by Lee. With which man do you agree?

Writing Workshop

1. Write a "study in contrasts" about two people you know well – two teachers, your parents, two relatives, two friends – or about two fictional characters you are very familiar with. Be sure to include a thesis statement.
2. Write a dialogue between two people you know that reveals their contrasting attitudes toward school, work, or any other subject.
3. **Working with Sources.** Using language and syntax appropriate for middle-school students, rewrite this essay for that audience, making the same points Catton makes about the differences between Grant and Lee. Be sure to include parenthetical documentation for any references to Catton's essay and also a works-cited page. (See Chapter 18 for information on MLA documentation.)

Combining the Patterns

In several places, Catton uses **exemplification** to structure a paragraph. For instance, in paragraph 7, he uses examples to support the topic sentence "Grant, the son of a tanner on the Western frontier, was everything Lee was not." Identify three paragraphs that use examples to support the topic sentence, and bracket the examples. How do these examples in these paragraphs reinforce the similarities and differences between Grant and Lee?

Thematic Connections

- "Ground Zero" (page 173)
- The Declaration of Independence (page 550)
- "Letter from Birmingham Jail" (page 558)
- "On Patriotism" (page 697)

JUAN WILLIAMS

Songs of the Summer of 1963 . . . and Today

Born in Panama in 1954, Juan Williams grew up in Brooklyn, New York, after his family came to the United States. He earned a B.A. from Haverford College. Williams has had a long and varied career in journalism, including a two-decade association with the *Washington Post*, where he not only wrote editorials and opinion columns but also covered the White House as a reporter. His books include *Eyes on the Prize: America's Civil Rights Years, 1954–1965* (1987) and *Muzzled: The Assault on Honest Debate* (2011). He has written for the *New York Times Sunday Magazine*, the *Atlantic Monthly*, *Ebony*, and other publications. For many years, he was a reporter and host for National Public Radio. Currently, he is a political analyst for Fox News.

Background on the 1963 March on Washington Although the August 28, 1963, March on Washington is primarily associated with the civil rights movement — and, in particular, with Martin Luther King Jr.'s famous "I Have a Dream" speech — the event was originally planned as a response to the high rate of unemployment among African Americans. In 1961, A. Philip Randolph, an African-American labor activist and civil rights pioneer, proposed a "Jobs Rights March and Mobilization." Over the course of the next two years, several organizations, including the National Association for the Advancement of Colored People (NAACP), the Congress for Racial Equality (CORE), the Negro American Labor Council (NALC), and King's Southern Christian Leadership Conference (SCLC), organized the event, which was ultimately called "The March on Washington for Jobs and Freedom." The platform of the march included calls for civil rights legislation; a national two-dollar-per-hour minimum wage; school desegregation; job training programs; and other political, social, and economic measures. More than 200,000 people took part in the march, a crowd that stretched from the Washington Monument to the Lincoln Memorial. Following the march, King and other civil rights leaders attended a meeting in the White House with President John Kennedy and Vice President Lyndon Johnson. Among the political legacies of the march are the Civil Rights Act of 1964 and the Voting Rights Act of 1965.

Fifty years after the March on Washington, mystical memories of that seminal moment in the civil-rights era are less likely to focus on movement politics than on the great poetry and great music. 1

The emotional uplift of the monumental march is a universe of time away from today's degrading rap music – filled with the n-word, bitches, and "hoes" – that confuses and depresses race relations in America now. 2

The poetry of August 28, 1963, is best on view when Martin Luther King Jr. went off his speech script and started using a musical, chanting reprise – "I have a dream." The transforming insight born of the power of 3 the interracial gathering at that time of turmoil, combined with the power of the spoken word, created an emotional message that still grips the American mind.

4 "I have a dream that one day on the red hills of Georgia, sons of former slaves and the sons of former slave owners will be able to sit down together at the table of brotherhood," King said, in verse that somehow spanned a history of slavery and the Founding Fathers' uniquely American promise of equality.

5 "I have a dream that one day even the state of Mississippi, a state sweltering with the heat of injustice, sweltering with the heat of oppression, will be transformed into an oasis of freedom and justice. I have a dream that my four little children will one day live in a nation where they will not be judged by the color of their skin, but the content of their character. I have a dream today!"

6 That poetry rose above the reality that as King spoke the civil-rights movement was stalled. Few schools had integrated after the Supreme Court's *Brown v. Board of Education* decision nine years earlier. One hundred years after the Emancipation Proclamation, the Civil Rights Act was stuck in Congress. NAACP leader Medgar Evers had been killed in June. After a violent April in Alabama, in which protest marchers were beaten and set upon by police dogs, an estimated fifteen thousand more civil-rights activists had been arrested at protests across the country that summer.

7 King sailed past all those sad realities to invoke his soaring vision of the nation at racial peace. When he finished speaking, the crowd spontaneously broke into singing "We Shall Overcome," holding hands and swaying as if in communal prayer.

> "That sense of unity, promise, and purpose was also evident in the music of the march. It's music that still stirs emotions to this day."

8 That sense of unity, promise, and purpose was also evident in the music of the march. It's music that still stirs emotions to this day.

9 Bob Dylan's "Blowin' in the Wind," written in 1962, hit number two on the Billboard charts just before the crowd gathered in Washington. When the folk-music trio Peter, Paul, and Mary sang the song for the 250,000 people in front of the Lincoln Memorial that day, it became an interracial anthem for change. The song itself drew inspiration from two others: The lyrics brought to mind Woody Guthrie's "Bound for Glory," which included an allegory about newspapers blowing down city streets, and its melody came from a slave protest song called "No More Auction Block."

10 And so they sang in Washington: "Yes, how many years can some people exist before they're allowed to be free? Yes, how many times can a man turn his head, pretending that he just doesn't see? The answer, my friend, is blowin' in the wind, the answer is blowin' in the wind."

11 Sam Cooke, the black gospel and rhythm-and-blues singer, began performing the Dylan song immediately after the march. He had been working

on a song about the hurt he felt as a black man living with racism yet also with hope for better times. In December 1963, Cooke recorded "A Change Is Gonna Come." The song became a hit on black radio, another anthem of yearning for a nation without racial rancor.

"I go to the movie and I go downtown, somebody keep telling me don't hang around," Cooke wrote. "It's been a long time coming, but I know a change is gonna come, oh yes it will." 12

The next year, in 1964, Curtis Mayfield – also openly inspired by the music of the march – wrote an even more hopeful song: "People Get Ready." It, too, picked up on a frequent image of American folklore, the train of salvation. 13

Just as Woody Guthrie and Johnny Cash had sung "This Train's Bound for Glory," Mayfield, a black Chicago singer steeped in church gospel music and the blues, sang about faith in the American struggle for racial justice. 14

"People get ready, there's a train a-comin'; you don't need no baggage, you just get on board . . . there ain't no room for the hopeless sinner who would hurt all mankind just to save his own. Have pity on those whose chances grow thinner, for there's no hiding place against the Kingdom's throne." 15

The uplifting lyrics made "People Get Ready" one of the earliest hits on both black and white radio. Bob Marley later used some of the words in his poignant song "One Love." Bruce Springsteen used the song as a healing anthem at concerts after the 9/11 terror attacks. 16

The songs by Dylan, Cooke, and Mayfield have been ranked fourteenth, twelfth, and twenty-fourth on *Rolling Stone* magazine's list of greatest songs of all time. All three have roots in the March on Washington. 17

Now, half a century after the lyrical promise of that inspiring music and poetry, there is the inescapable and heartbreaking contrast with the malignant, self-aggrandizing rap songs that define today's most popular music. 18

In Jay-Z's current hit, "Holy Grail," he sings about "psycho bitches" and uses the n-word seven times while bragging that he is "Living the life . . . Illest [n-word] alive." Another top rapper, Lil Wayne, released a song in the spring with an obscenity *in the title,* using the n-word repeatedly and depicting himself as abusing "hoes" and "bitches." 19

Similar examples abound in the rap-music world and have persisted for years with scarcely any complaint from today's civil-rights leaders. Their failure to denounce these lyrics for the damage they do to poor and minority families – words celebrating tattooed thugs and sexually indiscriminate women as icons of "keeping it real" – is a sad reminder of how long it has been since the world heard the sweet music of the March on Washington. 20

• • •

Comprehension

1. What is the "great poetry" that Williams alludes to in paragraph 1?
2. Williams says that when King delivered his "I Have a Dream" speech, "the civil-rights movement was stalled" (6). What does he mean?

3. How do the songs of 1962 and 1963 reflect the different moods of those two years? How would you define each of these two moods?
4. In his essay, Williams refers to songs by Bob Dylan, Sam Cooke, and Curtis Mayfield. According to Williams, what do these songs have in common?
5. How is today's mood different from that of the civil rights era? How does contemporary popular music reflect this difference?

Purpose and Audience

1. Does Williams assume his readers will be familiar with the events he discusses? How can you tell?
2. Do you think Williams expects readers to know the songs he refers to? Why or why not?
3. What is Williams's purpose in writing this essay? What effect does he want his essay to have on his readers?

Style and Structure

1. How do the first two paragraphs set up the discussion for the rest of the essay?
2. Write a one-sentence summary of Williams's thesis.
3. Throughout most of his essay, Williams discusses the music from the early 1960s. Only in paragraph 19 does he survey contemporary rap music. Should he have spent more time discussing current music? Why or why not?
4. This essay is organized as a subject-by-subject comparison. Where does Williams move from one subject to the other? What transition does he use to signal this shift?
5. What point does Williams emphasize in his conclusion? Does his conclusion reinforce his thesis statement? Explain.
6. **Vocabulary Project.** In paragraph 18, Williams talks about both the music of the early 1960s and more recent music. What adjectives does he use to describe each type of music? How do these adjectives convey Williams's attitude toward the two types of music?

Journal Entry

Do you think Williams's assessment of contemporary rap music is accurate, or do you think he exaggerates the harm it does (or misrepresents its effects)?

Writing Workshop

1. Compare the music you listened to when you were younger to the music you listen to now. What do the two types of music tell about you and how you have changed? Write a comparison-and-contrast essay in which you discuss your conclusions.

2. **Working with Sources.** Write an essay in which you compare and contrast two different popular songs, focusing on lyrics, music, or political or social messages. Be sure to quote lyrics from the songs and to include parenthetical documentation and a works-cited page. (See Chapter 18 for information on MLA documentation.)
3. **Working with Sources.** Find several of the songs Williams mentions on YouTube, and listen to them. Then, write an email to Williams in which you agree or disagree with his assessments. Make sure to structure your email as a comparison-and-contrast essay and to refer specifically to Williams's essay as well as to the lyrics of the songs. Include parenthetical documentation where necessary, as well as a works-cited page, and also include YouTube links to the performances you watched. (See Chapter 18 for information on MLA documentation.)

Combining the Patterns

Williams uses a number of **exemplification** paragraphs in his essay. Identify two or three of these exemplification paragraphs, and determine what they add to the essay.

Thematic Connections

- "Goodbye to My Twinkie Days" (page 169)
- "Once More to the Lake" (page 189)
- "Letter from Birmingham Jail" (page 558)

AMY CHUA

Why Chinese Mothers Are Superior

Amy Chua was born in Champaign, Illinois, in 1962. She graduated from Harvard College and earned her J.D. at Harvard Law School, where she was executive editor of the *Harvard Law Review*. Chua is now the John M. Duff Professor of Law at Yale Law School, where she focuses on international law and business, ethnic conflict, and globalization and the law. She has written two scholarly books, *World on Fire: How Exporting Free Market Democracy Breeds Ethnic Hatred and Global Instability* (2003) and *Days of Empire: How Hyperpowers Rise to Global Dominance—and Why They Fall* (2007). Today, however, Chua is best known for her parenting memoir, *Battle Hymn of the Tiger Mother* (2011).

Background on parenting styles Chua writes disapprovingly about contemporary "Western" parents who, she claims, are "extremely anxious about their children's self-esteem." Such anxieties are relatively new, especially when one surveys the history of parenting—from the ancient Greeks, who commonly left unwanted children in the woods to die of exposure, to seventeenth-century American Puritans, who practiced a philosophy of visual "Better whipt than damned." French Enlightenment figure Jean-Jacques Rousseau (1712–1778) proposed a more sympathetic view of the child, writing that when "children's wills are not spoiled by our fault, children want nothing uselessly." In the nineteenth and early twentieth centuries, however, American parenting philosophies usually focused on discipline, emotional detachment, and the wisdom of experts. As Dr. Luther Emmett Holt wrote in *The Care and Feeding of Children* (1894), "instinct and maternal love are too often assumed to be a sufficient guide for a mother." Pediatrician Benjamin Spock, who published his enormously influential *Baby and Child Care* in 1946, is often credited with—or blamed for—a social shift toward more permissive child-rearing, especially in the context of the baby-boom generation. Spock urged parents to trust their own judgment and to meet their children's needs rather than worrying about "spoiling" the child. In the decades that followed, this parenting approach accompanied an increasing emphasis on children's self-esteem, both at home and in school.

A lot of people wonder how Chinese parents raise such stereotypically successful kids. They wonder what these parents do to produce so many math whizzes and music prodigies, what it's like inside the family, and whether they could do it too. Well, I can tell them, because I've done it. Here are some things my daughters, Sophia and Louisa, were never allowed to do: 1

- attend a sleepover
- have a playdate
- be in a school play
- complain about not being in a school play
- watch TV or play computer games
- choose their own extracurricular activities

- get any grade less than an A
- not be the No. 1 student in every subject except gym and drama
- play any instrument other than the piano or violin
- not play the piano or violin.

2 I'm using the term "Chinese mother" loosely. I know some Korean, Indian, Jamaican, Irish, and Ghanaian parents who qualify too. Conversely, I know some mothers of Chinese heritage, almost always born in the West, who are not Chinese mothers, by choice or otherwise. I'm also using the term "Western parents" loosely. Western parents come in all varieties.

3 When it comes to parenting, the Chinese seem to produce children who display academic excellence, musical mastery, and professional success – or so the stereotype goes. *WSJ*'s* Christina Tsuei speaks to two moms raised by Chinese immigrants who share what it was like growing up and how they hope to raise their children.

4 All the same, even when Western parents think they're being strict, they usually don't come close to being Chinese mothers. For example, my Western friends who consider themselves strict make their children practice their instruments 30 minutes every day. An hour at most. For a Chinese mother, the first hour is the easy part. It's hours two and three that get tough.

5 Despite our squeamishness about cultural stereotypes, there are tons of studies out there showing marked and quantifiable differences between Chinese and Westerners when it comes to parenting. In one study of fifty Western American mothers and forty-eight Chinese immigrant mothers, almost 70 percent of the Western mothers said either that "stressing academic success is not good for children" or that "parents need to foster the idea that learning is fun." By contrast, roughly 0 percent of the Chinese mothers felt the same way. Instead, the vast majority of the Chinese mothers said that they believe their children can be "the best" students, that "academic achievement reflects successful parenting," and that if children did not excel at school then there was "a problem" and parents "were not doing their job." Other studies indicate that compared to Western parents, Chinese parents spend approximately ten times as long every day drilling academic activities with their children. By contrast, Western kids are more likely to participate in sports teams.

6 What Chinese parents understand is that nothing is fun until you're good at it. To get good at anything you have to work, and children on their own never want to work, which is why it is crucial to override their preferences. This often requires fortitude on the part of the parents because the child will resist; things are always hardest at the beginning, which is where Western parents tend to give up. But if done properly, the Chinese strategy produces a virtuous circle. Tenacious practice, practice, practice is crucial for excellence;

"What Chinese parents understand is that nothing is fun until you're good at it."

* Eds. note – *Wall Street Journal.*

rote repetition is underrated in America. Once a child starts to excel at something—whether it's math, piano, pitching, or ballet—he or she gets praise, admiration, and satisfaction. This builds confidence and makes the once not-fun activity fun. This in turn makes it easier for the parent to get the child to work even more.

Chinese parents can get away with things that Western parents can't. 7
Once when I was young—maybe more than once—when I was extremely disrespectful to my mother, my father angrily called me "garbage" in our native Hokkien dialect. It worked really well. I felt terrible and deeply ashamed of what I had done. But it didn't damage my self-esteem or anything like that. I knew exactly how highly he thought of me. I didn't actually think I was worthless or feel like a piece of garbage.

As an adult, I once did the same thing to Sophia, calling her "garbage" 8
in English when she acted extremely disrespectfully toward me. When I mentioned that I had done this at a dinner party, I was immediately ostracized. One guest named Marcy got so upset she broke down in tears and had to leave early. My friend Susan, the host, tried to rehabilitate me with the remaining guests.

The fact is that Chinese parents can do things that would seem unimag- 9
inable—even legally actionable—to Westerners. Chinese mothers can say to their daughters, "Hey fatty—lose some weight." By contrast, Western parents have to tiptoe around the issue, talking in terms of "health" and never ever mentioning the f-word, and their kids still end up in therapy for eating disorders and negative self-image. (I also once heard a Western father toast his adult daughter by calling her "beautiful and incredibly competent." She later told me that made her feel like garbage.)

Chinese parents can order their kids to get straight As. Western parents 10
can only ask their kids to try their best. Chinese parents can say, "You're lazy. All your classmates are getting ahead of you." By contrast, Western parents have to struggle with their own conflicted feelings about achievement, and try to persuade themselves that they're not disappointed about how their kids turned out.

I've thought long and hard about how Chinese parents can get away with 11
what they do. I think there are three big differences between the Chinese and Western parental mind-sets.

First, I've noticed that Western parents are extremely anxious about their 12
children's self-esteem. They worry about how their children will feel if they fail at something, and they constantly try to reassure their children about how good they are notwithstanding a mediocre performance on a test or at a recital. In other words, Western parents are concerned about their children's psyches. Chinese parents aren't. They assume strength, not fragility, and as a result they behave very differently.

For example, if a child comes home with an A-minus on a test, a Western 13
parent will most likely praise the child. The Chinese mother will gasp in horror and ask what went wrong. If the child comes home with a B on the test, some Western parents will still praise the child. Other Western parents

will sit their child down and express disapproval, but they will be careful not to make their child feel inadequate or insecure, and they will not call their child "stupid," "worthless," or "a disgrace." Privately, the Western parents may worry that their child does not test well or have aptitude in the subject or that there is something wrong with the curriculum and possibly the whole school. If the child's grades do not improve, they may eventually schedule a meeting with the school principal to challenge the way the subject is being taught or to call into question the teacher's credentials.

If a Chinese child gets a B – which would never happen – there would first be a screaming, hair-tearing explosion. The devastated Chinese mother would then get dozens, maybe hundreds of practice tests and work through them with her child for as long as it takes to get the grade up to an A. 14

Chinese parents demand perfect grades because they believe that their child can get them. If their child doesn't get them, the Chinese parent assumes it's because the child didn't work hard enough. That's why the solution to substandard performance is always to excoriate, punish, and shame the child. The Chinese parent believes that their child will be strong enough to take the shaming and to improve from it. (And when Chinese kids do excel, there is plenty of ego-inflating parental praise lavished in the privacy of the home.) 15

Second, Chinese parents believe that their kids owe them everything. The reason for this is a little unclear, but it's probably a combination of Confucian filial piety and the fact that the parents have sacrificed and done so much for their children. (And it's true that Chinese mothers get in the trenches, putting in long grueling hours personally tutoring, training, interrogating, and spying on their kids.) Anyway, the understanding is that Chinese children must spend their lives repaying their parents by obeying them and making them proud. 16

By contrast, I don't think most Westerners have the same view of children being permanently indebted to their parents. My husband, Jed, actually has the opposite view. "Children don't choose their parents," he once said to me. "They don't even choose to be born. It's parents who foist life on their kids, so it's the parents' responsibility to provide for them. Kids don't owe their parents anything. Their duty will be to their own kids." This strikes me as a terrible deal for the Western parent. 17

Third, Chinese parents believe that they know what is best for their children and therefore override all of their children's own desires and preferences. That's why Chinese daughters can't have boyfriends in high school and why Chinese kids can't go to sleepaway camp. It's also why no Chinese kid would ever dare say to their mother, "I got a part in the school play! I'm Villager Number Six. I'll have to stay after school for rehearsal every day from 3:00 to 7:00, and I'll also need a ride on weekends." God help any Chinese kid who tried that one. 18

Don't get me wrong: It's not that Chinese parents don't care about their children. Just the opposite. They would give up anything for their children. It's just an entirely different parenting model. 19

. . . Western parents worry a lot about their children's self-esteem. But as a parent, one of the worst things you can do for your child's self-esteem is to let them give up. On the flip side, there's nothing better for building confidence than learning you can do something you thought you couldn't. 20

There are all these new books out there portraying Asian mothers as scheming, callous, overdriven people indifferent to their kids' true interests. For their part, many Chinese secretly believe that they care more about their children and are willing to sacrifice much more for them than Westerners, who seem perfectly content to let their children turn out badly. I think it's a misunderstanding on both sides. All decent parents want to do what's best for their children. The Chinese just have a totally different idea of how to do that. 21

Western parents try to respect their children's individuality, encouraging them to pursue their true passions, supporting their choices, and providing positive reinforcement and a nurturing environment. By contrast, the Chinese believe that the best way to protect their children is by preparing them for the future, letting them see what they're capable of, and arming them with skills, work habits, and inner confidence that no one can ever take away. 22

• • •

Comprehension

1. What does Chua mean when she says, "What Chinese parents understand is that nothing is fun until you're good at it" (6)? Do you agree with her?
2. Does Chua's husband agree or disagree with her child-rearing methods? Why does he react the way he does?
3. According to Chua, why are Chinese parents able to do things that Western parents cannot?
4. How does Chua respond to the charge that Chinese parents don't care about their children?
5. According to Chua, how do Chinese child-rearing practices prepare children for life?

Purpose and Audience

1. What preconceptions about Chinese mothers does Chua think Westerners have? Do you think she is right?
2. Does Chua seem to expect her readers to be receptive, hostile, or neutral to her ideas? What evidence can you find to support your impression?
3. What is Chua's thesis? Where does she state it?
4. In an interview, Chua said that the editors of the *Wall Street Journal,* not she, chose the title of her essay. Why do you think the editors chose the title they did? What title do you think Chua would have chosen? What title would you give the essay?

Style and Structure

1. Why does Chua begin her essay with a list of things her two daughters were not allowed to do as they were growing up? How do you think she expects readers to react to this list? How do you react?
2. Is this essay a point-by-point comparison, a subject-by-subject comparison, or a combination of the two organizational strategies? Why does Chua arrange her comparison the way she does?
3. What evidence does Chua present to support her view that there are marked differences between the parenting styles of Chinese and Western parents?
4. Chua was born in the United States. Does this fact undercut her conclusions about the differences between Western and Chinese child-rearing? Explain.
5. What points does Chua emphasize in her conclusion? How else could she have ended her essay?
6. **Vocabulary Project.** In paragraph 2, Chua says she is using the terms "Chinese mother" and "Western parents" loosely. What does she mean? How does she define these two terms? How would you define them?

Journal Entry

Do you think Chua's essay perpetuates a cultural stereotype? Why or why not?

Writing Workshop

1. Write an essay in which you compare your upbringing to that of Chua's daughters. Were your parents "Western" or "Chinese" parents (or, were they a combination of the two)? In your thesis, take a stand on the question of which kind of parent is "superior." Use examples from your childhood to support your thesis.
2. **Working with Sources.** Read the poem "Suicide Note" by Janice Mirikitani (page 364). Then, write an essay in which you compare Chua's positive view of Asian child-rearing practices with the feelings expressed by the speaker in Mirikitani's poem. Be sure to include parenthetical documentation for any references to the two sources and a works-cited page. (See Chapter 18 for information on MLA documentation.)
3. When Chua's essay was published, it elicited thousands of responses, many of which were negative. For example, some readers thought her parenting methods were tantamount to child abuse, others admired Chua for her resolve and her emphasis on hard work, and still others said her methods reminded them of their own upbringings. Chua herself responded to readers' comments by saying her "tough love" approach was grounded in her desire to make sure her children were the best they could be. Write an email to Chua in which you respond to her essay. Be sure to address each of her major points and to compare your opinions to hers.

Combining the Patterns

Throughout her essay, Chua includes **exemplification** paragraphs. Identify two exemplification paragraphs, and explain how they help Chua make her point about the superiority of Chinese mothers.

Thematic Connections

- "Indian Education" (page 140)
- "Suicide Note" (page 364)
- "Mother Tongue" (page 458)

ELLEN LAIRD

I'm Your Teacher, Not Your Internet-Service Provider

An educator and essayist for more than thirty years, Ellen Laird believes that technology has forever changed both teaching and learning, as the following essay, originally published in the *Chronicle of Higher Education,* suggests. Laird teaches at Hudson Valley Community College in New York.

Background on distance learning Correspondence schools began to appear in the United States in the late nineteenth century, facilitated to a large degree by an extensive and efficient national postal service. These schools allowed students to receive study materials by mail and to complete examinations and other written work that they then submitted, again by mail, to a central departmental office for response and grading by instructors. For the most part, correspondence schools tended to focus on technical curricula, although some programs were geared toward a more traditional liberal arts curriculum. By the 1930s, correspondence schools had entered a period of decline because an increase in the number of high school graduates and the rise of junior colleges meant that students were more likely to have hands-on educational opportunities close to home. Then, beginning in the 1960s, the concept was revived through the broadcast of publicly funded televised courses, again with a mail-based system for transmitting written materials. Today, many universities have Internet-based distance-learning programs. They find that the Internet is a cost-effective, flexible, and efficient way to deliver courses to a large number of students, many of whom cannot commute to campus. Online education is not without problems, however. Some students complain that online classes do not provide the immediacy and intellectual stimulation of traditional classrooms. Moreover, students must be highly motivated and disciplined to complete online courses. Finally, discussion boards and email do not enable instructors to connect with students the way face-to-face settings do.

The honeymoon is over. My romance with distance teaching is losing its spark. Gone are the days when I looked forward to each new online encounter with students, when preparing and posting a basic assignment was a thrilling adventure, when my colleagues and friends were well-wishers, cautiously hopeful about my new entanglement. What remains is this instructor, alone, often in the dark of night, facing the reality of my online class and struggling to make it work. 1

After four years of Internet teaching, I must pause. When pressed to demonstrate that my online composition class is the equivalent of my classroom-based composition sections, I can do so professionally and persuasively. On the surface, course goals, objectives, standards, outlines, texts, Web materials, and so forth, are identical. But my fingers are crossed. 2

> "The honeymoon is over. My romance with distance teaching is losing its spark."

The two experiences are as different as a wedding reception and a rave. The nonlinear nature of online activity and the well-ingrained habits of Web use involve behavior vastly different from that which fosters success in the traditional college classroom. Last fall, my online students ranged from ages fifteen to fifty, from the home-schooled teen to the local union president. Yet all brought to class assumptions and habits that sometimes interfered with learning and often diminished the quality of the experience for all of us. As a seasoned online instructor, I knew what to expect and how to help students through the inevitable. But for the uninitiated, the reality of online teaching can be confounding and upsetting. It can make a talented teacher feel like an unmitigated failure. 3

If faculty members, whether well established or new, are to succeed in online teaching, they must be prepared for attitudes and behaviors that permeate Web use but undermine teaching and learning in the Web classroom. Potential online instructors are generally offered technical training in file organization, course-management software use, and the like. But they would be best served by an unfiltered look at what really happens when the student logs into class, however elegantly designed the course may be. A few declarative sentences drafted for my next online syllabus may suffice: 4

The syllabus is not a restaurant menu.

In sections offered in campus classrooms, my students regard the syllabus as a fixed set of requirements, not as a menu of choices. They accept the sequence and format in which course material is provided for them. They do not make selections among course requirements according to preference. 5

Online? Not so. Each semester, online students howl electronically about having to complete the same assignments in the same sequence required of my face-to-face students. Typical Internet users, these students are accustomed to choices online. They enjoy the nonlinear nature of Web surfing; they would be hard pressed to replicate the sequence of their activity without the down arrow beside the URL box on their browsers. 6

To their detriment, many of these students fail to consider that Web learning is different from Web use, particularly in a skills-based course like composition. They find it hard to accept, for example, that they must focus on writing a solid thesis before tackling a research paper. Most would prefer to surf from one module of material to the next and complete what appeals to them rather than what is required of them. 7

The difference between students' expectations and reality frustrates us all. In traditional classrooms, students do not pick up or download only the handouts that appeal to them; most do not try to begin the semester's final project without instruction in the material on which it is based. Yet, online students expect such options. 8

Even Cinderella had a deadline.

Students in my traditional classes certainly miss deadlines. But they generally regard deadlines as real, if not observable; they recognize an instructor's right to set due dates; and they accept the consequences of missing them to be those stated on the syllabus. 9

Not so with my online students. Neither fancy font nor flashing bullet can stir the majority to submit work by the published deadline. Students seem to extend the freedom to choose the time and place of their course work to every aspect of the class. Few request extensions in the usual manner. Instead, they announce them. One student, for example, emailed me days after a paper was due, indicating that he had traveled to New York for a Yankees' game and would submit the essay in a couple of weeks. 10

All course components do not function at the speed of the Internet.

As relaxed as my online students are about meeting deadlines, they begin the course expecting instantaneous service. The speed of Internet transmission seduces them into seeking and expecting speed as an element of the course. Naturally, students' emphasis on rapidity works against them. The long, hard, eventually satisfying work of thinking, doing research, reading, and writing has no relationship to bandwidth, processor speed, or cable modems. 11

At the same time, it takes me a long time to respond thoughtfully to students' work, particularly their writing. Each semester, online students require help in understanding that waiting continues to be part of teaching and learning, that the instructor is not another version of an Internet-service provider, to be judged satisfactory or not by processing speed and 24/7 availability. 12

There are no sick or personal days in cyberspace.

In my traditional classes, I refrain from informing students that I will be out of town for a weekend, that I need a root canal, or that my water heater failed before work. My face-to-face students can read my expression and bearing when they see me; thus, I can usually keep personal explanations to a professional minimum. 13

In my online class, however, students cannot see the bags under my eyes or the look of exuberance on my face. They cannot hear the calm or the shake in my voice. Thus, for the smooth functioning of the course, I willingly provide details about where I am and what I am doing, so students can know what to expect. 14

However, I am still troubled by the email message from an online student that began, "I know you are at your father's funeral right now, but I just wondered if you got my paper." Surely, he hesitated before pushing "send," but his need for reassurance prevailed. And so it goes, all semester long. There simply isn't room in an online class for the messiness of ordinary life, the students' or mine. Nor is there room for the extraordinary – the events of September 11, for example. As long as the server functions, the course is always on, bearing down hard on both students and instructor. 15

Still, students will register for online classes under circumstances that would prohibit them from enrolling in a course on the campus. The welder compelled to work mandatory overtime, the pregnant woman due before midsemester, and the newly separated security guard whose wife will not surrender the laptop all arrive online with the hope and the illusion that, in cyberspace, they can accomplish what is temporarily impossible for them on campus. 16

I am not on your buddy list.

The egalitarian atmosphere of the Internet chat room transfers rapidly and inappropriately to the online classroom. Faceless and ageless online, I am, at first, addressed as a peer. If students knew that I dress like many of their mothers, or that my hair will soon be more gray than brown, would their exchanges with me be different? I reveal what I want them to know—the date of my marathon, my now-deceased dog's consumption of a roll of aluminum foil, my one gig as a cocktail-lounge pianist—but little of what one good look at me, in my jumper and jewelry, would tell them. 17

They, on the other hand, hold back nothing. Confessional writing, always a challenge in composition, can easily become the norm online. So can racist, sexist, and otherwise offensive remarks—even admissions of crimes. The lack of a face to match with a rhetorical voice provides the illusion of anonymity, and thus the potential for a no-holds-barred quality to every discussion thread. The usual restraint characterizing conversation among classroom acquaintances evaporates online within about two weeks. Private conversations fuse with academic discussion before an instructor can log in. 18

Are there strategies to manage these and similar difficulties? Of course there are. Thus, I continue with online teaching and welcome both its challenges and its rewards. But educators considering online teaching need to know that instruction in person and online are day and night. They must brace themselves for a marriage of opposites, and build large reserves of commitment, patience, and wherewithal if the relationship is to succeed. 19

• • •

Comprehension

1. Why does Laird say that her "honeymoon" with online teaching is over (1)?
2. According to Laird, why are online teaching and classroom-based teaching different? How does she explain the differences?
3. What does Laird mean when she says that potential online instructors "would be best served by an unfiltered look at what really happens when the student logs into class" (4)?
4. In what way does classroom-based teaching limit students' choices? How is online teaching different?

5. In paragraph 11, Laird says, "The long, hard, eventually satisfying work of thinking, doing research, reading, and writing has no relationship to bandwidth, processor speed, or cable modems." What does she mean?

Purpose and Audience

1. What is the thesis of this essay?
2. To whom do you think Laird is addressing her essay? Instructors? Students? Both?
3. What do you think Laird is trying to accomplish in her essay? Is she successful?
4. Does Laird assume her readers are familiar with online teaching, or does she assume they are relatively unfamiliar with it? How can you tell?

Style and Structure

1. Is this essay a point-by-point or subject-by-subject comparison? Why do you think Laird chose this strategy?
2. Laird highlights a "few declarative sentences" (4) as boldfaced headings throughout her essay. What is the function of these headings?
3. Does Laird seem to favor one type of teaching over another? Is she optimistic or pessimistic about the future of online education? Explain.
4. Does Laird indicate how students feel about online teaching? Should she have spent more time exploring this issue?
5. In her conclusion, Laird asks, "Are there strategies to manage these and similar difficulties?" Her answer: "Of course there are" (19). Should she have listed some of these strategies in her conclusion? Why do you think she does not?
6. **Vocabulary Project.** In paragraph 3, Laird says, "The two experiences are as different as a wedding reception and a rave." What are the denotations and connotations of *wedding reception* and *rave*? What point is Laird trying to make with this comparison?

Journal Entry

Do you agree or disagree with Laird's assessment of distance learning and classroom-based learning? (If you have never taken an online course, discuss only her analysis of classroom-based learning.)

Writing Workshop

1. Write an essay in which you discuss whether you would like to take an online writing course. How do you think such a course would compare with a traditional classroom-based course? (If you are already taking such a course, compare it with a traditional writing course.)

2. **Working with Sources.** Write an email to Laird in which you explain that, like her, students also have difficulty adapting to online instruction. Address the specific difficulties students encounter in such courses, and compare these difficulties with those they experience when they take a classroom-based course. Include at least one quotation from Laird's essay, and be sure to include parenthetical documentation for the quotation and a works-cited page. (See Chapter 18 for information on MLA documentation.)
3. Read the following list of advantages of taking online courses:
   - A student who is ill will not miss classes.
   - Students who are employed and cannot come to campus can take courses.
   - Nontraditional students – people who are elderly or who have a disability, for example – can take courses.
   - Courses are taken at any time, day or night.
   - Guest speakers who cannot travel to campus can be integrated into the course.

   Then, make a list of disadvantages (for example, students never have face-to-face contact with an instructor). Finally, write an essay in which you discuss whether the advantages of online instruction outweigh the disadvantages.

Combining the Patterns

Laird begins her essay with two **narrative** paragraphs. What is the purpose of these paragraphs? What other strategy could Laird have used to introduce her essay?

Thematic Connections

- "Indian Education" (page 140)
- "What I Learned (and Didn't Learn) in College" (page 440)
- "The Dog Ate My Tablet, and Other Tales of Woe" (page 452)
- Debate: "Should Public Colleges and Universities Be Free?" (page 573)

DEBORAH TANNEN

Sex, Lies, and Conversation

Deborah Tannen was born in Brooklyn, New York, in 1945 and currently teaches at Georgetown University. Tannen has written and edited several scholarly books on the problems of communicating across cultural, class, ethnic, and sexual divides. She has also presented her research to the general public in newspapers and magazines and in her best-selling books *That's Not What I Meant!: How Conversational Style Makes or Breaks Relationships* (1986), *You Just Don't Understand: Women and Men in Conversation* (1990), and *Talking from 9 to 5: Women and Men at Work* (1994). Her most recent book is *You Were Always Mom's Favorite: Sisters in Conversation throughout Their Lives* (2009).

Background on men's and women's communication styles Tannen wrote "Sex, Lies, and Conversation" because the chapter in *That's Not What I Meant!* on the difficulties men and women have communicating with one another got such a strong response. She realized the chapter might raise some controversy — that discussing their different communication styles might be used to malign men or to put women at a disadvantage — and indeed, some critics have seen her work as reinforcing stereotypes. Still, her work on the subject, along with that of other writers (most notably John Gray in his *Men Are from Mars, Women Are from Venus* series), has proved enormously popular. Much of the research about male and female differences in terms of brain function, relational styles and expectations, and evolutionary roles continues to stir debate.

I was addressing a small gathering in a suburban Virginia living room – a 1
women's group that had invited men to join them. Throughout the evening, one man had been particularly talkative, frequently offering ideas and anecdotes, while his wife sat silently beside him on the couch. Toward the end of the evening, I commented that women frequently complain that their husbands don't talk to them. This man quickly concurred. He gestured toward his wife and said, "She's the talker in our family." The room burst into laughter; the man looked puzzled and hurt. "It's true," he explained. "When I come home from work I have nothing to say. If she didn't keep the conversation going, we'd spend the whole evening in silence."

This episode crystallizes the irony that although American men tend to 2
talk more than women in public situations, they often talk less at home. And this pattern is wreaking havoc with marriage.

The pattern was observed by political scientist Andrew Hacker in the 3
late '70s. Sociologist Catherine Kohler Riessman reports in her new book *Divorce Talk* that most of the women she interviewed – but only a few of the men – gave lack of communication as the reason for their divorces. Given the current divorce rate of nearly 50 percent, that amounts to millions of cases in the United States every year – a virtual epidemic of failed conversation.

In my own research, complaints from women about their husbands most often focused not on tangible inequities such as having given up the chance for a career to accompany a husband to his, or doing far more than their share of daily life-support work like cleaning, cooking, social arrangements, and errands. Instead, they focused on communication: "He doesn't listen to me," "He doesn't talk to me." I found, as Hacker observed years before, that most wives want their husbands to be, first and foremost, conversational partners, but few husbands share this expectation of their wives. 4

In short, the image that best represents the current crisis is the stereotypical cartoon scene of a man sitting at the breakfast table with a newspaper held up in front of his face, while a woman glares at the back of it, wanting to talk. 5

Linguistic Battle of the Sexes

> "How can women and men have such different impressions of communication in marriage? Why the widespread imbalance in their interests and expectations?"

How can women and men have such different impressions of communication in marriage? Why the widespread imbalance in their interests and expectations? 6

In the April issue of *American Psychologist,* Stanford University's Eleanor Maccoby reports the results of her own and others' research showing that children's development is most influenced by the social structure of peer interactions. Boys and girls tend to play with children of their own gender, and their sex-separate groups have different organizational structures and interactive norms. 7

I believe these systematic differences in childhood socialization make talk between women and men like cross-cultural communication, heir to all the attraction and pitfalls of that enticing but difficult enterprise. My research on men's and women's conversations uncovered patterns similar to those described for children's groups. 8

For women, as for girls, intimacy is the fabric of relationships, and talk is the thread from which it is woven. Little girls create and maintain friendships by exchanging secrets; similarly, women regard conversation as the cornerstone of friendship. So a woman expects her husband to be a new and improved version of a best friend. What is important is not the individual subjects that are discussed but the sense of closeness, of a life shared, that emerges when people tell their thoughts, feelings, and impressions. 9

Bonds between boys can be as intense as girls', but they are based less on talking, more on doing things together. Since they don't assume talk is the cement that binds a relationship, men don't know what kind of talk women want, and they don't miss it when it isn't there. 10

Boys' groups are larger, more inclusive, and more hierarchical, so boys must struggle to avoid the subordinate position in the group. This may play a role in women's complaints that men don't listen to them. Some men really 11 don't like to listen, because being the listener makes them feel one-down, like a child listening to adults or an employee to a boss.

12 But often when women tell men, "You aren't listening," and the men protest, "I am," the men are right. The impression of not listening results from misalignments in the mechanics of conversation. The misalignment begins as soon as a man and a woman take physical positions. This became clear when I studied videotapes made by psychologist Bruce Dorval of children and adults talking to their same-sex best friends. I found that at every age, the girls and women faced each other directly, their eyes anchored on each other's faces. At every age, the boys and men sat at angles to each other and looked elsewhere in the room, periodically glancing at each other. They were obviously attuned to each other, often mirroring each other's movements. But the tendency of men to face away can give women the impression they aren't listening even when they are. A young woman in college was frustrated: Whenever she told her boyfriend she wanted to talk to him, he would lie down on the floor, close his eyes, and put his arm over his face. This signaled to her, "He's taking a nap." But he insisted he was listening extra hard. Normally, he looks around the room, so he is easily distracted. Lying down and covering his eyes helped him concentrate on what she was saying.

13 Analogous to the physical alignment that women and men take in conversation is their topical alignment. The girls in my study tended to talk at length about one topic, but the boys tended to jump from topic to topic. The second-grade girls exchanged stories about people they knew. The second-grade boys teased, told jokes, noticed things in the room, and talked about finding games to play. The sixth-grade girls talked about problems with a mutual friend. The sixth-grade boys talked about fifty-five different topics, none of which extended over more than a few turns.

Listening to Body Language

14 Switching topics is another habit that gives women the impression men aren't listening, especially if they switch to a topic about themselves. But the evidence of the tenth-grade boys in my study indicates otherwise. The tenth-grade boys sprawled across their chairs with bodies parallel and eyes straight ahead, rarely looking at each other. They looked as if they were riding in a car, staring out the windshield. But they were talking about their feelings. One boy was upset because a girl had told him he had a drinking problem, and the other was feeling alienated from all his friends.

15 Now, when a girl told a friend about a problem, the friend responded by asking probing questions and expressing agreement and understanding. But the boys dismissed each other's problems. Todd assured Richard that his drinking was "no big problem" because "sometimes you're funny when you're off your butt." And when Todd said he felt left out, Richard responded, "Why should you? You know more people than me."

16 Women perceive such responses as belittling and unsupportive. But the boys seemed satisfied with them. Whereas women reassure each other by implying, "You shouldn't feel bad because I've had similar experiences,"

men do so by implying, "You shouldn't feel bad because your problems aren't so bad."

There are even simpler reasons for women's impression that men don't listen. Linguist Lynette Hirschman found that women make more listener-noise, such as "mhm," "uhuh," and "yeah," to show "I'm with you." Men, she found, more often give silent attention. Women who expect a stream of listener-noise interpret silent attention as no attention at all. 17

Women's conversational habits are as frustrating to men as men's are to women. Men who expect silent attention interpret a stream of listener-noise as overreaction or impatience. Also, when women talk to each other in a close, comfortable setting, they often overlap, finish each other's sentences, and anticipate what the other is about to say. This practice, which I call "participatory listenership," is often perceived by men as interruption, intrusion, and lack of attention. 18

A parallel difference caused a man to complain about his wife, "She just wants to talk about her own point of view. If I show her another view, she gets mad at me." When most women talk to each other, they assume a conversationalist's job is to express agreement and support. But many men see their conversational duty as pointing out the other side of an argument. This is heard as disloyalty by women, and refusal to offer the requisite support. It is not that women don't want to see other points of view, but that they prefer them phrased as suggestions and inquiries rather than as direct challenges. 19

In his book *Fighting for Life,* Walter Ong points out that men use "agonistic," or warlike, oppositional formats to do almost anything; thus discussion becomes debate, and conversation a competitive sport. In contrast, women see conversation as a ritual means of establishing rapport. If Jane tells a problem and June says she has a similar one, they walk away feeling closer to each other. But this attempt at establishing rapport can backfire when used with men. Men take too literally women's ritual "troubles talk," just as women mistake men's ritual challenges for real attack. 20

The Sounds of Silence

These differences begin to clarify why women and men have such different expectations about communication in marriage. For women, talk creates intimacy. Marriage is an orgy of closeness: you can tell your feelings and thoughts, and still be loved. Their greatest fear is being pushed away. But men live in a hierarchical world, where talk maintains independence and status. They are on guard to protect themselves from being put down and pushed around. 21

This explains the paradox of the talkative man who said of his silent wife, "She's the talker." In the public setting of a guest lecture, he felt challenged to show his intelligence and display his understanding of the lecture. But at home, where he has nothing to prove and no one to defend against, he is free to remain silent. For his wife, being home means she is free from the worry that something she says might offend someone, or spark disagreement, or appear to be showing off; at home she is free to talk. 22

The communication problems that endanger marriage can't be fixed by mechanical engineering. They require a new conceptual framework about the role of talk in human relationships. Many of the psychological explanations that have become second nature may not be helpful, because they tend to blame either women (for not being assertive enough) or men (for not being in touch with their feelings). A sociolinguistic approach by which male-female conversation is seen as cross-cultural communication allows us to understand the problem and forge solutions without blaming either party. 23

Once the problem is understood, improvement comes naturally, as it did to the young woman and her boyfriend who seemed to go to sleep when she wanted to talk. Previously, she had accused him of not listening, and he had refused to change his behavior, since that would be admitting fault. But then she learned about and explained to him the differences in women's and men's habitual ways of aligning themselves in conversation. The next time she told him she wanted to talk, he began, as usual, by lying down and covering his eyes. When the familiar negative reaction bubbled up, she reassured herself that he really was listening. But then he sat up and looked at her. Thrilled, she asked why. He said, "You like me to look at you when we talk, so I'll try to do it." Once he saw their differences as cross-cultural rather than right and wrong, he independently altered his behavior. 24

Women who feel abandoned and deprived when their husbands won't listen to or report daily news may be happy to discover their husbands trying to adapt once they understand the place of small talk in women's relationships. But if their husbands don't adapt, the women may still be comforted that for men, this is not a failure of intimacy. Accepting the difference, the wives may look to their friends or family for that kind of talk. And husbands who can't provide it shouldn't feel their wives have made unreasonable demands. Some couples will still decide to divorce, but at least their decisions will be based on realistic expectations. 25

In these times of resurgent ethnic conflicts, the world desperately needs cross-cultural understanding. Like charity, successful cross-cultural communication should begin at home. 26

• • •

Comprehension

1. What pattern of communication does Tannen identify at the beginning of her essay?
2. According to Tannen, what do women complain about most in their marriages?
3. What gives women the impression that men do not listen?
4. What characteristics of women's speech do men find frustrating?
5. According to Tannen, what can men and women do to remedy the communication problems that exist in most marriages?

Purpose and Audience

1. What is Tannen's thesis?
2. What is Tannen's purpose in writing this essay? Do you think she wants to inform or to persuade? On what do you base your conclusion?
3. Is Tannen writing for an expert audience or for an audience of general readers? To men, women, or both? How can you tell?

Style and Structure

1. What does Tannen gain by stating her thesis in paragraph 2 of the essay? Would there be any advantage in postponing the thesis statement until the end? Explain.
2. Is this essay a subject-by-subject or a point-by-point comparison? What does Tannen gain by organizing her essay the way she does?
3. Throughout her essay, Tannen cites scholarly studies and quotes statistics. How effectively does this information support her points? Could she have made a strong case without this material? Why or why not?
4. Would you say Tannen's tone is hopeful, despairing, sarcastic, angry, or something else? Explain.
5. Tannen concludes her essay with a far-reaching statement. What do you think she hopes to accomplish with this conclusion? Is she successful? Explain your reasoning.
6. **Vocabulary Project.** Where does Tannen use professional **jargon** in this essay? Would the essay be more effective or less effective without these words? Explain.

Journal Entry

Based on your own observations of male-female communication, how accurate is Tannen's analysis? Can you relate an anecdote from your own life that illustrates (or contradicts) her thesis?

Writing Workshop

1. **Working with Sources.** In another essay, Tannen contrasts the communication patterns of male and female students in classroom settings. After observing students in a few of your own classes, write an essay of your own that draws a comparison between the communication patterns of your male and female classmates. Include quotations from both male and female students. Be sure to include parenthetical documentation for these quotations as well as for any references to Tannen's essay; also include a works-cited page. (See Chapter 18 for information on MLA documentation.)
2. Write an essay comparing the way male and female characters speak (or behave) in films or on television. Use examples to support your points.

3. Write an essay comparing the vocabulary used in two different sports. Does one sport use more violent language than the other? For example, baseball uses the terms *bunt* and *sacrifice,* and football uses the terms *blitz* and *bomb.* Use as many examples as you can to support your thesis.

Combining the Patterns

Tannen begins her essay with an anecdote. Why does she begin with this paragraph of **narration**? How does this story set the tone for the rest of the essay?

Thematic Connections

- "The Myth of the Latin Woman: I Just Met a Girl Named Maria" (page 225)
- "Mother Tongue" (page 458)
- "I Want a Wife" (page 496)

ISABEL WILKERSON

Emmett Till and Tamir Rice, Sons of the Great Migration

A native of Washington, DC, and a graduate of Howard University, Isabel Wilkerson (b. 1961) is a distinguished journalist and academic. She won a 1994 Pulitzer Prize for Feature Writing for her work as Chicago bureau chief of the *New York Times*. She is also the recipient of a George S. Polk Award and a Guggenheim Fellowship. Wilkerson has taught journalism at Emory University, Princeton University, Northwestern University, and Boston University. Her 2010 book *The Warmth of Other Suns: The Epic Story of America's Great Migration* focuses on two historical waves of African Americans who left the South for the Midwest and other regions of the country.

Background on Emmett Till In her essay, Isabel Wilkerson refers to the 1955 murder of Emmett Till as "a turning point in the civil rights movement." A Chicago native, the fourteen-year-old Till was visiting relatives in segregated Money, Mississippi, when he spoke to a white, married woman, Carolyn Bryant, in a grocery store. The specifics of the exchange are unclear: according to some accounts, Till touched her arm, propositioned her, or whistled at her. A few days later, Bryant's husband, Roy Bryant, and his half-brother J. W. Milam abducted Till. They beat him, shot him, and dumped his body in the Tallahatchie River, where it was discovered three days later. Tens of thousands of people attended Till's funeral, which startled and unified the black community and drew sympathy from many whites across the country. Bryant and Milam were indicted for the murder, but were acquitted by an all-white Mississippi jury after only an hour of deliberation. Once acquitted — and immune from further prosecution — the two men admitted their guilt. Till's mother repeatedly tried to get prosecutors to reopen the case over the next several decades, but never succeeded. The brutal slaying of Emmett Till is still shocking, and it remains a foundational event of the early civil rights era.

In winter 1916, several hundred black families from the Selma, Ala., Cotton Belt began quietly defecting from the Jim Crow South, with its night rides and hanging trees, some confiding to *The Chicago Defender* in February that the "treatment doesn't warrant staying." It was the start of the Great Migration, a leaderless revolution that would incite six million black refugees over six decades to seek asylum within the borders of their own country. 1

> "The horrors they were fleeing would follow them in freedom and into the current day."

They could not know what was in store for them or their descendants, nor the hostilities they would face wherever they went. Consider the story of two mothers whose lives bookend the migration 2 and whose family lines would meet similar, unimaginable fates. The horrors they were fleeing would follow them in freedom and into the current day.

The first was Mamie Carthan Till, whose parents carried her from Missis- 3
sippi to Illinois early in the 1920s. In Chicago, she would marry and give birth to a son, Emmett. In the summer of 1955, she would send him to visit relatives back in Mississippi. Emmett had just turned 14, had been raised in the new world and was unschooled in the "yes, sir, no, sir" ways of the Southern caste system. That August, he was kidnapped, beaten, and shot to death, ostensibly for whistling at a white woman at a convenience store. His murder would become a turning point in the civil rights movement.

Around that year, another woman, Millie Lee Wylie, left the bottomlands 4
of Sumter County, Ala., near where the migration had begun, and settled in Cleveland. There, more than half a century later, just before Thanksgiving 2014, her 12-year-old great-grandson, bundled up in the cold, was playing with a friend's pellet gun at a park outside a recreation center. His name was Tamir Rice. A now familiar video shows a police officer shooting him seconds after arrival, and an officer tackling his sister to the ground as she ran toward her dying brother. Tamir's became one of the most recognizable names in a metronome of unarmed black people killed by the police in the last two years, further galvanizing the Black Lives Matter movement.

Tamir Rice would become to this young century what Emmett Till was 5
to the last. In pictures, the boys resemble each other, the same half-smiles on their full moon faces, the most widely distributed photographs of them taken from the same angle, in similar light, their clear eyes looking into the camera with the same male-child assuredness of near adolescence. They are now tragic symbols of the search for black freedom in this country.

It has been a century since the Great Migration that produced both boys 6
began. Our current era seems oddly aligned with that moment. The brutal decades preceding the Great Migration — when a black person was lynched on average every four days — were given a name by the historian Rayford Logan. He called them the Nadir. Today, in the era of the Charleston massacre, when, according to one analysis of F.B.I. statistics, an African-American is killed by a white police officer roughly every three and a half days, has the makings of a second Nadir.

Or perhaps, in the words of Eric Foner, the leading scholar of Reconstruc- 7
tion, a "second Redemption." That is what historians call the period of backlash against the gains made by newly freedmen that led to Jim Crow.

Today, with black advancement by an elite few extending as far as the 8
White House, we are seeing "a similar kind of retreat," Professor Foner said. "The attack on voting rights, incarceration, obviously but even more intellectually and culturally, a sort of exhaustion with black protest, an attitude of 'What are these people really complaining about? Look at what we've done for you.'"

The country seems caught in a cycle. We leap forward only to slip back. 9
"We have not made anywhere near the progress we think we have," said Bryan Stevenson of the Equal Justice Initiative in Alabama. "It's as if we're at halftime, and we started cheering as if we won the game."

What befell Emmett and Tamir reflects how racial interactions have mutated over time, from the overt hatreds now shunned by most Americans to the unspoken, unconscious biases that are no less lethal and may be harder to fight. For all of its changes, the country remains in a similar place, a caste system based on what people look like. 10

The men and women of the Great Migration were asking questions that remain unanswered today: What is to be the role of the people whom the country has marginalized by law and custom and with state-sanctioned violence for most of their time on this soil? How might these now 45 million people, still the most segregated of all groups in America, partake of the full fruits of citizenship? How can deeply embedded racial hierarchies be overcome? 11

Tamir Rice's great-grandmother, Millie Lee Wylie, was born into a family of farm hands and sawmill workers. She married young and was left a widow when her husband died after a fall in a crooked river. With dreams of a new life, she packed up her belongings and left the tenant shacks of Alabama for the smokestacks of Cleveland, later sending for her three young sons. Like many of the women new to the north, she found work as a housekeeper and later as a hospital janitor. She would have two more children and marry a man named Robert Petty, who worked at the old Republic Steel plant and whose family had arrived years before from Mississippi by way of Kentucky. 12

They found themselves hemmed into the worn-out, predominantly black east side of Cleveland, with other refugees from the South. He worked the 7 A.M. to 3 P.M. shift; she worked from 3 P.M. to 11 P.M. He played the numbers and bet the horses at Thistledown to help make the rent on their apartment, in a dilapidated four-flat owned by an Eastern European woman who saw no need to keep it up. 13

They finally saved up for a two-story house with aluminum siding in the suburbs. The white neighbors began moving out shortly thereafter, a common response to black efforts to move up in most every receiving station in the North. 14

Millie – now Mrs. Petty – went about recreating the things she missed from the "old country." She planted collard greens and watermelons and raised chickens in the backyard. She cooked neck bone and made hogshead cheese, singing hymns – "I'm coming up on the rough side of the mountain" – as she worked. Sundays, she ushered at a storefront Baptist church in her belted navy dress with white gloves and collar, perfumed with her one indulgence, Chanel No. 5. 15

After lives of work and want, both she and her husband died in their 50s, she of cancer and he of a heart attack after losing a lung from asbestos exposure at the plant. Their early deaths left the family ungrounded, without the close networks that had sustained their Southern ancestors. The daughter, Darlette Pinkston, suffered for it. Her marriage did not last, and she began living with a man who beat and threatened her until, fearing for her life, she killed him. Her daughter, Samaria, was 12 when she testified at 16 the trial to the abuse she had witnessed and then lost her mother to prison for 15 years.

Samaria moved between foster homes and then to the streets. She dropped out of school in ninth grade, worked odd jobs, cleaning and doing clerical work, and had four children, the youngest of whom was Tamir. 17

She got tutors for her children, managed to get the oldest through high school and the others on track to finish. Tamir had swimming and soccer lessons and "Iron Man" DVDs. He had suffered such separation anxiety that she had to send him to nursery school with a picture of herself so he would know he would see her again. 18

On the afternoon of Nov. 22, 2014, a Saturday, she let Tamir and his sister Tajai go to the recreation center by the park across the street before dinner. She was starting the lasagna when there was a knock at the door. Two children told her that Tamir had been shot. She didn't believe them. "No, not my kids," she told them. "My kids are in the park." A neighbor boy had let Tamir play with his pellet gun without her knowing it. "I hadn't seen the gun before," she told me. "They knew better than to let me see it." 19

When she arrived, the officers would not let her near her son to comfort him as he lay bleeding on the ground, she said. They told her they would put her in the squad car if she didn't stay back. 20

As in the majority of the twenty-first century cases of police shootings in the North, no one was prosecuted in the death of Tamir Rice. Late last December, a grand jury declined to indict the officer who killed him. Decades ago, in the Jim Crow South, Emmett Till's killers were acquitted by an all-white jury, but at least they had gone to trial. 21

I asked Michael Petty, Tamir's great-uncle and a retired chaplain's assistant in the Navy, how Millie, his mother, would have borne what happened to the great-grandson she never lived to see, in the place she traveled so far to reach. It would have crushed her, Mr. Petty said. "My mother would have carried that hurt," he said, "and felt the pain of the generations." 22

• • •

Comprehension

1. What is the "Great Migration"? Why did it occur?
2. In paragraph 1, Wilkerson mentions "night rides and hanging trees." Why do you think she doesn't explain these references? Should she have?
3. How were Mamie Carthan Till and Millie Lee Wylie alike? How were they different?
4. Wilkerson says, "Tamir Rice would become to this young century what Emmett Till was to the last" (5). What point is she making?
5. What does Wilkerson mean when she says that today "has the makings of a second Nadir" (6)? Why does she believe this?
6. How does Eric Foner define the "second Redemption" (7)? How, according to Wilkerson, is the United States "caught in a cycle" (9)?

Purpose and Audience

1. Is Wilkerson writing primarily for a white audience, an African-American audience, or both? How do you know?
2. Do you think Wilkerson expects her readers to be receptive or hostile to her ideas? How can you tell?
3. Where does Wilkerson state her thesis? In your own words, summarize this thesis.
4. What do you think Wilkerson hoped to accomplish with her essay? Is her purpose to persuade? To inform? To enlighten? Or, did she have some other motive? Explain.

Style and Structure

1. Wilkerson's introduction consists of two paragraphs. What does each of these paragraphs accomplish?
2. In comparing her two subjects, Wilkerson relies mainly on a point-by-point structure. What are the advantages and disadvantages of this organization?
3. Underline the transitional words and phrases that indicate the contrast between Wilkerson's two subjects in this essay. Should she have used more transitions, or does she have enough?
4. In paragraphs 19 and 20, Wilkerson tells how Tamir Rice's mother found out her son had been shot by police, but Wilkerson gives no details about the incident itself or its aftermath. Should she have? Why do you think she does not supply this information? (Before answering this question, do some research to find out more about Tamir Rice's killing.)
5. What points does Wilkerson emphasize in her conclusion? Is it an effective concluding strategy? Would another strategy have been better? Explain.
6. **Vocabulary Project.** In paragraph 10, Wilkerson says the United States remains "a caste system based on what people look like." What is a caste system? Do you think Wilkerson's use of this term is accurate?

Journal Entry

Wilkerson's essay discusses the families of both Emmett Till and Tamir Rice. What does each boy's upbringing tell you about his family?

Writing Workshop

1. Write an essay in which you compare Emmett Till's upbringing with Tamir Rice's.
2. **Working with Sources.** Wilkerson says that six million African Americans who took part in the Great Migration "could not know what was in store for them or their descendants" (2). Interview one of your grandparents (or an older relative) and find out what this person once envisioned for future

generations of his or her family. Did they accurately predict what lay ahead? Then, write an essay in which you compare your relative's expectations with what actually happened. Be sure to document your interview and include a works-cited page. (See Chapter 18 for information on MLA documentation.)

3. **Working with Sources.** Go to YouTube and listen to "The Death of Emmett Till" by Bob Dylan. Then, read the lyrics online. Write an essay in which you compare Wilkerson's treatment of Emmett Till to Dylan's. What does each hope to accomplish by telling Till's story? Do they each have the same purpose? Are they successful? Be sure to document all references to Wilkerson's essay and include a works-cited page. (See Chapter 18 for information on MLA documentation.)

Combining the Patterns

Much of this essay consists of **narrative** paragraphs. How do these narratives help Wilkerson develop her thesis?

Thematic Connections

- "Just Walk On By: A Black Man Ponders His Power to Alter Public Space" (page 233)
- "How to Tell a Mother Her Child Is Dead" (page 277)
- "My First Conk" (page 277)
- The Declaration of Independence (page 544)
- "Letter from Birmingham Jail" (page 558)

WILLIAM SHAKESPEARE

Shall I compare thee to a summer's day?

Generally considered the greatest writer in the English language, William Shakespeare (1564–1616) was a poet, playwright, actor, and theatrical businessman. Born and raised in Stratford-on-Avon, he wrote his plays between 1588 and 1613. His surviving works include roughly 38 plays and 154 sonnets, as well as two narrative poems, "Venus and Adonis" and "The Rape of Lucrece." Other texts exist as well, but their authorship remains uncertain. His comedies, tragedies, histories, and romances, from *A Midsummer Night's Dream* and *Hamlet* to *Henry the V* and *The Tempest*, are performed today more than any other playwright's work.

Background on the sonnet In "Scorn Not the Sonnet," the English poet William Wordsworth (1770–1850) writes that "with this key / Shakespeare unlocked his heart." By the time Shakespeare wrote his sonnets in the 1590s, the sonnet form was already centuries old. The sonnet — from *sonneto,* Italian for "little song" — originated in Italy in the thirteenth century; it was refined and innovated by writers like Dante (1265–1321) and Petrarch (1304–1374). The sonnet arrived in England in the 1500s when English writers such as Sir Thomas Wyatt (1503–1542) and Henry Howard, the Earl of Surrey (c. 1516–1547), began retooling it for the English language. Later in the century, it became a common form for poets, such as Sir Philip Sidney, Edmund Spenser, and William Shakespeare.

Consisting of three four-line stanzas followed by a rhymed couplet, Shakespeare's sonnets are timeless meditations on beauty, love, time, and death. They are thought to have been written in 1590 and were formally published in 1609. Their real-life historical characters of the sonnets remain mysterious. The first 126 are addressed to a "fair youth" or young man, whom the poet urges to marry and have children; the final 28, which are more overtly erotic, are thought to be directed at a woman, often referred to as the "dark lady." The sonnets have been translated into almost every written language and even now continue to fascinate and inspire contemporary readers and writers. As Virginia Woolf suggests in her novel *To the Lighthouse,* they are "beautiful and reasonable, clear and complete, the essence sucked out of life and rounded here."

Shall I compare thee to a summer's day?
Thou art more lovely and more temperate:
Rough winds do shake the darling buds of May,*
And summer's lease hath all too short a date;
Sometime too hot the eye of heaven shines,
And often is his gold complexion dimmed;
And every fair from fair sometimes declines,
By chance or nature's changing course untrimmed;**
But thy eternal summer shall not fade,
Nor lose possession of that fair thou ow'st;***
Nor shall death brag thou wand'rest in his shade,
When in eternal lines† to time thou grow'st:
    So long as men can breathe, or eyes can see,
    So long lives this, and this gives life to thee.

• • •

Reading Literature

1. What two subjects is Shakespeare comparing? How do you know when the speaker shifts from one subject to the other?
2. Is this poem a subject-by-subject or point-by-point comparison? Why do you think Shakespeare chose this organization?
3. What comment do you think the poem is making about a summer's day? About youth? About death? About poetry?

Journal Entry

Many people see this poem as celebrating love, but others see it differently. What do you think this poem is really about?

Thematic Connections

- "My Mother Never Worked" (page 121)
- "The Myth of the Latin Woman: I Just Met a Girl Named Maria" (page 225)

* Eds. note — At the time Shakespeare wrote, May was considered a summer month.
** Eds. note — Without decoration.
*** Eds. note — Own or ownest.
† Eds. note — Lines of poetry, lines of descent.

Writing Assignments for Comparison and Contrast

1. Find a description of the same news event in two different magazines or newspapers. Write a comparison-and-contrast essay discussing the similarities and differences between the two stories.
2. **Working with Sources.** In your local public library, locate two children's books on the same subject – one written in the 1950s and one written within the past ten years. Write an essay discussing which elements are the same and which are different. Include a thesis statement about the significance of the differences between the two books. Be sure to document all material you take from the two books, and include a works-cited page. (See Chapter 18 for information on MLA documentation.)
3. Write an essay about a relative or friend you have known since you were a child. Consider how your opinion of this person is different now from what it was then.
4. Write an essay comparing and contrasting the expectations that college professors and high school teachers have for their students. Cite your own experiences as examples.
5. Since you started college, how have you changed? Write a comparison-and-contrast essay that answers this question.
6. Taking careful notes, watch a local television news program and then a national news broadcast. Write an essay comparing the two programs, paying particular attention to the news content and to the journalists' broadcasting styles.
7. Write an essay comparing your own early memories of school with those of a parent or an older relative.
8. How are the attitudes toward education different among students who work to finance their own education and students who do not? Your thesis statement should indicate what differences exist and why.
9. Compare and contrast the college experiences of commuters and students who live in dorms on campus. Interview people in your classes to use as examples.
10. Write an essay comparing any two groups that have divergent values – vegetarians and meat eaters or smokers and nonsmokers, for example.
11. How is being a participant – playing a sport or acting in a play, for instance – different from being a spectator? Write a comparison-and-contrast essay in which you answer this question.

Collaborative Activity for Comparison and Contrast

Form groups of four students each. Assume your college has hired these groups as consultants to suggest solutions for several problems students have been complaining about. Select the four areas – food, campus safety, parking, and class scheduling, for example – you think need improvement. Then, as a group, write a short report to your college describing the present conditions in these areas, and compare them to the improvements you envision. (Be sure to organize your report as a comparison-and-contrast essay.) Finally, have one person from each group read the group's report to the class. Decide as a class which group has the best suggestion.

12

Classification and Division

What Is Classification and Division?

Division is the process of breaking a whole into parts; **classification** is the process of sorting individual items into categories. In the following paragraph from "Pregnant with Possibility," Gregory J. E. Rawlins divides Americans into categories based on their access to computer technology.

Topic sentence identifies categories

Today's computer technology is rapidly turning us into three completely new races: the superpoor, the rich, and the superrich. The superpoor are perhaps eight thousand in every ten thousand of us. The rich – me and you – make up most of the remaining two thousand, while the superrich are perhaps the last two of every ten thousand. Roughly speaking, the decisions of two superrich people control what almost two thousand of us do, and our decisions, in turn, control what the remaining eight thousand do. These groups are really like races since the group you're born into often determines which group your children will be born into.

Through **classification and division**, we can make sense of seemingly random ideas by putting scattered bits of information into useful, coherent order. By breaking a large group into smaller categories and assigning individual items to larger categories, we can identify relationships between a whole and its parts and relationships among the parts themselves. Keep in mind, though, that classification involves more than simply comparing two items or listing examples; when you classify, you sort individual examples into different categories.

In countless practical situations, classification and division bring order to chaos. For example, you can *classify* your music, sorting individual songs into distinct genres: alternative rock, hip-hop, country, ranchera, and so on. Similarly, phone numbers listed in your cell phone's address book are *divided* into four clearly defined categories: home, work, mobile, and other. Thus, order can be brought to your music and your phone numbers – just as it is brought to newspapers, department stores, supermarkets, biological hierarchies, and libraries – when a whole is divided into categories or sections and individual items are assigned to one or another of these subgroups.

Understanding Classification

Even though the interrelated processes of classification and division invariably occur together, they are two separate operations. When you **classify**, you begin with individual items and sort them into categories. Because a given item invariably has several different attributes, it can be classified in various ways. For example, the most obvious way to classify the students who attend your school might be according to their year. However, you could also classify students according to their major, grade-point average, or any number of other principles. The **principle of classification** that you choose – the quality your items have in common – depends on how you wish to approach the members of this large and diverse group.

Understanding Division

Division is the opposite of classification. When you **divide**, you start with a whole (an entire class) and break it into its individual parts. For example, you might start with the large general class *television shows* and divide it into categories: *sitcoms*, *action/adventure*, *reality shows*, and so forth. You could then divide each of these categories even further. *Action/adventure programs,* for example, might include *Westerns, crime dramas, spy dramas,* and so on – and each of these categories could be further divided as well. Eventually, you would need to identify a particular principle of classification to help you assign specific programs to one category or another – that is, to classify them.

Using Classification and Division

Whenever you write an essay, you use classification and division to bring order to the invention stage of the writing process. For example, when you brainstorm, as Chapter 2 explains, you begin with your topic and list all the ideas you can think of. Next, you *divide* your topic into logical categories and *classify* the items in your brainstorming notes into one category or another, perhaps narrowing, expanding, or eliminating some categories – or some ideas – as you go along. This sorting and grouping enables you to condense and shape your material until it eventually suggests a thesis and the main points your essay will develop.

More specifically, certain topics and questions, because of the way they are worded, immediately suggest a classification-and-division pattern. Suppose, for example, you are asked, "What kinds of policies can government implement to reduce the nation's budget deficit?" Here the word *kinds* suggests classification and division. Other words – such as *types, varieties, aspects,* and *categories* – can also indicate that this pattern of development is called for.

Planning a Classification-and-Division Essay

Once you decide to use a classification-and-division pattern, you need to identify a **principle of classification**. Every group of people, things, or ideas can be categorized in many different ways. For example, when deciding which textbooks to purchase first, you could classify books according to their usefulness, considering whether they are *required, recommended,* or *optional.* You could also classify books according to their relevance to your coursework, considering which books will be used in courses in your major, which will be used in other required courses, and which will be used in electives. Of course, if you have limited funds, you might want to classify books according to their cost, buying the less expensive ones first. In each case, your purpose would determine how you classify the items.

Selecting and Arranging Categories

After you define your principle of classification and apply it to your topic, you should decide on your categories by dividing a whole class into parts and grouping a number of different items together within each part. Next, you should decide how you will treat the categories in your essay. Just as a comparison-and-contrast essay makes comparable points about its subjects, so your classification-and-division essay should treat all categories similarly. When you discuss comparable points for each category, your readers are able to understand your distinctions among categories as well as your definition of each category.

Finally, you should arrange your categories in some logical order so that readers can see how the categories are related and what their relative importance is. Whatever order you choose, it should be consistent with your purpose and with your essay's thesis.

Developing a Thesis Statement

Like other kinds of essays, a classification-and-division essay should have a thesis. Your **thesis statement** should identify your subject, and perhaps introduce the categories you will discuss; it may also suggest the relationships of your categories to one another and to the subject as a whole. In addition,

CHECKLIST ESTABLISHING CATEGORIES

- ☐ **All the categories should derive from the same principle.** If you decide to divide *television shows* into *sitcoms, reality shows,* and the like, it is not logical to include *children's programs* because this category results from one principle (target audience), whereas the others result from another principle (genre). Similarly, if you were classifying undergraduates at your school according to their year, you would not include the category *students receiving financial aid*.
- ☐ **All the categories should be at the same level.** In the series *sitcoms, action/adventure,* and *Westerns,* the last item, *Westerns,* does not belong because it is at a lower level — that is, it is a subcategory of *action/adventure.* Likewise, *sophomores* (a subcategory of *undergraduates*) does not belong in the series *undergraduates, graduate students,* and *continuing education students.*
- ☐ **You should treat all categories that are significant and relevant to your discussion.** Include enough categories to make your point, with no important omissions and no overlapping categories. In a review of a network's fall television lineup, the series *sitcoms, reality shows, crime shows,* and *detective shows* is incomplete because it omits important categories such as *news programs, game shows,* and *documentaries;* moreover, *detective shows* may overlap with *crime shows.* In the same way, the series *freshmen, sophomores, juniors,* and *transfers* is illogical: the important group *seniors* has been omitted, and *transfers* may include *freshmen, sophomores,* and *juniors.*

your thesis statement should tell your readers why your classification is significant, and it might also establish the relative value of your categories. For example, if you were writing an essay about investment strategies, a thesis statement that simply listed different kinds of investments would be pointless. Instead, your thesis statement might note their relative strengths and weaknesses and perhaps make recommendations based on this assessment. Similarly, a research essay about a writer's major works would accomplish little if it merely categorized his or her writings. Instead, your thesis statement should communicate your evaluation of these different kinds of works, perhaps demonstrating that some deserve higher public regard than others.

Using Transitions

When you write a classification-and-division essay, you use transitional words and phrases both to introduce your categories (the *first category, one category,* and so on) and to move readers from one category to the next (*the second category, another category,* and so on). In addition, transitional words and expressions can show readers the relationships between categories – for example, whether one category is more important than another (*a more important category,* the *most important category,* and so on). A more complete list of transitions appears on page 55.

Structuring a Classification-and-Division Essay

Once you have drafted your essay's thesis statement and established your categories, you should plan your classification-and-division essay around the same three major sections that other essays have: *introduction, body,* and *conclusion.* Your **introduction** should orient your readers by identifying your topic, the principle for classifying your material, and the individual categories you plan to discuss; your thesis is also usually stated in the introduction. In the **body paragraphs**, you should discuss your categories one by one, in the same order in which you mentioned them in your introduction. Finally, your **conclusion** should restate your thesis in different words, summing up the points you have made and perhaps considering their implications.

Suppose you are preparing a research essay on Mark Twain's nonfiction works for an American literature course. You have read selections from *Roughing It, Life on the Mississippi,* and *The Innocents Abroad.* Besides these travel narratives, you have read parts of Twain's autobiography and some of his correspondence and essays. When you realize that the works you have studied can easily be classified as four different types of Twain's nonfiction – travel narratives, essays, letters, and autobiography – you decide to use classification and division to structure your essay. So, you first divide the large class *Twain's nonfiction prose* into major categories: his travel narratives, essays, autobiography, and letters. Then, you classify the individual works, assigning each work to one of these categories, which you will discuss one at a time. Your purpose is to persuade readers to reconsider the reputations of some of these works, and you word your thesis statement accordingly. You might then prepare a formal outline like the one that follows for the body of your essay.

SAMPLE OUTLINE: Classification and Division

INTRODUCTION
(thesis statement)
Most readers know Mark Twain as a novelist, but his nonfiction works — his travel narratives, essays, letters, and especially his autobiography — deserve more attention.

POINT 1: TRAVEL NARRATIVES
A. *Roughing It*
B. *The Innocents Abroad*
C. *Life on the Mississippi*

POINT 2: ESSAYS

A. "Fenimore Cooper's Literary Offenses"

B. "How to Tell a Story"

C. "The Awful German Language"

POINT 3: LETTERS

A. To W. D. Howells

B. To his family

POINT 4: AUTOBIOGRAPHY

Because this will be a long essay, each of the outline's divisions will have several subdivisions, and each subdivision might require several paragraphs.

This outline illustrates the characteristics of an effective classification-and-division essay. First, Twain's nonfiction works are classified according to a single principle of classification – literary genre. (Depending on your purpose, another principle – such as theme or subject matter – could work just as well.) The outline also reveals that the essay's four categories are on the same level (each is a different literary genre) and that all relevant categories are included. Had you left out *essays,* for example, you would have been unable to classify several significant works of nonfiction.

This outline also arranges the four categories so that they will support your thesis most effectively. Because you believe Twain's travel narratives are somewhat overrated, you plan to discuss them early in your essay. Similarly, because you think the autobiography would make your best case for the merit of the nonfiction works as a whole, you decide it should be placed last. (Of course, you could arrange your categories in several other orders, such as from shorter to longer works or from least to most popular, depending on the thesis your essay will support.)

Finally, this outline reminds you to treat all categories comparably in your essay. Your case would be weakened if, for example, you did not consider style in your discussion of Twain's letters while discussing style for every other category. This omission might lead your readers to suspect that you had not done enough research on the letters – or that the style of Twain's letters did not measure up to the style of his other works.

Revising a Classification-and-Division Essay

When you revise a classification-and-division essay, consider the items on the revision checklist on page 66. In addition, pay special attention to the items on the following checklist, which apply specifically to revising classification-and-division essays.

REVISION CHECKLIST **CLASSIFICATION AND DIVISION**

- ☐ Does your assignment call for classification and division?
- ☐ Have you identified a **principle of classification** for your material?
- ☐ Have you identified the categories you plan to discuss and decided how you will treat them?
- ☐ Have you arranged your categories in a logical order?
- ☐ Have you treated all categories similarly?
- ☐ Does your essay have a clearly stated thesis that identifies the subject of your classification (perhaps listing the categories you will discuss) and indicates why it is important?
- ☐ Have you used transitional words and phrases to show the relationships among categories?

Editing a Classification-and-Division Essay

When you edit your classification-and-division essay, you should follow the guidelines on the editing checklists on pages 83, 86, and 89. In addition, you should focus on the grammar, mechanics, and punctuation issues that are particularly relevant to classification-and-division essays. One of these issues – using a colon to introduce your categories – is discussed below.

GRAMMAR IN CONTEXT **USING A COLON TO INTRODUCE YOUR CATEGORIES**

When you state the thesis of a classification-and-division essay, you often give readers an overview by listing the categories you will discuss. You introduce this list of categories with a **colon**, a punctuation mark whose purpose is to direct readers to look ahead for a series, list, clarification, or explanation.

When you use a colon to introduce your categories, the colon must be preceded by a complete sentence.

CORRECT: Carolyn Foster Segal's essay identifies kinds of student excuses with five headings**:** The Family, The Best Friend, The Evils of Dorm Life, The Evils of Technology, and The Totally Bizarre.

INCORRECT: The headings that Carolyn Foster Segal uses to identify kinds of student excuses are: The Family, The Best Friend, The Evils of Dorm Life, The Evils of Technology, and The Totally Bizarre.

In any list or series of three or more categories, the categories should be separated by commas, with a comma preceding the *and* that separates the last two items. This last comma prevents confusion by ensuring that readers will be able to see at a glance exactly how many categories you are discussing.

CORRECT: The Family, The Best Friend, The Evils of Dorm Life, The Evils of Technology, and The Totally Bizarre (five categories)

INCORRECT: The Family, The Best Friend, The Evils of Dorm Life, The Evils of Technology and The Totally Bizarre (without the final comma, it might appear you are only discussing four categories)

NOTE: Items on a list or in a series are always expressed in **parallel** terms. See the Grammar in Context box on page 376.

LaunchPad

For more practice on using a colon to introduce categories, see the LearningCurve on Semicolons and Colons in the LaunchPad for *Patterns*.

EDITING CHECKLIST CLASSIFICATION AND DIVISION

- ☐ Do you introduce your list of categories with a colon preceded by a complete sentence?
- ☐ Are the items on your list of categories separated by commas?
- ☐ Do you include a comma before the *and* that connects the last two items on your list?
- ☐ Do you express the items on your list in parallel terms?

A STUDENT WRITER: Classification and Division

The following classification-and-division essay was written by Josie Martinez for an education course. Her assignment was to look back at her own education and to consider what she had learned so far, referring in her essay to Leon Wieseltier's "Perhaps Culture Is Now the Counterculture" (page 588). Josie's essay divides a whole – college classes – into four categories.

What I Learned (and Didn't Learn) in College

Introduction

1 In "Perhaps Culture Is Now the Counterculture," Leon Wieseltier writes in defense of the humanities, asking, "Has there ever been a moment in American life when the humanities were cherished less, and . . . needed more?" His essay goes on to stress the importance of balancing science and technology courses (which are increasingly popular with today's students) with humanities courses. Even though not every class will be rewarding or even enjoyable, taking a variety

of courses in different disciplines will expose students to a wide range of subjects, and also teach them about themselves.

Categories listed and explained

2 Despite the variety of experiences that different students have with different courses, most college classes can be classified into one of four categories: ideal classes, worthless classes, disappointing classes, and unexpectedly valuable classes. First are courses that students love — ideal learning environments in which they enjoy both the subject matter and the professor-student interaction. Far from these ideal courses are those that students find completely worthless in terms of subject matter, atmosphere, and teaching style. Somewhere between these two extremes are two kinds of courses that can be classified into another pair of opposites: courses that students expect to enjoy and to learn much from but are disappointing and courses that students are initially not interested in but that exceed their expectations. Understanding these four categories can help students accept the fact that one disappointing class is not a disaster and can encourage them to try classes in different disciplines as well as those with different instructors and formats.

Thesis statement

First category: ideal class

3 One of the best courses I have taken so far as a college student was my Shakespeare class. The professor who taught it had a great sense of humor and was liberal in terms of what she allowed in her classroom — for example, controversial Shakespeare adaptations and virtually any discussion, relevant or irrelevant. The students in the class — English majors and non-English majors, those who were interested in the plays as theater and those who preferred to study them as literature — shared an enthusiasm for Shakespeare, and they were eager to engage in lively discussions. This class gave us a thorough knowledge of Shakespeare's plays (tragedies, histories, comedies) as well as an understanding of his life. We also developed our analytical skills through our discussions of the plays and films as well as through special projects — for example, a character profile presentation and an abstract art presentation relating a work of art to one of the plays. This class was an ideal learning environment not only because of the wealth of material we were exposed to but also because of the respect with which our professor treated us: we were her colleagues, and she was as willing to learn from us as we were to learn from her.

Second category: worthless class

4 In contrast to this ideal class, one of the most worthless courses I have taken in college was Movement Education. As an education major, I expected to like this class, and several

other students who had taken it told me it was both easy and enjoyable. The class consisted of playing children's games and learning what made certain activities appropriate and inappropriate for children of various ages. The only requirement for this class was that we had to write note cards explaining how to play each game so that we could use them for reference in our future teaching experiences. Unfortunately, I never really enjoyed the games we played, and I have long since discarded my note cards and forgotten how to play the games — or even what they were.

Third category: disappointing class

5 Although I looked forward to taking Introduction to Astronomy, I was very disappointed in this class. I had hoped to satisfy my curiosity about the universe outside our solar system, but the instructor devoted most of the semester to a detailed study of the Earth and the other bodies in our own solar system. In addition, a large part of our work included charting orbits and processing distance equations — work that I found both difficult and boring. Furthermore, we spent hardly any class time learning how to use a telescope and how to locate objects in the sky. In short, I gained little information from the class, learning only how to solve equations I would never confront again and how to chart orbits that had already been charted.

Fourth category: unexpectedly valuable class

6 In direct contrast to my astronomy class, a religion class called Paul and the Early Church was much more rewarding than I had anticipated. Having attended Catholic school for thirteen years, I assumed this course would offer me little that was new to me. However, because the class took a historical approach to studying Paul's biblical texts, I found that I learned more about Christianity than I had in all my previous religion classes. We learned about the historical validity of Paul and other texts in the Bible and how they were derived from various sources and passed orally through several generations before being written down and translated into different languages. We approached the texts from a linguistic perspective, determining the significance of certain words and learning how various meanings can be derived from different translations of the same passage. This class was unlike any of my other religion classes in that it encouraged me to study the texts objectively, leaving me with a new and valuable understanding of material I had been exposed to for most of my life.

Conclusion

Although each student's learning experience in college will be different — because every student has a different learning style, is interested in different subjects, and takes courses at different schools taught by different professors — all college students' experiences are similar in one respect. All students will encounter the same kinds of courses: those that are ideal, those that are worthless, those that they learn little from despite their interest in the subject, and those that they learn from and become engaged in despite their low expectations. Understanding that these categories exist is important because it gives students the freedom and courage to try new things, as college students did years ago. After all, even if one course is a disappointment, another may be more interesting — or even exciting. For this reason, college students should not be discouraged by a course they do not like; the best classes are almost certainly still in their future. 7

Summary of four categories

Restatement of thesis

Work Cited

Works-cited list (begins new page)

Wieseltier, Leon. "Perhaps Culture Is Now the Counterculture: A Defense of the Humanities." *Patterns for College Writing: A Rhetorical Reader and Guide*, 14th ed., edited by Laurie G. Kirszner and Stephen R. Mandell, Bedford/St. Martin's, 2018, pp. 588–91.

Points for Special Attention

Working with Sources. Josie's teacher asked students to cite Leon Wieseltier's "Perhaps Culture Is Now the Counterculture," which they had just discussed, somewhere in their own essays. Josie knew that the passage she chose to quote or paraphrase would have to be directly relevant to her own essay's subject, so she knew it would have to focus on academic (rather than economic or social) issues. When she read Wieseltier's comments on the need for exposure to a wide variety of subjects, she knew she had found material that could give her essay a more global, less personal focus. For this reason, she decided to refer to Wieseltier in her essay's first paragraph. (Note that she includes parenthetical documentation and a separate work-cited page.)

Thesis and Support. Josie's purpose in writing this essay was to communicate to her professor and the other students in her education class what she had learned from the classes she had taken so far in college, and both the thesis she states in paragraph 2 and the restatement of this thesis in her conclusion make this point clear: what she has learned is to take a wide variety of courses. Knowing that few, if any, students in her class would have taken any of the courses she took, Josie realized she had to provide a lot of detail to show what these classes taught her.

Organization. As she reviewed the various courses she had taken and assessed their strengths and weaknesses, Josie saw a classification scheme emerging. As soon as she noticed it, she organized her material into four categories. Rather than discuss the four kinds of classes from best to worst or from worst to best, Josie decided to present them as two opposing pairs: ideal class and worthless class, and surprisingly disappointing class and unexpectedly worthwhile class. In paragraph 2, Josie lists the four categories she plans to discuss in her essay and gives readers an overview of these categories to help prepare them for her thesis.

Transitions between Categories. Josie uses clear topic sentences to move readers from one category to the next and to indicate the relationship of each category to another.

> One of the best courses I have taken so far as a college student was my Shakespeare class. (3)
>
> In contrast to this ideal class, one of the most worthless courses I have taken in college was Movement Education. (4)
>
> Although I looked forward to taking Introduction to Astronomy, I was very disappointed in this class. (5)
>
> In direct contrast to my astronomy class, a religion class called Paul and the Early Church was much more rewarding than I had anticipated. (6)

These four sentences distinguish the four categories from one another and also help to communicate Josie's direction and emphasis.

Focus on Revision

An earlier draft of Josie's essay, which she discussed with her instructor in a conference, did not include very specific topic sentences. Instead, the sentences were vague and unfocused:

> One class I took in college was a Shakespeare course.
>
> Another class I took was Movement Education.
>
> I looked forward to taking Introduction to Astronomy.
>
> My experience with a religion class was very different.

Although her essay's second paragraph listed the categories and explained how they differed, Josie's instructor advised her to revise her topic sentences so that it would be clear which category she was discussing in each body paragraph. Josie took his advice and revised these topic sentences. After reading her next draft, she felt confident that her categories – listed in paragraph 2 and repeated in her topic sentences and in her conclusion – were clear and distinct.

Even after making these revisions, however, Josie felt her essay needed some additional fine-tuning. For example, in her final draft, she planned to add some material to paragraphs 4 and 5. At first, because she had dismissed

Movement Education as completely worthless and Introduction to Astronomy as disappointing, Josie felt she did not have to say much about them. When she reread her essay, however, she realized she needed to explain the shortcomings of the two classes more fully so that her readers would understand why these classes had little value for her.

PEER-EDITING WORKSHEET: CLASSIFICATION AND DIVISION

1. Paraphrase the essay's thesis.
2. What whole is being divided into parts in this essay? Into what general categories is the whole divided?
3. Is each category clearly identified and explained? If not, what revisions can you suggest? (For example, can you suggest a different title for a particular category? A different topic sentence to introduce it?)
4. Where does the writer list the categories to be discussed? Is the list introduced by a colon (preceded by a complete sentence)? If not, suggest revisions.
5. Are the categories arranged in a logical order, one that indicates their relationships to one another and their relative importance? If not, how could they be rearranged?
6. Does the writer treat all relevant categories and no irrelevant ones? Which categories, if any, should be added, deleted, or combined?
7. Does the writer include all necessary items, and no unnecessary ones, within each category? What additional items could be added? Should any items be located elsewhere?
8. Does the writer treat all categories similarly, discussing comparable points for each? Should any additional points be discussed? If so, where?
9. Do topic sentences clearly signal the movement from one category to the next? Should any topic sentences be strengthened to mark the boundaries between categories more clearly? If so, which ones?
10. Could the writer use another pattern of development to structure this essay, or is classification and division the best choice? Explain.

Each of the following selections is developed by means of classification and division. In some cases, the pattern is used to explain ideas; in others, it is used to persuade the reader. The first selection, a visual text, is followed by questions designed to illustrate how classification and division can operate in visual form.

Coffee Types

lv_design/Getty Images

• • •

Reading Images

1. This image identifies twenty types of coffee. What principle of classification determines these twenty categories? Do any of these twenty categories overlap, or are they all distinct?
2. Rearrange the types of coffee illustrated here to create just four or five distinct categories. What principle of classification did you use?
3. At first glance, the twenty images look quite similar. Take a closer look, and determine how they are different.

Journal Entry

Classify your own favorite beverages or foods. Begin by listing your favorites; then, divide them into categories.

Thematic Connections

- "Getting Coffee Is Hard to Do" (page 283)
- "The Three Types of Happiness" (page 448)

OLGA KHAZAN

The Three Types of Happiness

A graduate of American University and the University of Southern California, Olga Khazan is a staff writer for the *Atlantic*, where she covers gender, health, and science. Previously, she was a reporter and blogger for the *Washington Post*, covering a range of issues, including business start-ups, health, and international affairs. Khazan's work has also appeared in the *Los Angeles Times, Forbes*, and *Wired*. She is an International Reporting Project fellowship recipient.

Background on "minimalism" and the tiny house movement "Minimalism is hot, culturally, and for years, science has assured us that it was also the path to maximal bliss," writes Olga Khazan in the following selection. Indeed, conspicuous opposition to materialism and the role of "things" in our lives has, in itself, become a powerful lifestyle signifier. One popular manifestation of the minimalism movement is the recent "tiny house" trend, in which people choose to live in homes that are smaller than 500 square feet. This trend, in part a response to the conspicuous spending of the first part of this century and the 2008 global financial crisis, has been popularized by the popular television show *Tiny House Hunters*. The tiny house movement has also been proposed as one possible solution to the homeless crises in many major cities. For example, the charity Starting Human has built and donated more than a dozen tiny houses for the homeless in and around Los Angeles. Of course, the idea of minimalism is not new: monasticism is part of the traditions of many different religious faiths, and the philosophy proposed by Henry David Thoreau's *Walden*, the antimaterialism of the beatniks of the 1950s and hippies of the 1960s, and the "voluntary simplicity" movement of the early 1980s are all examples of minimalism in action. These and other iterations suggest that minimalism is a newly branded version of an old principle. Recently, however, empirical science has appeared to support the minimalist philosophy. Research by psychologists and social scientists like Daniel Gilbert, author of *Stumbling on Happiness*, and Elizabeth Dunn and Michael Norton, authors of *Happy Money: The Science of Smarter Spending,* among others, indicate that "experiences" generally make us happier than "things." Although this view has gained acceptance over the past several years, it has also led to some pushback from those who find it glib and sexist to those who question the validity of "happiness" as a legitimate field of empirical or scientific study.

Stuff has gotten a bad rap of late – mostly for its incompatibility with other lifestyle trends. It won't fit in your tiny house. Marie Kondo thinks it should be eschewed entirely unless it sparks joy. And there won't be any need for all your whisks and woks once you switch over to Soylent for sustenance. 1

Minimalism is hot, culturally, and for years, science has assured us that it was also the path to maximal bliss. The prevailing wisdom is that people who want the most happiness for their buck should buy experiences, not things. 2

The idea is that the joy of an experience begins before it even starts, and continues when you look back on the fancy dinner/vacation/afternoon of LARPing fondly. Experiences provide, in other words, both more *anticipatory* happiness and *afterglow* happiness.

> "Minimalism is hot, culturally, and for years, science has assured us that it was also the path to maximal bliss."

3 But a recent study complicates that picture, suggesting that sweaters and iPhones might make you just as happy, in a way, as cruises and concerts do. There is a third type of happiness – momentary happiness – and it tends to last longer with material goods because people use them for more time than they typically experience their experiences for.

4 For the study, published in *Social Psychology and Personality Science,* researchers Aaron Weidman and Elizabeth Dunn from the University of British Columbia gave 67 participants $20 to spend on either an experiential or material purchase of their choice, and then to report one experiential or material gift they had recently received. Then they quizzed them about their happiness levels through text messages and questionnaires.

5 They found that the study subjects derived more frequent momentary happiness from material goods, but more intense momentary happiness from the experiences. In other words, they enjoyed their material goods on a greater number of occasions than they did their experiences, even though the happiness felt from the experiences was slightly more intense.

6 "Material purchases have an unsung advantage, in that they provide more frequent bouts of momentary happiness in the weeks after they are acquired," Weidman and Dunn wrote.

7 This isn't the only evidence suggesting that material possessions aren't as bleak as they're made out to be. This study somewhat echoes earlier work by Dunn and others finding that lots of small purchases make people happier than one big one. Because we psychologically adapt to the things we have, new things provide a positive jolt – which matters in the short run, if not in the long run. Five trips to H&M serve as tepid, but nevertheless welcome, distractions from the daily grind.

8 And another study found that things that *help us do* activities, like tennis rackets and musical instruments, can also generate happiness. But the difference between tennis rackets and jewelry is slight: Part of the fun of shopping, after all, is imagining the places you'll go with the stuff you get.

9 So should you splurge on the latest iThing or on *Hamilton* tickets? It depends on whether you are "seeking an intense but fleeting form of happiness that is accompanied by a rosy afterglow," Weidman and Dunn write, "or a more subtle, frequent form of happiness that will endure for weeks or months."

10 As someone who had a flip phone for far longer than was hip, I can only add that my feelings toward my smart phone every day for the first year I owned it were nothing short of the praise-hands emoji.

• • •

Comprehension

1. What is minimalism? What connection does Khazan make between minimalism and happiness?
2. According to Khazan, what are "the three types of happiness"? What distinguishes these three categories from one another?
3. Does Khazan ever define happiness? If so, where? Is such a definition necessary? Why or why not?
4. In addition to identifying types of happiness, Khazan also identifies two categories of purchases. Define these two types of purchases. Which one brings greater happiness? Why?
5. What other types of happiness can you suggest that Khazan does not mention? Should she have discussed additional categories? Why or why not?

Purpose and Audience

1. Khazan begins her essay by stating, "Stuff has gotten a bad rap of late" (1). How does she expect her audience to react to this informal opening? Do you think this opening strategy is effective?
2. Why does Khazan refer to minimalism guru Marie Kondo, who recommends discarding any item that does not bring its owner joy? Do you think she expects her readers to recognize the reference to Kondo? Explain.
3. What point about happiness does Khazan want to make? Given this purpose, why do you think she chooses classification and division to structure her essay? Was this a good choice? Why or why not?
4. In paragraphs 3 through 5, Khazan refers to a study by two researchers. What does this expert opinion add to her essay? In paragraph 8, she mentions "another study." Why do you think she does not identify this other study? Should she have?

Style and Structure

1. Do any of the three categories of happiness overlap, or are they mutually exclusive? Explain your reasoning.
2. This essay is written in the first person. Does Khazan's use of *I* strengthen or weaken her essay?
3. Create a brief outline that identifies each kind of happiness, supplying two or three examples for each category.
4. Does Khazan clearly introduce each type of happiness? If not, suggest phrases she could add to signal to readers that a new category will be discussed.
5. Does Khazan treat each category of happiness in similar fashion, devoting the same amount of attention to each? Does she suggest that any one type of happiness is more important than the others? Explain.

6. **Vocabulary Project.** Write a one-sentence definition of *happiness*. (See pages 481–82 for examples of how to construct a definition.)
7. Does Khazan introduce her three categories in any particular order? What, if anything, determines how she organizes her discussion?

Journal Entry

What makes you the happiest? Choose one of Khazan's three categories of happiness, and use examples to explain why this kind of happiness is the most important to you.

Writing Workshop

1. **Working with Sources.** Do some research on Marie Kondo, reading one or two articles about her, at least one interview with her, and a few excerpts from her international best-seller *The Life-Changing Magic of Tidying Up*. Then, write a classification-and-division essay in which you evaluate several different aspects of Kondo's philosophy. Which of the strategies and life-style changes that she recommends do you think have the power to make someone happy, and which do not? Be sure to document any references to information about Kondo and to include a works-cited list. (See Chapter 18 for information on MLA documentation.)
2. Write a classification-and-division essay entitled, "The Three Types of Unhappiness." Begin by identifying three or four categories of unhappiness, and then define and give examples from your own experiences, or from your reading, to explain and differentiate your categories for your readers. Include a thesis statement that explains what you mean by unhappiness.
3. Write a classification-and-division essay in which you expand on Khazan's two categories of purchases, which she discusses in paragraphs 3 through 6. Add examples and, if you like, add a category that focuses on another kind of purchase. Be sure to show how your categories are different from one another.

Combining the Patterns

Where in this essay does Khazan use **definition**? Where does she use **exemplification**? Where could she add more of each of these patterns of development?

Thematic Connections

- "Stability in Motion" (page 178)
- "Once More to the Lake" (page 189)
- "Why the Post Office Makes America Great" (page 220)
- "Tortillas" (page 500)
- "The Park" (page 671)

CAROLYN FOSTER SEGAL

The Dog Ate My Tablet, and Other Tales of Woe

Carolyn Foster Segal (b. 1950) is a professor emeritus of English at Cedar Crest College and currently teaches at Muhlenberg College in Allentown, Pennsylvania. Segal has published poetry, fiction, and essays in a number of publications, including the *Chronicle of Higher Education,* where the following essay originally appeared. She sums up her ideas about writing as follows: "Writing — and it does not matter if it is writing about a feature of the landscape, an aspect of human nature, or a work of literature — begins with observation. The other parts are curiosity, imagination, and patience." She has received hundreds of responses from other instructors corroborating the experiences she describes here.

Background on academic integrity and honor codes Although making up an excuse for being unprepared for class may seem like a minor infraction, it may still be considered a breach of academic integrity. At many colleges, honor codes define academic integrity and set penalties for those who violate its rules. The concept of college honor codes in the United States goes back to one developed by students at the University of Virginia in 1840, but reports of widespread cheating on college campuses in the early 1990s brought renewed interest in such codes. (Surveys show that more than three-quarters of college students have cheated at least once during their schooling, and an even greater number see cheating as the norm among successful students.) In 1992, the Center for Academic Integrity (known today as the International Center for Academic Integrity) was established to help colleges and universities find ways to promote "honesty, trust, fairness, respect, and responsibility" among students and faculty members. Its original twenty-five-member group has grown to include more than two hundred institutions, and many other colleges have adopted its goals as well. The main focus of most honor codes is on discouraging plagiarism — copying the work of others and presenting the work of others as one's own — and various forms of cheating on tests. The International Center for Academic Integrity sees promoting individual honesty as the fundamental issue underlying all of these concerns.

Taped to the door of my office is a cartoon that features a cat explaining to his feline teacher, "The dog ate my homework." It is intended as a gently humorous reminder to my students that I will not accept excuses for late work, and it, like the lengthy warning on my syllabus, has had absolutely no effect. With a show of energy and creativity that would be admirable if applied to the (missing) assignments in question, my students persist, week after week, semester after semester, year after year, in offering excuses about why their work is not ready. Those reasons fall into several broad categories: the 1 family, the best friend, the evils of dorm life, the evils of technology, and the totally bizarre.

"Those reasons fall into several broad categories: the family, the best friend, the evils of dorm life, the evils of technology, and the totally bizarre."

The Family

The death of the grandfather/grandmother is, of course, the grandmother of all excuses. What heartless teacher would dare to question a student's grief or veracity? What heartless student would lie, wishing death on a revered family member, just to avoid a deadline? Creative students may win extra extensions (and days off) with a little careful planning and fuller plot development, as in the sequence of "My grandfather/grandmother is sick"; "Now my grandfather/grandmother is in the hospital"; and finally, "We could all see it coming – my grandfather/grandmother is dead." 2

Another favorite excuse is "the family emergency," which (always) goes like this: "There was an emergency at home, and I had to help my family." It's a lovely sentiment, one that conjures up images of Louisa May Alcott's* little women rushing off with baskets of food and copies of *Pilgrim's Progress,*** but I do not understand why anyone would turn to my most irresponsible students in times of trouble. 3

The Best Friend

This heartwarming concern for others extends beyond the family to friends, as in, "My best friend was up all night and I had to (a) stay up with her in the dorm, (b) drive her to the hospital, or (c) drive to her college because (1) her boyfriend broke up with her, (2) she was throwing up blood [no one catches a cold anymore; everyone throws up blood], or (3) her grandfather/grandmother died." 4

At one private university where I worked as an adjunct, I heard an interesting spin that incorporated the motifs of both best friend and dead relative: "My best friend's mother killed herself." One has to admire the cleverness here: A mysterious woman in the prime of her life has allegedly committed suicide, and no professor can prove otherwise! And I admit I was moved, until finally I had to point out to my students that it was amazing how the simple act of my assigning a topic for a paper seemed to drive large numbers of otherwise happy and healthy middle-aged women to their deaths. I was careful to make that point during an off week, during which no deaths were reported. 5

* Eds. note – Nineteenth-century sentimental novelist, author of *Little Women*.
** Eds. note – Eighteenth-century allegory by John Bunyan describing a Christian's journey from the City of Destruction to the Celestial City.

The Evils of Dorm Life

These stories are usually fairly predictable; almost always feature the evil roommate or hallmate, with my student in the role of the innocent victim; and can be summed up as follows: My roommate, who is a horrible person, likes to party, and I, who am a good person, cannot concentrate on my work when he or she is partying. Variations include stories about the two people next door who were running around and crying loudly last night because (a) one of them had boyfriend/girlfriend problems; (b) one of them was throwing up blood; or (c) someone, somewhere, died. A friend of mine in graduate school had a student who claimed that his roommate attacked him with a hammer. That, in fact, was a true story; it came out in court when the bad roommate was tried for killing his grandfather. 6

The Evils of Technology

The computer age has revolutionized the student story, inspiring almost as many new excuses as it has Internet businesses. Here are just a few electronically enhanced explanations: 7

- The computer wouldn't let me save my work.
- The printer wouldn't print.
- The printer wouldn't print this file.
- The printer wouldn't give me time to proofread.
- The printer made a black line run through all my words, and I know you can't read this, but do you still want it, or wait, here, take my tablet. File name? I don't know what you mean.
- I swear I attached it.
- It's my roommate's computer, and she usually helps me, but she had to go to the hospital because she was throwing up blood.
- I did write to the listserv, but all my messages came back to me.
- I just found out that all my other listserv messages came up under a diferent name. I just want you to know that its really me who wrote all those messages, you can tel which ones our mine because I didnt use the spelcheck! But it was yours truely :) Anyway, just in case you missed those messages or dont belief its my writting. I'll repeat what I sad: I thought the last movie we watched in clas was borring.

The Totally Bizarre

I call the first story "The Pennsylvania Chain Saw Episode." A commuter student called to explain why she had missed my morning class. She had gotten up early so that she would be wide awake for class. Having a bit of extra time, she walked outside to see her neighbor, who was cutting some wood. She called out to him, and he waved back to her with the saw. Wouldn't you know it, the safety catch wasn't on or was broken, and the blade flew right out of the saw and across his lawn and over her fence and across her yard and severed a tendon in her right hand. So she was calling me from the hospital, where 8 she was waiting for surgery. Luckily, she reassured me, she had remembered to bring her paper and a stamped envelope (in a plastic bag, to avoid bloodstains) along with her in the ambulance, and a nurse was mailing everything to me even as we spoke.

That wasn't her first absence. In fact, this student had missed most of the class meetings, and I had already recommended that she withdraw from the course. Now I suggested again that it might be best if she dropped the class. I didn't harp on the absences (what if even some of this story were true?). I did mention that she would need time to recuperate and that making up so much missed work might be difficult. "Oh, no," she said, "I can't drop this course. I had been planning to go on to medical school and become a surgeon, but since I won't be able to operate because of my accident, I'll have to major in English, and this course is more important than ever to me." She did come to the next class, wearing—as evidence of her recent trauma—a bedraggled Ace bandage on her left hand. 9

You may be thinking that nothing could top that excuse, but in fact I have one more story, provided by the same student, who sent me a letter to explain why her final assignment would be late. While recuperating from her surgery, she had begun corresponding on the Internet with a man who lived in Germany. After a one-week, whirlwind Web romance, they had agreed to meet in Rome, to rendezvous (her phrase) at the papal Easter Mass. Regrettably, the time of her flight made it impossible for her to attend class, but she trusted that I—just this once—would accept late work if the pope wrote a note. 10

• • •

Comprehension

1. What exactly is Segal classifying in this essay?
2. In paragraph 3, Segal says, "I do not understand why anyone would turn to my most irresponsible students in times of trouble." Do you see this comment as fair? Is she making fun of her students?
3. Which of the excuses Segal discusses do you see as valid? Which do you see as just excuses? Why?
4. Do you see Segal as rigid and unsympathetic, or do you think her frustration is justified? Do you think her students are irresponsible procrastinators or simply overworked?
5. What lessons do you think Segal would like her students to learn from her? Would reading this essay teach them what she wants them to learn?

Purpose and Audience

1. This essay was originally published in the *Chronicle of Higher Education,* a periodical for college teachers and administrators. How do you think these readers responded to the essay? How do you respond?

2. Do you see Segal's purpose here as being to entertain, to let off steam, to warn, to criticize, or to change students' habits? Explain.
3. In paragraph 7, Segal lists some specific excuses in the "evils of technology" category, paraphrasing students' remarks and even imitating their grammar and style. Why does she do this? Considering her likely audience, is this an effective strategy?

Style and Structure

1. In paragraph 1, Segal lists the five categories she plans to discuss. Is this list necessary? Why or why not?
2. Are Segal's categories mutually exclusive, or do they overlap? Could she combine any categories? Can you think of any categories she does not include?
3. What determines the order in which Segal introduces her categories? Is this order logical, or should she present her categories in a different order?
4. Does Segal discuss comparable points for each category? What points, if any, need to be added?
5. Segal frequently uses **sarcasm** in this essay. Give some examples. Given her intended audience, do you think this tone is appropriate? How do you react to her sarcasm?
6. **Vocabulary Project.** Every profession has its own unique **jargon**. What words and expressions in this essay characterize the writer as a college professor?
7. Throughout her essay, Segal returns again and again to two excuses: "my grandfather/grandmother died" and "throwing up blood." Locate different versions of these excuses in the essay. Why do you think she singles out these two excuses?
8. Although Segal deals with a serious academic problem, she includes many expressions – such as "Wouldn't you know it" (8) – that give her essay an informal tone. Identify some other examples. What is your reaction to the essay's casual, offhand tone?
9. Review the category Segal calls "The Evils of Technology." Can you add to (and update) her list? Can you create subcategories?

Journal Entry

Do you think this essay is funny? Explain your reaction.

Writing Workshop

1. **Working with Sources.** Write an email to Segal explaining why your English paper will be late, presenting several different kinds of original excuses for your paper's lateness. Before you present your own superior excuses, be sure to acknowledge the inadequacies of the excuses Segal lists, quoting a few

and including parenthetical documentation and a works-cited page. (See Chapter 18 for information about MLA documentation.)

2. Write an essay identifying four or five categories of legitimate excuses for handing in work late. If you like, you can use narrative examples from your own life as a student to explain each category.
3. Using a humorous (or even sarcastic) tone, write an essay identifying several different categories of teachers in terms of their shortcomings – for instance, teachers who do not cover the assigned work or teachers who do not grade papers in a timely fashion. Be sure to give specific examples of teachers in each category.

Combining the Patterns

In paragraphs 8 through 10, Segal uses **narration** to tell two stories. What do these stories add to her essay? Do you think she should have added more stories like these to her essay? If so, where?

Thematic Connections

- "Cutting and Pasting: A Senior Thesis by (Insert Name)" (page 17)
- "The Price of Silence" (page 76)
- "Surrendering" (page 116)
- "Suicide Note" (page 364)
- "I'm Your Teacher, Not Your Internet-Service Provider" (page 409)
- "The Ways We Lie" (page 466)

AMY TAN

Mother Tongue

Amy Tan was born in 1952 in Oakland, California, the daughter of recent Chinese immigrants. When she began to write fiction, she started to explore the contradictions she faced as a Chinese American who was also the daughter of immigrant parents. In 1989, she published *The Joy Luck Club*, a best-selling novel about four immigrant Chinese women and their American-born daughters. Her most recent books are the novels *Saving Fish from Drowning* (2005), *Rules for Virgins* (2011), and *The Valley of Amazement* (2013). In the following 1990 essay, Tan considers her mother's heavily Chinese-influenced English, as well as the different "Englishes" she herself uses, especially in communicating with her mother. She then discusses the potential limitations of growing up with immigrant parents who do not speak fluent English.

Background on Asian Americans and standardized tests The children of Asian immigrants tend to be highly assimilated and are often outstanding students, in part because their parents expect them to work hard and do well. Most who were born in the United States speak and read English fluently, yet on standardized tests, they have generally scored much higher in math than in English. For example, the average SAT scores nationally in 2009 were 515 in math, 501 in critical reading, and 493 in writing. Asian-American students had average scores of 587 in math, 516 in critical reading, and 520 in writing. The verbal scores represent a recent improvement over previous years, in which Asian-American students generally scored lower than average in the verbal sections of the SAT. In some cases, as Tan suggests, the perception that Asian-American students have greater skill in math than in reading and writing, based on average standardized test scores, may lead teachers to discourage these students from pursuing degrees in fields outside of math and science.

I am not a scholar of English or literature. I cannot give you much more than personal opinions on the English language and its variations in this country or others. 1

I am a writer. And by that definition, I am someone who has always loved language. I am fascinated by language in daily life. I spend a great deal of my time thinking about the power of language—the way it can evoke an emotion, a visual image, a complex idea, or a simple truth. Language is the tool of my trade. And I use them all—all the Englishes I grew up with. 2

Recently, I was made keenly aware of the different Englishes I do use. I was giving a talk to a large group of people, the same talk I had already given to half a dozen other groups. The nature of the talk was about my writing, my life, and my book, *The Joy Luck Club*. The talk was going along well enough, until I remembered one major difference that made the whole talk sound wrong. My mother was in the room. And it was perhaps the first time she had 3 heard me give a lengthy speech, using the kind of English I have never used with her. I was saying things like, "The intersection of memory upon imagination" and "There is an aspect of my fiction that relates to thus-and-thus"—a speech filled with carefully wrought grammatical phrases, burdened, it suddenly seemed to me, with nominalized forms, past perfect tenses, conditional phrases, all the forms of standard English that I had learned in school and through books, the forms of English I did not use at home with my mother.

Just last week, I was walking down the street with my mother, and I again 4 found myself conscious of the English I was using, and the English I do use with her. We were talking about the price of new and used furniture and I heard myself saying this: "Not waste money that way." My husband was with us as well, and he didn't notice any switch in my English. And then I realized why. It's because over the twenty years we've been together I've often used that same kind of English with him, and sometimes he even uses it with me. It has become our language of intimacy, a different sort of English that relates to family talk, the language I grew up with.

So you'll have some idea of what this family talk I heard sounds like, I'll 5 quote what my mother said during a recent conversation which I videotaped and then transcribed. During this conversation my mother was talking about a political gangster in Shanghai who had the same last name as her family's, Du, and how the gangster in his early years wanted to be adopted by her family, which was rich by comparison. Later, the gangster became more powerful, far richer than my mother's family, and one day showed up at my mother's wedding to pay his respects. Here's what she said in part:

"Du Yusong having business like fruit stand. Like off the street kind. He 6 is Du like Du Zong—but not Tsung-ming Island people. The local people call putong, the river east side, he belong to that side local people. The man want to ask Du Zong father take him in like become own family. Du Zong father wasn't looking down on him, but didn't take seriously, until that man big like become a mafia. Now important person very hard to inviting him. Chinese way, come only to show respect, don't stay for dinner. Respect for making big celebration, he shows up. Mean gives lots of respect. Chinese custom. Chinese social life that way. If too important won't have to stay too long. He come to my wedding. I didn't see. I heard it. I gone to boy's side, they have YMCA dinner. Chinese age I was nineteen."

You should know that my mother's expressive command of English 7 belies how much she actually understands. She reads the *Forbes* report, listens to *Wall Street Week,* converses daily with her stockbroker, reads all of Shirley MacLaine's books with ease—all kinds of things I can't begin to understand. Yet some of my friends tell me they understand 50 percent of what my mother says. Some say they understand 80 to 90 percent. Some say they understand none of it, as if she were speaking pure Chinese. But to me, my mother's English is perfectly clear, perfectly natural. It's my mother's tongue. Her language, as I hear it, is vivid, direct, full of observation and imagery. This was the language that helped shape the way I saw things, expressed things, made sense of the world.

Lately, I've been giving more thought to the kind of English my mother speaks. Like others, I have described it to people as "broken" or "fractured" English. But I wince when I say that. It has always bothered me that I can think of no way to describe it other than "broken," as if it were damaged and needed to be fixed, as if it lacked a certain wholeness and soundness. I've heard other terms used, "limited English," for example. But they seem just as bad, as if everything is limited, including people's perceptions of the limited English speaker. 8

I know this for a fact, because when I was growing up, my mother's "limited" English limited *my* perception of her. I was ashamed of her English. I believed that her English reflected the quality of what she had to say. That is, because she expressed them imperfectly her thoughts were imperfect. And I had plenty of empirical evidence to support me: the fact that people in department stores, at banks, and at restaurants did not take her seriously, did not give her good service, pretended not to understand her, or even acted as if they did not hear her. 9

My mother has long realized the limitations of her English as well. When I was fifteen, she used to have me call people on the phone to pretend I was she. In this guise, I was forced to ask for information or even complain and yell at people who had been rude to her. One time it was a call to her stockbroker in New York. She had cashed out her small portfolio and it just so happened we were going to go to New York the next week, our very first trip outside California. I had to get on the phone and say in an adolescent voice that was not very convincing, "This is Mrs. Tan." 10

And my mother was standing in the back whispering loudly, "Why he don't send me check, already two weeks late. So mad he lie to me, losing me money." 11

And then I said in perfect English, "Yes, I'm getting rather concerned. You had agreed to send the check two weeks ago, but it hasn't arrived." 12

Then she began to talk more loudly. "What he want, I come to New York tell him front of his boss, you cheating me?" And I was trying to calm her down, make her be quiet, while telling the stockbroker, "I can't tolerate any more excuses. If I don't receive the check immediately I am going to have to speak to your manager when I'm in New York next week." And sure enough, the following week there we were in front of this astonished stockbroker, and I was sitting there red-faced and quiet, and my mother, the real Mrs. Tan, was shouting at his boss in her impeccable broken English. 13

We used a similar routine just five days ago, for a situation that was far less humorous. My mother had gone to the hospital for an appointment, to find out about a benign brain tumor a CAT scan had revealed a month ago. She said she had spoken very good English, her best English, no mistakes. Still, she said, the hospital did not apologize when they said they had lost the CAT scan and she had come for nothing. She said they did not seem to have any sympathy when she told them she was anxious to know the exact diagnosis, since her husband and son had both died of brain tumors. She said they would not give her any more information until the next time and she would have to make another appointment for that. So she said she would not 14 leave until the doctor called her daughter. She wouldn't budge. And when the doctor finally called her daughter, me, who spoke in perfect English – lo and behold – we had assurances the CAT scan would be found, promises that a conference call on Monday would be held, and apologies for any suffering my mother had gone through for a most regrettable mistake.

I think my mother's English almost had an effect on limiting my possi- 15
bilities in life as well. Sociologists and linguists probably will tell you that a person's developing language skills are more influenced by peers. But I do think that the language spoken in the family, especially in immigrant families which are more insular, plays a large role in shaping the language of the child. And I believe that it affected my results on achievement tests, IQ tests, and the SAT. While my English skills were never judged as poor, compared to math, English could not be considered my strong suit. In grade school I did moderately well, getting perhaps B's, sometimes B-pluses, in English and scoring perhaps in the sixtieth or seventieth percentile on achievement tests. But those scores were not good enough to override the opinion that my true abilities lay in math and science, because in those areas I achieved A's and scored in the ninetieth percentile or higher.

This was understandable. Math is precise; there is only one correct 16
answer. Whereas, for me at least, the answers on English tests were always a judgment call, a matter of opinion and personal experience. Those tests were constructed around items like fill-in-the-blank sentence completion, such as "Even though Tom was ________, Mary thought he was ________." And the correct answer always seemed to be the most bland combinations of thoughts, for example, "Even though Tom was shy, Mary thought he was charming," with the grammatical structure "even though" limiting the correct answer to some sort of semantic opposites, so you wouldn't get answers like, "Even though Tom was foolish, Mary thought he was ridiculous." Well, according to my mother, there were very few limitations as to what Tom could have been and what Mary might have thought of him. So I never did well on tests like that.

The same was true with word analogies, pairs of words in which you were 17
supposed to find some sort of logical, semantic relationship – for example, "*Sunset* is to *nightfall* as ________ is to ________." And here you would be presented with a list of four possible pairs, one of which showed the same kind of relationship: *red* is to *stoplight, bus* is to *arrival, chills* is to *fever, yawn* is to *boring.* Well, I could never think that way. I knew what the tests were asking, but I could not block out of my mind the images already created by the first pair, "*sunset* is to *nightfall*" – and I would see a burst of colors against a darkening sky, the moon rising, the lowering of a curtain of stars. And all the other pairs of words – red, bus, stoplight, boring – just threw up a mass of confusing images, making it impossible for me to sort out something as logical as saying: "A sunset precedes nightfall" is the same as "a chill precedes a fever." The only way I would have gotten that answer right would have been to imagine an associative situation, for example, my being disobedient and staying out past sunset, catching a chill at night, which turns into feverish pneumonia as punishment, which indeed did happen to me.

"Why are there few Asian Americans enrolled in creative writing programs? Why do so many Chinese students go into engineering?"

I have been thinking about all this 18
lately, about my mother's English, about achievement tests. Because lately I've been asked, as a writer, why there are not more Asian Americans represented in American literature. Why are there few Asian Americans enrolled in creative writing programs? Why do so many Chinese students go into engineering? Well, these are broad sociological questions I can't begin to answer. But I have noticed in surveys – in fact, just last week – that Asian students, as a whole, always do significantly better on math achievement tests than in English. And this makes me think that there are other Asian-American students whose English spoken in the home might also be described as "broken" or "limited." And perhaps they also have teachers who are steering them away from writing and into math and science, which is what happened to me.

Fortunately, I happen to be rebellious in nature and enjoy the challenge of 19
disproving assumptions made about me. I became an English major my first year in college, after being enrolled as pre-med. I started writing nonfiction as a freelancer the week after I was told by my former boss that writing was my worst skill and I should hone my talents toward account management.

But it wasn't until 1985 that I finally began to write fiction. And at first 20
I wrote using what I thought to be wittily crafted sentences, sentences that would finally prove I had mastery over the English language. Here's an example from the first draft of a story that later made its way into *The Joy Luck Club*, but without this line: "That was my mental quandary in its nascent state." A terrible line, which I can barely pronounce.

Fortunately, for reasons I won't get into today, I later decided I should 21
envision a reader for the stories I would write. And the reader I decided upon was my mother because these were stories about mothers. So with this reader in mind – and in fact she did read my early drafts – I began to write stories using all the Englishes I grew up with: the English I spoke to my mother, which for lack of a better term might be described as "simple"; the English she used with me, which for lack of a better term might be described as "broken"; my translation of her Chinese, which could certainly be described as "watered down"; and what I imagined to be her translation of her Chinese if she could speak in perfect English, her internal language, and for that I sought to preserve the essence, but neither an English nor a Chinese structure. I wanted to capture what language ability tests can never reveal: her intent, her passion, her imagery, the rhythms of her speech, and the nature of her thoughts.

Apart from what any critic had to say about my writing, I knew I had suc- 22
ceeded where it counted when my mother finished reading my book and gave me her verdict: "So easy to read."

• • •

Comprehension

1. What is Tan classifying in this essay? What individual categories does she identify?
2. Where does Tan identify the different categories she discusses in "Mother Tongue"? Should she have identified these categories earlier? Explain your reasoning.
3. Does Tan illustrate each category she identifies? Does she treat all categories equally? If she does not, do you see this as a problem? Explain.
4. In what specific situations does Tan say her mother's "limited English" was a handicap? In what other situations might Mrs. Tan face difficulties?
5. What effects has her mother's limited English had on Tan's life?
6. How does Tan account for the difficulty she had in answering questions on achievement tests, particularly word analogies? Do you think her problems in this area can be explained by the level of her family's language skills, or might other factors also be to blame? Explain.
7. In paragraph 18, Tan considers the possible reasons for the relatively few Asian Americans in the fields of language and literature. What explanations does she offer? What other explanations can you think of?

Purpose and Audience

1. Why do you suppose Tan begins her essay by explaining her qualifications? Why, for example, does she tell her readers she is "not a scholar of English or literature" (1) but rather a writer who is "fascinated by language in daily life" (2)?
2. Do you think Tan expects most of her readers to be Asian American? To be familiar with Asian-American languages and culture? How can you tell?
3. Is Tan's primary focus in this essay on language or on her mother? Explain your conclusion.

Style and Structure

1. This essay's style is relatively informal. For example, Tan uses *I* to refer to herself and addresses her readers as *you*. Identify other features that characterize her style as informal. Do you think a more formal style would strengthen her credibility? Explain your reasoning.
2. In paragraph 6, Tan quotes a passage of her mother's speech. What purpose does Tan say she wants this quotation to serve? What impression does it give of her mother? Do you think this effect is what Tan intended? Explain.
3. In paragraph 8, Tan discusses the different words and phrases that might be used to describe her mother's spoken English. Which of these terms seems

most accurate? Do you agree with Tan that these words are unsatisfactory? What other term for her mother's English would be both neutral and accurate?

4. In paragraphs 10 through 13, Tan juxtaposes her mother's English with her own. What point do these quoted passages make?
5. **Vocabulary Project.** Consider the expression *Mother Tongue* in Tan's title. What does this expression usually mean? What does it seem to mean here?
6. In paragraph 20, Tan quotes a "terrible line" from an early draft of part of her novel *The Joy Luck Club.* Why do you suppose she quotes this line? How is it different from the writing style she uses in "Mother Tongue"?

Journal Entry

In paragraph 9, Tan says that when she was growing up she was sometimes ashamed of her mother because of her limited English proficiency. Have you ever felt ashamed of a parent (or a friend) because of his or her inability to "fit in" in some way? How do you feel now about your earlier reaction?

Writing Workshop

1. What different "Englishes" (or other languages) do you use in your day-to-day life as a student, employee, friend, and family member? Write a classification-and-division essay identifying, describing, and illustrating each kind of language and explaining the purpose it serves.
2. **Working with Sources.** What kinds of problems does a person whose English is as limited as Mrs. Tan's face in the age of social media and instant communication? Write a classification-and-division essay that identifies and explains the kinds of problems you might encounter today if the level of your spoken English were comparable to Mrs. Tan's. Try to update some of the specific situations Tan describes, quoting Tan where necessary, and be sure to document any borrowed words or ideas and to include a works-cited page. (See Chapter 18 for information on MLA documentation.)
3. Tan's essay focuses on spoken language, but people also use different kinds of *written* language in different situations. Write a classification-and-division essay that identifies and analyzes three different kinds of written English that you might use: one appropriate for your parents, one for a teacher or employer, and one for a friend. Illustrate each kind of language with a few sentences directed at each audience about your plans for your future. In your thesis statement, explain why all three kinds of language are necessary.

Combining the Patterns

Tan develops her essay with a series of anecdotes about her mother and about herself. How does this use of **narration** strengthen her essay? Could she have made her point about the use of different "Englishes" without these anecdotes? What other strategy could she have used?

Thematic Connections

- "Surrendering" (page 116)
- "Midnight" (page 213)
- "Why Chinese Mothers Are Superior" (page 402)
- "The Park" (page 671)

STEPHANIE ERICSSON

The Ways We Lie

Stephanie Ericsson (b. 1953) grew up in San Francisco and began writing as a teenager. She has been a screenwriter and an advertising copywriter and has published several books based on her own life. *Shame Faced: The Road to Recovery* and *Women of AA: Recovering Together* (both 1985) focus on her experiences with addiction; *Companion through the Darkness: Inner Dialogues on Grief* (1993) deals with the sudden death of her first husband; and *Companion into the Dawn: Inner Dialogues on Loving* (1994) is a collection of essays.

Background on lies in politics and business The following piece originally appeared in the *Utne Reader* as the cover article of the January 1993 issue, which was devoted to the theme of lies and lying. The subject had particular relevance after a year when the honesty of Bill Clinton — the newly elected U.S. president — had been questioned. (It also followed the furor surrounding the confirmation hearings of U.S. Supreme Court nominee Clarence Thomas, who denied allegations by attorney Anita Hill of workplace sexual harassment; here the question was who was telling the truth and who was not.) Six years later, Clinton was accused of perjury and faced a Senate impeachment trial. In subsequent years, lying was featured prominently in the news as executives at a number of major corporations were charged with falsifying records at the expense of employees and shareholders, and George W. Bush's administration was accused of lying about the presence of weapons of mass destruction in Iraq to justify going to war.

More recently, major mortgage lenders were found to have lied about their reviews of documents justifying many thousands of foreclosures. In 2010, lying was again featured prominently in the news as investigations of the oil company BP found that the company was aware of problems with a safety device on the Deepwater Horizon oil rig prior to an explosion that killed eleven workers and spilled millions of gallons of oil, but covered up those concerns in an attempt to increase its profits. BP has also been accused of lying to Congress about its estimate of the extent of the spill.

The bank called today and I told them my deposit was in the mail, even 1
though I hadn't written a check yet. It'd been a rough day. The baby I'm pregnant with decided to do aerobics on my lungs for two hours, our three-year-old daughter painted the living-room couch with lipstick, the IRS put me on hold for an hour, and I was late to a business meeting because I was tired.

I told my client the traffic had been bad. When my partner came home, 2
his haggard face told me his day hadn't gone any better than mine, so when he asked, "How was your day?" I said, "Oh, fine," knowing that one more straw might break his back. A friend called and wanted to take me to lunch.

I said I was busy. Four lies in the course of a day, none of which I felt the least bit guilty about.

3 We lie. We all do. We exaggerate, we minimize, we avoid confrontation, we spare people's feelings, we conveniently forget, we keep secrets, we justify lying to the big-guy institutions. Like most people, I indulge in small falsehoods and still think of myself as an honest person. Sure I lie, but it doesn't hurt anything. Or does it?

4 I once tried going a whole week without telling a lie, and it was paralyzing. I discovered that telling the truth all the time is nearly impossible. It means living with some serious consequences: The bank charges me $60 in overdraft fees, my partner keels over when I tell him about my travails, my client fires me for telling her I didn't feel like being on time, and my friend takes it personally when I say I'm not hungry. There must be some merit to lying.

"I once tried going a whole week without telling a lie, and it was paralyzing."

5 But if I justify lying, what makes me any different from slick politicians or the corporate robbers who raided the S&L industry? Saying it's okay to lie one way and not another is hedging. I cannot seem to escape the voice deep inside me that tells me: When someone lies, someone loses.

6 What far-reaching consequences will I, or others, pay as a result of my lie? Will someone's trust be destroyed? Will someone else pay *my* penance because I ducked out? We must consider the *meaning of our actions.* Deception, lies, capital crimes, and misdemeanors all carry meanings. *Webster's* definition of *lie* is specific:

> 1: a false statement or action especially made with the intent to deceive;
> 2: anything that gives or is meant to give a false impression.

7 A definition like this implies that there are many, many ways to tell a lie. Here are just a few.

The White Lie

> A man who won't lie to a woman has very little consideration for her feelings.
>
> —BERGEN EVANS

8 The white lie assumes that the truth will cause more damage than a simple, harmless untruth. Telling a friend he looks great when he looks like hell can be based on a decision that the friend needs a compliment more than a frank opinion. But, in effect, it is the liar deciding what is best for the lied to. Ultimately, it is a vote of no confidence. It is an act of subtle arrogance for anyone to decide what is best for someone else.

9 Yet not all circumstances are quite so cut-and-dried. Take, for instance, the sergeant in Vietnam who knew one of his men was killed in action but listed him as missing so that the man's family would receive indefinite

compensation instead of the lump-sum pittance the military gives widows and children. His intent was honorable. Yet for twenty years this family kept their hopes alive, unable to move on to a new life.

Facades

Et tu, Brute?

—CAESAR*

We all put up facades to one degree or another. When I put on a suit to go to see a client, I feel as though I am putting on another face, obeying the expectation that serious businesspeople wear suits rather than sweatpants. But I'm a writer. Normally, I get up, get the kid off to school, and sit at my computer in my pajamas until four in the afternoon. When I answer the phone, the caller thinks I'm wearing a suit (though the UPS man knows better). 10

But facades can be destructive because they are used to seduce others into an illusion. For instance, I recently realized that a former friend was a liar. He presented himself with all the right looks and the right words and offered lots of new consciousness theories, fabulous books to read, and fascinating insights. Then I did some business with him, and the time came for him to pay me. He turned out to be all talk and no walk. I heard a plethora of reasonable excuses, including in-depth descriptions of the big break around the corner. In six months of work, I saw less than a hundred bucks. When I confronted him, he raised both eyebrows and tried to convince me that I'd heard him wrong, that he'd made no commitment to me. A simple investigation into his past revealed a crowded graveyard of disenchanted former friends. 11

Ignoring the Plain Facts

Well, you must understand that Father Porter is only human. . . .

—A MASSACHUSETTS PRIEST

In the '60s, the Catholic Church in Massachusetts began hearing complaints that Father James Porter was sexually molesting children. Rather than relieving him of his duties, the ecclesiastical authorities simply moved him from one parish to another between 1960 and 1967, actually providing him with a fresh supply of unsuspecting families and innocent children to abuse. After treatment in 1967 for pedophilia, he went back to work, this time in Minnesota. The new diocese was aware of Father Porter's obsession with children, but they needed priests and recklessly believed treatment had cured him. More 12

* Eds. note – "And you, Brutus?" (Latin). In Shakespeare's play *Julius Caesar,* Caesar asks this question when he sees Brutus, whom he has believed to be his friend, among the conspirators who are stabbing him.

children were abused until he was relieved of his duties a year later. By his own admission, Porter may have abused as many as a hundred children.

Ignoring the facts may not in and of itself be a form of lying, but consider the context of this situation. If a lie is *a false action done with the intent to deceive,* then the Catholic Church's conscious covering for Porter created irreparable consequences. The church became a co-perpetrator with Porter. 13

Deflecting

When you have no basis for an argument, abuse the plaintiff.

—CICERO

I've discovered that I can keep anyone from seeing the true me by being selectively blatant. I set a precedent of being up-front about intimate issues, but I never bring up the things I truly want to hide; I just let people assume I'm revealing everything. It's an effective way of hiding. 14

Any good liar knows that the way to perpetuate an untruth is to deflect attention from it. When Clarence Thomas exploded with accusations that the Senate hearings were a "high-tech lynching," he simply switched the focus from a highly charged subject to a radioactive subject. Rather than defending himself, he took the offensive and accused the country of racism. It was a brilliant maneuver. Racism is now politically incorrect in official circles – unlike sexual harassment, which still rewards those who can get away with it. 15

Some of the most skillful deflectors are passive-aggressive people who, when accused of inappropriate behavior, refuse to respond to the accusations. This you-don't-exist stance infuriates the accuser, who, understandably, screams something obscene out of frustration. The trap is sprung and the act of deflection successful, because now the passive-aggressive person can indignantly say, "Who can talk to someone as unreasonable as you?" The real issue is forgotten and the sins of the original victim become the focus. Feeling guilty of name-calling, the victim is fully tamed and crawls into a hole, ashamed. I have watched this fighting technique work thousands of times in disputes between men and women, and what I've learned is that the real culprit is not necessarily the one who swears the loudest. 16

Omission

The cruelest lies are often told in silence.

—R. L. STEVENSON

Omission involves telling most of the truth minus one or two key facts whose absence changes the story completely. You break a pair of glasses that are guaranteed under normal use and get a new pair, without mentioning that the first pair broke during a rowdy game of basketball. Who hasn't tried something like that? But what about omission of information that could make a difference in how a person lives his or her life? 17

For instance, one day I found out that rabbinical legends tell of another woman in the Garden of Eden before Eve. I was stunned. The omission of the Sumerian goddess Lilith from Genesis – as well as her demonization by ancient misogynists as an embodiment of female evil – felt like spiritual robbery. I felt like I'd just found out my mother was really my stepmother. To take seriously the tradition that Adam was created out of the same mud as his equal counterpart, Lilith, redefines all of Judeo-Christian history. 18

Some renegade Catholic feminists introduced me to a view of Lilith that had been suppressed during the many centuries when this strong goddess was seen only as a spirit of evil. Lilith was a proud goddess who defied Adam's need to control her, attempted negotiations, and when this failed, said adios and left the Garden of Eden. 19

This omission of Lilith from the Bible was a patriarchal strategy to keep women weak. Omitting the strong-woman archetype of Lilith from Western religions and starting the story with Eve the Rib has helped keep Christian and Jewish women believing they were the lesser sex for thousands of years. 20

Stereotypes and Clichés

> Where opinion does not exist, the status quo becomes stereotyped and all originality is discouraged.
>
> —BERTRAND RUSSELL

Stereotype and cliché serve a purpose as a form of shorthand. Our need for vast amounts of information in nanoseconds has made the stereotype vital to modern communication. Unfortunately, it often shuts down original thinking, giving those hungry for the truth a candy bar of misinformation instead of a balanced meal. The stereotype explains a situation with just enough truth to seem unquestionable. 21

All the "isms" – racism, sexism, ageism, et al. – are founded on and fueled by the stereotype and the cliché, which are lies of exaggeration, omission, and ignorance. They are always dangerous. They take a single tree and make it a landscape. They destroy curiosity. They close minds and separate people. The single mother on welfare is assumed to be cheating. Any black male could tell you how much of his identity is obliterated daily by stereotypes. Fat people, ugly people, beautiful people, old people, large-breasted women, short men, the mentally ill, and the homeless all could tell you how much more they are like us than we want to think. I once admitted to a group of people that I had a mouth like a truck driver. Much to my surprise, a man stood up and said, "I'm a truck driver, and I never cuss." Needless to say, I was humbled. 22

Groupthink

> Who is more foolish, the child afraid of the dark, or the man afraid of the light?
>
> —MAURICE FREEHILL

Irving Janis, in *Victims of GroupThink,* defines this sort of lie as a psychological phenomenon within decision-making groups in which loyalty to the group has become more important than any other value, with the result that dissent and the appraisal of alternatives are suppressed. If you've ever worked on a committee or in a corporation, you've encountered groupthink. It requires a combination of other forms of lying – ignoring facts, selective memory, omission, and denial, to name a few. 23

The textbook example of groupthink came on December 7, 1941. From as early as the fall of 1941, the warnings came in, one after another, that Japan was preparing for a massive military operation. The Navy command in Hawaii assumed Pearl Harbor was invulnerable – the Japanese weren't stupid enough to attack the United States' most important base. On the other hand, racist stereotypes said the Japanese weren't smart enough to invent a torpedo effective in less than 60 feet of water (the fleet was docked in 30 feet); after all, U.S. technology hadn't been able to do it. 24

On Friday, December 5, normal weekend leave was granted to all the commanders at Pearl Harbor, even though the Japanese consulate in Hawaii was busy burning papers. Within the tight, good-ole-boy cohesiveness of the U.S. command in Hawaii, the myth of invulnerability stayed well entrenched. No one in the group considered the alternatives. The rest is history. 25

Out-and-Out Lies

The only form of lying that is beyond reproach is lying for its own sake.

—OSCAR WILDE

Of all the ways to lie, I like this one the best, probably because I get tired of trying to figure out the real meanings behind things. At least I can trust the bald-faced lie. I once asked my five-year-old nephew, "Who broke the fence?" (I had seen him do it.) He answered, "The murderers." Who could argue? 26

At least when this sort of lie is told it can be easily confronted. As the person who is lied to, I know where I stand. The bald-faced lie doesn't toy with my perceptions – it argues with them. It doesn't try to refashion reality, it tries to refute it. *Read my lips. . . .* No sleight of hand. No guessing. If this were the only form of lying, there would be no such thing as floating anxiety or the adult-children of alcoholics movement. 27

Dismissal

Pay no attention to that man behind the curtain! I am the Great Oz!

—THE WIZARD OF OZ

Dismissal is perhaps the slipperiest of all lies. Dismissing feelings, perceptions, or even the raw facts of a situation ranks as a kind of lie that can do as much damage to a person as any other kind of lie. 28

The roots of many mental disorders can be traced back to the dismissal of reality. Imagine that a person is told from the time she is a tot that her perceptions are inaccurate. *"Mommy, I'm scared."* "No, you're not, darling." *"I don't like that man next door, he makes me feel icky."* "Johnny, that's a terrible thing to say, of course you like him. You go over there right now and be nice to him." 29

I've often mused over the idea that madness is actually a sane reaction to an insane world. Psychologist R. D. Laing supports this hypothesis in *Sanity, Madness & the Family,* an account of his investigations into families of schizophrenics. The common thread that ran through all of the families he studied was a deliberate, staunch dismissal of the patient's perceptions from a very early age. Each of the patients started out with an accurate grasp of reality, which, through meticulous and methodical dismissal, was demolished until the only reality the patient could trust was catatonia. 30

Dismissal runs the gamut. Mild dismissal can be quite handy for forgiving the foibles of others in our day-to-day lives. Toddlers who have just learned to manipulate their parents' attention sometimes are dismissed out of necessity. Absolute attention from the parents would require so much energy that no one would get to eat dinner. But we must be careful and attentive about how far we take our "necessary" dismissals. Dismissal is a dangerous tool, because it's nothing less than a lie. 31

Delusion

> We lie loudest when we lie to ourselves.
>
> —ERIC HOFFER

I could write the book on this one. Delusion, a cousin of dismissal, is the tendency to see excuses as facts. It's a powerful lying tool because it filters out information that contradicts what we want to believe. Alcoholics who believe that the problems in their lives are legitimate reasons for drinking rather than results of the drinking offer the classic example of deluded thinking. Delusion uses the mind's ability to see things in myriad ways to support what it wants to be the truth. 32

But delusion is also a survival mechanism we all use. If we were to fully contemplate the consequences of our stockpiles of nuclear weapons or global warming, we could hardly function on a day-to-day level. We don't want to incorporate that much reality into our lives because to do so would be paralyzing. 33

Delusion acts as an adhesive to keep the status quo intact. It shamelessly employs dismissal, omission, and amnesia, among other sorts of lies. Its most cunning defense is that it cannot see itself. 34

> The liar's punishment . . . is that he cannot believe anyone else.
>
> —GEORGE BERNARD SHAW

These are only a few of the ways we lie. Or are lied to. As I said earlier, it's not easy to entirely eliminate lies from our lives. No matter how pious we may 35 try to be, we will still embellish, hedge, and omit to lubricate the daily machinery of living. But there is a world of difference between telling functional lies and living a lie. Martin Buber* once said, "The lie is the spirit committing treason against itself." Our acceptance of lies becomes a cultural cancer that eventually shrouds and reorders reality until moral garbage becomes as invisible to us as water is to a fish.

How much do we tolerate before we become sick and tired of being sick and tired? When will we stand up and declare our *right* to trust? When do we stop accepting that the real truth is in the fine print? Whose lips do we read this year when we vote for president? When will we stop being so reticent about making judgments? When do we stop turning over our personal power and responsibility to liars? 36

Maybe if I don't tell the bank the check's in the mail I'll be less tolerant of the lies told me every day. A country song I once heard said it all for me: "You've got to stand for something or you'll fall for anything." 37

• • •

Comprehension

1. List and briefly define each of the ten kinds of lies Ericsson identifies.
2. Why, in Ericsson's view, is each kind of lie necessary?
3. According to Ericsson, what is the danger of each kind of lie?
4. Why does Ericsson like "out-and-out lies" (26–27) best?
5. Why is "dismissal" the "slipperiest of all lies" (28)?

Purpose and Audience

1. Is Ericsson's thesis simply that "there are many, many ways to tell a lie" (7)? Or, is she defending – or attacking – the practice of lying? Try to state her thesis in a single sentence.
2. Do you think Ericsson's choice of examples reveals a political bias? If so, do you think she expects her intended audience to share her political views? Explain your conclusion.

Style and Structure

1. Despite the seriousness of her subject matter, Ericsson's essay is informal; her opening paragraphs are especially personal and breezy. Why do you think she chose to use this kind of style, particularly in her introductory paragraphs? Do you think her decision makes sense?
2. Ericsson introduces each category of lie with a quotation. What function do these quotations serve? Do you think her essay would be less (or more) effective without them? Why or why not?

---

* Eds. note – Austrian-born Judaic philosopher (1878–1965).

3. In addition to a heading and a quotation, what other elements does Ericsson include in her treatment of each kind of lie? Are all the discussions parallel – that is, does her discussion of each category include the same elements? If not, do you think this lack of balance is a problem? Explain.
4. What, if anything, determines the order in which Ericsson arranges her categories in this essay? Do you think any category should be relocated? If so, why?
5. Throughout her essay, Ericsson uses **rhetorical questions**. Why do you suppose she uses this stylistic device?
6. **Vocabulary Project.** Ericsson uses many **colloquialisms** in this essay, such as "I could write the book on this one" (32). Identify as many of these informal expressions as you can. Why do you think she uses colloquialisms instead of more formal expressions? Do they have a positive or negative effect on your reaction to her ideas? Explain.
7. Ericsson occasionally cites the views of experts. Why does she include these references? If she wanted to cite additional experts, what professional backgrounds or fields of study do you think they should represent? Why?
8. In paragraph 29, Ericsson says, "Imagine that a person is told from the time she is a tot. . . ." Does she use *she* in similar contexts elsewhere in the essay? Do you find the feminine form of the personal pronoun appropriate or distracting? What other options does Ericsson have? Explain.
9. Paragraphs 35 through 37 constitute Ericsson's conclusion. How does this conclusion parallel the essay's introduction in terms of style, structure, and content?

Journal Entry

In paragraph 3, Ericsson says, "We lie. We all do." Later in the paragraph, she comments, "Sure I lie, but it doesn't hurt anything. Or does it?" Answer her question.

Writing Workshop

1. **Working with Sources.** Choose three or four of Ericsson's categories, and write a classification-and-division essay called "The Ways I Lie." Base your essay on personal experience, and include an explicit thesis statement that either defends your own lies or is sharply critical of their use. Be sure to document Ericsson's essay when you cite her categories and to include a works-cited page. (See Chapter 18 for information on MLA documentation.)
2. In paragraph 22, Ericsson condemns stereotypes. Write a classification-and-division essay with the following thesis statement: "Stereotypes are usually inaccurate, often negative, and always dangerous." In your essay, consider the stereotypes applied to three or four of the following groups: people who are disabled, overweight, or elderly; urban teenagers; politicians; housewives; and immigrants.

3. Using the thesis provided in question 2, write a classification-and division essay that considers the stereotypes applied to three or four of the following occupations: police officers, librarians, used-car dealers, flight attendants, lawyers, construction workers, rock musicians, accountants, and telemarketers.

Combining the Patterns

A dictionary **definition** is a familiar – even tired – strategy for an essay's introduction. Do you think Ericsson should delete the definition in paragraph 6 for this reason, or do you believe it is necessary? Explain.

Thematic Connections

- "'What's in a Name?'" (page 2)
- "The Money" (page 111)
- "Thirty-Eight Who Saw Murder Didn't Call the Police" (page 126)
- "The Hidden Life of Garbage" (page 184)
- "The Lottery" (page 304)

HENRY REED

Naming of Parts

Henry Reed (1914–1986) was an English poet, journalist, critic, teacher, translator, and broadcaster. He was born in Birmingham, England, and attended the University of Birmingham. After World War II, during which he served in the military as a Japanese translator, Reed published his best-known book, *A Map of Verona* (1946). Several of the poems in this work, including "Naming of Parts," focus on his experience in the army during the war.

Background on the problem of war Although there is a long tradition of literature that glorifies war, dating back to epics such as *The Iliad* and *The Odyssey*, literary works about World War I and World War II are distinguished by their depictions of the sheer horror of combat and the disillusion of its aftermath, with writers often retreating into irony or detachment. Three well-known examples are Ernest Hemingway's *In Our Time* (1925), Erich Maria Remarque's *All Quiet on the Western Front* (1929), and Norman Mailer's *The Naked and the Dead* (1948). This focus on the horrors of war may have stemmed, in part, from the advances in technology and weaponry that made modern warfare more destructive than its predecessors: the poison gas, along with other developments in firearms, artillery, aviation, and naval arms in World War I; the tanks, planes, bombs, and nuclear weapons of World War II. Over the years, various treaties have attempted to regulate the rules governing the practices and weaponry of military conflicts. For example, the 1925 Geneva Protocol, which has now been signed by 140 countries, banned the use of poisonous gases and bacterial agents, and the Geneva Convention of 1949 sought to codify the proper treatment prisoners of war and civilians, among other goals. These agreements generally evade addressing more fundamental questions about the morality of war. When is war justified? How can ethical rules of conduct exist in the context of warfare? Is it realistic to apply moral concepts such as "justice" to military conflict and international relations? These and other issues are addressed by poets and novelists as they struggle to make sense of war, as Henry Reed does in the poem that follows. On the surface, "Naming of Parts" focuses on the prosaic act of learning to handle a military rifle. A closer look, however, reveals that the poem wrestles with the meaning of war in a highly idiosyncratic — and evocative — way.

Today we have naming of parts. Yesterday,
We had daily cleaning. And tomorrow morning,
We shall have what to do after firing. But today,
Today we have naming of parts. Japonica
Glistens like coral in all the neighboring gardens,
And today we have naming of parts.

This is the lower sling swivel. And this
Is the upper sling swivel, whose use you will see,
When you are given your slings. And this is the piling swivel,

Which in your case you have not got. The branches
Hold in the gardens their silent, eloquent gestures,
Which in our case we have not got.

This is the safety-catch, which is always released
With an easy flick of the thumb. And please do not let me
See anyone using his finger. You can do it quite easy
If you have any strength in your thumb. The blossoms
Are fragile and motionless, never letting anyone see
Any of them using their finger.

And this you can see is the bolt. The purpose of this
Is to open the breech, as you see. We can slide it
Rapidly backwards and forwards: we call this
Easing the spring. And rapidly backwards and forwards
The early bees are assaulting and fumbling the flowers:
They call it easing the Spring.

They call it easing the Spring: it is perfectly easy
If you have any strength in your thumb: like the bolt,
And the breech, the cocking-piece, and the point of balance,
Which in our case we have not got; and the almond blossom
Silent in all of the gardens and the bees going backwards and forwards,
For today we have the naming of parts.

• • •

Reading Literature

1. This poem, published in 1942, is the first of a series of three poems, together called "Lessons of the War." What practical lesson does "Naming of Parts" teach? To what wider lesson might the poem also be referring?
2. The other two poems in this group are called "Judging Distances" and "Movement of Bodies." Based on these titles, can you suggest what principle of classification seems to have been used to divide the war's lessons into categories?
3. Why do you suppose the speaker keeps referring to the japonica blossoms? What is the connection, if any, between the actions described in the poem and the blooming flowers?

Journal Entry

Why does the speaker focus on naming each part of his weapon? What emotions does he convey to readers?

Thematic Connections

- "Shooting an Elephant" (page 131)
- "Ground Zero" (page 173)
- "A Peaceful Woman Explains Why She Carries a Gun" (page 350)
- Casebook: "Do Guns Have a Place on College Campuses?" (page 632)

Writing Assignments for Classification and Division

1. Choose a film you have seen recently, and list all the elements you consider significant: plot, direction, acting, special effects, and so on. Then, further subdivide each category (for instance, listing each of the major special effects). Using this list as an outline, write a review of the film.
2. Write an essay classifying the teachers or bosses you have had into several distinct categories, and form a judgment about the relative effectiveness of the individuals in each group. Give each category a name, and be sure your essay has a thesis statement.
3. What fashion styles do you observe on your college campus? Establish four or five distinct categories, and write an essay classifying students on the basis of how they dress. Give each group of students a descriptive title.
4. **Working with Sources.** Look through this book's thematic table of contents (page xxxiii), and choose three essays on the same general subject. Then, write a classification-and-division essay discussing the different ways writers can explore the same theme. Be sure your topic sentences clearly define your three categories. Include parenthetical documentation for all references to the essays you choose and a works-cited page. (See Chapter 18 for information on MLA documentation.)
5. Many consider violence in sports to be a serious problem. Write an essay expressing your views on this problem. Using a classification-and-division structure, categorize information according to sources of violence (such as the players, the nature of the game, and the fans).
6. **Working with Sources.** Review "Naming of Parts," and find the other two "Lessons of the War" poems online. Then, write a classification-and-division essay in which you discuss your reactions to these three poems and your view of what they say about war. In your essay, identify the three different kinds of lessons Reed explores. Are the three lessons equally important? Taken together, what larger lesson do the three poems communicate? Be sure to document all references to the three poems and to include a works-cited list. (See Chapter 18 for information on MLA documentation.)
7. Write a lighthearted classification-and-division essay discussing kinds of snack foods, cartoons, pets, status symbols, shoppers, vacations, weight-loss diets, hairstyles, or drivers.
8. Write a classification-and-division essay assessing the relative merits of several different politicians, websites, blogs, or academic majors.
9. What kinds of survival skills does a student need to get through college successfully? Write a classification-and-division essay identifying and discussing several kinds of skills and indicating why each category is important. If you like, you may write your essay in the form of an email to a beginning college student.
10. Divide your Facebook friends into categories according to some logical principle. Then, write a classification-and-division essay that includes a thesis statement indicating how different the various groups are.

Collaborative Activity for Classification and Division

Working in a group of four students, devise a classification system encompassing all the different kinds of popular music the members of your group favor. You may begin with general categories, such as country, pop, and rhythm and blues, but you should also include more specific categories, such as rap and heavy metal, in your classification system. After you decide on categories and subcategories that represent the tastes of all group members, fill in examples for each category. Then, devise several different options for arranging your categories into an essay.

13

Definition

What Is Definition?

A **definition** tells what a term means and how it differs from other terms in its class. In the following paragraph from "Altruistic Behavior," anthropologist Desmond Morris defines *altruism,* the key term of his essay.

Topic sentence	Altruism is the performance of an unselfish act.
Extended definition defines term by *enumeration* and *negation*	As a pattern of behavior, this act must have two properties: it must benefit someone else, and it must do so to the disadvantage of the benefactor. It is not merely a matter of being helpful; it is helpfulness at a cost to yourself.

Most people think of definition in terms of print or online dictionaries, which give brief, succinct explanations – called **formal definitions** – of what words mean, but a definition can also explain what something, or even someone, *is* – that is, its essential nature. Sometimes a definition requires a paragraph, an essay, or even a whole book. These longer, more complex definitions are called **extended definitions**.

Understanding Formal Definitions

Many definitions have a standard three-part structure. First, they present the *term* to be defined, then the general *class* it is a part of, and finally the *qualities that differentiate it* from the other terms in the same class.

TERM	CLASS	DIFFERENTIATION
behaviorism	a theory	that regards the objective facts of a subject's actions as the only valid basis for psychological study
cell	a unit of protoplasm	with a nucleus, cytoplasm, and an enclosing membrane

naturalism	a literary movement	whose original adherents believed writers should treat life with scientific objectivity
mitosis	a process	of nuclear division of cells, consisting of prophase, metaphase, anaphase, and telophase
authority	a power	to command and require obedience

For example, be sure to provide a true definition (like those illustrated above), not just a descriptive statement such as "Happiness is a four-day weekend." Also, remember that repetition is not definition, so don't include the term you are defining in your definition. For instance, the statement "Abstract art is a school of artists whose works are abstract" clarifies nothing for your readers. Finally, define as precisely as possible. Name the class of the term you are defining – "mitosis is *a process* of cell division" – and define this class as narrowly and as accurately as you can, clearly differentiating your term from other members of its class. Careful attention to the language and structure of your formal definition will help readers understand your meaning.

Understanding Extended Definitions

Many extended-definition essays include short formal definitions like those found in dictionaries. In such an essay, a brief formal definition can introduce readers to the extended definition, or it can help to support the essay's thesis. However, providing a formal definition of each term you use is seldom necessary or desirable. Readers will either already know what a word means or be able to look it up. Still, it is often helpful to provide a brief definition of any term that is key to your readers' understanding of your essay, especially if a key term has more than one meaning, if you are using it in an unusual way, or if you are fairly certain that the term will be unfamiliar to your readers.

An extended definition does not follow a set **pattern of development**. Instead, it uses whatever strategies best suit the writer's purpose, the term being defined, and the writing situation. In fact, any one (or more than one) of the essay patterns illustrated in this book can be used to structure a definition essay.

Using Definition

Many situations call for extended definitions. On an exam, for example, you might be asked to define *behaviorism*, tell what a *cell* is, explain the meaning of the literary term *naturalism*, include a comprehensive definition of *mitosis* in your answer, or define *authority*. Such exam questions cannot always be answered in a sentence or two. In fact, the definitions they call for often require a full paragraph or even several paragraphs.

Extended definitions are useful in many academic assignments besides exams. For example, definitions can explain abstractions such as *freedom,* controversial terms such as *right to life,* or **slang** terms (informal expressions whose meanings may vary from locale to locale or change as time passes).

Planning a Definition Essay

Developing a Thesis Statement

The thesis of a definition essay should do more than simply identify the term to be defined and more than just define it. The thesis statement needs to make clear to readers the larger purpose for which you are defining the term. For example, assume you set out to write an extended definition of *behaviorism.* If your goal is to show its usefulness for treating patients with certain psychological disorders, a statement like "This essay will define behaviorism" will not be very helpful. Even a formal definition – "Behaviorism is a theory that regards the objective facts of a subject's actions as the only valid basis for psychological study" – is not enough. Your thesis statement needs to suggest the *value* of this kind of therapy, not just tell what it is – for example, "Contrary to some critics' objections, behaviorism is a valid approach for treating a wide variety of psychological dysfunctions."

Deciding on a Pattern of Development

You can organize a definition essay according to one or more of the patterns of development described in this book. As you plan your essay and jot down your ideas about the term or subject you will define, you will see which of the patterns are most useful. For example, each of the formal definitions illustrated on pages 481–82 could be expanded with a different pattern of development:

- **Exemplification** To explain *behaviorism,* you could give **examples**. Carefully chosen cases could show exactly how behaviorism works and how this theory of psychology applies to different situations. Often, examples are the clearest way to explain something. For instance, defining dreams as "the symbolic representation of mental states" might convey little to readers who do not know much about psychology, but a few examples would help you make your meaning clear. Many students have dreams about taking exams – perhaps dreaming that they are late for the test, that they remember nothing about the course, or that they are writing their answers in disappearing ink. You might explain the nature of dreams by interpreting these particular dreams, which may reflect anxiety about a course or about school in general.

- **Description** You can explain the nature of something by **describing** it. For example, the concept of a *cell* is difficult to grasp from just a formal definition, but your readers would understand the concept more clearly if you were to describe what a cell looks like, possibly providing a diagram. Concentrating on the cell membrane, cytoplasm, and nucleus, you could detail each structure's appearance and function. These descriptions would enable readers to visualize the whole cell and understand its workings. Of course, description involves more than the visual: a definition of a tsunami might describe the sounds and the appearance of this enormous ocean wave, and a definition of Parkinson's disease might include a description of its symptoms.

- **Comparison and contrast** An extended definition of *naturalism* could use a **comparison-and-contrast** structure. Naturalism is one of several major movements in American literature, so its literary aims could be contrasted with those of other literary movements, such as romanticism or realism. Or, you might compare and contrast the plots and characters of several naturalistic works with those of romantic or realistic works. Anytime you need to define something unfamiliar, you can use an **analogy** to compare it to something that is likely to be familiar to your readers. For example, your readers may never have heard of the Chinese dish sweet-and-sour cabbage, but you can help them imagine it by saying it tastes something like coleslaw. You can also define a thing by contrasting it with something unlike it, especially if the two have some qualities in common. For instance, one way to explain the British sport of rugby might be to contrast it with American football, which is not as violent.

- **Process** Because mitosis is a process, an extended definition of *mitosis* can be organized as a **process explanation**. By tracing the process from stage to stage, you would clearly define this type of cell division for your readers. Process is also a suitable pattern for defining objects in terms of what they do. For example, because a computer carries out various processes, an extended definition of a computer would probably include a process explanation.

- **Classification and division** You could define *authority* by using **classification and division**. Basing your extended definition on the model developed by the German sociologist Max Weber, you could divide the class *authority* into the subclasses *traditional authority, charismatic authority,* and *legal-bureaucratic authority.* By explaining each type of authority, you could clarify this very broad term for your readers. In both extended and formal definitions, classification and division can be very useful. By identifying the class something belongs to, you are explaining what kind of thing it is. For instance, *monetarism* is an economic theory, *The Adventures of Huckleberry Finn* is a novel, and *emphysema* is a disease. Likewise, by dividing a class into subclasses, you are defining something more specifically. Emphysema, for instance, is a disease of the lungs and can therefore be classified with tuberculosis but not with appendicitis.

Structuring a Definition Essay

Like other essays, a definition essay should have an introduction, a body, and a conclusion. Although a formal definition strives for objectivity, an extended definition usually does not. Instead, it is likely to define a term in a way that reflects your attitude toward the subject or your reason for defining it. For example, your extended-definition essay about literary naturalism might argue that the significance of this movement's major works has been underestimated by literary scholars, or your definition of *authority* might criticize its abuses. In such cases, the **thesis statement** provides a focus for your definition essay, showing readers your approach to the definition.

The **introduction** identifies the term to be defined, perhaps presents a brief formal definition, and goes on to state the essay's thesis. The body of the essay expands the definition, using any one (or several) of the patterns of development explained and illustrated in this text.

In addition to using various patterns of development, you can expand the **body** of your definition by using any of the following strategies:

- You can define a term by using **synonyms** (words with similar meanings).
- You can define a term by using **negation** (telling what it is *not*).
- You can define a term by using **enumeration** (listing its characteristics).
- You can define a term by discussing its **origin and development** (the word's derivation, original meaning, and usages).

NOTE: If you are describing something that is unfamiliar to your readers, you can also include a **visual** – a drawing, painting, diagram, or photograph – to help them understand your definition.

Your essay's **conclusion** reminds readers why you have chosen to define the term, perhaps restating your thesis in different words.

Suppose your assignment is to write a short essay for your introductory psychology course. You decide to examine *behaviorism.* Of course, you can define the word in one or two sentences. To explain the *concept* of behaviorism and its status in the field of psychology, however, you must go beyond the dictionary.

Now, you have to decide what kinds of explanations are most suitable for your topic and for your intended audience. If you are trying to define *behaviorism* for readers who know very little about psychology, you might use analogies that relate behaviorism to your readers' experiences, such as how they were raised or how they train their pets. You might also use examples, but the examples would relate not to psychological experiments or clinical treatment but to experiences in everyday life. If, however, you are directing your essay to your psychology instructor, who obviously already knows what behaviorism is, your purpose is to show that you know, too. One way to do this is to compare behaviorism with other psychological theories, another way is to give examples of how behaviorism works in practice, and another way is to briefly summarize the background and history of the theory. (In a long essay, you might use all these strategies.)

After considering your essay's scope and audience, you might decide that because behaviorism is somewhat controversial, your best strategy is to supplement a formal definition with examples showing how behaviorist assumptions and methods are applied in specific situations. These examples, drawn from your class notes and textbook, would support your thesis that behaviorism is a valid approach for treating certain psychological dysfunctions. Together, your examples would define *behaviorism* as it is understood today.

An informal outline for your essay might look like the following.

SAMPLE OUTLINE: Definition

INTRODUCTION
(thesis statement)
Contrary to its critics' objections, behaviorism is a valid approach for treating a wide variety of psychological dysfunctions.

POINT 1
(background)
Definition of behaviorism, including its origins and evolution

POINT 2
(first example)
The use of behaviorism to help psychotic patients function in an institutional setting

POINT 3
(second example)
The use of behaviorism to treat neurotic behavior, such as chronic anxiety, a phobia, or a pattern of destructive acts

POINT 4
(third example)
The use of behaviorism to treat normal but antisocial or undesirable behavior, such as heavy smoking or overeating

CONCLUSION
Restatement of thesis (in different words) or review of key points

Notice how the three examples in this essay define behaviorism with the kind of complexity, detail, and breadth that a formal definition could not duplicate. This definition is more like a textbook explanation – and, in fact, textbook explanations are often written as extended definitions.

Revising a Definition Essay

When you revise a definition essay, consider the items on the revision checklist on page 66. In addition, pay special attention to the items on the following checklist, which apply specifically to revising definition essays.

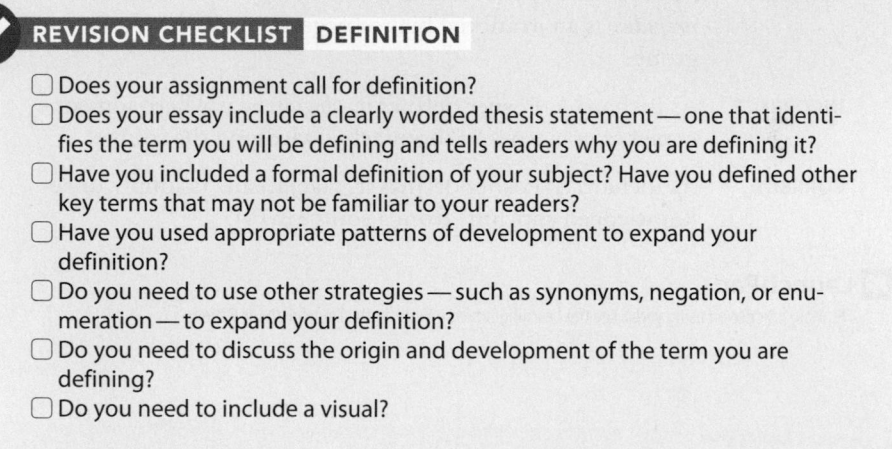

REVISION CHECKLIST DEFINITION

- ☐ Does your assignment call for definition?
- ☐ Does your essay include a clearly worded thesis statement — one that identifies the term you will be defining and tells readers why you are defining it?
- ☐ Have you included a formal definition of your subject? Have you defined other key terms that may not be familiar to your readers?
- ☐ Have you used appropriate patterns of development to expand your definition?
- ☐ Do you need to use other strategies — such as synonyms, negation, or enumeration — to expand your definition?
- ☐ Do you need to discuss the origin and development of the term you are defining?
- ☐ Do you need to include a visual?

Editing a Definition Essay

When you edit your definition essay, follow the guidelines on the editing checklists on pages 83, 86, and 89. In addition, focus on the grammar, mechanics, and punctuation issues that are particularly relevant to definition essays. One of these issues – avoiding the phrases *is when* and *is where* in formal definitions – is discussed below.

GRAMMAR IN CONTEXT AVOIDING *IS WHEN* AND *IS WHERE*

Many extended definitions include a one-sentence formal definition. As you have learned, such definitions must include the term you are defining, the class to which the term belongs, and the characteristics that distinguish the term from other terms in the same class.

Sometimes, however, when you are defining a term or concept, you may find yourself departing from this structure and using the phrase *is when* or *is where*. If so, your definition is not complete because it omits the term's class. (In fact, the use of *is when* or *is where* indicates that you are actually presenting an example of the term and not a definition.)

You can avoid this error by making certain that the form of the verb *be* in your definition is always followed by a noun.

INCORRECT: As described by Ajoy Mahtab in his essay "The Untouchable," *prejudice* is when someone forms an irrational bias or negative opinion of a person or group.

CORRECT: As described by Ajoy Mahtab in his essay "The Untouchable," *prejudice* is an irrational bias or negative opinion of a person or group.

INCORRECT: As Richard A. Posner defines it, *plagiarism* is where someone copies from a work without acknowledging the source.

CORRECT: As Richard A. Posner defines it, plagiarism "is simply unacknowledged copying" from a source (510).

LaunchPad

For more practice on using verbs, see the LearningCurve on Verbs in the LaunchPad for *Patterns*.

EDITING CHECKLIST DEFINITION

- ☐ Have you avoided using *is when* and *is where* in your formal definitions?
- ☐ Have you used the present tense for your formal definition — even if you have used the past tense elsewhere in your essay?
- ☐ In your formal definition, have you italicized the term you are defining and placed the definition itself in quotation marks?

A STUDENT WRITER: Definition

The following student essay, written by Ajoy Mahtab for a composition course, defines the untouchables, members of a caste that is shunned in India. In his essay, Ajoy, who grew up in Calcutta, presents a thesis that is sharply critical of the practice of ostracizing untouchables. Note that he includes a photograph to help readers understand the unfamiliar term he is defining.

The Untouchable

Introduction: background

A word that is extremely common in India yet uncommon to the point of incomprehension in the West is the word *untouchable*. It is a word that has had very sinister connotations throughout India's history. A rigorously worked-out caste system has traditionally existed in Indian society. At the top of the social ladder sat the Brahmins, the clan of the priesthood. These people had renounced the material world for a spiritual one. Below them came the Kshatriyas, or the warrior caste. This caste included the kings and all their nobles along with their armies. Third on the social ladder were the Vaishyas, who were the merchants of the land. Trade was their only form of livelihood. Last came the Shudras — the menials. Shudras were employed by the prosperous as sweepers and laborers. Originally a person's caste was determined only by his profession. Thus, if the son of a merchant joined the army, he automatically converted from a Vaishya to a Kshatriya. However, the system soon became hereditary and rigid. Whatever one's occupation, one's caste was determined from birth according to the caste of one's father. 1

Formal definition

Historical background

Outside of this structure were a group of people, human beings treated worse than dogs and shunned far more than lepers, people who were not considered even human, people who defiled with their very touch. These were the Achhoots: the untouchables, one of whom is shown in fig. 1. The word *untouchable* is commonly defined as "that which cannot or should not be touched." In India, however, it was taken to a far greater extreme. The untouchables of a village lived in a separate community downwind of the borders of the village. They had a separate water supply, for they would make the village water impure if they were to drink from it. When they walked, they were made to bang two sticks together continuously so that passersby could hear them coming and thus avoid an untouchable's shadow. Tied to their waists, trailing behind them, was a broom that would clean the ground they had walked on. The penalty for not following these or any other rules was death for the untouchable and, in many instances, for the entire untouchable community. 2

Present situation

One of the pioneers of the fight against untouchability was Mahatma Gandhi. Thanks to his efforts and those of many others, untouchability no longer presents anything like the horrific picture described above. In India today, in fact, recognition of untouchability is punishable by law. Theoretically, there is no such thing as untouchability anymore. But old traditions linger on, and a 3

Fig. 1. Sean Sprague. *Untouchable Woman Sweeping in Front of Her House in a Village in Tamil Nadu, India.* 2003. The Image Works, theimageworks.com/fotoweb/grid.fwx?SF_FIELD1=untouchable+woman+sweeping&SF_FIELD1_MATCHTYPE=all#Preview1.

deep-rooted fear passed down from generation to generation does not disappear overnight. Even today, caste is an important factor in most marriages. Most Indian surnames reveal a person's caste immediately, so it is a difficult thing to hide. The shunning of the untouchable is more prevalent in South India, where people are much more devout, than in the North. Some people would rather starve than share food and water with an untouchable. This concept is very difficult to accept in the West, but it is true all the same.

Example

I remember an incident from my childhood. I could not have been more than eight or nine at the time. I was on a holiday staying at my family's house on the river Ganges. A festival was going on, and, as is customary, we were giving the servants small presents. I was handing them out when an old woman, bent with age, slowly 4 hobbled into the room. She stood in the far corner of the room all alone, and no one so much as looked at her. When the entire line ended, she stepped hesitantly forward and stood in front of me, looking down at the ground. She then held a cloth stretched out in front of her. I was a little confused about how I was supposed to hand her her present, since both her hands were holding the cloth. Then, with the help of prompting from someone behind me, I learned that I was supposed to drop the gift into the cloth without touching the cloth itself. It was only later that I found out that she was an untouchable. This was the first time I had actually come face to face with such prejudice, and it felt like a slap in the face. That incident was burned into my memory, and I do not think I will ever forget it.

Conclusion begins

5 The word *untouchable* is not often used in the West, and when it is, it is generally used as a complimentary term. For example, an avid fan might say of an athlete, "He was absolutely untouchable. Nobody could even begin to compare with him." It seems rather ironic that a word could be so favorable in one culture and so negative in another. Why does a word that gives happiness in one part of the world cause pain in another? Why does the same word have different meanings to different people around the globe? Why do certain words cause rifts and others forge bonds? I do not think anyone can tell me the answers to these questions.

Conclusion continues

Thesis statement

6 No actual parallel can be found today that compares to the horrors of untouchability. For an untouchable, life itself was a crime. The day was spent just trying to stay alive. From the misery of the untouchables, the world should learn a lesson: isolating and punishing any group of people is dehumanizing and immoral.

Points for Special Attention

Thesis Statement. Ajoy Mahtab's assignment was to write an extended definition of a term he assumed would be unfamiliar to his audience. Because he had definite ideas about the unjust treatment of the untouchables, Ajoy wanted his essay to have a strong thesis that communicated his disapproval. Still, because he knew his American classmates would need a good deal of background information before they would understand the context for such a thesis, he decided not to present it in his introduction. Instead, he decided to lead up to his thesis gradually and state it at the end of his essay. When other students in the class reviewed his draft, this subtlety was one of the points they reacted to most favorably.

Structure. Ajoy's introduction establishes the direction of his essay by introducing the word he will define; he then places this word in context by explaining India's rigid caste system. In paragraph 2, he gives the formal definition of the word *untouchable* and goes on to sketch the term's historical background. Paragraph 3 explains the status of the untouchables in present-day India, and paragraph 4 gives a vivid example of Ajoy's first encounter with an untouchable. As he begins his conclusion in paragraph 5, Ajoy brings his readers back to the word his essay defines. Here he uses two strategies to add interest: he contrasts a contemporary American usage of *untouchable* with its pejorative meaning in India, and he asks a series of **rhetorical questions** (questions asked for effect and not meant to be answered). In paragraph 6, Ajoy presents a summary of his position to lead into his thesis statement.

Patterns of Development. This essay uses a number of strategies commonly incorporated into extended definitions: it includes a formal definition, explains the term's origin, and explores some of the term's connotations. The essay also uses several familiar patterns of development. For instance, paragraph 1 uses classification and division to explain India's caste system; paragraphs 2 and 3 use brief examples to illustrate the plight of the untouchable; and paragraph 4 presents a narrative. Each of these patterns enriches the definition.

Working with Sources. Ajoy includes a visual – a photograph of an untouchable – to supplement his passages of description and to help his readers understand this very unfamiliar concept. He places the photograph early in his essay, where it will be most helpful, and he refers to it in paragraph 2 with the phrase "one of whom is shown in fig. 1." In addition, he includes a caption below the photo with full source information.

Focus on Revision

Because the term Ajoy defined was so unfamiliar to his classmates, many of the peer-editing worksheets students filled in asked for more information. One suggestion in particular – that he draw an analogy between the unfamiliar term *untouchable* and a concept more familiar to American students – appealed to Ajoy as he planned his revision. Another student suggested that Ajoy could compare untouchables to other groups who have been shunned, such as people with AIDS. Although Ajoy states in his conclusion that no parallel exists, an attempt to find common ground between untouchables and other groups could make his essay more meaningful to his readers and bring home to them a distinctly unfamiliar idea.

PEER-EDITING WORKSHEET DEFINITION

1. What term is the writer defining? Does the essay include a formal definition? If so, where? If no formal definition is included, should one be added?
2. For what purpose is the writer defining the term? Does the essay include a thesis statement that makes this purpose clear? If not, suggest revisions.
3. What patterns does the writer use to develop the definition? What other patterns could be used? Would a visual be helpful?
4. Does the writer use analogies to develop the definition? If so, where? Do you find these analogies helpful? What additional analogies might help readers understand the term more fully?
5. Does the essay define the term in language and content appropriate for its audience? Does the definition help readers understand the meaning of the term?
6. Does the writer use synonyms to develop the definition? If so, where? If not, where could synonyms be used to help communicate the term's meaning?
7. Does the writer use negation to develop the definition? If so, where? If not, could the writer strengthen the definition by explaining what the term is not?
8. Does the writer use enumeration to develop the definition? If so, where? If not, where in the essay might the writer list the term's special characteristics?
9. Does the writer explain the term's origin and development? If so, where? If not, do you believe this information should be added?
10. Reread the essay's introduction. If the writer uses a formal definition as an opening strategy, try to suggest an alternative opening.

The selections that follow use exemplification, description, narration, and other methods of developing extended definitions. The first selection, a visual text, is followed by questions designed to illustrate how definition can operate in visual form.

U.S. CENSUS BUREAU

U.S. Census 2010 Form (Questionnaire)

→ **NOTE: Please answer BOTH Question 8 about Hispanic origin and Question 9 about race. For this census, Hispanic origins are not races.**

8. Is Person 1 of Hispanic, Latino, or Spanish origin?

- ☐ **No,** not of Hispanic, Latino, or Spanish origin
- ☐ Yes, Mexican, Mexican Am., Chicano
- ☐ Yes, Puerto Rican
- ☐ Yes, Cuban
- ☐ Yes, another Hispanic, Latino, or Spanish origin — *Print origin, for example, Argentinean, Colombian, Dominican, Nicaraguan, Salvadoran, Spaniard, and so on.*

9. What is Person 1's race? *Mark* ☒ *one or more boxes.*

- ☐ White
- ☐ Black, African Am., or Negro
- ☐ American Indian or Alaska Native — *Print name of enrolled or principal tribe.*
- ☐ Asian Indian
- ☐ Chinese
- ☐ Filipino
- ☐ Other Asian — *Print race, for example, Hmong, Laotian, Thai, Pakistani, Cambodian, and so on.*
- ☐ Japanese
- ☐ Korean
- ☐ Vietnamese
- ☐ Native Hawaiian
- ☐ Guamanian or Chamorro
- ☐ Samoan
- ☐ Other Pacific Islander — *Print race, for example, Fijian, Tongan, and so on.*
- ☐ Some other race — *Print race.*

U.S. Census Bureau

• • •

Reading Images

1. In a single complete sentence, define yourself in terms of your race, religion, or ethnicity (whatever is most important to you).
2. Look at the questions on the census form. Which boxes would you mark? Do you see this choice as an accurate expression of what you consider yourself to be? Explain.
3. Only recently has the Census Bureau permitted respondents to mark "one or more boxes" to indicate their ethnic identity. Do you think this option is a good idea?

Journal Entry

The U.S. Constitution requires that a census be taken every ten years. What do you think these questions might look like on the 2020 census form? What do you think they *should* look like? Why?

Thematic Connections

- "'What's in a Name?'" (page 2)
- "Indian Education" (page 140)
- "The Myth of the Latin Woman: I Just Met a Girl Named Maria" (page 225)
- "Mother Tongue" (page 458)

JUDY BRADY

I Want a Wife

Judy Brady has published articles on many social issues. Diagnosed with breast cancer in 1980, she became active in the politics of cancer and has edited *Women and Cancer* (1990) and *One in Three: Women with Cancer Confront an Epidemic* (1991). She also helped found the Toxic Links Coalition, an organization devoted to lobbying for cancer and environmental issues.

Background on the status of women Brady has been active in the women's movement since 1969, and "I Want a Wife" first appeared in the premiere issue of the feminist *Ms.* magazine in 1972. That year represented perhaps the height of the feminist movement in the United States. The National Organization for Women, established in 1966, had hundreds of chapters around the country. The Equal Rights Amendment, barring discrimination against women, passed in Congress (although it was ratified by only thirty-five of the necessary thirty-eight states), and Congress also passed Title IX of the Education Amendments of 1972, which required equal opportunity (in sports as well as academics) for all students in any school that receives federal funding. At that time, women accounted for just under 40 percent of the labor force (up from 23 percent in 1950), a number that has grown to almost 50 percent today, in part because of the severe recession that started in 2008, which has caused more job losses for men than for women. Of mothers with children under age eighteen, fewer than 40 percent were employed in 1970; today, three-quarters work, 38 percent of them full time and year-round. As for stay-at-home fathers, their numbers have increased from virtually zero to nearly two million.

I belong to that classification of people known as wives. I am A Wife. And, 1
not altogether incidentally, I am a mother.

Not too long ago a male friend of mine appeared on the scene fresh from 2
a recent divorce. He had one child, who is, of course, with his ex-wife. He is looking for another wife. As I thought about him while I was ironing one evening, it suddenly occurred to me that I, too, would like to have a wife. Why do I want a wife?

I would like to go back to school so that I can become economically inde- 3
pendent, support myself, and, if need be, support those dependent upon me. I want a wife who will work and send me to school. And while I am going to school I want a wife to take care of my children. I want a wife to keep track of the children's doctor and dentist appointments. And to keep track of mine, too. I want a wife to make sure my children eat properly and are kept clean. I want a wife who will wash the children's clothes and keep them mended. I want a wife who is a good nurturant attendant to my children, who arranges for their schooling, makes sure that they have an adequate social life with their peers, takes them to the park, the zoo, etc. I want a wife who takes care

of the children when they are sick, a wife who arranges to be around when the children need special care, because, of course, I cannot miss classes at school. My wife must arrange to lose time at work and not lose the job. It may mean a small cut in my wife's income from time to time, but I guess I can tolerate that. Needless to say, my wife will arrange and pay for the care of the children while my wife is working.

I want a wife who will take care of *my* physical needs. I want a wife who 4
will keep my house clean. A wife who will pick up after my children, a wife who will pick up after me. I want a wife who will keep my clothes clean, ironed, mended, replaced when need be, and who will see to it that my personal things are kept in their proper place so that I can find what I need the minute I need it. I want a wife who cooks the meals, a wife who is a *good* cook. I want a wife who will plan the menus, do the necessary grocery shopping, prepare the meals, serve them pleasantly, and then do the cleaning up while I do my studying. I want a wife who will care for me when I am sick and sympathize with my pain and loss of time from school. I want a wife to go along when our family takes a vacation so that someone can continue to care for me and my children when I need a rest and change of scene.

I want a wife who will not bother me with rambling complaints about 5
a wife's duties. But I want a wife who will listen to me when I feel the need to explain a rather difficult point I have come across in my course of studies. And I want a wife who will type my papers for me when I have written them.

I want a wife who will take care of the details of my social life. When my 6
wife and I are invited out by my friends, I want a wife who will take care of the babysitting arrangements. When I meet people at school that I like and want to entertain, I want a wife who will have the house clean, will prepare a special meal, serve it to me and my friends, and not interrupt when I talk about things that interest me and my friends. I want a wife who will have arranged that the children are fed and ready for bed before my guests arrive so that the children do not bother us. I want a wife who takes care of the needs of my guests so that they feel comfortable, who makes sure that they have an ashtray, that they are passed the hors d'oeuvres, that they are offered a second helping of the food, that their wine glasses are replenished when necessary, that their coffee is served to them as they like it. And I want a wife who knows that sometimes I need a night out by myself.

I want a wife who is sensitive to my 7
sexual needs, a wife who makes love passionately and eagerly when I feel like it, a wife who makes sure that I am satisfied. And, of course, I want a wife who will not demand sexual attention when I am not in the mood for it. I want a wife who assumes the complete responsibility for birth control, because I do not want more children. I want a wife who will remain sexually faithful to me so that I do not have to clutter up my intellectual life with jealousies. And I want a wife who understands that *my* sexual needs may entail more than strict adherence to monogamy. I must, after all, be able to relate to people as fully as possible.

> "My God, who *wouldn't* want a wife?"

If, by chance, I find another person more suitable as a wife than the wife I already have, I want the liberty to replace my present wife with another one. Naturally, I will expect a fresh new life; my wife will take the children and be solely responsible for them so that I am left free. 8

When I am through with school and have a job, I want my wife to quit working and remain at home so that my wife can more fully and completely take care of a wife's duties. 9

My God, who *wouldn't* want a wife? 10

• • •

Comprehension

1. In one sentence, define what Brady means by *wife*. Does this ideal wife actually exist? Explain.
2. List some of the specific duties of the wife Brady describes. Into what five general categories does Brady arrange these duties?
3. What complaints does Brady apparently have about the life she actually leads? To what does she seem to attribute her problems?
4. Under what circumstances does Brady say she would consider leaving her wife? What would happen to the children if she left?

Purpose and Audience

1. This essay was first published in *Ms.* magazine. In what sense is it appropriate for the audience of this feminist publication? Where might it appear if it were written today?
2. Does this essay have an explicitly stated thesis? If so, where is it? If the thesis is implied, paraphrase it.
3. Do you think Brady *really* wants the kind of wife she describes? Explain your response.

Style and Structure

1. Throughout the essay, Brady repeats the words "I want a wife." What is the effect of this repetition?
2. The first and last paragraphs of this essay are quite brief. Are these paragraphs effective, or should one or both be developed further?
3. In enumerating a wife's duties, Brady frequently uses the verb *arrange*. What other verbs does she use repeatedly? How do these verbs help her make her point?
4. Brady never uses the personal pronouns *he* or *she* to refer to the wife she defines. Why not?

5. **Vocabulary Project.** Going beyond the dictionary definitions, decide what Brady means to suggest by each of the following words. Is she using any of these terms sarcastically? Explain.

proper (4)	necessary (6)	suitable (8)
pleasantly (4)	demand (7)	free (8)
bother (6)	clutter up (7)	

Journal Entry

How accurate is Brady's 1972 characterization of a wife today? Which of the characteristics she describes have remained the same? Which have changed? Why?

Writing Workshop

1. Write an essay defining your ideal boss, parent, teacher, or pet.
2. Write an essay titled "I Want a Husband." Taking an **ironic** stance, use society's notions of the ideal husband to help you shape your definition.
3. **Working with Sources.** Find information online about the 1972 premiere issue of *Ms.* magazine. What articles and features appeared there? How did contemporary critics react to the magazine's content and philosophy at the time? Referring to the information you find, write an essay in which you define *Ms.* as a feminist magazine. Be sure to provide a clear definition of *feminist magazine* early in your essay. Be sure to cite your sources and to include a works-cited page. (See Chapter 18 for information on MLA documentation.)

Combining the Patterns

Like most definition essays, "I Want a Wife" uses several patterns of development. Which ones does it use? Which of these do you consider most important for supporting Brady's thesis? Why?

Thematic Connections

- "My Mother Never Worked" (page 121)
- "How to Build a Monster from Spare Parts" (page 287)
- "Sex, Lies, and Conversation" (page 415)
- "The Three Types of Happiness" (page 448)

JOSÉ ANTONIO BURCIAGA

Tortillas

José Antonio Burciaga (1940–1996) was the founder of *Diseños Literarios,* a publishing company in California, as well as one of the founders of the comedy troupe Culture Clash. He contributed fiction, poetry, and articles to many anthologies, as well as to journals and newspapers. He also published several books of poems, drawings, and essays, including the poetry collection *Undocumented Love* (1992) and the essay collection *Drink Cultura* (1993). "Tortillas," originally titled "I Remember Masa," was first published in *Weedee Peepo* (1988), a collection of essays in Spanish and English.

Background on tortillas Tortillas have been a staple of Mexican cooking for thousands of years. These thin, round griddlecakes made of cornmeal (*masa*) are often eaten with every meal, and the art of making them is still passed from generation to generation (although they now are widely available commercially as well). The earliest Mexican immigrants introduced them to the United States, and today, tortillas, along with many other popular items of Mexican cuisine, are part of the country's culinary landscape (as are a wide variety of other "ethnic" foods, such as pizza, egg rolls, bagels, sushi, and gyros). Still, tortillas have special meaning for Mexican Americans, and in this essay Burciaga discusses the role of the tortilla within his family's culture.

My earliest memory of *tortillas* is my *Mamá* telling me not to play with them. I had bitten eyeholes in one and was wearing it as a mask at the dinner table. 1

As a child, I also used *tortillas* as hand warmers on cold days, and my family claims that I owe my career as an artist to my early experiments with *tortillas.* According to them, my clowning around helped me develop a strong artistic foundation. I'm not so sure, though. Sometimes I wore a *tortilla* on my head, like a *yarmulke,* and yet I never had any great urge to convert from Catholicism to Judaism. But who knows? They may be right. 2

For Mexicans over the centuries, the *tortilla* has served as the spoon and the fork, the plate and the napkin. *Tortillas* originated before the Mayan civilizations, perhaps predating Europe's wheat bread. According to Mayan mythology, the great god Quetzalcoatl, realizing that the red ants knew the secret of using maize as food, transformed himself into a black ant, infiltrated the colony of red ants, and absconded with a grain of corn. (Is it any wonder that to this day, black ants and red ants do not get along?) Quetzalcoatl then put maize on the lips of the first man and woman, Oxomoco and Cipactonal, so that they would become strong. Maize festivals are still celebrated by many Indian cultures of the Americas. 3

When I was growing up in El Paso, *tortillas* were part of my daily life. I used to visit a *tortilla* factory in an ancient adobe building near the open *mercado* 4 in Ciudad Juárez. As I approached, I could hear the rhythmic slapping of the *masa* as the skilled vendors outside the factory formed it into balls and patted them into perfectly round corn cakes between the palms of their hands. The wonderful aroma and the speed with which the women counted so many dozens of *tortillas* out of warm wicker baskets still linger in my mind. Watching them at work convinced me that the most handsome and *deliciosas tortillas* are handmade. Although machines are faster, they can never adequately replace generation-to-generation experience. There's no place in the factory assembly line for the tender slaps that give each *tortilla* character. The best thing that can be said about mass-producing *tortillas* is that it makes it possible for many people to enjoy them.

> "For Mexicans over the centuries, the *tortilla* has served as the spoon and the fork, the plate and the napkin."

5 In the *mercado* where my mother shopped, we frequently bought *taquitos de nopalitos,* small tacos filled with diced cactus, onions, tomatoes, and *jalapeños.* Our friend Don Toribio showed us how to make delicious, crunchy *taquitos* with dried, salted pumpkin seeds. When you had no money for the filling, a poor man's *taco* could be made by placing a warm *tortilla* on the left palm, applying a sprinkle of salt, then rolling the *tortilla* up quickly with the fingertips of the right hand. My own kids put peanut butter and jelly on *tortillas,* which I think is truly bicultural. And speaking of fast foods for kids, nothing beats a *quesadilla,* a *tortilla* grilled-cheese sandwich.

6 Depending on what you intend to use them for, *tortillas* may be made in various ways. Even a run-of-the-mill *tortilla* is more than a flat corn cake. A skillfully cooked homemade *tortilla* has a bottom and a top; the top skin forms a pocket in which you put the filling that folds your *tortilla* into a taco. Paper-thin *tortillas* are used specifically for *flautas,* a type of taco that is filled, rolled, and then fried until crisp. The name *flauta* means *flute,* which probably refers to the Mayan bamboo flute; however, the only sound that comes from an edible *flauta* is a delicious crunch that is music to the palate. In México *flautas* are sometimes made as long as two feet and then cut into manageable segments. The opposite of *flautas* is *gorditas,* meaning *little fat ones.* These are very thick small *tortillas.*

7 The versatility of *tortillas* and corn does not end here. Besides being tasty and nourishing, they have spiritual and artistic qualities as well. The Tarahumara Indians of Chihuahua, for example, concocted a corn-based beer called *tesgüino,* which their descendants still make today. And everyone has read about the woman in New Mexico who was cooking her husband a *tortilla* one morning when the image of Jesus Christ miraculously appeared on it. Before they knew what was happening, the man's breakfast had become a local shrine.

8 Then there is *tortilla* art. Various Chicano artists throughout the Southwest have, when short of materials or just in a whimsical mood, used a dry *tortilla* as a small, round canvas. And a few years back, at the height of the Chicano movement, a priest in Arizona got into trouble with the Church after he

was discovered celebrating mass using a *tortilla* as the host. All of which only goes to show that while the *tortilla* may be a lowly corn cake, when the necessity arises, it can reach unexpected distinction.

• • •

Comprehension

1. What exactly is a tortilla?
2. List the functions – both practical and whimsical – that tortillas serve.
3. In paragraph 7, Burciaga cites the "spiritual and artistic qualities" of tortillas. Do you think he is being serious? Explain your reasoning.

Purpose and Audience

1. Burciaga states his thesis explicitly in his essay's final sentence. Paraphrase this thesis. Why do you think he does not state it sooner? Do you think it was the right decision? Why or why not?
2. Do you think Burciaga expects most of his readers to be of Hispanic descent? To be familiar with tortillas? How can you tell?
3. Why do you think Burciaga uses humor in this essay? Is it consistent with his essay's purpose? Could the humor have a negative effect on his audience? Explain.
4. Why are tortillas so important to Burciaga? Is it just their versatility he admires, or do they represent something more to him?

Style and Structure

1. Where does Burciaga provide a formal definition of *tortilla*? Why does he locate this formal definition where he does?
2. Burciaga uses many Spanish words, but he defines only some of them – for example, *taquitos de nopalitos* and *quesadilla* in paragraph 5 and *flautas* and *gorditas* in paragraph 6. Why do you think he defines some Spanish terms but not others? Should he have defined them all?
3. Does Burciaga use synonyms or negation to define *tortilla*? Does he discuss the word's origin and development? If so, where? If not, do you think any of these strategies would improve his essay? Explain.
4. **Vocabulary Project.** Look up each of the following words in a Spanish-English dictionary, and try to supply its English equivalent.

mercado (4)	deliciosas (4)
masa (4)	jalapeños (5)

Journal Entry

Explore some additional uses – practical or frivolous – for tortillas that Burciaga does not discuss.

Writing Workshop

1. **Working with Sources.** Find information about a food that is important to your family, ethnic group, or circle of friends, and write an essay that defines that food. Begin with your own "earliest memory" of the food, and then provide background information on the food's origin and history. As you develop your definition, use several patterns of development, as Burciaga does. Assume your audience is not familiar with the food you define. Your thesis should indicate why the food is so important to you. Be sure to document references to Burciaga's essay and to include a works-cited page. (See Chapter 18 for information on MLA documentation.)
2. Relying primarily on description and exemplification, define a food that is sure to be familiar to all your readers. Do not name the food until your essay's last sentence.
3. Write an essay defining a food – but include a thesis statement that paints a very favorable portrait of a much-maligned food (for example, Spam or brussels sprouts) or a very negative picture of a popular food (for example, chocolate or ice cream).

Combining the Patterns

Burciaga uses several patterns of development in his extended definition. Where, for example, does he use **description**, **narration**, **process**, and **exemplification**? Does he use any other patterns?

Thematic Connections

- "Goodbye to My Twinkie Days" (page 169)
- "Once More to the Lake" (page 189)
- "The Park" (page 671)

AMY WILENTZ

A Zombie Is a Slave Forever

Amy Wilentz is a writer and journalist who teaches literary journalism at the University of California, Irvine. Born in New Jersey in 1954, she graduated from Harvard University. She has worked at *Newsday*, *Time*, and the *New Yorker*. Currently, she is a contributing editor at the *Nation*. Wilentz is the author of several books, including *I Feel Earthquakes More Often than They Happen: Coming to California in the Age of Schwarzenegger* (2006) and *Farewell, Fred Voodoo: A Letter from Haiti* (2013), and her work has appeared in many publications, including the *New York Times*, the *New Republic*, *Vogue*, and *Harper's*.

Background on zombies "There are many reasons the zombie, sprung from the colonial slave economy, is returning now to haunt us," writes Amy Wilentz. Originating in Haiti and carrying a complex racial and ethnic history, zombies are, arguably, the most resonant monsters of our time. Film director George Romero helped bring them into the foreground of American pop culture with his 1968 horror movie hit, *Night of the Living Dead*, and he then revisited zombies in sequels that explored the monsters' allegorical implications. The slow march of the undead extends into movies such as *World War Z* (2013), television shows such as *The Walking Dead*; books such as *Pride and Prejudice and Zombies* (2009) and *Zone One* (2011), video games such as *All Zombies Must Die*, and countless websites and graphic novels. Even the U.S. government has taken part in the zombie craze: in 2011, the website of the Centers for Disease Control and Prevention published a humorous preparedness guide for responding to a zombie apocalypse. As zombies have proliferated in popular culture, so have theories to explain their current — and enduring — popularity. For example, cultural critic Chuck Klosterman has suggested that zombies resonate today because they are unavoidable and unstoppable, "like the Internet and the media and every conversation we don't want to have." Perhaps, however, the twenty-first-century preoccupation with zombies also speaks to our anxieties about life, disease, and death, as well as to our uneasiness about issues such as the rise of consumerism, the threats to our environment, the loss of community, and the speed of scientific progress.

Zombies will come to my door on Wednesday night – in rags, eye-sockets blackened, pumping devices that make fake blood run down their faces – asking for candies. There seem to be more and more zombies every Halloween, more zombies than princesses, fairies, ninjas, or knights. In all probability, none of them knows what a zombie really is. 1

Most people think of them as the walking dead, a being without a soul or someone with no free will. This is true. But the zombie is not an alien enemy who's been CGI-ed by Hollywood. He is a New World phenomenon that arose from the mixture of old African religious beliefs and the pain of slavery, 2 especially the notoriously merciless and coldblooded slavery of French-run, pre-independence Haiti. In Africa, a dying person's soul might be stolen and stoppered up in a ritual bottle for later use. But the full-blown zombie was a very logical offspring of New World slavery.

For the slave under French rule in Haiti—then Saint-Domingue—in the 3
seventeenth and eighteenth centuries, life was brutal: hunger, extreme overwork, and cruel discipline were the rule. Slaves often could not consume enough calories to allow for normal rates of reproduction; what children they did have might easily starve. That was not of great concern to the plantation masters, who felt that children were a waste of resources, since they weren't able to work properly until they reached 10 or so. More manpower could always be imported from the Middle Passage.

The only escape from the sugar plantations was death, which was seen 4
as a return to Africa, or lan guinée (literally Guinea, or West Africa). This is the phrase in Haitian Creole that even now means heaven. The plantation meant a life in servitude; lan guinée meant freedom. Death was feared but also wished for. Not surprisingly, suicide was a frequent recourse of the slaves, who were handy with poisons and powders. The plantation masters thought of suicide as the worst kind of thievery, since it deprived the master not only of a slave's service, but also of his or her person, which was, after all, the master's property. Suicide was the slave's only way to take control over his or her own body.

And yet, the fear of becoming a zombie 5
might stop them from doing so. The zombie is a dead person who cannot get across to lan guinée. This final rest—in green, leafy, heavenly Africa, with no sugarcane to cut and no master to appease or serve—is unavailable to the zombie. To become a zombie was the slave's worst nightmare: to be dead and still a slave, an eternal field hand. It is thought that slave drivers on the plantations, who were usually slaves themselves and sometimes Voodoo priests, used this fear of zombification to keep recalcitrant slaves in order and to warn those who were despondent not to go too far.

"To become a zombie was the slave's worst nightmare: to be dead and still a slave, an eternal field hand."

In traditional Voodoo belief, in order to get back to lan guinée, one must 6
be transported there by Baron Samedi, the lord of the cemetery and one of the darkest and most complicated of the religion's many complicated gods. Baron is customarily dressed in a business jacket, a top hat, and dark glasses; he's foul-mouthed and comic in a low, vicious way. One of Baron's spiritual functions, his most important, is to dig a person's grave and welcome him to the other side. If for some reason a person has thwarted or offended Baron, the god will not allow that person, upon his death, to reach guinée. Then you're a zombie. Some other lucky mortal can control you, it is believed. You'll do the bidding of your master without question.

Haiti's notorious dictator François Duvalier, known as Papa Doc, who 7
controlled Haiti with a viselike grip from 1957 until his death in 1971, well understood the Baron's role. He dressed like Baron, in a black fedora, business

suit, and heavy glasses or sunglasses. Like Baron at a ceremony, when Duvalier spoke publicly, it was often in a near whisper. His secret police, the Tontons Macoutes, behaved with the complete immorality and obedience of the undead, and were sometimes assumed to be zombies under the dictator's control. I once heard a Haitian radio announcer describe Klaus Barbie, a Nazi known as the Butcher of Lyon, as "youn ansyen Tonton Makout Hitler," or one of Hitler's Tontons Macoutes: a zombie of the Reich.

The only way for a zombie to have his will and soul return is for him to eat salt – a smart boss of a zombie keeps the creature's food tasteless. In the 1980s, with Duvalier's son ousted from power and the moment ripe for reform, the literacy primer put out by the liberation theologians' wing of the Roman Catholic Church in Haiti was called "A Taste of Salt." 8

There are many reasons the zombie, sprung from the colonial slave economy, is returning now to haunt us. Of course, the zombie is scary in a primordial way, but in a modern way, too. He's the living dead, but he's also the inanimate animated, the robot of industrial dystopias. He's great for fascism: one recent zombie movie (and there have been many) was called *The Fourth Reich*. The zombie is devoid of consciousness and therefore unable to critique the system that has entrapped him. He's labor without grievance. He works free and never goes on strike. You don't have to feed him much. He's a Foxconn worker in China; a maquiladora seamstress in Guatemala; a citizen of North Korea; he's the man, surely in the throes of psychosis and under the thrall of extreme poverty, who, years ago, during an interview, told me he believed he had once been a zombie himself. 9

So when kids come to your door this Halloween wearing costumes called Child Zombie Doctor or Shopko's Fun World Zombie, offer them a sprinkling of salt along with their candy corn. 10

• • •

Comprehension

1. What inspired Wilentz to write this essay?
2. What do most people think a zombie is? How are they wrong?
3. In paragraph 4, Wilentz says that for slaves, "Death was feared but also wished for." Why?
4. Why was becoming a zombie "the slave's worst nightmare" (5)?
5. Who is Baron Samedi? Why is he so important?
6. Who was François Duvalier? What is the connection between Duvalier and Baron Samedi?
7. According to Wilentz, why is the figure of the zombie "returning now to haunt us" (9)?
8. In what sense is a zombie "a slave forever"?

Purpose and Audience

1. Why did Wilentz write her essay? Did she write it primarily to warn, educate, debunk, mock, or entertain?
2. Write a one-sentence thesis statement for this essay. Is this thesis stated anywhere in the essay? If so, how is it different from the thesis statement you wrote?
3. Why does Wilentz include so much background about Haiti and its slaves? Do you think she provides *too much* background? If so, why?

Style and Structure

1. This essay's introduction and conclusion are very different in content and tone from the rest of the essay. Is this a problem? Should the introduction and conclusion be revised so they are consistent with the rest of the essay? Why or why not?
2. Where does Wilentz use description to develop her definition? Where does she use cause and effect? What other patterns of development does she use?
3. Where does Wilentz use an **analogy**? Where does she use **enumeration**? What does each of these strategies add to her essay?
4. Where in this essay does Wilentz provide a formal definition of the term *zombie*? Where does she use negation to tell readers what a zombie is *not*?
5. Do you think Wilentz should have quoted historians or scholars? Should she have provided statistics about slavery in Haiti? Explain your reasoning.
6. **Vocabulary Project.** In paragraph 2, Wilentz uses the term *enemy alien*. What connotations does this term have? How is the word *alien* generally used today?
7. Does Wilentz need to define any additional terms? For example, should she have defined *Voodoo* (5)? Why or why not?

Journal Entry

Why do you think the idea of encountering (or becoming) a zombie is so frightening to so many people today?

Writing Workshop

1. Write an essay in which you define another frightening creature, such as a werewolf or a vampire. Use exemplification, cause and effect, and description to develop your definition.
2. **Working with Sources.** In paragraph 3, Wilentz mentions the Middle Passage. Do some research to learn about this term, and then write an essay defining it for an audience of middle-school students. Be sure to

acknowledge your sources and to include a works-cited page. (See Chapter 18 for information on MLA documentation.)

3. **Working with Sources.** Watch the 1943 movie *I Walked with a Zombie* (loosely based on the novel *Jane Eyre*) or another zombie movie. Then, write a review of the film you chose, including an extended definition of *zombie* in your essay. If you quote dialogue from the movie, be sure to document your source and to include a works-cited page.

Combining the Patterns

Reread paragraph 9. What **argument** is Wilentz making here?

Thematic Connections

- "'What's in a Name?'" (page 2)
- "'Girl'" (page 254)
- "How to Build a Monster from Spare Parts" (page 287)
- "The Untouchable" (page 489)

RICHARD POSNER

On Plagiarism

Richard Posner (b. 1939) is a legal scholar, judge, and expert in the field of law and economics. Since graduating from Yale University and Harvard Law School, Posner has had a long and distinguished career: he has taught at Stanford University Law School and the University of Chicago School of Law; he served as chief judge of the United States Court of Appeals for the Seventh Circuit; and he was a founding editor of the *Journal of Legal Studies*. An enormously influential legal theorist, Posner has written dozens of books and scholarly articles as well as pieces for general-interest publications such as the *Atlantic*, the *New Republic*, and the *Wall Street Journal*.

Background on recent plagiarism scandals In this 2002 essay, Posner refers to then-recent scandals in which "two popular historians were discovered to have lifted passages from other historians' books." Most likely, he is alluding to popular historians Stephen Ambrose and Doris Kearns Goodwin: in 2002, both were found to have borrowed passages from other writers. In the years since Posner's article appeared, the issue of plagiarism has persisted, although its consequences have varied. Popular science writer Jonah Lehrer, a rising star and journalism phenom, severely damaged his career when he not only plagiarized other writers, but also plagiarized himself and fabricated quotations in his work. In contrast, columnist, author, and CNN television host Fareed Zakaria weathered accusations — and admissions — of plagiarism with minimal consequences. Of course, plagiarism is not merely a problem for journalists, academics, or students. In 2014, former Montana senator John Walsh had his master's degree from the U.S. Army War College revoked when it was discovered that he had plagiarized in a 2007 research paper. Likewise, senator and former presidential candidate Rand Paul faced accusations of plagiarism in his books and speeches; in 2013, he effectively defended himself in part by dismissing his critics as pedants, saying, "The footnote police have really been dogging me." As Posner notes, plagiarism is ultimately an "ambiguous term," which perhaps explains why responses to it are so inconsistent.

Recently two popular historians were discovered to have lifted passages 1
from other historians' books. They identified the sources in footnotes, but they failed to place quotation marks around the purloined passages. Both historians were quickly buried under an avalanche of criticism. The scandal will soon be forgotten, but it leaves in its wake the questions What is "plagiarism"? and Why is it reprobated? These are important questions. The label "plagiarist" can ruin a writer, destroy a scholarly career, blast a politician's chances for election, and cause the expulsion of a student from a college or university. New computer search programs, though they may in the long run deter plagiarism, will in the short run lead to the discovery of more cases of it.

"The label 'plagiarist' can ruin a writer."

We must distinguish in the first place between a plagiarist and a copyright infringer. They are both copycats, but the latter is trying to appropriate revenues generated by property that belongs to someone else – namely, the holder of the copyright on the work that the infringer has copied. A pirated edition of a current best seller is a good example of copyright infringement. There is no copyright infringement, however, if the "stolen" intellectual property is in the public domain (in which case it is not property at all), or if the purpose is not appropriation of the copyright holder's revenue. The doctrine of "fair use" permits brief passages from a book to be quoted in a book review or a critical essay; and the parodist of a copyrighted work is permitted to copy as much of that work as is necessary to enable readers to recognize the new work as a parody. A writer may, for that matter, quote a passage from another writer just to liven up the narrative; but to do so without quotation marks – to pass off another writer's writing as one's own – is more like fraud than like fair use. 2

"Plagiarism," in the broadest sense of this ambiguous term, is simply unacknowledged copying, whether of copyrighted or uncopyrighted work. (Indeed, it might be of uncopyrightable work – for example, of an idea.) If I reprint *Hamlet* under my own name, I am a plagiarist but not an infringer. Shakespeare himself was a formidable plagiarist in the broad sense in which I'm using the word. The famous description in *Antony and Cleopatra* of Cleopatra on her royal barge is taken almost verbatim from a translation of Plutarch's life of Mark Antony: "on either side of her, pretty, fair boys apparelled as painters do set forth the god Cupid, with little fans in their hands, with which they fanned wind upon her" becomes "on each side her / Stood pretty dimpled boys, like smiling Cupids, / With divers-colour'd fans, whose wind did seem / To glow the delicate cheeks which they did cool." (Notice how Shakespeare improved upon the original.) In *The Waste Land*, T. S. Eliot "stole" the famous opening of Shakespeare's barge passage, "The barge she sat in, like a burnish'd throne, / Burn'd on the water" becoming "The Chair she sat in, like a burnished throne, / Glowed on the marble." 3

Mention of Shakespeare brings to mind that *West Side Story* is just one of the links in a chain of plagiarisms that began with Ovid's Pyramus and Thisbe and continued with the forgotten Arthur Brooke's *The Tragical History of Romeus and Juliet,* which was plundered heavily by Shakespeare. Milton in *Paradise Lost* plagiarized Genesis, as did Thomas Mann in *Joseph and His Brothers*. Examples are not limited to writing. One from painting is Edouard Manet, whose works from the 1860s "quote" extensively from Raphael, Titian, Velásquez, Rembrandt, and others, of course without express acknowledgment. 4

If these are examples of plagiarism, then we want more plagiarism. They show that not all unacknowledged copying is "plagiarism" in the pejorative sense. Although there is no formal acknowledgment of copying in my examples, neither is there any likelihood of deception. And the copier has added value to the original – this is not slavish copying. Plagiarism is also innocent when no value is attached to originality; so judges, who try to conceal originality and pretend that their decisions are foreordained, "steal" freely from one another without attribution or any ill will. 5

But all that can be said in defense of a writer who, merely to spice up his work, incorporates passages from another writer without acknowledgment is that the readability of his work might be impaired if he had to interrupt a 6 fast-paced narrative to confess that "a predecessor of mine, ___, has said what I want to say next better than I can, so rather than paraphrase him, I give you the following passage, indented and in quotation marks, from his book ___." And not even that much can be said in defense of the writer who plagiarizes out of sheer laziness or forgetfulness, the latter being the standard defense when one is confronted with proof of one's plagiarism.

Because a footnote does not signal verbatim incorporation of material from the source footnoted, all that can be said in defense of the historians with whom I began is that they made it easier for their plagiarism to be discovered. This is relevant to how severely they should be criticized, because one of the reasons academic plagiarism is so strongly reprobated is that it is normally very difficult to detect. (In contrast, Eliot and Manet *wanted* their audience to recognize their borrowings.) This is true of the student's plagiarized term paper, and to a lesser extent of the professor's plagiarized scholarly article. These are particularly grave forms of fraud, because they may lead the reader to take steps, such as giving the student a good grade or voting to promote the professor, that he would not take if he knew the truth. But readers of popular histories are not professional historians, and most don't care a straw how original the historian is. The public wants a good read, a good show, and the fact that a book or a play may be the work of many hands – as, in truth, most art and entertainment are – is of no consequence to it. The harm is not to the reader but to those writers whose work does not glitter with stolen gold. 7

• • •

Comprehension

1. What two "important questions" does Posner ask in paragraph 1? Does his essay answer these two questions?
2. In paragraph 1, Posner mentions "new computer search programs" that can detect plagiarism. What prediction does he make about this kind of "new" plagiarism-detection software? Has this prediction turned out to be correct?
3. What possible consequences of plagiarism does Posner identify?
4. According to Posner, what is the difference between a plagiarist and a copyright infringer? How are they alike?
5. Why does Posner see academic plagiarism as a "particularly grave [form] of fraud" (7)? Do you agree with him? Why or why not?

Purpose and Audience

1. This essay was published in 2002. Does it still seem timely, or would its examples have to be updated to make it relevant to today's readers? Explain.
2. Richard Posner is a federal judge. How might this position affect his perspective on the issue of plagiarism? How does it affect his credibility?
3. What central point about plagiarism does Posner make in this essay? Given this central idea, is definition a logical pattern of development? Why or why not?

4. Reread the first paragraph of this essay, and circle any words whose definitions you are not sure of. What does Posner's use of this level of vocabulary tell you about how he sees his audience?

Style and Structure

1. Where does Posner give a formal definition of *plagiarism*? In one sentence, paraphrase this definition.
2. What patterns does Posner use to develop his extended definition of *plagiarism*?
3. **Vocabulary Project.** Posner uses the word *copying* in place of *plagiarism*. What other expressions could be used instead of *copying*?
4. Evaluate the examples Posner gives in paragraphs 3 and 4. What point do these examples support? Is it a problem that these examples are all drawn from literature and art? Why or why not?
5. Analyze the last sentence of this essay. What does Posner mean by "harm . . . to the reader"? What does he mean by "stolen gold"?

Journal Entry

Do you think unintentional plagiarism – for example, a student carelessly pasting the words of a source into an essay – is less serious that intentional plagiarism? Or, do you think both kinds of plagiarism should be dealt with in the same way?

Writing Workshop

1. Read the student essay "The Price of Silence" (p. 76). Then, write a definition essay about an experience of your own that defines what plagiarism is and what it is not.
2. **Working with Sources.** Search online for the texts of the plagiarism policies of four or five schools. Using their policies as source material, write an essay that defines *plagiarism* and outlines a plagiarism policy for your school. Be sure to cite information you borrow from your sources and to include a works-cited page. (See Chapter 18 for information on MLA documentation.)
3. Write an essay in which you define *Internet plagiarism*. How is it different from plagiarizing from print sources? Include a process paragraph explaining how a student might accidentally incorporate borrowed material into an essay, and develop your definition with exemplification and cause and effect.

Combining the Patterns

Do you think Posner should have spent more time in this essay on developing the **cause-and-effect** relationship behind *students* choosing to plagiarize? What additional information could he have provided?

Thematic Connections

- "Cutting and Pasting: A Senior Thesis by (Insert Name)" (page 17)
- "Surrendering" (page 116)

EMILY DICKINSON

"Hope" is the thing with feathers

Emily Dickinson (1830–1886) is one of the most distinctive voices in all American poetry. Dickinson was born in Amherst, Massachusetts, to a well-known and public-spirited family (her father served in Congress as a representative from Massachusetts). Although she was well-read and well-educated for a woman of her time, she spent much of her life as a recluse in Amherst, reading, corresponding, spending time with her family, and writing nearly eighteen hundred poems. She was not recognized for her writing in her lifetime: nearly all Dickinson's poems were discovered — and published — after her death. Along with the unmistakable style of her work, its timeless themes — nature, love, personal identity, mortality — continue to startle and fascinate readers.

Background on the idea of hope Many of our earliest myths and stories explore the idea of hope. In Greek mythology, for example, Pandora opens a forbidden box (or jar), releasing evils into the world; after the lid is closed, only hope is left behind. Among early philosophers, Greek and Roman stoics believed hope was dangerous and misleading. In the Christian tradition, hope is one of the three theological virtues (faith, hope, and charity), bound up with the certainty of salvation: "By whom also we have access by faith into this grace wherein we stand, and rejoice in hope of the glory of God" Romans 5:2. Buddhists believe hope must be liberated from personal desires and discontent with the present, even if it aims toward enlightenment in the next earthly life. Of course, hope is also significant outside religious traditions. Marxist thinkers, for example, have placed hope in the utopian transformation of society. A perennial theme of self-help and motivational experts, hope — as a function of cognition and culture — has also become a focus of study for neurologists, anthropologists, and psychologists. In an influential essay, the psychologist Richard Lazarus wrote, "To hope is to believe that something positive, which does not presently apply to one's life, could still materialize, and so we yearn for it."

"Hope" is the thing with feathers –
That perches in the soul –
And sings the tune without the words –
And never stops – at all –

And sweetest – in the Gale – is heard –
And sore must be the storm –
That could abash the little Bird
That kept so many warm –

I've heard it in the chillest land –
And on the strangest Sea –
Yet – never – in Extremity,
It asked a crumb – of me.

Reading Literature

1. This poem defines *hope* by drawing an **analogy** between hope and a bird. What does the poem suggest these two things have in common?
2. How does hope "perch" in the soul? What other words could you substitute for "perches" (line 2)?
3. What kind of "tune" (3) does hope sing? What kind of "Gale" (5) and "storm" (6) might threaten hope?

Journal Entry

Write a one-paragraph definition of *hope*. Develop your paragraph with examples and analogies.

Thematic Connections

- "My Field of Dreams" (page 104)
- "My Mother Never Worked" (page 121)
- "Why the Post Office Makes America Great" (page 220)
- "How to Tell a Mother Her Child Is Dead" (page 277)
- "The Three Types of Happiness" (page 448)
- The Declaration of Independence (page 550)

Writing Assignments for Definition

1. Choose a document or ritual that is a significant part of your religious or cultural heritage. Define it, using any pattern or combination of patterns you choose, but be sure to include a formal definition somewhere in your essay. Assume your readers are not familiar with the term you are defining.
2. Define an abstract term – for example, *stubbornness, security, courage,* or *fear* – by making it concrete. You can develop your definition with a series of brief examples or with an extended narrative that illustrates the characteristic you are defining.
3. The readings in this chapter define (among other things) a food, a family role, and an item of clothing. Write an essay using examples and description to define one of these topics, such as ramen noodles (food), a stepmother (family role), or a chador (item of clothing).
4. **Working with Sources.** Visit webmd.com (for adult health issues) or kidshealth.org (for children's health issues) to learn about one of these medical conditions: angina, migraine, Down syndrome, attention deficit disorder, schizophrenia, autism, or Alzheimer's disease. Then, write an extended definition essay explaining the condition to an audience of high school students. Be sure to include parenthetical documentation for references to your source and a works-cited page. (See Chapter 18 for information on MLA documentation.)
5. Use a series of examples to support a thesis in an essay that defines *racism, sexism, ageism, homophobia,* or another type of bigotry.
6. Choose a term that is central to one of your courses – for instance, *naturalism, behaviorism,* or *authority* – and write an essay defining the term. Assume your audience is made up of students who have not yet taken the course. You may begin with an overview of the term's origin if you believe this information is appropriate. Then, develop your essay with examples and analogies that will facilitate your audience's understanding of the term. Your purpose is to convince readers that understanding the term you are defining is important.
7. Assume your audience is from a culture unfamiliar with present-day American children's pastimes. Write a definition essay for this audience describing the form and function of a Frisbee, a Barbie doll, an action figure, a skateboard, or a video game.
8. Review any one of the following narrative essays in Chapter 6, and use it to help you develop an extended definition of one of the following terms.

   - "The Money" – revenge
   - "Surrendering" – bullying
   - "My Mother Never Worked" – work
   - "Thirty-Eight Who Saw Murder Didn't Call the Police" – apathy
   - "Shooting an Elephant" – power

   Be sure to document any words or ideas you borrow from a source and to include a works-cited page. (See Chapter 18 for information on MLA documentation.)

9. What constitutes an education? Define the term *education* by identifying several different sources of knowledge, formal or informal, and explaining what each contributes. To get ideas for your essay, look at the excerpt from *Persepolis II* (page 109) or "Indian Education" (page 140).
10. What qualifies someone as a hero? Developing your essay with a series of examples, define the word *hero*. Include a formal definition, and try to incorporate at least one paragraph defining the term by explaining and illustrating what a hero is *not*.

Collaborative Activity for Definition

Working as a group, choose one of the following words to define: *pride, hope, sacrifice,* or *justice*. Then, define the term with a series of extended examples drawn from films your group members have seen, with each of you developing an illustrative paragraph based on a different film. (Before beginning, your group may decide to focus on one particular genre of film.) When everyone in the group has read each paragraph, work together to formulate a thesis that asserts the vital importance of the quality your examples have defined. Finally, write suitable opening and closing paragraphs for the essay, and arrange the body paragraphs in a logical order, adding transitions where necessary.

14

Argumentation

What Is Argumentation?

Argumentation is a logical way of asserting the soundness of a debatable position, belief, or conclusion. Argumentation takes a stand — supported by evidence — and urges people to share the writer's perspective and insights. In the following paragraph from *To Sell Is Human: The Surprising Truth about Moving Others*, Daniel Pink argues that the impact of the smartphone has been much greater than most people realize.

Topic sentence (takes a stand)

Background presents both sides of issue

Evidence (examples)

While the Web has enabled more microentrepreneurs to flourish, its overall impact might seem quaint compared with the smartphone. As Marc Andreessen, the venture capitalist who in the early 1990s created the first Web browser, has said, "The smartphone revolution is *under*hyped." These handheld mini-computers certainly can destroy certain aspects of sales. Consumers can use them to conduct research, comparison-shop, and bypass salespeople altogether. But once again, the net effect is more creative than destructive. The same technology that renders certain types of salespeople obsolete has turned even more people into potential sellers. For instance, the existence of smartphones has birthed an entire app economy that didn't exist before 2007, when Apple shipped its first iPhone. Now the production of apps itself is responsible for nearly half a million jobs in the United States alone, most of them created by bantamweight entrepreneurs. Likewise, an array of new technologies, such as Square from one of the founders of Twitter, PayHere from eBay, and GoPayment from Intuit, make it easier for individuals to accept credit card payments directly on their mobile devices — allowing anyone with a phone to become a shopkeeper.

Argumentation can be used to convince other people to accept (or at least acknowledge the validity of) your position; to defend your position, even if you cannot convince others to agree; or to question or refute a position you believe to be misguided, untrue, dangerous, or evil (without necessarily offering an alternative).

Understanding Argumentation and Persuasion

Although the terms *persuasion* and *argumentation* are frequently used interchangeably, they do not mean the same thing. **Persuasion** is a general term that refers to how a writer influences an audience to adopt a belief or follow a course of action. To persuade an audience, a writer relies on various kinds of appeals – appeals based on emotion (***pathos***), appeals based on logic (***logos***), and appeals based on the character reputation of the writer (***ethos***).

Argumentation is the appeal to reason (*logos*). In an argument, a writer connects a series of statements so that they lead logically to a conclusion. Argumentation is different from persuasion in that it does not try to move an audience to action; its primary purpose is to demonstrate that certain ideas are valid and others are not. Moreover, unlike persuasion, argumentation has a formal structure: an argument makes points, supplies evidence, establishes a logical chain of reasoning, refutes opposing arguments, and accommodates the audience's views.

As the selections in this chapter demonstrate, however, most effective arguments combine two or more appeals: even though their primary appeal is to reason, they may also appeal to emotions. For example, you could use a combination of logical and emotional appeals to argue against lowering the drinking age in your state from twenty-one to eighteen. You could appeal to *reason* by constructing an argument leading to the conclusion that the state should not condone policies that have a high probability of injuring or killing citizens.

You could support your conclusion by presenting statistics showing that alcohol-related traffic accidents kill more teenagers than disease does. You could also cite a study showing that when the drinking age was raised from eighteen to twenty-one, fatal accidents declined. In addition, you could include an appeal to the *emotions* by telling a particularly poignant story about an eighteen-year-old alcoholic or by pointing out how an increased number of accidents involving drunk drivers would cost some innocent people their lives. Keep in mind, however, that although appeals to your audience's emotions may reinforce the central point of your argument, they do not take the place of sound logic and compelling evidence. The appeals you choose and how you balance them depend on your purpose and your sense of your audience.

As you consider what strategies to use, remember that some extremely effective appeals are unfair. Although most people would agree that lies, threats, misleading statements, and appeals to greed and prejudice are unacceptable ways of reaching an audience, such appeals are used in daily conversation, in political campaigns, and even in international diplomacy. Nevertheless, in your college writing you should use only those appeals that most people would consider fair. To do otherwise will undercut your audience's belief in your trustworthiness and weaken your argument.

Planning an Argumentative Essay

Choosing a Topic

In an argumentative essay, as in all writing, choosing the right topic is important. Ideally, you should have an intellectual or emotional stake in your topic. Still, you should be open-minded and willing to consider all sides of a question. In other words, you should be able, from the outset, to consider your topic from other people's viewpoints; doing so will help you determine what their beliefs are and how they are likely to react to your argument. You can then use this knowledge to build your case and to refute opposing viewpoints. If you cannot be open-minded, you should choose another topic you can deal with more objectively.

Other factors should also influence your selection of a topic. First, you should be well informed about your topic. In addition, you should choose an issue narrow enough to be treated in the space available to you or be willing to confine your discussion to one aspect of a broad issue. It is also important to consider what you expect your argument to achieve. If your topic is so far-reaching that you cannot identify what point you want to make, or if your position is overly idealistic or unreasonable, your essay will suffer.

Developing a Thesis

After you have chosen your topic, you are ready to state the position you will argue in the form of a **thesis**. Keep in mind that in an argumentative essay, your thesis must take a stand – in other words, it must be **debatable**. A good argumentative thesis states a proposition that at least some people will object to. Arguing a statement of fact or an idea that most people accept as self-evident is pointless. Consider the following thesis statement:

> Education is the best way to address the problem of increased drug use among teenagers.

This thesis statement presents ideas that some people might take issue with: it says that increased drug use is a problem among teenagers, that more than one possible solution to this problem exists, and that education is a better solution than any other. Your argumentative essay will go on to support each of these three points logically and persuasively.

A good way to test the suitability of your thesis for an argumentative essay is to formulate an **antithesis**, a statement that asserts the opposite position. If you think that some people would support the antithesis, you can be certain your thesis is indeed debatable.

Thesis:	Education is the best way to address the problem of increased drug use among teenagers.
Antithesis:	Education is not the best way to address the problem of increased drug use among teenagers.

Analyzing Your Audience

Before writing any essay, you should analyze the characteristics, values, and interests of your audience. In argumentation, it is especially important to consider what beliefs or opinions your readers are likely to have and whether your audience is likely to be friendly, neutral, or hostile to your thesis.

In an argumentative essay, you face a dual challenge. You must appeal to readers who are neutral or even hostile to your position, and you must influence those readers so that they are more receptive to your viewpoint. For example, it would be relatively easy to convince college students that tuition should be lowered or to convince instructors that faculty salaries should be raised. You could be reasonably sure, in advance, that each group would agree with your position. But argument requires more than just telling people what they already believe. It would be much harder to convince college students that tuition should be raised to pay for an increase in instructors' salaries or to persuade instructors to forgo raises so that tuition can remain the same. Remember that your audience will not just take your word for the claims you make. You must provide evidence that will support your thesis and establish a line of reasoning that will lead logically to your conclusion.

It is probably best to assume that some, if not most, of your readers are **skeptical** – that they are open to your ideas but need to be convinced. This assumption will keep you from making claims you cannot support. If your position is controversial, you should assume an informed (and possibly determined) opposition is looking for holes in your argument.

Gathering and Documenting Evidence

All the points you make in your essay must be supported. If they are not, your audience will dismiss them as unfounded, irrelevant, or unclear. Sometimes you can support a statement with appeals to emotion, but most of the time you support your argument's points by appealing to reason – by providing **evidence**: facts and opinions in support of your position.

As you gather evidence and assess its effectiveness, keep in mind that evidence in an argumentative essay never proves anything conclusively. If it did, there would be no debate – and hence no point in arguing. The best that evidence can do is convince your audience that an assertion is reasonable and worth considering.

Kinds of Evidence. Evidence can be *fact* or *opinion*. **Facts** are statements that people generally agree are true and that can be verified independently. For example, it is a fact that fewer people were killed in U.S. automobile accidents in 2016 than in 1975. It is also a fact that this decrease came about, in part, because of better-engineered cars.

Facts are often accompanied by **opinions** – judgments or beliefs that are not substantiated by proof. Opinions do not carry the same weight as facts, but they can be quite persuasive, particularly when they are the opinions of experts in a relevant field. For example, you could offer the opinion that automobile deaths could be reduced if all vehicles were equipped with crash-avoidance systems. You could then make this statement more persuasive by supporting it with **expert opinion** – for example, by saying that David Zuby, the chief researcher at the Insurance Institute for Highway Safety, believes crash-avoidance systems should be standard equipment for all automobiles.

Keep in mind that not all opinions are equally convincing. The opinions of experts are more convincing than are those of individuals who have limited knowledge of an issue. Your personal opinions can be evidence (provided you are knowledgeable about your subject), but they are usually less convincing to your audience than an expert's opinion. In the final analysis, what is important is not just the quality of the evidence but also the **credibility** (or believability) of the person offering it.

What kind of evidence might change readers' minds? That depends on the readers, the issue, and the facts at hand. Put yourself in the place of your readers, and ask what would make them receptive to your thesis. Why, for example, should a student agree to pay higher tuition? You might concede that tuition is high but point out that it has not been raised for three years while the college's costs have kept going up. The cost of heating and maintaining the buildings has increased, and professors' salaries have not, with the result that several excellent teachers have recently left the college for higher-paying jobs. Furthermore, cuts in federal and state funding have already caused a reduction in the number of courses offered. Similarly, how could you convince a professor to agree to accept no raise at all, especially because faculty salaries have not kept up with inflation? You could say that because cuts in government funding have already reduced course offerings and because the government has also reduced funds for student loans, any further increase in tuition to pay faculty salaries would cause some students to drop out, which in turn would eventually cost some instructors their jobs. As you can see, the evidence you use in an argument depends to a great extent on whom you want to convince and what you know about them.

Criteria for Evidence. As you select and review material, choose your evidence with the following three criteria in mind.

1. Your evidence should be **relevant**. It should support your thesis and be pertinent to your argument. As you present evidence, be careful not to concentrate so much on a single example that you lose sight of the broader position you are supporting. Such digressions may confuse your readers. For example, in arguing for more medical aid to Central and South America, one student made the point that the Zika virus epidemic is spreading to many countries in this region. To support his point, he discussed the recent spread of dengue fever. Although interesting, this example is not relevant. To show its relevance, the student would have to link his discussion to his assertions about the Zika epidemic, possibly by pointing out that both diseases are tropical, transmitted by mosquitoes, and relatively recent in origin.

2. Your evidence should be **representative**. It should represent the full range of opinions about your subject, not just one side. For example, in an essay arguing against the use of animals in medical experimentation, you would not just use information provided by animal rights activists. You would also use information supplied by medical researchers, pharmaceutical companies, and medical ethicists.

The examples and expert opinions you include should also be **typical**, not aberrant. Suppose you are writing an essay in support of creating bike lanes on your city's streets. To support your thesis, you present the example of Philadelphia, which has a successful bike-lane program. As you consider your evidence, ask yourself if Philadelphia's experience with bike lanes is typical. Did other cities have less success? Take a close look at the opinions that disagree with the position you plan to take. If you understand your opposition, you can refute it effectively when you write your paper.

3. Your evidence should be **sufficient**. It should include enough facts, opinions, and examples to support your claims. The amount of evidence you need depends on the length of your essay, your audience, and your thesis. It stands to reason that you would use fewer examples in a two-page essay than in a ten-page essay. Similarly, an audience that is favorably disposed to your thesis might need only one or two examples to be convinced, whereas a skeptical or hostile audience would need many more. As you develop your thesis, think about the amount of support you will need to write your essay. You may decide that a narrower, more limited thesis will be easier to support than a more inclusive one.

Documentation of Evidence. After you decide on a topic, you should begin to gather evidence. Sometimes you can use your own ideas and observations to support your claims. Most of the time, however, you will have to use the print and electronic resources of the library or search the Internet to locate the information you need.

Whenever you use such evidence in your essay, you have to **document** it by providing the source of the information. (When documenting sources, follow the MLA documentation format explained in Chapter 18 of this book.) If you don't document your sources, your readers are likely to question or dismiss your evidence, thinking that it may be inaccurate, unreliable, or simply false. **Documentation** gives readers the ability to evaluate the sources you cite and to consult them if they wish. When you document sources, you establish credibility by showing readers that you are honest and have nothing to hide.

Documentation also helps you avoid **plagiarism** – presenting the ideas or words of others as if they were your own. Certainly you don't have to document every idea you use in your paper. For example, **common knowledge** – information you could easily find in several reference sources – can be presented without documentation, and so can your own ideas. You must, however, document any use of a direct quotation and any ideas, statistics, charts, diagrams, or pictures that you obtain from your source. (See Chapter 17 for information on plagiarism.)

Dealing with the Opposition

When gathering evidence, you should always try to identify the most obvious – and even the not-so-obvious – objections to your position. By directly addressing these objections in your essay, you will help convince readers that your own position is valid. This part of an argument, called **refutation**, is essential to making the strongest case possible.

You can **refute** opposing arguments by showing that they are unsound, unfair, or inaccurate. Frequently, you will present evidence to show the weakness of your opponent's points and to reinforce your own case. Careful use of definition and cause-and-effect analysis may also prove effective. In the following passage from the classic essay "Politics and the English Language," George Orwell refutes an opponent's argument:

> I said earlier that the decadence of our language is probably curable. Those who deny this would argue, if they produced an argument at all, that language merely reflects existing social conditions, and that we cannot influence its development by any direct tinkering with words and constructions. So far as the general tone or spirit of a language goes, this may be true, but it is not true in detail. Silly words and expressions have often disappeared, though not through any evolutionary process but owing to the conscious actions of a minority.

In the excerpt above, Orwell begins by stating the point he wants to make, goes on to define the argument against his position, and then identifies the weakness of this opposing argument. Later in the essay, Orwell strengthens his argument by presenting examples that support his point.

When an opponent's argument is so compelling that it cannot be easily dismissed, you should **concede** its strength (admit that it is valid). By acknowledging that a point is well taken, you reinforce the impression that you are a fair-minded person. After conceding the strength of the opposing argument, try to identify its limitations and then move your argument to more solid ground. (Often an opponent's strong point addresses only *one* facet of a multifaceted problem.) Notice in the example above that Orwell concedes an opposing argument when he says, "So far as the general tone or spirit of a language goes, this may be true." Later in his discussion, he refutes this argument by pointing out its shortcomings.

When planning an argumentative essay, write down all the arguments against your thesis you can think of. Then, as you gather your evidence, decide which points you will refute, keeping in mind that careful readers will expect you to refute the most compelling of your opponent's arguments. Be careful, however, not to distort an opponent's argument by making it seem weaker than it actually is. This technique, called creating a **straw man**, can backfire and actually turn fair-minded readers against you.

Understanding Rogerian Argument

Not all arguments are (or should be) confrontational. Psychologist Carl Rogers has written about how to argue without assuming an adversarial relationship. According to Rogers, traditional strategies of argument rely on confrontation – trying to prove that an opponent's position is wrong. With this method of arguing, one person is "wrong" and one is "right." By attacking an opponent and repeatedly hammering home the message that his or her arguments are incorrect or misguided, a writer forces the opponent into a defensive position. The result is conflict, disagreement, and frequently ill will and hostility.

Rogers recommends that you think of those who disagree with you as colleagues, not adversaries. With this approach, now known as **Rogerian argument**, you enter into a cooperative relationship with opponents. Instead of aggressively refuting opposing arguments, you emphasize points of agreement and try to find common ground. You thus collaborate to find mutually satisfying solutions. By adopting a conciliatory attitude, you demonstrate your respect for opposing viewpoints and your willingness to compromise and work toward a position that both you and those who disagree with you will find acceptable. To use a Rogerian strategy in your writing, follow the guidelines below.

CHECKLIST GUIDELINES FOR USING ROGERIAN ARGUMENT

- ☐ Begin by summarizing opposing viewpoints.
- ☐ Carefully consider the position of those who disagree with you. What are their legitimate concerns? If you were in their place, how would you react?
- ☐ Present opposing viewpoints accurately and fairly. Demonstrate your respect for the ideas of those who disagree with you.
- ☐ Concede the strength of a compelling opposing argument.
- ☐ Acknowledge the concerns you and your opposition share.
- ☐ Point out to readers how they will benefit from the position you are defining.
- ☐ Present the evidence that supports your viewpoint.

Using Deductive and Inductive Arguments

In an argument, you move from evidence to a conclusion in two ways. One method, called **deductive reasoning**, proceeds from a general premise or assumption to a specific conclusion. Deduction is what most people mean when they speak of logic. Using strict logical form, deduction holds that if all the statements in the argument are true, the conclusion must also be true.

The other method of moving from evidence to conclusion is called **inductive reasoning**. Induction proceeds from individual observations to a more general conclusion and uses no strict form. It requires only that all the relevant evidence be stated and that the conclusion fit the evidence better than any other conclusion would.

Most written arguments use a combination of deductive and inductive reasoning, but it is simpler to discuss and illustrate them separately.

Using Deductive Arguments

The basic form of a deductive argument is a **syllogism**. A syllogism consists of a **major premise**, which is a general statement; a **minor premise**, which is a related but more specific statement; and a **conclusion**, which is drawn from those premises. Consider the following example.

Major premise:	All Olympic runners are fast.
Minor premise:	Jesse Owens was an Olympic runner.
Conclusion:	Therefore, Jesse Owens was fast.

As you can see, if you grant both the major and minor premises, you must also grant the conclusion. In fact, it is the only conclusion you can properly draw. You cannot reasonably conclude that Jesse Owens was slow, because that conclusion contradicts the premises. Nor can you conclude (even if it is true) that Jesse Owens was tall, because that conclusion includes information that was not in the premises.

Of course, this argument seems obvious, and it is much simpler than an argumentative essay would be. In fact, a deductive argument's premises can be fairly elaborate. The Declaration of Independence, which appears later in this chapter, has at its core a deductive argument that could be summarized in this way:

Major premise:	Tyrannical rulers deserve no loyalty.
Minor premise:	King George III is a tyrannical ruler.
Conclusion:	Therefore, King George III deserves no loyalty.

The major premise is a statement that the Declaration claims is **self-evident** – so obvious it needs no proof. Much of the Declaration consists of evidence to support the minor premise that King George is a tyrannical ruler. The conclusion, because it is drawn from those premises, has the force of irrefutable logic: the king deserves no loyalty from his American subjects, who are therefore entitled to revolt against him.

When a conclusion follows logically from the major and minor premises, the argument is said to be **valid**. But if the syllogism is not logical, the argument is not valid, and the conclusion is not sound. For example, the following syllogism is not logical:

Major premise:	All dogs are animals.
Minor premise:	All cats are animals.
Conclusion:	Therefore, all dogs are cats.

Of course, the conclusion is absurd. But how did we wind up with such a ridiculous conclusion when both premises are obviously true? The answer is that the syllogism actually contains two major premises. (Both the major and minor premises begin with *all*.) Therefore, the syllogism is defective, and the argument is invalid. Consider the following example of an invalid argument:

Major premise:	All dogs are animals.
Minor premise:	Ralph is an animal.
Conclusion:	Therefore, Ralph is a dog.

Here, an error in logic occurs because the minor premise refers to a term in the major premise that is **undistributed** – that is, it covers only some of the items in the class it denotes. (To be valid, the minor premise must refer to the term in the major premise that is **distributed** – that is, it covers *all* the items in the class it denotes.) In the major premise, *dogs* is the distributed term; it designates *all dogs.* The minor premise, however, refers to *animals,* which is undistributed because it refers only to animals that are dogs. As the minor premise establishes, Ralph is an animal, but it does not logically follow that he is a dog. He could be a cat, a horse, or even a human being.

Even if a syllogism is valid – that is, correct in its form – its conclusion will not necessarily be **true**. The following syllogism draws a false conclusion:

Major premise:	All dogs are brown.
Minor premise:	My poodle Toby is a dog.
Conclusion:	Therefore, Toby is brown.

As it happens, Toby is black. The conclusion is false because the major premise is false: many dogs are *not* brown. If Toby were actually brown, the conclusion would be correct, but only by chance, not by logic. To be **sound**, a syllogism must be both logical and true.

The advantage of a deductive argument is that if your audience accepts your major and minor premises, they must grant your conclusion. Therefore, you should try to select premises that you know your audience accepts or that are self-evident – that is, premises most people believe to be true. Do not assume, however, that "most people" refers only to your friends and acquaintances. Consider those who may hold different views. If you think your premises are too controversial or difficult to establish firmly, you should use inductive reasoning.

Using Inductive Arguments

Unlike deduction, induction has no distinctive form, and its conclusions are less definitive than those of syllogisms. Still, much inductive thinking (and writing based on that thinking) tends to follow a particular process.

- First, you decide on a question to be answered or, especially in the sciences, a tentative answer to such a question, called a **hypothesis**.
- Then, you gather the evidence that is relevant to the question and that may be important to finding the answer.
- Finally, you move from your evidence to your conclusion by making an **inference** – a statement about the unknown based on the known – that answers the question and takes the evidence into account.

Here is a very simple example of the inductive process:

Question:	How did that living-room window get broken?
Evidence:	There is a baseball on the living-room floor. The baseball was not there this morning. Some children were playing baseball this afternoon. They were playing in the vacant lot across from the window. They stopped playing a little while ago. They aren't in the vacant lot now.
Conclusion:	One of the children hit or threw the ball through the window; then, they all ran away.

The conclusion, because it takes all the evidence into account, seems obvious, but if it turned out that the children had been playing volleyball, not baseball, this additional piece of evidence would undercut the conclusion. Even if the conclusion is believable, you cannot necessarily assume it is true: after all, the window could have been broken in some other way. For example, perhaps a bird flew against it, and perhaps the baseball in the living room had gone unnoticed for days, making the second piece of "evidence" on the list not true.

Because inductive arguments tend to be more complicated than the example above, it is not always easy to move from the evidence you have collected to a sound conclusion. The more pertinent information you gather, the smaller the gap between your evidence and your conclusion; the less pertinent evidence you have, the larger the gap and the weaker your conclusion. To bridge this gap, you have to make what is called an **inductive leap** – a stretch of the imagination that enables you to draw a sound conclusion. Remember, however, that inductive conclusions are only probable, never certain. The more evidence you provide, the stronger your conclusion. When the gap between your evidence and your conclusion is too great, you reach a weak conclusion that is not supported by the facts. This well-named error is called **jumping to a conclusion** because it amounts to a premature inductive leap. You can avoid reaching an unjustified or false conclusion by making sure you have collected enough evidence to justify your conclusion.

Using Toulmin Logic

Another approach for structuring arguments has been advanced by philosopher Stephen Toulmin. Known as **Toulmin logic**, this method tries to describe how the argumentative strategies a writer uses lead readers to respond the way they do. Toulmin puts forth a model that divides arguments into three parts: the *claim,* the *grounds,* and the *warrant.*

- The **claim** is the main point of the essay. Usually the claim is stated directly as the thesis, but in some arguments it may be implied.
- The **grounds** – the material a writer uses to support the claim – can be evidence (facts or expert opinion) or appeals to the emotions or values of the audience.
- The **warrant** is the inference that connects the claim to the grounds. It can be a belief that is taken for granted or an assumption that underlies the argument.

In its simplest form, an argument following Toulmin logic would look like this example.

Claim:	Carol should be elected class president.
Grounds:	Carol is an honor student.
Warrant:	A person who is an honor student would make a good class president.

When you formulate an argument using Toulmin logic, you can still use inductive and deductive reasoning. You derive your claim inductively from facts and examples, and you connect the grounds and warrant to your claim deductively. For example, the deductive argument in the Declaration of Independence that was summarized on page 525 can be represented as shown here.

Claim:	King George III deserves no loyalty.
Grounds:	King George III is a tyrannical ruler.
Warrant:	Tyrannical rulers deserve no loyalty.

As Toulmin points out, the clearer your warrant, the more likely readers will be to agree with it. Notice that in the two preceding examples, the warrants are very explicit.

Recognizing Fallacies

Fallacies are flaws in reasoning that undermine your argument's logic. They may sound reasonable or true but are actually deceptive and dishonest. When readers detect them, such statements can turn even a sympathetic audience against your position. Here are some of the more common fallacies that you should avoid.

Begging the Question. This fallacy assumes that a statement is true when it actually requires proof. It requires readers to agree that certain points are self-evident when in fact they are not.

> Unfair and shortsighted policies that limit free trade are a threat to the U.S. economy.

Restrictions against free trade may or may not be unfair and shortsighted, but emotionally loaded language does not constitute proof. The statement begs the question because it assumes what it should be proving – that policies that limit free trade are unfair and shortsighted.

Argument from Analogy. An **analogy** explains something unfamiliar by comparing it to something familiar. Although analogies can help explain abstract or unclear ideas, they do not constitute proof. An argument based on an analogy frequently ignores important dissimilarities between the two things being compared. When this occurs, the argument is fallacious.

> Overcrowded conditions in some parts of our city have forced people together like rats in a cage. Like rats, they will eventually turn on one another, fighting and killing until a balance is restored. It is therefore necessary that we vote to appropriate funds to build low-cost housing.

No evidence is offered to establish that people behave like rats under these or any other conditions. Just because two things have some characteristics in common, you should not assume they are alike in other respects.

Personal Attack (Argument *Ad Hominem*). This fallacy tries to divert attention from the facts of an argument by attacking the motives or character of the person making the argument.

> The public should not take seriously Dr. Mason's plan for improving county health services. He is overweight and a smoker.

This attack on Dr. Mason's character says nothing about the quality of his plan. Sometimes a connection exists between a person's private and public lives – for example, in a case of conflict of interest. However, no evidence of such a connection is presented here.

Jumping to a Conclusion. Sometimes called a *hasty* or *sweeping generalization,* this fallacy occurs when a conclusion is reached on the basis of too little evidence.

> Because our son benefited from home schooling, every child should be educated in this way.

Perhaps other children would benefit from home schooling, and perhaps not, but no conclusion about children in general can be reached on the basis of just one child's experience.

False Dilemma (Either/Or Fallacy). This fallacy occurs when a writer suggests that only two alternatives exist even though there may be others.

> We must choose between life and death, between intervention and genocide. No one can be neutral on this issue.

An argument like this oversimplifies an issue and forces people to choose between extremes instead of exploring more moderate positions.

Equivocation. This fallacy occurs when the meaning of a key term changes at some point in an argument. Equivocation makes it seem as if a conclusion follows from premises when it actually does not.

> As a human endeavor, computers are a praiseworthy and even remarkable accomplishment. But how human can we hope to be if we rely on computers to make our decisions?

The use of *human* in the first sentence refers to the entire human race. In the second sentence, *human* means "merciful" or "civilized." By subtly shifting this term to refer to qualities characteristic of people as opposed to machines, the writer makes the argument seem more sound than it is.

Red Herring. This fallacy occurs when the focus of an argument is shifted to divert the audience from the actual issue.

> The mayor has proposed building a new sports stadium. How can he consider allocating millions of dollars to this scheme when so many professional athletes are being paid such high salaries?

The focus of this argument should be the merits of the sports stadium. Instead, the writer shifts to the irrelevant issue of athletes' high salaries.

You Also (*Tu Quoque*). This fallacy asserts that an opponent's argument has no value because the opponent does not follow his or her own advice.

> How can that judge favor stronger penalties for convicted drug dealers? During his confirmation hearings, he admitted to smoking marijuana when he was in college.

Appeal to Doubtful Authority. Often people will attempt to strengthen an argument with references to experts or famous people. These appeals have merit when the person referred to is an expert in the area being discussed. They do not have merit, however, when the individuals cited have no expertise on the issue.

> According to Jenny McCarthy, childhood vaccines cause autism in children.

Although Jenny McCarthy is a model, actress, and radio host, she is not a physician or a research scientist. Therefore, her pronouncements about vaccines are no more than personal opinions or, at best, educated guesses.

Misleading Statistics. Although statistics are a powerful form of factual evidence, they can be misrepresented or distorted in an attempt to influence an audience.

> Women will never be competent firefighters; after all, 50 percent of the women in the city's training program failed the exam.

Here, the writer has neglected to mention that there were only two women in the program. Because this statistic is not based on a large enough sample, it cannot be used as evidence to support the argument.

***Post Hoc, Ergo Propter Hoc* (After This, Therefore Because of This).** This fallacy, known as ***post hoc* reasoning**, assumes that because two events occur close together in time, the first must be the cause of the second.

> Every time a Republican is elected president, a recession follows. If we want to avoid another recession, we should elect a Democrat.

Even if it were true that recessions always occur during the tenure of Republican presidents, no causal connection has been established. (See pages 321–22.)

***Non Sequitur* (It Does Not Follow).** This fallacy occurs when a statement does not logically follow from a previous statement.

> Disarmament weakened the United States after World War I. Disarmament also weakened the United States after the Vietnam War. For this reason, the city's efforts to limit gun sales will weaken the United States.

The historical effects of disarmament have nothing to do with current efforts to control the sale of guns. Therefore, the conclusion is a *non sequitur.*

Using Transitions

Transitional words and **phrases** are extremely important in argumentative essays. Without these words and phrases, readers could easily lose track of your argument.

Argumentative essays use transitions to signal a shift in focus. For example, paragraphs that present the specific points in support of your argument can signal this purpose with transitions such as *first, second, third, in addition,* and *finally.* In the same way, paragraphs that refute opposing arguments can signal this purpose with transitions such as *still, nevertheless, however,* and *yet.* Transitional words and phrases – such as *therefore* and *for these reasons* – can indicate that you are presenting your argument's conclusions.

USEFUL TRANSITIONS FOR ARGUMENTATION

all in all	in conclusion
as a result	in other words
finally	in short
first, second, third	in summary
for example	nevertheless
for instance	on the one hand . . . on the other hand
for these reasons	still
however	therefore
in addition	thus
in brief	yet

A more complete list of transitions appears on page 55.

Structuring an Argumentative Essay

An argumentative essay, like other kinds of essays, has an **introduction**, a **body**, and a **conclusion**. However, an argumentative essay has its own special structure, one that ensures that ideas are presented logically and convincingly. The Declaration of Independence follows the typical structure of many classic arguments.

SAMPLE OUTLINE: Argumentation

INTRODUCTION

Introduces the issue

States the thesis

BODY

Induction — offers evidence to support the thesis

Deduction — uses syllogisms to support the thesis

States the arguments against the thesis and refutes them

CONCLUSION

Restates the thesis in different words

Makes a forceful closing statement

Jefferson begins the Declaration by presenting the issue that the document addresses: the obligation of the people of the American colonies to tell the world why they must separate from Great Britain. Next, Jefferson states his thesis that because of the tyranny of the British king, the colonies must replace his rule with another form of government. In the body of the Declaration, he offers as evidence twenty-eight examples of injustice endured by the colonies. Following the evidence, Jefferson refutes counterarguments by explaining how again and again the colonists have appealed to the British for redress, but without result. In his concluding paragraph, he restates the thesis and reinforces it one final time. He ends with a flourish: speaking for the representatives of the United States, he explicitly dissolves all political connections between England and America.

Not all arguments, however, follow this pattern. Your material, your thesis, your purpose, your audience, the type of argument you are writing, and the limitations of your assignment all help you determine the strategies you use. If your thesis is especially novel or controversial, for example, the refutation of opposing arguments may come first. In this instance, opposing positions might even be mentioned in the introduction – provided they are discussed more fully later in the argument.

Suppose your journalism instructor gives you the following assignment:

> Select a controversial topic that interests you, and write a brief editorial about it. Direct your editorial to readers who do not share your views, and try to convince them that your position is reasonable. Be sure to acknowledge the view your audience holds and to refute possible criticisms of your argument.

You are well informed about one local issue because you have just read a series of articles on it. A citizens' group is lobbying for a local ordinance that would authorize government funding for religious schools. Because you have also recently studied the doctrine of separation of church and state in your American government class, you know you could argue fairly and strongly against the position taken by this group.

An informal outline of your essay might look like the following:

SAMPLE OUTLINE: Argumentation

INTRODUCTION

Introduce the issue: Should public tax revenues be spent on aid to religious schools?

State the thesis: Despite the pleas of citizen groups like Religious School Parents United, using tax dollars to support church-affiliated schools violates the U.S. Constitution.

POINT 1

Explain the general principle of separation of church and state.

Evidence (deduction)

POINT 2

Present recent examples of court cases interpreting and applying this principle.

Evidence (induction)

POINT 3

Explain how the court cases apply to your community's situation.

Evidence (deduction)

OPPOSITING ARGUMENTS REFUTED

Identify and refute arguments used by Religious School Parents United. Concede the point that religious schools educate many children who would otherwise have to be educated in public schools at taxpayers' expense. Then, explain the limitations of this argument.

CONCLUSION

Restate the thesis (in different words); end with a strong closing statement.

Revising an Argumentative Essay

When you revise an argumentative essay, consider the items on the revision checklist on page 66. In addition, pay special attention to the items on the following checklist, which apply specifically to argumentative essays.

REVISION CHECKLIST ARGUMENTATION

- ☐ Does your assignment call for argumentation?
- ☐ Have you chosen a topic you can argue about effectively?
- ☐ Do you have a debatable thesis?
- ☐ Have you considered the beliefs and opinions of your audience?
- ☐ Is your evidence relevant, representative, and sufficient?
- ☐ Have you documented evidence you have gathered from sources? Have you included a works-cited page?
- ☐ Have you made an effort to address your audience's possible objections to your position?
- ☐ Have you refuted opposing arguments?
- ☐ Have you used inductive or deductive reasoning (or a combination of the two) to move from your evidence to your conclusion?
- ☐ Have you avoided logical fallacies?
- ☐ Have you used appropriate transitional words and phrases?

Editing an Argumentative Essay

When you edit your argumentative essay, follow the guidelines on the editing checklists on pages 83, 86, and 89. In addition, focus on the grammar, mechanics, and punctuation issues that are particularly relevant to argumentative essays. One of these issues—using coordinating and subordinating conjunctions to link ideas—is discussed in the pages that follow.

GRAMMAR IN CONTEXT USING COORDINATING AND SUBORDINATING CONJUNCTIONS

When you write an argumentative essay, you often have to use **conjunctions** – words that join other words or groups of words – to express the logical and sequential relationships between ideas in your sentences. Conjunctions are especially important because they help readers follow the logic of your argument. For this reason, you should be certain the conjunctions you select clearly and accurately communicate the connections between the ideas you are discussing.

Using Coordinating Conjunctions A **compound sentence** is made up of two or more independent clauses (simple sentences) connected by a coordinating conjunction. **Coordinating conjunctions** join two independent clauses that express ideas of equal importance, and they also indicate how those ideas are related.

independent clause *independent clause*
[People can disobey unjust laws], or [they can be oppressed by them].

COORDINATING CONJUNCTIONS

and (*indicates addition*)
but, yet (*indicate contrast or contradiction*)
or (*indicates alternatives*)
nor (*indicates an elimination of alternatives*)
so, for (*indicate a cause-and-effect connection*)

According to Thomas Jefferson, the king has refused to let governors pass important laws, and he has imposed taxes without the consent of the people.

Rachel Carson says human beings use pesticides to control insects, but these chemicals damage the environment.

Martin Luther King Jr. does not believe that all laws are just, nor does he believe that it is wrong to protest unjust laws.

When you use a coordinating conjunction to join together two independent clauses, you should always place a comma before the coordinating conjunction.

Using Subordinating Conjunctions A **complex sentence** is made up of one independent clause (simple sentence) and one or more dependent clauses. (A dependent clause cannot stand alone as a sentence.) Subordinating conjunctions link dependent and independent clauses that express ideas of unequal importance, and they also indicate how those ideas are related.

independent clause
[According to Martin Luther King Jr., he led protests]
dependent clause
[so that he could fight racial injustice].

SUBORDINATING CONJUNCTIONS

SUBORDINATING CONJUNCTION	RELATIONSHIP BETWEEN CLAUSES
after, before, since, until, when, whenever, while	Time
as, because, since, so that	Cause or effect
even if, if, unless	Condition
although, even though, though	Contrast

"All segregation statutes are unjust because segregation distorts the soul and damages the personality" (King 562).

"If this philosophy had not emerged, by now many streets of the South would, I am convinced, be flowing with blood" (King 566).

"Before the pen of Jefferson etched the majestic words of the Declaration of Independence across the pages of history, we were here" (King 569).

When you use a subordinating conjunction to join two clauses, place a comma after the dependent clause when it comes *before* the independent clause. Do not use a comma when the dependent clause comes *after* the independent clause.

When they signed the Declaration of Independence, Thomas Jefferson and the others knew they were committing treason. (*comma*)

Thomas Jefferson and the others knew they were committing treason when they signed the Declaration of Independence. (*no comma*)

LaunchPad

For more practice on using coordinating and subordinating conjunctions, see the LearningCurve on Coordination and Subordination in the LaunchPad for *Patterns*.

EDITING CHECKLIST ARGUMENTATION

- ☐ Have you used coordinating conjunctions correctly to connect two or more independent clauses?
- ☐ Do the coordinating conjunctions accurately express the relationship between the ideas in the independent clauses?
- ☐ Have you placed a comma before the coordinating conjunction?
- ☐ Have you used subordinating conjunctions correctly to connect an independent clause and one or more dependent clauses?
- ☐ Do the subordinating conjunctions accurately express the relationship between the ideas in the dependent and independent clauses?
- ☐ Have you placed a comma after the dependent clause when it comes before the independent clause?
- ☐ Have you remembered not to use a comma when the dependent clause comes after the independent clause?

A STUDENT WRITER: Argumentation

The following essay, written by Marta Ramos for her composition course, illustrates the techniques discussed earlier in this chapter.

Just Say No

Introduction

Recently, the increase in the use of so-called study drugs has become a hotly debated subject. Many students now routinely take prescription medications such as Ritalin or Adderall to improve their academic performance (Brennan). On the one hand, students who take these medications say that they help them concentrate and improve their ability to study and to get high grades. On the other hand, medical professionals warn that the effects of prolonged exposure to these drugs can be harmful and in some cases even fatal. Unfortunately, these warnings have not stopped an ever-increasing number of students — both in high school and in college — from taking such drugs. They argue that parental pressure and the need to succeed have forced them to take extreme measures. In the final analysis, however, the risks that these drugs present far outweigh their supposed advantages. 1

Summary of controversy

Thesis statement

Argument (inductive)

Despite the claims of users, there is little empirical evidence to show that study drugs actually improve attention or enhance memory. A recent article in the *Daily Beast* examined a range of research on the effectiveness of Ritalin and Adderall. It concluded, "In study after study examining the effect of the drugs on so-called healthy subjects, the findings have been underwhelming. At best, the drugs show a small effect; more often, researchers come up with negative findings. . . ." Moreover, researchers have concluded that Adderall, in particular, "makes you think you're doing better than you actually are" (Schwartz). This probably accounts for the anecdotal evidence of the drug's effectiveness. In short, even though students who take study drugs think they work, there is little hard evidence to suggest they actually do. 2

Evidence

Argument (inductive)

Adding to the problem, study drugs are often obtained illegally or under false pretenses. Students either buy them from friends or fake conditions such as Attention Deficit Disorder (ADD) to get doctors to prescribe them. Because Adderall is an amphetamine, its side effects are unpredictable — especially when it is abused or mixed with alcohol. For this reason, taking drugs like Adderall without proper medical supervision can — and often does — have severe physical and mental consequences. For example, a student 3

Evidence

named Steven Roderick, cited in a *New York Times* article about study drugs, began taking Adderall during his first year in college. In the beginning, a small amount of the drug seemed to improve his academic performance, but as time went on, he needed to increase the dosage to experience the same effect. By his senior year, Roderick was taking large amounts of Adderall in the morning before classes and taking other drugs at night to get to sleep. Eventually, the Adderall stopped working, and because he could not concentrate without it, he was forced to drop out of school (Cohen).

Argument (inductive)

Even though the physical effects of study drugs are obvious, other negative effects can be subtle and quite insidious. Current research suggests that study drugs can "alter personality and constrain the very self that should be supported to live authentically" (Graf et al. 1257). In other words, study drugs provide a false sense of self to students at a time when they should be testing their abilities and pursuing authenticity. It goes without saying that college is a time of self-discovery and that any substance that interferes with this process is, therefore, harmful and should be avoided. Unfortunately, the temptation to take study drugs is encouraged by a society that values superficiality over depth, instant gratification over determination, and winning at all costs over fairness and personal development. 4

Refutation of opposing argument

Of course, not everyone agrees with this assessment of study drugs. Some argue that concerns about these medications are overblown and that they are more like caffeinated drinks than steroids or amphetamines. In an article on *Slate.com,* Will Oremus asks, "What if Adderall turns out to be the new coffee—a ubiquitous, mostly harmless little helper that enables us to spend more time poring over spreadsheets and less time daydreaming or lolling about in bed?" The answer to this question is simple. Unlike drinking coffee, the abuse of illicitly obtained prescription drugs is not "mostly harmless." On the contrary, it can undermine the academic mission of colleges; it can damage the physical and mental well-being of students; and it can hurt society as a whole by compromising its core values. 5

Conclusion

Because of the dangers of study drugs, educators, medical professionals, and parents should inform students of the risks and discourage their use. Medical professionals should be on the lookout for students who are trying to fool them into prescribing Adderall. Parents should be educated to recognize the behavior associated with 6 the excessive use of study drugs. Finally, colleges should make it clear to students that the use of study drugs is unacceptable and will not be tolerated. Only by adopting these measures can the use of study drugs be curtailed — and, eventually, eliminated.

Works-cited list (begins new page)

Works Cited

Brennan, Collin. "Popping Pills: Examining the Use of 'Study Drugs' during Finals." *USA Today College*, 16 Dec. 2015, college.usatoday.com/2015/12/16/popping-pills-examining-the-use-of-study-drugs-during-fnals/.

Cohen, Roger. "The Competition Drug." *The New York Times*, 4 Mar. 2013, www.nytimes.com/2013/03/05/opinion/global/roger-cohen-adderall-the-academic-competition-drug.html?_r=0.

Graf, William D., et al. "Pediatric Neuroenhancement: Ethical, Legal, Social, and Neurodevelopmental Implications." *Neurology*, vol. 80, no. 13, 26 Mar. 2013, pp. 1251–60.

Oremus, Will. "The New Stimulus Package." *Slate*, 27 Mar. 2013, www.slate.com/articles/technology/superman/2013/03/adderall_ritalin_vyvanse_do_smart_pills_work_if_you_don_t_have_adhd.html.

Schwartz, Casey. "Busting the Adderall Myth." *The Daily Beast*, 20 Dec. 2010, www.thedailybeast.com/articles/2010/12/21/adderall-concentration-benefits-in-doubt-new-study.html.

Points for Special Attention

Choosing a Topic. For her composition course, Marta Ramos was asked to write an argumentative essay on a topic of her choice. Because her college newspaper had recently run an editorial on the use of study drugs, she decided to explore this topic. Although Marta had no direct experience with study drugs, such as Adderall and Ritalin, she knew people who used them. Given the timeliness and seriousness of the issue, Marta thought it would be a good topic for her to write about. Because she had read the article in her school newspaper, as well as the many responses (both pro and con) that it elicited, she thought she understood both sides of the controversy. She knew she was against the use of study drugs, but even so, she believed she could approach the topic with an open mind and would be able to reconsider her opinion if the evidence led her in a different direction.

Gathering Evidence. Marta realized she could not rely on personal experience to support her position. For this reason, she used information from several outside sources to develop her argument. For example, she found an article in the academic journal *Neurology* that increased her understanding of her subject. She also found a newspaper article about a student whose story illustrated the practical dangers of study drugs. In addition, she decided to address Will Oremus's 2013 defense of study drugs, which she found both interesting and troubling. She took notes on her sources and recorded their bibliographic information for her works-cited page.

Organization. Marta begins her essay by supplying the context for her argument and then stating her thesis:

> In the final analysis, however, the risks that these drugs present far outweigh their supposed advantages.

In her first body paragraph, Marta addresses the misconception that study drugs are effective. She includes material from an article by Casey Schwartz that summarizes several studies on the use of Ritalin and Adderall by college students, and she combines this information with her own ideas to make the point that study drugs give users a false sense of confidence.

Marta goes on to discuss the harmful physical and psychological effects of study drugs. She begins by saying that because study drugs are often obtained illegally or under false pretenses, their use is extremely risky. She illustrates this point with an anecdote about a student who began taking Adderall to improve his academic performance but eventually had to drop out of college because he could no longer concentrate.

Finally, Marta explains how study drugs have insidious effects on users. In this paragraph, she presents a deductive argument:

Major premise:	Students should discover their authentic selves in college.
Minor premise:	Any substance that interferes with this discovery process is harmful to students.
Conclusion:	Therefore, study drugs are harmful and should be avoided.

Refuting Opposing Arguments. Marta spends one paragraph addressing Will Oremus's point that taking study drugs may be no more harmful than drinking coffee. She refutes this claim by pointing out that unlike coffee, study drugs can do real harm to students as well as to colleges and to society. Here, as in the rest of her essay, Marta is careful to appear both reasonable and respectful. She makes her points clearly and concisely, taking care to avoid name-calling, personal attacks, and jumping to conclusions.

Focus on Revision

When Marta's instructor returned her essay along with his comments, he told her that she had made a very strong argument but that the argument would have been even stronger had she refuted more than one opposing argument. For example, she could have addressed the argument that taking study drugs is not unethical because these medications only help you if you have studied in the first place. Marta could also have considered other issues related to this controversy. For instance, is it unfair for some students to use study drugs while others do not? Does the increasing use of study drugs indicate a problem with the educational system? Does pressure to excel put students under too much pressure? Should colleges be doing more to limit the number of courses that students can carry? Would more student aid enable students to concentrate more on studying and less on earning money to pay tuition?

PEER-EDITING WORKSHEET ARGUMENTATION

1. Does the essay take a stand on an issue? What is it? At what point does the writer state his or her thesis? Is the thesis debatable?
2. What evidence does the writer include to support his or her position? What additional evidence could the writer supply?
3. Has the writer used information from outside sources? If so, is documentation included? Identify any information the writer should have documented but did not.
4. Does the essay summarize and refute the opposing arguments? List these arguments.
5. How effective are the writer's refutations? Should the writer address any other arguments?
6. Does the essay use inductive reasoning? Deductive reasoning? Both? Provide an example of each type of reasoning used in the essay.
7. Does the essay include any logical fallacies? How would you correct these fallacies?
8. Do coordinating and subordinating conjunctions convey the logical and sequential connections between ideas?
9. How could the introduction be improved?
10. How could the conclusion be improved?

The essays that follow represent a wide variety of topics, and the purpose of each essay is to support a debatable thesis. In addition to three classic arguments, this chapter also includes two debates and two casebooks that focus on current issues. Each of the debates pairs two essays that take opposing stands on the same issue. In the casebooks, four essays on a single topic offer a greater variety of viewpoints. The first selection, a visual text, is followed by questions designed to illustrate how argumentation can operate in visual form.

STOPTEXTSSTOPWRECKS.ORG

You Don't Want Them Responding to Your Text (Ad)

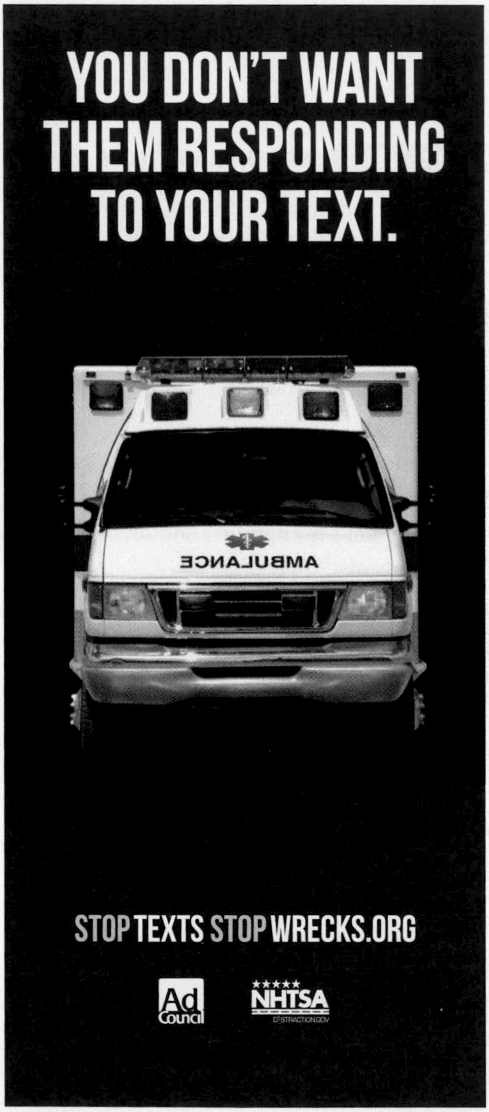

National Highway Traffic Safety Administration and the Ad Council

• • •

Reading Images

1. At whom is this ad directed?
2. What point does the headline make? How does the image support this point?
3. Does this ad appeal primarily to logic, to emotion, or to both? Explain.
4. Visit the website StopTextsStopWrecks.org. What additional information does the site include that supports the message of the advertisement?

Journal Entry

Do you have additional suggestions about how to address the problem of texting while driving? Post your comments in the "Talk to Us" box on StopTextsStopWrecks.org.

Thematic Connections

- "The YouTube Effect" (page 20)
- "Ten Ways We Get the Odds Wrong" (page 245)
- "The Embalming of Mr. Jones" (page 297)

THOMAS JEFFERSON

The Declaration of Independence

Thomas Jefferson was born in 1743 in what is now Albemarle County, Virginia. A lawyer, he was elected to Virginia's colonial legislature in 1768 and began a distinguished political career that strongly influenced the early development of the United States. In addition to his participation in the Second Continental Congress of 1775–1776, which ratified the Declaration of Independence, he served as governor of Virginia; as minister to France; as secretary of state under President George Washington; as vice president under John Adams; and, finally, as president from 1801 to 1809. After his retirement, he founded the University of Virginia. He died on July 4, 1826.

Background on the struggle for American independence By the early 1770s, many residents of the original thirteen American colonies were convinced that King George III and his ministers wielded too much power over the colonists. In particular, they objected to a series of taxes imposed on them by the British Parliament, and, being without political representation, they asserted that "taxation without representation" amounted to tyranny. In response to a series of laws Parliament passed in 1774 to limit the political and geographic freedom of the colonists, representatives of each colony met at the Continental Congress of 1774 to draft a plan of reconciliation, but it was rejected.

As cries for independence increased, British soldiers and state militias began to engage in armed conflict, which by 1776 had become a full-fledged war. On June 11, 1776, the Second Continental Congress chose Jefferson, Benjamin Franklin, and several other delegates to draft a declaration of independence. The draft was written by Jefferson, with suggestions and revisions contributed by other commission members. Jefferson's Declaration of Independence challenges a basic assumption of its time — that the royal monarch ruled by divine right — and, in so doing, it became one of the most important political documents in world history.

As you read, keep in mind that to the British, the Declaration of Independence was a call for open rebellion. For this reason, the Declaration's final sentence, in which the signatories pledge their lives, fortunes, and honor, is no mere rhetorical flourish. Had England defeated the colonists, everyone who signed the Declaration of Independence would have been arrested, charged with treason or sedition, stripped of his property, and probably hanged.

When in the course of human events, it becomes necessary for one people 1
to dissolve the political bonds which have connected them with another, and to assume among the powers of the earth, the separate and equal station to which the Laws of Nature and of Nature's God entitle them, a decent respect to the opinions of mankind requires that they should declare the causes which impel them to the separation.

2 We hold these truths to be self-evident, that all men are created equal, that they are endowed by their Creator with certain unalienable rights, that among these are life, liberty, and the pursuit of happiness. That to secure these rights, governments are instituted among men, deriving their just powers from the consent of the governed. That whenever any form of government becomes destructive to these ends, it is the right of the people to alter or to abolish it, and to institute new government, laying its foundation on such principles and organizing its powers in such form, as to them shall seem most likely to effect their safety and happiness. Prudence, indeed, will dictate that governments long established should not be changed for light and transient causes; and accordingly all experience hath shown, that mankind are more disposed to suffer, while evils are sufferable, than to right themselves by abolishing the forms to which they are accustomed. But when a long train of abuses and usurpations, pursuing invariably the same object, evinces a design to reduce them under absolute despotism, it is their right, it is their duty, to throw off such government, and to provide new guards for their future security. Such has been the patient sufferance of these Colonies; and such is now the necessity which constrains them to alter their former systems of government. The history of the present king of Great Britain is a history of repeated injuries and usurpations, all having in direct object the establishment of an absolute tyranny over these States. To prove this, let facts be submitted to a candid world.

"We hold these truths to be self-evident, that all men are created equal. . . ."

3 He has refused his assent to laws, the most wholesome and necessary for the public good.

4 He has forbidden his Governors to pass laws of immediate and pressing importance, unless suspended in their operation till his assent should be obtained; and when so suspended, he has utterly neglected to attend to them.

5 He has refused to pass other laws for the accommodation of large districts of people, unless those people would relinquish the right of representation in the legislature, a right inestimable to them and formidable to tyrants only.

6 He has called together legislative bodies at places unusual, uncomfortable, and distant from the depository of their public records, for the sole purpose of fatiguing them into compliance with his measure.

7 He has dissolved representative houses repeatedly, for opposing with manly firmness his invasions on the rights of people.

8 He has refused for a long time, after such dissolutions, to cause others to be elected; whereby the legislative powers, incapable of annihilation, have returned to the people at large for their exercise; the State remaining in the meantime exposed to all the dangers of invasion from without, and convulsions within.

9 He has endeavoured to prevent the population of these states; for that purpose obstructing the laws for naturalization of foreigners; refusing to pass

others to encourage their migration hither, and raising the conditions of new appropriations of lands.

He has obstructed the administration of justice, by refusing his assent to 10
laws for establishing judiciary powers.

He has made judges dependent on his will alone, for the tenure of their 11
offices, and the amount and payment of their salaries.

He has erected a multitude of new offices, and sent hither swarms of offi- 12
cers to harass our people, and eat out their substance.

He has kept among us, in times of peace, standing armies without the 13
consent of our legislatures.

He has affected to render the military independent of and superior to the 14
civil power.

He has combined with others to subject us to a jurisdiction foreign to our 15
constitution, and unacknowledged by our laws; giving his assent to their acts of pretended legislation:

For quartering large bodies of troops among us: 16

For protecting them, by a mock trial, from punishment for any murders 17
which they should commit on the inhabitants of these States:

For cutting off our trade with all parts of the world: 18

For imposing taxes on us without our consent: 19

For depriving us in many cases, of the benefits of trial by jury: 20

For transporting us beyond seas to be tried for pretended offences: 21

For abolishing the free system of English laws in a neighbouring Province, 22
establishing therein an arbitrary government, and enlarging its boundaries so as to render it at once an example and fit instrument for introducing the same absolute rule into these Colonies:

For taking away our Charters, abolishing our most valuable laws, and 23
altering fundamentally the forms of our governments:

For suspending our own legislatures, and declaring themselves invested 24
with power to legislate for us in all cases whatsoever.

He has abdicated government here, by declaring us out of his protection 25
and waging war against us.

He has plundered our seas, ravaged our coasts, burnt our towns, and 26
destroyed the lives of our people.

He is at this time transporting large armies of foreign mercenaries to com- 27
plete the works of death, desolation and tyranny, already begun with circumstances of cruelty and perfidy scarcely paralleled in the most barbarous ages, and totally unworthy the head of a civilized nation.

He has constrained our fellow citizens taken captive on the high seas to 28
bear arms against their country, to become the executioners of their friends and brethren, or to fall themselves by their hands.

He has excited domestic insurrections amongst us, and has endeavoured 29
to bring on the inhabitants of our frontiers, the merciless Indian savages, whose known rule of warfare, is an undistinguished destruction of all ages, sexes, and conditions.

In every stage of these oppressions we have petitioned for redress in 30
the most humble terms: our repeated petitions have been answered only by

repeated injury. A prince whose character is thus marked by every act which may define a tyrant, is unfit to be the ruler of a free people.

Nor have we been wanting in attentions to our British brethren. We have 31
warned them from time to time of attempts by their legislature to extend an unwarrantable jurisdiction over us. We have reminded them of the circumstances of our emigration and settlement here. We have appealed to their native justice and magnanimity, and we have conjured them by the ties of our common kindred to disavow these usurpations, which would inevitably interrupt our connections and correspondence. They too have been deaf to the voice of justice and of consanguinity. We must, therefore, acquiesce in the necessity, which denounces our separation, and hold them, as we hold the rest of mankind, enemies in war, in peace friends.

We, therefore, the Representatives of the United States of America, in 32
General Congress, assembled, appealing to the Supreme Judge of the world for the rectitude of our intentions, do, in the name, and by authority of the good people of these Colonies, solemnly publish and declare, That these United Colonies are, and of right ought to be Free and Independent States; that they are absolved from all allegiance to the British Crown, and that all political connection between them and the state of Great Britain, is and ought to be totally dissolved; and that as Free and Independent States, they have full power to levy war, conclude peace, contract alliances, establish commerce, and to do all other acts and things which Independent States may of right do. And for the support of this declaration, with a firm reliance on the protection of divine Providence, we mutually pledge to each other our lives, our fortunes, and our sacred honor.

• • •

Comprehension

1. What "truths" does Jefferson say are "self-evident" (2)?
2. What does Jefferson say is the source from which governments derive their powers?
3. What reasons does Jefferson give to support his premise that the United States should break away from Great Britain?
4. What conclusions about British rule does Jefferson draw from the evidence he presents?

Purpose and Audience

1. What is the major premise of Jefferson's argument? Should Jefferson have done more to establish the truth of this premise?
2. The Declaration of Independence was written during a period now referred to as the Age of Reason. In what ways has Jefferson tried to make his document appear reasonable?

3. For what audience (or audiences) was the document intended? Which groups of readers would have been most likely to accept it? Explain.
4. How effectively does Jefferson anticipate and refute the opposition?
5. In paragraph 31, following the list of grievances, why does Jefferson address his "British brethren"?
6. At what point does Jefferson state his thesis? Why does he state it where he does?

Style and Structure

1. Does the Declaration of Independence rely primarily on inductive reasoning or deductive reasoning? Identify examples of each.
2. What techniques does Jefferson use to create smooth and logical transitions from one paragraph to another?
3. Why does Jefferson list his twenty-eight grievances? Why doesn't he just summarize them or mention a few representative grievances?
4. Jefferson begins the last paragraph of the Declaration of Independence with "We, therefore." How effective is this conclusion? Explain.
5. **Vocabulary Project.** Underline ten words that have negative connotations. How does Jefferson use these words to help him make his point? Do you think words with more neutral connotations would strengthen or weaken his case? Why?
6. **Vocabulary Project.** What words does Jefferson use that are rarely used today? Would the Declaration of Independence be more meaningful to today's readers if it were updated, with more familiar words substituted? To help you formulate your response, try rewriting a paragraph or two, and assess your updated version. Look up any unfamiliar words in an online dictionary such as dictionary.com.

Journal Entry

Do you think Jefferson is being fair to the king? Do you think he should be?

Writing Workshop

1. Following Jefferson's example, write a declaration of independence from your school, job, family, or any other institution with which you are associated.
2. **Working with Sources.** Go to the website ushistory.org/declaration/document/, and look at the revisions Congress made to Jefferson's original draft of the Declaration of Independence. Decide which version you think is better. Then, write an essay in which you present your case. Be sure to document references to both versions of the Declaration and to include a works-cited page. (See Chapter 18 for information on MLA documentation.)

3. **Working with Sources.** In an argumentative essay written from the viewpoint of King George III, answer Jefferson. Try to convince the colonists that they should not break away from Great Britain. If you can, refute some of the points Jefferson makes. Be sure to include parenthetical documentation for all references to the Declaration and to include a works-cited page. (See Chapter 18 for information on MLA documentation.)

Combining the Patterns

The middle section of the Declaration of Independence is developed by means of **exemplification**: it presents a series of examples to support Jefferson's assertion that the colonists have experienced "repeated injuries and usurpations" (2). Are these examples relevant? Representative? Sufficient? What other pattern of development could Jefferson have used to support his assertion?

Thematic Connections

- "Why the Post Office Makes America Great" (page 220)
- "Grant and Lee: A Study in Contrasts" (page 392)
- "Letter from Birmingham Jail" (page 558)
- "On Patriotism" (page 697)

RACHEL CARSON

The Obligation to Endure

A marine biologist, conservationist, and author, Rachel Carson (1907–1964) was a foundational figure in the modern environmental movement. While working for the U.S. Bureau of Fisheries in the 1930s, she began writing for general-interest publications and newspapers like the *Baltimore Sun*, the *Atlantic*, and *Colliers*. Her first book, an accessible but scientifically accurate work about fish and seabirds, was published in 1941. After World War II, she became more focused on nature conservation and the widespread use of synthetic and chemical pesticides like DDT (dichlorodiphenyltrichloroethane). Those preoccupations led to Carson's most famous work, *Silent Spring*, which was serialized in the *New Yorker* magazine and then published as a book in 1962. *Silent Spring* not only raised awareness of environmental issues, but also influenced national policy. Her other works include *The Edge of the Sea* (1955) and *Lost Woods: The Discovered Writing of Rachel Carson* (1998).

Background on the environmental movement in the United States The history of environmental awareness in the United States stretches back to the nation's founding. For example, Thomas Jefferson was a naturalist, botanist, and farmer who envisioned the United States as an agrarian republic. Industrialization and urbanization in the nineteenth century, however, spurred both skepticism about progress and a more urgent sense that nature needed protection. Henry David Thoreau published *Walden*, a philosophical manifesto about living close to nature, in 1854; President Ulysses S. Grant established Yellowstone National Park as protected wilderness in 1872. Author and activist John Muir, the most important American conservationist of the late nineteenth and early twentieth centuries, founded the Sierra Club — the largest environmental organization in the United States — in 1892. During his term as president, Theodore Roosevelt created the United States Forest Service and established several national parks, forests, and reserves. Wisconsin Senator Gaylord Nelson founded Earth Day in 1970, the beginning of a decade that witnessed the creation of the Environmental Protection Agency, Clean Air Act, and other initiatives. But writers, in particular, have played a significant role in conservation and environmentalism. For example, ecologist Aldo Leopold's *Sand County Almanac* (1949) and activist and writer Edward Abbey's *Desert Solitaire* (1968) shaped public attitudes about nature and influenced government policies toward the environment. Perhaps no single book was as influential as Carson's *Silent Spring*, however, from which the following selection is excerpted.

The history of life on earth has been a history of interaction between living things and their surroundings. To a large extent, the physical form and the habits of the earth's vegetation and its animal life have been molded by the environment. Considering the whole span of earthly time, the opposite effect, 1 in which life actually modifies its surroundings, has been relatively slight. Only within the moment of time represented by the present century has one species—man—acquired significant power to alter the nature of his world.

During the past quarter century this power has not only increased to one of disturbing magnitude but it has changed in character. The most alarming of all man's assaults upon the environment is the contamination of air, earth, rivers, and sea with dangerous and even lethal materials. This pollution is for the most part irrecoverable; the chain of evil it initiates not only in the world that must support life but in living tissues is for the most part irreversible. In this now universal contamination of the environment, chemicals are the sinister and little-recognized partners of radiation in changing the very nature of the world—the very nature of its life. Strontium 90, released through nuclear explosions into the air, comes to earth in rain or drifts down as fall-out, lodges in soil, enters into the grass or corn or wheat grown there, and in time takes up its abode in the bones of a human being, there to remain until his death. Similarly, chemicals sprayed on croplands or forests or gardens lie long in soil, entering into living organisms, passing from one to another in a chain of poisoning and death. Or they pass mysteriously by underground streams until they emerge and, through the alchemy of air and sunlight, combine into new forms that kill vegetation, sicken cattle, and work unknown harm on those who drink from once pure wells. As Albert Schweitzer has said, "Man can hardly even recognize the devils of his own creation." 2

It took hundreds of millions of years to produce the life that now inhabits the earth—eons of time in which that developing and evolving and diversifying life reached a state of adjustment and balance with its surroundings. The environment, rigorously shaping and directing the life it supported, contained elements that were hostile as well as supporting. Certain rocks gave out dangerous radiation; even within the light of the sun, from which all life draws its energy, there were short-wave radiations with power to injure. Given time—time not in years but in millennia—life adjusts, and a balance has been reached. For time is the essential ingredient; but in the modern world there is no time. 3

The rapidity of change and the speed with which new situations are created follow the impetuous and heedless pace of man rather than the deliberate pace of nature. Radiation is no longer merely the background radiation of rocks, the bombardment of cosmic rays, the ultraviolet of the sun that have existed before there was any life on earth; radiation is now the unnatural creation of man's tampering with the atom. The chemicals to which life is asked to make its adjustment are no longer merely the calcium and silica and copper and all the rest of the minerals washed out of the rocks and carried in rivers to the sea; they are the synthetic creations of man's inventive mind, brewed in his laboratories, and having no counterparts in nature. 4

"The rapidity of change and the speed with which new situations are created follow the impetuous and heedless pace of man rather than the deliberate pace of nature."

To adjust to these chemicals would require time on the scale that is nature's; it would require not merely the years of a man's life but the life of generations. And even this, were it by some miracle possible, would be futile, for the new chemicals come from our laboratories in an endless stream; almost five hundred annually find their way into actual use in the United States alone. The figure is staggering and its implications are not easily grasped—500 new chemicals to which the bodies of men and animals are required somehow to adapt each year, chemicals totally outside the limits of biologic experience. 5

Among them are many that are used in man's war against nature. Since the mid-1940s over 200 basic chemicals have been created for use in killing insects, weeds, rodents, and other organisms described in the modern vernacular as "pests"; and they are sold under several thousand different brand names. 6

These sprays, dusts, and aerosols are now applied almost universally to farms, gardens, forests, and homes—nonselective chemicals that have the power to kill every insect, the "good" and the "bad," to still the song of birds and the leaping of fish in the streams, to coat the leaves with a deadly film, and to linger on in soil—all this though the intended target may be only a few weeds or insects. Can anyone believe it is possible to lay down such a barrage of poisons on the surface of the earth without making it unfit for all life? They should not be called "insecticides," but "biocides." 7

The whole process of spraying seems caught up in an endless spiral. Since DDT was released for civilian use, a process of escalation has been going on in which ever more toxic materials must be found. This has happened because insects, in a triumphant vindication of Darwin's principle of the survival of the fittest, have evolved super races immune to the particular insecticide used, hence a deadlier one has always to be developed—and then a deadlier one than that. It has happened also because, for reasons to be described later, destructive insects often undergo a "flareback," or resurgence, after spraying, in numbers greater than before. Thus the chemical war is never won, and all life is caught in its violent crossfire. 8

Along with the possibility of the extinction of mankind by nuclear war, the central problem of our age has therefore become the contamination of man's total environment with such substances of incredible potential for harm—substances that accumulate in the tissues of plants and animals and even penetrate the germ cells to shatter or alter the very material of heredity upon which the shape of the future depends. 9

Some would-be architects of our future look toward a time when it will be possible to alter the human germ plasm by design. But we may easily be doing so now by inadvertence, for many chemicals, like radiation, bring about gene mutations. It is ironic to think that man might determine his own future by something so seemingly trivial as the choice of an insect spray. 10

All this has been risked—for what? Future historians may well be amazed by our distorted sense of proportion. How could intelligent beings seek to control a few unwanted species by a method that contaminated the entire environment and brought the threat of disease and death even to their own kind? Yet this is precisely what we have done. We have done it, moreover, for reasons that collapse the moment we examine them. We are told that the enormous and expanding use of pesticides is necessary to maintain farm production. 11

Yet is our real problem not one of *overproduction*? Our farms, despite measures to remove acreages from production and to pay farmers *not* to produce, have yielded such a staggering excess of crops that the American taxpayer in 1962 is paying out more than one billion dollars a year as the total carrying cost of the surplus-food storage program. And is the situation helped when one branch of the Agriculture Department tries to reduce production while another states, as it did in 1958, "It is believed generally that reduction of crop acreages under provisions of the Soil Bank will stimulate interest in use of chemicals to obtain maximum production on the land retained in crops."

All this is not to say there is no insect problem and no need of control. 12
I am saying, rather, that control must be geared to realities, not to mythical situations, and that the methods employed must be such that they do not destroy us along with the insects.

The problem whose attempted solution has brought such a train of disas- 13
ter in its wake is an accompaniment of our modern way of life. Long before the age of man, insects inhabited the earth—a group of extraordinarily varied and adaptable beings. Over the course of time since man's advent, a small percentage of the more than half a million species of insects have come into conflict with human welfare in two principal ways: as competitors for the food supply and as carriers of human disease.

Disease-carrying insects become important where human beings are 14
crowded together, especially under conditions where sanitation is poor, as in time of natural disaster or war or in situations of extreme poverty and deprivation. Then control of some sort becomes necessary. It is a sobering fact, however, as we shall presently see, that the method of massive chemical control has had only limited success, and also threatens to worsen the very conditions it is intended to curb.

Under primitive agricultural conditions the farmer had few insect prob- 15
lems. These arose with the intensification of agriculture—the devotion of immense acreages to a single crop. Such a system set the stage for explosive increases in specific insect populations. Single-crop farming does not take advantage of the principles by which nature works; it is agriculture as an engineer might conceive it to be. Nature has introduced great variety into the landscape, but man has displayed a passion for simplifying it. Thus he undoes the built-in checks and balances by which nature holds the species within bounds. One important natural check is a limit on the amount of suitable habitat for each species. Obviously then, an insect that lives on wheat can build up its population to much higher levels on a farm devoted to wheat than on one in which wheat is intermingled with other crops to which the insect is not adapted.

The same thing happens in other situations. A generation or more ago, 16
the towns of large areas of the United States lined their streets with the noble elm tree. Now the beauty they hopefully created is threatened with complete destruction as disease sweeps through the elms, carried by a beetle that would have only limited chance to build up large populations and to spread from tree to tree if the elms were only occasional trees in a richly diversified planting.

Another factor in the modern insect problem is one that must be viewed 17
against a background of geologic and human history: the spreading of

thousands of different kinds of organisms from their native homes to invade new territories. This worldwide migration has been studied and graphically described by the British ecologist Charles Elton in his recent book *The Ecology of Invasions*. During the Cretaceous Period, some hundred million years ago, flooding seas cut many land bridges between continents and living things found themselves confined in what Elton calls "colossal separate nature reserves." There, isolated from others of their kind, they developed many new species. When some of the land masses were joined again, about 15 million years ago, these species began to move out into new territories—a movement that is not only still in progress but is now receiving considerable assistance from man.

The importation of plants is the primary agent in the modern spread of species, for animals have almost invariably gone along with the plants, quarantine being a comparatively recent and not completely effective innovation. The United States Office of Plant Introduction alone has introduced almost 200,000 species and varieties of plants from all over the world. Nearly half of the 180 or so major insect enemies of plants in the United States are accidental imports from abroad, and most of them have come as hitchhikers on plants. 18

In new territory, out of reach of the restraining hand of the natural enemies that kept down its numbers in its native land, an invading plant or animal is able to become enormously abundant. Thus it is no accident that our most troublesome insects are introduced species. 19

These invasions, both the naturally occurring and those dependent on human assistance, are likely to continue indefinitely. Quarantine and massive chemical campaigns are only extremely expensive ways of buying time. We are faced, according to Dr. Elton, "with a life-and-death need not just to find new technological means of suppressing this plant or that animal"; instead we need the basic knowledge of animal populations and their relations to their surroundings that will "promote an even balance and damp down the explosive power of outbreaks and new invasions." 20

Much of the necessary knowledge is now available but we do not use it. We train ecologists in our universities and even employ them in our governmental agencies but we seldom take their advice. We allow the chemical death rain to fall as though there were no alternative, whereas in fact there are many, and our ingenuity could soon discover many more if given opportunity. 21

Have we fallen into a mesmerized state that makes us accept as inevitable that which is inferior or detrimental, as though having lost the will or the vision to demand that which is good? Such thinking, in the words of the ecologist Paul Shepard, "idealizes life with only its head out of water, inches above the limits of toleration of the corruption of its own environment. . . . Why should we tolerate a diet of weak poisons, a home in insipid surroundings, a circle of acquaintances who are not quite our enemies, the noise of motors with just enough relief to prevent insanity? Who would want to live in a world which is just not quite fatal?" 22

Yet such a world is pressed upon us. The crusade to create a chemically sterile, insect-free world seems to have engendered a fanatic zeal on the part of many specialists and most of the so-called control agencies. On every hand there is evidence that those engaged in spraying operations exercise a ruthless 23 power. "The regulatory entomologists . . . function as prosecutor, judge and jury, tax assessor and collector and sheriff to enforce their own orders," said Connecticut entomologist Neely Turner. The most flagrant abuses go unchecked in both state and federal agencies.

It is not my contention that chemical insecticides must never be used. 24
I do contend that we have put poisonous and biologically potent chemicals indiscriminately into the hands of persons largely or wholly ignorant of their potentials for harm. We have subjected enormous numbers of people to contact with these poisons, without their consent and often without their knowledge. If the Bill of Rights contains no guarantee that a citizen shall be secure against lethal poisons distributed either by private individuals or by public officials, it is surely only because our forefathers, despite their considerable wisdom and foresight, could conceive of no such problem.

I contend, furthermore, that we have allowed these chemicals to be used 25
with little or no advance investigation of their effect on soil, water, wildlife, and man himself. Future generations are unlikely to condone our lack of prudent concern for the integrity of the natural world that supports all life.

There is still very limited awareness of the nature of the threat. This is an era 26
of specialists, each of whom sees his own problem and is unaware of or intolerant of the larger frame into which it fits. It is also an era dominated by industry, in which the right to make a dollar at whatever cost is seldom challenged. When the public protests, confronted with some obvious evidence of damaging results of pesticide applications, it is fed little tranquilizing pills of half truth. We urgently need an end to these false assurances, to the sugar coating of unpalatable facts. It is the public that is being asked to assume the risks that the insect controllers calculate. The public must decide whether it wishes to continue on the present road, and it can do so only when in full possession of the facts. In the words of Jean Rostand, "The obligation to endure gives us the right to know."

• • •

Comprehension

1. How, according to Carson, have people "acquired significant power to alter the nature of [the] world" (1)?
2. What does Carson mean when she says that "in the modern world there is no time" (3)?
3. Why does Carson think that "insecticides" should be called "biocides" (7)? What new problems do pesticides create?
4. What does Carson see as "the central problem of our age" (9)?
5. How do increased human populations create the conditions for increased insect populations? Why, according to Carson, is this situation a problem?
6. Why is single-crop farming dangerous? What effect does it have on the environment? On insect populations?
7. What are the "false assurances" (26) to which Carson refers in her conclusion? What does she say we should we do to end them?

Purpose and Audience

1. What is Carson's thesis? At what point does she state it? Why does she state it where she does?
2. What is Carson's purpose? Do you think she expects to change people's ideas or behavior, or does she have some other idea in mind?
3. Does Carson see her audience as receptive, hostile, or neutral? How can you tell?

Style and Structure

1. What is the significance of the essay's title?
2. Why does Carson begin her essay by discussing the history of life on earth? How does this introduction set up the discussion to follow?
3. Throughout her essay, Carson cites statistics and includes the opinions of experts. How effective is this support?
4. Where in her essay does Carson appeal to logic? To emotions? To ethics? What does each of these appeals accomplish?
5. In paragraph 12, Carson concedes the point that insects can cause problems. Does she adequately refute this point? Explain your answer.
6. What points does Carson emphasize in her conclusion? Why?
7. **Vocabulary Project.** In paragraph 13, Carson uses the metaphor "train of disaster" to describe the impact of using pesticides to destroy insects. What does she mean? How effective is this use of **figurative language**?

Journal Entry

What environmental issue today is as serious as the one Carson discusses in her essay?

Writing Workshop

1. In paragraph 6, Carson says that she thinks man "is in a war against nature." Write an argumentative essay in which you take a stand for and against her position.
2. Do you think this essay is as relevant today as it was when it appeared in 1962? Write an argumentative essay in which you answer this question.
3. **Working with Sources.** *Silent Spring*, the book from which this essay is excerpted, is credited with launching the modern environmental movement. This book is not without its critics, however. Some, such as the entomologist J. Gordon Edwards, have asserted that it is full of omissions, faulty logic, and fabrications. Go online and read Edwards's 1992 essay, "The Lies of Rachel Carson." Then, do further research on the accuracy of Carson's claims. Finally, write an essay in which you argue whether Carson's legacy has been positive or negative. Be sure to document all your sources and to include a works-cited page. (See Chapter 18 for information on MLA documentation.)

Combining the Patterns

Carson uses **cause and effect** extensively in this essay, especially when she discusses the detrimental effects of using "nonselective chemicals" (7). Find two examples of her use of cause and effect, and consider what each cause-and-effect discussion adds to her essay.

Thematic Connections

- "The Hidden Life of Garbage" (page 184)
- "Once More to the Lake" (page 189)
- "Ten Ways We Get the Odds Wrong" (page 245)
- "On Dumpster Diving" (page 676)

MARTIN LUTHER KING JR.

Letter from Birmingham Jail

Martin Luther King Jr. was born in Atlanta, Georgia, in 1929. After receiving his doctorate in theology from Boston University in 1955, he became pastor of the Dexter Avenue Baptist Church in Montgomery, Alabama. There, he organized a 382-day bus boycott that led to the 1956 Supreme Court decision outlawing segregation on Alabama's buses. As leader of the Southern Christian Leadership Conference, he was instrumental in securing the civil rights of black Americans, using methods based on a philosophy of nonviolent protest. His books include *Stride toward Freedom* (1958) and *Why We Can't Wait* (1964). In 1964, King was awarded the Nobel Peace Prize. He was assassinated in 1968 in Memphis, Tennessee.

Background on racial segregation In 1896, the Supreme Court ruled in *Plessy v. Ferguson* that "separate but equal" accommodations on railroad cars gave African Americans the equal protection guaranteed by the Fourteenth Amendment of the United States Constitution. This decision was used to justify separate public facilities — including schools — for blacks and whites well into the twentieth century.

In the mid-1950s, state support for segregation and discrimination against blacks had begun to be challenged. Supreme Court decisions in 1954 and 1955 declared segregation in public schools and other publicly financed venues unconstitutional, while blacks and whites alike were calling for an end to discrimination. Their actions took the form of marches, boycotts, and sit-ins (organized protests whose participants refuse to move from a public area). Many whites, however, particularly in the South, vehemently resisted any change in race relations.

By 1963, when King organized a campaign against segregation in Birmingham, Alabama, tensions ran deep. He and his followers met fierce opposition from the police, as well as from white moderates, who considered him an "outside agitator." During the demonstrations, King was arrested and jailed for eight days. While imprisoned, he wrote his "Letter from Birmingham Jail" to white clergymen to explain his actions and to answer those who urged him to call off the demonstrations.

April 16, 1963

My Dear Fellow Clergymen:

While confined here in the Birmingham city jail, I came across your recent statement calling my present activities "unwise and untimely." Seldom do I pause to answer criticism of my work and ideas. If I sought to answer all the criticisms that cross my desk, my secretaries would have little time for anything other than such correspondence in the course of the day, and I would have no time for constructive work. But since I feel that you are men of genuine good will and that your criticisms are sincerely set forth, I want to try to answer your statement in what I hope will be patient and reasonable terms. 1

I think I should indicate why I am here in Birmingham, since you have been influenced by the view which argues against "outsiders coming in." I have the honor of serving as president of the Southern Christian Leadership Conference, an organization operating in every southern state, with headquarters in Atlanta, Georgia. We have some eighty-five affiliated organizations across the South, and one of them is the Alabama Christian Movement for Human Rights. Frequently we share staff, educational, and financial resources with our affiliates. Several months ago the affiliate here in Birmingham asked us to be on call to engage in a nonviolent direct-action program if such were deemed necessary. We readily consented, and when the hour came we lived up to our promise. So I, along with several members of my staff, am here because I was invited here. I am here because I have organizational ties here. 2

But more basically, I am in Birmingham because injustice is here. Just as the prophets of the eighth century B.C. left their villages and carried their "thus saith the Lord" far beyond the boundaries of their home towns, and just as the Apostle Paul left his village of Tarsus and carried the gospel of Jesus Christ to the far corners of the Greco-Roman world, so am I compelled to carry the gospel of freedom beyond my own home town. Like Paul, I must constantly respond to the Macedonian call for aid. 3

Moreover, I am cognizant of the interrelatedness of all communities and states. I cannot sit idly by in Atlanta and not be concerned about what happens in Birmingham. Injustice anywhere is a threat to justice everywhere. We are caught in an inescapable network of mutuality, tied in a single garment of destiny. Whatever affects one directly, affects all indirectly. Never again can we afford to live with the narrow, provincial, "outside agitator" idea. Anyone who lives inside the United States can never be considered an outsider anywhere within its bounds. 4

You deplore the demonstrations taking place in Birmingham. But your statement, I am sorry to say, fails to express a similar concern for the conditions that brought about the demonstrations. I am sure that none of you would want to rest content with the superficial kind of social analysis that deals merely with effects and does not grapple with underlying causes. It is unfortunate that demonstrations are taking place in Birmingham, but it is even more unfortunate that the city's white power structure left the Negro community with no alternative. 5

In any nonviolent campaign there are four basic steps: collection of the facts to determine whether injustices exist; negotiation; self-purification; and direct action. We have gone through all these steps in Birmingham. There can be no gainsaying the fact that racial injustice engulfs this community. Birmingham is probably the most thoroughly segregated city in the United States. Its ugly record of brutality is widely known. Negroes have experienced grossly unjust treatment in courts. There have been more unsolved bombings of Negro homes and churches in Birmingham than in any other city in the nation. These are the hard, brutal facts of the case. On the basis of these conditions, Negro leaders sought to negotiate with the city fathers. But the latter consistently refused to engage in good-faith negotiation. 6

Then, last September, came the opportunity to talk with leaders of Birmingham's economic community. In the course of the negotiations, certain promises were made by the merchants—for example, to remove the stores' humiliating racial signs. On the basis of these promises, the Reverend Fred Shuttlesworth and the leaders of the Alabama Christian Movement for Human Rights agreed to a moratorium on all demonstrations. As the weeks and months went by, we realized that we were the victims of a broken promise. A few signs, briefly removed, returned; the others remained. 7

As in so many past experiences, our hopes had been blasted, and the shadow of deep disappointment settled upon us. We had no alternative except to prepare for direct action, whereby we would present our very bodies as means of laying our case before the conscience of the local and the national community. Mindful of the difficulties involved, we decided to undertake a process of self-purification. We began a series of workshops on nonviolence, and we repeatedly asked ourselves: "Are you able to accept blows without retaliating?" "Are you able to endure the ordeal of jail?" We decided to schedule our direct-action program for the Easter season, realizing that except for Christmas, this is the main shopping period of the year. Knowing that a strong economic-withdrawal program would be the by-product of direct action, we felt that this would be the best time to bring pressure to bear on the merchants for the needed change. 8

Then it occurred to us that Birmingham's mayoral election was coming up in March, and we speedily decided to postpone action until after election day. When we discovered that the Commissioner of Public Safety, Eugene "Bull" Connor, had piled up enough votes to be in the run-off, we decided again to postpone action until the day after the run-off so that the demonstrations could not be used to cloud the issues. Like many others, we waited to see Mr. Connor defeated, and to this end we endured postponement after postponement. Having aided in this community need, we felt that our direct-action program could be delayed no longer. 9

You may well ask, "Why direct action? Why sit-ins, marches, and so forth? Isn't negotiation a better path?" You are quite right in calling for negotiation. Indeed, this is the very purpose of direct action. Nonviolent direct action seeks to create such a crisis and foster such a tension that a community which has constantly refused to negotiate is forced to confront the issue. It seeks so to dramatize the issue that it can no longer be ignored. My citing the creation of tension as part of the work of the nonviolent-resister may sound rather shocking. But I must confess that I am not afraid of the word "tension." I have earnestly opposed violent tension, but there is a type of constructive, nonviolent tension which is necessary for growth. Just as Socrates felt that it was necessary to create a tension in the mind so that individuals could rise from the bondage of myths and half-truths to the unfettered realm of creative analysis and objective appraisal, so must we see the need for nonviolent gadflies to create the kind of tension in society that will help men rise from the dark depths of prejudice and racism to the majestic heights of understanding and brotherhood. 10

The purpose of our direct-action program is to create a situation so crisis-packed that it will inevitably open the door to negotiation. I therefore concur with you in your call for negotiation. Too long has our beloved Southland been bogged down in a tragic effort to live in monologue rather than dialogue. 11

One of the basic points in your statement is that the action that I and my associates have taken in Birmingham is untimely. Some have asked: "Why didn't you give the new city administration time to act?" The only answer that I can give to this query is that the new Birmingham administration must be prodded about as much as the outgoing one, before it will act. We are sadly mistaken if we feel that the election of Albert Boutwell as mayor will bring the millennium to Birmingham. While Mr. Boutwell is a much more gentle person than Mr. Connor, they are both segregationists, dedicated to maintenance of the status quo. I have hoped that Mr. Boutwell will be reasonable enough to see the futility of massive resistance to desegregation. But he will not see this without pressure from devotees of civil rights. My friends, I must say to you that we have not made a single gain in civil rights without determined legal and nonviolent pressure. Lamentably, it is an historical fact that privileged groups seldom give up their privileges voluntarily. Individuals may see the moral light and voluntarily give up their unjust posture; but, as Reinhold Niebuhr* has reminded us, groups tend to be more immoral than individuals. 12

We know through painful experience that freedom is never voluntarily given by the oppressor; it must be demanded by the oppressed. Frankly, I have yet to engage in a direct-action campaign that was "well timed" in the view of those who have not suffered unduly from the disease of segregation. For years now I have heard the word "Wait!" It rings in the ear of every Negro with piercing familiarity. This "Wait" has almost always meant "Never." We must come to see, with one of our distinguished jurists, that "justice too long delayed is justice denied." 13

We have waited for more than 340 years for our constitutional and God-given rights. The nations of Asia and Africa are moving with jetlike speed toward gaining political independence, but we still creep at horse-and-buggy pace toward gaining a cup of coffee at a lunch counter. Perhaps it is easy for those who have never felt the stinging darts of segregation to say, "Wait." But when you have seen vicious mobs lynch your mothers and fathers at will and drown your sisters and brothers at whim; when you have seen hate-filled policemen curse, kick, and even kill your black brothers and sisters; when you see the vast majority of 14

> "We must come to see, with one of our distinguished jurists, that 'justice too long delayed is justice denied.'"

* Eds. note—American religious and social thinker (1892–1971).

your twenty million Negro brothers smothering in an airtight cage of poverty in the midst of an affluent society; when you suddenly find your tongue twisted and your speech stammering as you seek to explain to your six-year-old daughter why she can't go to the public amusement park that has just been advertised on television, and see tears welling up in her eyes when she is told that Funtown is closed to colored children, and see ominous clouds of inferiority beginning to form in her little mental sky, and see her beginning to distort her personality by developing an unconscious bitterness toward white people; when you have to concoct an answer for a five-year-old son who is asking, "Daddy, why do white people treat colored people so mean?"; when you take a cross-country drive and find it necessary to sleep night after night in the uncomfortable corners of your automobile because no motel will accept you; when you are humiliated day in and day out by nagging signs reading "white" and "colored"; when your first name becomes "nigger," your middle name becomes "boy" (however old you are), and your last name becomes "John," and your wife and mother are never given the respected title "Mrs."; when you are harried by day and haunted at night by the fact that you are a Negro, living constantly at tiptoe stance, never quite knowing what to expect next, and are plagued with inner fears and outer resentments; when you are forever fighting a degenerating sense of "nobodiness" – then you will understand why we find it difficult to wait. There comes a time when the cup of endurance runs over, and men are no longer willing to be plunged into the abyss of despair. I hope, sirs, you can understand our legitimate and unavoidable impatience.

You express a great deal of anxiety over our willingness to break laws. This 15
is certainly a legitimate concern. Since we so diligently urge people to obey the Supreme Court's decision of 1954 outlawing segregation in the public schools, at first glance it may seem rather paradoxical for us consciously to break laws. One may well ask: "How can you advocate breaking some laws and obeying others?" The answer lies in the fact that there are two types of laws: just and unjust. I would be the first to advocate obeying just laws. One has not only a legal but a moral responsibility to obey just laws. Conversely, one has a moral responsibility to disobey unjust laws. I would agree with St. Augustine* that "an unjust law is no law at all."

Now, what is the difference between the two? How does one determine 16
whether a law is just or unjust? A just law is a man-made code that squares with the moral law or the law of God. An unjust law is a code that is out of harmony with the moral law. To put it in the terms of St. Thomas Aquinas:** An unjust law is a human law that is not rooted in eternal law and natural law. Any law that uplifts human personality is just. Any law that degrades human personality is unjust. All segregation statutes are unjust because segregation distorts the soul and damages the personality. It gives the segregator a false

* Eds. note – Early church father and philosopher (354–430).
** Eds. note – Italian philosopher and theologian (1225–1274).

sense of superiority and the segregated a false sense of inferiority. Segregation, to use the terminology of the Jewish philosopher Martin Buber, substitutes an "I-it" relationship for an "I-thou" relationship and ends up relegating persons to the status of things. Hence segregation is not only politically, economically, and sociologically unsound, it is morally wrong and sinful. Paul Tillich* has said that sin is separation. Is not segregation an existential expression of man's tragic separation, his awful estrangement, his terrible sinfulness? Thus it is that I can urge men to obey the 1954 decision of the Supreme Court, for it is morally right; and I can urge them to disobey segregation ordinances, for they are morally wrong.

Let us consider a more concrete example of just and unjust laws. An 17
unjust law is a code that a numerical or power majority group compels a minority group to obey but does not make binding on itself. This is *difference* made legal. By the same token, a just law is a code that a majority compels a minority to follow and that it is willing to follow itself. This is *sameness* made legal.

Let me give another explanation. A law is unjust if it is inflicted on a 18
minority that, as a result of being denied the right to vote, had no part in enacting or devising the law. Who can say that the legislature of Alabama which set up that state's segregation laws was democratically elected? Throughout Alabama all sorts of devious methods are used to prevent Negroes from becoming registered voters, and there are some counties in which, even though Negroes constitute a majority of the population, not a single Negro is registered. Can any law enacted under such circumstances be considered democratically structured?

Sometimes a law is just on its face and unjust in its application. For 19
instance, I have been arrested on a charge of parading without a permit. Now, there is nothing wrong in having an ordinance which requires a permit for a parade. But such an ordinance becomes unjust when it is used to maintain segregation and to deny citizens the First-Amendment privilege of peaceful assembly and protest.

I hope you are able to see the distinction I am trying to point out. In no 20
sense do I advocate evading or defying the law, as would the rabid segregationist. That would lead to anarchy. One who breaks an unjust law must do so openly, lovingly, and with a willingness to accept the penalty. I submit that an individual who breaks a law that conscience tells him is unjust, and who willingly accepts the penalty of imprisonment in order to arouse the conscience of the community over its injustice, is in reality expressing the highest respect for law.

Of course, there is nothing new about this kind of civil disobedi- 21
ence. It was evidenced sublimely in the refusal of Shadrach, Meshach, and

* Eds. note—American philosopher and theologian (1886–1965).

Abednego* to obey the laws of Nebuchadnezzar, on the ground that a higher moral law was at stake. It was practiced superbly by the early Christians, who were willing to face hungry lions and the excruciating pain of chopping blocks rather than submit to certain unjust laws of the Roman Empire. To a degree, academic freedom is a reality today because Socrates practiced civil disobedience. In our own nation, the Boston Tea Party represented a massive act of civil disobedience.

We should never forget that everything Adolph Hitler did in Germany was "legal" and everything the Hungarian freedom fighters did in Hungary was "illegal." It was "illegal" to aid and comfort a Jew in Hitler's Germany. Even so, I am sure that, had I lived in Germany at the time, I would have aided and comforted my Jewish brothers. If today I lived in a Communist country where certain principles dear to the Christian faith are suppressed, I would openly advocate disobeying that country's antireligious laws. 22

I must make two honest confessions to you, my Christian and Jewish brothers. First, I must confess that over the past few years I have been gravely disappointed with the white moderate. I have almost reached the regrettable conclusion that the Negro's great stumbling block in his stride toward freedom is not the White Citizens Counciler or the Ku Klux Klanner, but the white moderate, who is more devoted to "order" than to justice; who prefers a negative peace which is the absence of tension to a positive peace which is the presence of justice; who constantly says, "I agree with you in the goal you seek, but I cannot agree with your methods of direct action"; who paternalistically believes he can set the timetable for another man's freedom; who lives by a mythical concept of time and who constantly advises the Negro to wait for a "more convenient season." Shallow understanding from people of good will is more frustrating than absolute misunderstanding from people of ill will. Lukewarm acceptance is much more bewildering than outright rejection. 23

I had hoped that the white moderate would understand that law and order exist for the purpose of establishing justice and that when they fail in this purpose they become the dangerously structured dams that block the flow of social progress. I had hoped that the white moderate would understand that the present tension in the South is a necessary phase of the transition from an obnoxious negative peace, in which the Negro passively accepted his unjust plight, to a substantive and positive peace, in which all men will respect the dignity and worth of human personality. Actually, we who engage in nonviolent direct action are not the creators of tension. We merely bring to the surface the hidden tension that is already alive. We bring it out in the open, where it can be seen and dealt with. Like a boil that can never be cured so long as it is covered up but must be opened with all its ugliness to the natural medicines of air and light, injustice must be exposed, with all the tension its exposure creates, to the light of human conscience and the air of national opinion, before it can be cured. 24

* Eds. note – In the Book of Daniel, three men who were thrown into a blazing fire for refusing to worship a golden statue.

In your statement you assert that our actions, even though peaceful, must be condemned because they precipitate violence. But is this a logical assertion? Isn't this like condemning a robbed man because his possession of money precipitated the evil act of robbery? Isn't this like condemning Socrates because his unswerving commitment to truth and his philosophical inquiries precipitated the act by the misguided populace in which they made him drink hemlock? Isn't this like condemning Jesus because his unique God-consciousness and never-ceasing devotion to God's will precipitated the evil act of crucifixion? We must come to see that, as the federal courts have consistently affirmed, it is wrong to urge an individual to cease his efforts to gain his basic constitutional rights because the quest may precipitate violence. Society must protect the robbed and punish the robber. 25

I had also hoped that the white moderate would reject the myth concerning time in relation to the struggle for freedom. I have just received a letter from a white brother in Texas. He writes: "All Christians know that the colored people will receive equal rights eventually, but it is possible that you are in too great a religious hurry. It has taken Christianity almost two thousand years to accomplish what it has. The teachings of Christ take time to come to earth." Such an attitude stems from a tragic misconception of time, from the strangely irrational notion that there is something in the very flow of time that will inevitably cure all ills. Actually, time itself is neutral; it can be used either destructively or constructively. More and more I feel that the people of ill will have used time much more effectively than have the people of good will. We will have to repent in this generation not merely for the hateful words and actions of the bad people, but for the appalling silence of the good people. Human progress never rolls in on wheels of inevitability; it comes through the tireless efforts of men willing to be coworkers with God, and without this hard work, time itself becomes an ally of the forces of social stagnation. We must use time creatively, in the knowledge that the time is always ripe to do right. Now is the time to make real the promise of democracy and transform our pending national elegy into a creative psalm of brotherhood. Now is the time to lift our national policy from the quicksand of racial injustice to the solid rock of human dignity. 26

You speak of our activity in Birmingham as extreme. At first I was rather disappointed that fellow clergymen would see my nonviolent efforts as those of an extremist. I began thinking about the fact that I stand in the middle of two opposing forces in the Negro community. One is a force of complacency, made up in part of Negroes who, as a result of long years of oppression, are so drained of self-respect and a sense of "somebodiness" that they have adjusted to segregation; and in part of a few middle-class Negroes who, because of a degree of academic and economic security and because in some ways they profit by segregation, have become insensitive to the problems of the masses. The other force is one of bitterness and hatred, and it comes perilously close to advocating violence. It is expressed in the various black nationalist groups that are springing up across the nation, the largest and best-known being Elijah Muhammad's Muslim movement. Nourished by the Negro's frustration over the continued existence of racial discrimination, this movement is 27 made up of people who have lost faith in America, who have absolutely repudiated Christianity, and who have concluded that the white man is an incorrigible "devil."

I have tried to stand between these two forces, saying that we need emulate neither the "do-nothingism" of the complacent nor the hatred and despair of the black nationalist. For there is the more excellent way of love and nonviolent protest. I am grateful to God that, through the influence of the Negro church, the way of nonviolence became an integral part of our struggle. 28

If this philosophy had not emerged, by now many streets of the South would, I am convinced, be flowing with blood. And I am further convinced that if our white brothers dismiss as "rabble-rousers" and "outside agitators" those of us who employ nonviolent direct action, and if they refuse to support our nonviolent efforts, millions of Negroes will, out of frustration and despair, seek solace and security in black-nationalist ideologies—a development that would inevitably lead to a frightening racial nightmare. 29

Oppressed people cannot remain oppressed forever. The yearning for freedom eventually manifests itself, and that is what has happened to the American Negro. Something within has reminded him of his birthright of freedom, and something without has reminded him that it can be gained. Consciously or unconsciously, he has been caught up by the *Zeitgeist,* and with his black brothers of Africa and his brown and yellow brothers of Asia, South America, and the Caribbean, the United States Negro is moving with a sense of great urgency toward the promised land of racial justice. If one recognizes this vital urge that has engulfed the Negro community, one should readily understand why public demonstrations are taking place. The Negro has many pent-up resentments and latent frustrations, and he must release them. So let him march; let him make prayer pilgrimages to the city hall; let him go on freedom rides—and try to understand why he must do so. If his repressed emotions are not released in nonviolent ways, they will seek expression through violence; this is not a threat but a fact of history. So I have not said to my people, "Get rid of your discontent." Rather, I have tried to say that this normal and healthy discontent can be channeled into the creative outlet of nonviolent direct action. And now this approach is being termed extremist. 30

But though I was initially disappointed at being categorized as an extremist, as I continued to think about the matter I gradually gained a measure of satisfaction from the label. Was not Jesus an extremist for love: "Love your enemies, bless them that curse you, do good to them that hate you, and pray for them which despitefully use you, and persecute you." Was not Amos an extremist for justice: "Let justice roll down like waters and righteousness like an everflowing stream." Was not Paul an extremist for the Christian gospel: "I bear in my body the marks of the Lord Jesus." Was not Martin Luther an extremist: "Here I stand; I cannot do otherwise, so help me God." And John Bunyan: "I will stay in jail to the end of my days before I make a butchery of my conscience." And Abraham Lincoln: "This nation cannot survive half slave and half free." And Thomas Jefferson: "We hold these truths to be self-evident, that all men are created equal. . . ." So the question is not 31 whether we will be extremists, but what kind of extremists we will be. Will we be extremists for hate or for love? Will we be extremists for the preservation of injustice or for the extension of justice? In that dramatic scene of Calvary's hill three men were crucified. We must never forget that all three were crucified for the same crime – the crime of extremism. Two were extremists for immorality, and thus fell below their environment. The other, Jesus Christ, was an extremist for love, truth, and goodness, and thereby rose above his environment. Perhaps the South, the nation, and the world are in dire need of creative extremists.

I hoped that the white moderate would see this need. Perhaps I was too 32
optimistic; perhaps I expected too much. I suppose I should have realized that few members of the oppressor race can understand the deep groans and passionate yearnings of the oppressed race, and still fewer have the vision to see that injustice must be rooted out by strong, persistent, and determined action. I am thankful, however, that some of our white brothers in the South have grasped the meaning of this social revolution and committed themselves to it. They are still all too few in quantity, but they are big in quality. Some – such as Ralph McGill, Lillian Smith, Harry Golden, James McBride Dabbs, Ann Braden, and Sarah Patton Boyle – have written about our struggle in eloquent and prophetic terms. Others have marched with us down nameless streets of the South. They have languished in filthy, roach-infested jails, suffering the abuse and brutality of policemen who view them as "dirty nigger-lovers." Unlike so many of their moderate brothers and sisters, they have recognized the urgency of the movement and sensed the need for powerful "action" antidotes to combat the disease of segregation.

Let me take note of my other major disappointment. I have been so greatly 33
disappointed with the white church and its leadership. Of course, there are some notable exceptions. I am not unmindful of the fact that each of you has taken some significant stands on this issue. I commend you, Reverend Stallings, for your Christian stand on this past Sunday, in welcoming Negroes to your worship service on a nonsegregated basis. I commend the Catholic leaders of this state for integrating Spring Hill College several years ago.

But despite these notable exceptions, I must honestly reiterate that I have 34
been disappointed with the church. I do not say this as one of those negative critics who can always find something wrong with the church. I say this as a minister of the gospel, who loves the church; who was nurtured in its bosom; who has been sustained by its spiritual blessings and who will remain true to it as long as the cord of life shall lengthen.

When I was suddenly catapulted into the leadership of the bus protest in 35
Montgomery, Alabama, a few years ago, I felt we would be supported by the white church. I felt that the white ministers, priests, and rabbis of the South would be among our strongest allies. Instead, some have been outright opponents, refusing to understand the freedom movement and misrepresenting its leaders; all too many others have been more cautious than courageous and have remained silent behind the anesthetizing security of stained-glass windows.

In spite of my shattered dreams, I came to Birmingham with the hope that the white religious leadership of this community would see the justice of our cause and, with deep moral concern, would serve as the channel through which our just grievances could reach the power structure. I had hoped that each of you would understand. But again I have been disappointed. 36

There was a time when the church was very powerful—in the time when the early Christians rejoiced at being deemed worthy to suffer for what they believed. In those days the church was not merely a thermometer that recorded the ideas and principles of popular opinion; it was a thermostat that transformed the mores of society. Whenever the early Christians entered a town, the people in power became disturbed and immediately sought to convict the Christians for being "disturbers of the peace" and "outside agitators." But the Christians pressed on, in the conviction that they were "a colony of heaven," called to obey God rather than man. Small in number, they were big in commitment. They were too God-intoxicated to be "astronomically intimidated." By their effort and example they brought an end to such ancient evils as infanticide and gladiatorial contests. 37

Things are different now. So often the contemporary church is a weak, ineffectual voice with an uncertain sound. So often it is an archdefender of the status quo. Far from being disturbed by the presence of the church, the power structure of the average community is consoled by the church's silent—and often even vocal—sanction of things as they are. 38

But the judgment of God is upon the church as never before. If today's church does not recapture the sacrificial spirit of the early church, it will lose its authenticity, forfeit the loyalty of millions, and be dismissed as an irrelevant social club with no meaning for the twentieth century. Every day I meet young people whose disappointment with the church has turned into outright disgust. 39

Perhaps I have once again been too optimistic. Is organized religion too inextricably bound to the status quo to save our nation and the world? Perhaps I must turn my faith to the inner spiritual church, the church within the church, as the true *ekklesia** and the hope of the world. But again I am thankful to God that some noble souls from the ranks of organized religion have broken loose from the paralyzing chains of conformity and joined us as active partners in the struggle for freedom. They have left their secure congregations and walked the streets of Albany, Georgia, with us. They have gone down the highways of the South on tortuous rides for freedom. Yes, they have gone to jail with us. Some have been dismissed from their churches, have lost the support of their bishops and fellow ministers. But they have acted in the faith that right defeated is stronger than evil triumphant. Their witness has been the spiritual salt that has preserved the true meaning of the gospel in these troubled times. They have carved a tunnel of hope through the dark mountain of disappointment. 40

I hope the church as a whole will meet the challenge of this decisive hour. But even if the church does not come to the aid of justice, I have no despair 41

* Eds. note—Greek word for the early Christian church.

about the future. I have no fear about the outcome of our struggle in Birmingham, even if our motives are at present misunderstood. We will reach the goal of freedom in Birmingham and all over the nation, because the goal of America is freedom. Abused and scorned though we may be, our destiny is tied up with America's destiny. Before the pilgrims landed at Plymouth, we were here. Before the pen of Jefferson etched the majestic words of the Declaration of Independence across the pages of history, we were here. For more than two centuries our forebears labored in this country without wages; they made cotton king; they built the homes of their masters while suffering gross injustice and shameful humiliation—and yet out of a bottomless vitality they continued to thrive and develop. If the inexpressible cruelties of slavery could not stop us, the opposition we now face will surely fail. We will win our freedom because the sacred heritage of our nation and the eternal will of God are embodied in our echoing demands.

Before closing I feel impelled to mention one other point in your statement that has troubled me profoundly. 42 You warmly commended the Birmingham police for keeping "order" and "preventing violence." I doubt that you would have so warmly commended the police force if you had seen its dogs sinking their teeth into unarmed, nonviolent Negroes. I doubt that you would so quickly commend the policemen if you were to observe their ugly and inhumane treatment of Negroes here in the city jail; if you were to watch them push and curse old Negro women and young Negro girls; if you were to see them slap and kick old Negro men and young boys; if you were to observe them, as they did on two occasions, refuse to give us food because we wanted to sing our grace together. I cannot join you in your praise of the Birmingham police department.

It is true that the police have exercised a degree of discipline in handling 43 the demonstrators. In this sense they have conducted themselves rather "nonviolently" in public. But for what purpose? To preserve the vile system of segregation. Over the past few years I have consistently preached that nonviolence demands that the means we use must be as pure as the ends we seek. I have tried to make clear that it is wrong to use immoral means to attain moral ends. But now I must affirm that it is just as wrong, or perhaps even more so, to use moral means to preserve immoral ends. Perhaps Mr. Connor and his policemen have been rather nonviolent in public, as was Chief Pritchett in Albany, Georgia, but they have used the moral means of nonviolence to maintain the immoral end of racial injustice. As T. S. Eliot has said, "The last temptation is the greatest treason: To do the right deed for the wrong reason."

I wish you had commended the Negro sit-inners and demonstrators of 44 Birmingham for their sublime courage, their willingness to suffer, and their amazing discipline in the midst of great provocation. One day the South will recognize its real heroes. They will be the James Merediths,* with the noble sense of purpose that enables them to face jeering and hostile mobs, and with

* Eds. note—James Meredith was the first African American to enroll at the University of Mississippi.

the agonizing loneliness that characterizes the life of the pioneer. They will be old, oppressed, battered Negro women, symbolized in a seventy-two-year-old woman in Montgomery, Alabama, who rose up with a sense of dignity and with her people decided not to ride segregated buses, and who responded with ungrammatical profundity to one who inquired about her weariness: "My feets is tired, but my soul is at rest." They will be the young high school and college students, the young ministers of the gospel and a host of their elders, courageously and nonviolently sitting in at lunch counters and willingly going to jail for conscience's sake. One day the South will know that when these disinherited children of God sat down at lunch counters, they were in reality standing up for what is best in the American dream and for the most sacred values in our Judaeo-Christian heritage, thereby bringing our nation back to those great wells of democracy which were dug deeply by the founding fathers in their formulation of the Constitution and the Declaration of Independence.

Never before have I written so long a letter. I'm afraid it is much too long 45 to take your precious time. I can assure you that it would have been much shorter if I had been writing from a comfortable desk, but what else can one do when he is alone in a narrow jail cell, other than write long letters, think long thoughts, and pray long prayers?

If I have said anything in this letter that overstates the truth and indicates 46 an unreasonable impatience, I beg you to forgive me. If I have said anything that understates the truth and indicates my having a patience that allows me to settle for anything less than brotherhood, I beg God to forgive me.

I hope this letter finds you strong in the faith. I also hope that circum- 47 stances will soon make it possible for me to meet each of you, not as an integrationist or a civil-rights leader but as a fellow clergyman and a Christian brother. Let us all hope that the dark clouds of racial prejudice will soon pass away and the deep fog of misunderstanding will be lifted from our fear-drenched communities, and in some not too distant tomorrow the radiant stars of love and brotherhood will shine over our great nation with all their scintillating beauty.

Yours for the cause of Peace and Brotherhood,
Martin Luther King Jr.

• • •

Comprehension

1. King says he seldom answers criticism. Why not? Why, then, does he decide to do so in this instance?
2. Why do the other clergymen consider King's activities to be "'unwise and untimely'" (1)?
3. What reasons does King give for the demonstrations? Why does he think it is too late for negotiations?
4. What does King say *wait* means to black people?

5. What are the two types of laws King defines? What is the difference between the two?
6. What does King find illogical about the claim that the actions of his followers precipitate violence?
7. Why is King disappointed in the white church?

Purpose and Audience

1. Why, in the first paragraph, does King establish his setting (the Birmingham city jail) and define his intended audience?
2. Why does King begin his letter with a reference to his audience as "men of genuine good will" (1)? Is this phrase **ironic** in light of his later criticism of them? Explain.
3. What indicates that King is writing his letter to an audience other than his fellow clergymen?
4. What is the thesis of this letter? Is it stated or implied?

Style and Structure

1. Where does King seek to establish that he is a reasonable person?
2. Where does King address the objections of his audience?
3. As in the Declaration of Independence, transitions are important in King's letter. Identify the transitional words and phrases that connect the different parts of his argument.
4. Why does King cite Jewish, Catholic, and Protestant philosophers to support his position?
5. Throughout his letter, King cites theologians and philosophers (Augustine, Aquinas, Buber, Tillich, and others). Why do you think he does this?
6. King uses both induction and deduction in his letter. Find an example of each, and explain how they function in his argument.
7. Throughout the body of his letter, King criticizes his audience of white moderates. In his conclusion, however, he seeks to reestablish a harmonious relationship with them. How does he do this? Is he successful?
8. **Vocabulary Project.** Locate five **allusions** to the Bible in this essay. Look up these allusions online. Then, determine how these allusions help King express his ideas.
9. In paragraph 14, King refers to his "cup of endurance." What is this a reference to? How is the original phrase worded?

Journal Entry

Do you believe King's remarks go too far? Do you believe they do not go far enough? Explain.

Writing Workshop

1. Write an argumentative essay supporting a deeply held belief of your own. Assume your audience, like King's, is not openly hostile to your position.
2. **Working with Sources.** Assume you are a militant political leader responding to Martin Luther King Jr. Argue that King's methods do not go far enough. Be sure to address potential objections to your position. You might want to consult a website such as mlk-kpp01.stanford.edu or read some newspapers and magazines from the 1960s to help you prepare your argument. Be sure to document all references to your sources and to include a works-cited page. (See Chapter 18 for information on MLA documentation.)
3. **Working with Sources.** Read your local newspaper for several days, collecting articles about a controversial subject that interests you. Using information from the articles, take a position on the issue, and write an essay supporting it. Be sure to document all references to your sources and to include a works-cited page. (See Chapter 18 for information on MLA documentation.)

Combining the Patterns

In "Letter from Birmingham Jail," King includes several passages of **narration**. Find two of these passages, and discuss what use King makes of narration. Why do you think narration plays such an important part in King's argument?

Thematic Connections

- "Indian Education" (page 140)
- "Just Walk On By: A Black Man Ponders His Power to Alter Public Space" (page 233)
- "Photos That Change History" (page 356)
- "Emmett Till and Tamir Rice, Sons of the Great Migration" (page 422)
- "On Patriotism" (page 697)

★DEBATE

Should Public Colleges and Universities Be Free?

AP Photo/Bloomington Herald-Times, Jeremy Hogan

A student at Indiana University protests the high debt that he has incurred in order to finance his education.

• • •

The progress of American higher education is, in a sense, a history of widening accessibility and democratization. Beginning with state-chartered public universities in Georgia and North Carolina, America's public higher education system was designed to provide — in the words of North Carolina's 1776 state constitution — the "convenient instruction of youth, with such salaries to the masters, paid by the public, as may enable them to instruct at low prices." This principle of expanding access was extended by nineteenth-century land-grant universities, "free" institutions like the City of College of New York, the post–World War II GI Bill, the community college system, and widely available Stafford Loans. Not surprisingly, then, the number of Americans with two- and four-year degrees has risen consistently; for example, the percentage of people with a bachelor's degree or higher increased from 25 percent to 36 percent over the past two decades. This history reflects an American belief that education is the key to socioeconomic mobility as well as a necessity for an informed citizenry and a workforce that will be competitive in the global marketplace.

More recent headlines, however, tell another story about higher education in the United States. The costs of attending college have increased by more than 1000% over the last four decades. Most colleges and universities in the United States are private, but even at public institutions, tuitions have risen faster than inflation. The total in-state annual price tag for a public university now averages around $24,000. At private schools, the costs have risen even faster. Although many debate the causes of this increase – from state budget cuts and overpaid administrators to inflation driven by easy access to student loans – no one disputes that overall student debt now tops $1 trillion. The average college senior now graduates with almost $30,000 in loans to repay. Many seeking higher education face a choice between being priced out and left behind or submitting to what the research institute Demos has called a "debt-for-diploma system."

Politicians, reformers, and others have proposed many remedies to this problem. Some argue that states need to increase funding to public universities and bring their costs down; others suggest reconfiguring the entire system of private and public student financial aid; still others advocate a system in which student debt repayment would be limited to a certain percentage of a graduate's earnings. Among these and many other solutions, however, perhaps the most provocative proposal is to make public colleges and universities tuition free. Although this idea may seem radical, it is not unprecedented: schools in the University of California system were free for many decades, as was the City College of New York. Moreover, other countries – such as Germany, Norway, and Sweden – offer tuition-free college to citizens. Supporters of this position assert that colleges and universities function as a public good that drives economic mobility and other social benefits. Opponents, however, are quick to point out that "free" colleges are not literally free: the financial burden is merely transferred from students to taxpayers.

The following two selections take opposing points of view on this issue. In "Public Universities Should Be Free," Aaron Bady sees the current system of public higher education as "public" in name only given that these colleges charge tuition. He asks, "If an education is available only to those who can afford it – if an education is a commodity to be purchased in the marketplace – in what sense can it really be called public?" While Bady focuses on the word *public,* Matt Bruenig, in "The Case against Free College, "focuses on the word *free.* Bruenig argues that "free college" would, paradoxically, undermine egalitarian social goals by "giving far more money to students from richer families than from poorer ones."

AARON BADY

Public Universities Should Be Free

Aaron Bady is a postdoctoral fellow at the University of Texas, where he teaches African literature. He is an editor at the *New Inquiry* as well as a blogger at zunguzungu. His work has also appeared in the *New Republic*, the *Nation, Pacific Standard*, and other publications.

Background on public education in the United States The history of public schooling in the United States predates the official founding of the country. In 1647, for example, the Massachusetts Bay Colony passed the Old Deluder Act, which (among other provisions) mandated "that every township . . . after the Lord hath increased them to fifty households shall forthwith appoint one within their town to teach all such children as shall resort to him to write and read." Later, both George Washington and Thomas Jefferson also advocated public education. Jefferson unsuccessfully proposed various policies throughout his lifetime, including the tax-funded Bill for the More General Diffusion of Knowledge (1779) and the Elementary School Act (1817). In his view, an educated populace was necessary to preserve a democratic republic. (Of course, Jefferson's notion of public schooling limited access to white males, and he generally opposed compulsory education.) In the nineteenth century, Horace Mann, a member of the Massachusetts Congress, helped establish secular, standardized public schools in his state that were soon emulated in New York State and elsewhere. At the college level, the University of Georgia and the University of North Carolina were established as public institutions in the late eighteenth century. However, a more comprehensive public university system was not created until the passage of the Morrill Land-Grant Acts, starting in 1862: these statutes provided public lands for the creation of state- and federally-funded universities throughout the United States, such as Kansas State University, Michigan State University, and Pennsylvania State University. In addition, public junior colleges and "normal schools," two-year postsecondary institutions that began training students in the nineteenth century, have evolved into a community college system that now educates more than seven million students a year.

Public education should be free. If it isn't free, it isn't public education. 1

This should not be a controversial assertion. This should be common 2 sense. But Americans have forgotten what the "public" in "public education" actually means (or used to mean). The problem is that the word no longer has anything to refer to: This country's public universities have been radically transformed. The change has happened so slowly and so gradually—bit by bit, cut by cut over half a century—that it can be seen really only in retrospect. But with just a small amount of historical perspective, the change is dramatic: public universities that once charged themselves to open their doors to all who could benefit by attending—that were, by definition, the public property of the entire state—have become something entirely different.

"What we still call public universities would be more accurately described as state-controlled private universities—corporate entities that think and behave like businesses."

3 What we still call public universities would be more accurately described as state-controlled private universities—corporate entities that think and behave like businesses. Whereas there once was a public mission to educate the republic's citizens, there is now the goal of satisfying the educational needs of the market, aided by PR departments that brand degrees as commodities and build consumer interest, always with an eye to the bottom line. And while public universities once sought to advance the industry of the state as a whole, with an eye to the common good, shortfalls in public funding have led to universities' treating their research capacity as a source of primary fundraising, developing new technologies and products for the private sector, explicitly to raise the money they need to operate. Conflicts of interest are now commonplace.

4 Should public universities be free? Only because our public universities have been so fundamentally privatized over the last 40 years does the sentence "Public universities should be free" even make sense. Of course they should be free! If an education is available only to those who can afford it—if an education is a commodity to be purchased in the marketplace—in what sense can it really be called public?

Let There Be Light

5 In the early 1960s, California formulated a master plan for higher education—a single name for a set of interlocking policies developed by University of California president Clark Kerr. The idea was that any Californian who wanted a postsecondary education would have a place to go in the state's three-tiered system. Students could go to a community college for free, and from there they could transfer to a California State University or a University of California—where no tuition was charged, only course fees that were intended to be nominal. New universities were swiftly planned and built to meet the dramatic increase in demand expected from baby boomers and the state's growing population; as more and more citizens aspired to higher education, California opened more and more classrooms and universities to give them that opportunity. The master plan was not a blank check, but it was a commitment: any Californian who wanted a postsecondary education could get one.

6 Today that is simply not true. For one thing, institutions like the University of California have not grown to meet the rising demand; year by year, bit by bit, as the state's population has continued to grow, a larger percentage of California students have been turned away or replaced by out-of-state students

(who pay much higher tuition). In fact, university officials are quite explicit about the fact that they are admitting more out-of-state and international students (and fewer Californians) in order to raise money. Historically, about 10 percent of the U.C.'s student population was from out of state, but that number has more than doubled since the 2008 financial crisis. (In Michigan, which has been hit even harder than California, out-of-state enrollment in the University of Michigan system is closer to 40 percent.)

Most important, as tuition steadily rises to the level of comparable private universities, the word "public" comes to mean less and less. Indeed, when Mark Yudof was appointed president of the University of California in 2008, he was known as an advocate of what he had called in 2002 the hybrid university: an institution that retained some of the characteristics of a public university but would draw the bulk of its revenue from student tuition. 7

Yudof's vision of the "public" university would have been unrecognizable to the architects of the master plan: instead of providing the tools for the state's citizens to better themselves, state universities are to survive by thinking like a business, selling their product for as much as the market will bear. From the point of view of higher-education consumers — which are what its students have effectively become — the claim that the U.C. system is public rings increasingly false with every passing year. 8

For my parents, by contrast, distinction between public and private was very clear. Both baby boomers and the first in their families to get college degrees, they went to public universities because they were affordable and private universities were not. By that definition, are there any public universities left? Schools that are at least partially funded and controlled by elected officials, usually at the state level, are nominally public, and the broad range of universities that are not owned by the government — from nonprofit corporations like Harvard to explicitly for-profit corporations like the University of Phoenix or Udacity — truly inhabit the private sector. But if the price tag is the same, if the product is the same, and if the experience is the same, what difference does a university's tax status make? A university that thinks and behaves like a private-sector corporation — charging its consumers what the market will bear, cutting costs wherever it can, and using competition with its peers as its measure of success — is a public university in name only. 9

Open Roads and Toll Roads

A better way to compare public and private would be to consider the difference between public roads and toll roads. Some toll roads are owned and operated by state governments and some by the private sector. But does the driver care who owns the road? I doubt it; the important thing is whether the road is free and open to all or whether it can be used only by those who can afford to drive on it. The same is true of public and private universities: A university is public only if those who need to use it can do so. 10

In this sense, it seems to me that the malaise that afflicts our public universities is not really about dollars and cents. If this country can build the world's largest military and fight open-ended wars in multiple theaters across 11 the globe, it can find a way to pay for public education, as it once did in living memory. But doing so has ceased to be a real priority. Affordable public education is no longer something we expect, demand, or take for granted; to argue that public education should be free makes you sound like an absurd and unrealistic utopian. Meanwhile, we take it for granted that roads should be free to drive on, a toll road here or there not withstanding. You provide the car and the gas; the state provides the road.

This used to be how we thought about our public universities, before they became exorbitant toll roads. If you had the grades and the ambition, there was a classroom open to you. But if every road were a toll road, no one would expect to drive for free. If every road were a toll road, the very idea that the government would build and maintain a massive system of roads and highways—and then let anyone use it (for free!)—would seem fantastical, ridiculous, even perverse. People expecting the right to drive anywhere they pleased, for free, would be branded utopian, socialist, and deluded, soft-hearted liberals demanding a free lunch. That's the world we live in when it comes to highways. When the roads that drive our economy and make modern life possible get too crowded or too congested, we expect the state to build new roads. When the old roads wear out, they are repaved. When a tree or a landslide obstructs a thoroughfare, the state clears the way. When there are not enough classrooms, on the other hand, the state no longer builds new universities; it simply charges more. 12

For most of the twentieth century, when the overwhelming majority of this country's public universities were built, it was simply common sense that a growing college-age population had to be matched by a growing system of accessible higher education, something that—as everyone agreed—only the government could provide and that only the government did provide. They were explicitly chartered to bring a college degree within the reach of as many citizens as possible and to advance the greater good by disseminating knowledge as widely as possible. Without that common sense, that bipartisan consensus, our public universities would never have been built in the first place. And judged by that original standard, there are few, if any, public universities left. 13

• • •

Comprehension

1. Bady notes that we still use the term *public universities*. In his view, what might be a more accurate description of these institutions?
2. List the elements of the causal chain Bady traces in paragraph 3.
3. According to Bady, how has public higher education in California changed in recent decades?
4. What is the "hybrid university" (7)? How is it different from Bady's idea of a public university?
5. In Bady's view, how do state universities now "survive"? How is their mission today different from what it was in the past?

Purpose and Audience

1. What is Bady's purpose in writing this essay?
2. Bady writes, "Only because our public universities have been so fundamentally privatized over the last 40 years does the sentence 'Public universities should be free' even make sense" (4). Why is this claim important to his purpose? What does it suggest about his understanding of his readers?
3. In paragraph 5, Bady focuses on the history of public higher education in California. Why do you think he chose this example?
4. How does Bady seem to characterize his audience? For example, does he think readers will be receptive to his argument? Does he see them as skeptical? As hostile? Explain your answer.

Style and Structure

1. What is Bady's thesis? Where is it stated? Why do you think he chose to place it where he does?
2. Where in this essay does Bady use **definition**? Why is definition so important to his argument?
3. Bady writes that if public education "isn't free, it isn't public education" (1). Is he committing the false dilemma fallacy by presenting his argument in this way? Explain.
4. **Vocabulary Project.** Bady writes that "to argue that public education should be free makes you sound like [a] . . . utopian" (11). What does he mean here by *utopian*? Why is the connotation of *utopian* in this context important to his argument?
5. Does Bady address counterarguments in this essay? If so, where and how effectively? If he does not address opposing arguments, do you think he should have? Why or why not?

Journal Entry

Bady writes that public universities were "chartered to bring a college degree within the reach of as many citizens as possible and to advance the greater good by disseminating knowledge as widely as possible" (13). Do you think this goal has been achieved? Do you think this goal still makes sense? Why or why not?

Writing Workshop

1. **Working with Sources.** After reading both Bady's argument and Matt Bruenig's "The Case against Free College" (page 581), where do you stand on the issue of whether public colleges and universities should be free? Write an argumentative essay that presents and supports your position. You should cite these two essays as sources, but you can also do further research. Be sure to document all the sources you use and to include a works-cited page. (See Chapter 18 for information on MLA documentation.)

2. In paragraph 3, Bady claims that, increasingly, public universities present "degrees as commodities." Later in the essay, he writes, "From the point of view of higher-education consumers – which are what its students have effectively become – the claim that the U.C. system is public rings increasingly false with every passing year" (8). Does it make sense to view college degrees as "commodities"? Is it logical to see students, ultimately, as "consumers"? Do you see any problems with this consumer model of higher education? Where do we draw the line between "student" and "consumer"? Write an essay that explores and addresses these questions.
3. Bady uses paragraphs 10 through 12 to develop an analogy between private and public universities and toll roads. Write an argumentative essay that develops an analogy of your own for public higher education. For example, you might consider comparisons within health care, recreation, public utilities, or consumer goods.

Combining the Patterns

How does Bady use **comparison and contrast** in this essay? Why are comparison and contrast so central to his purpose and main idea? How does he combine comparison and contrast with definition?

Thematic Connections

- "Indian Education" (page 140)
- "Why the Post Office Makes America Great" (page 220)
- "Get It Right: Privatize Executions" (page 292)
- "I'm Your Teacher, Not Your Internet-Service Provider" (page 409)

MATT BRUENIG

The Case against Free College

Matt Bruenig is a writer, blogger, and activist who focuses on poverty, inequality, and welfare. Formerly a blogger at *Demos*, a liberal research and policy institute, Bruenig has written for *Jacobin, Salon,* and the *Washington Post*, among other publications.

Background on the rising cost of college and student debt According to most accounts, the cost of attending college over the last 60 years was relatively stable until the late 1970s and early 1980s. Indeed, observers at the time noticed a shift, as indicated by a 1981 *New York Times* article entitled "The $10,000-a-Year College Education Has Arrived." It may have arrived, but it was only just getting started. Between 1978 and 2012, tuitions and fees increased 1,120 percent, dwarfing increases in the consumer price index, health-care expenses, and the price of food. Politicians, critics, and policy specialists cite various reasons for the increase, including the rising salaries of administrators; the heightened expectations of students, who now expect campus amenities as part of their college experience; a prevailing view that universities should be run like corporations; a decrease in public funding for state schools; and even inflation caused by the wide availability of student aid. Regardless of the cause, overall student debt now is now well over $1 trillion and rising, and the average graduate now leaves college with almost $30,000 in loans to repay. The student loan default rate appears to have peaked at 13.7 percent in 2014, but it remains well over 10 percent today.

In the United States, as in much of the rest of the world, college students receive three kinds of public benefits: tuition subsidies, living grants, and public loans. Through various combinations of this benefit troika, almost all students are able to finance their college education. Some on the left are very unhappy with the precise mix of student benefits currently on offer. Student debt activists, among others, complain that tuition subsidies and living grants make up too little of the student benefit bundle, while public loans make up too much of it. 1

Recently, this complaint has begun to coalesce into a number of movements and proposals for "free college." I put the phrase in quotes because it means different things to different people. For some, "free college" means subsidizing tuition to zero. For others, it means subsidizing tuition to zero and providing living grants high enough to completely cover room and board. For still others, it appears to mean putting in place some mix of means-tested tuition subsidies, living grants, and even subsidized work-study jobs that, combined with expected parental assistance, allow nearly all students to leave college with little to no debt. 2

One could write at great length about these different conceptions of "free" and the policy proposals that have formed around them. For instance, 3 since people who do not attend college also have housing and food costs, is it really correct to say room and board is a cost of attending college? Why do none of these conceptions consider as a cost of college all of the potential wages students forego by choosing to study rather than work? Does parental assistance with college really help to make it free or is it more properly understood as a family wealth transfer that students then pay towards their higher education?

"Of greater importance than all of those questions, however, is the more basic question about the fairness of free college as an idea."

4 Of greater importance than all of those questions, however, is the more basic question about the fairness of free college as an idea. Those clamoring for free college make normative claims about the nature of a just and good society. As currently argued, however, these claims are largely uncompelling. Without a dramatic overhaul of how we understand student benefits, making college more or entirely free would most likely boost the wealth of college attendees without securing any important egalitarian gains.

5 The main problem with free college is that most students come from disproportionately well-off backgrounds and already enjoy disproportionately well-off futures, which makes them relatively uncompelling targets for public transfers. At age nineteen, only around 20 percent of children from the poorest 2 percent of families in the country attend college. For the richest 2 percent of families, the same number is around 90 percent. In between these two extremes, college attendance rates climb practically straight up the income ladder: the richer your parents are, the greater the likelihood that you are in college at age nineteen. The relatively few poor kids who do attend college heavily cluster in two-year community colleges and cheaper, less selective four-year colleges, while richer kids are likely to attend more expensive four-year institutions. At public colleges (the type we'd likely make free), students from the poorest fourth of the population currently pay no net tuition at either two-year or four-year institutions, while also receiving an average of $3,080 and $2,320 respectively to offset some of their annual living expenses. Richer students currently receive much fewer tuition and living grant benefits.

6 Given these class-based differences in attendance levels, institutional selection, and current student benefit levels, making college free for everyone would almost certainly mean giving far more money to students from richer families than from poorer ones. Of course, providing more generous student benefits might alter these class-based skews a bit by encouraging more poor and middle-class people to go to college or to attend more expensive institutions. But even reasonably accounting for those kinds of responses, the primary result of such increased student benefit generosity would be to fill the pockets of richer students and their families.

7 Student benefit campaigners tend not to focus on these sorts of distributive questions, preferring instead to gesture towards a supposed student debt crisis to prove that those who attended college really are a hurting class

needing higher benefits. While there are certain extreme cases of students with very high debts, and certain college sectors such as for-profits that are truly immiserating specific groups of students, the reality remains that college graduates are generally on track for much better financial outcomes than non-attendees. Even in the wake of the Great Recession, which hit young people harder than anyone else, those with bachelor's degrees had median personal incomes $17,500 higher than young high school graduates. Just one year of this income premium would be enough to wipe out the median debt of a public four-year-college graduate, which currently stands slightly above $10,000.

Although extending extra benefits to such a disproportionately well-off group is a deeply suspicious idea, the way American student benefit campaigners talk about it is somehow worse still. Due to the toxic American mix of aversion to welfare benefits, love of individual rights, and faith in meritocracy, the typical line you hear about free college is that it should be a right of students because they have worked hard and done everything right. The implicit suggestion of such rhetoric is that students are really owed free college as the reward for not being like those less virtuous high school graduates who refuse to do what it takes to better themselves through education. 8

Needless to say, such thinking is extremely damaging to a broader egalitarian project, even more so in some ways than its goal of setting aside a part of our national income for the inegalitarian aim of making college free. If we are actually going to push a free college agenda, it should not be under a restrictive students' rights banner, but instead under a general pro-welfare banner. The goal of free college should not be to help students *per se*, but instead to bind them to a broader welfare benefit system. By presenting their tuition subsidies and living grants as indistinguishable from benefits for the disabled, the poor, the elderly, and so on, it may be possible to encourage wealthier students to support the welfare state and to undermine students' future claims of entitlement to the high incomes that college graduates so often receive. After all, the college income premium would only be possible through the welfare benefits to which the rest of society – including those who never went to college – has contributed. 9

Without understanding and presenting student benefits as welfare handouts, a free college agenda has no real egalitarian purpose. Giving extra money to a class of disproportionately well-off people without securing any reciprocal benefit to poor and working-class people who so often do not attend college, all while valorizing the college student as a virtuous person individually deserving of such benefits, would be at worst destructive, and at best, totally pointless. 10

• • •

Comprehension

1. Why does Bruenig place quotation marks around "free college" in paragraph 2?
2. In paragraph 2, Bruenig refers to "means-tested tuition subsidies." What does the term *means-tested* mean?

3. According to Bruenig, what is the primary problem with free college?
4. Bruenig believes current "student benefit campaigners" are focusing on the wrong issue. What does he mean?
5. What is Bruenig's attitude toward the "welfare state"? Do you agree with his view? Why or why not?

Purpose and Audience

1. Restate the thesis of this essay in your own words.
2. In paragraph 9, Bruenig cites "a broader egalitarian project." What does this project seem to be? How is it related to the overall purpose of this essay?
3. Bruenig takes a critical view of advocates seeking to make college more affordable and alleviate the burden of student debt. Is his purpose in this essay to persuade these "benefit campaigners"? Do they seem to be part of his primary audience? Explain.
4. What preconceptions does Bruenig think his readers might have? How does he address these preconceptions?

Style and Structure

1. Describe the relationship between paragraphs 2 and 3. What purpose does each of these paragraphs serve?
2. What causal relationships does Bruenig suggest in paragraph 5? Why are these relationships important for his argument?
3. **Vocabulary Project.** In paragraph 8, Bruenig refers to the American "faith in meritocracy." What is a meritocracy? What connotations does this word have? Does Bruenig's use of this term make sense within the context of his overall argument?
4. What kind of reasoning – **inductive** or **deductive** – does Bruenig use in paragraph 9? Explain your answer.

Journal Entry

How does Bruenig's argument apply to your own experience as a student, particularly in the context of funding your education? For example, is college "free" for you in any of the senses he describes? Should it be?

Writing Workshop

1. **Working with Sources.** According to Bruenig, free college "means different things to different people" (2). What does it mean to you? Write an essay in which you define "free college," and take a position on whether higher education should be "free." Document all references to Bruenig and to any other sources you use, and be sure to include a works-cited page. (See Chapter 18 for information on MLA documentation.)

2. **Working with Sources.** In paragraph 8, Bruenig writes, "Due to the toxic American mix of aversion to welfare benefits, love of individual rights, and faith in meritocracy, the typical line you hear about free college is that it should be a right of students because they have worked hard and done everything right." Do you agree with his generalizations about Americans and this "toxic American mix" of attitudes? Do you agree with his suggestions about welfare benefits, individual rights, and meritocracy? Write an argumentative essay that responds to these related claims, using Bruenig's essay as a source and quoting from it in your own essay. Be sure to document references to Bruenig and to any other sources you use, and include a works-cited page. (See Chapter 18 for information on MLA documentation.)
3. In Bruenig's view, people "clamoring for free college make normative claims about the nature of a just and good society" (4). A "normative claim" is a statement about the way things should be or ought to be. In your view, what is the relationship between access to higher education and "a just and good society"? For example, is a society in which more people can afford to go to college necessarily more "just" and "good" than one in which fewer people have access to higher education? Write an argumentative essay that explores this normative claim.

Combining the Patterns

Where in this essay does Bruenig use **classification and division**? How does his use of this pattern of development support his overall argument?

Thematic Connections

- "Why the Post Office Makes America Great" (page 220)
- "Ten Ways We Get the Odds Wrong" (page 245)
- "The Lottery" (page 304)
- "Free Expression in Peril" (page 609)

✶DEBATE

Does It Pay to Study the Humanities?

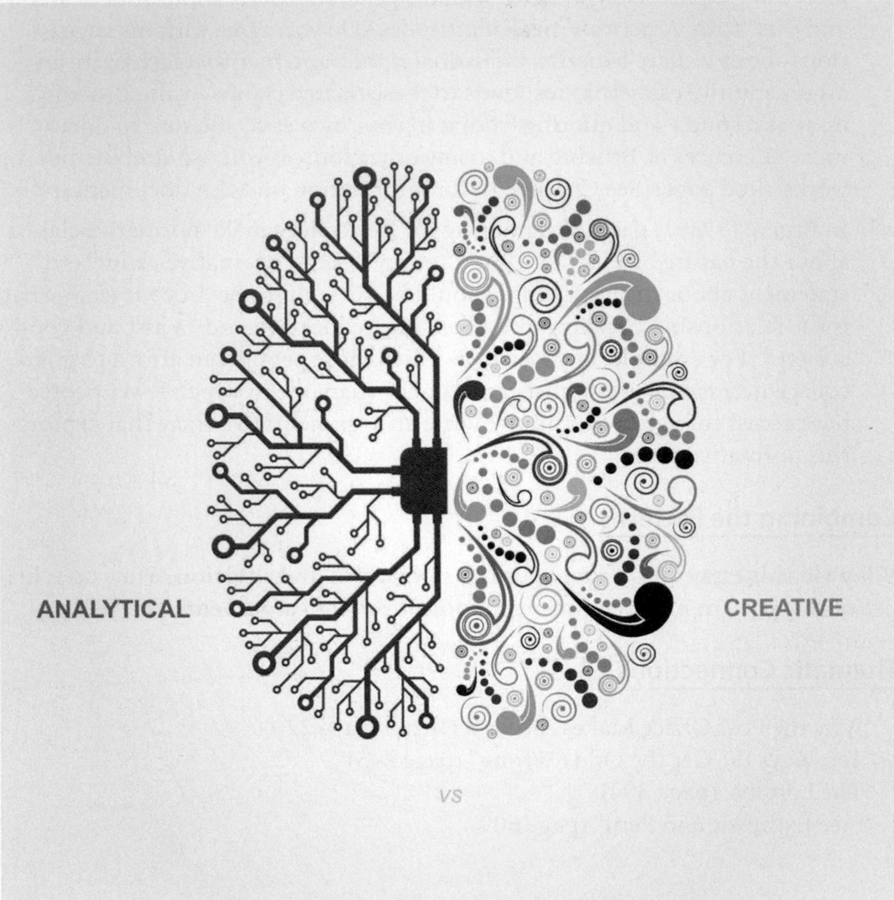

© Shai_Halud/Shutterstock

Artist Shai Halud represents the two sides of the brain visually. These same categories of analytical and creative thinking are often viewed as the crux of the debate between STEM subjects (science, technology, engineering, and math) versus the humanities.

• • •

The rising costs of higher education, the effects of the 2008 economic crisis, and the pressures of finding employment in a competitive global economy have caused many people to question the value of majoring in the humanities in college. As former Republican presidential nominee Marco Rubio bluntly asserted in a 2015 primary debate, "We need more welders and less philosophers." That skepticism has gone beyond mere political rhetoric. In Kentucky, for example, Governor Matt Bevin proposed that colleges and universities receive more public funding for fields like engineering and less public funding for liberal arts and the humanities. According to Bevin, "All the people in the world that want to study French literature can do so. They are just not going to be subsidized by the taxpayer." At the national level, former President Barack Obama proposed initiatives that emphasize the primacy of science, technology, engineering, and mathematics.

Career-minded college students seem to have accepted this shift toward a utilitarian view of higher education. Indeed, the number of bachelor's degrees granted in subjects like literature, history, classics, and philosophy has fallen overall in the past decade. That is probably because the demand for—and starting salaries of—those who graduate with degrees in accounting and engineering are much higher than those who graduate with degrees in English or philosophy. As a result, some institutions have eliminated specific humanities departments; in other cases, smaller liberal arts colleges, such as Sweet Briar College, have closed altogether.

Defenders of the humanities say reports of the death of the liberal arts have been greatly exaggerated. They note that the major decline in the relative number of humanities degrees actually occurred in the 1970s. Others argue that by sharpening reading, writing, and critical thinking skills, the humanities provide relevant training for the contemporary economy. They point out that humanities majors succeed in law, marketing, education, government, and business and that employers actually want flexible, sociable, adaptable, and versatile employees who can think critically and learn new skills. Finally, advocates of the humanities say the emphasis on specialization and practicality misses a larger point: people grounded in the humanities are not only ready for careers, but they are also ready to take their place as citizens in a democracy.

The tension between the humanities and utilitarian learning is not new. For example, in his treatise *The Idea of a University* (1852), the English theologian and educator John Henry Newman addressed those who questioned the "market" value of a liberal arts education. For Newman, narrow minds are born out of narrow specialization, and a utilitarian education is no education at all. The two essays in this debate address the tension between learning for the sake of learning and learning to gain job skills. For Leon Wieseltier, those who study the humanities are not merely learning about art or literature; they are "uphold[ing] the honor of a civilization that was founded upon the quest for the true and the good and the beautiful." In contrast, Vinod Khosla sees the traditional liberal arts curriculum as outdated and unsuited for the problems and opportunities of the twenty-first century.

LEON WIESELTIER

Perhaps Culture Is Now the Counterculture: A Defense of the Humanities

American writer and critic Leon Wieseltier (b. 1952) was a long-time literary editor at the *New Republic* magazine. He is currently a fellow at the Brookings Institution, a social science research organization, as well as a contributing editor at the *Atlantic*. He is the author of *Against Identity* (1996) and *Kaddish* (1998), and the editor of *The Moral Obligation to Be Intelligent: Selected Essays* (2000), a collection of essays by the literary critic Lionel Trilling.

Background on C. P. Snow's *The Two Cultures* The cultural divide that separates two great areas of intellectual activity — the sciences and the humanities — has long been a source of debate. In 1959, for example, the English scientist and novelist C. P. Snow gave a lecture at Cambridge University in which he identified a divide between two groups in modern intellectual life: "Literary intellectuals at one pole — at the other, scientists, and as the most representative, physical scientists." In between, Snow saw a "gulf of mutual incomprehension — sometimes . . . hostility and dislike." He especially lamented the lack of appreciation among elite humanists for the physical sciences, which (in his view) were "the most beautiful and wonderful collective work of the mind of man." Snow argued that part of the problem was an English educational system that emphasized (and privileged) the humanities over engineering and the sciences. The lecture was well received and was subsequently published as a book under the title *The Two Cultures and the Scientific Revolution*. It also provoked a scathing attack from the eminent English literary critic F. R. Leavis, who found Snow "portentously ignorant." Leavis's response merely reaffirmed the gulf between humanists and scientists, even as he conceded that scientific education needed to be improved.

Has there ever been a moment in American life when the humanities were cherished less, and has there ever been a moment in American life when the humanities were needed more? I am genuinely honored to be addressing you this morning, because in recent years I have come to regard a commitment to the humanities as nothing less than an act of intellectual defiance, of cultural dissidence. 1

For decades now in America we have been witnessing a steady and sickening denigration of humanistic understanding and humanistic method. We live in a society inebriated by technology, and happily, even giddily governed by the values of utility, speed, efficiency, and convenience. The technological mentality that has become the American worldview instructs us to prefer practical questions to questions of meaning—to ask of things not if they are true or false, or good or evil, but how they work. Our reason has 2 become an instrumental reason, and is no longer the reason of the philosophers, with its ancient magnitude of intellectual ambition, its belief that the proper subjects of human thought are the largest subjects, and that the mind, in one way or another, can penetrate to the very principles of natural life and human life. Philosophy itself has shrunk under the influence of our weakness for instrumentality – modern American philosophy was in fact one of the causes of that weakness – and generally it, too, prefers to tinker and to tweak.

3 The machines to which we have become enslaved, all of them quite astonishing, represent the greatest assault on human attention ever devised: they are engines of mental and spiritual dispersal, which make us wider only by making us less deep. There are thinkers, reputable ones if you can believe it, who proclaim that the exponential growth in computational ability will soon take us beyond the finitude of our bodies and our minds so that, as one of them puts it, there will no longer be any difference between human and machine. La Mettrie* lives in Silicon Valley. This, of course, is not an apotheosis of the human but an abolition of the human; but Google is very excited by it.

"The machines to which we have become enslaved, all of them quite astonishing, represent the greatest assault on human attention ever devised..."

4 In the digital universe, knowledge is reduced to the status of information. Who will any longer remember that knowledge is to information as art is to kitsch** – that information is the most inferior kind of knowledge, because it is the most external? A great Jewish thinker of the early Middle Ages wondered why God, if He wanted us to know the truth about everything, did not simply tell us the truth about everything. His wise answer was that if we were merely told what we need to know, we would not, strictly speaking, know it. Knowledge can be acquired only over time and only by method. And the devices that we carry like addicts in our hands are disfiguring our mental lives also in other ways: for example, they generate a hitherto unimaginable number of numbers, numbers about everything under the sun, and so they are transforming us into a culture of data, into a cult of data, in which no human activity and no human expression is immune to quantification, in which happiness is a fit subject for economists, in which the ordeals of the human heart are inappropriately translated into mathematical expressions, leaving us with new illusions of clarity and new illusions of control.

5 Our glittering age of technologism is also a glittering age of scientism. Scientism is not the same thing as science. Science is a blessing, but scientism is a curse. Science, I mean what practicing scientists actually do, is acutely and

* Eds. note – Julien Offray de La Mettrie (1709–1751), French materialist philosopher who conceived of human beings as machines.

** Eds. note – Artistic objects, texts, decorations, or music considered tasteless and sentimental, but still appreciated in an ironic or knowing way.

admirably aware of its limits, and humbly admits to the provisional character of its conclusions; but scientism is dogmatic, and peddles certainties. It is always at the ready with the solution to every problem, because it believes that the solution to every problem is a scientific one, and so it gives scientific answers to non-scientific questions. But even the question of the place of science in human existence is not a scientific question. It is a philosophical, which is to say, a humanistic, question.

Owing to its preference for totalistic explanation, scientism transforms 6
science into an ideology, which is of course a betrayal of the experimental and empirical spirit. There is no perplexity of human emotion or human behavior that these days is not accounted for genetically or in the cocksure terms of evolutionary biology. It is true that the selfish gene has lately been replaced by the altruistic gene, which is lovelier, but it is still the gene that tyrannically rules. Liberal scientism should be no more philosophically attractive to us than conservative scientism, insofar as it, too, arrogantly reduces all the realms that we inhabit to a single realm, and tempts us into the belief that the epistemological eschaton has finally arrived, and at last we know what we need to know to manipulate human affairs wisely. This belief is invariably false and occasionally disastrous. We are becoming ignorant of ignorance.

So there is no task more urgent in American intellectual life at this hour 7
than to offer some resistance to the twin imperialisms of science and technology, and to recover the old distinction – once bitterly contested, then generally accepted, now almost completely forgotten – between the study of nature and the study of man. As Bernard Williams* once remarked, "'humanity' is a name not merely for a species but also for a quality." You who have elected to devote yourselves to the study of literature and languages and art and music and philosophy and religion and history – you are the stewards of that quality. You are the resistance. You have had the effrontery to choose interpretation over calculation, and to recognize that calculation cannot provide an accurate picture, or a profound picture, or a whole picture, of self-interpreting beings such as ourselves; and I commend you for it.

Do not believe the rumors of the obsolescence of your path. If Proust 8
was a neuroscientist,** then you have no urgent need of neuroscience, because you have Proust. If Jane Austen was a game theorist, then you have no reason to defect to game theory, because you have Austen. There is no greater bulwark against the twittering acceleration of American consciousness than the encounter with a work of art, and the experience of a text or an image. You are the representatives, the saving remnants, of that encounter and that experience, and of the serious study of that encounter and that experience – which is to say, you are the counterculture. Perhaps culture is now the counterculture.

---

* Eds. note – English philosopher (1929–2003).

** Eds. note – Wieseltier refers to the 2007 book *Proust Was a Neuroscientist* and the 2013 book *Jane Austen, Game Theorist,* which consider the value of these writers in the context of contemporary science.

So keep your heads. Do not waver. Be very proud. Use the new technologies for the old purposes. Do not be rattled by numbers, which will never be the springs of wisdom. In upholding the humanities, you uphold the honor of a civilization that was founded upon the quest for the true and the good and the beautiful. For as long as we are thinking and feeling creatures, creatures who love and imagine and suffer and die, the humanities will never be dispensable. From this day forward, then, act as if you are indispensable to your society, because – whether it knows it or not – you are. 9

Congratulations. 10

• • •

Comprehension

1. What is the difference between the "reason of the philosophers" and "instrumental reason" (2)?
2. How does Wieseltier distinguish between "knowledge" and "information"? Which one, according to him, is superior? Why?
3. Why does Wieseltier call science and technology "twin imperialisms," and why is resisting them the most urgent task "in American intellectual life" (7)?
4. According to Wieseltier, what is civilization founded upon? Do you agree? Explain.
5. In paragraph 8, Wieseltier says, "Perhaps culture is now the counterculture." In what sense is this statement a **paradox**?

Purpose and Audience

1. This selection was originally a speech given at a Brandeis University commencement ceremony. Wieseltier address his remarks to his "fellow humanists." What does he assume about his audience, and how are these assumptions reflected in his speech?
2. What is Wieseltier's thesis? Restate it in your own words.
3. Wieseltier spends part of his speech criticizing certain uses of "reason." Is he rejecting appeals to logic in his argument? Why or why not?
4. What is Wieseltier's purpose in making his speech? Is he trying to change people's minds? Move them to action? Something else?

Style and Structure

1. Wieseltier begins his speech with a question. Does he eventually answer this question? If not, should he have?
2. Does Wieseltier address – or make concessions to – opposing points of view? If not, should he have? Why or why not?

3. In paragraph 4, Wieseltier asks, "Who will any longer remember that knowledge is to information as art is to kitsch"? What two things does he compare in his analogy? What point is he making?
4. **Vocabulary Project.** Wieseltier uses several words that may be unfamiliar, including *kitsch* (4), *technologism* (5), *scientism* (5), and *eschaton* (6). If you do not know what these terms mean, look up their definitions. Would it be possible to replace any of these unusual words with more accessible and familiar language and still retain the writer's meaning? Explain.
5. Find examples of Wieseltier's use of **hyperbole**. Why do you think he uses hyperbole? Does the use of this figure of speech help or hurt his argument?
6. What point does Wieseltier make in his conclusion? Do you think he should have emphasized something else? Explain.

Journal Entry

Assume you are the parent of a member of the graduating class at Brandeis, where this talk was first given. How would you respond to Wieseltier's speech? Would his argument influence or change your thinking about the humanities and their value? Why or why not?

Writing Workshop

1. **Working with Sources.** Wieseltier claims we live in "a glittering age of scientism" (5). For the most part, however, he does not include specific examples to support his point. What contemporary examples of "scientism" can you find? Do you agree with Wieseltier's negative view of scientism? Are his claims about it fair? Write an argumentative essay that answers these questions. Be sure to document all references to your sources and to include a works-cited page. (See Chapter 18 for information on MLA documentation.)
2. In paragraph 3, Wieseltier says, "The machines to which we have become enslaved, all of them quite astonishing, represent the greatest assault on human attention ever devised: they are engines of mental and spiritual dispersal, which make us wider only by making us less deep." Do you agree with the charge that technology is, in some ways, harmful to humanity? Write an argumentative essay that agrees or disagrees with his assertion. Be sure to discuss some of the "machines" with which you are familiar, such as smartphones, computers, and video game consoles.
3. **Working with Sources.** Wieseltier writes about the power and importance of our "encounter[s] with a work of art, and the experience[s] of a text or an image" (8). For him, they are a defense against the scattering and dehumanizing effects of "scientism" and "technologism." Write an essay about your own experiences or encounters with art, literature, or any other form of the humanities. Do you agree or disagree that these encounters serve

the purpose Wieseltier claims they do? (You may want to write about a specific text or image.) Be sure to document all references to your sources and to include a works-cited page. (See Chapter 18 for information on MLA documentation.)

Combining the Patterns

Where does Wieseltier use **comparison and contrast** in this essay? Why do you think this pattern is important to his argument as well as to his overall purpose?

Thematic Connections

- "Ten Ways We Get the Odds Wrong" (page 245)
- "The Three Types of Happiness" (page 448)
- "Warning: The Literary Canon Could Make Students Squirm" (page 621)

VINOD KHOSLA

Is Majoring in Liberal Arts a Mistake for Students?

Born in New Delhi, India, in 1955, Vinod Khosla was educated at the Indian Institute of Technology, Carnegie Mellon University, and the Stanford University Graduate School of Business. He cofounded the computer and information technology company Sun Microsystems in 1982; he also served as its chief executive officer and chairman. In 2004, he founded Khosla Ventures, a venture capital firm focused on the technology and space sectors.

Background on college majors Although people argue about the value of a four-year liberal arts degree, this debate can be misleading because it implies that such majors are more popular than they actually are. For more than two decades, the most popular undergraduate major has been business. In 2012 and 2013, for example, 361,000 business-related undergraduate degrees were conferred, about 20 percent of all college graduates. This major is followed in popularity by the health professions, which currently account for about 10 percent of all graduates. If these figures are compared with the percentage of students getting degrees in humanities (less than 3 percent), foreign languages (less than 2 percent), or philosophy (less than 1 percent), the disparity seems to support the assertion that the liberal arts are in decline. This narrative of decline is misleading, however. The percentage of English, philosophy, history, and other, similar majors has remained steady for more than three decades. Moreover, the increasing popularity of visual and performing arts majors seems to indicate that many students still believe they should "pursue their passion."

Critical Thinking and the Scientific Process First — Humanities Later

If luck favors the prepared mind, as Louis Pasteur is credited with saying, we're in danger of becoming a very unlucky nation. Little of the material taught in Liberal Arts programs today is relevant to the future. 1

Consider all the science and economics that has been updated, the shifting theories of psychology, the programming languages and political theories that have been developed, and even how many planets our solar system has. Much, like literature and history, should be evaluated against updated, relevant priorities in the twenty-first century. 2

I feel that liberal arts education in the United States is a minor evolution of eighteenth century European education. The world needs something more than that. Non-professional undergraduate education needs a new system that teaches students how to learn and judge using the scientific process on issues relating to science, society, and business. 3

Though Jane Austen and Shakespeare might be important, they are far less important than many other things that are more relevant to make an 4 intelligent, continuously learning citizen, and a more adaptable human being in our increasingly more complex, diverse, and dynamic world.

I would coin a new term, "the liberal sciences," as this basic education, the test for which would be quite simple: at the end of an undergraduate education, is a student roughly able to understand and discuss the *Economist,** end-to-end, every week. This modern, non-professional education would meet the original "Greek life purpose" of a liberal arts education, updated for today's world. 5

The most important things for a general, non-professional, or vocational education are critical thinking and problem-solving skills, familiarity with logic and the scientific process, and the ability to use these in forming opinions, discourse, and in making decisions. Other general skills that are also important include – but are not limited to – interpersonal skills and communication skills. 6

So What Is Wrong with Today's Typical Liberal Arts Degree?

Neither the old definition of liberal arts nor the current implementation of it is the best use of four years of somebody's education (if it is to be non-professional). The hardest (and most lucrative) problems to solve are non-technical problems. In my opinion, getting a STEM degree gives you the tools to think about those problems more effectively than a liberal arts degree today; though it is far from a complete way of thinking, and a liberal science degree will do this in an even more complete form. 7

Some of you will point to very successful people who've gone to Yale and done well, but you don't understand statistics. A lot of successful people have started out as liberal arts majors. A lot haven't. If you're very driven and intelligent or lucky, you'll probably be successful in life, even with today's liberal arts degree. Then again, if you're that driven and intelligent, you could probably find success with any degree, or even no degree. Apple's Steve Jobs and Joi Ito (Director of the MIT media lab) are both college dropouts. Joi is a largely self-taught computer scientist, disc jockey, nightclub entrepreneur, and technology investor. The top 20 percent of people in any cohort will do well independent of what curriculum their education follows, or if they had any education at all. If we want to maximize the potential of the other 80 percent, then we need a new Liberal Sciences curriculum. 8

Yale just decided that Computer Science was important and I like to ask, "if you live in France, shouldn't you learn French? If you live in the computer world, shouldn't you learn Computer Science?" What should be the second required language in schools today if we live in a computer world? And if you live in a technology world what must you understand? Traditional education is far behind and the old world tenured professors at our universities with their parochial views and interests will keep dragging them back. My 9

* Eds. note – London-based magazine that covers globalism, world politics, economics, current events, and other issues from the perspective of economic liberalism and laissez-faire economics.

"Many adults have little understanding of important science and technology issues or, more importantly, how to approach them."

disagreement is not with the goals of a liberal arts education but its implementation and evolution (or lack thereof) from eighteenth century European education and its purpose. There is too little emphasis on teaching critical thinking skills in schools, even though that was the original goal of such education. Many adults have little understanding of important science and technology issues or, more importantly, how to approach them, which leaves them open to poor decision-making on matters that will affect both their families and society in general.

10 Connections matter and many Ivy League colleges are worth it just to be an alumnus. There are people with the view that liberal arts broadened their vision and gave them great conversational topics. There are those who argue that the humanities are there to teach us what to do with knowledge. As one observer commented: "They should get lawyers to think whether an unjust law is still law. An engineer could contemplate whether Artificial Intelligence is morally good. An architect could pause to think on the merit of building a house fit for purpose. A doctor could be taught whether and how to justify using scarce medical resources for the benefit of one patient and not another. This is the role of humanities – a supplement to STEM and the professions." In my view creativity, humanism, and ethics are very hard to teach, whereas worldliness and many other skills supposedly taught through the liberal arts are more easily self-taught in a continuously updating fashion if one has a good quantitative, logical, and scientific process-oriented base education.

11 The argument goes that a scientific/engineering education lacks enough training in critical thinking skills, creativity, inspiration, innovation, and holistic thinking. On the contrary, I argue that the scientific and logical basis of a better liberal sciences education would allow some or all of this – and in a more consistent way. The argument that being logical makes one a linear problem solver and ill prepared for professions that require truly creative problem solving has no merit in my view. The old version of the Liberal Arts curriculum was reasonable in . . . the far less complex eighteenth century Euro-centric world and an elitist education focused on thinking and leisure. Since the twentieth century, despite its goals, it has evolved as the "easier curriculum" to get through college and may now be the single biggest reason students pursue it.

12 I do not believe that today's typical liberal arts degree turns you into a more complete thinker; rather, I believe they limit the dimensionality of your thinking since you have less familiarity with mathematical models (to me it's the dimensionality of thinking that I find deficient in many people without a rigorous education), and worse statistical understanding of anecdotes and data (which liberal arts was supposedly good at preparing students for but is actually highly deficient at). People in the humanities fields are told that they get taught analytical skills, including how to digest large volumes of

information, but I find that by and large such education is poor at imparting these skills. Maybe, that was the intent but the reality is very far from this idealization (again, excluding the top 20 percent).

There is a failing in many college programs that are not pragmatic enough 13 to align and relate liberal arts programs to the life of a working adult. From finance to media to management and administration jobs, necessary skills like strategic-thinking, finding trends, and big-picture problem-solving have all evolved in my view to need the more quantitative preparation than today's degrees provide.

Such skills, supposedly the purview of liberal arts education, are best 14 learnt through more quantitative methods today. Many vocational programs from engineering to medicine also need these same skills and need to evolve and broaden to add to their training. But if I could only have one of a liberal arts or an engineering/science education, I'd pick the engineering even if I never intended to work as an engineer and did not know what career I wanted to pursue.

I have in fact almost never worked as an engineer but deal exclusively with 15 risk, evolution of capability, innovation, people evaluation, creativity, and vision formulation. That is not to say that goal setting, design, and creativity are not important or even critical. In fact these need to be added to most professional and vocational degrees, which are also deficient for today's practical careers.

More and more fields are becoming very quantitative, and it's becoming 16 harder and harder to go from majoring in English or history to having optionality on various future careers and being an intelligent citizen in a democracy. Math, statistics, and science are hard, and school is a great time to learn those areas, whereas many of the liberal arts courses can be pursued after college on the base of a broad education. But without training in the scientific process, logic, and critical thinking, discourse and understanding are both made far more difficult.

A good illustrative example of the problems of today's liberal arts edu- 17 cation can be found in the writing of well-known author, Malcolm Gladwell, a history major and a one-time writer for the *New Yorker*. Gladwell famously argued that stories were more important than accuracy or validity without even realizing it. The *New Republic* called the final chapter of Gladwell's *Outliers,* "impervious to all forms of critical thinking" and said that Gladwell believes "a perfect anecdote proves a fatuous rule." Referencing a Gladwell reporting mistake in which Gladwell refers to "eigenvalue" as "Igon Value," Harvard professor and author Steven Pinker criticizes his lack of expertise: "I will call this the Igon Value Problem: when a writer's education on a topic consists in interviewing an expert, he is apt to offer generalizations that are banal, obtuse, or flat wrong." Unfortunately too many in today's media are similarly "uneducated" in their interpretation of experts. Storytelling and quotes become a misleading factor instead of being an aid to communicating the accurate facts more easily. His assertions around "10,000 hours" may or may not be true but his arguments for it carry very little weight with me because of the quality of his thinking.

Though one example of Malcolm Gladwell does not prove the invalidity of arguments for a Liberal Arts degree, I find this kind of erroneous thinking (anecdotally) true of many humanities and liberal arts graduates. In fact I see the inconsistencies that Gladwell failed to understand (giving him the benefit of the doubt that these were unintentional) in the writings of many authors of articles in supposedly elite publications like the *New Yorker* and the *Atlantic*. Again this is not a statistically valid conclusion but the impression across hundreds or thousands of examples of one person. When I do occasionally read articles from these publications, I make a sport of judging the quality of thinking of the writers as I read, based on false arguments, unsupported conclusions, confusion of story telling with factual assertions, mistaking quotes from interviews as facts, misinterpreting statistics, etc. Similar lack of cogent thinking leads to bad decisions, uninformed rhetoric, and lack of critical thinking around topics like nuclear power and GMOs. 18

Unfortunately in an increasingly complex world, all these topics are skills that many liberal arts majors even at elite universities fail to muster. The topic of risk and risk assessment from simple personal financial planning to societal topics like income inequality is so poorly understood and considered by most liberal arts majors as to make me pessimistic. I am not arguing that engineering or STEM education is good at these topics but rather that this is not the intent of STEM or professional education. The intent of Liberal Arts education is what Steven Pinker called a "building a self" and I would add "for the technological and dynamically evolving twenty-first century." 19

Learning new areas as career paths and interests evolve becomes harder. Traditional European liberal arts education was for the few and the elite. Is that still the goal today? People spend years and a small fortune or lifelong indebtedness to obtain it and employability should be a criterion in addition to an education's contribution to intelligent citizenry. 20

Wikipedia defines "the liberal arts as those subjects or skills that in classical antiquity were considered essential for a free person to know in order to take an active part in civic life, something that (for Ancient Greece) included participating in public debate, defending oneself in court, serving on juries, and most importantly, military service. Grammar, logic, and rhetoric were the core liberal arts, while arithmetic, geometry, the theory of music, and astronomy also played a (somewhat lesser) part in education." Today's ideal list, not anchored in "classical antiquity" would be more expansive and more prioritized in my view. 21

Idealists and those who perceive liberal arts education today as meeting these goals are wrong not in its intent but in assessing how well it does this function (and that is an assertion/opinion). I agree that we need a more humanistic education but it is hard to agree or disagree with the current curriculum without defining what humanistic means. Does it really teach critical thinking, logic, or the scientific process, things every citizen should know in order to participate in society? Does it allow for intelligent discourse or decision-making across a diverse set of beliefs, situations, preferences, and assumptions? 22

Should we teach our students what we already know, or prepare them to discover more? Memorizing the Gettysburg address is admirable but ultimately worthless; understanding history is interesting, even useful, but not as relevant as topics from the *Economist*. A student who can apply the scientific process or employ critical thinking skills to solve a big problem has the potential to change the world (or at minimum get a better-paying job). They can actually debate a topic like #blacklivesmatter, income inequality, or Climate Change without being subject to "Trumpism" or emotion and biases-based distortions. No wonder half the college graduates who fill jobs as some studies indicate, actually fill jobs that don't need a college degree! Their degree is not relevant to adding value to an employer (though that is not the only purpose of a degree). 23

Further, even if an ideal curriculum can be stitched together, most liberal arts majors infrequently do it. If the goal is not professional education then it must be general education, which requires many more must-have requirements for me to consider a university degree respectable. Of course others are entitled to their own opinion, though the right answer is testable if one agrees that the goals of such an education are intelligent citizenry and/or employability. 24

For now I am mostly leaving aside matters related to professional, vocational, or technical curriculum. I'm also ignoring the not irrelevant and pragmatic issues of education affordability and the burden of student debt, which would argue for a more employment-enabling type of education. The failure[s] I am referring to are two-fold: (1) the failure of curriculums to keep up with the changing needs of modern society and (2) liberal arts becoming the "easy curriculum" for those who shy away from the more demanding majors and prefer an easier, often (but not always) more socially-oriented college life. Ease, not value, or interest instead of value become key criteria in designing a curriculum for many students today. And for those of you who think this is not true, I am asserting based on my experience this is true for the majority of today's students, but not for every liberal arts student. 25

Not every course is for every student but the criteria need to match the needs of the student and not their indulgences, taking interests and capability into account. "Pursue your passion" even if it increases the probability of getting you into unemployment or homelessness later is advice I have seldom agreed with (yes there are occasions this is warranted, especially for the top or the bottom 20 percent of students). More on passions later but I'm not saying passions are unimportant. What I am saying is with today's implementation of a liberal arts curriculum, even at elite universities like Stanford and Yale, I find that many liberal arts majors (excluding roughly the top 20 percent of students) lack the ability to rigorously defend ideas, make compelling, persuasive arguments, or discourse logically. 26

Steven Pinker – in addition to refuting Gladwell – has a brilliant, clarion opinion on what education ought to be, writing in the *New Republic*, "It seems to me that educated people should know something about the 13-billion-year prehistory of our species and the basic laws governing the physical and living world, including our bodies and brains. They should grasp the timeline 27 of human history from the dawn of agriculture to the present. They should be exposed to the diversity of human cultures, and the major systems of belief and value with which they have made sense of their lives. They should know about the formative events in human history, including the blunders we can hope not to repeat. They should understand the principles behind democratic governance and the rule of law. They should know how to appreciate works of fiction and art as sources of aesthetic pleasure and as impetuses to reflect on the human condition."

Though I agree, I am not sure this curriculum is more important than the ideas below. Based on the skills defined below any gaps in the above education can be filled in by students post-graduation. 28

So What Should Non-Professional Elite Education Entail?

If we had enough time in school, I would suggest we do everything. Sadly that is not realistic, so we need a prioritized list of basic requirements because every subject we do cover excludes some other subject given the fixed time we have available. We must decide what is better taught during the limited teaching time we have, and what subjects are easier learnt during personal time or as post-education or graduate pursuits. 29

In the new Liberal Science curriculum I propose, students would master: 30

1. The fundamental tools of learning and analysis, primarily critical thinking, the scientific process or methodology, and approaches to problem solving and diversity.
2. Knowledge of a few generally applicable topics and knowledge of the basics such as logic, mathematics, and statistics to judge and model conceptually almost anything one might run into over the next few decades.
3. The skills to "dig deep" into their areas of interest in order to understand how these tools can be applied to one domain and to be equipped to change domains every so often.
4. Preparation for jobs in a competitive and evolving global economy or preparation for uncertainty about one's future direction, interest, or areas where opportunities will exist.
5. Preparation to continuously evolve and stay current as informed and intelligent citizens of a democracy.

Critical subject matter should include economics, statistics, mathematics, logic and systems modeling, psychology, computer programming, and current (not historical) cultural evolution (Why rap? Why ISIS? Why suicide bombers? Why the Kardashians and Trump? Why environmentalism and what matters and what does not? And of course the question, are the answers to these questions expert opinions or have some other validity?). 31

Furthermore, certain humanities disciplines such as literature and history should become optional subjects, in much the same way that physics is today (and, of course, I advocate mandatory basic physics study along with the other sciences). And one needs the ability to think through many, if not most, of the 32 social issues we face (which the softer liberal arts subjects ill-prepare one for in my view).

Imagine a required course each semester where every student is asked to analyze and debate topics from every issue of a broad publication such as the *Economist* or *Technology Review*. And imagine a core curriculum that teaches the core skills to have the discussions above. Such a curriculum would not only provide a platform for understanding in a more relevant context how the physical, political, cultural, and technical worlds function, but would also impart instincts for interpreting the world, and prepare students to become active participants in the economy. 33

It would be essential to understand psychology because human behavior and human interaction are important and will continue to be so. I'd like people who are immune to the fallacies and agendas of the media, politicians, advertisers, and marketers because these professions have learned to hack the human brain's biases (a good description of which are described in Dan Kannehman's *Thinking Fast & Slow* and in Dan Gardner's *The Science of Fear*). I'd like to teach people how to understand history but not to spend time getting the knowledge of history, which can be done after graduation. 34

I'd like people to read a *New York Times* article and understand what is an assumption, what's an assertion by the writer, what are facts, and what are opinions, and maybe even find the biases and contradictions inherent in many articles. We are far beyond the days of the media simply reporting news, shown by the different versions of the "news" that liberal and conservative newspapers in the US report, all as different "truths" of the same event. Learning to parse this media is critical. I'd like people to understand what is statistically valid and what is not. What is a bias or the color of the writer's point of view. 35

Students should learn the scientific method, and most importantly how to apply its mental model to the world. The scientific method requires that hypotheses be tested in controlled conditions; this can diminish the effects of randomness and, often, personal bias. This is very valuable in a world where too many students fall victim to confirmation biases (people observe what they expect to observe), appeal to new and surprising things, and narrative fallacies (once a narrative has been built, its individual elements are more accepted). There are many, many types of human biases defined in psychology that people fall victim to. Failure to understand mathematical models and statistics makes it substantially more difficult to understand critical questions in daily life, from social sciences to science and technology, political issues, health claims, and much more. 36

I'd also suggest tackling several general and currently relevant topic areas such as genetics, computer science, systems modeling, econometrics, linguistics modeling, traditional and behavioral economics, and genomics/bioinformatics (not an exhaustive list) which are quickly becoming critical issues for everyday decisions from personal medical decisions to understanding minimum pay, economics of taxes and inequality, immigration, or climate change. E. O. Wilson argues in his book *The Meaning of Human Existence* that it is hard to understand social behavior without understanding multi-level selection theory and the mathematical optimization that nature performed through 37 years of evolutionary iterations. I am not arguing that every educated person should be able to build such a model but rather that they should be able to "think" such a model qualitatively.

Not only do these topics expose students to a lot of useful and current information, theories, and algorithms, they may in fact become platforms to teach the scientific process – a process that applies to (and is desperately needed for) logical discourse as much as it applies to science. The scientific process critically needs to be applied to all the issues we discuss socially in order to have intelligent dialog. Even if the specific information becomes irrelevant within a decade (who knows where technology will head next; hugely important cultural phenomena and technologies like Facebook, Twitter, and the iPhone didn't exist before 2004, after all), it's incredibly useful to understand the current frontiers of science and technology as building blocks for the future. 38

It's not that history or Kafka* are not important, but rather it is even more critical to understand if we change the assumptions, environmental conditions, and rules that applied to historical events, that would alter the conclusions we draw from historical events today. Every time a student takes one subject they exclude the possibility of taking something else. I find it ironic that those who rely on "history repeating itself" often fail to understand the assumptions that might cause "this time" to be different. The experts we rely on for predictions have about the same accuracy as dart-throwing monkeys according to at least one very exhaustive study by Prof Phil Tetlock. So it is important to understand how to rely on "more likely to be right" experts, as defined in the book *Superforecasters*. We make a lot of judgments in everyday life and we should be prepared to make them intelligently. 39

Students can use this broad knowledge base to build mental models that will aid them in both further studies and vocations. Charlie Munger, the famous investor from Berkshire Hathaway, speaks about mental models and what he calls "elementary, worldly wisdom." Munger believes a person can combine models from a wide range of disciplines (economics, mathematics, physics, biology, history, and psychology, among others) into something that is more valuable than the sum of its parts. I have to agree that this cross-disciplinary thinking is becoming an essential skill in today's increasingly complex world. 40

"The models have to come from multiple disciplines because all the wisdom of the world is not to be found in one little academic department," Munger explains. "That's why poetry professors, by and large, are so unwise in a worldly sense. They don't have enough models in their heads. So you've got to have models across a fair array of disciplines.... These models generally fall into two categories: (1) ones that help us simulate time (and predict the future) and better understand how the world works (e.g., understanding a useful idea from like autocatalysis), and (2) ones that help us better understand how our mental processes lead us astray (e.g., availability bias)." I would add that they provide the "common truth" in discussions where the well-educated discussants disagree. 41

---

* Eds. note – Franz Kafka (1883–1924), Czech-born German language novelist and short-story writer who is a major figure in twentieth-century literature and literary modernism.

After grasping the fundamental tools of learning and some broad topical exposure, it's valuable to "dig deep" in one or two topic areas of interest. For this, I prefer some subject in science or engineering rather than literature or history (bear with me before you have an emotional reaction; I'll explain in a minute). Obviously, it's best if students are passionate about a specific topic, but it's not critical as the passion may develop as they dig in (some students will have passions, but many won't have any at all). The real value for digging deep is to learn how to dig in; it serves a person for the duration of their life: in school, work, and leisure. As Thomas Huxley said, "learn something about everything and everything about something," though his saying that does not make it true. Too often, students don't learn that a quote is not a fact. 42

If students choose options from traditional liberal-education subjects, they should be taught in the context of the critical tools mentioned above. If students want jobs, they should be taught skills where future jobs will exist. If we want them as intelligent citizens, we need to have them understand critical thinking, statistics, economics, how to interpret technology and science developments, and how global game theory applies to local interests. Traditional majors like international relations and political science are passé as base skills and can easily be acquired once a student has the basic tools of understanding. And they and many other traditional liberal arts subjects like history or art will be well served in graduate level work. I want to repeat that this is not to claim those "other subjects" are not valuable. I think they are very appropriate for graduate level study. 43

Back to history and literature for a moment – these are great to wrestle with once a student has learned to think critically. My contention is not that these subjects are unimportant, but rather that they are not basic or broad enough "tools for developing learning skills" as they were in the 1800s, because the set of skills needed today has changed. Furthermore, they are topics easily learned by someone trained in the basic disciplines of thinking and learning that I've defined above. This isn't as easy the other way around. A scientist can more easily become a philosopher or writer than a writer or philosopher can become a scientist. 44

If subjects like history and literature are focused on too early, it is easy for someone not to learn to think for themselves and not to question assumptions, conclusions, and expert philosophies. This can do a lot of damage. 45

Separating the aspirational claims by universities from the reality of today's typical liberal arts education I tend to agree with the views of William Deresiewicz. He was an English professor at Yale from 1998–2008 and recently published the book *Excellent Sheep: The Miseducation of the American Elite and the Way to a Meaningful Life*. Deresiewicz writes on the current state of liberal arts, "At least the classes at elite schools are academically rigorous, demanding on their own terms, no? Not necessarily. In the sciences, usually; in other disciplines, not so much. There are exceptions, of course, but professors and students have largely entered into what one observer called a 'nonaggression pact.'" Easy is often the reason students pick liberal arts subjects today. 46

Lots of Things Are Important but What Are the Most Important Goals of an Education?

To repeat, school is a place where every student should have the opportunity to become a potential participant in whatever they might want to tackle in the future, with an appropriate focus not only on what they want to pursue but also, pragmatically, what they will need to do to be productively employed or a productive and thinking member of society. By embracing thinking and learning skills, and adding a dash of irreverence and confidence that comes from being able to tackle new arenas (creative writing as a vocational skill, not a liberal arts education, may have a role here, but *Macbeth* does not make my priority list; we can agree to disagree but if we discourse I want to understand the assumptions that cause us to disagree, something many students are unable to do), hopefully they will be lucky enough to help shape the next few decades or at least be intelligent voters in a democracy and productive participants in their jobs. 47

With the right critical lens, history, philosophy, and literature can help creativity and breadth by opening the mind to new perspectives and ideas. Still, learning about them is secondary to learning the tools of learning except possibly the right approach to philosophy education. Again I want to remind you that none of this applies to the top 20 percent of students who learn all these skills independent of their education or major. Passions like music or literature (leaving aside the top few students who clearly excel at music or literature) and its history may be best left to self-pursuit, while exploring the structure and theory of music or literature may be a way to teach the right kind of thinking about music and literature! 48

For some small subset of the student body, pursuing passions and developing skills in subjects such as music or sports can be valuable, and I am a fan of schools like Juilliard, but in my view this must be in addition to a required general education especially for the "other 80 percent." It's the lack of balance in general education which I am suggesting needs to be addressed (including for engineering, science, and technology subjects' students. Setting music and sports aside, with the critical thinking tools and exposure to the up-and-coming areas mentioned above, students should be positioned to discover their first passion and begin to understand themselves, or at the least be able to keep up with the changes to come, get (and maintain) productive jobs, and be intelligent citizens. 49

At the very least they should be able to evaluate how much confidence to place in a *New York Times* study of 11 patients on a new cancer treatment from Mexico or a health supplement from China and to assess the study's statistical validity and whether the treatment's economics make sense. And they should understand the relationship between taxes, spending, balanced budgets, and growth better than they understand fifteenth century English history in preparation for "civic life" to quote the original purpose of a liberal arts education. And if they are to study language or music, Dan Levitin's book *This Is Your Brain on Music: The Science of a Human Obsession* should be first reading or its equivalent in linguistics. It can teach you about a human obsession 50 but also teach you how to build a mathematical model in your head and why and how Indian music is different than Latin music. In fact, these should be required for all education, not just liberal arts education, along with the other books mentioned above.

The role of passion and emotion in life is best epitomized by a quote (unknown source) I once saw that says the most important things in life are best decided by the heart and not logic. For the rest we need logic and consistency. The "what" may be emotion and passion based but the "how" often (yes, sometimes the journey is the reward) needs a different approach that intelligent citizens should possess and education should teach. 51

• • •

Comprehension

1. What, according to Khosla, should be the "most important" elements taught in a "general, non-professional, or vocational education" (6)? Do you agree?
2. In Khosla's view, what is the "single biggest reason students pursue" (11) liberal arts degrees?
3. According to Khosla, what misleading claims are made about the benefits of a liberal arts education?
4. In paragraphs 17 and 18, Khosla discusses the author Malcolm Gladwell. What point does Gladwell's example support?
5. What objection does Khosla have to the advice, "Pursue your passion"? Do you think he is correct? Explain your answer.

Purpose and Audience

1. What is the thesis of this essay, and where is it located?
2. What does Khosla want to accomplish by writing this essay? How do you know?
3. What preconceptions about his subject does Khosla expect readers to have? Explain.

Style and Structure

1. Khosla begins his essay by referring to the nineteenth-century French scientist Louis Pasteur. Why?
2. At several points in the essay, including paragraphs 21 and 32, Khosla uses **anecdotal evidence** – evidence based or hearsay rather than facts – and assertions based on "personal experience." How effectively do these types of evidence support his argument? Explain.
3. In paragraph 9, Khosla writes, "I like to ask, 'if you live in France, shouldn't you learn French? If you live in the computer world, shouldn't you learn Computer Science?' " Is this analogy persuasive? What are its strengths and weaknesses?

4. In paragraph 21, Khosla includes a definition of liberal arts from *Wikipedia*, a website many instructors consider unsuitable for academic research. Is his use of *Wikipedia* effective? Why or why not?
5. **Vocabulary Project.** In paragraph 4, Khosla refers to the need to create "continuously learning citizen[s]." Why do you think he uses the term *citizen* rather than a term such as *graduate* or *professional*? What does *citizen* mean, and what connotations does it have that are important to Khosla's argument?

Journal Entry

At several points in his essay, Khosla refers to "critical thinking." Find some of these references. Then, write your own definition of the term.

Writing Workshop

1. In paragraph 35, Khosla says, "I'd like people to read a *New York Times* article and understand what is an assumption, what's an assertion by the writer, what are facts, and what are opinions, and maybe even find the biases and contradictions inherent in many articles." Using Khosla's criteria, identify these different elements in his article. Then, write an argumentative essay in which you discuss if his writing lives up to his own standards of critical thinking.
2. According to Khosla, "understanding history is interesting, even useful, but not as relevant as topics from the *Economist*" (23). Write an essay in which you agree or disagree with this assertion. Use examples from you own experience to support your points.
3. **Working with Sources.** Which writer, Wieseltier or Khosla, makes a better case the value of a liberal arts education? Using their essays as well as some of your own research, write an argumentative essay that takes a position on this issue. Be sure to document all references to your sources and to include a works-cited page. (See Chapter 18 for information on MLA documentation.)

Combining the Patterns

Where does Khosla use **definition** in this essay? Are his definitions clear, precise, and thorough enough to support his overall purpose?

Thematic Connections

- "Surrendering" (page 116)
- "Ten Ways We Get the Odds Wrong" (page 245)
- "Why Rational People Buy into Conspiracy Theories" (page 338)
- "Why Chinese Mothers Are Superior" (page 402)
- "What I Learned (and Didn't Learn) in College" (page 440)

✶CASEBOOK

Do College Students Need Trigger Warnings?

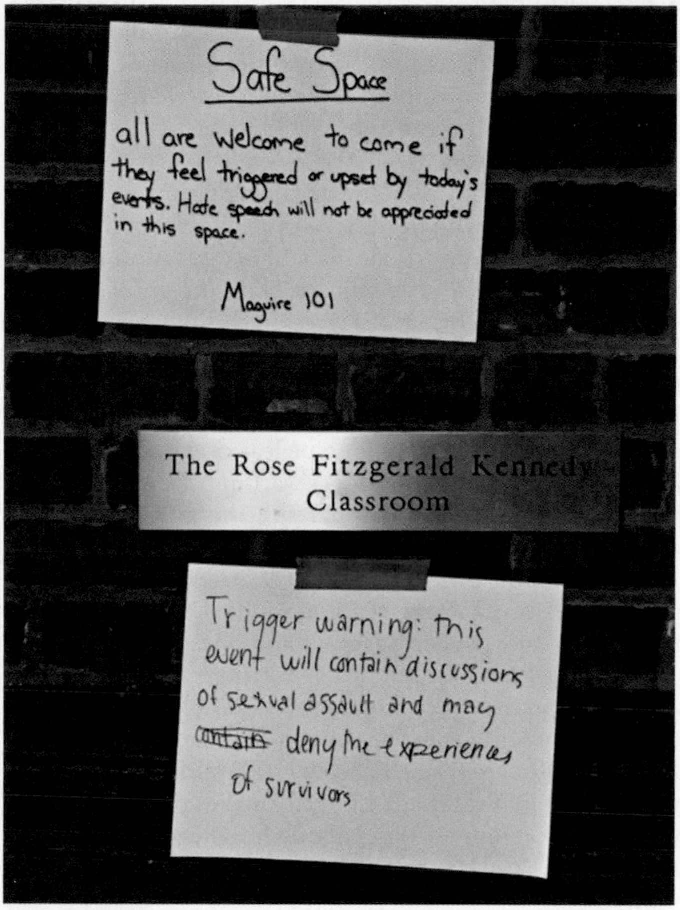

These signs were posted outside the classroom where Dr. Christina Hoff Sommers, an author and speaker for the Luce Institute, was giving a lecture called "What's Right (and Badly Wrong) with Feminism?"

• • •

Before the fall 2016 semester at the University of Chicago, John Ellison, dean of students, sent incoming students a letter that affirmed the school's dedication to open discussion and rigorous intellectual debate on campus. In his letter, Ellison wrote, "Our commitment to academic freedom means that we do not support so-called 'trigger warnings,' we do not cancel invited speakers because their topics might prove controversial, and we do not condone the creation of intellectual 'safe spaces' where individuals can retreat from ideas and perspectives at odds with their own."

Ellison's assertions – particularly with regard to "trigger warnings" – are not without their detractors. For example, some critics point out that victims of sexual violence, physical abuse, or other traumas often suffer from posttraumatic stress disorder. As a result, vivid texts and graphic images can trigger panic attacks and other physical reactions. For this reason, instructors need to provide trigger warnings (a note on the syllabus, for example) letting students know that a book, a class discussion, or any other aspect of a course could possibly provoke painful or disturbing responses. These warnings enable students to prepare for – or, in some cases, avoid – potentially traumatic material.

Critics such as Ellison disagree, however, saying that trigger warnings treat students as if they are children who need to be protected from ideas that may upset or offend them. They point out that the aim of education is to build independent thinking by pushing students out of their comfort zones and exposing them to ideas with which they disagree. In this sense, trigger warnings as well as so-called safe spaces, speech codes, and microaggressions (unintentional slights to marginalized groups), undercut the educational mission of a university. They encourage conformity, stifle free speech, and discourage the open inquiry that is necessary for true learning to take place.

The selections in this casebook examine trigger warnings from a number of different perspectives. Geoffrey R. Stone charts the history of free speech on college campuses in America and expresses his concern that this hard-fought right might be slipping away. In "Trigger Warnings, Safe Spaces, and Free Speech, Too," University of Chicago senior Sophie Downes defines important terms in the debate over trigger warnings and questions the motivations behind the Ellison letter. Jennifer Medina's "Warning: The Literary Canon Could Make Students Squirm" provides an overview of the debate, focusing on the role of trigger warnings in the context of course material such as Shakespeare's *The Merchant of Venice*, F. Scott Fitzgerald's *The Great Gatsby*, and Greek mythology. Finally, Soraya Chemaly makes the point that trigger warnings are central to ongoing debates about "privilege" and what constitutes the core canon.

GEOFFREY R. STONE

Free Expression in Peril

Geoffrey R. Stone is an author and educator. He graduated from the University of Chicago Law School before serving as a law clerk for the U.S. Court of Appeals for the D.C. Circuit and to Supreme Court Justice William J. Brennan Jr. He returned to teaching at the University of Chicago, where he is currently the Edward H. Levi Distinguished Service Professor at the University of Chicago. He is the editor of the *Supreme Court Review* and has authored a number of books, including *Top Secret: When Our Government Keeps Us in the Dark* (2007) and *Speaking Out: Reflections of Law, Liberty and Justice* (2015).

Background on the Report of the Committee on Freedom of Expression In 2014, Robert Zimmer, the president of the University of Chicago, appointed a Committee on Freedom of Expression at his school. This committee was asked to create a statement "articulating the University's overarching commitment to free, robust, and uninhibited debate and deliberation among all members of the University's community." Geoffrey R. Stone was the chair of this committee, which included six other University of Chicago professors. The three-page report was lauded by some in the press, in part because it was published only a day before the 2016 attacks on the offices of French satirical magazine *Charlie Hebdo*, which were viewed by many as a direct assault on freedom of speech. The editorial board at the University of Chicago student newspaper, however, criticized the report for failing to differentiate "between acceptable and unacceptable speech."

Until recently, and for roughly half a century, American universities enjoyed an era of relatively robust academic freedom. In the past few years, though, that has changed. Ironically, the threat to academic freedom in the United States today comes not from government and not from the institutions themselves but from a new generation of students who do not understand the nature, the fragility, and the importance of this principle. 1

Universities must educate our students to understand that academic freedom is not a law of nature. It is not something to be taken for granted. It is, rather, a hard-won acquisition in a lengthy struggle for academic integrity. 2

Students today seem not to understand that, until well into the 19th century, real freedom of thought was neither practiced nor professed in American universities. Before then, any freedom of inquiry or expression in American colleges was smothered by the prevailing theory of "doctrinal moralism," which assumed that the worth of an idea must be judged by what the institution's leaders considered its moral value. Through the first half of the 19th century, American higher education squelched any notion of free discussion or intellectual curiosity. Indeed, as the nation moved toward the Civil War, any professor or student in the North who defended slavery, or any professor or student in the South who challenged slavery, could readily be dismissed, disciplined, or expelled. 3

Between 1870 and 1900, however, there was a genuine revolution in American higher education. With the battle over Darwinism, new academic goals came to be embraced. For the first time, to criticize as well as to preserve traditional moral values and understandings became an accepted function of higher education. 4

In 1892, William Rainey Harper, the first president of the University of Chicago, could boldly assert: "When for any reason the administration of a university attempts to dislodge a professor or punish a student because of his political or religious sentiments, at that moment the institution has ceased to be a university." But, despite such sentiments, the battle for academic freedom has been a contentious and a continuing one. 5

For example, in the closing years of the 19th century, businessmen who had accumulated vast industrial wealth began to support universities on an unprecedented scale. But that support was not without strings, and professors who offended wealthy trustees by criticizing the ethics of their business practices were dismissed from such leading universities as Cornell and Stanford. 6

Then, during World War I, when patriotic zealots persecuted and even prosecuted those who questioned the wisdom or the morality of the war, universities collapsed almost completely in their defense of academic freedom. Students and professors were systematically expelled or fired at even such distinguished institutions as Columbia University and the University of Virginia merely for "encouraging a spirit of indifference toward the war." 7

Similar issues arose again, with a vengeance, during the post–World War II Red Scare. In the late 1940s and the 1950s, most universities excluded from academic life those even suspected of entertaining Communist sympathies. Yale's president, Charles Seymour, went so far as to boast that "there will be no witch hunts at Yale, because there will be no witches. We will neither admit nor hire anyone with Communist sympathies." 8

We now face a similar set of challenges. We live today in an era of political correctness in which students themselves demand censorship, and colleges, afraid to offend those students, too often surrender academic freedom. 9

In recent years, student pressure thwarted speakers' scheduled appearances at Brown University, Johns Hopkins, Williams, and elsewhere. Colorado College suspended a student for making a joke considered antifeminist and racist. William & Mary, De Paul University, and the University of Colorado all disciplined students for criticizing affirmative action, and the University of Kansas disciplined a professor for condemning the National Rifle Association. 10

At Wesleyan University, after the school newspaper published a student op-ed criticizing the Black Lives Matter movement, students demanded that administrators defund the paper. At Amherst College, students demanded that the administration remove posters stating that "All Lives Matter." At Emory University, students demanded that the university punish whoever had chalked "Trump 2016" on campus sidewalks because, in the words of one, "I'm supposed to feel comfortable and safe. . . . I don't deserve to feel afraid at my school." And at Harvard, African-American students demanded that a professor be taken to the woodshed for saying in class that he would be "lynched" if he gave a closed-book examination. 11

The latter is an example of a so-called "microaggression" – words or phrases that may make students feel uncomfortable or "unsafe." Such microaggressions, whether uttered by students or faculty members, have been deemed punishable by colleges and universities across the nation. A recent survey revealed that 72 percent of current college students support disciplinary action against any student or faculty member who expresses views that they deem "racist, sexist, homophobic, or otherwise offensive." 12

Another recent innovation is the much-discussed "trigger warning." A trigger warning is a requirement that before professors assign readings or hold classes that might make some students feel uncomfortable, they must warn students that the readings or the class will deal with sensitive topics like rape, affirmative action, abortion, murder, slavery, the Holocaust, religion, homosexuality, or immigration. 13

And then there's disruption: If students who disagree with a speaker's views can't get a speech canceled, they disrupt the event to silence that speaker. Too often, college administrators, fearful of seeming unsympathetic to the protesters, terminate the events because of the disruptions and then fail to discipline the disrupters for their behavior. 14

How did we get here? It was not long ago when college students were demanding the right to free speech. Now they demand the right to be free from speech that they find offensive or upsetting. 15

One often-expressed theory is that students of this generation, unlike their predecessors, are weak, fragile, and emotionally unstable. They've been raised, the argument goes, by parents who have protected, rewarded, and celebrated them in every way from the time they were infants. Therefore they've never learned to deal with challenge, defeat, uncertainty, anxiety, stress, insult, or fear. They are emotionally incapable of dealing with challenge. 16

But if that is so, then the proper role of a university is not to protect and pamper them but to prepare them for the difficulties of the real world. The goal should not be to shield them from discomfort, insult, and insecurity, but to enable them to be effective citizens. If their parents have, indeed, failed them, then their colleges and universities should save them from themselves. 17

There is, however, another possibility. It is that students, or at least some students, have always felt this way, but until now they were too intimidated, too shy, too deferential to speak up. If so, this generation of college students deserves credit, because instead of remaining silent and oppressed, they have the courage to demand respect, equality, and safety. 18

I think there is an element of truth in both of these perspectives, but I am inclined to think that the former explains more than the latter. 19

Faced with the continuing challenges to academic freedom at American universities, the University of Chicago's president, Robert J. Zimmer, charged a faculty committee last year with the task of drafting a formal statement on freedom of expression. The goal of that committee, which I chaired, was to stake out Chicago's position on these issues. That statement has since become a model for a number of other universities. Here are some examples of its central principles. 20

- "It is not the proper role of the University to attempt to shield individuals from ideas and opinions they find unwelcome, disagreeable, or even deeply offensive."
- "Concerns about civility and mutual respect can never be used as a justification for closing off discussion of ideas, however offensive or disagreeable those ideas may be to some members of our community."
- "The University may restrict expression that violates the law, that falsely defames a specific individual, that constitutes a genuine threat or harassment, that unjustifiably invades substantial privacy or confidentiality interests, or that is otherwise directly incompatible with the core functioning of the university. But these are narrow exceptions to the general principle of freedom of expression."
- "The university's fundamental commitment is to the principle that robust debate and deliberation may not be suppressed because the ideas put forth are thought by some or even by most members of the University community to be offensive, unwise, immoral, or wrong-headed. It is for the individual members of the community, not for the university as an institution, to make those judgments for themselves, and to act on those judgments not by seeking to suppress speech, but by openly and vigorously contesting the ideas that they oppose."
- "Although members of the university are free to criticize and contest the views expressed on campus, and to criticize and contest speakers who are invited to express their views on campus, they may not obstruct or otherwise interfere with the freedom of others to express views they reject or even loathe."

Why should a university embrace these principles? 21

First, bitter experience has taught that even the ideas we hold to be most certain often turn out to be wrong. As confident as we might be in our own wisdom, certainty is different from truth. The core obligation of a university is to invite challenge to the accepted wisdom. 22

Second, history shows that suppression of speech breeds suppression of speech. If today I am permitted to silence those whose views I find distasteful, I have then opened the door to allow others down the road to silence me. The neutral principle, no suppression of ideas, protects us all. 23

> "Should students be allowed to express whatever views they want, however offensive? Yes. Absolutely."

Third, a central precept of free expression is the possibility of a chilling effect. That problem is especially acute today because of social media. Students and faculty members used to be willing to take controversial positions because the risks were relatively modest. After all, one could say something provocative, and the statement soon disappeared from view. But now, every comment you make can be circulated to the world and called up with a click by prospective employers or graduate schools or neighbors. The potential costs of speaking courageously, of taking 24 controversial positions, of taking risks, is greater than ever. Indeed, according to a recent survey, about half of American college students now say that it is unsafe for them to express unpopular views. Many faculty members clearly share that sentiment. In this climate, it is especially important for universities to stand up for free expression.

How should this work in practice? Should students and faculty be allowed to express whatever views they want, however offensive they might be to others? 25

Yes. Absolutely. 26

Should those who disagree and who are offended be allowed to condemn that speech and those speakers in the most vehement terms? Yes. Absolutely. 27

Should those who are offended and who disagree be allowed to demand that the university punish those who have offended them? Yes. Absolutely. 28

Should the university punish those whose speech annoys, offends, and insults others? Absolutely not. 29

That is the core meaning of academic freedom. 30

Does that mean the university's hands are tied? No. 31

A university should educate its students about the importance of civility and mutual respect. These values should be reinforced by education and example, not by censorship. 32

A university should encourage disagreement, argument, and debate. It should instill in its students and faculty members the importance of winning the day by facts, by ideas, and by persuasion, rather than by force, obstruction, or censorship. For a university to fulfill its most fundamental mission, it must be a safe space for even the most loathsome, odious, offensive, disloyal arguments. Students should be encouraged to be tough, fearless, rigorous, and effective advocates and critics. 33

At the same time, a university has to recognize that in our society, flawed as it is, the costs of free speech will fall most heavily on those who feel the most marginalized and unwelcome. All of us feel that way sometimes, but the individuals who bear the brunt of free speech – at least of certain types of free speech – often include racial minorities; religious minorities; women; gay men, lesbians, and transsexuals; and immigrants. Universities must be sensitive to that reality. 34

Although they should not attempt to "solve" this problem by censorship, universities should support students who feel vulnerable, marginalized, silenced, and demeaned. They should help them learn how to speak up, how to respond effectively, how to challenge those whose attitudes, whose words, and whose beliefs offend and appall them. The world is not a safe space, and we must enable our graduates to win the battles they'll have to fight in years to come. 35

But hard cases remain. As simple as it may be to state a principle, it is always much more difficult to apply it to concrete situations. So let me leave you with a few cases to ponder. 36

A sociology professor gives a talk on campus condemning homosexuality as immoral and calling on "normal" students to steer clear of "fags, perverts, and sexual degenerates." What, if anything, should the chair of the sociology 37 department do? In my judgment, this is a classic case of academic freedom. The professor is well within his rights to offer such opinions, however offensive others might find them.

A student hangs a Confederate flag, a swastika, an image of an aborted fetus, or a "Vote for Trump" sign on the door of his dorm room. What, if anything, should administrators do? The university should not pick and choose which messages to permit and which to ban. That is classic censorship. But in the context of a residence hall, where students are a bit of a captive audience, the university can have a content-neutral rule that bans all signs on dorm-room doors. 38

The dean of a university's law school goes on Fox News and says "Abortion is murder. We should fire any female faculty member and expel any female student who has had an abortion." The university president is then inundated with complaints from alumni saying, in effect, "I'll never give another nickel to your damn school as long as she remains dean." What should the president do? A dean or other administrator at a university has distinctive responsibilities. If she engages in behavior, including expression, that renders her effectively incapable of fulfilling her administrative responsibilities, then she can be removed from her position. This is necessary to the core functioning of the institution. At the same time, though, if the dean is also a faculty member, she cannot be disciplined as a faculty member for the exercise of academic freedom. 39

We needn't rely solely on hypotheticals. There was the situation at DePaul University in which a student group invited a highly controversial speaker who maintains, among other things, that there is no wage gap for women, that as a gay man he can attest that one's sexual orientation is purely a matter of choice, and that white men have fewer advantages than women and African-Americans. A group of student protesters disrupted the event by shouting, ultimately causing the talk to be canceled. They maintained that their shouting was merely the exercise of free speech. 40

What should the university do in such circumstances? Should it permit the protest? Arrest the protesters on the spot? Allow them to protest and then punish them after the fact? 41

Such a disruption is not in any way an exercise of free expression. Although students can protest the event in other ways, they cannot prevent either speakers or listeners from engaging in a dialogue they wish to engage in without obstruction. In such circumstances, the protesters should be removed and disciplined for their behavior. (DePaul's president, the Rev. Dennis H. Holtschneider, apologized to the speaker but also criticized "speakers of his ilk" for being "more entertainers and self-serving provocateurs than the public intellectuals they purport to be.") 42

Or consider the incident last year at the University of Oklahoma when a group of fraternity brothers, in a private setting, chanted a racist song. Someone who was present at the time filmed the event and circulated it online. Was the university's president, David Boren, right to expel the students? In my judgment, no. 43

As these examples attest, there are, in fact, marginal cases. But we should not let them obscure the clarity of our commitment to academic freedom. That commitment is now seriously and dangerously under attack. It will be interesting to see whether our universities today have the courage, the integrity, and the fortitude – sometimes lacking in the past – to live up to the highest ideals of a "true" university. 44

• • •

Comprehension

1. According to Stone, what kind of intellectual climate do colleges create by sanctioning "safe space[s]" and "trigger warnings"?
2. What theories does Stone propose to explain why students are demanding safe spaces and trigger warnings?
3. In paragraph 23, Stone says that "suppression of speech breeds suppression of speech." What does he mean?
4. Stone implies that the debates about free speech in higher education have implications for all Americans. What are these implications?
5. What does Stone mean when he says that "the costs of free speech will fall most heavily on those who feel the most marginalized and unwelcome" (34)? Do you agree?

Purpose and Audience

1. Does Stone expect his audience to be in favor of free speech? Does he expect them to be sympathetic to the rest of his argument, or more neutral? How can you tell?
2. Where does Stone state his thesis? Why do you think he places it where he does?
3. Does Stone appeal mainly to logic, to emotions, or to character and authority? Explain.
4. Stone concedes in paragraph 36 that "hard cases remain" and presents several examples of controversy over free speech. How might this information undermine his case? How might it support his case?

Style and Structure

1. Why does Stone quote some central principles from the University of Chicago's statement on freedom of expression?
2. Stone presents a brief history of free speech on college campuses, including the rise of Darwinism and the Red Scare. How do these historical examples support his overall point? What other examples might he have chosen?
3. In paragraphs 15 through 18, Stone presents two possible causes for recent student movements in favor of safe spaces and trigger warnings. In paragraph 19, he acknowledges that he finds truth in both options, but feels

that the first one is a stronger explanation. Why do you think he presented both of these causes?

4. **Vocabulary Project.** In his closing paragraph, Stone calls on schools "to live up to the highest ideals of a 'true' university." Write a paragraph-length definition of a *true university* according to Stone's view.

Journal Entry

Do you think students in your class are able to "express whatever views they want" (paragraph 25)? Or do you think that your school is one of those that "too often surrender academic freedom" (9)?

Writing Workshop

1. According to Stone, colleges are "fearful of seeming unsympathetic" (14) and so they inhibit free speech. Do you think that students should be allowed to say anything they want to in class, or do you think faculty and administrators should place limits on speech? Write an argumentative essay that presents your position. Be sure to include specific examples to support your thesis.
2. **Working with Sources.** Stone refers to the University of Chicago's 2015 Report of the Committee on Freedom of Expression as a model for administrators and faculty. Find this document online and read it, paying close attention to the restrictions on expression that it allows. If your university has such a statement, read it. If not, find two similar documents from other schools. Then, using these statements as source material, write your own statement on principles of free expression. Be sure to document all references to your sources and to include a works-cited page. (See Chapter 18 for information on MLA documentation.)
3. In paragraph 25, Stone argues that "students and faculty be allowed to express whatever views they want, however offensive they might be to others." Do you think that faculty members should be allowed to say anything they want in class? Or, do you think that there should be limits? Write an argumentative essay that presents your opinion. Be sure to include specific examples to support your thesis.

Combining the Patterns

Where in this essay does Stone use **exemplification**? Does he provide enough examples to support his claims? Explain your answer.

Thematic Connections

- "Why Looks Are the Last Bastion of Discrimination" (page 239)
- "I'm Your Teacher, Not Your Internet-Service Provider" (page 409)
- "On Plagiarism" (page 509)
- "On Patriotism" (page 697)

SOPHIE DOWNES

Trigger Warnings, Safe Spaces, and Free Speech, Too

Sophie Downes is a recent graduate from the University of Chicago, where she was a senior English major at the time she wrote this article. While there, she was a head editor and contributor for the *Chicago Maroon*, a student newspaper.

Background on the 2016 welcome letter from the University of Chicago In August of 2016, John "Jay" Ellison, the Dean of Students at the University of Chicago, sent a letter to the incoming class of 2020. In part, this letter contained a message of welcome and congratulated students on their acceptance to the school. The communication then outlined the university's "commitment to freedom of inquiry and expression," inviting members of the campus community "to speak, write, listen, challenge, and learn, without feat of censorship." This touched off a flurry of response, as supporters held up the letter as a robust defense of free speech. Critique of the letter focused around its controversial second paragraph, which stated, "Our commitment to academic freedom means that we do not support so-called 'trigger warnings,' we do not cancel invited speakers because their topics might prove controversial, and we do not condone the creation of intellectual 'safe spaces' where individuals can retreat from ideas and perspectives at odds with their own." The letter was not officially published by the University of Chicago, but the *Chicago Maroon*, the university's independent student newspaper, shared a photo of it on their Twitter feed.

I didn't get the University of Chicago welcome letter that made the rounds 1 on the internet earlier this summer. I'm a senior this year, and the message from Jay Ellison, the dean of undergraduate students, was for the incoming class: Don't expect trigger warnings or safe spaces here. The university, he said, was committed to free expression and would not shield students from ideas they disagreed with or found offensive.

The implication was that students who support trigger warnings and safe 2 spaces are narrow-minded, oversensitive, and opposed to dialogue. The letter betrayed a fundamental misunderstanding of what the terms "trigger warnings" and "safe spaces" mean, and came across as an embarrassing attempt to deflect attention from serious issues on campus.

A trigger warning is pretty simple: It consists of a professor's saying in 3 class, "The reading for this week includes a graphic description of sexual assault," or a note on a syllabus that reads, "This course deals with sensitive material that may be difficult for some students."

A safe space is an area on campus where students – especially but not 4 limited to those who have endured trauma or feel marginalized – can feel comfortable talking about their experiences. This might be the Office of Multicultural Student Affairs or it could be Hillel House, but in essence, it's a place for support and community.

5 This spring, I was in a seminar that dealt with gender, sexuality, and disability. Some of the course reading touched on disturbing subjects, including sexual violence and child abuse. The instructor told us that we could reach out to her if we had difficulty with the class materials, and that she'd do everything she could to make it easier for us to participate. She included a statement to this effect on the syllabus and repeated it briefly at the beginning of each class. Nobody sought to "retreat from ideas and perspectives at odds with their own," as Dean Ellison put it in the letter, nor did these measures hinder discussion or disagreement, both of which were abundant.

"Support systems can be a lifeline in the tumultuous environment of college."

6 Of course, not every class calls out for trigger warnings—I've never heard of them for an economics course. Likewise, plenty of students will never need to visit a safe space. But for those who do, support systems can be a lifeline in the tumultuous environment of college, and are important precisely because they encourage a free exchange of ideas.

7 A little heads-up can help students engage with uncomfortable and complex topics, and a little sensitivity to others, at the most basic level, isn't coddling. Civic discourse in this country has become pretty ugly, so maybe it's not surprising that students are trying to create ways to have compassionate, civil dialogue.

8 The really strange thing about the Ellison letter, though, is that it positioned itself in opposition to resources the University of Chicago has already built: Instructors already choose whether to use trigger warnings in their classes, and there are many safe spaces on campus. Dean Ellison is even listed as a "safe space ally" on the website of one program run by the Office of L.G.B.T.Q. Student Life.

9 If, as a university spokesman says, no program or policy is set to change, why release this condemnation at all?

10 The administration wants to appear as an intellectual force beating back destabilizing waves of political correctness that have rocked college campuses. But the focus of student protests hasn't been the lack of trigger warnings and safe spaces. Instead, many protesters want the university to evaluate how it invests its money, improve access for students with mental illnesses and disabilities, support low-income and first-generation students, and pay its employees fair wages. They have been pushing for more transparency in the school's private police force, which has resisted making most of its policies public in the face of complaints. The university is also under federal investigation over its handling of sexual assault cases.

11 Yet, the administration has refused to meet with student groups who have asked to discuss these issues, and it has threatened to discipline students who staged a sit-in protest. The university even hired a provost who specializes in corporate crisis management and dealing with "activist pressure." While the university accuses students of silencing opposing voices, it continues to insulate itself against difficult questions.

12 In this context, it's hard to see the dean's letter as anything other than a public relations maneuver. While students are being depicted as coddled and fragile, the administration is stacking bricks in its institutional wall to avoid engaging with their real concerns.

It's too bad, because there are certainly legitimate debates to be had over speech in academic settings. The Ellison letter, for example, included a denunciation of attempts by students to disrupt university-sponsored events featuring controversial speakers. But that has little to do with trigger warnings and safe spaces. 13

Regardless of the posturing of academic administrations, in trigger warnings and safe spaces, students have carved out ways to help, accommodate, and listen to those around them. Campus advocacy groups will not be deterred by a letter, as their goals have nothing to do with censorship and everything to do with holding universities accountable to the communities they are supposed to foster. 14

• • •

Comprehension

1. Downes argues that the Ellison letter "came across as an embarrassing attempt to deflect attention from serious issues on campus" (2). What does she mean? How does this claim set up her main argument?
2. Why does Downes mention that Dean Ellison is listed as a "safe space ally" (8) on a school website?
3. In what sense could the Ellison letter be seen as "a public relations maneuver" (12)? Why does Downes consider this a bad thing?
4. Why does Downes argue that denouncing "attempts by students to disrupt university-sponsored events . . . has little to do with trigger warnings and safe spaces" (13)? Do you agree?
5. How does Downes think students on campus will respond to the Ellison letter?

Purpose and Audience

1. Why does Downes mention that she did not receive Jay Ellison's welcome letter? How does her status as a senior at the University of Chicago strengthen or weaken her *ethos*?
2. What is Downes's purpose in writing this article? What does she want to accomplish?
3. Does Downes consider her audience friendly, hostile, or neutral? How can you tell?

Style and Structure

1. Where does Downes present her thesis? Why do you think she chose to place it there?
2. Downes offers a personal anecdote from her seminar on gender, sexuality, and disability. How does this example support her argument? What other information from the seminar could she have included?
3. In paragraph 12, Downes says the administration at the University of Chicago "is stacking bricks in its institutional wall to avoid engaging with their real concerns." To what logical fallacy is she referring? Why does Downes imply that the university might actually prefer to take on the wrong issues?

4. How would Downes's essay be different if she structured it as a Rogerian argument? What changes would she have to make? Do you think that this strategy would be more or less effective than the one she uses?
5. How does Downes use transitions to move readers through her essay? Where might additional transitions have helped you follow her argument more easily?

Journal Entry

How do you define "free speech"? Does this term have a different meaning on college campuses than it does in the "real world"?

Writing Workshop

1. According to Downes, "support systems can be a lifeline in the tumultuous environment of college, and are important precisely because they encourage a free exchange of ideas" (6). She also says, "Civic discourse in this country has become pretty ugly, so maybe it's not surprising that students are trying to create ways to have compassionate, civil dialogue" (7). How do you respond to these statements? Do you think that civic discourse has become "ugly"? Do you think that the support systems Downes outlines are the solution? Write an essay in which you agree or disagree with Downes's point.
2. **Working with Sources.** According to Downes, the University of Chicago "hired a provost who specializes in corporate crisis management and dealing with 'activist pressure.'" Do some research on the field of corporate crisis management. Then, write an essay explaining why a provost with this focus would or would not be a benefit for the school. Be sure to document all references to your sources and to include a works-cited page. (See Chapter 18 for information on MLA documentation.)
3. **Working with Sources.** Downes agrees that "there are certainly legitimate debates to be had over speech in academic settings" (13). Do some research on one of these other "legitimate debates," and write an argument for why this issue would have been a stronger focus for administrators at the University of Chicago. Include quotations from your research to support your argument and document them in a works-cited page. (See Chapter 18 for information on MLA documentation.)

Combining the Patterns

Where does Downes use definition in this essay? How do these definitions support her main argument?

Thematic Connections

- "Why Looks Are the Last Bastion of Discrimination" (page 239)
- "Get It Right: Privatize Executions" (page 292)
- "Public Universities Should Be Free" (page 575)
- "Perhaps Culture Is Now the Counterculture: A Defense of the Humanities" (page 588)

JENNIFER MEDINA

Warning: The Literary Canon Could Make Students Squirm

Jennifer Medina is a Los Angeles–based reporter for the *New York Times* who has covered a broad range of topics, including education, politics, race, labor, and immigration. Born in Riverside, California, she earned a bachelor's degree in journalism and political science from University of Southern California. In 2006, Medina won a Front Page Award from the Newswomen's Club of New York for her coverage of the aftermath of Hurricane Katrina.

Background on the AUUP and trigger warnings In 2014, the American Association of University Professors (AAUP) released a report addressing both the academic and free-speech implications of adding trigger warnings to classroom syllabi. Although acknowledging that calls for trigger warnings coincided with an increase in violence on college campuses, the AAUP nonetheless advised against such a step. Its report questioned the reductive nature of trigger warnings and put concerns about posttraumatic stress disorder in the same category as concerns about other medical conditions. In doing so, the report noted that "the Americans with Disabilities Act contains recommendations for reasonable accommodation to be made on an individual basis. This should be done without affecting other students' exposure to material that has educational value." As an organization whose central mission is to advance the cause of academic freedom, the AAUP not only expressed the prevailing opinions of university professors, but also influenced future conversations on the topic of trigger warnings in the classroom.

Should students about to read *The Great Gatsby* be forewarned about "a variety of scenes that reference gory, abusive, and misogynistic violence," as one Rutgers student proposed? Would any book that addresses racism—like *The Adventures of Huckleberry Finn* or *Things Fall Apart*—have to be preceded by a note of caution? Do sexual images from Greek mythology need to come with a viewer-beware label? 1

Colleges across the country this spring have been wrestling with student requests for what are known as "trigger warnings," explicit alerts that the material they are about to read or see in a classroom might upset them or, as some students assert, cause symptoms of post-traumatic stress disorder in victims of rape or in war veterans. 2

The warnings, which have their ideological roots in feminist thought, have gained the most traction at the University of California, Santa Barbara, where the student government formally called for them. But there have been similar requests from students at Oberlin College, Rutgers University, the University of Michigan, George Washington University, and other schools. 3

> "Trigger warnings, they say, suggest a certain fragility of mind that higher learning is meant to challenge, not embrace."

The debate has left many academics fuming, saying that professors should be trusted to use common sense and that being provocative is part of their mandate. Trigger warnings, they say, suggest a certain fragility of mind that higher learning is meant to challenge, not embrace. The warnings have been widely debated in intellectual circles and largely criticized in opinion magazines, newspaper editorials, and academic email lists. 4

"Any kind of blanket trigger policy is inimical to academic freedom," said Lisa Hajjar, a sociology professor at the university here, who often uses graphic depictions of torture in her courses about war. "Any student can request some sort of individual accommodation, but to say we need some kind of one-size-fits-all approach is totally wrong. The presumption there is that students should not be forced to deal with something that makes them uncomfortable is absurd or even dangerous." 5

Bailey Loverin, a sophomore at Santa Barbara, said the idea for campuswide trigger warnings came to her in February after a professor showed a graphic film depicting rape. She said that she herself had been a victim of sexual abuse, and that although she had not felt threatened by the film, she had approached the professor to suggest that students should have been warned. 6

Ms. Loverin draws a distinction between alerting students to material that might truly tap into memories of trauma – such as war and torture, since many students at Santa Barbara are veterans – and slapping warning labels on famous literary works, as other advocates of trigger warnings have proposed. 7

"We're not talking about someone turning away from something they don't want to see," Ms. Loverin said in a recent interview. "People suddenly feel a very real threat to their safety – even if it is perceived. They are stuck in a classroom where they can't get out, or if they do try to leave, it is suddenly going to be very public." 8

The most vociferous criticism has focused on trigger warnings for materials that have an established place on syllabuses across the country. Among the suggestions for books that would benefit from trigger warnings are Shakespeare's "The Merchant of Venice" (contains anti-Semitism) and Virginia Woolf's "Mrs. Dalloway" (addresses suicide). 9

"Frankly it seems this is sort of an inevitable movement toward people increasingly expecting physical comfort and intellectual comfort in their lives," said Greg Lukianoff, president of the Foundation for Individual Rights in Education, a nonprofit group that advocates free speech. "It is only going to get harder to teach people that there is a real important and serious value to being offended. Part of that is talking about deadly serious and uncomfortable subjects." 10

The term "trigger warning" has its genesis on the Internet. Feminist blogs and forums have used the term for more than a decade to signal that readers, particularly victims of sexual abuse, might want to avoid certain articles or pictures online. 11

On college campuses, proponents say similar language should be used in class syllabuses or before lectures. The issue arose at Wellesley College this year after the school installed a lifelike statue of a man in his underwear, and hundreds of students signed a petition to have it removed. Writing in the *Huffington Post*, one Wellesley student called it a "potentially triggering sculpture," and petition signers cited "concerns that it has triggered memories of sexual assault amongst some students." 12

Here at the University of California, Santa Barbara, in March there was a confrontation when a group of anti-abortion protesters held up graphic pictures of aborted fetuses and a pregnant professor of feminist studies tried to destroy the posters, saying they triggered a sense of fear in her. After she was arrested on vandalism, battery, and robbery charges, more than 1,000 students signed a petition of support for her, saying the university should impose greater restrictions on potentially trigger-inducing content. (So far, the faculty senate has promised to address the concerns raised by the petition and the student government but has not made any policy changes.) 13

At Oberlin College in Ohio, a draft guide was circulated that would have asked professors to put trigger warnings in their syllabuses. The guide said they should flag anything that might "disrupt a student's learning" and "cause trauma," including anything that would suggest the inferiority of anyone who is transgender (a form of discrimination known as cissexism) or who uses a wheelchair (or ableism). 14

"Be aware of racism, classism, sexism, heterosexism, cissexism, ableism, and other issues of privilege and oppression," the guide said. "Realize that all forms of violence are traumatic, and that your students have lives before and outside your classroom, experiences you may not expect or understand." For example, it said, while "Things Fall Apart" by Chinua Achebe – a novel set in colonial-era Nigeria – is a "triumph of literature that everyone in the world should read," it could "trigger readers who have experienced racism, colonialism, religious persecution, violence, suicide, and more." 15

After several professors complained, the draft was removed from a campus website, pending a more thorough review by a faculty-and-student task force. Professors and campus administrators are expected to meet with students next fall to come up with a more comprehensive guide. 16

Meredith Raimondo, Oberlin's associate dean of the College of Arts and Sciences, said the guide was meant to provide suggestions, not to dictate to professors. An associate professor of comparative American studies and a co-chairwoman of the task force, Ms. Raimondo said providing students with warnings would simply be "responsible pedagogical practice." 17

"I quite object to the argument of 'Kids today need to toughen up,'" she said. "That absolutely misses the reality that we're dealing with. We have students coming to us with serious issues, and we need to deal with that respectfully and seriously." 18

But Marc Blecher, a professor of politics and East Asian studies at Oberlin and a major critic of trigger warnings at Oberlin, said such a policy would have a chilling effect on faculty members, particularly those without the job security of tenure. 19

"If I were a junior faculty member looking at this while putting my syllabus together, I'd be terrified," Mr. Blecher said. "Any student who felt triggered by something that happened in class could file a complaint with the various procedures and judicial boards, and create a very tortuous process for anyone." 20

• • •

Comprehension

1. According to Medina, why has the concept of a "trigger warning" made some academics angry? Do you think their anger is justified? Why or why not?
2. What caused students at Wellesley to ask for trigger warnings? Does their request seem reasonable? Explain.
3. What distinction is made in paragraphs 7 and 8? Why is it important, given the debate over the issue of trigger warnings?
4. According to Medina, in what context have trigger warnings drawn the "most vociferous criticism" (9) from academics? Why do you think that is the case?
5. Where does the term *trigger warning* come from? Why does Meredith Raimondo, associate dean of the College of Arts and Sciences, object to the argument that "kids today need to toughen up" (18)?

Purpose and Audience

1. Does Medina's article seem balanced, or does it seem biased toward one particular side of the issue? Explain.
2. What preconceived ideas about trigger warnings does Medina assume her audience have? How do you know?
3. What is Medina's purpose in writing this essay? Does she want to change people's minds? Move them to action? Something else? Explain.
4. Where does Medina state her thesis? Why does she state it where she does?

Style and Structure

1. What is the purpose of the rhetorical questions in paragraph 1? Does Medina answer these questions in her essay? If not, should she have?
2. **Vocabulary Project.** According to Medina, Marc Blecher, a professor at Oberlin College, is concerned that trigger warnings could have "a chilling effect on faculty members" (19). What is a chilling effect, and why is it a problem? How is a chilling effect different from censorship?
3. What specific examples does Medina use to support her thesis? What other kinds of evidence does she use?
4. At what point in her essay does Medina address opposing viewpoints? How effectively does she refute these counterarguments?

5. In what respects is Medina's essay a definition essay? What is being defined? How is this definition developed?

Journal Entry

After reading this article, what is your opinion of trigger warnings? In your own words, how would you define this term?

Writing Workshop

1. Medina quotes an opponent of trigger warnings who worries that "it is only going to get harder to teach people that there is a real important and serious value to being offended" (10). Do you agree? If so, think of examples – from personal experience or otherwise – that illustrate the educational value of "being offended." If you disagree, think of examples that refute this claim.
2. **Working with Sources.** Medina briefly recounts two controversies from 2014: one at Wellesley College and one at the University of California, Santa Barbara. Investigate both of these events. What do they reveal about trigger warnings? Does Medina accurately present the facts of these stories? Use these examples, along with any relevant material you find, and write an argument that presents your view of this issue. Be sure to document all references to your sources and to include a works-cited page. (See Chapter 18 for information on MLA documentation.)
3. **Working with Sources.** Survey some students, instructors, and administrators at your school. What range of opinion do you find regarding trigger warnings? How does your school handle this issue? Then, using your research, write an essay in which you argue for or against the use of trigger warnings at your school. Be sure to document all references to your sources and to include a works-cited page. (See Chapter 18 for information on MLA documentation.)

Combining the Patterns

Where does Medina use **cause and effect** in this article? Do you find the causal connections convincing? Why or why not?

Thematic Connections

- "Thirty-Eight Who Saw Murder Didn't Call the Police" (page 126)
- "Photos That Change History" (page 356)
- "I'm Your Teacher, Not Your Internet-Service Provider" (page 409)
- "Emmett Till and Tamir Rice, Sons of the Great Migration" (page 422)

SORAYA CHEMALY

What's Really Important about "Trigger Warnings"

Soraya Chemaly is an activist, media critic, and journalist who writes about gender in the context of politics, culture, media, and religion. She is the director of the Women's Media Center Speech Project and creator of the Safety and Free Speech Coalition, a group of organizations focused on expanding women's freedom of expression, stopping online abuse, and increasing diversity in media. Her work has appeared in the *Atlantic*, the *Huffington Post*, the *National*, *Role/Reboot*, and other publications.

Background on the origin of trigger warnings A trigger warning is a sentence or phrase at the beginning of a piece of writing or video to alert readers or viewers that what follows is potentially disturbing. These warnings allow readers, viewers, or listeners to avoid potentially upsetting or provocative content. The term — and the practice — originated in the late 1990s and early 2000s on feminist blogs and online forums where issues such as rape, sexual abuse, eating disorders, and mental illness were discussed. The idea of a "trigger" has its roots in psychiatry and clinical psychology, however. In their 1921 book *Psycho-Analysis and the War Neuroses*, for example, psychoanalysts Karl Abraham and Sándor Ferenczi described seemingly innocuous events that triggered memories of traumatic experiences in shell-shocked war veterans. More recently, triggers and trigger warnings have moved from the purview of clinical psychiatry, online support groups, and discussions of posttraumatic stress disorder to fan fiction, magazines, social networking sites, and — most controversially — college classrooms. Many instructors include trigger warnings on their syllabi to alert students to disturbing materials so that they can prepare themselves to encounter it or avoid it altogether. For some faculty and students, such warnings are simply common courtesy. For others, however, trigger warnings are synonymous with overprotection, coddling, and censorship.

In an article title "Warning: The Literary Canon Could Make Students Squirm," the *New York Times* yesterday described ongoing debates on college and university campuses about whether or not trigger warnings should be used in advance of discussions that include, among other things, violent, racist, and misogynistic content. This argument is a repeat of a long-standing one about the uses and efficacy of warnings regarding possibly disturbing and re-traumatizing content. Conversations about trigger warnings, however, seem more and more like superficial proxies for ones about deeper problems on campuses regarding diversity, equity, the corporatization of education, and, the dreaded word, privilege. 1

Triggers, images, sounds, smells, and, yes, texts, that provoke specific emotional and physical responses in people, are not about "squirming." They 2 are complex, unpredictable, and highly individual reactions to material that evokes pain and fear. The idea of trigger warnings started in feminist spaces because experiences with, for example, sexual and domestic violence, are so common that it made sense, out of compassion, to warn participants before revealing graphic descriptions of incest, rape, sexual assault, domestic violence, self-harm, and suicide. In recent years, however, the use of trigger warnings has expanded from feminist spaces into broader public discourse. While there are legitimate concerns about how and when trigger warnings should be used, and whether or not their use has been degraded past the point of usefulness, the primary objections cited in the *New York Times* article should not be among them.

3 The first objection raised in the article is that professors should be able to use "common sense." Common to whom? Academic cultures are legacy cultures. Until relatively recently, classrooms were largely comprised of young, elite, mostly white men who were not frequently on the receiving end of sex, race, or sexuality based violence and threats. The core canon was built around the same constituency. These were not spaces, historically, where conversations about "women's issues," for example, either took place or were considered vitally important. As we all know, campuses today are much more diverse places and students have more direct experiences of racism, sexism, colonialism, and more, including well-documented multi-generational trauma.

4 Many academics express the belief that their "common sense" judgment, when it comes to material that might cause genuine harm, should be respected. However, history, and the current composition of academia, which remains dominated by white men in most fields of study, suggests that trusting professors to know what will traumatize students is *not* a wise assumption. Additionally, revelations regarding widespread institutional tolerance for sexual assault on campuses, brought to public attention primarily by students, rarely professors or administrators, do little to inspire confidence in the common sense of either.

5 Despite good intentions and individual professors' interests, implicit biases are a legitimate and serious problem in academia. There is no reason to think these biases would not inform judgment and reduce empathy. Trigger warnings are fundamentally about empathy, which is informed by epistemology, status, and stereotypes. People with higher status, wealth, race, and/or sex, for example, have the least amount. This is a consequence of living in a culture optimized to reflect their perspectives and address their needs. When it comes to trigger warnings, the prediction and acknowledgement of pain are salient.

> "Despite good intentions and individual professors' interests, implicit biases are a legitimate and serious problem in academia."

6 What this objection to warnings ignores is well-documented race and sex-based biases in the assessment and recognition of pain. People in the United

States actually feel more empathy when they see a white person in pain than a black person. In their study, "The Girl Who Cried Pain: A Bias Against Women in the Treatment of Pain," researchers Diane E. Hoffmann and Anita J. Tarzian documented the degree to which women's pain is routinely dismissed in these ways as the "not real," "emotional," response of "fragile" females. Not only are women who experience pain less likely to be taken seriously when they describe it, but they are less likely to be treated by medical professionals.

"Squirm," and "discomfort," for example, do not accurately capture the sensation of white heat, rapid heartbeat, the feeling that you are about to die, or vivid flashbacks of assault. Many administrators and professors feel that students need to grow a "thicker skin." A marginalizing "sticks and stones" understanding of what "counts" as "real" pain is evident not only in the statements of many professors, but in the large number of comments that quickly followed the *Times* piece, where readers categorized trigger warnings as "coddling" a "weak" "victim-mentality." 7

Additionally, the idea that any trigger warnings constitute censorship is not only incorrect but also definitively misleading. In most cases, no one is saying professors cannot teach texts or show videos. Nor do warnings imply some sort of apology for lessons to follow. Nor, in the interesting choice of words of one professor quoted in the *Times* piece, do trigger warnings mean that students "should not be forced to deal with something that makes them uncomfortable." Warnings seek mainly to give students information they need in order to decide whether or not to take or stay in a class. 8

There are examples, however, that, as the *Atlantic*'s Conor Friedersdorf points out, are broad enough to become meaningless and harmful to the actual purpose of warnings. Putting trigger warning labels on literary works, for example, have a decidedly chilling effect given the history and meaning of burned and banned books. Likewise, blanket warnings, which would result in labeling "classroom material more tame than much of what [students] encounter in daily life . . . huge chunk[s] of network TV shows, hip hop albums, standup comics and Hollywood films . . . they'd need to be taped all over campus." Blanket trigger warnings do no one any good and would have a negative effect on campus speech. 9

Ironically, given the chorus of "free speech!" complaints even against narrowly defined warnings, trigger warnings were, in their origins, a sign of the *liberation of speech*. They are a civil adaptation to the important acknowledgement and public discussion of stories long suppressed by a culture and a mainstream media either not interested in hearing them or that actively benefits from keeping them hidden. Trigger warnings exist *because* deadly serious and uncomfortable subjects previously not explored are now on the table and not relegated to a distant past or being discussed primarily by people largely unaffected negatively by them. Exaggerated objections to warnings based on free speech arguments attest to how profoundly integral our free speech norms are to maintaining and changing social structures. 10

Another way of thinking about trigger warnings, in the context of hierarchy and status on campus, is that the people to whom trigger warnings are important are legitimately saying, "I am here, acknowledge me and my 11 experiences." That statement goes far beyond warnings. It is essentially the crux of ongoing debates about what constitutes our core canon and what we do about "privilege." That is why there is particular objection to demands for trigger warnings on "materials that have an established place on syllabuses."

To that end, what the *New York Times* article, and much of the conversation regarding the use of trigger warnings on campuses, did not talk about and should have was power, especially institutionalized power and the role it plays in deciding what and who are important on campus. Tressie McMillan Cottom argues clearly that concerns for students' feelings often act not to "silence power so much as stifle any discourse about how power acts on people." The results can undermine attempts, among other things, to diversify the canon and its analysis. This was absolutely what happened in the case of Professor Shannon Gibney whose in-class discussion of structural racism "alienated" three white male students who then filed a discrimination suit, was sanctioned as the result of... structural racism and education as a capitalist enterprise. 12

However, Gibney's perspective is not the primary one being espoused by the loudest challengers to trigger warnings. Those most inclined to resist on the basis of "censorship" appear to frequently be the same people who take their free speech and autonomy for granted and their truth as normative and universal. The speech norms they seem to be espousing, mainly our mainstream ones, are stubbornly tied to discriminatory status quo hierarchies uninterested in "harm." 13

Having said all of this, I do not think that trigger warnings on campus should be mandated in any way, shape, or form. As Professor Brittany Cooper says in describing why she does not employ them, "Encountering material that you have never encountered before, being challenged, and learning strategies for both understanding and engaging the material is what it means to get an education." Warnings, originally not about being "offended," narrowly defined, and a reflection of compassion, are not in-and-of themselves inimical to this idea or academic freedom. 14

In the end, the most important fact about trigger warnings isn't whether they are formalized or not, narrow or not, but that they are being discussed on campuses and in mainstream media, and no longer limited to the feminist blogs that understood why they were necessary in the first place. The words themselves, like others before them such as "domestic violence," "sexual assault," "rape culture," signal a shift in the culture towards better understanding of broader perspectives. That empathy and diversity, which is what so much of trigger warnings comes down to, is a topic of debate on campuses, even by proxy, is a good thing. 15

• • •

Comprehension

1. Chemaly claims that arguments about trigger warnings are proxies for discussions of "deeper problems" (1). What are these problems?
2. According to Chemaly, what is the problem with "common sense" (3)?

3. Chemaly writes that our sense of empathy is "informed by epistemology, status, and stereotypes" (5). What does *epistemology* mean? How is this term related to empathy?
4. According to Chemaly, "the idea that any trigger warnings constitute censorship is not only incorrect but also definitively misleading" (8). Why?
5. What are trigger warnings fundamentally "about"? Do you agree or disagree with Chemaly's point?

Purpose and Audience

1. Chemaly states her thesis at the end of her first paragraph. Why do you think she states it so early in her essay? What does this placement tell readers about Chemaly's assessment of her readers and their preconceptions?
2. Where does Chemaly address opposing arguments? How effectively does she refute them?
3. Does Chemaly make concessions to those with opposing points of view? If so, how do these concessions affect your view of her argument?
4. What does Chemaly want to accomplish with her essay? How do you know?

Style and Structure

1. Chemaly begins her argument by mentioning Jennifer Medina's essay "Warning: The Literary Canon Could Make Students Squirm." Why do you think Chemaly begins this way?
2. Chemaly says that "revelations regarding widespread institutional tolerance for sexual assault on campuses" are "brought to public attention primarily by students" (4). What does she mean? Why is this point important?
3. How does Chemaly use **cause-and-effect** in her essay? Point to specific examples.
4. **Vocabulary Project.** In paragraph 1, Chemaly says, "Conversations about trigger warnings, however, seem more and more like superficial proxies for ones about deeper problems on campuses regarding diversity, equality, the corporatization of education, and, the dreaded word, privilege." What is a *proxy*? Where else in the essay does Chemaly use this term? In each instance, what point is she trying to make?
5. In paragraph 13, Chemaly says, "Those most inclined to resist on the basis of 'censorship' appear to frequently be the same people who take their free speech and autonomy for granted and their truth as normative and universal." Does she provide enough evidence to support this generalization? Explain.

Journal Entry

Chemaly says trigger warnings are a way to address "complex, unpredictable, and highly individual reactions to material that evokes pain and fear" (2). Are there any images, sounds, or texts that have – or could have – this effect on you? If so, what are they?

Writing Workshop

1. **Working with Sources.** In paragraph 5, Chemaly says, "People with higher status, wealth, race, and/or sex, for example, have the least amount [of empathy]." She does not support this assertion with evidence, however. What research has been done on the relationship between empathy and status, wealth, race, and sex? What insight does this research provide on the debate about trigger warnings? Write an argumentative essay in which you either agree or disagree with Chemaly's point. Be sure to document all references to your sources and to include a works-cited page. (See Chapter 18 for information on MLA documentation.)
2. **Working with Sources.** In her essay "Trigger or Not, Warnings Matter," Julie A. Winterich makes the following comment, "Not giving students a heads-up risks a return to the status quo of intellectualizing violence and trauma as something that happens only outside the classroom. And those in the classroom who have suffered such trauma may needlessly suffer even more." Write an essay in which you either agree or disagree with Winterich's statement. Be sure to look at Winterich's essay online and also to use material from one or two of the essays in this casebook to support your points. Be sure to document all references to your sources and to include a works-cited page. (See Chapter 18 for information on MLA documentation.)
3. **Working with Sources.** What is your own position on trigger warnings? Do you think they are a reasonable response to provocative texts and images? Or, do you think they stifle free speech or unnecessarily "coddle" students? Write an argumentative essay that takes a position on the issue of trigger warnings. Refer to the essays in this casebook, as well as to your own experiences and (if you choose) other outside sources. Be sure to document all references to your sources and to include a works-cited page. (See Chapter 18 for information on MLA documentation.)

Combining the Patterns

How does Chemaly use **definition** in this essay? Why is it important to her argument that certain terms and concepts are defined in particular ways? Why does she disapprove of the use of certain words in the debate about trigger warnings?

Thematic Connections

- "My Mother Never Worked" (page 121)
- "Just Walk On By: A Black Man Ponders His Power to Alter Public Space" (page 233)
- "Why Looks Are the Last Bastion of Discrimination" (page 239)
- "Sex, Lies, and Conversation" (page 415)

★CASEBOOK

Do Guns Have a Place on College Campuses?

Ralph Barrera/Austin American-Statesman via AP

In this photo, taken on October 21, 2015, students at the University of Texas at West Mall gather on the steps of one of the campus buildings to protest a state law making it legal for those with permits to carry firearms on campus. Another student, in favor of the law, joined the protest.

• • •

Statistically, colleges and universities are relatively safe environments for students, faculty, and administrators. Indeed, they are probably among the safest public spaces in the United States. According to some studies, the homicide rate on campuses is one in one million students, as compared to fifty-seven deaths per million people in the general population. On average, there are fewer than twenty homicides a year on the grounds of American colleges and universities. This general pattern holds true across a range of crimes even when researchers take into account the lengthy semester breaks that leave campuses sparsely populated. The pattern also remains consistent regardless of a college's location. "Contrary to the concerns of many parents... about sending their children to college in some 'dangerous big city,' campuses in urban centers do not tend to have higher rates of victimization than do those in remote, rural locations," writes Northeastern University criminology professor James Alan Fox.

Of course, colleges and universities are not crime- or violence-free, although suicides are one hundred times more likely on campus than homicides. And despite their relative rarity, recent high-profile mass shootings on campuses have captured – and horrified – the public imagination. In a horrific 2007 shooting at Virginia Tech, a student killed thirty-two people and injured seventeen others. In 2008, an undergraduate at Louisiana Technical College killed two people and herself in a classroom. Also in 2008, a former graduate student at Northern Illinois University killed five people and injured twenty-one. Since 1990, there have been more than twenty multiple-victim shooting incidents on college campuses.

These and similar incidents have led to a nationwide conversation among public officials, college administrators, students, and others about how to make colleges safer. The discussion often boils down to two issues: how to prevent such events and how to respond to such events. Solutions include a range of measures, from profiling troubled individuals and focusing on the general psychological health of students to improving communications during emergencies and setting up procedures for locking down campuses. Perhaps the most controversial response to these events, however, involves the status of firearms and policies banning – or allowing – students and others to carry guns on campuses. As always, the discussion of gun rights touches on fundamental issues of personal freedom and public safety. These issues come into even sharper focus in the context of college and university campuses, which tend to be seen as orderly, peaceful places.

The four essays in this casebook illuminate the complex – and often polarizing – aspects of this discussion. In "Why I Wouldn't Go to the University of Texas Law School," law student Andrew Wilson explains not only how a Texas law permitting concealed handguns on campuses influenced his own decision, but also how it might detract from intellectual life and personal safety on campuses. The essay by Students for Gun-Free Schools, an advocacy organization that emerged in the wake of the Virginia Tech shootings, makes a comprehensive case (in "Why Our Campuses Are Safer without Concealed Handguns") against allowing guns on campus; among other points, the writers suggest that the presence of concealed firearms will detract from a free and open learning environment. In "Why Our Campuses Are *Not* Safer without Concealed Handguns," Students for Concealed Carry, another advocacy organization, offers point-by-point counterarguments to the claims made by Students for Gun-Free Schools. Finally, in "There's a Reason They Choose Schools," Timothy Wheeler, a retired physician and gun-rights activist, criticizes public policy experts, medical professionals, and "timid" college bureaucrats for restricting the rights of those who wish to carry guns on campus and elsewhere.

ANDREW WILSON

Why I Wouldn't Go to the University of Texas Law School

Andrew Wilson is a student at the University of Pennsylvania School of Law. He earned his undergraduate degree at the University of Texas at Austin.

Background on the Charles Whitman shooting As Wilson notes in his essay, the history of the University of Texas has a unique role in the debate about guns on campus. On August 1, 1966, Charles Whitman, a twenty-five-year-old engineering student there, barricaded himself in the observation deck in the iconic tower of the university's Main Building. Within about an hour and a half, he had killed fourteen people and wounded thirty-two using multiple firearms before being killed by the police. Many have speculated about what compelled Whitman's actions, from academic and family problems to a brain tumor discovered during his autopsy. In his suicide note, Whitman himself professed not to understand. Ultimately, investigators discovered that Whitman had previously sought counseling at the university's health center, where a physician had described him as "oozing with hostility." He was also an avid hunter and a marine veteran with sniper training. During Whitman's siege, armed students and other Austin residents attempted to aid the authorities. One of these civilians was the university's bookstore manager, Allen Crum, who armed himself and reached the observation tower with the police. Although he was lauded for his efforts, some have suggested that the presence of armed civilians might also have complicated the police response.

It's that time of year again. Prospective law students around the country must choose which school they will attend. They will compare costs, job prospects, location, and other deciding factors. But, for the first time, students looking at public law schools in Texas must compare a new factor: their safety on campus in light of Senate Bill 11, permitting concealed handguns on public college campuses. 1

Not long ago, I was one of those prospective students. My law school strategy was simple: cast a wide net and hope something sticks. I applied to a handful of schools, including the University of Texas Law School. My relationship with UT-Austin runs deep. During my time as an undergrad on the Forty Acres, the school gave me a number of opportunities I never imagined possible growing up in rural East Texas. Besides my emotional connection, Texas Law also appealed to me because in the face of rising law school tuition across the nation, it remains a great value compared to private schools. 2

In an exercise of naïve optimism, I thought SB 11 would not pass, or that the administration might circumvent it, and the issue of concealed carrying would not factor in my decision-making. I was wrong. 3

4 The inscription on the UT Tower celebrates the freedom to learn in universities. It reads, "Ye shall know the truth and the truth shall make you free." The UT Tower is a symbol of learning, freedom of expression, and intellectual discovery. It is also the site of the 1966 Charles Whitman shootings, which left 15 people dead and 32 wounded. Now, campus carry stands to threaten these values, putting students' minds and bodies at risk, and with them, the future success of UT-Austin.

5 I have experienced two school shootings in my life: once in middle school when gunfire broke out at the neighboring high school, and once as a freshman at UT-Austin when an unstable student shot at random on campus before taking his own life. I would never wish these harrowing experiences on anyone. Unfortunately, state governments around the country are considering bills similar to SB 11. Other states considering this legislation should look to Texas, and see the fear and frustration facing students and faculty, even before the law has gone into effect.

6 As an undergraduate, I had many diverse and at times provocative perspectives shape my learning. I learned most by listening to viewpoints different from my own. This freedom of expression makes universities ideal for the safe exchange of ideas. Campus carry corrupts this marketplace and threatens to undermine its very integrity. How can professors teach courses or assign grades with the possibility of violent retaliation one pull of a trigger away? How can students engage one another if the fear of offense is now informed by the fear of safety? Come August 1, the concept of trigger warnings will take on a literal meaning in Texas college campuses.

"How can professors teach courses or assign grades with the possibility of violent retaliation one pull of a trigger away?"

7 These concerns heighten when considering graduate and professional programs, particularly the law school.

8 Two major concerns inform my opposition to campus carry at the law school. The first, numbers. Only students 21 and older will be able to obtain a concealed-handgun license, a fact proponents of the bill love to cite. While these older students make up only a small fraction of undergraduate programs, they make up the majority of the law school. Realizing most of my classmates could potentially be carrying lethal weapons would increase my fear of speaking freely.

9 These numbers apply to all graduate programs, but my second concern pertains to the environment of law school specifically. Students must grapple with the stress of grades and careers, but also with topics like abortion and marriage equality, adding fuel to the fire. The potential for offense in legal classrooms is high, and adding guns in the mix is dangerous.

10 SB 11 was only one reason I turned down Texas Law, but it was an important one. Over the past months, UT has felt the impact of campus carry as prominent faculty members have left the school and other recruits have turned it down, citing the new law as a factor. From personal conversations,

I know other admitted students express concern over the law, and I imagine the legislation will continue to pose problems as the university tries to recruit exceptional students and faculty.

SB 11 threatens the future of higher education in Texas. As a Longhorn and a Texan, this possibility frightens me, and I hope it does you, too. 11

• • •

Comprehension

1. Why did the University of Texas Law School originally appeal to Wilson?
2. What does Texas's Senate Bill 11 allow? What did Wilson incorrectly assume about this legislation?
3. In paragraph 4, Wilson writes about the "UT Tower." Why, from his perspective, is the tower's meaning complicated?
4. The writer suggests that Senate Bill 11 might make law school classes especially dangerous, more so than undergraduate – or even other graduate – classes. What is his reasoning?

Purpose and Audience

1. The title of this essay is "Why I Wouldn't Go to the University of Texas Law School," and Wilson writes about his own personal experience and decision-making process. Do you think he has a broader aim beyond explaining a personal choice? If so, what is that broader purpose?
2. Although Wilson briefly touches on the substance of Senate Bill 11 in his essay, he does not provide a thorough summary of the bill or give the history, rationale, or context of the legislation. Do you think the essay would benefit from more information about the law? Would providing that information better serve the writer's purpose? Why or why not?
3. This essay appeared on the website of the *Nation,* a publication generally identified with a progressive, left-leaning point of view. Does Wilson seem to be addressing an audience who already agrees with him, or is he trying to change the minds of his readers? Explain your reasoning.
4. Does Wilson address counterarguments in this essay? If so, where – and how effectively – does he do so? If not, should he have addressed alternative points of view?

Style and Structure

1. Where does the writer use **cause-and-effect** to make his argument? What causal relationships does he identify?
2. Would you consider Wilson's essay a **Rogerian argument**? Why or why not?
3. Where does Wilson appeal to *ethos*? Do you find this kind of appeal persuasive and effective? Why or why not?
4. In paragraph 6, Wilson asks: "How can professors teach courses or assign grades with the possibility of violent retaliation one pull of a trigger away?

How can students engage one another if the fear of offense is now informed by the fear of safety?" Do you consider these questions alarmist? Do they seem reasonable? Explain.

5. **Vocabulary Project.** The writer argues that campus carry "corrupts" the "marketplace" of free expression and "threatens to undermine its very integrity" (6). What does the word *integrity* mean in this context? How is its meaning here similar to – or different from – its meaning when it is used to denote a person's honesty or virtue?

Journal Entry

Clearly, Wilson believes that the possible presence of guns on campus would threaten freedom of expression, both in himself and in others. Do you agree? For example, if you were aware that some of your fellow students might be carrying concealed firearms in classrooms, would that awareness affect your behavior, speech, or attitude?

Writing Workshop

1. **Working with Sources.** What is the firearms policy on your college campus? Find out the rules, and learn whether they are determined by the state or by the school. Then, talk to campus security, college officials, students, and other people to gather a range of views on this topic, and write an essay that takes a position on the appropriateness of your school's firearms policy. Be sure to document all the sources you use and to include a works-cited page. (See Chapter 18 for information on MLA documentation.)
2. Texas Senate Bill 11 allows individuals with a concealed handgun license to carry a handgun while on Texas public university campuses (with certain restrictions). In signing the legislation, Texas governor Greg Abbott explicitly said the measure protected Second Amendment rights identified by the United States Constitution. Do you agree that these rights should extend to college campuses? For example, who should be the final authority on a university's firearms policies? College officials? Students? The state? The federal government? Write an essay that takes a position on this issue.
3. Expanding your journal entry above, write an essay that explores the effects of (potentially) having more guns on campus. Do you think their presence would inhibit speech, change behavior, or increase danger? What benefits might the presence of more guns on campus have? Before you begin, decide how you will frame the issue. For example, do you see it primarily as a matter of Second Amendment rights and personal freedom? Or, do you view the issue primarily as a matter of keeping students as safe as possible?

Combining the Patterns

How does Wilson use **comparison and contrast** in this essay? How does this strategy help him develop his main idea and convey his overall purpose?

Thematic Connections

- "What Motivates Terrorists?" (page 344)
- "A Peaceful Woman Explains Why She Carries a Gun" (page 350)
- "Naming of Parts" (page 476)
- "Free Expression in Peril" (page 609)

STUDENTS FOR GUN-FREE SCHOOLS

Why Our Campuses Are Safer without Concealed Handguns

Students for Gun-Free Schools is a public advocacy organization founded by a number of people, including Omar Samaha and Randa Samaha, whose sister Reema was killed in the 2007 Virginia Tech massacre. The organization, which now has dozens of chapters at universities across the United States, opposes laws that allow students to carry concealed firearms on college campuses. In 2009, a chapter at the University of Texas at Austin organized a large rally and walkout protesting state legislation allowing guns on campuses. SGFS's motto is "Armed with knowledge, not guns."

Background on campus crime and safety Generally, colleges are relatively safe places. For example, a student is much less likely to die in a homicide on his or her campus than away from it. Recent work by researchers such as professor James Alan Fox at Northeastern University indicates that college campuses have low rates of violence and violent crimes overall, a reality that holds true at both urban and rural institutions. Horrific events like the Virginia Tech massacre understandably capture the public imagination and lead to concerns about the safety of students. However, the more common dangers of campus life are tied to binge drinking and to suicide (almost 1,200 college students commit suicide every year).

In the wake of tragic shootings at Virginia Tech and Northern Illinois University, a group called Students for Concealed Carry on Campus formed to advocate for the "right" of students and faculty to carry concealed handguns at colleges and universities in the United States. This group was quickly joined by the National Rifle Association and other progun organizations that had been lobbying for years to liberalize America's concealed carry laws. 1

Frequently lost in the national debate that ensued was the fact that our nation's colleges and universities are some of the safest places in our country in large part because their campuses, in almost all cases, have remained gun-free. 2

The overwhelming majority of the 4,314 colleges and universities in the United States prohibit students and faculty from carrying concealed handguns on campus (the exceptions include public colleges and universities in Utah; Blue Ridge Community College in Weyers Cave, Virginia; and Colorado State University in Fort Collins, Colorado). Despite high-profile shootings like the ones mentioned above, homicides at American colleges and universities remain rare events. 3

A 2001 study by the U.S. Department of Education found that the overall homicide rate at postsecondary education institutions was 0.07 per 100,000 of enrollment in 1999. By comparison, the criminal homicide rate in the United States was 5.7 per 100,000 persons overall in 1999, and 14.1 per 100,000 for 4 persons ages seventeen to twenty-nine. Another study, conducted by the Department of Justice, found that 93 percent of violent crimes that victimize college students occur off campus. This research demonstrates conclusively that students on the campuses of postsecondary institutions are significantly safer than both their off-campus counterparts and the nation as a whole.

Students for Gun-Free Schools (SGFS) believes these results can be attributed largely to strict policies that have kept firearms off our nation's campuses. Our colleges and universities are safe sanctuaries for learning, and we believe they would be endangered by the presence of concealed handguns for the following reasons: 5

1. Concealed handguns would detract from a healthy learning environment;
2. More guns on campus would create additional risk for students;
3. Shooters would not be deterred by concealed carry permit holders;
4. Concealed carry permit holders are not always "law-abiding" citizens; and
5. Concealed carry permit holders are not required to have law enforcement training.

1. Concealed Handguns Would Detract from a Healthy Learning Environment

In order to foster a healthy learning environment at America's colleges and universities, it is critical that students and faculty feel safe on campus. If concealed carry were allowed on America's campuses, there is no doubt that many students would feel uncomfortable about not knowing whether their professors and/or fellow students were carrying handguns. Students and teachers must be able to express themselves freely in classroom environments, where discussions frequently touch on controversial topics that arouse passion. The introduction of handguns on our campuses would inhibit this dialogue by creating fear of possible retaliation. Whether it's a classroom debate, a student-teacher conversation about a grade, or an informal interaction in a dormitory, the presence of hidden handguns would restrain the open exchange of ideas that is so critical to the college experience. 6

Americans, in overwhelming numbers, believe that guns have no place at our colleges and universities. In one national survey, 94 percent of Americans answered "No" when asked, "Do you think regular citizens should be allowed to bring their guns [onto] college campuses?" 7

2. More Guns on Campus Would Create Additional Risk for Students

Allowing concealed carry permit holders to bring handguns onto college campuses would raise a host of public safety concerns for institutions that have a legal duty to provide secure environments for their students, faculty, and visitors. As noted in a 2007 report by the Brady Campaign to Prevent Gun Violence, there are four reasons why gun violence would be likely to increase if more guns were present on college campuses: (1) The prevalence of drugs and 8 alcohol; (2) The risk of suicide and mental health issues; (3) The likelihood of gun thefts; and (4) An increased risk of accidental shootings.

A 2007 study by the National Center on Addiction and Substance Abuse at Columbia University found that "[N]early half of America's 5.4 million full-time college students abuse drugs or drink alcohol on binges at least once a month." Another study found that alcohol is involved in 95 percent of the violent crime on campus. The combination of alcohol, drugs, and guns is a dangerous mix that could lead to additional, and more lethal, violence on campus. A 2002 study by the Harvard School of Public Health compared students who have a firearm at college with those who do not have a firearm. They found that students who have a firearm at college are more likely to binge drink, drive a motor vehicle after binge drinking, use illegal drugs, vandalize property, and get into trouble with the police. 9

Suicide and mental health are also substantial issues on college campuses. One study found that 24 percent of college students had thought about attempting suicide and 5 percent had actually attempted to kill themselves. Firearms, of course, make many types of violence more lethal. Suicide attempts are successful more than 90 percent of the time when a firearm is used. By comparison, such attempts are fatal only 3 percent of the time when a drug overdose is the method used. One study that examined college student suicide from 1920–2004 found that, "It is the reduced use of firearms as a method of suicide that is responsible for virtually all of the benefit associated with being a student . . . and that the relationship between student status and firearms may be the key to understanding why students commit suicide at a lower rate than does the general U.S. population." 10

Allowing concealed handguns on campus would also increase the risk of gun theft and accidental shootings. College dorm rooms are typically small, with few places available to lock up or secure a handgun. They also experience considerable numbers of visitors who could gain unauthorized access to these firearms. 11

3. Shooters Would Not Be Deterred by Concealed Carry Permit Holders

The gun lobby frequently advances the argument that shooters target gun-free zones such as college campuses for their attacks because they are unlikely to receive initial resistance. 12

This ignores the fact that homicides and shootings at American colleges and universities are rare events in large part because of these institutions' current policies regarding firearms on campus. In 2003, for example, there were 11,920 total gun homicides in the United States, but only ten total murders on the nation's college campuses. 13

Campus shooters are also frequently suicidal. Most of the campus shootings in America in recent years (i.e., Virginia Tech, Northern Illinois University, Louisiana Technical College, etc.) were murder-suicides. These shooters left home on the morning of their attacks knowing they were going to die by gunfire before the day was over — their goal was simply to take as many people with them as they could. It is unlikely these shooters would have been deterred 14 by the knowledge that their fellow students (or campus faculty) might be armed. In fact, it is possible that a college campus that allows staff and faculty to carry concealed handguns might provide a more attractive target to such shooters. Lacking any fear of death, they might welcome the opportunity to provoke shootouts and crossfire among relatively untrained concealed carry permit holders in order to increase casualties.

There have also been numerous incidents in recent years where shooters have targeted what might be deemed "gun-full zones" for their attacks, including: 15

> May 8, 2006 – Michael Kennedy, eighteen, attacks Fairfax County Police Sully District Station in Virginia, firing more than seventy rounds and killing two officers before police are able to take him down. Kennedy is armed with five handguns and two rifles, including a semiautomatic AK-47 assault rifle, and carries more than three hundred rounds of ammunition.
>
> May 19, 2007 – Jason Hamilton shoots and kills his wife at home and then attacks a sheriff's department at Latah County Courthouse and a church in Moscow, Idaho. Hamilton kills a total of three people, including a police officer, before taking his own life. He is armed with an AK-47 assault rifle and an M1 carbine despite a long history of domestic violence, mental illness, and run-ins with the police. Local resident and University of Idaho student Pete Hussmann, twenty, races to the courthouse on his bike armed with a .45 caliber handgun and is shot four times by Hamilton. "It was like a war zone," says Hussmann. Two other law enforcement officers are wounded.

There is no evidence that suicidal shooters would be deterred from attacks on college campuses by concealed carry permit holders. To the extent that they could provoke firefights with such individuals in crowded college classrooms and create additional mayhem, they might even seek out such confrontations. 16

"There is no evidence that suicidal shooters would be deterred from attacks on college campuses by concealed carry permit holders."

4. Concealed Carry Permit Holders Are Not Always "Law-Abiding" Citizens

The gun lobby frequently claims that those with permits to carry concealed handguns are "law-abiding citizens," or even the most law-abiding citizens in their communities. This is not always true. Two states, Alaska and Vermont, do not even require residents to obtain a permit to carry a concealed weapon. Individuals in these states can buy a handgun through an unregulated private sale (no background check required) and then carry it in public. 17

Thirty-eight states have a "shall-issue" policy for concealed carry permits, meaning that officials may not arbitrarily deny an application to those who meet a basic set of requirements. The primary requirement for obtaining a permit in these states is to pass a background check through the National Instant Criminal Background Check System (NICS). The purpose of the 18 background check is to ascertain whether the applicant is prohibited under federal law from owning and purchasing firearms. Those with felony convictions are automatically prohibited. The only misdemeanor convictions that would prohibit someone from owning and purchasing firearms, however, are those related to incidents of domestic violence. Someone who obtains a concealed carry permit in a shall-issue state could have a rap sheet with other types of misdemeanor convictions, including violent offenses.

The National Instant Criminal Background Check System is also not foolproof. A recent study found that the NICS database is "deeply flawed" and missing millions of disqualifying records. Most troubling, nine out of ten mental health records that would disqualify individuals from purchasing firearms are not currently in the database. One-fourth of felony conviction records have also not been submitted to NICS by the states. 19

The bottom line is that even if someone passes a background check and qualifies for a concealed carry permit (if their state requires one), that person is not necessarily a law-abiding citizen. They could have a substantial criminal record involving misdemeanor offenses, or a history of mental illness. It is notable that campus shooters including Gang Lu, Wayne Lo, Robert Flores, Biswanath Halder, Seung-Hui Cho, Latina Williams, and Steven Kazmierczak passed background checks in acquiring the firearms used in their attacks. Some possessed a concealed carry permit in their home states; others would have qualified had they applied. Finally, individuals who are prohibited under federal law from owning or purchasing firearms can still pass a background check (and potentially qualify for a concealed carry permit) if their disqualifying records have not been transferred to NICS. 20

Research has demonstrated that those who obtain concealed carry permits can pose a threat to public safety. 21

A Violence Policy Center study found that Texas concealed handgun license holders were arrested for weapon-related offenses at a rate 81 percent higher than the general population of Texas aged twenty-one and older (offenses included 279 assaults, 671 unlawfully carrying a weapon, and 172 deadly conduct/discharge of a firearm). Between January 1, 1996, and August 31, 2001, Texas concealed handgun license holders were arrested for 5,314 crimes—including murder, rape, kidnapping, and theft. 22

A 2007 investigation by the Florida *Sun-Sentinel* found that the state's permit system had granted concealed carry permits to more than 1,400 individuals who pled guilty or no contest to a felony, 216 individuals with outstanding warrants, 128 individuals with active domestic violence restraining orders, and 6 registered sex offenders. 23

5. Concealed Carry Permit Holders Are Not Required to Have Law Enforcement Training

The forty-eight states in the U.S. that allow residents to carry concealed handguns do not require them to have any formal law enforcement training. The training requirement to obtain a concealed carry permit in a "shall-issue" state is typically a day class. Many shall-issue states do not even require the 24 applicant to fire his/her handgun at a range to demonstrate proficiency or even basic competency with the weapon. An example would be Virginia, where a four-hour sit-down session in a classroom is sufficient to meet the state's training requirement.

This is in direct contrast to the intensive training required of law enforcement officers who are currently called on to safeguard our nation's colleges and universities. These officers start receiving training in how to safely handle a sidearm – and in demonstrating discretion in using lethal force – long before they ever see actual duty in their communities. This training then continues throughout their career in law enforcement. Police departments typically require their officers to qualify one to four times a year with their duty weapon. 25

Nonetheless, even trained law enforcement officers rarely hit their targets when firing at other human beings. One 2006 study examined three decades of bullet hit rates among larger U.S. police departments and found that officers hit their targets approximately 20 percent of the time. The New York City Police Department's Firearms Discharge report for 2006 showed similar results. That year, their officers intentionally fired a gun at a person 364 times, hitting their target only 103 times – a success rate of 28.3 percent. Commenting on that success rate, New York City Police Commissioner Ray Kelly said, "When you factor in all of the other elements that are involved in shooting at an adversary, that's a high hit rate. The adrenaline flow, the movement of the target, the movement of the shooter, the officer, the lighting conditions, the weather . . . I think it is a high rate when you consider all of the variables." 26

Given the record of trained law enforcement officers, how often would relatively untrained concealed carry permit holders hit their targets when opening fire on college campuses? Recent shootings on America's campuses have occurred in crowded classrooms and involved a great deal of chaos, with students panicked and running for their lives. Concealed carry permit holders discharging their weapons in such situations would be unlikely to have clear lines of fire. If multiple students drew handguns, just identifying the actual "shooter" or target would be challenging. The potential for collateral damage is enormous, even assuming that concealed carry permit holders would make sound decisions about when to discharge their handguns. 27

Law enforcement officers responding to such emergencies would also face enormous difficulties. If police arrived on the scene of a campus shooting and found multiple students with handguns drawn, how would they know who their target is? This scenario was contemplated by the Virginia Tech Review Panel, which commented: "If numerous people had been rushing around with handguns outside Norris Hall on the morning of April 16, [2007,] the possibility of accidental or mistaken shootings would have increased significantly. The campus police said that the probability would have been high that anyone emerging from a classroom at Norris Hall holding a gun would have been shot." 28

Despite the fact that there are more than 200 million firearms in private hands in the United States and forty-eight states now allow some form of concealed carry, instances in which law-abiding citizens successfully shoot 29 and kill criminals are exceedingly rare. In 2005, there were a total of 12,352 gun-related homicides in the United States. Yet, during the same year, the FBI reported only 143 justifiable homicides involving a firearm. A 2000 study by the Harvard School of Public Health concluded that, "Guns are used to threaten and intimidate far more often than they are used in self-defense. Most self-reported self-defense gun uses may well be illegal and against the interests of society." This is no doubt partially due to the lack of formal training among those purchasing firearms and receiving permits to carry concealed handguns in the United States.

The notion that individuals with concealed carry permits are going to 30
make prudent decisions about when to discharge their firearms on school campuses is dubious at best, as is the notion that these individuals would successfully take down active shooters while avoiding collateral damage in chaotic situations. The safest policy to limit potential violence is to prohibit students and faculty from keeping handguns on campus and allow trained law enforcement officers to provide for campus security.

• • •

Comprehension

1. According to the writers, what often gets "lost in the national debate" (2) about gun laws after high-profile school shootings? Why is this important to the writers' main point?
2. According to the 2007 Brady Campaign report cited by the writers, why will gun violence likely increase if guns are allowed on campuses? What four reasons does the report give?
3. The writers discuss "shall-issue" policies (18) for concealed carry permits. What is a "shall-issue" policy?
4. According to the writers, what is the "bottom line" with regard to "law-abiding" (20) concealed carry permit holders? Why are the writers skeptical of the "gun lobby" on this issue?

Purpose and Audience

1. Students for Gun-Free Schools is a national organization devoted to keeping guns off campuses. For example, it works to influence legislation and policy directly. How do you think this mission affects the writers' purpose in this essay?
2. Before the writers list their reasons for keeping guns off campus, they establish that campuses are relatively safe places. Why do you think they do so?
3. Restate the essay's thesis in your own words.
4. The writers often refer to claims made by the "gun lobby," but they do not define this term. Should they have done so? Why or why not?
5. Why do the writers bring up the "bullet hit rate" (26) of the New York City Police Department? How is this statistic related to their main argument?

Style and Structure

1. In their opening paragraph, why do the writers put the word *right* in quotation marks?
2. In paragraph 7, the writers cite an unnamed "national survey" indicating that 94 percent of Americans think citizens should not be allowed to bring guns on campuses. Is this information convincing? Is it relevant to the main issue?
3. What is the purpose of the two examples used in paragraph 15?
4. **Vocabulary Project.** In paragraph 27, the writers discuss the "potential for collateral damage" if more students are armed on campus. What connotations does the expression *collateral damage* have? What connotations do you think the writers want it to have in this essay?

Journal Entry

The writers argue that guns on campus would encourage an unhealthy learning environment, restraining exchanges of ideas, inhibiting discussions, making students uncomfortable, and discouraging passionate debate by "creating fear of possible retaliation" (6). Does this seem like a reasonable concern? Why or why not?

Writing Workshop

1. The writers argue that college campuses are relatively safe places. Do you agree? Do you feel safe at your school? Do you think allowing students to carry guns on campus would make colleges less safe? Would you feel more secure knowing your fellow students and professors might be armed? Write an essay that presents your position on these questions.
2. **Working with Sources.** In the first paragraph, the writers refer to the National Rifle Association and "other pro-gun organizations" that lobby to "liberalize America's concealed carry laws." Do you think gun laws should be "liberalized" or made more restrictive? Write an essay that takes a position on this issue. Before you begin, consult the NRA's website at nra.org and the website of the Brady Campaign to Prevent Gun Violence at bradycampaign.org or Everytown for Gun Safety at everytown.org to get an overview of the opposing positions on this issue. Be sure to document any sources you use and to include a works-cited page. (See Chapter 18 for information on MLA documentation.)
3. Students for Gun-Free Schools was founded in the wake of the Virginia Tech shootings in 2007, and much of the discussion and activism in the aftermath of Virginia Tech and other shootings has focused on guns. Do you believe guns are the central problem in these events, or even a main cause? Or, do you think the emphasis on firearms and gun laws is misplaced in the context of other issues, such as mental health? Write an essay that answers these questions.

Combining the Patterns

Where in this essay do the writers use **comparison and contrast**? How does this pattern help them develop their main argument?

Thematic Connections

- “Shooting an Elephant” (page 131)
- “Just Walk On By: A Black Man Ponders His Power to Alter Public Space” (page 233)
- “Naming of Parts” (page 476)

STUDENTS FOR CONCEALED CARRY

Why Our Campuses Are *Not* Safer without Concealed Handguns

Founded in 2007, Students for Concealed Carry is a national organization of U.S. college students, faculty, staff, and others who support allowing those with concealed handgun licenses to carry their guns on college campuses. The group seeks to raise public awareness about the issue of campus safety and to persuade legislators and college administrators to (in the words of the organization's website) "grant concealed handgun license holders the same rights on college campuses that those licensees currently enjoy in most other unsecured locations." Students for Concealed Carry is known for its national campus "empty holster" protests, in which members visibly wear empty holsters and distribute literature in support of their cause.

Background on concealed carry The phrase *concealed carry* refers to the practice of carrying a concealed gun or other weapon. Concealed carry laws are determined by individual states, not federal law; in 2012, however, a federal court overturned a long-standing Illinois ban on concealed weapons as unconstitutional. Generally, concealed carry laws fall into several categories, including "shall-issue" and "may-issue." In "shall-issue" states, such as Idaho and Pennsylvania, permits are granted to those who meet specific requirements. In "may-issue" states, such as Massachusetts and Maryland, the issuing of permits remains at the discretion of local or state authorities even if the applicant meets basic requirements. In some cases, those applying for concealed carry licenses must demonstrate "good cause" for desiring a permit. States generally require applicants to meet basic criteria. For example, those who have been judged mentally incompetent in court or who have been committed to a mental institution are ineligible. Over the last two decades, more states have become "shall-issue" jurisdictions, which suggests an easing of gun restrictions.

In response to the unprecedented media attention and public support 1 generated by Students for Concealed Carry (SCC), the organization leading the charge to extend concealed carry (of handgun) rights to college campuses, a counter-movement has emerged, operating under the banner Students for Gun-Free Schools (SGFS). SGFS recently released an essay titled "Why Our Campuses Are Safer without Concealed Handguns." This attack on the positions of SCC brings few, if any, new arguments to the table and relies instead on the well-worn arguments put forth by groups like the Brady Campaign to Prevent Gun Violence.

The crux of the SGFS essay is the undeniable fact that college campuses 2 typically have lower crime rates than the cities in which they reside. Tossing academic standards of research and citation to the wind, the essay's introduction simply points out this fact and concludes, "Students for Gun-Free

Schools (SGFS) believes these results can be attributed largely to strict policies that have kept firearms off our nation's campuses." Without citing corroborating facts or research, the same gun control advocates who want us to believe that lax gun control laws in nearby states negate the effectiveness of strict gun control laws in the District of Columbia and other tightly regulated cities/states now want us to believe that strict gun control regulations on college campuses are able to stand up against the lax gun control laws in the very cities in which those campuses reside.

To assume a cause-and-effect relationship between the unenforceable gun control regulations on college campuses and the relative safety of college campuses constitutes an astoundingly naïve leap in logic. A similar disparity can be found between the relatively low crime rates in affluent neighborhoods and the higher crime rates in the cities in which those neighborhoods exist. After all, what are college campuses but, essentially, large, affluent neighborhoods? 3

After making the unsubstantiated claim that strict gun control regulations make college campuses safer, the essay moves on to present five reasons why SGFS believes that allowing concealed carry on college campuses would make colleges less safe: 4

1. Concealed handguns would detract from a healthy learning environment;
2. More guns on campus would create additional risk for students;
3. Shooters would not be deterred by concealed carry permit holders;
4. Concealed carry permit holders are not always "law-abiding" citizens; and
5. Concealed carry permit holders are not required to have law enforcement training.

1. Concealed Handguns Would Not Detract from a Healthy Learning Environment

An opponent of concealed carry on campus isn't doing his or her job unless he or she argues, "Concealed handguns would detract from a healthy learning environment." The SGFS essay contends, "If concealed carry were allowed on America's campuses, there is no doubt that many students would feel uncomfortable about not knowing whether their professors and/or fellow students were carrying handguns." This argument not only ignores the fact that, in the absence of metal detectors and X-ray machines at every campus entrance, students already have no way of knowing who, if anyone, is carrying a gun; it also assumes that students would be made more uncomfortable by the presence of guns on campus than they are by the presence of guns off campus. 5

In most U.S. states approximately 1 percent of the population (one person out of a hundred) is licensed to carry a concealed handgun. Are students afraid to sit in three-hundred-seat movie theaters knowing that, statistically speaking, as many as three of their fellow moviegoers may be legally carrying concealed handguns? Are they afraid to walk through crowded shopping malls knowing that one out of every hundred shoppers they pass is potentially carrying a legally concealed handgun? Or do they go through their daily 6 routines, both on and off campus, never giving much thought to what is concealed beneath the clothing and within the handbags of the people they pass? Does SGFS honestly contend that students on the one hundred U.S. college campuses where concealed carry is currently allowed, including all public colleges in the states of Utah, Colorado, Mississippi, and recently Idaho, are afraid to engage in intelligent debate for fear that somebody nearby might have a gun? Does concealed carry discourage debate on the floor of the state legislatures in Texas and Virginia and the other states where it is allowed in the state capitol?

The SGFS essay points to a 1999 survey that asked 1,500 respondents, "Do you think regular citizens should be allowed to bring their guns [onto] college campuses?" This survey, which asked only about "regular citizens" and made no distinction for concealed handgun license holders, took place ten years ago, when America's right-to-carry laws were still in their infancy and before many current right-to-carry states adopted "shall-issue" licensing laws. At that time very few Americans were familiar with the process or even the notion of obtaining a concealed handgun license, and it is absurd to suggest that this outdated poll reflects current national opinion on the rights of trained, licensed adults. However, accepting for the sake of argument that a majority of the general public does oppose allowing concealed carry on college campuses, what does that prove? Beyond the 1 percent who possess concealed handgun licenses, what percentage of Americans can tell you the requirements to obtain a concealed handgun license in their state, much less accurately comment on whether or not concealed carry leads to more or less crime? Public opinion does not always dictate public policy on complicated issues of public safety. The FDA does not poll the public on acceptable procedures for sanitizing meatpacking plants. 7

2. More Guns on Campus Would Create Little If Any Additional Risk for Students

The SGFS essay goes on to assert, "More guns on campus would create additional risk for students." Citing a study by the Brady Campaign, the essay points to "(1) The prevalence of drugs and alcohol; (2) The risk of suicide and mental health issues; (3) The likelihood of gun thefts; and (4) An increased risk of accidental shootings." The essay doesn't mention that after allowing concealed carry on campus for a combined total of one hundred semesters, none of the aforementioned twelve U.S. colleges have seen a single resulting incident of a student under the influence of drugs or alcohol using or brandishing a weapon on campus, a single resulting suicide, a single resulting gun theft, or a single resulting gun accident. 8

The essay points to a 2007 Columbia University study that concluded, "[N]early half of America's 5.4 million full-time college students abuse drugs or drink alcohol on binges at least once a month"; however, the essay fails to differentiate between underclassmen and upperclassmen. Since the age limit to obtain a concealed handgun license in most states is twenty-one, it seems only fair to note that a three-year study by the Task Force on College Drinking, 9 commissioned by the National Institute on Alcohol Abuse and Alcoholism (NIAAA), found that ages eighteen through twenty-one is the period of heaviest alcohol consumption for most drinkers in the United States, that college students under the age of twenty-one are more likely than older students to binge drink and have alcohol-related problems, and that the average levels of drinking drop off significantly by the age of twenty-three. In July of 2008 more than one hundred university chancellors and college presidents, recognizing that binge drinking is primarily a problem among students under the age of twenty-one and convinced that college binge drinking occurs because students under the age of twenty-one are not allowed to drink in the same safe, controlled environments as students over the age of twenty-one, signed on to the Amethyst Initiative, a movement aimed at creating a dialogue over the wisdom of the national drinking age.

According to Dr. Robert D. Foss, manager of alcohol studies at the Uni- 10
versity of North Carolina Highway Safety Research Center (HSRC), "Almost everybody misperceives how much college students actually drink. When people are asked to estimate it, they almost always way overshoot the reality." Between 1999 and 2003, HSRC conducted a study that used breathalyzers (as opposed to the anonymous surveys used in the studies cited by SGFS) to gauge the drinking habits of students at the University of North Carolina. According to Dr. Foss, "Our findings ran counter to reports in the national media that portrayed excessive college student drinking as a rampant epidemic." The study found that two out of three students returning to their residences on Friday and Saturday nights had not had anything to drink and that many of the remaining one-third had only had a few drinks. The rate of alcohol consumption during the rest of the week was found to be much lower.

The SGFS essay also points to a 2002 Harvard University study that found 11
that students who have firearms at college are more likely to binge drink, drive while under the influence, use illegal drugs, vandalize property, and get into trouble with the police. What the essay doesn't point out is that a comparison of the Harvard study's data to concealed handgun licensing data from that same period of time suggests that fewer (most likely far fewer) than 5 percent of the gun owners surveyed were concealed handgun license holders. Studies[1] show that concealed handgun license holders, unlike unlicensed gun owners, are significantly less likely than the general population to engage in criminal behavior.

Despite all of these statistics, the issue of alcohol consumption and reck- 12
less behavior by college students is a moot point – this is not a debate about keeping guns out of the hands of college students. Allowing concealed carry on college campuses would not change the rules about who can purchase a firearm or who can obtain a concealed handgun license. It also wouldn't change the rules at off-campus parties and bars, the places where individuals over the age of twenty-one are most likely to consume alcohol. And it would not make it legal to carry a handgun while under the influence of drugs or alcohol. Changing the rules would simply allow the same trained, licensed adults who carry concealed handguns, without incident when not on campus, to do so on campus. There is no reason to assume that the same individuals

who aren't getting drunk and shooting people outside of college campuses would suddenly get drunk and start shooting people on college campuses.

SGFS's arguments about suicide and the vulnerability of dorm rooms to theft carry very little weight when viewed in light of the fact that this is not a debate about who can own or carry a gun. The overwhelming majority of suicides are committed in the victim's home. Under current regulations, the only students prohibited from keeping firearms in their homes are students living in on-campus housing. At most colleges, on-campus housing is occupied primarily by freshmen and sophomores, students typically too young to obtain a concealed handgun license. A comparison of housing statistics at the University of Texas (a major university with over fifty thousand students) to Texas concealed handgun licensing statistics shows a probability of only ten to twenty concealed handgun license holders living in on-campus housing. Statistically speaking, how many of those ten to twenty individuals are likely to commit suicide in a given year? As for theft, the vulnerability of dorms to theft does not necessitate a campus-wide ban on concealed carry. There are a multitude of security options, from floor safes to safes that bolt to bed frames to community gun lockups. 13

Concerns about accidental discharges are overblown, to say the least. Accidental discharges of concealed firearms are very rare — particularly because modern firearms are designed with safety in mind and because a handgun's trigger is typically not exposed when it is concealed — and only a small fraction of accidental discharges result in injury. It is silly to suggest that citizens should be denied a right simply because that right is accompanied by a negligible risk. 14

3. Shooters May or May Not Be Deterred by Concealed Carry Permit Holders, but Deterring Shooting Sprees Is Only One of Several Potential Benefits

SGFS goes on to argue, "Shooters would not be deterred by concealed carry permit holders." To quote Louisiana State Representative Ernest D. Wooton, speaking at the 2008 SCC (then Students for Concealed Carry on Campus) National Conference in Washington, D.C., "If we don't try it, are we going to know?" 15

Though campus shooters are frequently suicidal, they are not simply suicidal — if they were, they would simply shoot themselves at home and leave everyone else alone. Campus shooters go on armed rampages because they misguidedly seek to make a point or attain infamy. It's hard to attain infamy if a concealed handgun license holder ends your shooting spree before it begins. Even if the knowledge that concealed handgun license holders might be present isn't enough to deter all would-be gunmen, an attempted shooting spree thwarted by a licensee might be enough to deter a few. 16

The SGFS essay points to two attacks on facilities where the shooters knew that law enforcement officers would be present, as evidence that suicidal gunmen are not deterred by armed resistance. Those particular shooters may not have been deterred, but they also didn't cause nearly as great a loss of life 17 as is often caused by shooters in "gun-free zones." In those two incidents, the shooters killed a combined total of five people, less than one-sixth the total body count from the Virginia Tech massacre.

The issue of concealed carry on college campuses is not just about preventing campus shooting sprees. Though it's the mass shootings that get the headlines, college campuses play host to assaults, rapes, and every type of criminal activity found in the rest of society. The question of whether or not concealed carry would deter would-be mass-shooters should not be the determining factor in whether or not it is allowed on college campuses. Why should a 105-pound woman who is allowed the means to defend herself against a 250-pound would-be rapist outside of campus not be afforded that same right on campus? Why should a professor who is allowed the means to defend himself at the local bank and at his neighborhood church be forced to hide under his desk listening to gunshots getting closer, with no recourse but to hope and pray the gunman doesn't find him? 18

4. Concealed Carry Permit Holders Are Not Always "Law-Abiding" Citizens, but They're Statistically More Law-Abiding Than Most

Students for Gun-Free Schools unnecessarily points out, "Concealed carry permit holders are not always 'law-abiding' citizens." This is true. Likewise, law enforcement officers, elected officials, and clergy members are not always "law-abiding" citizens. Every segment of society has its bad apples, but statistically speaking, concealed carry has fewer than most. Numerous studies[1] by independent researchers and state agencies suggest that concealed handgun license holders are five times less likely than non-license holders to commit violent crimes. A comparison of statistics[2] in the mid-nineties, when Florida was still one of the few shall-issue states, found that Florida concealed handgun license holders were three times less likely to be arrested than were New York City police officers. 19

Despite the fact that Students for Concealed Carry on Campus does not advocate concealed carry by unlicensed individuals, SGFS finds it necessary to point out that Alaska and Vermont do not require (though Alaska offers) a license to carry a concealed handgun. The essay then goes on to erroneously suggest, "The primary requirement for obtaining a permit in [the thirty-eight shall-issue] states is to pass a background check through the National Instant Criminal Background Check System." In reality, many states, such as Texas, require applicants to submit to extensive state and federal fingerprint and background checks that often take one to three months (far from instant) to complete. 20

The essay further blurs the line between the requirements to purchase a firearm and the requirements to obtain a concealed handgun license by stating, "The only misdemeanor convictions that would prohibit someone from owning and purchasing firearms, however, are those related to incidents of domestic violence. Someone who obtains a concealed carry permit in a shall-issue state could have a rap sheet with other types of misdemeanor convictions, including violent offenses." The factors that can disqualify an individual 21 from obtaining a concealed handgun license vary from state to state, but most states place certain restrictions and time limits on misdemeanor offenders. For instance, in the state of Texas you cannot obtain a concealed handgun license if you have had any misdemeanor convictions greater than a traffic citation in the past five years. A current license holder who commits a misdemeanor greater than a traffic violation would immediately have his or her license revoked.

> "Contrary to the claims of SGFS, mental health rulings are commonly considered by states when deciding whether or not to issue a concealed handgun license."

22 The SGFS essay refers to several mass-shooters and erroneously suggests that several of them either possessed or would have qualified for concealed handgun licenses. For example, the essay mentions Seung-Hui Cho, the Virginia Tech shooter, even though his adjudication as a danger to himself and others would have disqualified him from obtaining a concealed handgun license in most shall-issue states. Contrary to the claims of SGFS, mental health rulings are commonly considered by states when deciding whether or not to issue a concealed handgun license.

23 Perhaps most discrediting of SGFS's many claims is its citation of a widely discredited 2001 study by the Violence Policy Center, a highly biased gun control advocacy group. The study claims that Texas concealed handgun license holders were arrested for weapon-related offenses at a rate 81 percent higher than the general population of Texas age twenty-one and older, between January 1, 1996, and December 31, 2000 (SGFS mistakenly lists the end date as August 31, 2001). This study, which took place during the first five years of Texas's concealed handgun licensing program, when police officers were not always clear on the new weapons laws and often took a "better safe than sorry" approach to making arrests, focused solely on arrests, not convictions. According to Texas Department of Corrections statistics from that same period of time, Texas concealed handgun license holders were 7.6 times *less* likely than non-license holders to be arrested for *violent* crimes (as opposed to the weapons crimes – which can include non-violent offenses such as attempting to carry a concealed handgun into a federal building – researched by the Violence Policy Center). A four-year study by engineering statistician William E. Sturdevant found that Texas concealed handgun license holders were 5.5 times less likely than non-license holders to be *convicted* of violent crimes. According to statistics from the Texas Department of Public Safety and the U.S. Census Bureau, reported by the *San Antonio Express-News* in September 2000, Texas concealed handgun license holders were 14 times less likely than the non-license holders to commit a crime of any kind and 5 times less likely to commit a violent crime. The SGFS essay mentions murder as one of the crimes for which Texas concealed handgun license holders were arrested during the course of the VPC study, but the essay fails to mention that in the first ten years of Texas's concealed handgun licensing program (during which

time over a quarter of a million concealed handgun licenses were issued), only eight Texas concealed handgun license holders were convicted of murder. As of January 1, 2007, no Texas concealed handgun license holder had ever been convicted of capital murder. The discrepancy between arrests and convictions is caused, in large part, by the way law enforcement officers respond to a self-defense shooting. If the facts of a self-defense shooting are not immediately evident, a shooter who acted within the letter of the law may still be arrested for murder and held until investigators are able to sort out the sequence of events.

The SGFS essay concludes its attack on the integrity of concealed hand- 24 gun license holders by pointing to a 2007 investigation by the Florida *Sun-Sentinel* that purportedly found more than 1,400 convicted felons in possession of Florida concealed handgun licenses. Though the Florida licensing system may have a few cracks in its screening process, the cracks appear to be relatively minor. Those 1,400 convicted felons constitute only about 0.1 percent of all Florida concealed handgun license holders. And the cracks apparently aren't causing problems. Statistics show that Florida concealed handgun license holders are still significantly less likely than non-license holders to commit violent crimes. In fact, according to Florida state agencies, you are more than twice as likely to be attacked by an alligator than by a concealed handgun license holder in the state of Florida.

The truth is that possessing a concealed handgun license and/or having 25 the right to legally carry a firearm does not enable a person to carry a gun or commit a crime. There are no checkpoints where officials screen for guns and check licenses. A person intent on carrying a gun can easily do so throughout modern American society, including on college campuses, regardless of whether or not he or she is licensed to do so. An individual engaged in criminal activity is typically not concerned with the prospect of committing a misdemeanor (carrying a concealed handgun without a license) on his or her way to commit a felony (armed robbery, assault, rape, murder, etc.).

5. Concealed Carry Permit Holders Are Not Required to Have Law Enforcement Training Because They're Not Law Enforcement Officers

For its final argument, the essay points out, "Concealed carry permit 26 holders are not required to have law enforcement training." This is true. Concealed carry permit holders are not required to have law enforcement training because they are not law enforcement officers. Law enforcement officers do not go through academy training to learn to carry concealed handguns for self-defense; they go through academy training to learn to be law enforcement officers. Concealed handgun license holders have no need of most of the training received by law enforcement officers. Concealed handgun license holders don't need to know how to drive police cars at high speeds or how to kick down doors or how to conduct traffic stops or how to make arrests or how to use handcuffs. And concealed handgun license holders definitely don't need to spend weeks memorizing radio codes and traffic laws.

Contrary to what SGFS and other opponents of concealed carry might 27 claim, concealed handgun license holders don't need extensive tactical training because they are not charged with protecting the public. Concealed handgun license holders don't go looking for bad guys – it's not their job to act like amateur, one-man SWAT teams. All a concealed handgun license holder needs to know is how to use his or her concealed handgun to stop an immediate threat of death or serious bodily harm. That type of training *can* be accomplished in the one-day training courses required to obtain a concealed handgun license in most states.

The SGFS essay accurately points out that police officers in the field typically hit their intended targets approximately 25 percent of the time. What it fails to point out is that police officers frequently encounter scenarios that a concealed handgun license holder would never encounter. License holders do not chase bad guys down dark alleys or raid drug labs or engage in standoffs with criminals barricaded inside buildings. According to experts on the issue, most self-defense shootings occur at close range and are over in a matter of seconds. 28

Interestingly enough, law enforcement officers in most states are only required to requalify with their weapons once a year, and in some states, such as Texas, the requalification test for law enforcement officers varies very little from the shooting test that must be passed by concealed handgun license applicants. 29

Not surprisingly, the SGFS essay presents the typical far-fetched scenarios of self-defense shootings resulting in "collateral damage" and of multiple students drawing weapons and finding themselves unable to identify the actual "shooter" in prolonged shootouts. This ignores both the findings of a 1997 FBI study[3] that concluded that most shootouts last less than ten seconds and the fact that the rate of concealed carry among individuals in their twenties is typically about one half of one percent. How nine seconds of exchanged gunfire between two armed individuals could possibly lead to greater loss of life than a nine-minute, uncontested execution-style massacre, such as the one that occurred at Virginia Tech, is something Students for Gun-Free Schools, like most opponents of concealed carry on campus, doesn't attempt to explain. Likewise, they make no attempt to explain how one of these brief shootouts could lead to multiple students drawing their weapons and losing track of the shooter, when statistically speaking, only about one out of every two hundred students would be armed. Given the fact that even a huge four-hundred-seat lecture hall would statistically contain only two students with concealed handgun licenses, the chance of one of those armed students losing track of the actual shooter during a few seconds of exchanged gunfire is highly unlikely. 30

Students for Gun-Free Schools concludes its essay by suggesting that the relatively small number of justified shooting deaths each year somehow proves that concealed carry is ineffective. Like many opponents of concealed carry, they fail to realize that the key factor is not the number of bad guys killed but, rather, the number of good guys saved. According to a 1991 FBI study,[4] less than one out of a thousand lawful defensive uses of a firearm results in the death of the attacker. By that estimate, firearms are used almost five times more frequently to save lives than to take lives in the U.S. 31

In the end, Students for Gun-Free Schools' arguments against concealed carry on campus, like all arguments against concealed carry on campus, rely entirely on speculation, false assumptions, and emotion. Most college 32 campuses in America are surrounded by neighborhoods where concealed handgun license holders, including college students, lawfully carry concealed handguns at movie theaters, grocery stores, shopping malls, office buildings, restaurants, churches, banks, etc. Yet, we don't hear of spates of accidental discharges or alcohol-fueled shootings by licensees in those places. If the majority of college campuses are safer than their surrounding areas because they don't allow concealed carry on campus, why don't we see higher crime rates at the twelve U.S. colleges that do allow concealed carry on campus? After a combined total of one hundred semesters, why haven't we seen *any* negative results on those twelve campuses? There is absolutely no verifiable evidence to suggest that allowing concealed carry on college campuses makes campuses any less safe; therefore, reason dictates that current school policies and state laws against concealed carry on campus serve only to stack the odds in favor of dangerous criminals who have no regard for school policy or state law. SCC simply seeks to take the advantage away from those who seek to harm the innocent.

SCC
Better armed because we're armed with knowledge and *guns!*

Endnotes

1. "Crime, Deterrence, and Right-to-Carry Concealed Handguns," John Lott and David Mustard, *Journal of Legal Studies* (v. 26, no. 1, pages 1–68, January 1997); "An Analysis of the Arrest Rate of Texas Concealed Handgun License Holders as Compared to the Arrest Rate of the Entire Texas Population," William E. Sturdevant, September 1, 2000; Florida Department of Justice statistics, 1998; Florida Department of State, "Concealed Weapons/Firearms License Statistical Report," 1998; Texas Department of Public Safety and the U.S. Census Bureau, reported in *San Antonio Express-News,* September 2000; Texas Department of Corrections data, 1996–2000, compiled by the Texas State Rifle Association.
2. A comparison of statistics on arrests of police officers, published by the *Washington Post* on 08/28/94, to Florida Department of Law Enforcement statistics submitted to the governor on 03/15/95.
3. "In the Line of Fire: Violence against Law Enforcement," U.S. Department of Justice, Federal Bureau of Investigation, National Institute of Justice, 1997.
4. "Critical Incidents in Policing," Federal Bureau of Investigation, 1991.

• • •

Comprehension

1. Why do the writers discuss the Texas and Virginia state legislatures? What is significant about them?
2. According to the writers, what misperception do people generally have about the drinking habits of college students? Why do the writers discuss students' drinking habits in this essay?

3. What kind of training do the writers say can be "accomplished in the one-day training courses required to obtain a concealed handgun license in most states" (27)?
4. The writers claim that arguments against concealed carry on campus rely entirely on three premises. What are these three premises?

Purpose and Audience

1. Paraphrase the thesis of this essay.
2. In paragraphs 2 and 3, the writers accuse their opponents of committing a logical **fallacy**. What is this fallacy? Why do you think the writers choose to make this claim near the beginning of their essay? How does it serve their overall purpose?
3. Do you think the writers are primarily trying to persuade those who disagree with them or addressing those who already agree with their position? How can you tell?
4. How do the writers characterize the views of the American public on the issues of guns and gun control? What is their opinion of the general population? Do you think this opinion influences their argument? Why or why not?
5. The writers accuse opponents of concealed carry on campus of relying on emotion to make their arguments. Do the writers of this essay use any emotional arguments to build their own case? If so, point to an example, and explain how this kind of emotional appeal supports (or does not support) their overall purpose.

Style and Structure

1. This essay is structured as a point-by-point rebuttal of arguments made by Students for Gun-Free Schools (page 639). Do you find this approach effective? Would this essay be as convincing to those who have not read the original SGFS article that prompted this response? Why or why not?
2. Where in the essay do the writers use **analogies**? Do you find the comparisons logical? Persuasive? Explain.
3. **Vocabulary Project.** The writers claim that the "issue of alcohol consumption and reckless behavior by college students is a moot point" (12). What is a "moot point"? Do you agree that this issue is a "moot point"?
4. In paragraph 23, the writers address a study by the Violence Policy Center, referring to the organization as a "highly biased gun control advocacy group." Is this characterization fair? What are the writers trying to accomplish by labeling the Violence Policy Center in this way? Do they achieve their goal?
5. Where in this essay do the writers use expert opinion? Where do they cite statistics? Do you find these kinds of support persuasive? Why or why not?

Journal Entry

In paragraph 13, the writers discuss the security options of those who wish to keep their guns while living on campus, including "safes that bolt to bed frames" and "community gun lockups." Would you feel less safe (or safer) living in a college dorm or residence with guns on the premises?

Writing Workshop

1. **Working with Sources.** Referring to accidental gun discharges, the writers claim, "It is silly to suggest that citizens should be denied a right simply because that right is accompanied by a negligible risk" (14). Indeed, arguments about gun laws and policies invariably lead to debates about the meaning of the noun *right*. How do you view the right of an individual to possess firearms? What are its limits? In what ways, if any, should public safety be balanced against the individual's right to own a gun? Write an essay that explores and tries to answer these questions. Be sure to document any sources you use (for example, the United States Constitution) and to include a works-cited page. (See Chapter 18 for information on MLA documentation.)
2. The writers discuss the general public's opinion of concealed carry laws, but they also suggest that the public is uninformed. Moreover, they argue that public opinion may be irrelevant in this context, saying, "Public opinion does not always dictate public policy on complicated issues of public safety. The FDA does not poll the public on acceptable procedures for sanitizing meatpacking plants" (7). Do you think these arguments are valid? Do you share the writers' overall view of the public and the public's ability to understand complex policies or issues? Write an essay that addresses these questions.
3. In their last paragraph, the writers say that all arguments against concealed carry on campus "rely entirely on speculation, false assumptions, and emotion." Do you agree? After reading both this essay and the essay by Students for Gun-Free Schools (page 639), consider where you stand on the issue of guns on campus. Write an essay that presents and supports your position.

Combining the Patterns

The writers examine several **cause-and-effect** relationships in this essay. Point to a specific example, and explain how it supports their overall argument or purpose.

Thematic Connections

- "A Peaceful Woman Explains Why She Carries a Gun" (page 350)
- The Declaration of Independence (page 544)

TIMOTHY WHEELER

There's a Reason They Choose Schools

A retired surgeon, Timothy Wheeler is the director of Doctors for Responsible Gun Ownership, a national group of physicians, medical students, scientists, and others who support — and advocate for — gun rights as well as the safe and lawful use of firearms. DRGO is associated with the Claremont Institute, a conservative think tank. Wheeler's writing has appeared in the *Washington Times*, the *National Review Online*, and other publications.

Background on gun violence as a public health issue More than thirty thousand people are killed every year by gun violence. As Wheeler's essay suggests, many physicians and health-care experts view this problem as a public health issue — and even a public health crisis. Wheeler cites the 2007 issue of the American Medical Association's *Disaster Medicine and Public Health Preparedness*, which focused on the Virginia Tech massacre. The AMA, the largest association of physicians in the United States, has long viewed the problem in a public health context. After the 2012 shootings at Sandy Hook Elementary School in Connecticut, the AMA and fifty-two other medical organizations sent a letter to President Barack Obama. The signatories advocated several proposals, including an assault weapons ban, increased mental health services, and more research on violence prevention. In the past, the government funded extensive research for studying (and reducing) gun violence at the Centers for Disease Control and Prevention, but gun-rights advocates, including the NRA, lobbied for legal restrictions on the CDC, requiring that "none of the funds made available . . . may be used to advocate or promote gun control." Such public health research is not limited to the public sector, of course. For example, the University of Chicago Crime Lab, founded in 2008, explores the causes and effects of gun violence in the United States. For gun-rights activists such as Wheeler, these physicians, researchers, and health-care experts too often put the "emphasis on guns and not on the humans who misuse them."

Wednesday's shooting at yet another school has a better outcome than most in recent memory. No one died at Cleveland's Success Tech Academy except the perpetrator. The two students and two teachers he shot are in stable condition at Cleveland hospitals. 1

What is depressingly similar to the mass murders at Virginia Tech and Nickel Mines, Pennsylvania,* and too many others was the killer's choice of venue – that steadfastly gun-free zone, the school campus. Although murderer Seung-Hui Cho at Virginia Tech and Asa Coon, the Cleveland shooter, were both students reported to have school-related grudges, other school killers have proved to be simply taking advantage of the lack of effective security at 2

* Eds. note – On October 2, 2006, Charles Carl Roberts shot ten students, killing five and injuring five others in an Amish one-room schoolhouse.

schools. The Bailey, Colorado, multiple rapes and murder of September 2006, the Nickel Mines massacre of October 2006, and Buford Furrow's murderous August 1999 invasion of a Los Angeles Jewish day-care center were all committed by adults. They had no connection to the schools other than being drawn to the soft target a school offers such psychopaths.

This latest shooting comes only a few weeks after the American Medical Association released a theme issue of its journal *Disaster Medicine and Public Health Preparedness*. This issue is dedicated to analyzing the April 2007 Virginia Tech shootings, in which thirty-two people were murdered. The authors are university officials, trauma surgeons, and legal analysts who pore over the details of the incident, looking for "warning signs" and "risk factors" for violence. They rehash all the tired rhetoric of bureaucrats and public-health wonks, including the public-health mantra of the 1990s that guns are the root cause of violence. 3

Sheldon Greenberg, a dean at Johns Hopkins, offers this gem: "Reinforce a 'no weapons' policy and, when violated, enforce it quickly, to include expulsion. Parents should be made aware of the policy. *Officials should dispel the politically driven notion that armed students could eliminate an active shooter*" (emphasis added). Greenberg apparently isn't aware that at the Appalachian School of Law in 2002 another homicidal Virginia student was stopped from shooting more of his classmates when another student held him at gunpoint. The Pearl High School murderer Luke Woodham was stopped cold when vice principal Joel Myrick got his Colt .45 handgun out of his truck and pointed it at the young killer. 4

Virginia Tech's 2005 no-guns-on-campus policy was an abject failure at deterring Seung-Hui Cho. Greenberg's audacity in ignoring the obvious is typical of arrogant school officials. What the AMA journal authors studiously avoid are on one hand the repeated failures of such feel-good steps as no-gun policies, and on the other hand the demonstrated success of armed first responders. These responders would be the students themselves, such as the trained and licensed law student, or their similarly qualified teachers. 5

In Cleveland this week and at Virginia Tech the shooters took time to walk the halls, searching out victims in several rooms, and then shooting them. Virginia Chief Medical Examiner Marcella Fierro describes the locations of the dead in Virginia Tech's Norris Hall. Dead victims were found in groups ranging from one to thirteen, scattered throughout four rooms and a stairwell. If any one of the victims had, like the Appalachian School of Law student, used armed force to stop Cho, lives could have been saved. 6

The people of Virginia actually had a chance to implement such a plan last year. House Bill 1572 was introduced in the legislature to extend the state's concealed-carry provisions to college campuses. But the bill died in committee, opposed by the usual naysayers, including the Virginia Association of Chiefs of Police and the university itself. Virginia Tech spokesman Larry Hincker was quoted in the *Roanoke Times* as saying, "I'm sure the university community is appreciative of the General Assembly's actions because this will help parents, students, faculty, and visitors feel safe on our campus." 7

> "It is encouraging that college students themselves have a much better grasp on reality than their politically correct elders."

8 It is encouraging that college students themselves have a much better grasp on reality than their politically correct elders. During the week of October 22–26, Students for Concealed Carry on Campus will stage a nationwide "empty holster" demonstration (peaceful, of course) in support of their cause.

9 School officials typically base violence-prevention policies on irrational fears more than real-world analysis of what works. But which is more horrible, the massacre that timid bureaucrats fear might happen when a few good guys (and gals) carry guns on campus, or the one that actually did happen despite Virginia Tech's progressive violence-prevention policy? Can there really be any more debate?

10 AMA journal editor James J. James, M.D., offers up this nostrum:

> We must meaningfully embrace all of the varied disciplines contributing to preparedness and response and be more willing to be guided and informed by the full spectrum of research methodologies, including not only the rigid application of the traditional scientific method and epidemiological and social science applications but also the incorporation of observational/empirical findings, as necessary, in the absence of more objective data.

11 Got that?

12 I prefer the remedy prescribed by self-defense guru Massad Ayoob. When good people find themselves in what he calls "the dark place," confronted by the imminent terror of a gun-wielding homicidal maniac, the picture becomes clear. Policies won't help. Another federal gun law won't help. The only solution is a prepared and brave defender with the proper lifesaving tool—a gun.

• • •

Comprehension

1. What does Wheeler see as "depressingly similar" (2) about the sites of recent mass shootings?
2. The American Medical Association devoted an entire issue of one of its journals to dealing with tragedies such as school shootings. How does Wheeler view the AMA's reaction and policy proposals?
3. According to Wheeler, what do the AMA journal authors "studiously avoid" (5)?
4. In Wheeler's view, what is the basis of most antiviolence policies on school campuses?
5. According to Wheeler, what is the only effective way to deal with the "imminent terror of a gun-wielding homicidal maniac" (12)?

Purpose and Audience

1. Wheeler, a doctor, is the director of Doctors for Responsible Gun Ownership. How does your knowledge of his professional background affect your view of his argument? Do you think he should have mentioned his background in the essay? Why or why not?
2. This article originally appeared in the *National Review Online,* a conservative publication. Given Wheeler's likely audience, what do you think his purpose is? For example, do you think he wants to change readers' minds? To reinforce what they already believe? Explain.
3. How would you restate Wheeler's thesis in your own words?
4. Wheeler writes about the positions and policies of school officials and public health experts. If they read this article, how do you think they would react?
5. In paragraph 8, Wheeler refers to an "encouraging" sign. What is this sign? How does it support his overall purpose?
6. In paragraph 10, Wheeler includes a passage by AMA journal editor James J. James, M.D. Why does he include this long quotation?

Style and Structure

1. Where does Wheeler address opposing points of view? How does he respond to these arguments against his position? Are his responses effective? Explain.
2. How does Wheeler characterize those with opposing viewpoints? What specific words does he use? How do you respond to this characterization?
3. In paragraph 3, why does Wheeler place quotation marks around the terms "warning signs" and "risk factors"? How does this use of quotation marks affect the meanings and connotations of those phrases?
4. **Vocabulary Project.** In paragraph 3, Wheeler refers to a "public health mantra." What is a mantra? What connotations does this word have? Why do you think Wheeler chose to use *mantra* in this context?
5. What purpose does paragraph 4 serve? How does it help support Wheeler's thesis?

Journal Entry

In his conclusion, Wheeler discusses the "imminent terror" of a "gun-wielding homicidal maniac." Mass shootings have captured the public imagination; they understandably evoke fear and horror. Do you think the public tends to overreact to mass shootings, or do you think their reactions are appropriate? Explain.

Writing Workshop

1. Wheeler writes: "Policies won't help. Another federal law won't help. The only solution is a prepared and brave defender with the proper lifesaving tool – a gun" (12). Do you agree that policies and laws "won't help"? Is

the solution to the problem as clear-cut as the one Wheeler presents in his conclusion? Write an essay that addresses these questions.

2. The writer seems to have little use for school officials. For example, in paragraph 8, he suggests that college students "have a much better grasp on reality than their politically correct elders," and in paragraph 9, he refers to college administrators as "timid bureaucrats." Consider your own college or university. What are your school's policies with regard to firearms on campus and emergency procedures? Do you think administrators and officials are making policies based on "irrational fears" instead of "real-world analysis" (9)? Write an essay that examines and evaluates your school's policies.
3. **Working with Sources.** The title of this essay is "There's a Reason They Choose Schools." The writer refers to colleges as "soft targets" for shooters because campuses are usually gun-free zones. How safe are the elementary schools, high schools, and colleges in your community? Do you see these schools as "soft targets"? Why or why not? Write an argumentative essay that answers these questions and makes recommendations that address the problems you identify. Be sure to document any sources you cite and to include a works-cited page. (See Chapter 18 for information on MLA documentation.)

Combining the Patterns

Where does the writer use **comparison and contrast** in this essay? How does the pattern work to support his main point?

Thematic Connections

- "Thirty-Eight Who Saw Murder Didn't Call the Police" (page 126)
- "Ground Zero" (page 173)

Writing Assignments for Argumentation

1. Write an argumentative essay discussing whether parents have a right to spank their children. If your position is that they do, under what circumstances? What limitations should exist? If your position is that they do not, how should parents discipline children? How should they deal with inappropriate behavior?
2. Visit the American Library Association's website at ala.org, and read the list of banned and challenged books of the twenty-first century. Choose a book from the list that you have read. Assume a library in your town has decided that the book you have chosen is objectionable and has removed it from the shelves. Write an email to your local newspaper arguing for or against the library's actions. Make a list of the major arguments that might be advanced against your position, and try to refute some of them in your email.
3. In Great Britain, cities began installing video surveillance systems in public areas in the 1970s. Police departments claim these cameras help them do their jobs more efficiently. For example, such cameras enabled police to identify and capture the two terrorists who bombed the Boston Marathon in 2013. Opponents of the cameras say the police are creating a society that severely compromises the right of personal privacy. How do you feel about this issue? Assume the police department in your city is proposing to install cameras in the downtown and other pedestrian areas. Write an editorial for your local paper presenting your views on the topic.
4. Write an essay discussing under what circumstances, if any, animals should be used for scientific experimentation.
5. **Working with Sources.** Each year, a growing number of high school graduates are choosing to take a year off before going to college. The idea of this kind of "gap year" has been the source of some debate. Proponents say a gap year gives students time to mature, time to decide what they want to get out of their education. It also gives them the opportunity to travel or to save some money for college. Detractors of a gap year point out that some students have trouble getting back into the academic routine when the year is over. In addition, students who take a year off are a year behind their classmates when they return. Research the pros and cons of the gap year. Then, write an essay in which you argue for or against taking a year off before college. Be sure to document your sources and to include a works-cited page. (See Chapter 18 for information on MLA documentation.)
6. **Working with Sources.** Visit the website deathpenalty.org, and research some criminal cases that resulted in the death penalty. Write an essay using these accounts to support your arguments either for or against the death penalty. Be sure to document your sources and to include a works-cited page. (See Chapter 18 for information about MLA documentation.)
7. Write an argumentative essay discussing under what circumstances a nation has an obligation to go (or not to go) to war.

8. **Working with Sources.** Gasoline-powered cars account for more than half the oil consumed in the United States and almost 25 percent of the greenhouse gasses. As a result, carmakers, such as Tesla, BMW, and General Motors, have spent considerable time and money trying to develop practical and efficient electric vehicles. Supporters say these electric-driven vehicles could reduce pollution significantly over the next ten years. Detractors say electric cars come with a cost, one that cancels out any possible benefits they may have. Research the pros and cons of electric vehicles. Then, write an essay in which you argue for or against the move toward electric cars. Be sure to document your sources and to include a works-cited page. (See Chapter 18 for information on MLA documentation.)
9. In the Declaration of Independence, Jefferson says all individuals are entitled to "life, liberty and the pursuit of happiness." Write an essay arguing that these rights are not absolute.
10. Write an argumentative essay on one of these topics:
    - Should high school students be required to recite the Pledge of Allegiance at the start of each school day?
    - Should college students be required to do community service?
    - Should public school teachers be required to pass periodic competency tests?
    - Should the legal drinking age be raised (or lowered)?
    - Should the children of undocumented immigrants qualify for in-state tuition rates at public colleges?
    - Should sugary drinks be banned in all public schools and government workplaces?
    - Do Facebook and other social networking sites do more harm than good?

Collaborative Activity for Argumentation

Working with three other students, select a controversial topic—one not covered in any of the debates in this chapter—that interests all of you. (You can review the Writing Assignments for Argumentation to get ideas.) State your topic the way a topic is stated in a formal debate:

Resolved: The federal government should censor Internet content.

Then, divide into two-member teams, and decide which team will take the pro position and which will take the con. Each team should list the arguments on its side of the issue and then write two or three paragraphs summarizing its position. Finally, the teams should stage a ten-minute debate—five minutes for each side—in front of the class. (The pro side presents its argument first.) At the end of each debate, the class should decide which team has presented the stronger arguments.

15

Combining the Patterns

Many paragraphs combine several patterns of development. In the following paragraph, for example, Paul Hoffman uses narration, exemplification, and cause and effect to explain why we tend to see numbers as more than "instruments of enumeration."

Topic sentence / **Narration** / **Exemplification** / **Cause and effect**

The idea that numbers are not mere instruments of enumeration but are sacred, perfect, friendly, lucky, or evil goes back to antiquity. In the sixth century B.C. Pythagoras, whom schoolchildren associate with the famous theorem that in a right triangle the square of the hypotenuse always equals the sum of the squares of its sides, not only performed brilliant mathematics but made a religion out of numbers. In numerology, the number 12 has always represented completeness, as in the 12 months of the year, the 12 signs of the zodiac, the 12 hours of the day, the 12 gods of Olympus, the 12 labors of Hercules, the 12 tribes of Israel, the 12 apostles of Jesus, the 12 days of Christmas, and, more recently perhaps, the 12 eggs in an egg carton. Since 13 exceeds 12 by only one, the number lies just beyond completeness and, hence, is restless to the point of being evil.

Like paragraphs, essays do not usually follow a single pattern of development; in fact, nearly every essay, including the ones in this text, combines a variety of patterns. Even though an essay may be organized according to one dominant pattern, it is still likely to include paragraphs, and even groups of paragraphs, shaped by other patterns of development. For example, a process essay can use **cause and effect** to show the results of the process, and a cause-and-effect essay can use **exemplification** to illustrate possible causes or effects. In many cases, a dominant pattern is supported by other patterns;

in fact, combining various patterns in a single essay gives writers the flexibility to express their ideas most effectively. For this reason, each essay in Chapters 6 through 14 of this text is followed by a Combining the Patterns question that focuses on how the essay uses (or might use) other patterns of development along with its dominant pattern.

Structuring an Essay by Combining the Patterns

Essays that combine various patterns of development, like essays structured primarily by a single pattern, include an **introduction**, several **body paragraphs**, and a **conclusion**. The introduction typically ends with the thesis statement that gives the essay its focus, and the conclusion often restates that thesis in different words or summarizes the essay's main points. Each body paragraph (or group of paragraphs) is structured according to the pattern of development that best suits the material it develops.

Suppose you are planning your answer to the following question on a take-home essay exam for a sociology of religion course.

> For what reasons are people attracted to cults? Why do they join? Support your answer with specific examples that illustrate how cults recruit and retain members.

The wording of this exam question ("for what reasons") suggests that the essay's dominant pattern of development will be **cause and effect**; the wording also suggests that this cause-and-effect structure will include **exemplification** ("specific examples"). In addition, you may decide to develop your essay with **definition** and **process**.

An informal outline for your essay might look like this one.

SAMPLE OUTLINE: Combining the Patterns

INTRODUCTION

Definition of *cult* (defined by negation — telling what it is *not* — and by comparison and contrast with *religion*).

Thesis statement (suggests cause and effect): Using aggressive recruitment tactics and isolating potential members from their families and past lives, cults appeal to new recruits by offering them a highly structured environment.

CAUSE AND EFFECT

Why people join cults

PROCESS

How cults recruit new members

EXEMPLIFICATION
Tactics various cults use to retain members (series of brief examples)

CONCLUSION
Restatement of thesis or review of key points

Combining the Patterns: Revising and Editing

When you revise an essay that combines several patterns of development, consider the items on the revision checklist on page 66, as well as any of the more specific revision checklists in Chapters 6 through 14 that apply to the patterns in your essay. As you edit your essay, refer to the editing checklists on pages 83, 86, and 89 and to the individual editing checklists in Chapters 6 through 14. You may also wish to consult the Grammar in Context sections that appear throughout the book, as well as the one that follows.

GRAMMAR IN CONTEXT AGREEMENT WITH INDEFINITE PRONOUNS

A **pronoun** is a word that takes the place of a noun or another pronoun in a sentence. Unlike most pronouns, an **indefinite pronoun** (*anyone, either, each,* and so on) does not refer to a specific person or thing.

Subject-Verb Agreement Pronoun subjects must agree in number with their verbs: singular pronouns (*I, he, she, it,* and so on) take singular verbs, and plural pronouns (*we, they,* and so on) take plural verbs.

"I have learned much as a scavenger" (Eighner 677).

We were super ninjas one day and millionaires the next; we became the heroes we idolized and lived the lives we dreamed about (Truong 672).

Indefinite pronoun subjects must also agree in number with their verbs: singular indefinite pronouns take singular verbs, and plural indefinite pronouns take plural verbs. Most indefinite pronouns are singular, but some are plural.

SINGULAR INDEFINITE PRONOUNS

another	anyone	everyone	one	each
either	neither	anything	everything	

"Everyone was darker or lighter than we were" (Truong 673).

"Everything seems to stink" (Eighner 682).

PLURAL INDEFINITE PRONOUNS

both many few several others

"Many are discarded for minor imperfections that can be pared away" (Eighner 679).

NOTE: A few indefinite pronouns – *some, all, any, more, most,* and *none* – may be either singular or plural, depending on their meaning in the sentence.

SINGULAR: According to David Kirby, some of the history of tattoos is surprising. (*Some* refers to *history,* so the verb is singular.)

PLURAL: Some of the tattoos David Kirby discusses serve as a kind of "record book," while others create a "canvas" (694). (*Some* refers to *tattoos,* so the verb is plural.)

Pronoun-Antecedent Agreement An **antecedent** is the noun or pronoun that a pronoun refers to in a sentence. Pronouns must agree in number with their antecedents.

Use a singular pronoun to refer to a singular indefinite pronoun antecedent.

Each day has its surprises for Lars Eighner and his dog, Lizbeth.

Use a plural pronoun to refer to a plural indefinite pronoun antecedent.

Many of the people who pass Eighner and Lizbeth avert their eyes.

NOTE: Although the indefinite pronoun *everyone* is singular, it is often used with a plural pronoun in everyday speech and informal writing.

INFORMAL: Everyone turns their heads when Eighner and Lizbeth walk by.

This usage is generally acceptable in informal situations, but college writing requires correct pronoun-antecedent agreement.

CORRECT: People turn their heads when Eighner and Lizbeth walk by.

The essays in this chapter illustrate how different patterns of development work together in a single piece of writing. The first two essays – "The Park" by Michael Huu Truong, a student, and "On Dumpster Diving" by Lars Eighner – include marginal annotations that identify the various patterns these writers use. Truong's essay relies primarily on narration, but he also uses description and exemplification to convey his memories of childhood. Eighner's essay combines sections of definition, exemplification, classification and division, cause and effect, comparison and contrast, and process; at the same time, he tells the story (narration) and provides vivid details (description) of his life as a homeless person.

Following these annotated essays are three additional selections that combine patterns: David Kirby's "Inked Well," Donald Kagan's "On Patriotism," and Jonathan Swift's classic satire "A Modest Proposal." Each of the essays in this chapter is followed by the same types of questions that accompany the reading selections that appear elsewhere in the text.

A STUDENT WRITER: Combining the Patterns

This essay was written by Michael Huu Truong for a first-year composition course in response to the assignment "Write an essay about the person and/or place that defined your childhood."

The Park

Background

1 My childhood did not really begin until I came to this country from the jungle of Vietnam. I can't really remember much from this period, and the things I do remember are vague images that I have no desire or intention to discuss. However, my childhood in the States was a lot different, especially after I met my friend James. While it lasted, it was paradise.

Thesis statement

Narrative begins

Description: effects of cold

Comparison and contrast: U.S. vs. Vietnam

2 It was a cold wintry day in February after a big snowstorm — the first I'd ever seen. My lips were chapped, my hands were frozen stiff, and my cheeks were burning from the biting wind, and yet I loved it. I especially loved the snow. I had come from a country where the closest things to snow were white paint and cotton balls. But now I was in America. On that frosty afternoon, I was determined to build a snowman. I had seen them in books, and I had heard they could talk. I knew they could come alive, and I couldn't wait.

Description: James

Narration: the first day

3 "Eyryui roeow ierog," said a voice that came out of nowhere. I turned around, and right in my face was a short, red-faced (probably from the cold wind) Korean kid with a dirty, runny nose. I responded, "Wtefkjkr ruyjft gsdfr" in my own tongue. We understood each other perfectly, and we expressed our understanding with a smile. Together, we built our first snowman. We were disappointed that evening when the snowman just stood there; however, I was happy because I had made my first friend.

Analogies

4 Ever since then we've been a team like Abbott and Costello (or, when my cousin joined us, the Three Stooges). The two of us were inseparable. We could've made the greatest Krazy Glue commercial ever.

Narration: what they did that summer

5 The summer that followed the big snowstorm, from what I can recall, was awesome. We were free like comets in the heavens, and we did whatever our hearts wanted. For the most part, our desires were fulfilled in a little park across the street. This park was ours; it was like our own planet guarded by our own robot army (disguised as trees). Together we fought against the bigger people who always tried to invade and take over our world. The enemy could never conquer our fortress because they would have to destroy our robots, penetrate our force field, and then defeat us; this last feat would be impossible.

Narrative continues

Examples: what they banished

6 This park was our fantasy land where everything we wished for came true and everything we hated was banished forever. We banished vegetables, cheese, bigger people, and — of course — girls. The land was enchanted, and we could be whatever we felt like. We were super ninjas one day and millionaires the next; we became the heroes we idolized and lived the lives we dreamed about.

Examples: superhero fantasies

I had the strength of Bruce Lee and Superman; James possessed the power of Clint Eastwood and the Bionic Man. My weapons were the skills of Bruce and a cape. James, however, needed a real weapon for Clint, and the weapon he made was awesome. The Death Ray could destroy a building with one blast, and it even had a shield so that James was always protected. Even with all his mighty weapons and gadgets, though, he was still no match for Superman and Bruce Lee. Every day, we fought until death (or until our parents called us for dinner).

Narrative continues

Examples: new worlds and planets

7 When we became bored with our super powers, the park became a giant spaceship. We traveled all over the Universe, conquering and exploring strange new worlds and mysterious planets. Our ship was a top-secret indestructible space warship called the X-007. We went to Mars, Venus, Pluto, and other alien planets, destroying all the monsters we could find. When necessary, our spacecraft was transformed into a submarine for deep-sea adventures. We found lost cities, unearthed treasures, and saved Earth by destroying all the sea monsters that were plotting against us. We became heroes — just like Superman, Bruce Lee, the Bionic Man, and Clint Eastwood.

Cause and effect: prospect of school leads to problems

8 James and I had the time of our lives in the park that summer. It was great — until we heard about the horror of starting school. Shocked and terrified, we ran to our fortress to escape. For some reason, though, our magic kingdom had lost its powers. We fought hard that evening, trying to keep the bigger people out of our planet, but the battle was soon lost. Bruce Lee, Superman, the Bionic Man, and Clint Eastwood had all lost their special powers.

Narrative continues

9 School wasn't as bad as we'd thought it would be. The first day, James and I sat there with our hands folded. We didn't talk or move, and we didn't dare look at each other (we would've cracked up because we always made these goofy faces). Even though we had pens that could be transformed into weapons, we were still scared.

Description: school

10 Everyone was darker or lighter than we were, and the teacher was speaking a strange language (English). James and I giggled as she talked. We giggled softly when everyone else talked, and they laughed out loud when it was our turn to speak.

Narrative continues

11 The day dragged on, and all we wanted to do was go home and rebuild our fortress. Finally, after an eternity, it was almost three o'clock. James and I sat at the edge of our seats as we counted under our breath: "10, 9, 8, 7, 6, 5, 4, 3, 2, 1." At last, the bell sounded. We dashed for the door and raced home and across the street — and then we stopped. We stood still in the middle of the street with our hearts pounding like the beats of a drum. The cool September wind began to pick up, and everything became silent. We stood there and watched the metal of the fence reflect the beautiful colors of the sun. It was beautiful, and yet we hated everything about it. The new metal fence separated us from our fortress, our planet, our spaceship, our submarine — and, most important of all, from our heroes and our dreams.

Description: the fence

12 We stood there for a long time. As the sun slowly turned red and sank beneath the ground, so did our dreams, heroes, and hearts. Darkness soon devoured the park, and after a while we walked home with only the memories of the summer that came after the big snowstorm.

Points for Special Attention

Writing a Personal Experience Essay. Michael's instructor specified that he was to write an essay about a person or place to help his readers – other students – understand what his childhood was like. Because the assignment called for a personal experience essay, Michael was free to use the first-person pronouns *I* and *we,* as well as contractions, although neither would be acceptable in a more formal essay.

Thesis Statement. Because Michael's primary purpose in this essay was to communicate personal feelings and impressions, an argumentative thesis statement (such as "If every cell phone and video game in the United States disappeared, more people would have childhoods like mine") would have been inappropriate. Still, Michael states his thesis explicitly in order to unify his essay around the dominant impression he wants to convey: "While it lasted, it was paradise."

Combining the Patterns. Michael also had more specific purposes, and they determined the patterns that shape his essay. His essay's dominant pattern is *narration,* but to help students visualize the person (James) and the place (the park) he discusses, he includes sections that *describe* and give concrete, specific *examples* as well as summarize his daily routine. These patterns work together to create an essay that conveys the nature of his childhood to readers.

Transitions. The transitional words and phrases that connect the individual sentences and paragraphs of Michael's essay – "But now," "Ever since," "The summer that followed the big snowstorm" – serve primarily to move readers through time. Such transitions are appropriate because narration is the dominant pattern of this essay.

Detail. "The Park" is full of specific detail – for example, the quoted bits of dialogue in paragraph 3 and the names of Michael's heroes and of particular games (and related equipment and weapons) elsewhere. The descriptive details that re-create the physical scenes – in particular, the snow, cold, frost, and wind of winter and the sun reflected on the fence – are vivid enough to help readers visualize the places Michael writes about.

Figures of Speech. Michael's essay describes a time when his imagination wandered without the restraints of adulthood. Appropriately, he uses **simile**, **metaphor**, and **personification** – "We were free like comets in the heavens"; "the park became a giant spaceship"; "We found lost cities, unearthed treasures, and saved Earth"; "Darkness soon devoured the park" – to evoke the time and place he describes.

Working with Sources. Michael's assignment did not require him to consult any outside sources. If it had, he could have included background information about immigration from Vietnam to the United States – particularly data about when Vietnamese people came to the United States, where immigrants settled, how children adjusted to school and learned English, and how quickly they assimilated. Such information could have provided some context for his childhood memories.

Focus on Revision

Michael's assignment asked him to write about his childhood, and he chose to focus on his early years in the United States. When his peer-editing group discussed his essay, however, a number of students were curious about his life in Vietnam. Some of them thought he should add a paragraph summarizing the "vague images" he remembered of his earlier childhood, perhaps contrasting it with his life in the United States, as he does in passing in paragraph 2. When Michael discussed this idea with his instructor, she suggested instead that he consider deleting the sentence in paragraph 1 that states he has "no desire or intention to discuss" this part of his life because it raises issues his essay does not address. After thinking about these suggestions, Michael decided to delete this sentence in his next draft but also to add a brief paragraph about his life in Vietnam, contrasting the park and his friendship with James with some of his earlier, less idyllic memories.

PEER-EDITING WORKSHEET **COMBINING THE PATTERNS**

1. Using the annotations for "The Park" (page 671) or "On Dumpster Diving" (page 676) as a guide, annotate the essay to identify the patterns of development it uses.
2. What is the essay's thesis? If it is not explicitly stated, state it in your own words. What pattern or patterns of development are suggested by the wording of the thesis statement?
3. What dominant pattern of development determines the essay's overall structure?
4. What patterns does the writer use to develop the body paragraphs of the essay? Explain why each pattern is used in a particular paragraph or group of paragraphs.
5. What patterns are *not* used? Where, if anywhere, might using one of these patterns serve the writer's purpose?
6. Review the essay's topic sentences. Is the wording of each topic sentence consistent with the particular pattern that structures the paragraph? If not, suggest possible ways some of the topic sentences might be reworded.

Each of the following essays combines several patterns, blending strategies to achieve the writer's purpose.

LARS EIGHNER

On Dumpster Diving

Lars Eighner (b. 1948) dropped out of the University of Texas at Austin after his third year and took a job at a state mental hospital. After leaving his job over a policy dispute in 1988 and falling behind in his rent payments, Eighner became homeless. For three years, he traveled between Austin and Los Angeles with his dog, Lizbeth, earning what money he could from writing stories for magazines. Eighner's memories of his experiences living on the street, *Travels with Lizbeth* (1993), was written on a computer he found in a Dumpster. The following chapter from that book details the practical dangers as well as the many possibilities he discovered in his "Dumpster diving." Eighner now lives in Austin and works as a freelance writer and writing coach.

Background on the homeless Although the number of homeless people in the United States is difficult to measure accurately, homelessness has become a highly visible issue in the past two decades. It is estimated, for example, that as many as ten million people experienced homelessness in the United States in the late 1980s alone. This surge in homelessness had a number of causes. Perhaps most important was a booming real estate market that led to a significant drop in affordable housing in many areas of the country. In several cities, single-room-occupancy hotels, which had long provided cheap lodging, were demolished or converted into luxury apartments. At the same time, new technologies left many unskilled workers jobless. Government policies against detaining the nondangerous mentally ill against their will also played a significant role. (About a quarter of all homeless people are thought to be mentally ill.) More recently, a real estate bubble and the subsequent foreclosure crisis forced hundreds of thousands out of their houses, leading many cities to report increased demand for emergency shelter. Currently, the U.S. Department of Health and Human Services estimates that homelessness affects two to three million Americans each year, of which approximately 40 percent are children.

This chapter was composed while the author was homeless. The present tense has been preserved.

***Definition:* Dumpster**

1 Long before I began Dumpster diving I was impressed with Dumpsters, enough so that I wrote the Merriam-Webster research service to discover what I could about the word *Dumpster*. I learned from them that it is a proprietary word belonging to the Dempsey Dumpster company. Since then I have dutifully capitalized the word, although it was lowercased in almost all the citations Merriam-Webster photocopied for me. Dempsey's word is too apt. I have never heard these things called anything but

Dumpsters. I do not know anyone who knows the generic name for these objects. From time to time I have heard a wino or hobo give some corrupted credit to the original and call them Dipsy Dumpsters.

Narration: Eighner's story begins

2 I began Dumpster diving about a year before I became homeless.

***Definition:* Dumpster diving**

3 I prefer the word *scavenging* and use the word *scrounging* when I mean to be obscure. I have heard people, evidently meaning to be polite, use the word *foraging,* but I prefer to reserve that word for gathering nuts and berries and such, which I do also according to the season and the opportunity. *Dumpster diving* seems to me to be a little too cute and, in my case, inaccurate because I lack the athletic ability to lower myself into the Dumpsters as the true divers do, much to their increased profit.

4 I like the frankness of the word *scavenging,* which I can hardly think of without picturing a big black snail on an aquarium wall. I live from the refuse of others. I am a scavenger. I think it a sound and honorable niche, although if I could I would naturally prefer to live the comfortable consumer life, perhaps—and only perhaps—as a slightly less wasteful consumer, owing to what I have learned as a scavenger.

Narration: story continues

5 While Lizbeth and I were still living in the shack on Avenue B as my savings ran out, I put almost all my sporadic income into rent. The necessities of daily life I began to extract from Dumpsters. Yes, we ate from them. Except for jeans, all my clothes came from Dumpsters. Boom boxes, candles, bedding, toilet paper, a virgin male love doll, medicine, books, a typewriter, dishes, furnishings, and change, sometimes amounting to many dollars—I acquired many things from Dumpsters.

Exemplification: things found in Dumpsters

Thesis statement

6 I have learned much as a scavenger. I mean to put some of what I have learned down here, beginning with the practical art of Dumpster diving and proceeding to the abstract.

7 What is safe to eat?

8 After all, the finding of objects is becoming something of an urban art. Even respectable employed people will sometimes find something tempting sticking out of a Dumpster or standing beside one. Quite a number of people, not all of them of the bohemian type, are willing to brag that they found this or that piece of trash. But eating from Dumpsters is what separates the dilettanti from the professionals. Eating safely from the Dumpsters involves three principles: using the senses and common sense to

evaluate the condition of the found materials, knowing the Dumpsters of a given area and checking them regularly, and seeking always to answer the question "Why was this discarded?"

Comparison and contrast: Dumpster divers vs. others

Perhaps everyone who has a kitchen and a regular supply of groceries has, at one time or another, made a sandwich and eaten half of it before discovering mold on the bread or got a mouthful of milk before realizing the milk had turned. Nothing of the sort is likely to happen to a Dumpster diver because he is constantly reminded that most food is discarded for a reason. Yet a lot of perfectly good food can be found in Dumpsters. 9

Classification and division: different kinds of food found in Dumpsters and their relative safety

Canned goods, for example, turn up fairly often in the Dumpsters I frequent. All except the most phobic people will be willing to eat from a can, even if it came from a Dumpster. Canned goods are among the safest foods to be found in Dumpsters but are not utterly foolproof. 10

Although very rare with modern canning methods, botulism is a possibility. Most other forms of food poisoning seldom do lasting harm to a healthy person, but botulism is almost certainly fatal and often the first symptom is death. Except for carbonated beverages, all canned goods should contain a slight vacuum and suck air when first punctured. Bulging, rusty, and dented cans and cans that spew when punctured should be avoided, especially when the contents are not very acidic or syrupy. 11

Heat can break down the botulin, but this requires much more cooking than most people do to canned goods. To the extent that botulism occurs at all, of course, it can occur in cans on pantry shelves as well as in cans from Dumpsters. Need I say that home-canned goods are simply too risky to be recommended. 12

From time to time one of my companions, aware of the source of my provisions, will ask, "Do you think these crackers are really safe to eat?" For some reason it is most often the crackers they ask about. 13

This question has always made me angry. Of course I would not offer my companion anything I had doubts about. But more than that, I wonder why he cannot evaluate the condition of the crackers for himself. I have no special knowledge and I have been wrong before. Since he knows where the food comes from, it seems to me he ought to assume some of the responsibility for deciding what he will put in his mouth. For myself I have few qualms about dry foods such as crackers, cookies, cereal, chips, and pasta if they are free of visible contaminates and still dry and crisp. Most often such things are found 14 in the original packaging, which is not so much a positive sign as it is the absence of a negative one.

Raw fruits and vegetables with intact skins seem perfectly safe to me, excluding of course the obviously rotten. Many are discarded for minor imperfections that can be pared away. Leafy vegetables, grapes, cauliflower, broccoli, and similar things may be contaminated by liquids and may be impractical to wash. 15

Candy, especially hard candy, is usually safe if it has not drawn ants. Chocolate is often discarded only because it has become discolored as the cocoa butter de-emulsified. Candying, after all, is one method of food preservation because pathogens do not like very sugary substances. 16

All of these foods might be found in any Dumpster and can be evaluated with some confidence largely on the basis of appearance. Beyond these are foods that cannot be correctly evaluated without additional information. 17

I began scavenging by pulling pizzas out of the Dumpster behind a pizza delivery shop. In general, prepared food requires caution, but in this case I knew when the shop closed and went to the Dumpster as soon as the last of the help left. 18

Such shops often get prank orders; both the orders and the products made to fill them are called *bogus*. Because help seldom stays long at these places, pizzas are often made with the wrong topping, refused on delivery for being cold, or baked incorrectly. The products to be discarded are boxed up because inventory is kept by counting boxes: A boxed pizza can be written off; an unboxed pizza does not exist. 19

I never placed a bogus order to increase the supply of pizzas and I believe no one else was scavenging in this Dumpster. But the people in the shop became suspicious and began to retain their garbage in the shop overnight. While it lasted I had a steady supply of fresh, sometimes warm pizza. Because I knew the Dumpster I knew the source of the pizza, and because I visited the Dumpster regularly I knew what was fresh and what was yesterday's. 20

Cause and effect: why Eighner visits certain Dumpsters; why students throw out food

The area I frequent is inhabited by many affluent college students. I am not here by chance; the Dumpsters in this area are very rich. Students throw out many good things, including food. In particular they tend to throw everything out when they move at the end of a semester, before and after breaks, and around midterm, when many of them despair of college. So I find it advantageous to keep an eye on the academic calendar. 21

Students throw food away around breaks because they do not know whether it has spoiled or will spoil before they return. A typical discard is a half jar of peanut butter. In fact, nonorganic peanut butter does not require refrigeration and is unlikely to spoil in any reasonable time. The student does not know that, and since it is Daddy's money, the student decides not to take a chance. Opened containers require caution and some attention to the question "Why was this discarded?" But in the case of discards from student apartments, the answer may be that the item was thrown out through carelessness, ignorance, or wastefulness. This can sometimes be deduced when the item is found with many others, including some that are obviously perfectly good. 22

Some students, and others, approach defrosting a freezer by chucking out the whole lot. Not only do the circumstances of such a find tell the story, but also the mass of frozen goods stays cold for a long time and items may be found still frozen or freshly thawed. 23

Yogurt, cheese, and sour cream are items that are often thrown out while they are still good. Occasionally I find cheese with a spot of mold, which of course I just pare off, and because it is obvious why such a cheese was discarded, I treat it with less suspicion than an apparently perfect cheese found in similar circumstances. Yogurt is often discarded, still sealed, only because the expiration date on the carton had passed. This is one of my favorite finds because yogurt will keep for several days, even in warm weather. 24

Students throw out canned goods and staples at the end of semesters and when they give up college at midterm. Drugs, pornography, spirits, and the like are often discarded when parents are expected—Dad's Day, for example. And spirits also turn up after big party weekends, presumably discarded by the newly reformed. Wine and spirits, of course, keep perfectly well even once opened, but the same cannot be said of beer. 25

Examples: liquids that require care

My test for carbonated soft drinks is whether they still fizz vigorously. Many juices or other beverages are too acidic or too syrupy to cause much concern, provided they are not visibly contaminated. I have discovered nasty molds in the vegetable juices, even when the product was found under its original seal; I recommend that such products be decanted slowly into a clear glass. Liquids always require some care. One hot day I found a large jug of Pat O'Brien's Hurricane mix. The jug had been opened but was still ice cold. I drank three large glasses before it 26 became apparent to me that someone had added rum to the mix, and not a little rum. I never tasted the rum, and by the time I began to feel the effects I had already ingested a very large quantity of the beverage. Some divers would have considered this a boon, but being suddenly intoxicated in a public place in the early afternoon is not my idea of a good time.

I have heard of people maliciously contaminating discarded food and even handouts, but mostly I have heard of this from people with vivid imaginations who have had no experience with Dumpsters themselves. Just before the pizza shop stopped discarding its garbage at night, jalapeños began showing up on most of the thrown-out pizzas. If indeed this was meant to discourage me, it was a wasted effort because I am a native Texan. 27

For myself, I avoid game, poultry, pork, and egg-based foods, whether I find them raw or cooked. I seldom have the means to cook what I find, but when I do I avail myself of plentiful supplies of beef, which is often in very good condition. I suppose fish becomes disagreeable before it becomes dangerous. Lizbeth is happy to have any such thing that is past its prime and, in fact, does not recognize fish as food until it is quite strong. 28

Home leftovers, as opposed to surpluses from restaurants, are very often bad. Evidently, especially among students, there is a common type of personality that carefully wraps up even the smallest leftover and shoves it into the back of the refrigerator for six months or so before discarding it. Characteristic of this type are the reused jars and margarine tubs to which the remains are committed. I avoid ethnic foods I am unfamiliar with. If I do not know what it is supposed to look like when it is good, I cannot be certain I will be able to tell if it is bad. 29

No matter how careful I am I still get dysentery at least once a month, oftener in warmer weather. I do not want to paint too romantic a picture. Dumpster diving has serious drawbacks as a way of life. 30

Process: how to scavenge

I learned to scavenge gradually, on my own. Since then I have initiated several companions into the trade. I have learned that there is a predictable series of stages a person goes through in learning to scavenge. 31

At first the new scavenger is filled with disgust and self-loathing. He is ashamed of being seen and may lurk around, trying to duck behind things, or he may try to dive at night. (In fact, most people instinctively look away from a scavenger. By skulking around, the novice calls attention 32 to himself and arouses suspicion. Diving at night is ineffective and needlessly messy.)

Every grain of rice seems to be a maggot. Everything seems to stink. He can wipe the egg yolk off the found can, but he cannot erase from his mind the stigma of eating garbage. 33

That stage passes with experience. The scavenger finds a pair of running shoes that fit and look and smell brand-new. He finds a pocket calculator in perfect working order. He finds pristine ice cream, still frozen, more than he can eat or keep. He begins to understand: People throw away perfectly good stuff, a lot of perfectly good stuff. 34

At this stage, Dumpster shyness begins to dissipate. The diver, after all, has the last laugh. He is finding all manner of good things that are his for the taking. Those who disparage his profession are the fools, not he. 35

He may begin to hang on to some perfectly good things for which he has neither a use nor a market. Then he begins to take note of the things that are not perfectly good but are nearly so. He mates a Walkman with broken earphones and one that is missing a battery cover. He picks up things that he can repair. 36

At this stage he may become lost and never recover. Dumpsters are full of things of some potential value to someone and also of things that never have much intrinsic value but are interesting. All the Dumpster divers I have known come to the point of trying to acquire everything they touch. Why not take it, they reason, since it is all free? This is, of course, hopeless. Most divers come to realize that they must restrict themselves to items of relatively immediate utility. But in some cases the diver simply cannot control himself. I have met several of these pack-rat types. Their ideas of the values of various pieces of junk verge on the psychotic. Every bit of glass may be a diamond, they think, and all that glisters,* gold. 37

Cause and effect: why Eighner gains weight when he scavenges

I tend to gain weight when I am scavenging. Partly this is because I always find far more pizza and doughnuts than water-packed tuna, nonfat yogurt, and fresh vegetables. Also I have not developed much faith in the reliability of Dumpsters as a food source, although it has been proven to me many times. I tend to eat as if I have no idea where my next meal is coming from. But mostly I just hate to see food go to waste and so I eat much more than I should. Something like this drives the obsession to collect junk. 38

* Eds. note – Glitters.

As for collecting objects, I usually restrict myself to collecting one kind of small object at a time, such as pocket calculators, sunglasses, or campaign buttons. To live on the street I must anticipate my needs to a certain extent: I must pick up and save warm bedding I find in August because it will not be found in Dumpsters in November. As I have no access to health care, I often hoard essential drugs, such as antibiotics and antihistamines. (This course can be recommended only to those with some grounding in pharmacology. Antibiotics, for example, even when indicated are worse than useless if taken in insufficient amounts.) But even if I had a home with extensive storage space, I could not save everything that might be valuable in some contingency. 39

Cause and effect: why Eighner saves items

I have proprietary feelings about my Dumpsters. As I have mentioned, it is no accident that I scavenge from ones where good finds are common. But my limited experience with Dumpsters in other areas suggests to me that even in poorer areas, Dumpsters, if attended with sufficient diligence, can be made to yield a livelihood. The rich students discard perfectly good kiwi fruit; poorer people discard perfectly good apples. Slacks and Polo shirts are found in one place; jeans and T-shirts in the other. The population of competitors rather than the affluence of the dumpers most affects the feasibility of survival by scavenging. The large number of competitors is what puts me off the idea of trying to scavenge in places like Los Angeles. 40

Comparison and contrast: Dumpsters in rich and poorer areas

Curiously, I do not mind my direct competition, other scavengers, so much as I hate the can scroungers. 41

People scrounge cans because they have to have a little cash. I have tried scrounging cans with an able-bodied companion. Afoot a can scrounger simply cannot make more than a few dollars in a day. One can extract the necessities of life from the Dumpsters directly with far less effort than would be required to accumulate the equivalent value in cans. (These observations may not hold in places with container redemption laws.) 42

Cause and effect: why people scrounge cans

Can scroungers, then, are people who must have small amounts of cash. These are drug addicts and winos, mostly the latter because the amounts of cash are so small. Spirits and drugs do, like all other commodities, turn up in Dumpsters and the scavenger will from time to time have a half bottle of a rather good wine with his dinner. But the wino cannot survive on these occasional finds; he must have his daily dose to stave off the DTs. All the cans he can carry will buy about three bottles of Wild Irish Rose. 43

Comparison and contrast: can scroungers vs. true scavengers

I do not begrudge them the cans, but can scroungers tend to tear up the Dumpsters, mixing the contents and littering the area. They become so specialized that they can see only cans. They earn my contempt by passing up change, canned goods, and readily hockable items. 44

There are precious few courtesies among scavengers. But it is common practice to set aside surplus items: pairs of shoes, clothing, canned goods, and such. A true scavenger hates to see good stuff go to waste, and what he cannot use he leaves in good condition in plain sight. 45

Can scroungers lay waste to everything in their path and will stir one of a pair of good shoes to the bottom of a Dumpster, to be lost or ruined in the muck. Can scroungers will even go through individual garbage cans, something I have never seen a scavenger do. 46

Cause and effect: why scavengers do not go through individual garbage cans

Individual garbage cans are set out on the public easement only on garbage days. On the other days going through them requires trespassing close to a dwelling. Going through individual garbage cans without scattering litter is almost impossible. Litter is likely to reduce the public's tolerance of scavenging. Individual cans are simply not as productive as Dumpsters; people in houses and duplexes do not move so often and for some reason do not tend to discard as much useful material. Moreover, the time required to go through one garbage can that serves one household is not much less than the time required to go through a Dumpster that contains the refuse of twenty apartments. 47

But my strongest reservation about going through individual garbage cans is that this seems to me a very personal kind of invasion to which I would object if I were a householder. Although many things in Dumpsters are obviously meant never to come to light, a Dumpster is somehow less personal. 48

I avoid trying to draw conclusions about the people who dump in the Dumpsters I frequent. I think it would be unethical to do so, although I know many people will find the idea of scavenger ethics too funny for words. 49

Examples: things found in Dumpsters

Dumpsters contain bank statements, correspondence, and other documents, just as anyone might expect. But there are also less obvious sources of information. Pill bottles, for example. The labels bear the name of the patient, the name of the doctor, and the name of the drug. AIDS drugs and antipsychotic medicines, to name but two groups, are specific and are seldom prescribed for any other disorders. The plastic compacts for birth-control pills usually have complete label information. 50

Despite all of this sensitive information, I have had only one apartment resident object to my going through the Dumpster. In that case it turned out the resident was a university athlete who was taking bets and who was afraid I would turn up his wager slips. 51

Occasionally a find tells a story. I once found a small paper bag containing some unused condoms, several partial tubes of flavored sexual lubricants, a partially used compact of birth-control pills, and the torn pieces of a picture of a young man. Clearly she was through with him and planning to give up sex altogether. 52

Dumpster things are often sad – abandoned teddy bears, shredded wedding books, despaired-of sales kits. I find many pets lying in state in Dumpsters. Although I hope to get off the streets so that Lizbeth can have a long and comfortable old age, I know this hope is not very realistic. So I suppose when her time comes she too will go into a Dumpster. I will have no better place for her. And after all, it is fitting, since for most of her life her livelihood has come from the Dumpster. When she finds something I think is safe that has been spilled from a Dumpster, I let her have it. She already knows the route around the best ones. I like to think that if she survives me she will have a chance of evading the dog catcher and of finding her sustenance on the route. 53

Silly vanities also come to rest in the Dumpsters. I am a rather accomplished needleworker. I get a lot of material from the Dumpsters. Evidently sorority girls, hoping to impress someone, perhaps themselves, with their mastery of a womanly art, buy a lot of embroider-by-number kits, work a few stitches horribly, and eventually discard the whole mess. I pull out their stitches, turn the canvas over, and work an original design. Do not think I refrain from chuckling as I make gifts from these kits. 54

I find diaries and journals. I have often thought of compiling a book of literary found objects. And perhaps I will one day. But what I find is hopelessly commonplace and bad without being, even unconsciously, camp. College students also discard their papers. I am horrified to discover the kind of paper that now merits an A in an undergraduate course. I am grateful, however, for the number of good books and magazines the students throw out. 55

In the area I know best I have never discovered vermin in the Dumpster, but there are two kinds of kitty surprise. One is alley cats whom I meet as they leap, claws first, out of Dumpsters. This is especially thrilling when I have Lizbeth in tow. The other kind of kitty surprise is a plastic 56 garbage bag filled with some ponderous, amorphous mass. This always proves to be used cat litter.

City bees harvest doughnut glaze and this makes the Dumpster at the doughnut shop more interesting. My faith in the instinctive wisdom of animals is always shaken whenever I see Lizbeth attempt to catch a bee in her mouth, which she does whenever bees are present. Evidently some birds find Dumpsters profitable, for birdie surprise is almost as common as kitty surprise of the first kind. In hunting season all kinds of small game turn up in Dumpsters, some of it, sadly, not entirely dead. Curiously, summer and winter, maggots are uncommon. 57

The worst of the living and near-living hazards of the Dumpsters are the fire ants. The food they claim is not much of a loss, but they are vicious and aggressive. It is very easy to brush against some surface of the Dumpster and pick up half a dozen or more fire ants, usually in some sensitive area such as the underarm. One advantage of bringing Lizbeth along as I make Dumpster rounds is that, for obvious reasons, she is very alert to ground-based fire ants. When Lizbeth recognizes a fire-ant infestation around our feet, she does the Dance of the Zillion Fire Ants. I have learned not to ignore this warning from Lizbeth, whether I perceive the tiny ants or not, but to remove ourselves at Lizbeth's first *pas de bourée*.* All the more so because the ants are the worst in the summer months when I wear flip-flops if I have them. (Perhaps someone will misunderstand this. Lizbeth does the Dance of the Zillion Fire Ants when she recognizes more fire ants than she cares to eat, not when she is being bitten. Since I have learned to react promptly, she does not get bitten at all. It is the isolated patrol of fire ants that falls in Lizbeth's range that deserves pity. She finds them quite tasty.) 58

Process: how to go through a Dumpster

By far the best way to go through a Dumpster is to lower yourself into it. Most of the good stuff tends to settle at the bottom because it is usually weightier than the rubbish. My more athletic companions have often demonstrated to me that they can extract much good material from a Dumpster I have already been over. 59

To those psychologically or physically unprepared to enter a Dumpster, I recommend a stout stick, preferably with some barb or hook at one end. The hook can be used to grab plastic garbage bags. When I find canned goods or other objects loose at the bottom of a Dumpster, I lower 60

* Eds. note – A ballet step.

a bag into it, roll the desired object into the bag, and then hoist the bag out – a procedure more easily described than executed. Much Dumpster diving is a matter of experience for which nothing will do except practice.

Dumpster diving is outdoor work, often surprisingly pleasant. It is not entirely predictable; things of interest turn up every day and some days there are finds of great value. I am always very pleased when I can turn up exactly the thing I most wanted to find. Yet in spite of the element of chance, scavenging more than most other pursuits tends to yield returns in some proportion to the effort and intelligence brought to bear. It is very sweet to turn up a few dollars in change from a Dumpster that has just been gone over by a wino. 61

The land is now covered with cities. The cities are full of Dumpsters. If a member of the canine race is ever able to know what it is doing, then Lizbeth knows that when we go around to the Dumpsters, we are hunting. I think of scavenging as a modern form of self-reliance. In any event, after having survived nearly ten years of government service, where everything is geared to the lowest common denominator, I find it refreshing to have work that rewards initiative and effort. Certainly I would be happy to have a sinecure again, but I am no longer heartbroken that I left one. 62

Cause and effect: results of Eighner's experiences as a scavenger

I find from the experience of scavenging two rather deep lessons. The first is to take what you can use and let the rest go by. I have come to think that there is no value in the abstract. A thing I cannot use or make useful, perhaps by trading, has no value however rare or fine it may be. I mean useful in some broad sense – some art I would find useful and some otherwise. 63

I was shocked to realize that some things are not worth acquiring, but now I think it is so. Some material things are white elephants that eat up the possessor's substance. The second lesson is the transience of material being. This has not quite converted me to a dualist,* but it has made some headway in that direction. I do not suppose that ideas are immortal, but certainly mental things are longer lived than other material things. 64

Once I was the sort of person who invests objects with sentimental value. Now I no longer have those objects, but I have the sentiments yet. 65

* Eds. note – Someone who believes that the world consists of two opposing forces, such as mind and matter.

Many times in our travels I have lost everything but the clothes I was wearing and Lizbeth. The things I find in Dumpsters, the love letters and rag dolls of so many lives, remind me of this lesson. Now I hardly pick up a thing without envisioning the time I will cast it aside. This I think is a healthy state of mind. Almost everything I have now has already been cast out at least once, proving that what I own is valueless to someone. 66

Anyway, I find my desire to grab for the gaudy bauble has been largely sated. I think this is an attitude I share with the very wealthy—we both know there is plenty more where what we have came from. Between us are the rat-race millions who nightly scavenge the cable channels looking for they know not what. 67

I am sorry for them. 68

• • •

Comprehension

1. In your own words, give a one-sentence definition of *Dumpster diving*.
2. List some of Eighner's answers to the question "Why was this discarded?" (8). What additional reasons can you think of?
3. What foods does Eighner take particular care to avoid? Why?
4. In paragraph 30, Eighner comments, "Dumpster diving has serious drawbacks as a way of life." What drawbacks does he cite in his essay? What additional drawbacks are implied? Can you think of others?
5. Summarize the stages in the process of learning to scavenge.
6. In addition to food, what else does Eighner scavenge for? Into what general categories do these items fall?
7. Why does Eighner hate can scroungers?
8. What lessons has Eighner learned as a Dumpster diver?

Purpose and Audience

1. In paragraph 6, Eighner states his purpose: to record what he has learned as a Dumpster diver. What additional purposes do you think he had in setting his ideas down on paper?
2. Do you think most readers are apt to respond to Eighner's essay with sympathy? Pity? Impatience? Contempt? Disgust? How do you react? Why?
3. Why do you think Eighner chose not to provide much background about his life—his upbringing, education, or work history—before he became homeless? Do you think this decision was a wise one? How might such information (for example, any of the details in the headnote that precedes the essay) have changed readers' reactions to his discussion?

4. In paragraph 8, Eighner presents three principles one must follow to eat safely from a Dumpster; in paragraphs 59 and 60, he explains how to go through a Dumpster; and throughout the essay, he includes many cautions and warnings. Clearly, he does not expect his audience to take up Dumpster diving. What, then, is his purpose in including such detailed explanations?
5. When Eighner begins paragraph 9 with "Perhaps everyone who has a kitchen," he encourages readers to identify with him. Where else does he make efforts to help readers imagine themselves in his place? Are these efforts successful? Explain your response.
6. What effect do you think the essay's last sentence is calculated to have on readers? What effect does it have on you?

Style and Structure

1. Eighner opens his essay with a fairly conventional strategy: extended definitions of *Dumpster* and *Dumpster diving*. What techniques does he use in paragraphs 1 through 3 to develop these definitions? Is beginning with definitions the best strategy for this essay? Explain your answer.
2. **Vocabulary Project.** In paragraph 3, Eighner suggests several alternative words for *diving* as he uses it in his essay. Consult an unabridged dictionary to determine the connotations of each of his alternatives. What are the pros and cons of substituting one of these words for *diving* in Eighner's title and throughout the essay?
3. This long essay contains three one-sentence paragraphs. Why do you think Eighner isolates these three sentences? Do you think any of them should be combined with an adjacent paragraph? Explain your reasoning.
4. As the introductory note explains, Eighner chose to retain the present tense even though he was no longer homeless when the essay was published. Why do you think he decided to preserve the present tense?
5. Eighner's essay includes a number of lists that catalog items he came across (for example, in paragraphs 5 and 50). Identify as many of these lists as you can. Why do you think Eighner includes such extensive lists?

Journal Entry

In paragraphs 21 through 25, Eighner discusses the discarding of food by college students. Does your own experience support his observations? Do you think he is being too hard on students, or does his characterization seem accurate?

Writing Workshop

1. Write an essay about a homeless person you have seen in your community. Use any patterns you like to structure your paper. When you have finished, annotate your essay to identify the patterns you have used.
2. Write an email to your school's dean of students recommending steps that can be taken on your campus to redirect discarded (but edible) food to the

homeless. Use process and exemplification to structure your message, and use information from Eighner's essay to support your points. (Be sure to acknowledge your source.)

3. **Working with Sources.** Taking Eighner's point of view and using information from his essay, as well as information (for example, statistics) you find online, write an argumentative essay with a thesis statement that takes a strong stand against homelessness and recommends government or private measures to end it. If you like, you may write your essay in the form of a statement by Eighner to a congressional committee. Be sure to document any words or ideas you borrow from Eighner or from other sources and to include a works-cited page. (See Chapter 18 for information on MLA documentation.)

Combining the Patterns

Review the annotations that identify each pattern of development used in this essay. Which patterns seem to be most effective in helping you understand and empathize with the life of a homeless person? Why?

Thematic Connections

- "Stability in Motion" (page 178)
- "Photos That Change History" (page 356)
- "The Untouchable" (page 489)
- The Declaration of Independence (page 544)

DAVID KIRBY

Inked Well

Poet David Kirby is a longtime professor of English at Florida State University, where he teaches nineteenth-century American literature and creative writing. He has authored or coauthored twenty-nine books, including the poetry collections *The Ha-Ha* (2003) and *The House on Boulevard Street* (2007), literary studies such as *Mark Strand and the Poet's Place in Contemporary Culture* (1990) and *Herman Melville* (1993), and the essay collection *Ultra-Talk: Johnny Cash, the Mafia, Shakespeare, Drum Music, St. Teresa of Avila, and 17 Other Colossal Topics of Conversation* (2007).

Background on tattoos People have sported tattoos for more than five thousand years. In some cultures, tattoos have marked a rite of passage into adulthood. They have also symbolized spiritual protection, status within a clan, fertility, and social ostracism, among other things. (Interestingly, the teachings of both Judaism and Islam specifically prohibit tattooing.) In modern Western culture, tattoos primarily serve as body adornment, although there are some exceptions — for example, the Nazis forcibly tattooed identifying numbers on many Jews, and members of some street gangs wear tattoos that signify membership. In the United States today, the most popular tattoos include skulls, hearts, eagles, and crosses as well as abstract tribal designs based on motifs that originated among Polynesian Islanders (historically, some of the most heavily tattooed people in the world). Celtic designs, flowers and butterflies, angels, stars, dragons, Chinese characters, and swallows are also popular, and anchors, once staples among sailors, are now making a comeback. Increasingly, tattoo artists are being taken seriously, and an original design may be worth thousands of dollars, or even more. Today, conventions of tattoo enthusiasts, such as the traveling Bodyart Expo, draw millions of participants each year. The cost of getting a tattoo can be as much as two hundred dollars an hour. (Getting rid of a tattoo can cost considerably more.)

Some tattooed people are easier to read than others. 1

When Richard Costello tried to sell stolen motorcycle parts on eBay earlier this year, he put the items on the floor and photographed them, though the photos also included his bare feet, with the word *White* tattooed on one and *Trash* on the other. The bike's lawful owner did a Web search, found what appeared to be the stolen parts, and notified the Clearwater, Florida, police department. Since jail records typically include identifying marks, it didn't take long for local detectives to identify Mr. Costello and set up a sting. He was arrested after showing up with a van full of stolen parts and is now facing trial. According to Sgt. Greg Stewart, Mr. Costello "just tiptoed his way back to jail." 2

L'Affaire White Trash confirmed just about everything that I thought about tattoos until recently; namely, that in addition to being nasty and unsanitary, tattoos only grace the skins of either bottom feeders or those who want to pretend they are. Richard Costello's phenomenal act of self-betrayal wouldn't have been a surprise at all to modernist architect Adolph Loos, whose influential 1908 essay "Ornament and Crime" is still cited today as a potent argument against frills and fancy stuff. Mr. Loos wrote in effect a manifesto opposing decoration, which he saw as a mark of primitive cultures, and in favor of simplicity, which is a sign of, well, modernism. Thus, Mr. Loos reasoned, it's OK for a Pacific Islander to cover himself and all his possessions with ink and carvings, whereas "a modern person [i.e., a European] who tattoos himself is either a criminal or a degenerate. . . . People with tattoos not in prison are either latent criminals or degenerate aristocrats." 3

So, presuming the kid with a Tweety Bird tattoo on his forearm who delivered your pizza last night isn't a down-on-his-luck baronet who's trying to earn enough money to return to his ancestral estate in Northumberland and claim his seat on the Queen's Privy Council, does the fact that he's slinging pies mean that he simply hasn't lived long enough to commit his first murder? Not necessarily: tattoos have a richer social history than one might think. 4

Tattoos were brought to Europe from Polynesia by eighteenth-century British explorers, as Margo DeMello writes in *Bodies of Inscription: A Cultural History of the Modern Tattoo Community* (2000). Europeans who had tattoos in those days were not social bottom dwellers. And as Charles C. Mann points out in *1491* (2005), Americans first saw tattoos in the New World on their conflicted Indian hosts as early as 1580. To Protestants of ascetic temperaments, these exotic displays were of a piece with the colonists' propensity to see Indians as primeval savages. 5

Perhaps predictably, however, tattoos came ultimately to signify patriotism rather than exoticism in the United States. The first known professional tattoo artist in the United States was one Martin Hildebrandt, who set up shop in New York City in 1846. Mr. Hildebrandt became instrumental in establishing the tradition of the tattooed serviceman by practicing his craft on soldiers and sailors on both sides in the Civil War as he migrated from one camp to another. 6

And then occurred one of those curious little shifts that make history so delicious. Tattoos became fashionable among members of the European aristocracy, who encountered the practice during nineteenth-century trips to the Far East. 7

By the beginning of World War I, though, the lords and ladies had all but abandoned bodily decoration. Why? Because by then, anybody could get a tattoo. The laborious process involving hand-tapping ink into the skin with a single needle was made obsolete with the invention of the electric tattoo machine in 1891. Tattooing suddenly became easier, less painful, and, mainly, cheaper. This led to the speedy spread of the practice throughout the working class and its abandonment by the rich. 8

By the middle of the twentieth century, tattooing seemed largely the province of bikers, convicts, and other groups on the margins of society, much as 9

Mr. Loos had predicted. Except for all those patriotic servicemen, a century ago tattoos were the tribal marks that you paid somebody to cut into your skin so that everyone would know you belonged to a world populated by crooks and creeps, along with a few bored aristocrats who would probably have been attracted to living a life of crime had their trust funds not rendered it redundant. And if things had stayed that way, I wouldn't be writing this essay: tattoos would be simply one more way of differentiating "Them" from "Us."

But "We" are the ones who are tattooed now: in the late twentieth century, the middle class began showing up in droves at tattoo parlors. A study in the June 2006 issue of the *Journal of the American Academy of Dermatology* reveals that as many as 24 percent of men and women between the ages of eighteen and fifty have one or more tattoos – up from just 15 to 16 percent in 2003. Men and women are equally likely to be tattooed, though the women surveyed are more likely to have body piercings, as well. 10

How did this change come to pass? Those of us who are certain we'll never get a tattoo will always shudder with joy when we read about knuckleheads like Richard Costello. But more and more people who wouldn't have dreamed of being tattooed a few years back are paying good money to have sketches of boom boxes, court jesters, and spider webs incised into their hides. Why, and what does it say about the world we live in? 11

To answer these questions, I walked the streets of Tallahassee, Florida, accosting total and sometimes menacing-looking strangers with the intent of asking them questions about the most intimate parts of their bodies. Any stereotypes of tattooed "victims" I had fell by the wayside rather quickly. 12

One of my first lessons was that people can get the biggest, most colorful tattoos either for exceedingly complex reasons or none at all. Jen (I'll use first names only), a pretty, slender brunette in her late twenties, said getting a tattoo was simply on a list of things she wanted to do. Melissa, a grad student in modern languages whom I spied in a bookstore wearing a pair of low-slung jeans, got a black and blue love knot high on one hip because she and her friend wanted identical tattoos, "even though she's not my friend anymore." Becky wanted a tattoo that would be a means of "making a promise to myself that I would become the person I wanted to be, that I would improve my life through hard work." 13

Of the dozen or so subjects I interviewed, Jodie was the sweetest, the most articulate, and the most heavily inked – her arms were fully sleeved in tattoos, and she was making plans to get started on her hands and neck. Jodie explained that she had been a "cutter" who "was having a lot of trouble with hurting myself physically for various reasons, so I began to get tattooed. It didn't take me long to realize that getting tattooed was quite comparable to cutting myself; it was a way for me to 'bleed out' the emotional pains which I was unable to deal with otherwise." 14

Jodie is smart as well as troubled. She knew she was hurting herself and would continue to do so, so she sublimated her self-destruction and made art of it, as surely as, say, poet Sylvia Plath* did – temporarily, anyway. 15

* Eds. note – American confessional poet who committed suicide in 1963 at the age of thirty.

It seems that more and more people from every walk of life in these United States are getting tattooed. These pioneers are "deterritorializing" tattoos, in Ms. DeMello's words, liberating them from patriotic sailors and dim-bulb motorcycle thieves and making them available to soccer moms and dads. 16

Tattoos have always been a means of identifying oneself, notes Ms. DeMello, and are always meant to be read – even a tattoo that's hidden becomes a secret book of sorts. When you get a tattoo, you write yourself, in a manner of speaking, and make it possible for others to read you, which means that every tattoo has a story. 17

There are primarily two types of tattoo narratives, the Record Book and the Canvas. Melissa, the young woman who got her tattoo to signify bonding with a friend, was capturing a relationship as one might with a photograph. In the pop music world, rap artists and other musicians sometimes get tattoos of friends or relatives who have died violently or merely passed away. The Dixie Chicks agreed to get a little chick footprint on the insteps of their feet for every No. 1 album they had. 18

If your body is a Record Book, then you and everyone who sees you is looking back at the events depicted there. But if you see your body as a Canvas, then the story you tell is, at least in its conception and execution, as inner-driven as any by Faulkner or Hemingway. Jodie, for example, is going over every inch of her body, using it as a way to tell herself a story she's beginning to understand only gradually. The more she understands, the more she "revises," just as any other artist might: her first tattoo was "a horrible butterfly thing," she told me, "which has since been covered up with a lovely raven." 19

Every person with a tattoo is a link in a chain of body modification that goes back to the dawn of human history. Researchers have found sharpened pieces of manganese dioxide – black crayons, really – that Neanderthals may have used to color animal skins as well as their own. The ancient Egyptians practiced simple tattooing. Today, radically different cultures share an obsession with body remodeling that goes far beyond mere tattooing. African tribes pierce and scar the body routinely; weightlifters pump their pecs until they bulge like grapefruit; women pay for cosmetic breast enlargement or reduction. And if that's not enough evidence that body modification is endemic, I have one word for you: *Botox*. 20

> "In a word, tattoos are now officially OK by me."

The point of all this is self-expression – and we seem to be living in a time where that's what nearly everybody (word carefully chosen) wants to do, in one way or another. As with all lifestyle changes, the tricky part is knowing when to stop. 21

As I said, I used to think tattoos were for either lowlifes or those who wanted to pretend they were, but my mind now stands changed by the thoughtful, articulate people I talked to and the spectacular designs that had been inked into their bodies. In a word, tattoos are now officially OK by me. 22

Does that mean I'd get one? Not on your life. 23

• • •

Comprehension

1. Explain the possible meanings of "Inked Well," the essay's title.
2. Kirby opens his essay with a narrative that recounts "L'Affaire White Trash" (3). Why does he begin with this narrative? What does it illustrate about tattoos?
3. Where does Kirby present information on the history of tattoos? Why does he include this background? Is it necessary? Why does he return to this historical background in paragraph 20?
4. According to Kirby, how has the tattooed population changed over the years? What factors explain these changes?
5. What does Kirby mean when he says, " 'We' are the ones who are tattooed now" (10)?
6. What two kinds of "tattoo narratives" does Kirby identify? How are they different?
7. According to Kirby, for what reasons do people get tattoos? Can you think of additional reasons?
8. How have Kirby's ideas about tattoos changed over the years? *Why* have they changed?

Purpose and Audience

1. Is Kirby's primary purpose to provide information about tattoos, to entertain readers, to explore his own feelings about tattoos, or to persuade readers to consider getting (or not getting) tattoos? Explain.
2. In paragraph 4, Kirby says that "tattoos have a richer social history than one might think." Is this his essay's thesis? If not, what is the thesis of "Inked Well"?
3. Why do you think Kirby mentions the universal "obsession with body remodeling" in paragraph 20? How do you think he expects this reference to affect his audience's reactions to his thesis? How do you react?

Style and Structure

1. **Vocabulary Project.** What is the origin of the word *tattoo*? Check an online dictionary to find out. Then, visit a tattoo website such as tattoos.com, and list some words and phrases that are part of the vocabulary of the tattoo industry. Define several of these words and expressions in layperson's terms.
2. What do you see as this essay's dominant pattern of development? Why?
3. Kirby's first and last paragraphs are each just one sentence long. Are his short introduction and conclusion effective? If you were to expand them, what would you add? Why?
4. Where does Kirby cite experts? Where does he include statistics? What do these kinds of information add to his essay?

Journal Entry

Do you see tattoos as art or as a kind of defacement or self-mutilation? Explain your feelings.

Writing Workshop

1. **Working with Sources.** Find some pictures of tattoos online. Then, write a classification-and-division essay that discusses the kinds of tattoos you find there. (You might want to begin by looking at "Four Tattoos," page 218.) Be sure your essay has a thesis statement that makes a point about tattoos, and use exemplification, description, and comparison and contrast to support your thesis. If you like, you may illustrate your essay with photos or drawings you find on the Web, but if you do, remember to document your sources and to include a works-cited page. (See Chapter 18 for information on MLA documentation.)
2. In paragraph 11, Kirby asks what the prevalence of tattoos says about the world we live in. Using cause and effect as your dominant pattern of development, write an essay that tries to explain what accounts for this phenomenon. Use description and exemplification to support your points.
3. In paragraph 17, Kirby says, "When you get a tattoo, you write yourself, in a manner of speaking, and make it possible for others to read you, which means that every tattoo has a story." What story would you like your own tattoo (or tattoos) to tell? Write an essay that answers this question, using description, exemplification, and cause and effect as well as narration.

Combining the Patterns

What patterns of development does Kirby use in his essay? Annotate the essay to identify each pattern. Use the annotations accompanying "On Dumpster Diving" (page 676) as a guide.

Thematic Connections

- "Four Tattoos" (page 218)
- "Why Looks Are the Last Bastion of Discrimination" (page 239)
- "Medium Ash Brown" (page 270)

DONALD KAGAN

On Patriotism

Historian and classical scholar Donald Kagan (b. 1932) was born in Lithuania but grew up in Brooklyn, New York, after his family immigrated to the United States. He was educated at Brooklyn College and Brown University before receiving his Ph.D. from Ohio State University. A classicist known for his work on ancient Greece and the Peloponnesian War, Kagan spent much of his career teaching at Yale University, where he was Sterling Professor of Classics and History. His books include *The Outbreak of the Peloponnesian War* (1969) and *On the Origins of War and the Preservation of Peace* (1995). He is a 2002 winner of the National Humanities Medal, among many other honors.

Background on patriotism versus nationalism "The encouragement of patriotism is no longer a part of our public educational system, and the cost of that omission is now making itself felt," writes Donald Kagan in the essay that follows. In simple terms, *patriotism* means love of — or devotion to — one's country and usually has a positive connotation. It is often used synonymously with *nationalism*, however, which in both its denotation and connotation suggests rigid support for one's own country to the detriment of other countries. It implies a national chauvinism that asserts superiority and inspires conflict. As the late political writer Joseph Sobran wrote, "While patriotism is a form of affection, nationalism . . . is grounded in resentment and rivalry; it's often defined by its enemies and traitors, real or supposed." When we view *patriotism* and *nationalism* as abstract ideas, the difference between the two is easy to spot. At times of national crisis or threat, however, such distinctions can become blurred — especially when manipulative political leaders and demagogues seek to erase them. At the Nuremberg trials after World War II, for example, the infamous Nazi official and military leader Hermann Göring asserted that dragging a reluctant population to war was a simple task: "All you have to do is tell them they are being attacked and denounce the pacifists for lack of patriotism and exposing the country to danger." One way to distinguish *patriotism* and *nationalism* is in terms of their contrasting attitudes toward dissent: generally speaking, the former can tolerate criticism, but the latter cannot. Keep this difference in mind as you read Kagan's essay.

In October 2001, without dissent, Congress requested that the president designate September 11 "Patriot Day," a national day of remembrance of the attacks by international terrorists on two American cities that killed thousands of innocent civilians. When they had recovered from their shock after the attacks, most Americans reacted in two ways: They clearly and powerfully supported their government's determination to use military force to prevent future attacks by capturing or killing the perpetrators and tearing out their organizations root and branch. And, to this end, they supported the 1 removal of the leaders of states that supported, abetted, or gave refuge to terrorists unless those leaders abandoned such practices. Most Americans also expressed a new sense of unity and an explicit love for their country that had not been seen for a long time.

Not every country deserves the devotion and patriotic support of its citizens. Dictatorships of whatever kind have no right to these commitments, for they rule over unfree, often unwilling, people as if over slaves; they lack moral legitimacy. But citizens of free countries like the United States can vote in elections with real choices for lawmakers and leaders, and those who don't approve of their country's laws and way of life have the right and opportunity to change them by legal process. Failing in such an attempt, they are free to leave the country with all their property. By staying they are tacitly accepting the laws of the country and the principles on which those laws are based. They are free to doubt them and even to denounce them, but they are morally bound to observe them. For Americans, as for citizens of any free country, there really is a social contract like those imagined by the political philosophers, and that contract provides legitimacy. People who tacitly accept that contract have the moral obligation to defend and support the country they have chosen as their own—that is, to be patriotic. 2

It seems to me, moreover, that Americans have especially good reasons for belief in and devotion to their country. America has been a beacon of liberty to the world since its creation, and was especially so in the twentieth century. The September 11 attacks produced a wave of vilification against America from "intellectuals" at home and abroad, but it is worth remembering what Americans did in the twentieth century. They helped save Europe from German domination in two world wars. After World War II they rebuilt the continent from the ashes. They stood against and helped defeat the Soviet Communist government, which along with Nazi Germany and Maoist China, was among the most brutal regimes in history. They stopped the slaughter in the Balkans while Europeans stood by and watched, and they drove Saddam Hussein from Kuwait and ultimately from his seat of power as he prepared to resume his goal of dominating the Middle East. 3

"People should think," the late David Halberstam* said from New York following the attacks, "what the world would be like without the backdrop of American leadership with all its flaws over the past sixty years. Probably, I think, a bit like hell." In my view it doesn't take an American chauvinist to suggest that there is some virtue in a country that has helped save the world from Wilhelmian Germany's right-wing imperialism, Hitler's Nazi regime, Japan's militaristic domination, and Stalin's totalitarianism. Yet voices here and abroad from the world of "intellectual" orthodoxy continue to condemn and blame the United States, as they did throughout the Cold War. 4

These dissenters' ideas have a wide currency and reflect a serious flaw in American education that should especially concern those of us who take some 5

* Eds. note—Popular Pulitzer Prize–winning historian and journalist (1934–2007) who wrote about the civil rights movement and the Vietnam War, among many other subjects.

part in it. The encouragement of patriotism is no longer a part of our public educational system, and the cost of that omission is now making itself felt. In the intellectual climate of our time the very suggestion brings contemptuous sneers or outrage, depending on the mood of the listener. Many have been the attacks on patriotism for its alleged intolerance, arrogance, and bellicosity, but that is to equate it with its bloated distortion, chauvinism. My favorite dictionary defines the latter as "militant and boastful devotion to and glorification of one's country," but a patriot as "one who loves, supports, and defends his country." That does not require us to hate, contemn, denigrate, or attack any other country, nor does it require us to admire our own uncritically. Few countries have been subjected to as much criticism and questioning, even from its patriotic citizens, as our own.

So distant are we from a proper understanding of patriotism that I some- 6
times hear people say, "It is silly to be patriotic. Why should I love, support, and defend a country just because, quite by chance, I happened to be born there?" In fact, there should be a presupposition in favor of patriotism, for human beings are not solitary creatures but require organized societies if they are to flourish or even survive. Just as individuals must have an appropriate self-love in order to perform well, and an appropriate love of their families if both are to prosper, so, too, must they love their country if it is to survive. Neither family nor nation can flourish without love, support, and defense, and individuals who have benefited from those institutions not only serve their self-interest in defending them but also have a moral responsibility to give them that support.

The assaults on patriotism, therefore, are failures of character. They are 7
made by privileged people who enjoy the full benefits offered by the country they deride and detest – its opportunities, its freedom, its riches – but lack the basic decency to pay the allegiance and respect that honor demands. For the rest of us, our own honor and our devotion to our nation's special virtues require us to respect and defend these privileged people's opportunity to be irresponsible and subversive of our safety – but nothing forbids us from pointing out the despicable nature of their behavior.

Free countries like our own, it seems 8
to me, have an even greater need of patriotic citizens than others. Every country requires a high degree of cooperation and unity among its people if it is to achieve the internal harmony that every good society requires. These must rest on something shared and valued in common. Most countries have relied on the common ancestry and traditions of their people as the basis of their unity, but the United States of America can rely on no such commonality. We are an enormously diverse and varied people, composed almost entirely of immigrants or the descendants of immigrants. We come from almost every continent, our forebears spoke – and many of us still speak – many different languages, and all the races and religions of the world are to be found among us. The great strengths provided by this diversity are matched by great dangers. We are

> "Free countries like our own . . . have an even greater need of patriotic citizens than others."

always vulnerable to divisions that can be exploited to set one group against another and destroy the unity and harmony that have allowed us to flourish.

We live in a time when civic devotion has been undermined and national unity is under attack. The individualism that is so crucial a part of our tradition is often used to destroy civic responsibility. The idea of a common American culture, enriched by the diverse elements that compose it but available equally to all, is also under assault, and some are trying to replace it with narrower and politically divisive programs that are certain to set one group of Americans against another. The answer to these problems, and our only hope for the future, must lie in a proper education, which philosophers have long put at the center of the consideration of justice and the good society. We rightly look to education to solve the pressing current problems of our economic and technological competition with other nations, but we must not neglect the inescapable political and ethical effects of education. We in the academic community have too often engaged in miseducation. If we ignore civic education, the forging of a single people, the building of a legitimate patriotism, we will have selfish individuals, heedless of the needs of others, reluctant to work toward the common good and to defend our country when defense is needed. In telling the story of the American experience we must insist on the honest search for truth; we must permit no comfortable self-deception or evasion. The story of this country's vision of a free, democratic republic and of its struggle to achieve it need not fear the most thorough examination and can proudly stand comparison with that of any other land. It provides the basis for the civic devotion and love of country we so badly need. 9

Some critics of America's efforts to defend itself against its current enemies, who insist that our wars in Afghanistan and Iraq are too costly and that success is unattainable, who demand that we withdraw from one or both of these battlefronts whatever the cost, claim that they are no less patriotic than others. To be sure, a patriot may disagree with the policy and strategy of the government and legitimately try to argue for change. He or she may not, however, attempt to justify opposition to that policy and gain political advantage from so doing by tendentiously mis-describing the facts, by insisting that the war has been lost when it plainly has not. The war in Iraq was not lost, although opponents of that war, even as the situation improved, rushed to declare America defeated. They offered no plausible alternative to what turned out to be the successful strategy and took no serious notice of the dreadful consequences of swift withdrawal in defeat. They seemed to be panicked by the possibility of success and eager to bring about withdrawal and defeat before success could get in the way. Such are the actions of defeatists and political opportunists; they can never be called patriotic. 10

Americans have miraculously been spared another attack on their homeland since 2001, and this has made many of us complacent and helped us forget the kind of threat we face. The best evidence for the character of that threat is provided by the words of our enemies themselves. In February 1998, Osama bin Laden published his declaration of a holy war against America in which he said, "To kill Americans and their allies, both civil and military, is an individual duty of every Muslim who is able." 11

In countless statements he and others have made it clear that the United States is "the great Satan," the enemy of all they hold dear. That includes the establishment of an extreme and reactionary Islamic fundamentalism at least in all current Islamic lands – a considerable portion of the globe. It would impose a totalitarian theocracy that would subjugate the mass of the people, especially women. Radical Islamicists hate the United States not only because its power stands in the way of the achievement of their vision but because its free, open, democratic, tolerant, liberal, and prosperous society is a powerful competitor for the allegiance of millions of Muslims around the world. No change of U.S. policy, no retreat from the world, no repentance or increase of modesty can alter these things. Only the destruction of the United States and its way of life will do. In one of his public statements bin Laden said that the only way to peace was for Americans to abandon democracy and convert to his perverted brand of Islam. 12

A couple of months after the attacks I suggested that we were at war, 13

> a war waged against us by angry and determined men who will not let us escape, a war that will be more difficult and longer than most of us understand. If America is defeated in this war or driven into a cowering isolationism, liberty's brightest light will go out, and a terrible darkness will descend on the whole world.
>
> We must face the fact that our people and our friends around the world are in great danger from people who make it plain that they are determined to kill us, to destroy our country and our way of life. Betraying our friends, retreating from the world, expressing our guilt, our shame, our repentance for anything and everything they claim we have done, will neither appease nor deter them. It is our existence that troubles them. We seek not vengeance but only safety and the establishment of an order in the world that is secure against wanton violence and that allows people freely to choose the way of life that pleases them.

I would say the same today, with much more evidence.

Since the attacks of 2001, U.S. and allied forces have driven out the Taliban regime that provided a haven for al-Qaeda in Afghanistan. They have dethroned the murderous dictator Saddam Hussein from Iraq, where he had launched wars against his neighbors, terrorized and brutalized his own people, and threatened the security of the entire region. In May U.S. forces killed Osama bin Laden. These were valuable and important steps, but they have not brought an end to the struggle. Both wars continue, and ultimate success seems distant and difficult. The costs and duration of the fighting have made the war and the government conducting that war unpopular. Opponents of the war continue to claim that victory is impossible and demand an early withdrawal of our forces, regardless of the horrendous consequences of such an irresponsible action. 14

In this they have been typical of citizens of democracies engaged in long painful wars that do not promise swift victory. On the eve of the Peloponnesian War, for example, Pericles told the Athenians that "men are not moved by the same feeling when they are already at war as when they make the decision to fight but change their minds in the face of misfortunes," and so it turned out. 15

The Athenians were suffering and the strategy for victory was not working, so defeatists and those who had opposed the war from the first demanded that Athens make peace at once. As Thucydides tells us, "They began to find fault with Pericles, as the author of the war and the cause of all their misfortunes, and became eager to come to terms with Sparta, and actually sent ambassadors there, who did not however succeed in their mission. Their despair was now complete and all vented itself upon Pericles" (*History of the Peloponnesian War*). He, in response, called for patriotism in time of trouble: "Since a republic can support the misfortunes of private citizens, while they cannot support hers, it is surely the duty of everyone to be forward in her defense.... The apparent error of my policy lies in the infirmity of your resolution, since...your mind is too much depressed to persevere in your resolves.... Cease then to grieve for your private afflictions, and address yourselves instead to the safety of the republic." Ultimately, the Athenians continued the fight, recovering from what seemed certain defeat, until the enemy offered a peace they could accept.

So it was, too, in the midst of America's Civil War. As late as 1864, after 16 three years of fearful casualties, victory for the Union forces was not in sight. Lincoln was determined to continue the fight to restore the integrity of the Union and to abolish slavery. Those who had opposed the war from the beginning were joined by great numbers of civilians who were simply weary of the war and others who were ready to seek peace at any price: for some the persistence of slavery and for others the dissolution of the Union. One English friend of the Union cause expected the politicians to compromise with the South – to take the southern states back slavery and all. Such an event would be shameful, he said, but still "it would leave the question to be settled by a similar process of blood by another generation."

In 1864, Lincoln changed generals and undertook a more aggressive 17 strategy, but the war continued to drag on. A hostile newspaper editorialized that "perhaps it is time to agree to a peace without victory." Like Pericles, Lincoln was assailed by attacks on his policies and by personal vituperation. At the Democratic convention in August 1864 a speaker told a crowd in the streets that Lincoln and the Union armies had " 'Failed! Failed!! FAILED!!! FAILED!!!!' The loss of life 'has never been seen since the destruction of Sennacherib by the breath of the Almighty and still the monster usurper wants more men for his slaughter pens.' "

The Democrats nominated a rabidly antiwar candidate for vice president, 18 adopted a platform that called the war a "failure," and demanded "immediate efforts" to end hostilities. Their platform statement would permit abandonment not only of emancipation but of the most basic war aim, reunion. Even New York's Republican Party boss declared that Lincoln's reelection was widely regarded as an "impossibility.... The People are wild for Peace."

At the end of August, defeat for the Republicans and the Union cause 19 seemed inevitable, but Lincoln refused to seek peace without victory, saying that he was not prepared to "give up the Union for a peace which, so achieved, could not be of much duration."

No one would have predicted that within a matter of months the war 20 would end with a total victory for the Federal forces, slavery abolished, and the Union restored, but events took an unexpected turn. A series of Union military victories changed the course of the war. The Democrats, having declared or predicted defeat, were, as the historian Jennifer L. Weber noted, "tarred as traitors, regardless of their actual positions on the war"; "Democrats were... roundly thrashed in November. In fact, the stench of treason clung to the Democrats for years; nearly a generation would pass before another Democrat, Grover Cleveland, occupied the White House" (*Copperheads*).

Lincoln remains an American icon and hero for many reasons, but not least of them is his steadfast patriotism. In the face of political defeat and personal humiliation he would not abandon the integrity and security of his country nor would he abandon its most treasured principle, freedom, to escape his troubles. 21

In spite of the shock caused by the attacks on New York and Washington and the years of war that have followed, I am not sure that we yet understand how serious is the challenge that now faces us. Early in the Iraq War I noted that "we are only at the beginning of a long and deadly war that will inflict loss and pain, that will require sacrifice and steady commitment and determination even during very dark hours to come. We must be powerfully armed, morally as well as materially, if we are to do what must be done. That will take courage and unity, and these must rest on a justified and informed patriotism to sustain us through the worst times." I think those words are still relevant. 22

A verse by Edna St. Vincent Millay provides a clear answer to the question of why Americans should love their country and make the sacrifices needed to defend it and its principles: 23

> Not for the flag
> Of any land because myself was born there
> Will I give up my life.
> But will I love that land where man is free,
> And that will I defend.

Ours is such a land, and it will need the legitimate patriotism of its people in the long, dangerous, and difficult struggle that lies ahead.

• • •

Comprehension

1. What immediate reactions did most Americans have after the September 11, 2001, terrorist attacks?
2. According to Kagan, under what circumstances does a country not have the right to its citizens' support? Do you agree with him? Why or why not?
3. Why does Kagan think Americans should be patriotic?
4. Why, according to Kagan, do "free countries" (8) like the United States need patriotic citizens more than other countries do? What does our being such a diverse nation have to do with why we need to be patriotic?
5. What is Kagan's opinion of critics of the Iraq war? Does he consider them to be patriotic? Why or why not? Do you find his explanation convincing?
6. What specific dangers does Kagan believe "Radical Islamicists" (12) pose? What is the relationship between these dangers and American patriotism?

7. In this essay, written in 2011, Kagan says he considers the United States to be "at war" (13). What evidence does he present to support this statement? Is this evidence convincing? Why or why not?

Purpose and Audience

1. Why does Kagan open his essay with a discussion of the September 11, 2001, terrorist attacks? What connection does he make between September 11 and patriotism?
2. What is Kagan's definition of *patriotism*? Where does he state it? Could this definition serve as his essay's thesis? If so, why? If not, why not?
3. What preconceptions about patriotism does Kagan seem to expect his readers to have? Do you think he expects them to share his political philosophy? Explain your answer.
4. In paragraph 5, Kagan says, "The encouragement of patriotism is no longer a part of our public educational system, and the cost of that omission is now making itself felt." What does he mean by that statement? Do you think he is right?
5. In paragraph 9, Kagan identifies himself as part of "the academic community." How might his role as an academic have influenced his purpose for writing this essay?

Style and Structure

1. In paragraph 6, Kagan draws an **analogy**, comparing *nation* to *family*. Is this analogy valid? Why or why not?
2. Although this essay is relatively formal, Kagan uses the first person throughout. What does this strategy – particularly his use of *we* – achieve?
3. **Vocabulary Project.** In paragraph 5, Kagan discusses *chauvinism*. What is *chauvinism*? How is it different from *patriotism*?
4. Evaluate Kagan's concluding paragraph. What do the lines by Edna St. Vincent Millay add to his essay? How do these lines reinforce the point Kagan is making about patriotism?

Journal Entry

Do you see "On Patriotism" as optimistic or pessimistic? Explain your position.

Writing Workshop

1. **Working with Sources.** Reread the lines by Edna St. Vincent Millay that Kagan quotes in paragraph 23. Then, search online for poems about the American flag and for images that include the flag. Now, write an essay that examines the relationship between patriotism and the flag, including references to the poems and images you find. You can use description, exemplification, and definition as well as comparison and contrast.

Include one or two of the key images in your essay. Be sure to document all references to poems and images and to include a works-cited page. (See Chapter 18 for information on MLA documentation.)

2. **Working with Sources.** Quoting from Kagan at least once, write an essay about the importance of patriotism from the point of view of writers in this book – for example, Zeynep Tufekci – who were not born in the United States. (You can find this information in the headnotes that precede the essays.) Be sure to document all references to Kagan and other essays and to include a works-cited page. (See Chapter 18 for information on MLA documentation.)

3. Using several different patterns of development, write an essay called "On Loyalty," "On Friendship," or "On Ambition."

Combining the Patterns

What patterns of development does Kagan use in this essay? Annotate the essay to identify each pattern. Use the annotations accompanying "On Dumpster Diving" (page 676) as a guide.

Thematic Connections

- "Ground Zero" (page 173)
- "Why the Post Office Makes America Great" (page 220)
- The Declaration of Independence (page 544)
- "Letter from Birmingham Jail" (page 558)

JONATHAN SWIFT

A Modest Proposal

Jonathan Swift (1667–1745) was born in Dublin, Ireland, and spent much of his life journeying between his homeland, where he had a modest income as an Anglican priest, and England, where he wished to be part of the literary establishment. The author of many satires and political pamphlets, he is best known today for *Gulliver's Travels* (1726), a sharp satire that, except among academics, is now read primarily as a fantasy for children.

Background on the English-Irish conflict At the time Swift wrote "A Modest Proposal," Ireland had been essentially under British rule since 1171, with the British often brutally suppressing rebellions by the Irish people. When Henry VIII of England declared a Protestant Church of Ireland, many of the Irish remained fiercely Roman Catholic, which led to even greater contention. By the early 1700s, the English-controlled Irish Parliament had passed laws that severely limited the rights of Irish Catholics, and British trade policies had begun to seriously depress the Irish economy. A fierce advocate for the Irish people in their struggle under British rule, Swift published several works supporting the Irish cause. The following sharply ironic essay was written during the height of a terrible famine in Ireland, when the British were proposing a devastating tax on the impoverished Irish citizenry. Note that Swift does not write in his own voice here but adopts the persona of one who does not recognize the barbarity of his "solution."

It is a melancholy object to those who walk through this great town* or travel in the country, when they see the streets, the roads, and cabin doors, crowded with beggars of the female sex, followed by three, four, or six children, all in rags and importuning every passenger for an alms. These mothers, instead of being able to work for their honest livelihood, are forced to employ all their time in strolling to beg sustenance for their helpless infants, who, as they grow up, either turn thieves for want of work, or leave their dear native country to fight for the Pretender in Spain, or sell themselves to the Barbadoes.** 1

I think it is agreed by all parties that this prodigious number of children in the arms, or on the backs, or at the heels of their mothers, and frequently of their fathers, is in the present deplorable state of the kingdom a very great additional grievance; and therefore whoever could find out a fair, cheap, and easy method of making these children sound, useful members of the commonwealth would deserve so well of the public as to have his statue set up for a preserver of the nation. 2

* Eds. note — Dublin.

** Eds. note — Many young Irishmen left their country to fight as mercenaries in Spain's civil war or to work as indentured servants in the West Indies.

But my intention is very far from being confined to provide only for the children of professed beggars; it is of a much greater extent, and shall take in the whole number of infants at a certain age who are born of parents in effect as little able to support them as those who demand our charity in the streets. 3

As to my own part, having turned my thoughts for many years upon this important subject, and maturely weighed the several schemes of the other projectors, I have always found them grossly mistaken in their computation. It is true, a child just dropped from its dam may be supported by her milk for a solar year, with little other nourishment; at most not above the value of two shillings, which the mother may certainly get, or the value in scraps, by her lawful occupation of begging; and it is exactly at one year old that I propose to provide for them in such a manner as instead of being a charge upon their parents or the parish, or wanting food and raiment for the rest of their lives, they shall on the contrary contribute to the feeding, and partly to the clothing, of many thousands. 4

There is likewise another great advantage in my scheme, that it will prevent those involuntary abortions, and that horrid practice of women murdering their bastard children, alas, too frequent among us, sacrificing the poor innocent babies, I doubt, more to avoid the expense than the shame, which would move tears and pity in the most savage and inhuman breast. 5

The number of souls in this kingdom being usually reckoned one million and a half, of these I calculate there may be about two hundred thousand couples whose wives are breeders, from which number I subtract thirty thousand couples who are able to maintain their own children, although I apprehend there cannot be so many under the present distress of the kingdom; but this being granted, there will remain an hundred and seventy thousand breeders. I again subtract fifty thousand for those women who miscarry, or whose children die by accident or disease within the year. There only remain an hundred and twenty thousand children of poor parents annually born. The question therefore is, how this number shall be reared and provided for, which, as I have already said, under the present situation of affairs, is utterly impossible by all the methods hitherto proposed. For we can neither employ them in handicraft nor agriculture; we neither build houses (I mean in the country) nor cultivate land. They can very seldom pick up livelihood by stealing till they arrive at six years old, except where they are of towardly parts,* although I confess they learn the rudiments much earlier, during which time they can however be looked upon only as probationers, as I have been informed by a principal gentleman in the country of Cavan, who protested to me that he never knew above one or two instances under the age of six, even in a part of the kingdom so renowned for the quickest proficiency in that art. 6

I am assured by our merchants that a boy or a girl before twelve years old is no salable commodity; and even when they come to this age, they will not yield above three pounds, or three pounds and half a crown at most on the Exchange; which cannot turn to account either to the parents or the kingdom, the charge of nutriment and rags having been at least four times that value. 7

* Eds. note — Precocious.

8 I shall now therefore humbly propose my own thoughts, which I hope will not be liable to the least objection.

9 I have been assured by a very knowing American of my acquaintance in London, that a young healthy child well nursed is at a year old a most delicious, nourishing, and wholesome food, whether stewed, roasted, baked, or boiled; and I make no doubt that it will equally serve in fricassee or a ragout.

10 I do therefore humbly offer it to public consideration that of the hundred and twenty thousand children, already computed, twenty thousand may be reserved for breed, whereof only one fourth part to be males, which is more than we allow to sheep, black cattle, or swine; and my reason is that these children are seldom the fruits of marriage, a circumstance not much regarded by our savages, therefore one male will be sufficient to serve four females. That the remaining hundred thousand may at a year old be offered in sale to the persons of quality and fortune through the kingdom, always advising the mother to let them suck plentifully in the last month, so as to render them plump and fat for a good table. A child will make two dishes at an entertainment for friends; and when the family dines alone, the fore or hind quarter will make a reasonable dish, and seasoned with a little pepper or salt, will be very good boiled on the fourth day, especially in winter.

11 I have reckoned upon a medium that a child just born will weigh twelve pounds, and in a solar year if tolerably nursed increaseth to twenty-eight pounds.

12 I grant this food will be somewhat dear, and therefore very proper for landlords, who, as they have already devoured most of the parents, seem to have the best title to the children.

"I grant this food will be somewhat dear, and therefore very proper for landlords, who, as they have already devoured most of the parents, seem to have the best title to the children."

13 Infant's flesh will be in season throughout the year, but more plentiful in March, and a little before and after. For we are told by a grave author, an eminent French physician,* that fish being a prolific diet, there are more children born in Roman Catholic countries about nine months after Lent, than at any other season; therefore, reckoning a year after Lent, the markets will be more glutted than usual, because the number of popish infants is at least three to one in this kingdom; and therefore it will have one other collateral advantage, by lessening the number of Papists** among us.

14 I have already computed the charge of nursing a beggar's child (in which list I reckon all cottagers, laborers, and four fifths of the farmers) to be about two shillings per annum, rags included; and I believe no gentleman would repine to give ten shillings for the carcass of a good fat child, which, as I have said, will make four dishes of excellent nutritive meat, when he hath only

* Eds. note—François Rabelais, a sixteenth-century satirical writer.
** Eds. note—Roman Catholics.

some particular friend or his own family to dine with him. Thus the squire will learn to be a good landlord, and grow popular among the tenants; the mother will have eight shillings net profit, and be fit for work till she produces another child.

Those who are more thrifty (as I must confess the times require) may flay the carcass; the skin of which artificially* dressed will make admirable gloves for ladies, and summer boots for fine gentlemen. 15

As to our city of Dublin, shambles** may be appointed for this purpose in the most convenient parts of it, and butchers we may be assured will not be wanting; although I rather recommend buying the children alive, and dressing them hot from the knife as we do roasting pigs. 16

A very worthy person, a true lover of his country, and whose virtues I highly esteem, was lately pleased in discoursing on this matter to offer a refinement upon my scheme. He said that many gentlemen of his kingdom, having of late destroyed their deer, he conceived that the want of venison might be well supplied by the bodies of young lads and maidens, not exceeding fourteen years of age nor under twelve, so great a number of both sexes in every county being now ready to starve for want of work and service; and these to be disposed of by their parents, if alive, or otherwise by their nearest relations. But with due deference to so excellent a friend and so deserving a patriot I cannot be altogether in his sentiments; for as to the males, my American acquaintance assured me from frequent experience that their flesh was generally tough and lean, like that of our schoolboys, by continual exercise, and their taste disagreeable; and to fatten them would not answer the charge. Then as to the females, it would, I think with humble submission, be a loss to the public, because they soon would become breeders themselves; and besides, it is not improbable that some scrupulous people might be apt to censure such a practice (although indeed very unjustly) as a little bordering upon cruelty; which, I confess, hath always been with me the strongest objection against any project, how well soever intended. 17

But in order to justify my friend, he confessed that this expedient was put into his head by the famous Psalmanazar,*** a native of the island Formosa, who came from thence to London above twenty years ago, and in conversation told my friend that in his country when any young person happened to be put to death, the executioner sold the carcass to the persons of quality as a prime dainty; and that in his time the body of a plump girl of fifteen, who was crucified for an attempt to poison the emperor, was sold to the Imperial Majesty's prime minister of state, and other great mandarins of the court, in joints from the gibbet, at four hundred crowns. Neither indeed can I deny that if the same use were made of several plump young girls in this town, who without one 18

* Eds. note – Skillfully.

** Eds. note – A slaughterhouse or meat market.

*** Eds. note – Frenchman who passed himself off as a native of Formosa (present-day Taiwan).

single groat to their fortunes cannot stir abroad without a chair,* and appear at the playhouse and assemblies in foreign fineries which they never will pay for, the kingdom would not be the worse.

Some persons of a desponding spirit are in great concern about the vast number of poor people who are aged, diseased, or maimed, and I have been desired to employ my thoughts what course may be taken to ease the nation of so grievous an encumbrance. But I am not in the least pain upon that matter, because it is very well known that they are every day dying and rotting by cold and famine, and filth and vermin, as fast as can be reasonably expected. And as to the younger laborers, they are now in almost as hopeful a condition. They cannot get work, and consequently pine away for want of nourishment to a degree that if any time they are accidentally hired to common labor, they have not strength to perform it; and thus the country and themselves are happily delivered from the evils to come. 19

I have too long digressed, and therefore shall return to my subject. I think the advantages by the proposal which I have made are obvious and many, as well as of the highest importance. 20

For first, as I have already observed, it would greatly lessen the number of Papists, with whom we are yearly overrun, being the principal breeders of the nation as well as our most dangerous enemies; and who stay at home on purpose to deliver the kingdom to the Pretender, hoping to take their advantage by the absence of so many good Protestants, who have chosen rather to leave their country than to stay at home and pay tithes against their conscience to an Episcopal curate. 21

Secondly, the poorer tenants will have something valuable of their own, which by law may be made liable to distress,** and help to pay their landlord's rent, their corn and cattle being already seized and money a thing unknown. 22

Thirdly, whereas the maintenance of an hundred thousand children, from two years old and upwards, cannot be computed at less than ten shillings a piece per annum, the nation's stock will be thereby increased fifty thousand pounds per annum, besides the profit of a new dish introduced to the tables of all gentlemen of fortune in the kingdom who have any refinement in taste. And the money will circulate among ourselves, the goods being entirely of our own growth and manufacture. 23

Fourthly, the constant breeders, besides the gain of eight shillings sterling per annum by the sale of their children, will be rid of the charge for maintaining them after the first year. 24

Fifthly, this food would likewise bring great custom to taverns, where the vintners will certainly be so prudent as to procure the best receipts*** for dressing it to perfection, and consequently have their houses frequented by all the fine gentlemen, who justly value themselves upon their knowledge in 25

* Eds. note – A sedan chair; that is, a portable covered chair designed to seat one person and then to be carried by two men.

** Eds. note – Property could be seized by creditors.

*** Eds. note – Recipes.

good eating; and a skillful cook, who understands how to oblige his guests, will contrive to make it as expensive as they please.

Sixthly, this would be a great inducement to marriage, after which all wise nations have either encouraged by rewards or enforced by laws and penalties. It would increase the care and tenderness of mothers toward their children, when they were sure of a settlement for life to the poor babes, provided in some sort by the public, to their annual profit instead of expense. We should see an honest emulation among the married women, which of them could bring the fattest child to the market. Men would become as fond of their wives during the time of pregnancy as they are now of their mares in foal, their cows in calf, or sows when they are ready to farrow; nor offer to beat or kick them (as is too frequent a practice) for fear of miscarriage. 26

Many other advantages might be enumerated. For instance, the addition of some thousand carcasses in our exportation of barreled beef, the propagation of swine's flesh, and improvements in the art of making good bacon, so much wanted among us by the great destruction of pigs, too frequent at our tables, which are no way comparable in taste or magnificence to a well-grown, fat, yearling child, which roasted whole will make a considerable figure at a lord mayor's feast or other public entertainment. But this and many others I omit, being studious of brevity. 27

Supposing that one thousand families in this city would be constant customers for infants' flesh, besides others who might have it at merry meetings, particularly weddings and christenings, I compute that Dublin would take off annually about twenty thousand carcasses, and the rest of the kingdom (where probably they will be sold somewhat cheaper) the remaining eighty thousand. 28

I can think of no one objection that will possibly be raised against this proposal, unless it should be urged that the number of people will be thereby much lessened in the kingdom. This I freely own, and it was indeed one principal design in offering it to the world. I desire the reader will observe; that I calculate my remedy for this one individual kingdom of Ireland and for no other that ever was, is, or I think ever can be upon earth. Therefore, let no man talk to me of other expedients: of taxing our absentees at five shillings a pound: of using neither clothes nor household furniture except what is of our own growth and manufacture: of utterly rejecting the materials and instruments that promote foreign luxury: of curing the expensiveness of pride, vanity, idleness, and gaming in our women: of introducing a vein of parsimony, prudence, and temperance: of learning to love our country, in the want of which we differ even from Lowlanders and the inhabitants of Topinamboo:* of quitting our animosities and factions, nor acting any longer like the Jews,** who were murdering one another at the very moment their city was taken: of being a little cautious not to sell our country and conscience for nothing: of teaching landlords to have at least one degree of mercy toward their tenants: lastly, of putting a spirit of honesty, industry, and skill into our shopkeepers; 29

* Eds. note—A place in the Brazilian jungle.

** Eds. note—In the first century B.C., the Roman general Pompey could conquer Jerusalem in part because the citizenry was divided among rival factions.

who, if a resolution could now be taken to buy only our native goods, would immediately unite to cheat and exact upon us in the price, the measure, and the goodness, nor could ever yet be brought to make one fair proposal of just dealing, though often and earnestly invited to it.

Therefore, I repeat, let no man talk to me of these and the like expedients, till he hath at least some glimpse of hope that there will ever be some hearty and sincere attempt to put them in practice.* 30

But as to myself, having been wearied out for many years with offering vain, idle, visionary thoughts, and at length utterly despairing of success, I fortunately fell upon this proposal, which, as it is wholly new, so it hath something solid and real, of no expense and little trouble, full in our own power, and whereby we can incur no danger in disobliging England. For this kind of commodity will not bear exploration, the flesh being of too tender a consistence to admit a long continuance in salt, although perhaps I could name a country which would be glad to eat up our whole nation without it. 31

After all, I am not so violently bent upon my own opinion as to reject any offer proposed by wise men, which shall be found equally innocent, cheap, easy, and effectual. But before something of that kind shall be advanced in contradiction to my scheme, and offering a better, I desire the author or authors will be pleased maturely to consider two points. First, as things now stand, how they will be able to find food and raiment for an hundred thousand useless mouths and backs. And secondly, there being a round million of creatures in human figure throughout this kingdom, whose sole subsistence put into a common stock would leave them in debt two million of pounds sterling, adding those who are beggars by profession to the bulk of farmers, cottagers, and laborers, with their wives and children who are beggars in effect; I desire those politicians who dislike my overture, and may perhaps be so bold to attempt an answer, that they will first ask the parents of these mortals whether they would not at this day think it a great happiness to have been sold for food at a year old in this manner I prescribe, and thereby have avoided such a perpetual scene of misfortunes as they have since gone through by the oppression of landlords, the impossibility of paying rent without money or trade, the want of common sustenance, with neither house nor clothes to cover them from the inclemencies of the weather, and the most inevitable prospect of entailing the like or greater miseries upon their breed forever. 32

I profess, in the sincerity of my heart, that I have not the least personal interest in endeavoring to promote this necessary work, having no other motive than the public good of my country, by advancing our trade, providing for infants, relieving the poor, and giving some pleasure to the rich. I have no children by which I can propose to get a single penny; the youngest being nine years old, and my wife past childbearing. 33

• • •

* Eds. note—Note that these measures represent Swift's true proposal.

Comprehension

1. What problem does Swift identify? What general solution does he recommend?
2. What advantages does Swift see in his plan?
3. What does he see as the alternative to his plan?
4. What clues indicate that Swift is not serious about his proposal?
5. In paragraph 29, Swift lists and rejects a number of "other expedients." What are they? Why do you think he presents and rejects these ideas?

Purpose and Audience

1. Swift's target here is the British government, in particular its poor treatment of the Irish. How would you expect British government officials to have responded to his proposal at the time? How would you expect Irish readers to have reacted?
2. What do you think Swift hoped to accomplish in this essay? Do you think his purpose was simply to amuse and shock, or do you think he wanted to change people's minds or even inspire them to take some kind of action? Explain.
3. In paragraphs 6, 14, 23, and elsewhere, Swift presents a series of mathematical calculations. What effect do you think he expected these computations to have on his readers?
4. Explain why each of the following groups might have been offended by this essay: women, Catholics, butchers, the poor.
5. How do you think Swift expected the appeal in his conclusion to affect his audience?

Style and Structure

1. **Vocabulary Project.** In paragraph 6, Swift uses the word *breeders* to refer to fertile women. What connotations does this word have? Why does he use this word rather than a more neutral alternative?
2. What purpose does paragraph 8 serve in the essay? Do the other short paragraphs have the same function? Explain.
3. Swift's remarks are presented as an argument. Where, if anywhere, does Swift anticipate and refute his readers' objections?
4. **Vocabulary Project.** Swift applies to infants many words usually applied to animals who are slaughtered to be eaten – for example, *fore or hind quarter* (10) and *carcass* (15). Identify as many examples of this kind of usage as you can. Why do you think Swift uses such words?
5. Throughout his essay, Swift cites the comments of others – "our merchants" (7), "a very knowing American of my acquaintance" (9), and "an eminent French physician" (13), for example. Find some additional examples. What, if anything, does he accomplish by referring to these people?

6. A **satire** is a piece of writing that uses wit, **irony**, and ridicule to attack foolishness, incompetence, or evil. How does "A Modest Proposal" fit this definition of satire?
7. Evaluate the strategy Swift uses to introduce each advantage he cites in paragraphs 21 through 26.
8. Swift uses a number of parenthetical comments in his essay – for example, in paragraphs 14, 17, and 26. Identify as many of these parenthetical comments as you can, and consider what they contribute to the essay.
9. Swift begins paragraph 20 with "I have too long digressed, and therefore shall return to my subject." Has he in fact been digressing? Explain.
10. The title of this essay states that Swift's proposal is a "modest" one; elsewhere, he says he proposes his ideas "humbly" (8). Why do you think he chooses these words? Does he really mean to present himself as modest and humble?

Journal Entry

What is your emotional reaction to this essay? Do you find it amusing or offensive? Why?

Writing Workshop

1. Write a "modest proposal," either straightforward or satirical, for solving a problem in your school or community.
2. Write a "modest proposal" for achieving one of these national goals:
   - Banning assault weapons
   - Eliminating binge drinking on college campuses
   - Promoting sexual abstinence among teenagers
3. **Working with Sources.** Write a letter to an executive of the tobacco industry, a television network, or an industry that threatens the environment. In your letter, set forth a "modest proposal" for making the industry more responsible. Begin by researching industry statements and newspaper editorials on the issue you select. Be sure to cite the sources of all borrowed material and to include a works-cited page. (See Chapter 18 for information on MLA documentation.)

Combining the Patterns

What patterns of development does Swift use in his argument? Annotate the essay to identify each pattern. Use the annotations accompanying "On Dumpster Diving" (page 676) as a guide.

Thematic Connections

- "The Embalming of Mr. Jones" (page 297)
- "The Irish Famine, 1845–1849" (page 327)
- "I Want a Wife" (page 496)

Writing Assignments for Combining the Patterns

1. Reread Michael Huu Truong's essay at the beginning of this chapter. Responding to the same assignment he was given ("Write an essay about the person and/or place that defined your childhood"), use several different patterns of development to communicate to readers what your own childhood was like.
2. Write an essay about the political, social, or economic events (local, national, or international) that you believe have dominated and defined your life (or a stage of your life). Use cause and effect and any other patterns you think are appropriate to explain and illustrate why these events were important to you and how they affected you.
3. **Working with Sources.** Develop a thesis statement that draws a general conclusion about the nature, quality, or effectiveness of advertising in online media or in print media (in newspapers or magazines or on billboards). Write an essay that supports this thesis statement with specific references to particular ads. Include some of the ads in your essay, and be sure to document all the ads you cite and to include a works-cited page. (See Chapter 18 for information on MLA documentation.)
4. Exactly what do you think it means to be an American? Write a definition essay that answers this question, developing your definition with whatever patterns best serve your purpose.
5. Many of the essays in this text recount the writers' personal experiences. Identify one essay that describes experiences that are either similar to your own or in sharp contrast to your own. Then, write a comparison-and-contrast essay *either* comparing *or* contrasting your experiences with those of the writer. Use several different patterns to develop your essay.

Collaborative Activity for Combining the Patterns

Working in pairs, choose an essay from Chapters 6 through 14 of this text. Then, working individually, identify the various patterns of development used in the essay. When you have finished, compare notes with your classmate. Have both of you identified the same patterns in the essay? If not, try to reach a consensus. Working together, write a paragraph summarizing why each pattern is used and explaining how the various patterns combine to support the essay's thesis.

PART THREE

Working with Sources

Some students see research as a complicated, time-consuming process that seems to have no obvious benefit. They wonder why instructors assign topics that involve research or why they have to spend so much time considering other people's ideas. These are fair questions that deserve straightforward answers.

For one thing, doing research enables you to become part of an academic community—one that attempts to answer some of the most interesting and profound questions being asked today. For example, what steps should be taken to ensure privacy on the Internet? What is the value of a college education, and how should it be paid for? How do we define free speech? How much should the government be involved in people's lives? These and other questions need to be addressed not just because they are interesting, but also because the future of our society depends on the answers.

In addition, research teaches sound methods of inquiry. By doing research, you learn to ask questions, to design a research plan, to meet deadlines, to collect and analyze information, and to present your ideas in a well-organized essay. Above all, research encourages you to **think critically**—to consider different sources of information, to evaluate conflicting points of view, to understand how the information you discover fits in with your own ideas about your subject, and to reach logical conclusions. Thus, doing research helps you become a more thoughtful writer as well as a more responsible, more informed citizen—one who is capable of sorting through the vast amount of information you encounter each day and of making informed decisions about the important issues that confront us all.

When you use sources in an essay, you follow the same process that guides you when you write any essay. However, in addition to using your own ideas to support your points, you use information that you find in the library and online. Because working with sources presents special challenges, there are certain issues that you should be aware of before you engage in research. The chapters in Part Three identify these issues and give you practical suggestions for dealing with them. Chapter 16 discusses how to find sources and how to determine if those sources are authoritative, accurate, objective, current, and comprehensive. Chapter 17 discusses how to paraphrase, summarize, and quote sources and how to avoid committing plagiarism. Finally, Chapter 18 explains how to use the documentation style recommended by the Modern Language Association (MLA) to acknowledge the source information you use in your papers. (The documentation style recommended by the American Psychological Association [APA] is illustrated in the Appendix.)

16

Finding and Evaluating Sources

In some essays you write—personal narratives or descriptions, for example—you can use your own ideas and observations to support the points you make. In other essays, however, you will have to supplement your own ideas with **research**, looking for information in magazines, newspapers, journals, and books as well as in the library's electronic databases or on the Internet.

Finding Information in the Library

Although many students turn first to the Internet, the best place to begin your research is in your college library, which contains electronic and print resources that you cannot find anywhere else. Of course, your college library houses books, magazines, and journals, but it also gives you access to the various **databases** to which it subscribes as well as to reference works that contain facts and statistics.

THE RESOURCES OF THE LIBRARY

The Online Catalog

An **online catalog** enables you to search all the resources of the library. You can access the online catalog in the library or remotely through an Internet portal. By typing in keywords related to your topic, you can find articles, books, or other sources of information to use in your research.

Electronic Databases

Libraries subscribe to **electronic databases**—for example, *Expanded Academic ASAP* and *LexisNexis Academic Universe*. These electronic databases enable you to access information from hundreds of newspapers, magazines, and journals. Some contain lists of bibliographic citations as well as **abstracts** (summaries of articles); many others enable you to retrieve entire articles or books.

Reference Works

Libraries also contain **reference works** — in print and in electronic form — that can give you an overview of your topic as well as key facts, dates, and names. **General encyclopedias** — such as the *New Encyclopaedia Britannica* — include articles on a wide variety of topics. **Specialized encyclopedias** — such as the *Encyclopedia of Law Enforcement* — contain articles that give you detailed information about a specific field (sociology or criminal justice, for example).

Sources for Facts and Statistics

Reference works such as *Facts on File*, the *Information Please Almanac*, and the *Statistical Abstract of the United States* can help you locate reliable facts or statistics that you may need to support your points. (These resources are available online as well as in the reference section of your college library.)

Much of the information in library databases – for example, the full text of many scholarly articles – cannot be found on the Internet. In addition, because your college librarians oversee all material coming into the library, the sources you find there are generally more reliable, more focused, and more useful than many you will find on the Internet.

INTERNET	LIBRARY DATABASES
Coverage is general, haphazard	Coverage is focused and often discipline-specific
Sources may not contain bibliographic information	Sources will contain bibliographic information
Web postings are not filtered	Databases are created by librarians and scholars
Material is posted by anyone, regardless of qualifications	Material is checked for accuracy and quality

Exercise 1

Assume that you are writing a three- to five-page essay on one of the general topics listed below.

Eating disorders	The student-loan bubble
Alternative medicine	Green construction projects
Government health care	Legalizing marijuana
Hydraulic fracturing	Self-driving cars

Using your college library's online catalog, see how much information you can find. How easy was this system to use? Where did you have difficulty? Did you try asking a librarian for help?

Finding Information on the Internet

When using a search engine such as Google or Yahoo!, you have access to millions of documents online. Although that guarantees you will find a great deal of information, it also means you need to limit your search to information that specifically addresses your topic. There are two ways to search for information on the Internet: doing a keyword search and doing a subject search.

Doing a keyword search. All search engines enable you to do a **keyword search**. You type a search term into a box, and the search engine looks for documents that contain the term. If you type in a broad term like *civil war,* you will get millions of hits – many more than you could possibly consider. If you narrow your search by using a more specific search term – *Battle of Gettysburg,* for example – you will get fewer hits. You can focus your search even further by connecting search terms with *and* (in capital letters) – for example, *Battle of Gettysburg* AND *military strategy*. The documents you retrieve will contain both these search terms, not just one or the other. You can also put quotation marks around a search term – for example, "Lee's surrender at Appomattox." If you do this, the search engine will retrieve only documents that contain this specific phrase.

Doing a subject search. Some search engines, such as Excite.com and Yahoo!, enable you to do a **subject search** (also called a *directory search*). First, you choose a subject from a list of general subjects: *The Arts, Business, Computers, Science,* and so on. Each of these general subjects leads you to more specific subjects and, eventually, to the subtopic you want. For example, you could start your search by selecting the general topic *Science*. Clicking on this topic would lead you to *Environment* and then to *Forests and Rainforests*. Finally, you would get a list of websites that could be useful to you.

Finding Useful Information

Whether you search using keywords or by subject, you will have many more results than you need for your essay. These results will help you get a broad sense of your topic, but they are only a starting point for your research. By skimming the search results, you should get an idea of any major trends concerning your topic and who the leading experts are.

When you have found a source that seems promising for your research, be sure to visit the pages in the works-cited section (or to copy the information for any print resources) and to click through any links the author may have added to the work. This step will lead you to other material on your topic that has already been vetted by the author of the article and will save you time in your own search. Looking at the sources and links will also help you to *evaluate* the source (see page 723).

Online publications will often contain multiple articles or pages on a single topic. If you find a source that is not quite what you are looking for, navigate to the home page of the website where you found the source. From there, you can do a keyword search to see what other material may be available on your topic.

AVOID BACKTRACKING

Open promising articles in new tabs or separate windows so that you can easily return to your original search results or to your original source. This strategy will allow you to follow leads and to avoid losing track of your sources as you do further research. You can also keep track of your sources by clicking on the "history" tab at the top of your browser.

If you find a source that does not address your topic or one that does not seem credible, return to your original search results and try again. If you find that many of your results do not fit the topic you intend to address, try using a different set of search terms or broadening or narrowing your search.

Exercise 2

Carry out an Internet search of the topic you chose for Exercise 1. How much useful information were you able to find? How does this information compare with the information you found when you used the library's online catalog?

ACCESSING WEBSITES: TROUBLESHOOTING

Sometimes you will be unable to connect to the site you want. Before giving up, try these strategies:

- **Check to make sure the URL is correct.** Any error in typing the URL — an extra space or an added letter — will send you to the wrong site or to no site at all.
- **Try using part of the URL.** If the URL is long, try deleting everything after the last slash. If that doesn't work, use just the part of the URL that ends in .com or .gov. If this part of the URL doesn't work, you have an incorrect (or inoperable) URL.
- **Try revisiting the site later.** Sometimes websites experience technical problems that prevent you from accessing them. Wait a while, and then try accessing your site again.

Evaluating Sources

Not every source contains trustworthy information. For this reason, even after you find information (either in print or online), you still have to **evaluate** it – that is, determine its suitability. When you use print information from your college library, you can be reasonably certain that it has been evaluated in some way. Material from the Web presents special problems, however, because so much of it is either anonymous or written by people who have little or no knowledge of their subject.

To evaluate any source, whether print or digital, ask the following questions.

Is the source authoritative? A source is **authoritative** when it is written by an expert. Given the volume and variety of information online, it is particularly important to determine if it is written by a well-respected scholar or expert in the field. To determine if the author has the expertise to write about a subject, find out what else he or she has written on the same subject, and then do a search to see if other authorities recognize the author as an expert.

Trying to determine the legitimacy of information on websites, online publications, and blogs can often be difficult or impossible. Even some print resources, such as unattributed magazine articles without the necessary publication information, can be difficult to verify. Some sites do not list authors, and if they do, they do not always include their credentials. In addition, you may not be able to determine how a website decides what to publish. (Does one person decide, or does an editorial board make decisions?) Finally, you might have difficulty evaluating (or even identifying) the sponsoring organization. If you cannot determine if a website or other source is authoritative, do not use it as a source.

Is the source accurate? A source is **accurate** if its information is factual, correct, detailed, and up-to-date. If a university press or scholarly journal published a book or article, you can be reasonably certain that experts in the field reviewed it to confirm its accuracy. Books published by commercial presses or articles in high-level magazines, such as the *Atlantic* and the *Economist*, may also be suitable for your research – provided experts wrote them. The same is true for newspaper articles. Articles in respected newspapers, such as the *New York Times* or the *Wall Street Journal*, have much more credibility than articles in tabloids, such as the *National Enquirer* or the *Globe*.

You can judge the accuracy of a source by comparing specific information it contains to the same information in several other sources. If you find discrepancies, you should assume the source contains other errors as well. You should also check to see if an author includes citations for the information he or she uses. Such documentation can help readers determine the accuracy (and the quality) of the information in the source. Perhaps the best (and safest) course to follow is that if you can't verify the information you find on a website, don't use it.

Is the source objective? A source is **objective** when it is not unduly influenced by personal opinions or feelings. Of course, all sources reflect the **biases** of their authors, regardless of how impartial they may try to be. Some sources — such as those that support one political position over another — make no secret of their biases. In fact, bias does not automatically disqualify a source. At the very least, it should alert you to the fact that you are seeing just one side of an issue and that you have to look elsewhere to get a fuller picture. Bias becomes a problem, however, when it is so extreme that a source distorts an issue or misrepresents opposing points of view.

As a researcher, you should ask yourself if a writer's conclusions are supported by evidence or if they are the result of emotional reactions or preconceived ideas. You can make this determination by looking at the writer's choice of words and seeing if the language is slanted and also by seeing if the writer ignores (or attacks) opposing points of view.

With websites, you should try to determine if the advertising that appears on the site affects the site's objectivity. Also try to determine if the site has a commercial purpose. If it does, the writer may have a conflict of interest. (Sometimes, commercially motivated content is not easy to recognize. Critics have recently charged that individuals were paid to write favorable *Wikipedia* articles to promote companies or products.) The same need to assess objectivity exists when a political group or special-interest group sponsors a site. These organizations have agendas, and you should make sure they are not manipulating facts to promote their own goals.

Is the source current? A source is **current** if the information it contains is up-to-date. It is relatively easy to find out how current a print source is. You can find the publication date of a book on the page that lists its publication information, and you can find the publication date of a periodical on its front cover.

Websites and blogs, however, may present problems. First, check to see when a website was last updated. (Some Web pages automatically display the current date, and you should not confuse this date with the date when the site was last updated.) Then, check the dates of individual articles. Even if a site has been updated recently, it may include information that is out-of-date. You should also see if the links on a site are still live. If a number of links are not functioning, you should question the currency of the site.

Is the source comprehensive? A source is **comprehensive** if it covers a subject in sufficient breadth and depth. How comprehensive a source needs to be depends on your purpose and your audience as well as on your assignment. For a short essay, an op-ed from a newspaper or a short article might give you enough information to support your points. A longer essay, however, would call for sources that treat your subject in depth, such as scholarly articles or even whole books.

You can determine the comprehensiveness of a source by seeing if it devotes a great deal of coverage to your subject. Does it discuss your topic in one or two paragraphs, or does it devote much more space to it – say, a chapter in a book or a major section of an article? You should also try to determine the level of the source. Although a source may be perfectly acceptable for high school research, it may not be comprehensive enough for college research.

USING *WIKIPEDIA* AS A SOURCE

Wikipedia — the most popular encyclopedia on the Web — has no single editor who checks entries for accuracy, credibility, objectivity, currency, and comprehensiveness. In many cases, the users themselves write and edit entries. For this reason, many college instructors do not consider *Wikipedia* to be a credible source of information.

Exercise 3

Choose one source from the library and one from the Internet. Then, evaluate each source to determine if it is authoritative, accurate, objective, current, and comprehensive.

17

Integrating Sources and Avoiding Plagiarism

After you have gathered and evaluated your sources, it is time to think about how you can use this material in your essay. As you take notes, you should record relevant information in a computer file or in a note-taking application. These notes should be in the form of *paraphrase, summary*, and *quotation*. When you actually write your paper, you will **synthesize** this source material, blending it with your own ideas and interpretations – but making sure that your own ideas, not those of your sources, dominate your discussion. Finally, you should make certain that you do not inadvertently commit plagiarism.

Paraphrasing

When you **paraphrase**, you use your own words to restate a source's ideas in some detail, presenting the source's main idea, its key supporting points, and possibly an example or two. For this reason, a paraphrase may be only slightly shorter than the original.

You paraphrase when you want to present the information from a source without using its exact words. Paraphrasing is useful when you want to make a difficult discussion easier to understand while still giving readers a good sense of the original.

Keep in mind that when you paraphrase, you do not use the exact language or syntax of the original source, and you do not include your own analysis or opinions. The idea is to convey the ideas and emphasis of the source but not to mirror the order of its ideas or reproduce its exact words or sentence structure. If you decide to include a particularly memorable word or phrase from the source, be sure to put it in quotation marks. Finally, remember that because a paraphrase relies on a writer's original ideas, *you must document the source.*

GUIDELINES FOR WRITING A PARAPHRASE

- Read the source you intend to paraphrase until you understand it.
- Jot down the main points of the source.
- As you write, retain the purpose and emphasis of the original.
- Make sure to use your own words and phrases, not the language or syntax of your source.
- Do not include your own analysis or opinions.
- Be sure to provide documentation.

Here is a passage from page 22 of the article "*Wikipedia* and Beyond: Jimmy Wales's Sprawling Vision" by Katherine Mangu-Ward, followed by a paraphrase.

ORIGINAL

An obvious question troubled, and continues to trouble, many people: how could an "encyclopedia that anyone can edit" possibly be reliable? Can truth be reached by a consensus of amateurs? Can a community of volunteers aggregate and assimilate knowledge . . . ?

PARAPHRASE

According to Katherine Mangu-Ward, there are serious questions about the reliability of *Wikipedia*'s articles because any user can add, change, or delete information. There is some doubt about whether *Wikipedia*'s unpaid and nonprofessional writers and editors can work together to create an accurate encyclopedia (22).

Exercise 1

Select one or two paragraphs from any essay in this book, and then paraphrase them. Make sure your paraphrase communicates the main ideas and key supporting points of the passage you selected.

Summarizing

Unlike a paraphrase, which restates the ideas of a source in detail, a **summary** is a brief restatement, in your own words, of a passage's main idea. Because it is so general, a summary is always much shorter than the original.

When you summarize (as when you paraphrase), you use your own words, not the words of your source. Keep in mind that a summary can be one sentence or several sentences in length, depending on the length and complexity of the original passage. Your summary expresses just the main idea of your source, not your own opinions or conclusions. Remember that because a summary expresses a writer's original idea, *you must document your source.*

GUIDELINES FOR WRITING A SUMMARY

- Read the source you intend to summarize until you understand it.
- Jot down the main idea of the source.
- Make sure to use your own words and phrases, not the words and sentence structure of your source.
- Do not include your own analysis or opinions.
- Be sure to provide documentation.

Here is a summary of the passage from the article "*Wikipedia* and Beyond: Jimmy Wales's Sprawling Vision" by Katherine Mangu-Ward.

SUMMARY

According to Katherine Mangu-Ward, *Wikipedia*'s reliability is open to question because anyone can edit its articles (22).

Exercise 2

Write a summary of the material you paraphrased for Exercise 1. How is your summary different from your paraphrase?

Quoting

When you **quote**, you use a writer's exact words as they appear in the source, including all punctuation, capitalization, and spelling. Enclose all words from your source in quotation marks—*followed by appropriate documentation*. Because quotations distract readers, use a quotation only when you think a writer's exact words will add something to your discussion. In addition, too many quotations will make your paper look like a collection of other people's words. As a rule, unless you have a definite reason to quote a source, you should paraphrase or summarize it instead.

WHEN TO QUOTE SOURCES

1. Quote when the original language is so memorable that paraphrasing would lessen the impact of the writer's ideas.
2. Quote when a paraphrase or summary would change the meaning of the original.

3. Quote when the original language adds authority to your discussion. The exact words of an expert on your topic can help you make your point convincingly.

GUIDELINES FOR QUOTING

- Put all words and phrases that you take from your source in quotation marks.
- Make sure to use the *exact* words of your source.
- Do not include too many quotations.
- Be sure to provide documentation.

Exercise 3

Reread the passage you chose to paraphrase in Exercise 1, and identify one or two quotations you could include in your paraphrase. Which words or phrases did you decide to quote? Why?

Integrating Source Material into Your Writing

When you use source material in your writing, your goal is to integrate this material smoothly into your discussion. To distinguish your own ideas from those of your sources, you should always introduce source material and follow it with appropriate documentation.

Introduce paraphrases, summaries, and quotations with a phrase that identifies the source or its author. You can place this **identifying phrase** (also called a *signal phrase*) at the beginning, in the middle, or at the end of a sentence. Instead of always using the same words to introduce your source material—*says* or *states,* for example—try using different words and phrases—*points out, observes, comments, notes, remarks*, or *concludes*.

IDENTIFYING PHRASE AT THE BEGINNING

According to Jonathan Dee, *Wikipedia* is "either one of the noblest experiments of the Internet age or a nightmare embodiment of relativism and the withering of intellectual standards" (36).

IDENTIFYING PHRASE IN THE MIDDLE

Wikipedia is "either one of the noblest experiments of the Internet age," Jonathan Dee comments, "or a nightmare embodiment of relativism and the withering of intellectual standards" (36).

IDENTIFYING PHRASE AT THE END

Wikipedia is "either one of the noblest experiments of the Internet age or a nightmare embodiment of relativism and the withering of intellectual standards," Jonathan Dee observes (36).

Synthesizing

When you write a **synthesis**, you combine paraphrases, summaries, and quotations with your own ideas. It is important to keep in mind that a synthesis is not simply a collection of your sources' ideas. On the contrary, a synthesis uses source material to support *your* ideas and to help readers see the topic *you* are writing about in a new way. For this reason, when you write a synthesis, it is important to differentiate your ideas from those of your sources and to clearly show which piece of information comes from which source.

The following synthesis is a paragraph from the model MLA paper that begins on page 750. This paragraph synthesizes several sources to present an overview of *Wikipedia*, focusing on the ease with which its text can be edited. The paragraph begins with the student's own ideas, and the rest of the paragraph includes source material that supports these ideas.

A wiki allows multiple users to collaborate in creating the content of a website. With a wiki, anyone with a browser can edit, modify, rearrange, or delete content. It is not necessary to know HTML (hypertext mark-up language). The word *wiki* comes from the word *wikiwiki*, which means "quick" or "fast" in Hawaiian. The most popular wiki is *Wikipedia*, a free, Internet-based encyclopedia that relies on the collaboration of those who post and edit entries. Anyone can write a *Wikipedia* article by using the "*Wikipedia* Article Wizard" or edit an entry by clicking on the "Edit" tab. Readers can easily view the revision history of an entry by clicking on "View History" ("Help: Page History"). For its many advocates, *Wikipedia*'s open and collaborative nature makes it a "collectively brilliant creation" (Chozick). This collaboration enables *Wikipedia* to publish a wide variety of entries on timely, unusual, and specialized topics (see fig. 1). According to Casper Grathwohl, President, Dictionaries Division, and Director, Global Business Development at Oxford University Press, it "has become increasingly clear that [*Wikipedia*] functions as a necessary layer in the Internet knowledge system, a layer that was not needed in the analog age." At this time, the site contains 40 million articles in 293 languages ("*Wikipedia*").

GUIDELINES FOR WRITING A SYNTHESIS

1. Identify the key points discussed in each of your sources.
2. Identify the evidence your sources use to support their views.
3. Clearly report what each source says, using summaries, paraphrases, and quotations. (Be sure to document your sources.)
4. Show how the sources are related to one another. For instance, do they agree on everything? Do they show directly opposite views, or do they agree on some points and disagree on others?
5. Decide on your own viewpoint, and show how the sources relate to your viewpoint.

Exercise 4

Look at the Model Student Research Paper that begins on page 750. Choose a paragraph (other than the one on page 731) that synthesizes source material. What kind of information (summary, paraphrase, or quotation) is being synthesized?

Avoiding Plagiarism

Plagiarism – whether intentional or unintentional – occurs when a writer passes off the words or ideas of others as his or her own. (Ideas can also be in the form of visuals, such as charts and graphs, or statistics.) Students plagiarize for a number of reasons. Some take the easy way out and buy a paper and submit it as if it were their own. This **intentional plagiarism** compromises a student's education as well as the educational process as a whole. Instructors assign essays for a reason, and if you do not do the work, you miss a valuable opportunity to learn. For most students, however, plagiarism is **unintentional**.

Plagiarism can be the result of carelessness, poor time management, not knowing the conventions of documentation, laziness, or simply panic. For example, some students do not give themselves enough time to do an assignment, fail to keep track of their sources, inadvertently include the exact words of a source without using quotation marks, forget to include documentation, or cut and paste information from the Internet directly into their essays. In addition, some students have the mistaken belief that if information they find online does not have an identifiable author, it is all right to use it without documentation. Whatever the reason, whenever you present information from a source as if it were your own (either intentionally or unintentionally), you are committing plagiarism – and ***plagiarism is theft***.

TIPS FOR AVOIDING PLAGIARISM

You can avoid plagiarism by keeping careful notes and by following these guidelines:

- **Give yourself enough time to do your research and to write your paper.** Do not put yourself in a position where you do not leave enough time to give your assignment the attention it requires.
- **Begin with a research plan.** Make a list of the steps you intend to follow, and estimate how much time they will take.
- **Ask for help.** If you run into trouble, don't panic. Ask your instructor or a reference librarian for help.
- **Do not cut and paste downloaded text directly into your paper.** Summarize and paraphrase this source material first. Boldface or highlight quotation marks so that you will recognize quotations when you are ready to include them in your paper.
- **Set up a system that enables you to keep track of your sources.** Create computer files where you can store downloaded source information. (If you photocopy print sources, maintain a file for this material.) Create another set of files for your notes. Be sure to clearly name and date these files so that you know what is in them and when they were created. You can also use note-taking software tools, such as Zotero, Evernote, or Awesome Note, to keep track of your research sources.
- **Include full source information for all paraphrases and summaries as well as for quotations.** As you write, clearly differentiate between your ideas and those of your sources. Do not forget to include documentation. If you try to fill in documentation later, you may not remember where your information came from.
- **Keep a list of all the sources you have downloaded or have taken information from.** Be sure to always have an up-to-date list of the sources you are using.

The easiest way to avoid plagiarism is simple – give credit where credit is due. In other words, document *all* information you borrow from your sources (print or electronic) – not just paraphrases, summaries, and quotations but also statistics, images, and charts and graphs. It is not necessary, however, to document **common knowledge** – information that most people will probably know or factual information that is available in several different reference works. (Keep in mind that even though *information* might be common knowledge, you cannot use the exact *words* of a reference source without quoting the source and providing appropriate documentation.)

WHAT TO DOCUMENT

You Must Document

- All word-for-word quotations from a source
- All summaries and paraphrases of material from a source
- All ideas — opinions, judgments, and insights — that are not your own
- All tables, graphs, charts, statistics, and images you get from a source

You Do Not Need to Document

- Your own ideas
- Common knowledge
- Familiar quotations

Avoiding Common Errors That Lead to Plagiarism

The following paragraph is from *The Cult of the Amateur: How Today's Internet Is Killing Our Culture* by Andrew Keen. This paragraph, and the four rules listed after it, will help you understand and avoid the most common causes of plagiarism.

ORIGINAL

The simple ownership of a computer and an Internet connection doesn't transform one into a serious journalist any more than having access to a kitchen makes one into a serious cook. But millions of amateur journalists think that it does. According to a June 2006 study by the Pew Internet and American Life Project, 34 percent of the 12 million bloggers in America consider their online "work" to be a form of journalism. That adds up to millions of unskilled, untrained, unpaid, unknown "journalists" – a thousandfold growth between 1996 and 2006 – spewing their (mis)information out in the cyberworld. (Andrew Keen. *The Cult of the Amateur: How Today's Internet Is Killing Our Culture*. Double Day, 2007. p. 47.)

1. Identify Your Source

PLAGIARISM

One-third of the people who post material on Internet blogs think of themselves as serious journalists.

The writer does not quote Keen directly, but he still must identify Keen as the source of his paraphrased material. He can do this by adding an identifying phrase and parenthetical documentation.

CORRECT

According to Andrew Keen, one-third of the people who post material on Internet blogs think of themselves as serious journalists (47).

2. Place Borrowed Words in Quotation Marks

PLAGIARISM

According to Andrew Keen, the simple ownership of a computer and an Internet connection doesn't transform one into a serious journalist any more than having access to a kitchen makes one into a serious cook (47).

Although the writer cites Keen as his source, the passage incorrectly uses Keen's exact words without putting them in quotation marks. The writer must either place the borrowed words in quotation marks or paraphrase them.

CORRECT (BORROWED WORDS IN QUOTATION MARKS)

According to Andrew Keen, "The simple ownership of a computer and an Internet connection doesn't transform one into a serious journalist any more than having access to a kitchen makes one into a serious cook" (47).

3. Use Your Own Wording

PLAGIARISM

According to Andrew Keen, having a computer that can connect to the Internet does not make someone a real reporter, just as having a kitchen does not make someone a real cook. However, millions of these people think they are real journalists. A Pew Internet and American Life study in June 2006 showed that about 4 million bloggers think they are journalists when they write on their blogs. Thus, millions of people who have no training may be putting erroneous information on the Internet (47).

Even though the writer acknowledges Keen as his source and provides parenthetical documentation, and even though he does not use Keen's exact words, his passage closely follows the order, emphasis, and phrasing of the original. In the following passage, the writer uses his own wording, quoting one distinctive phrase from his source.

CORRECT

According to Andrew Keen, although millions of American bloggers think of themselves as journalists, they are wrong. As Keen notes, "The simple ownership of a computer and an Internet connection doesn't transform one into a serious journalist any more than having access to a kitchen makes one into a serious cook" (47).

4. Distinguish Your Own Ideas from Your Source's Ideas

PLAGIARISM

The anonymous writers of *Wikipedia* articles are, in some ways, similar to those who put material on personal blogs. Although millions of American bloggers think of themselves as journalists, they are wrong. "The simple ownership of a computer and an Internet connection doesn't transform one into a serious journalist any more than having access to a kitchen makes one into a serious cook" (Keen 47).

In the preceding passage, it appears that only the quotation in the last sentence is borrowed from Keen's book. In fact, the ideas in the second sentence are also Keen's. The writer should use an identifying phrase (such as "According to Keen") to acknowledge the borrowed material in this sentence and to indicate where it begins.

CORRECT

The anonymous writers of *Wikipedia* articles are, in some ways, similar to those who put material on personal blogs. According to Andrew Keen, although millions of American bloggers think of themselves as journalists, they are wrong. As Keen notes, "The simple ownership of a computer and an Internet connection doesn't transform one into a serious journalist any more than having access to a kitchen makes one into a serious cook" (47).

Avoiding Plagiarism with Online Sources

Most students know that using long passages (or entire articles) from a print source without documenting the source is plagiarism. Unfortunately, many students assume that borrowing material found on a website or elsewhere online without documentation is acceptable. However, such borrowing is also plagiarism. Just as you do for print sources, you must always document words, ideas, or visuals you get from online sources.

USING PLAGIARISM CHECKERS

If you are concerned that you may have accidentally plagiarized material from one of your Web sources, there are a number of online tools that can help you identify and correct this problem. These plagiarism checkers, such as the free options available at SmallSEOTools.com or Grammarly.com, allow you to check your work. Once you paste the text of your essay into the application, it will highlight and identify content that you should consider documenting. Remember that you cannot simply depend on a computer application to detect possible plagiarism, however. It is your responsibility to keep track of your sources and to document the information you borrow from your sources.

Exercise 5

Select an essay you have written this semester that refers to a reading selection in this book. Reread both your essay and the selection in the book, and then decide where you could add each of the following:

- A quotation
- A summary of a paragraph
- A paraphrase of a paragraph

Exercise 6

Insert a quotation, a summary, and a paraphrase into the essay you reviewed for Exercise 5. Then, check to make sure you have not committed plagiarism. Finally, consult Chapter 18 to help you document your sources correctly.

18

Documenting Sources: MLA

When you **document**, you tell readers where you have found the information you have used in your essay. The Modern Language Association (MLA) recommends the following documentation style for essays that use outside sources.* This format consists *of parenthetical references* in the body of the essay that refer to a *works-cited* list at the end of the essay.

Parenthetical References in the Text

A **parenthetical reference** should include enough information to guide readers to a specific entry in your works-cited list.

A typical parenthetical reference consists of the author's last name and the page number: (Mangu-Ward 21). If you use more than one work by the same author, include a shortened form of the title in the parenthetical reference: (Mangu-Ward, "*Wikipedia* and Beyond" 25). Notice that the parenthetical references do not include a comma after the title or "p." before the page number.

Whenever possible, introduce information with a phrase that includes the author's name. (If you do so, include only the page number in parentheses.)

> According to Andrew Keen, the absence of professional reporters and editors leads to erroneous information on *Wikipedia* (4).

Place documentation so that it does not interrupt the flow of your ideas, preferably at the end of a sentence.

---

* For further information, see the eighth edition of the *MLA Handbook* (Modern Language Association, 2016) or the MLA website at mla.org.

The format for parenthetical references departs from these guidelines in the following special situations:

1. When you are citing a work by two authors

It is impossible to access all websites by means of a single search engine (Sherman and Price 53).

2. When you are citing a work without a listed author

The technology of wikis is important, but many users are not aware of it ("7 Things").

3. When you are citing an indirect source

If you use a statement by one author that is quoted in the work of another author, indicate it by including the abbreviation qtd. in ("quoted in").

Marshall Poe notes that information on *Wikipedia* is "not exactly expert knowledge; it's common knowledge" (qtd. in Keen 39).

4. When you are citing a source without page numbers

Sources from the Internet or from library databases often do not include page numbers. If the source uses paragraph, section, or screen numbers, use the abbreviation par. or sec., or the full word screen, followed by the corresponding number, in your documentation. (If the citation includes an author's name, place a comma after the name.)

On its website, *Wikipedia* warns its writers and editors to inspect sources carefully when they make assertions that are not generally held in academic circles ("Verifiability," sec. 3).

If the electronic source has no page numbers or markers of any kind, include just the name(s) of the author(s). Readers will learn more about the source when they consult the works-cited list.

A *Wikipedia* entry can be very deceptive, but some users may not realize that its information may not be reliable (McHenry).

GUIDELINES FOR FORMATTING QUOTATIONS

Short Quotations

Quotations of no more than four typed lines are run in with the text. End punctuation comes after the parenthetical reference (which follows the quotation marks).

> According to Andrew Keen, on *Wikipedia*, "the voice of a high school kid has equal value to that of an Ivy League scholar of a trained profession" (42).

Long Quotations

Quotations of more than four lines are set off from the text. Indent a long quotation half of an inch from the left-hand margin, and do not enclose the passage in quotation marks. The first line of a long quotation is not indented even if it is the beginning of a paragraph. If a quoted passage has more than one paragraph, indent the first line of each subsequent paragraph one-quarter inch. Introduce a long quotation with a colon, and place the parenthetical reference one space after the end punctuation.

> According to Katherine Mangu-Ward, *Wikipedia* has changed the world:
>
> > *Wikipedia* was born as an experiment in aggregating information. But the reason it works isn't that the world was clamoring for a new kind of encyclopedia. It took off because of the robust, self-policing community it created. . . . Despite its critics, it is transforming our everyday lives; as with Amazon, Google, and eBay, it is almost impossible to remember how much more circumscribed our world was before it existed. (21)

NOTE: Ellipses indicate that the writer has deleted some words from the quotation.

The Works-Cited List

The works-cited list includes all the works you **cite** (refer to) in your essay. Use the following guidelines to help you prepare your list.

GUIDELINES FOR PREPARING THE WORKS-CITED LIST

- Begin the works-cited list on a new page after the last page of text.
- Number the works-cited page as the next page.
- Center the heading Works Cited one inch from the top of the page; do not underline the heading or put it in quotation marks.
- Double-space the list.
- List entries alphabetically according to the author's last name.
- Alphabetize unsigned articles according to the first major word of the title.
- Begin each entry flush with the left-hand margin.
- Indent second and subsequent lines of each entry one-half inch.
- Follow the author name and title with a period and one space. Follow each element of the publication information with a comma and one space, and end with a period.

CONTAINERS

The MLA recognizes that changing technology and the overwhelming number of sources you may encounter make it impossible to create rules that cover every citation situation. Instead, when you come upon a source for which you do not find a citation model in the guidelines, the MLA suggests using this generic "container" model as a starting point, adapting it as necessary for each new source.

In this model, any larger work that contains the source you are citing might be considered a container. For instance, each of the readings in *Patterns* would have two containers: the first is the reading itself, and the second is the larger book that contains the reading.

Vuong, Ocean. "Surrendering." *Patterns for College Writing*, 14th ed., edited by Laurie G. Kirszner and Stephen R. Mandell, Bedford/St. Martin's, 2018, pp. 116–18.

Below are some generic models for citing sources with only one container (entire books, websites, poems, or films, for example) or for sources with two containers (selections from a book, a single named page on a website, or a film streamed through a repository such as Netflix, for example).

One Container

________. ________. ________, ________,
Author Title Title of Container Publisher/Source

________, ________.
Date Location/pages

Two Containers

________. ________. ________, ________,
Author Title Title of Container 1 volume number if applicable

________, ________. ________, ________.
Date Location/pages Title of Container 2 Location

The following sample works-cited entries cover the situations you will encounter most often. Follow the formats exactly as they appear here.

Articles

GUIDELINES FOR MLA ARTICLE CITATIONS

To cite a periodical article in MLA style, follow these guidelines:

1. List the author, last name first.
2. Put the title of the article in quotation marks and italicize the title of the periodical.
3. Include the volume and issue number (when applicable), the year and date of publication, and the pages on which the full article appears (without the abbreviation *p.* or *pp.*).

Journal Articles. A **journal** is a publication aimed at readers who know a lot about a particular subject, such as English or history.

ARTICLE IN A JOURNAL

Provide the volume number and issue number preceded by vol. and no. List the date of publication and the pages of the article.

Long, Hoyt, and Richard Jean So. "Turbulent Flow: A Computational Model of World Literature." *Modern Language Quarterly,* vol. 77, no. 3, Sept. 2016, pp. 345–67.

ARTICLE IN A JOURNAL THAT USES ONLY ISSUE NUMBERS

For a journal that uses only issue numbers, cite the issue number, publication date, and page numbers.

Adelt, Ulrich. "Black, White, and Blue: Racial Politics in B. B. King's Music from the 1960s." *Journal of Popular Culture,* vol. 44, 2011, pp. 195–216.

Magazine Articles. A **magazine** is a publication aimed at general readers. For this reason, it contains articles that are easier to understand than those in journals.

ARTICLE IN A MONTHLY OR BIMONTHLY MAGAZINE

Frequently, an article in a magazine does not appear on consecutive pages; for example, it might begin on page 43, skip to page 47, and continue on page 49. If that is the case, include only the first page followed by a plus sign.

Edwards, Owen. "Kilroy Was Here." *Smithsonian,* Oct. 2004, pp. 40+.

ARTICLE IN A WEEKLY OR BIWEEKLY MAGAZINE (SIGNED OR UNSIGNED)

Schley, Jim. "Laid Off, and Working Harder than Ever." *Newsweek,* 20 Sept. 2004, p. 16.

"Real Reform Post-Enron." *Nation,* 4 Mar. 2002, p. 3.

ARTICLE IN A NEWSPAPER

Sherry, Allison. "Volunteers' Personal Touch Turns High-Tech Data into Votes." *The Denver Post,* 30 Oct. 2012, pp. 1A+.

EDITORIAL OR LETTER TO THE EDITOR

"Cheers to a New University Circle Music Festival." Editorial. *Plain Dealer* [Cleveland], 19 Aug. 2016, p. A5.

REVIEW IN A NEWSPAPER

Scott, A. O. "Forever Obsessing about Obsession." Review of *Adaptation,* directed by Spike Jonze, *The New York Times,* 6 Dec. 2002, pp. F1+.

REVIEW IN A WEEKLY OR BIWEEKLY MAGAZINE

Walton, James. "Noble, Embattled Souls." Review of *The Bone Clocks* and *Slade House*, by David Mitchell, *The New York Review of Books*, 3 Dec. 2015, pp. 55–58.

REVIEW IN A MONTHLY MAGAZINE

Jones, Kent. "The Lay of the Land." Review of *Sunshine State*, directed by John Sayles, *Film Commentary*, May/June 2002, pp. 22–24.

Books

GUIDELINES FOR MLA BOOK CITATIONS

To cite a print book in MLA style, follow these guidelines:

1. List the author with last name first.
2. Italicize the title.
3. Include the publisher's name. Use the abbreviation *UP* for *University Press*, as in *Princeton UP* and *U of Chicago P*.
4. Include the year of publication, followed by a period.

The two illustrations that follow show where to find the information you need for your book citations.

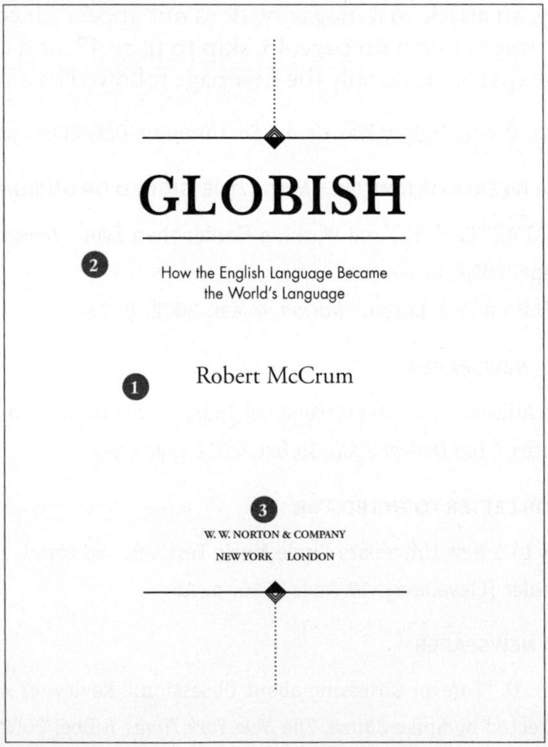

GLOBISH
2
How the English Language Became the World's Language
1
Robert McCrum
3
W. W. NORTON & COMPANY
NEW YORK LONDON

Title Page

4

Copyright © 2010 by Robert McCrum

All rights reserved
Printed in the United States of America
First Edition

For information about permission to reproduce selections from this book, write to Permissions, W. W. Norton & Company, Inc., 500 Fifth Avenue, New York, NY 10110

For information about special discounts for bulk purchases, please contact W. W. Norton Special Sales at specialsales@wwnorton.com or 800-233-4830

Manufacturing by Courier Westford
Book design by Ellen Cipriano
Production manager: Devon Zahn

Library of Congress Cataloging-in-Publication Data

McCrum, Robert.
Globish : how the English language became the world's language / Robert McCrum, — 1st ed.
p. cm.
Includes bibliographical references and index.
ISBN 978-0-393-06255-7
1. English language—History. 2. English language—Globalization.
I. Title.
PE1075.M57 2010
420.9—dc22

2010008157

W. W. Norton & Company, Inc.
500 Fifth Avenue, New York, NY 10110
www.wwnorton.com

W. W. Norton & Company Ltd.
Castle House, 75/76 Wells Street, London W1T3QT

1 2 3 4 5 6 7 8 9 0

Copyright Page

1 — 2

McCrum, Robert. *Globish: How the English Language Became the World's Language*. W. W. Norton & Company, 2010.

3 — 4

BOOKS BY ONE AUTHOR

McCrum, Robert. *Globish: How the English Language Became the World's Language*. W. W. Norton & Company, 2010.

BOOKS BY TWO AUTHORS

List authors in the order in which they are listed on the book's title page. List second and subsequent authors with first names first.

Gardner, Dan, and Philip E. Tetlock. *Super Forecasting: The Art and Science of Prediction*. Penguin Random House, 2015.

BOOKS BY MORE THAN TWO AUTHORS

List only the first author, followed by the abbreviation *et al.* ("and others").

Hoffer, Peter Charles, et al. *The Federal Courts: An Essential History*. Oxford UP, 2016.

TWO OR MORE BOOKS BY THE SAME AUTHOR

List two or more books by the same author in alphabetical order according to title. In each entry after the first, use three unspaced hyphens (followed by a period) instead of the author's name.

García, Cristina. *Dreams of Significant Girls.* Simon and Schuster, 2011.

---. *The Lady Matador's Hotel.* Scribner, 2010.

EDITED BOOK

Horner, Avril, and Anne Rowe, editors. *Living on Paper: Letters from Iris Murdoch.* Princeton UP, 2016.

TRANSLATION

Ullmann, Regina. *The Country Road: Stories.* Translated by Kurt Beals, New Directions Publishing, 2015.

REVISED EDITION

Eagleton, Terry. *Literary Theory: An Introduction.* 3rd ed., U of Minnesota P, 2008.

ANTHOLOGY

Kirszner, Laurie G., and Stephen R. Mandell, editors. *Patterns for College Writing: A Rhetorical Reader and Guide.* 14th ed., Bedford/St. Martin's, 2018.

ESSAY IN AN ANTHOLOGY

Gansberg, Martin. "Thirty-Eight Who Saw Murder Didn't Call the Police." *Patterns for College Writing: A Rhetorical Reader and Guide,* 14th ed., edited by Laurie G. Kirszner and Stephen R. Mandell, Bedford/St. Martin's, 2018, pp. 126–29.

MORE THAN ONE ESSAY IN THE SAME ANTHOLOGY

List each essay separately with a cross-reference to the entire anthology.

Gansberg, Martin. "Thirty-Eight Who Saw Murder Didn't Call the Police." Kirszner and Mandell, pp. 126–29.

Kirszner, Laurie G., and Stephen R. Mandell, editors. *Patterns for College Writing: A Rhetorical Reader and Guide.* 14th ed., Bedford/St. Martin's, 2018.

Staples, Brent. "Just Walk On By: A Black Man Ponders His Power to Alter Public Space." Kirszner and Mandell, pp. 233–36.

SECTION OR CHAPTER OF A BOOK

Rizga, Kristina. "Mr. Hsu." *Mission High: One School, How Experts Tried to Fail It, and the Students and Teachers Who Made It Triumph*, Nation Books, 2015, pp. 89–114.

INTRODUCTION, PREFACE, FOREWORD, OR AFTERWORD

Dunham, Lena. Foreword. *The Liars' Club*, by Mary Karr, Penguin Classics, 2015, pp. xi–xiii.

MULTIVOLUME WORK

Stark, Freya. *Letters.* Edited by Lucy Moorehead, Compton Press, 1974–82. 8 vols.

ARTICLE IN A REFERENCE WORK

For familiar reference works that publish new editions regularly, include only the edition (if given) and the year of publication.

"Civil Rights." *The World Book Encyclopedia*. 2016 ed.

For less familiar reference works, provide a full citation.

"Ball's in Your Court, The." *The American Heritage Dictionary of Idioms*, 2nd ed., Houghton Mifflin Harcourt, 2013.

Internet Sources

GUIDELINES FOR MLA INTERNET CITATIONS

When citing an Internet source, include the following information:

1. The name of the author or editor of the site
2. The title of the site (italicized)
3. The site's sponsor or publisher
4. The date of electronic publication (if no publication date is available, include the date you accessed the site at the end of the citation instead)
5. The URL of the site or, preferably, the Digital Object Identifier (DOI). (The DOI is a unique code assigned to a digital object, such as a research paper. No matter where on the Internet the paper or other object appears, the DOI is the same.)

ENTIRE INTERNET SITE

The Dickens Project. Edited by Jon Michael Varese, U of California, Santa Cruz, 2004, dickens.ucsc.edu/.

Women of Protest: Photographs from the Records of the National Woman's Party. Library of Congress, www.loc.gov/collections/women-of-protest/. Accessed 1 May 2015.

DOCUMENT WITHIN A WEBSITE

Enzinna, Wes. "Syria's Unknown Revolution." *Pulitzer Center on Crisis Reporting,* 24 Nov. 2015, pulitzercenter.org/projects/middle-east-syria-enzinna-war-rojava.

ENTIRE ONLINE BOOK

Milton, John. *Paradise Lost: Book I. Poetry Foundation,* 2014, www.poetryfoundation.org/poem/174987.

Piketty, Thomas. *Capital in the Twenty-First Century.* Translated by Arthur Goldhammer, Harvard UP, 2014. *Google Books,* books.google.com/books?isbn=0674369556.

PART OF AN ONLINE BOOK

Radford, Dollie. "At Night." *Poems.* London, 1910. *Victorian Women Writers Project,* webapp1.dlib.indiana.edu/vwwp/view?docId=VAB7138.xml&chunk.id=d1e1027&brand=vwwp&doc.view=0&anchor.id=#VAB7138-022.

ARTICLE IN AN ONLINE JOURNAL

Amao, Olumuyiwa Babatunde, and Ufo Okeke-Uzodike. "Nigeria, Afrocentrism, and Conflict Resolution: After Five Decades — How Far, How Well?" *African Studies Quarterly,* vol. 15, no. 4, Sept. 2015, pp. 1–23, asq.africa.ufl.edu/files/Volume-15-Issue-4-OLUMUYIWA-BABATUNDE-AMAO.pdf.

ARTICLE IN AN ONLINE REFERENCE BOOK OR ENCYCLOPEDIA

Durante, Amy M. "Finn Mac Cumhail." *Encyclopedia Mythica,* 17 Apr. 2011, www.pantheon.org/articles/f/finn_mac_cumhail.html.

ARTICLE IN AN ONLINE NEWSPAPER

Crowell, Maddy. "How Computers Are Getting Better at Detecting Liars." *The Christian Science Monitor,* 12 Dec. 2015, www.csmonitor.com/Science/Science-Notebook/2015/1212/How-computers-are-getting-better-at-detecting-liars.

ONLINE EDITORIAL

"City's Blight Fight Making Difference." *The Columbus Dispatch*, 17 Nov. 2015, www.dispatch.com/content/stories/editorials/2015/11/17/1-citys-blight-fight-making-difference.html. Editorial.

ARTICLE IN AN ONLINE MAGAZINE

Greenstone, Dan. "Down with Classroom Icebreakers." *Salon*, 6 Sept. 2016, http://www.salon.com/2016/09/06/down-with-classroom-icebreakers-can-we-all-just-start-teaching-instead/.

REVIEW IN AN ONLINE PERIODICAL

Della Subin, Anna. "It Has Burned My Heart." Review of *The Lives of Muhammad*, by Kecia Ali, *London Review of Books*, 22 Oct. 2015, www.lrb.co.uk/v37/n20/anna-della-subin/it-has-burned-my-heart.

POSTING TO A DISCUSSION LIST

Yen, Jessica. "Quotations within Parentheses (Study Measures)." *Copyediting-L*, 18 Mar. 2016, list.indiana.edu/sympa/arc/copyediting-l/2016-03/msg00492.html.

BLOG POST

Caryl, Christian. "Burma: How Much Change?" *NYR Daily*, NYREV, 17 Nov. 2015, www.nybooks.com/daily/2015/11/17/burma-election-how-much-change/.

YOUTUBE VIDEO

Nayar, Vineet. "Employees First, Customers Second." *YouTube*, 9 June 2015, www.youtube.com/watch?v=cCdu67s_C5E.

Other Internet Sources

A PAINTING ON THE INTERNET

Clough, Charles. *January Twenty-First*. 1988–89, Joslyn Art Museum, Omaha, www.joslyn.org/collections-and-exhibitions/permanent-collections/modern-and-contemporary/charles-clough-january-twenty-first/.

A PHOTOGRAPH ON THE INTERNET

Hura, Sohrab. *Old Man Lighting a Fire*. 2015, *Magnum Photos*, www.magnumphotos.com/C.aspx?VP3=SearchResult&ALID=2K1HRG681B_Q.

A CARTOON ON THE INTERNET

Zyglis, Adam. "City of Light." Cartoon. *Buffalo News*, 8 Nov. 2015, adamzyglis.buffalonews.com/2015/11/08/city-of-light/.

A MAP OR CHART ON THE INTERNET

"Map of Sudan." *Global Citizen*, Citizens for Global Solutions, 2011, globalsolutions.org/blog/bashir#.VthzNMfi_FI.

SOCIAL MEDIA POST

For posts to social media sites, the content often does not have a specific title. Instead, write out the comment or tweet in its entirety (or use the first line for particularly long comments), and cite the platform as the publisher. Be sure to include the date of the post and a URL.

Bedford English. "Stacey Cochran explores Reflective Writing in the classroom and as a writer: http://ow.ly/YkjVB." *Facebook*, 15 Feb. 2016, www.facebook.com/BedfordEnglish/posts/10153415001259607.

Curiosity Rover. "Can you see me waving? How to spot #Mars in the night sky: https://youtu.be/hv8hVvJlcJQ." *Twitter*, 5 Nov. 2015, 11:00 a.m., twitter.com/marscuriosity/status/672859022911889408.

EMAIL

Thornbrugh, Caitlin. "Coates Lecture." Received by Rita Anderson, 20 Oct. 2017.

COMPUTER SOFTWARE OR VIDEO GAME

Provide the name of the author or developer of the software, if available; the title of the software, italicized; the publisher or distributor and publication date; and the version (if relevant).

Firaxis Games. *Sid Meier's Civilization Revolution*. Take-Two Interactive, 2008.

Words with Friends. Version 5.84. Zynga, 2013.

MATERIAL FROM A LIBRARY DATABASE

For material retrieved from a library database such as *InfoTrac*, *LexisNexis*, *ProQuest*, or *EBSCOhost*, list the publication information for the source, and provide the name of the database (such as *LexisNexis Academic*), italicized, and the URL of the database or the DOI.

Coles, Kimberly Anne. "The Matter of Belief in John Donne's Holy Sonnets." *Renaissance Quarterly*, vol. 68, no. 3, Fall 2015, pp. 899–931. *JSTOR*, doi:10.1086/683855.

Macari, Anne Marie. "Lyric Impulse in a Time of Extinction." *American Poetry Review*, vol. 44, no. 4, July/Aug. 2015, pp. 11–14. *General OneFile*, go.galegroup.com/.

Rosenbaum, Ron. "The Last Renaissance Man." *Smithsonian*, Nov. 2012, pp. 39–44. *OmniFile Full Text Select*, web.b.ebscohost.com .ezproxy.bpl.org/.

Other Nonprint Sources

ELECTRONIC BOOK

Whitehead, Colson. *The Underground Railroad*. Nook. Penguin Random House, 2016.

TELEVISION OR RADIO PROGRAM

"Federal Role in Support of Autism." *Washington Journal*, narrated by Robb Harleston, C-SPAN, 1 Dec. 2012.

FILM, DVD, OR CD

Blige, Mary J. "Don't Mind." *Life II: The Journey Continues (Act 1)*, Geffen, 2011.

The Martian. Directed by Ridley Scott, performances by Matt Damon, Jessica Chastain, Kristen Wiig, and Kate Mara, Twentieth Century Fox, 2015.

PERSONAL INTERVIEW

Huffington, Arianna. Personal interview, 7 May 2013.

Model Student Research Paper in MLA Style

The following research paper, "The Limitations of *Wikipedia*," by Philip Lau, follows MLA format as outlined in the previous pages.

Lau 1

Philip Lau

Professor Carroll

English 101

5 December 2016

The Limitations of *Wikipedia*

Introduction

When students get a research assignment, many immediately go to the Internet to find sources. Searching the Web, they may discover a *Wikipedia* article on their topic. But is *Wikipedia* a reliable reference source for a research paper? There is quite a controversy over the use of *Wikipedia* as a source, but the consensus seems to be that it is not. Although *Wikipedia* can be a good starting point for general information about a topic, it is not suitable for college-level research.

Thesis statement

Paragraph combines factual information found in more than one source: information and statistics from* Wikipedia *articles, quotations from Chozick and Grathwohl

A wiki allows multiple users to collaborate in creating the content of a website. With a wiki, anyone with a browser can edit, modify, rearrange, or delete content. It is not necessary to know HTML (hypertext mark-up language). The word *wiki* comes from the word *wikiwiki*, which means "quick" or "fast" in Hawaiian. The most popular wiki is *Wikipedia*, a free, Internet-based encyclopedia that relies on the collaboration of those who post and edit entries. Anyone can write a *Wikipedia* article by using the "*Wikipedia* Article Wizard" or edit an entry by clicking on the "Edit" tab. Readers can also view the revision history of an entry by clicking on "View History" ("Help: Page History"). For its many advocates, *Wikipedia*'s open and collaborative nature makes it a "collectively brilliant creation" (Chozick). This collaboration enables *Wikipedia* to publish a wide variety of entries on timely, unusual, and specialized topics (see fig. 1). According to Casper Grathwohl, President, Dictionaries Division, and Director, Global Business Development at Oxford University Press, it "has become increasingly clear that [*Wikipedia*] functions as a necessary layer in the Internet knowledge system, a layer that was not needed in the analog age." At this time, the site contains 40 million articles in 293 languages ("*Wikipedia*").

Lau 2

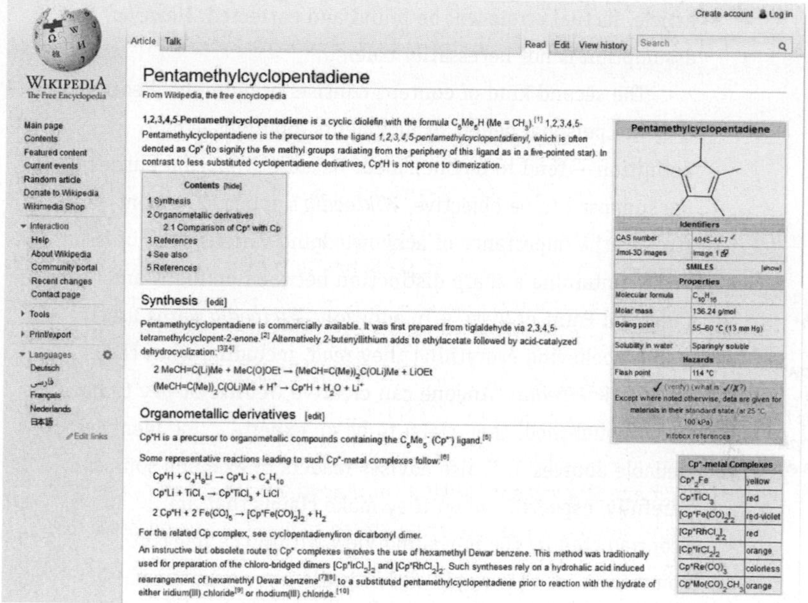
Create account Log in

Article Talk Read Edit View history Search

WIKIPEDIA
The Free Encyclopedia

Main page
Contents
Featured content
Current events
Random article
Donate to Wikipedia
Wikimedia Shop

Interaction
Help
About Wikipedia
Community portal
Recent changes
Contact page

Tools
Print/export
Languages
Deutsch
فارسی
Français
Nederlands
日本語
Edit links

Pentamethylcyclopentadiene

From Wikipedia, the free encyclopedia

1,2,3,4,5-Pentamethylcyclopentadiene is a cyclic diolefin with the formula C_5Me_5H (Me = CH_3).[1] 1,2,3,4,5-Pentamethylcyclopentadiene is the precursor to the ligand *1,2,3,4,5-pentamethylcyclopentadienyl*, which is often denoted as Cp* (to signify the five methyl groups radiating from the periphery of this ligand as in a five-pointed star). In contrast to less substituted cyclopentadiene derivatives, Cp*H is not prone to dimerization.

Contents [hide]
1 Synthesis
2 Organometallic derivatives
2.1 Comparison of Cp* with Cp
3 References
4 See also
5 References

Synthesis [edit]

Pentamethylcyclopentadiene is commercially available. It was first prepared from tiglaldehyde via 2,3,4,5-tetramethylcyclopent-2-enone.[2] Alternatively 2-butenyllithium adds to ethylacetate followed by acid-catalyzed dehydrocyclization:[3][4]

2 MeCH=C(Li)Me + MeC(O)OEt → $(MeCH{=}C(Me))_2C(OLi)Me$ + LiOEt

$(MeCH{=}C(Me))_2C(OLi)Me + H^+ \rightarrow Cp^*H + H_2O + Li^+$

Organometallic derivatives [edit]

Cp*H is a precursor to organometallic compounds containing the $C_5Me_5^-$ (Cp*) ligand.[5]

Some representative reactions leading to such Cp*-metal complexes follow:[6]

$Cp^*H + C_4H_9Li \rightarrow Cp^*Li + C_4H_{10}$

$Cp^*Li + TiCl_4 \rightarrow Cp^*TiCl_3 + LiCl$

$2\ Cp^*H + 2\ Fe(CO)_5 \rightarrow [Cp^*Fe(CO)_2]_2 + H_2$

For the related Cp complex, see cyclopentadienyliron dicarbonyl dimer.

An instructive but obsolete route to Cp* complexes involves the use of hexamethyl Dewar benzene. This method was traditionally used for preparation of the chloro-bridged dimers $[Cp^*IrCl_2]_2$ and $[Cp^*RhCl_2]_2$. Such syntheses rely on a hydrohalic acid induced rearrangement of hexamethyl Dewar benzene[7][8] to a substituted pentamethylcyclopentadiene prior to reaction with the hydrate of either iridium(III) chloride[9] or rhodium(III) chloride.[10]

Pentamethylcyclopentadiene	
Identifiers	
CAS number	4045-44-7 ✓
Jmol-3D images	image 1
SMILES	[show]
Properties	
Molecular formula	$C_{10}H_{16}$
Molar mass	136.24 g/mol
Boiling point	55–60 °C (13 mm Hg)
Solubility in water	Sparingly soluble
Hazards	
Flash point	114 °C
✓ (verify) (what is: ✓/✗?) Except where noted otherwise, data are given for materials in their standard state (at 25 °C, 100 kPa)	
Infobox references	

Cp*-metal Complexes	
Cp^*_2Fe	yellow
Cp^*TiCl_3	red
$[Cp^*Fe(CO)_2]_2$	red-violet
$[Cp^*RhCl_2]_2$	red
$[Cp^*IrCl_2]_2$	orange
$Cp^*Re(CO)_3$	colorless
$Cp^*Mo(CO)_2CH_3$	orange

Fig. 1. *Wikipedia* entry for a chemical compound. "Pentamethylcyclopentadiene." *Wikipedia*. Wikimedia Foundation, 3 July 2016, en.wikipedia.org/wiki/Pentamethylcyclopentadiene.

Paragraph combines student's ideas with quotations from "No Original Research"

Wikipedia contains two kinds of content. The first kind of content is factual—that is, information that can be verified or proved true. Factual material from reliable sources is more trustworthy than material from other sources. *Wikipedia's* own site states, "In general, the most reliable sources are peer-reviewed journals and books published in university presses; university-level textbooks; magazines, journals, and books published by respected publishing houses; and mainstream newspapers" ("No Original Research"). Most reliable publications have staff whose job it is to check factual content. However, because *Wikipedia* relies on a community of contributors to write articles, no single person or group of people is responsible for checking facts. The theory is that if enough people work on an article, factual errors will be found and corrected. However, this assumption is not necessarily true.

The second kind of content consists of opinions. Because they are personal beliefs or judgments, opinions — by definition — tend to be one-sided. Because *Wikipedia* entries are supposed to be objective, *Wikipedia's* policy statement stresses the importance of acknowledging various sides of issues and maintaining a sharp distinction between opinions and facts ("Neutral Point of View"). In addition, *Wikipedia* warns users against believing everything they read, including what they read on *Wikipedia*: "Anyone can create a website or pay to have a book published, then claim to be an expert . . ." ("Identifying Reliable Sources"). It also advises readers to examine sources carefully, especially when they make claims that are "contradicted by the prevailing view within the relevant community, or that would significantly alter mainstream assumptions, especially in science, medicine, history, politics, and biographies of living people" ("Verifiability"). However, everything is up to users; no editor at *Wikipedia* checks to make sure that these guidelines are followed.

Paragraph combines student's own ideas with quotations from multiple Wikipedia *entries*

In spite of its stated policies, *Wikipedia* remains susceptible to certain problems. One problem is the assumption that the knowledge of the community is more valuable than the knowledge of acknowledged experts in a field. In other words, *Wikipedia* values crowd-sourced information more than the knowledge of an individual specialist. In his book *You Are Not a Gadget*, computer scientist and pioneer of virtual reality Jaron Lanier argues that *Wikipedia's* authors "implicitly celebrate the ideal of intellectual mob rule" (144). According to Lanier, "Wikipedians always act out the ideal that the collective is closer to the truth and the individual voice is dispensable" (144). Adherence to this ideal can have serious consequences for the accuracy of *Wikipedia* entries. For example, historian Timothy Messer-Kruse, an expert on American labor history,

Lau 4

Paragraph combines quotations from two Wikipedia *entries and Lanier, as well as a long quotation from Messer-Kruse; it includes student's summary of Messer-Kruse's story and student's own ideas*

attempted to edit a *Wikipedia* article to correct a factual error in the entry on the 1886 Chicago Haymarket Riot. Although Messer-Kruse has published extensively on the subject, his correction was rejected. Messer-Kruse's subsequent attempts to correct the entry — which had multiple errors — were dismissed as well. In an article he wrote for *The Chronicle of Higher Education*, Messer-Kruse recounted the experience, including a telling comment from one of the site's editors, with whom he had an online exchange:

> If all historians save one say that the sky was green in 1888, our policies require that we write, "Most historians write that the sky was green, but one says the sky was blue." As individual editors, we're not in the business of weighing claims, just reporting what reliable sources write.

In other words, *Wikipedia*'s policy is to present all views, even incorrect ones, provided they are published in a reliable source ("Neutral Point of View").

Paragraph contains student's summary of Seigenthaler's story from Torrenzano and Davis's Digital Assassination, *as well as paraphrases and quotations from the book*

Another problem with *Wikipedia* is the ease with which entries can be edited. Because anyone can edit entries, individuals can vandalize content by inserting incorrect information, obscene language, or even nonsense into articles. For example, entries for controversial people, such as President George W. Bush, financier George Soros, or Scientology founder L. Ron Hubbard, or for controversial subjects, such as abortion, are routinely vandalized. Sometimes the vandalism can be extremely harmful. One notorious case of vandalism involved John Seigenthaler, a journalist and former administrative assistant to Attorney General Robert Kennedy, who was falsely accused in *Wikipedia* of being involved in the assassinations of John F. Kennedy and Robert Kennedy. Ultimately, Seigenthaler contacted *Wikipedia* founder Jimmy Wales, threatened legal action, and even tracked down the writer who had inserted the libelous accusation. If a friend had not alerted Seigenthaler to the vandalized entry, it would have likely remained in place, with its false claim that Seigenthaler was "a suspected assassin who had defected to the Soviet Union for 13 years" (Torrenzano and Davis 60–63).

Paragraph contains paraphrase from "Examples of Bias in Wikipedia,*" quotations from Scarborough and Cohen, and the student's own conclusions*

In addition to misinformation and vandalism, bias is another problem for *Wikipedia*. Some critics have accused the site of having a liberal bias. Writing for the Web publication *Human Events*, Rowan Scarborough notes that observers on the right have "long complained of *Wikipedia*'s liberal bias that infects voters with unflattering profiles of their candidates." In fact, a competitor, *Conservapedia*, lists many examples of this skewed coverage in *Wikipedia* entries ("Examples of Bias in *Wikipedia*"). Other critics have identified different kinds of biases on the site. For example, a 2010 survey of *Wikipedia* contributors suggested that "less than 15 percent of its hundreds of thousands of contributors are women" (Cohen). This imbalance indicates a significant lack of women's perspectives on the site. In response, Sue Gardner, the executive director of the Wikimedia Foundation, "set a goal to raise the share of female contributors to 25 percent by 2015" (Cohen).[1]

As Gardner indicates, *Wikipedia* has tried to correct some of the problems that its critics have noted. For example, in response to criticism of its policy of allowing writers and editors to remain anonymous, Wales changed this policy. Now, writers and editors have to provide their user names and thus take responsibility for the content they contribute. In addition, *Wikipedia* has made it possible for administrators to block edits originating from certain Internet domains and to prevent certain writers and editors from posting or changing information. However, authorship is still a problem. Most readers have no idea who has written an article that they are reading or whether or not the writer can be trusted. Given *Wikipedia*'s basic philosophy, there is no way to solve this problem.

---

[1] In 2013, Gardner acknowledged that matters had not improved and that "[t]he solution won't come from the Wikimedia Foundation" ("Gender Bias"), which raises questions about the credibility of *Wikipedia*.

Of course, even traditional encyclopedias have shortcomings. For example, a 2005 study by the journal *Nature* found that although *Wikipedia* included errors, the *Encyclopædia Britannica* also did (Giles). *Britannica* — the oldest English-language encyclopedia still in print at the time — ceased print publication in 2012 after 244 years (Rousseau). However, this venerable source of information persists online because people still value its expertise and trust its credibility. As Jorge Cauz, the president of Encyclopædia Britannica, Inc., observes, "While *Wikipedia* has become ubiquitous, *Britannica* remains a consistently more reliable source. In other words, *Britannica* brings scholarly knowledge to an editorial process" (qtd. in Rousseau). Although that editorial process is not a 100 percent guarantee of accuracy, *Britannica's* staff of dedicated experts and specialists is more reliable than anonymous *Wikipedia* posters. Moreover, conscientious and knowledgeable editors work to make sure that entries are clear, logical, coherent, and grammatically correct. The same cannot be said for *Wikipedia*, which is known for its inconsistent treatment of subjects and its ungrammatical and awkward prose.

Paragraph contains ideas found in several sources and the student's own ideas

Supporters of *Wikipedia* defend the site against charges of bias and errors, pointing out that even respected peer-reviewed journals have problems. For example, some reviewers of articles submitted for publication in peer-reviewed journals may have conflicts of interest. A reviewer might reject an article that challenges his or her own work, or editors may favor certain authors over others. Also, it may be possible for a reviewer to identify the work of a rival, especially if the number of people working in a field is relatively small, and let bias influence his or her evaluation of an article. Another problem is that it takes a long time for articles in peer-reviewed journals to get into print. Critics point out that by the time an article in a peer-reviewed journal appears, it may be outdated. In short, peer-reviewed journals may not be either as objective or as up-to-date as many readers think they are.

Conclusion

Despite their problems, articles that appear in an edited encyclopedia or journal are more trustworthy than those that appear in *Wikipedia*. These articles are thoroughly reviewed by editors or go through a peer-review process (that is, they are screened by experts in a field), and for this reason, they can be considered reliable sources of information. *Wikipedia*, however, is not a reliable research source. The fact that almost anyone can contribute an article or edit one at any time raises serious questions about *Wikipedia*'s reliability. In addition, many articles contain factual errors. Although some errors are found and corrected immediately, others remain for a long time or go entirely unnoticed. Finally, articles frequently reflect the biases or political agendas of contributors and, as a result, present a one-sided or inaccurate view of a subject. All in all, *Wikipedia*'s open-source philosophy makes it more prone to errors, inconsistencies, poor writing, and even vandalism, and for this reason, it should be used with caution. Perhaps the best that can be said of *Wikipedia* is that it is a good starting point for research. Although it is a useful site for getting an overview of a subject before doing in-depth research, it should not be considered a credible or authoritative academic source.

Works Cited

Chozick, Amy. "Jimmy Wales Is Not an Internet Billionaire." *The New York Times*, 30 June 2013, www.nytimes.com/2013/06/30/magazine/jimmy-wales-is-not-an-internet-billionaire.html?_r=0.

Cohen, Noam. "Define Gender Gap? Look Up Wikipedia's Contributor List." *The New York Times*, 31 Jan. 2011, pp. A1+.

"Examples of Bias in Wikipedia." *Conservapedia*, 18 Oct. 2016, www.conservapedia.com/Examples_of_Bias_in_Wikipedia.

"Gender Bias on Wikipedia." *Wikipedia*, Wikimedia Foundation, 7 Feb. 2016, en.wikipedia.org/wiki/Gender_bias_on_Wikipedia.

Giles, Jim. "Internet Encyclopædias Go Head to Head." *Nature*, vol. 438, 15 Dec. 2005, pp. 900–901.

Grathwohl, Casper. "Wikipedia Comes of Age." *The Chronicle of Higher Education*, 7 Jan. 2011, chronicle.com/article/article-content/125899.

"Help: Page History." *Wikipedia*, Wikimedia Foundation, 16 Oct. 2016, en.wikipedia.org/wiki/Help:Page_history.

"Identifying Reliable Sources." *Wikipedia*, Wikimedia Foundation, 29 Nov. 2016, en.wikipedia.org/wiki/Wikipedia:Identifying_reliable_sources.

Lanier, Jaron. *You Are Not a Gadget: A Manifesto*. Allen Lane, 2010.

Messer-Kruse, Timothy. "The 'Undue Weight' of Truth on Wikipedia." *The Chronicle of Higher Education*, 12 Feb. 2012, chronicle.com/article/The-Undue-Weight-of-Truth-on/130704.

"Neutral Point of View." *Wikipedia*, Wikimedia Foundation, 3 Dec. 2016, en.wikipedia.org/wiki/Wikipedia:Neutral_point_of_view.

"No Original Research." *Wikipedia*, Wikimedia Foundation, 15 Nov. 2016, en.wikipedia.org/wiki/Wikipedia:No_original_research.

Rousseau, Caryn. "Encyclopædia Britannica to End Print Editions." *Yahoo! News*, 13 Mar. 2012, www.yahoo.com/news/encyclopaedia-britannica-end-print-editions-234637805.html.

Scarborough, Rowan. "Wikipedia Whacks the Right." *Human Events*, 27 Sep. 2010, humanevents.com/2010/09/27/wikipedia-whacks-the-right/.

Torrenzano, Richard, and Mark Davis. *Digital Assassination: Protecting Your Reputation, Brand, or Business against Online Attacks*. St. Martin's Press, 2011.

"Verifiability." *Wikipedia*, Wikimedia Foundation, 26 Nov. 2016, en.wikipedia.org/wiki/Wikipedia:Verifiability.

"Wikipedia." *Wikipedia*, Wikimedia Foundation, 3 Dec. 2016, en.wikipedia.org/wiki/Wikipedia.

APPENDIX

Documenting Sources: APA

APA style was developed by the American Psychological Association and is commonly used in the social sciences. Sources are cited to help readers in the social sciences understand new ideas in the context of previous research and show them how current the sources are.*

There are several reasons to cite sources. Readers expect arguments to be well supported by evidence and want to be able to locate those sources if they decide to delve deeper. Citing sources is also important to give credit to writers and to avoid plagiarism.

Using Parenthetical References

In APA style, parenthetical references refer readers to sources in the list of references at the end of the essay. In general, parenthetical references should include the author and year of publication. You may also include page numbers if you are quoting directly from a source. Here are some more specific guidelines:

- Refer to the author's name in the text, or cite it, along with the year of publication, in parentheses: Vang asserted . . . (2004) or (Vang, 2004). When quoting words from a source, include the page number: (Vang, 2004, p. 33). Once you have cited a source, you can refer to the author a second time without the publication date as long as it is clear you are referring to the same source: Vang also found . . .
- If no author is identified, use a shortened version of the title: ("Mind," 2007).
- If you are citing multiple works by the same author or authors published in the same year, add a lowercase letter with the year: (Peters, 2004a), (Peters, 2004b), and so on.

*American Psychological Association, *Publication Manual of the American Psychological Association*, Sixth Edition (2010).

- When a work has two authors, cite both names and the year: (Tabor & Garza, 2006). For three to five authors, cite all authors in the first reference, with the year; for subsequent references, use the first author followed by et al. When a work has six or more authors, use the first author's name followed by et al. and the year: (McCarthy et al., 2010).
- Omit page numbers or dates if the source does not include them. (Try to find a .pdf version of an online source if it is an option; it will usually include page numbers.)
- If you quote a source found in another source, indicate the original author and the source in which you found it: Psychologist Gary Wells asserted . . . (as cited in Doyle, 2005, p. 122).
- Include in-text references to personal communications and interviews by providing the person's name, the phrase "personal communication," and the date: (J. Smith, personal communication, February 12, 2014). Do not include these sources in your reference list.

Parenthetical citations must be included for all sources that are not common knowledge, whether you are paraphrasing, summarizing, or quoting directly from a source. If a direct quotation is forty words or less, include it within quotation marks without separating it from the rest of the text. When quoting a passage that is more than forty words long, indent the entire block of quoted text one-half inch from the left margin, and do not enclose it in quotation marks. It should be double-spaced, like the rest of the essay.

GUIDELINES FOR PREPARING THE REFERENCE LIST

Start your list of references on a separate page at the end of your essay. Center the title References at the top of the page.

- Begin each reference flush with the left margin, and indent subsequent lines one-half inch.
- List your references alphabetically by the author's last name (or by the first major word of the title if no author is identified).
- If the list includes references for two or more sources by the same author, list them in order by the year of publication, starting with the earliest.
- Italicize titles of books and periodicals. Do not italicize article titles or enclose them in quotation marks.
- For titles of books and articles, capitalize the first word of the title and subtitle as well as any proper nouns. Capitalize words in a periodical title as in the original.

When you have completed your reference list, go through your essay and make sure every reference cited is included in the list in the correct order.

Examples of APA Citations

The following are examples of APA citations.

Periodicals

ARTICLE IN A JOURNAL PAGINATED BY VOLUME

Nussbaum, M. C. (2016). Women's progress and women's human rights. *Human Rights Quarterly, 38,* 589–622.

ARTICLE IN A JOURNAL PAGINATED BY ISSUE

Lamb, B., & Keller, H. (2007). Understanding cultural models of parenting: The role of intracultural variation and response style. *Journal of Cross-Cultural Psychology, 38*(1), 50–57.

MAGAZINE ARTICLE

Lasdun, J. (2016, April 11). Alone in the alps. *The New Yorker*, 34–39.

NEWSPAPER ARTICLE

DeParle, J. (2009, April 19). Struggling to rise in suburbs where failing means fitting in. *The New York Times,* pp. A1, A20–A21.

Books

BOOKS BY ONE AUTHOR

McCrum, R. (2010). *Globish: How the English language became the world's language*. New Yoik, NY: Norton.

BOOKS BY TWO TO SEVEN AUTHORS

Cottler, S., Sambrook, R., & Mosdell, N. (2016). *Reporting dangerously: Journalist killings, intimidation, and security*. London: Palgrave Macmillan.

BOOKS BY EIGHT OR MORE AUTHORS

Mulvaney, S. A., Mudasiru, E., Schlundt, D. G., Baughman, C. L., Fleming, M., VanderWoude, A., . . . Rothman, R. (2008). Self-management in Type 2 diabetes:
The adolescent perspective. *The Diabetes Educator*, *34*, 118–127.

EDITED BOOK

Brummett, B. (Ed.). (2008). *Uncovering hidden rhetorics: Social issues in disguise*. Los Angeles, CA: Sage.

ESSAY IN AN EDITED BOOK

Alberts, H. C. (2006). The multiple transformations of Miami. In H. Smith & O. J. Furuseth (Eds.), *Latinos in the new south: Transformations of place* (pp. 135–151). Burlington, VT: Ashgate.

TRANSLATION

Courville, S. (2008). *Quebec: A historical geography* (R. Howard, Trans.). Vancouver, Canada: UBC.

REVISED EDITION

Johnson, B., & Christensen, L. B. (2008). *Educational research: Quantitative, qualitative, and mixed approaches* (3rd ed.). Los Angeles, CA: Sage.

Internet Sources

ENTIRE WEBSITE

Paris 2015 UN Climate Change Conference COP21 CMP11. (2015). *UN climate change conference*. Retrieved from http://www.cop21.gouv.fr/en/

WEB PAGE WITHIN A WEBSITE

The great divide: How Westerners and Muslims view each other. (2006, July 6). In *Pew global attitudes project*. Retrieved from http://pewglobal.org/reports/display.php?ReportID=253

UNIVERSITY PROGRAM WEBSITE

National security archive. (2009). Retrieved from George Washington University website: http://www.gwu.edu/~nsarchiv/

JOURNAL ARTICLE FOUND ON THE WEB WITH A DOI

Because websites change and disappear without warning, many publishers have started adding a digital object identifier (DOI) to their articles. A DOI is a unique number that can be retrieved no matter where the article ends up on the Web.

To locate an article with a known DOI, go to the DOI system website at http://dx.doi.org/, and type in the DOI number. When citing an article that has a DOI (usually found on the first page of the article), you do not need to include a URL in your reference or the name of the database in which you may have found the article.

Geers, A. L., Wellman, J. A., & Lassiter, G. D. (2009). Dispositional optimism and engagement: The moderating influence of goal prioritization. *Journal of Personality and Social Psychology, 94*, 913–932. doi:10.1037/a0014746

JOURNAL ARTICLE FOUND ON THE WEB WITHOUT A DOI

Bendetto, M. M. (2008). Crisis on the immigration bench: An ethical perspective. *Brooklyn Law Review, 73,* 467–523. Retrieved from http://brooklaw.edu/students/journals/blr.php/

JOURNAL ARTICLE FROM AN ELECTRONIC DATABASE

The name and URL of the database are not required for citations if a DOI is available. If no DOI is available, provide the home page URL of the journal or of the book or report publisher.

Staub, E., & Pearlman, L. A. (2009). Reducing intergroup prejudice and conflict: A commentary. *Journal of Personality and Social Psychology, 11,* 3–23. Retrieved from http://www.apa.org/journals/psp/

ELECTRONIC BOOK

Katz, R. N. (Ed.). (2008). *The tower and the cloud: Higher education in an era of cloud computing.* Retrieved from http://net.educause.edu/ir/library/pdf/PUB7202.pdf

VIDEO BLOG POST

Vlogbrothers. (2016, August 4). How to vote in every state [Video file]. Retrieved from https://www.youtube.com/watch?v=bFnI25Pu19k

PRESENTATION SLIDES

Hall, M. E. (2009) *Who moved my job!? A psychology of job-loss "trauma"* [Presentation slides]. Retrieved from http://www.cew.wisc.edu/docs/WMMJ%20PwrPt-Summry2.ppt

Model Student Paper in APA Style

The following research paper follows APA format as outlined in the preceding pages. Note that this paper has the same content as the MLA paper on pages 750–58 but follows APA conventions. For this reason, it includes an abstract, a title page, and internal headings.

The Limitations of *Wikipedia*

Philip Lau
English 101
Professor Carroll
December 5, 2016

Abstract

Wikipedia is an online encyclopedia with entries that are created and updated by users rather than by editors. This essay examines the benefits and drawbacks associated with *Wikipedia*'s open-forum approach. *Wikipedia* contains information about a great number of topics and could be a good resource for students who are trying to narrow the focus of their essays. However, many educators believe that this information is unreliable and therefore should not be used for scholarly research. They are concerned that entries that can be edited by anyone, regardless of their expertise on the subject, might not be accurate. Although *Wikipedia* strives to be as accurate as a traditional encyclopedia, there has been at least one case in which inflammatory and untrue information remained on the site for months and was disseminated through other outlets as fact. Because there is no way to determine the expertise of the authors or the validity of the information on *Wikipedia*, it should not be considered a reliable source.

The Limitations of *Wikipedia*

Introduction

When students get a research assignment, many immediately go to the Internet to find sources. Searching the Web, they may discover a *Wikipedia* article on their topic. But is *Wikipedia* a reliable reference source for a research paper? There is quite a controversy over the use of *Wikipedia* as a source, but the consensus seems to be that it is not. Although *Wikipedia* can be a good starting point for general information about a topic, it is not suitable for college-level research.

Thesis statement

Paragraph combines factual information found in more than one source: information and statistics from Wikipedia *articles, quotations from Chozick and Grathwohl*

A wiki allows multiple users to collaborate in creating the content of a website. With a wiki, anyone with a browser can edit, modify, rearrange, or delete content. It is not necessary to know HTML (hypertext mark-up language). The word *wiki* comes from the word *wikiwiki*, which means "quick" or "fast" in Hawaiian. The most popular wiki is *Wikipedia*, a free, Internet-based encyclopedia that relies on the collaboration of those who post and edit entries. Anyone can write a *Wikipedia* article by using the "*Wikipedia* Article Wizard" or edit an entry by clicking on the "Edit" tab. Readers can easily view the revision history of an entry by clicking on "View History" ("Help: page history," 2016). For its many advocates, *Wikipedia*'s open and collaborative nature makes it a "collectively brilliant creation" (Chozick, 2016). This collaboration enables *Wikipedia* to publish a wide variety of entries on timely, unusual, and specialized topics (see Figure 1). It has certainly altered the way people think about research. Moreover, *Wikipedia* has increasingly become a "necessary layer in the Internet knowledge system, a layer that was not needed in the analog age" (Grathwohl, 2011). At this time, the site contains 40 million articles in 293 languages ("*Wikipedia*," 2016).

Wikipedia's Two Kinds of Content

Wikipedia contains two kinds of content. The first kind of content is factual—that is, information that can be verified

THE LIMITATIONS OF *WIKIPEDIA* 4

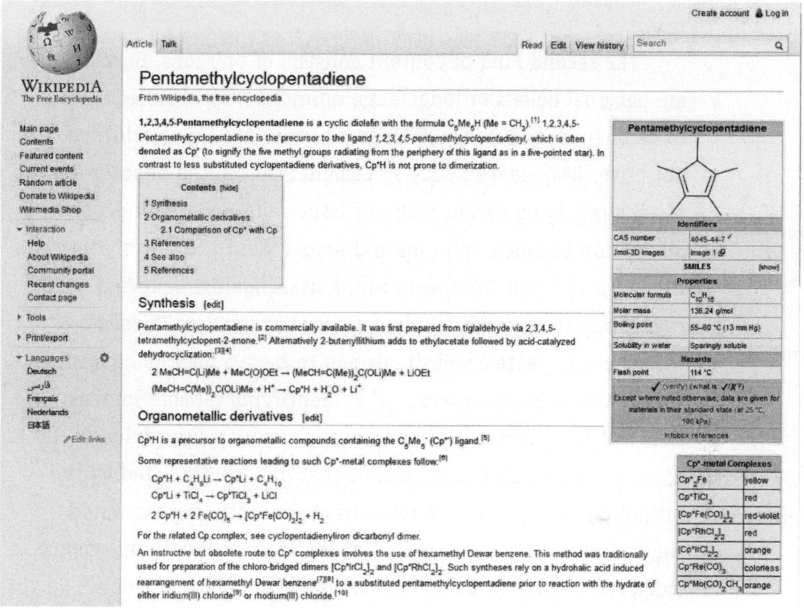

Figure 1. *Wikipedia* entry for a chemical compound. Pentamethylcyclopentadiene (2016, July 5). *Wikipedia*. Retrieved from http://en.wikipedia.org/wiki/Pentamethylcyclopentadiene

Paragraph combines student's ideas with quotations from "No Original Research"

or proved true. Factual material from reliable sources is more trustworthy than material from other sources. *Wikipedia's* own site states, "In general, the most reliable sources are peer-reviewed journals and books published in university presses; university-level textbooks; magazines, journals, and books published by respected publishing houses; and mainstream newspapers" ("No Original Research," 2016). Most reliable publications have staff whose job it is to check factual content. However, because *Wikipedia* relies on a community of contributors to write articles, no single person or group of people is responsible for checking facts. The theory is that if enough people work on an article, factual errors will be found and corrected. However, this assumption is not necessarily true.

Paragraph combines student's own ideas with quotations from multiple Wikipedia *entries*

The second kind of content consists of opinions. Because they are personal beliefs or judgments, opinions—by definition—tend to be one-sided. Because *Wikipedia* entries are supposed to be objective, *Wikipedia*'s policy statement stresses the importance of acknowledging various sides of issues and maintaining a sharp distinction between opinions and facts ("Neutral Point of View," 2016). In addition, *Wikipedia* warns users against believing everything they read, including what they read on *Wikipedia*: "Anyone can create a website or pay to have a book published, then claim to be an expert . . ." ("Identifying reliable sources," 2016). It also advises readers to examine sources carefully, especially when they make claims that are "contradicted by the prevailing view within the relevant community, or that would significantly alter mainstream assumptions, especially in science, medicine, history, politics, and biographies of living people" ("Verifiability," 2016). However, everything is up to users; no editor at *Wikipedia* checks to make sure that these guidelines are followed.

Errors and Other Problems with *Wikipedia*

In spite of its stated policies, *Wikipedia* remains susceptible to certain problems. One problem is the assumption that the knowledge of the community is more valuable than the knowledge of acknowledged experts in a field. In other words, *Wikipedia* values crowd-sourced information more than the knowledge of an individual specialist. In his book *You Are Not a Gadget,* Lanier (2010) argues that *Wikipedia*'s authors "implicitly celebrate the ideal of intellectual mob rule" (p. 144). According to Lanier, "Wikipedians always act out the ideal that the collective is closer to the truth and the individual voice is dispensable" (p. 144). Adherence to this ideal can have serious consequences for the accuracy of *Wikipedia* entries. For example, historian Timothy Messer-Kruse, an expert on American labor history, attempted to edit a *Wikipedia* article to correct a factual error in the entry on

Paragraph combines quotations from two Wikipedia *entries and Lanier, as well as a long quotation from Messer-Kruse; it includes student's summary of Messer-Kruse's story and student's own ideas*

the 1886 Chicago Haymarket Riot. Although Messer-Kruse has published extensively on the subject, his correction was rejected. Messer-Kruse's subsequent attempts to correct the entry—which had multiple errors—were dismissed as well. In an article he wrote for *The Chronicle of Higher Education*, Messer-Kruse recounted the experience, including a telling comment from one of the site's editors, with whom he had an online exchange:

> If all historians save one say that the sky was green in 1888, our policies require that we write, "Most historians write that the sky was green, but one says the sky was blue." As individual editors, we're not in the business of weighing claims, just reporting what reliable sources write. (Messer-Kruse, 2012)

In other words, *Wikipedia*'s policy is to present all views, even incorrect ones, provided they are published in a reliable source ("Neutral Point of View," 2016).

Paragraph contains student's summary of Seigenthaler's story from Torrenzano and Davis's Digital Assassination, *as well as paraphrases and quotations from the book*

Another problem with *Wikipedia* is the ease with which entries can be edited. Because anyone can edit entries, individuals can vandalize content by inserting incorrect information, obscene language, or even nonsense into articles. For example, entries for controversial people, such as President George W. Bush, financier George Soros, or Scientology founder L. Ron Hubbard, or for controversial subjects, such as abortion, are routinely vandalized. Sometimes the vandalism can be extremely harmful. One notorious case of vandalism involved John Seigenthaler, a journalist and former administrative assistant to Attorney General Robert Kennedy, who was falsely accused in *Wikipedia* of being involved in the assassinations of John F. Kennedy and Robert Kennedy. Ultimately, Seigenthaler contacted *Wikipedia* founder Jimmy Wales, threatened legal action, and even tracked down the writer who had inserted the libelous accusation. If a friend had not alerted Seigenthaler to the vandalized entry, it would have likely remained in place, with its false claim that Seigenthaler was "a suspected assassin who had defected to the Soviet Union for 13 years" (Torrenzano & Davis, 2011, pp. 60–63).

Paragraph contains paraphrase from "Examples of Bias in Wikipedia," quotations from Scarborough and Cohen, and the student's own conclusions

In addition to misinformation and vandalism, bias is another problem for *Wikipedia*. Some critics have accused the site of having a liberal bias. Writing for the Web publication *Human Events,* Scarborough (2010) noted that observers on the right have "long complained of *Wikipedia*'s liberal bias that infects voters with unflattering profiles of their candidates." In fact, a competitor, *Conservapedia,* lists many examples of this skewed coverage in *Wikipedia* entries ("Examples of Bias in *Wikipedia*," 2016). Other critics have identified different kinds of biases on the site. For example, a 2010 survey of *Wikipedia* contributors suggested that "less than 15 percent of its hundreds of thousands of contributors are women" (Cohen, 2011). This imbalance indicates a significant lack of women's perspectives on the site. In response, Sue Gardner, the executive director of the Wikimedia Foundation, "set a goal to raise the share of female contributors to 25 percent by 2015" (Cohen, 2011).[1]

As Gardner indicates, *Wikipedia* has tried to correct some of the problems that its critics have noted. For example, in response to criticism of its policy of allowing writers and editors to remain anonymous, Wales changed this policy. Now, writers and editors have to provide their user names and thus take responsibility for the content they contribute. In addition, *Wikipedia* has made it possible for administrators to block edits originating from certain Internet domains and to prevent certain writers and editors from posting or changing information. However, authorship is still a problem. Most readers have no idea who has written an article that they are reading or whether or not the writer can be trusted. Given *Wikipedia*'s basic philosophy, there is no way to solve this problem.

Of course, even traditional encyclopedias have shortcomings. For example, a study by the journal *Nature* found that although

[1]In 2013, Gardner acknowledged that matters had not improved and that "[t]he solution won't come from the Wikimedia Foundation" ("Gender Bias," 2016), which raises questions about the credibility of *Wikipedia*.

Wikipedia included errors, the *Encyclopædia Britannica* also did (Giles, 2005). *Britannica*—the oldest English-language encyclopedia still in print at the time—ceased print publication in 2012 after 244 years (Rousseau, 2012). However, this venerable source of information persists online because people still value its expertise and trust its credibility. As Jorge Cauz, the president of Encyclopædia Britannica, Inc., observes, "While *Wikipedia* has become ubiquitous, *Britannica* remains a consistently more reliable source. In other words, *Britannica* brings scholarly knowledge to an editorial process" (Rousseau, 2012). Although that editorial process is not a 100 percent guarantee of accuracy, *Britannica*'s staff of dedicated experts and specialists is more reliable than anonymous *Wikipedia* posters. Moreover, conscientious and knowledgeable editors work to make sure that entries are clear, logical, coherent, and grammatically correct. The same cannot be said for *Wikipedia*, which is known for its inconsistent treatment of subjects and its ungrammatical and awkward prose.

Comparison to Traditional Sources

Paragraph contains ideas found in several sources and the student's own ideas

Supporters of *Wikipedia* defend the site against charges of bias and errors, pointing out that even respected peer-reviewed journals have problems. For example, some reviewers of articles submitted for publication in peer-reviewed journals may have conflicts of interest. A reviewer might reject an article that challenges his or her own work, or editors may favor certain authors over others. Also, it may be possible for a reviewer to identify the work of a rival, especially if the number of people working in a field is relatively small, and let bias influence his or her evaluation of an article. Another problem is that it takes a long time for articles in peer-reviewed journals to get into print. Critics point out that by the time an article in a peer-reviewed journal appears, it may be outdated. In short, peer-reviewed journals may not be either as objective or as up-to-date as many readers think they are.

Conclusion

Conclusion

Despite their problems, articles that appear in an edited encyclopedia or journal are more trustworthy than those that appear in *Wikipedia*. These articles are thoroughly reviewed by editors or go through a peer-review process (that is, they are screened by experts in a field), and for this reason, they can be considered reliable sources of information. *Wikipedia*, however, is not a reliable research source. The fact that almost anyone can contribute an article or edit one at any time raises serious questions about *Wikipedia*'s reliability. In addition, many articles contain factual errors. Although some errors are found and corrected immediately, others remain for a long time or go entirely unnoticed. Finally, articles frequently reflect the biases or political agendas of contributors and, as a result, present a one-sided or inaccurate view of a subject. All in all, *Wikipedia*'s open-source philosophy makes it more prone to errors, inconsistencies, poor writing, and even vandalism, and for this reason, it should be used with caution. Perhaps the best that can be said of *Wikipedia* is that it is a good starting point for research. Although it is a useful site for getting an overview of a subject before doing in-depth research, it should not be considered a credible or authoritative academic source.

THE LIMITATIONS OF *WIKIPEDIA* 10

References

Chozick, A. (2013, June 30). Jimmy Wales is not an Internet billionaire. *The New York Times*. Retrieved from http://nytimes.com/2013/06/30/magazine/jimmy-wales-is-not-an-internet-billionaire.html?_r=0

Cohen, N. (2011, January 31). Define gender gap? Look up *Wikipedia*'s contributor list. *The New York Times,* p. A1+.

Examples of bias in *Wikipedia*. (2016, October 18). *Conservapedia.* Retrieved December 3, 2016, from http://www.conservapedia.com/Examples_of_Bias_in_Wikipedia

Gender Bias. (2016, November 7). *Wikipedia.* Retrieved December 2, 2016, from en.wikipedia.org/wiki/Gender_bias_on_Wikipedia

Giles, J. (2005). Internet encyclopaedias go head to head. *Nature, 438*, 900–901.

Grathwohl, C. (2011, January 11). *Wikipedia* comes of age. *Chronicle of Higher Education.* Retrieved from http://chronicle.com/article/article-content/125899

Help: page history. (2016, October 16). *Wikipedia.* Retrieved December 1, 2016, from http://en.wikipedia.org/wiki/Help:Page_history

Identifying reliable sources. (2016, November 29). *Wikipedia.* Retrieved December 3, 2016, from http://en.wikipedia.org/wiki/Wikipedia:Identifying_reliable_sources

Lanier, J. (2010). *You are not a gadget: A manifesto.* London, England: Allen Lane.

Messer-Kruse, T. (2012, February 12). The "undue weight" of truth on *Wikipedia*. *Chronicle of Higher Education.* Retrieved from http://chronicle.com/article/The-Undue-Weight-of-Truth-on/130704

Neutral point of view. (2016, December 3). *Wikipedia*. Retrieved December 5, 2016, from http://en.wikipedia.org/wiki/Wikipedia:Neutral_point_of_view

No original research. (2016, November 15). *Wikipedia.* Retrieved December 1, 2016, from http://en.wikipedia.org/wiki/Wikipedia:No_original_research

Rousseau, C. (2012, March 13). *Encyclopædia Britannica* to end print editions. *Yahoo! News.* Retrieved from http://news.yahoo.com/encyclopaedia-britannica-end-print-editions-234637805.html

Scarborough, R. (2010, September 27). *Wikipedia* whacks the right. *Human Events.* Retrieved from http://www.humanevents.com/2010/09/27/wikipedia-whacks-the-right

Torrenzano, R., & Davis, M. (2011). *Digital assassination: Protecting your reputation, brand, or business against online attacks.* New York, NY: St. Martin's Press.

Verifiability. (2016, November 26). *Wikipedia.* Retrieved December 2, 2016, from http://en.wikipedia.org/wiki/Wikipedia:Verifiability

Wikipedia. (2016, December 3). *Wikipedia*. Retrieved December 5, 2016, from http://en.wikipedia.org/wiki/Wikipedia

GLOSSARY

Abstract/Concrete language Abstract language names concepts or qualities that cannot be directly seen or touched: *love, emotion, evil, anguish*. Concrete language denotes objects or qualities that the senses can perceive: *fountain pen, leaky, shouting, rancid*. Abstract words are sometimes needed to express ideas, but they are very vague unless used with concrete supporting detail. The abstract phrase "The speaker was overcome with emotion" could mean almost anything, but the addition of concrete language clarifies the meaning: "He clenched his fist and shook it at the crowd" (anger).

Active reading Approaching a reading with a clear understanding of your purpose and marking or otherwise highlighting the text to help you understand what you are reading.

Allusion A brief reference to literature, history, the Bible, mythology, popular culture, and so on that readers are expected to recognize. An allusion evokes a vivid impression in very few words. "The gardener opened the gate, and suddenly we found ourselves in Eden" suggests in one word (*Eden*) the stunning beauty of the garden.

Analogy A form of comparison that explains an unfamiliar element by comparing it to another that is more familiar. Analogies also enable writers to put abstract or technical information in simpler, more concrete terms: "The effect of pollution on the environment is like that of cancer on the body."

Annotating The technique of recording one's responses to a reading selection by writing notes in the margins of the text. Annotating a text might involve asking questions, suggesting possible parallels with other selections or with the reader's own experience, arguing with the writer's points, commenting on the writer's style, or defining unfamiliar terms or concepts.

Antithesis A viewpoint opposite to one expressed in a *thesis*. In an argumentative essay, the thesis must be debatable. If no antithesis exists, the writer's thesis is not debatable. (See also **Thesis**.)

Antonym A word opposite in meaning to another word. *Beautiful* is the antonym of *ugly*. *Synonym* is the antonym of *antonym*.

Argumentation The form of writing that takes a stand on an issue and attempts to convince readers by presenting a logical sequence of points supported by evidence. Unlike *persuasion,* which uses a number of different appeals, argumentation is primarily an appeal to reason. (See Chapter 14.)

Audience The people "listening" to a writer's words. Writers who are sensitive to their audience will carefully choose a tone, examples, and allusions that their readers will understand and respond to. For instance, an effective article attempting to persuade high school students not to drink alcohol would use examples and allusions pertinent to a teenager's life. Different examples would be chosen if the writer were addressing middle-aged members of Alcoholics Anonymous.

Basis for comparison A fundamental similarity between two or more things that enables a writer to compare them. In a comparison of how two towns react to immigrants, the basis of comparison might be that both towns have a rapidly expanding immigrant population. (If one of the towns did not have any immigrants, this comparison would be illogical.)

Biases Preferences or prejudices in favor of or against a stance.

Body paragraphs The paragraphs that develop and support an essay's thesis.

Brainstorming An invention technique that can be done individually or in a group. When writers brainstorm on their own, they jot down every fact or idea that relates to a particular topic. When they brainstorm in a group, they discuss a topic with others and write down the useful ideas that come up.

Causal chain A sequence of events when one event causes another event, which in turn causes yet another event.

Cause and effect The pattern of development that discusses either the reasons for an occurrence or the observed or predicted consequence of an occurrence. Often, both causes and effects are discussed in the same essay. (See Chapter 10.)

Causes The reasons for an event, situation, or phenomenon. An *immediate cause* is an obvious one; a *remote cause* is less easily perceived. The *main cause* is the most important cause, whether it is immediate or remote. Other, less important causes that nevertheless encourage the effect in some way (for instance, by speeding it up or providing favorable circumstances for it) are called *contributory causes.*

Chronological order The time sequence of events. Chronological order is often used to organize a narrative; it is also used to structure a process essay.

Claim In Toulmin logic, the thesis or main point of an essay. Usually the claim is stated directly, but sometimes it is implied. (See also **Toulmin logic**.)

Classification and division The pattern of development that uses these two related methods of organizing information. *Classification* involves searching for common characteristics among various items and grouping them accordingly, thereby imposing order on randomly organized information. *Division* breaks up an entity into smaller groups or elements. Classification generalizes; division specifies. (See Chapter 12.)

Cliché An overused expression, such as *beauty is in the eye of the beholder, the good die young,* or *a picture is worth a thousand words.*

Clustering A method of invention whereby a writer groups ideas visually by listing the main topic in the center of a page, circling it, and surrounding it with words or phrases that identify the major points to be addressed. The writer then circles these words or phrases, creating new clusters or ideas for each of them.

Coherence The tight relationship between all the parts of an effective piece of writing. Such a relationship ensures that the writing will make sense to readers. For a piece of writing to be coherent, it must be logical and orderly, with effective *transitions* making the movement between sentences and paragraphs clear. Within and between paragraphs, coherence may also be enhanced by the repetition of key words and ideas, by the use of pronouns to refer to nouns mentioned previously, and by the use of parallel sentence structure.

Colloquialisms Expressions that are generally appropriate for conversation and informal writing but not usually acceptable for the writing you do in college, business, or professional settings. Examples of colloquial language include contractions; clipped forms (*fridge* for *refrigerator*); vague expressions such as *kind of* and *sort of;* conversation fillers such as *you know;* and other informal words and expressions, such as *get across* for *communicate* and *kids* for *children*.

Common knowledge Factual information that is widely available in reference sources, such as the dates of important historical events. Writers do not need to document common knowledge.

Comparison and contrast The pattern of development that focuses on similarities and differences between two or more subjects. In a general sense, *comparison* shows how two or more subjects are alike; *contrast* shows how they are different. (See Chapter 11; see also **Point-by-point comparison**; **Subject-by-subject comparison**.)

Conclusion The group of sentences or paragraphs that brings an essay to a close. To *conclude* means not only "to end" but also "to resolve." Although a conclusion does not review all the issues discussed in an essay, the conclusion is the place to show that those issues have been resolved. An effective conclusion indicates that the writer is committed to what has been expressed, and it is the writer's last chance to leave an impression or idea with readers.

Concrete language See **Abstract/Concrete language**.

Connotation The associations, meanings, or feelings a word suggests beyond its literal meaning. Literally, the word *home* means "one's place of residence," but *home* also connotes warmth and a sense of belonging. (See also **Denotation**.)

Contributory cause See **Causes**.

Deductive reasoning The method of reasoning that moves from a general premise to a specific conclusion. Deductive reasoning is the opposite of *inductive reasoning*. (See also **Syllogism**.)

Definition An explanation of a word's meaning; the pattern of development in which a writer explains what something or someone is. (See Chapter 13; see also **Extended definition**; **Formal definition**.)

Denotation The literal meaning of a word. The denotation of *home* is "one's place of residence." (See also **Connotation**.)

Description The pattern of development that presents a word picture of a thing, a person, a situation, or a series of events. (See Chapter 7; see also **Objective description**; **Subjective description**.)

Digression A remark or series of remarks that wanders from the main point of a discussion. In a personal narrative, a digression may be entertaining because of its irrelevance, but in other kinds of writing, it is likely to distract and confuse readers.

Division See **Classification and division**.

Documentation The formal way of giving credit to the sources a writer borrows words or ideas from. Documentation allows readers to evaluate a writer's sources and to consult them if they wish. Essays written for literature and writing classes use the documentation style recommended by the Modern Language Association (MLA). (See Chapter 18.)

Dominant impression The mood or quality that is central to a piece of writing.

Essay A short work of nonfiction writing on a single topic that usually expresses the author's impressions or opinions. An essay may be organized around one of the patterns of development presented in Chapters 6 through 14 of this book, or it may combine several of these patterns.

Ethos An appeal based on the character reputation of the writer.

Euphemism A polite term for an unpleasant concept. (*Passed away* is a euphemism for *died*.)

Evidence Facts and opinions used to support a statement, position, or idea. *Facts,* which may include statistics, may be drawn from research or personal experience; *opinions* may represent the conclusions of experts or the writer's own ideas.

Example A concrete illustration of a general point.

Exemplification The pattern of development that uses a single extended *example* or a series of shorter examples to support a thesis. (See Chapter 8.)

Extended definition A paragraph-, essay-, or book-length definition developed by means of one or more of the rhetorical strategies discussed in this book.

Fallacy A statement that resembles a logical argument but is actually flawed. Logical fallacies are often persuasive, but they unfairly manipulate readers to win agreement. Fallacies include begging the question; argument from analogy; personal (*ad hominem*) attacks; jumping to a conclusion (hasty or sweeping generalizations); false dilemmas (the either/or fallacy); equivocation; red herrings; you also (*tu quoque*); appeals to doubtful authority; misleading statistics; *post hoc* reasoning; and *non sequiturs*. See the section on "Recognizing Fallacies" (page 528) for explanations and examples.

Figures of speech (also known as *figurative language*) Imaginative language used to suggest a special meaning or create a special effect. Three of the most common figures of speech are *similes, metaphors,* and *personification*.

Formal definition A brief explanation of a word's meaning as it appears in the dictionary.

Formal outline A detailed construction that uses headings and subheadings to indicate the order in which key points and supporting details are presented in an essay.

Freewriting A method of invention that involves writing without stopping for a fixed period – perhaps five or ten minutes – without paying attention to spelling, grammar, or punctuation. The goal of freewriting is to let ideas flow and record them.

Grounds In Toulmin logic, the material that a writer uses to support a claim. Grounds may be evidence (facts or expert opinions) or appeals to the emotions or values of an audience. (See also **Toulmin logic**.)

Highlighting A technique used by a reader to record responses to a reading selection by marking the text with symbols. Highlighting a text might involve underlining important ideas, boxing key terms, numbering a series of related points, circling unfamiliar words (or placing question marks next to them), drawing vertical lines next to an interesting or important passage, drawing arrows to connect related points, or placing asterisks next to discussions of the selection's central issues or themes.

Hyperbole Deliberate exaggeration for emphasis or humorous effect: "I froze to death out in the storm"; "She has hundreds of boyfriends"; "Senior year passed by in a second." The opposite of hyperbole is *understatement*.

Imagery A set of verbal pictures of sensory experiences. These pictures, conveyed through concrete details, make a description vivid and immediate to the reader. Some images are literal ("The cows were so white they almost glowed in the dark"); others are more figurative ("The black-and-white cows looked like maps, with the continents in black and the seas in white"). A pattern of imagery (repeated images of, for example, shadows, forests, or fire) may run through a piece of writing.

Immediate cause See **Causes**.

Implied thesis An essay that conveys its main focus without explicitly stating it.

Inductive reasoning The method of reasoning that moves from specific evidence to a general conclusion based on this evidence. Inductive reasoning is the opposite of *deductive reasoning*.

Informal outline A list of points to be developed in an essay.

Instructions A kind of process essay whose purpose is to enable readers to *perform* a process. Instructions use the present tense and speak directly to readers: "Walk at a moderate pace for twenty minutes."

Introduction An essay's opening. Depending on the length of an essay, the introduction may be one paragraph or several paragraphs. In an introduction, a writer tries to encourage the audience to read the essay that follows. Therefore, the writer must choose tone and diction carefully, indicate what the essay is about, and suggest to readers what direction it will take.

Invention (also known as *prewriting*) The stage of writing when a writer explores the writing assignment, focuses ideas, and ultimately decides on a thesis for an essay. A writer might begin by thinking through the requirements of the assignment – the essay's purpose, length, and audience. Then, using one or more methods of invention – such as *freewriting, questions for probing, brainstorming, clustering,* and *journal writing* – the writer can formulate a tentative thesis and begin to write the essay.

Irony Language that points to a discrepancy between two different levels of meaning. *Verbal irony* is characterized by a gap between what is stated and what is really meant, which often has the opposite meaning – for instance, "his humble abode" (referring to a millionaire's estate). *Situational irony* points to a discrepancy between what actually happens and what readers expect will happen. This kind of irony is present, for instance, when a character, trying to frighten a rival, ends up frightening himself. *Dramatic irony* occurs when the reader understands more about what is happening in a story than the character who is telling the story does. For example, a narrator might tell an anecdote that he intends to illustrate how clever he is, while it is obvious to the reader from the story's events that the narrator has made a fool of himself because of his gullibility. (See also **Sarcasm**.)

Jargon The specialized vocabulary of a profession or academic field. Although the jargon of a particular profession is an efficient means of communication within that field, it may not be clear or meaningful to readers outside that profession.

Journal writing A method of invention that involves recording ideas that emerge from reading or other experiences and then exploring them in writing.

Literacy narrative A personal account focusing on the author's experiences with reading and writing.

Logos An appeal based on logic.

Looping A method of invention that involves isolating one idea from a piece of freewriting and using this idea as a focus for a new piece of freewriting.

Main cause See **Causes**.

Mapping See **Clustering**.

Metaphor A comparison of two dissimilar things that does not use the words *like* or *as* ("The small waves were the same, chucking the rowboat under the chin . . ." – E. B. White).

Narration The pattern of development that tells a story. (See Chapter 6.)

Objective description A detached, factual picture presented in a plain and direct manner. Although pure objectivity is impossible to achieve, writers of science papers, technical reports, and news articles, among others, strive for precise language that is free of value judgments.

Occasion The situation (or situations) that leads someone to write about a topic. For academic writing, it will almost always be a specific assignment from an instructor. The occasion helps a writer determine the purpose, audience, and format of the piece.

Outline See **Formal outline**; **Informal outline**.

Paradox A statement that seems self-contradictory or absurd but is nonetheless true.

Paragraph The basic unit of an essay. A paragraph is composed of related sentences that together express a single idea. This main idea is often stated in a single *topic sentence*. Paragraphs are also graphic symbols on the page, mapping the progress of the ideas in the essay and providing visual breaks for readers.

Parallelism The use of similar grammatical elements within a sentence or sentences. "I like hiking, skiing, and to cook" is not parallel because *hiking* and *skiing* are gerund forms (*-ing*), whereas *to cook* is an infinitive form. Revised for parallelism, the sentence could read either "I like hiking, skiing, and cooking" or "I like to hike, to ski, and to cook." As a stylistic technique, parallelism can provide emphasis through repetition, "Walk groundly, talk profoundly, drink roundly, sleep soundly" (William Hazlitt). Parallelism is also a powerful oratorical technique: "Until justice is blind to color, until education is unaware of race, until opportunity is unconcerned with the color of men's skins, emancipation will be a proclamation but not a fact" (Lyndon B. Johnson). Finally, parallelism can increase *coherence* within a paragraph or an essay.

Paraphrase The restatement of another person's words in one's own words, following the order and emphasis of the original. Paraphrase is frequently used in source-based essays, where the purpose is to use information gathered during research to support the ideas in the essay. For example, Bruce Catton's "Grant was the modern man emerging; beyond him, ready to come on the stage, was the great age of steel and machinery, of crowded cities and a restless burgeoning vitality" (page 394) might be paraphrased as, "Grant was a man of a new era; following him, glimpsed but not fully seen, was the time of new technologies, with its crowded urban life and growing restlessness."

Pathos An appeal based on emotion.

Personification Describing concepts or objects as if they were human ("the chair slouched"; "the wind sighed outside the window").

Persuasion The method a writer uses to move an audience to adopt a belief or follow a course of action. To persuade an audience, a writer relies on the various appeals — to the emotions, to reason, or to ethics. Persuasion is different from *argumentation,* which appeals primarily to reason.

Plagiarism Presenting the words or ideas of someone else as if they were actually one's own (whether intentionally or unintentionally). Plagiarism should always be avoided.

Point-by-point comparison A comparison in which the writer first makes a point about one subject and then follows it with a comparable point about the other subject. (See also **Subject-by-subject comparison**.)

***Post hoc* reasoning** A logical fallacy that involves looking back at two events that occurred in chronological sequence and wrongly assuming that the first event caused the second. For example, just because a car will not start after a thunderstorm, one cannot automatically assume that the storm caused the problem.

Prewriting See **Invention**.

Principle of classification In a classification-and-division essay, the quality the items have in common. For example, if a writer were classifying automobiles, one principle of classification might be "repair records."

Process The pattern of development that presents a series of steps in a procedure in chronological order and shows how this sequence of steps leads to a particular result. (See Chapter 9.)

Process explanation A kind of process essay whose purpose is to enable readers to understand a process rather than perform it.

Purpose A writer's reason for writing. A writer's purpose may, for example, be to entertain readers with an amusing story, to inform them about a dangerous disease, to move them to action by enraging them with an example of injustice, or to change their perspective by revealing a hidden dimension of a person or situation.

Quotation The exact words of a source, enclosed in quotation marks. A quotation should be used only to present a particularly memorable statement or to avoid a paraphrase that would change the meaning of the original.

Refutation The attempt to counter an opposing argument by revealing its weaknesses. Three of the most common weaknesses are logical flaws in the argument, inadequate evidence, and irrelevance. Refutation greatly strengthens an argument by showing that the writer is aware of the complexity of the issue and has considered opposing viewpoints.

Remote cause See **Causes**.

Rhetorical question A question asked for effect and not meant to be answered.

Rogerian argument A strategy put forth by psychologist Carl Rogers that rejects the adversarial approach that characterizes many arguments. Rather than attacking the opposition, Rogers suggests acknowledging the validity of opposing positions. By finding areas of agreement, a Rogerian argument reduces conflict and increases the chance that the final position will satisfy all parties.

Sarcasm Deliberately insincere and biting irony – for example, "That's okay – I love it when you borrow things and don't return them."

Satire Writing that uses wit, irony, and ridicule to attack foolishness, incompetence, or evil in a person or idea. Satire has a different purpose from comedy, which usually intends simply to entertain. For a classic example of satire, see Jonathan Swift's "A Modest Proposal," page 706.

Sexist language Language that stereotypes people according to gender. Writers often use plural constructions to avoid sexist language. For example, *the doctors . . . they* can be used instead of *the doctor . . . he*. Words such as *police officer* and *firefighter* can be used instead of *policeman* and *fireman*.

Simile A comparison of two dissimilar things using the words *like* or *as* ("Hills Like White Elephants" – Ernest Hemingway).

Slang Informal words whose meanings vary from locale to locale or change as time passes. Slang is frequently associated with a particular group of people – for example, bikers, musicians, or urban youth. Slang is inappropriate in college writing.

Subject-by-subject comparison A comparison that discusses one subject in full and then goes on to discuss the next subject. (See also **Point-by-point comparison**.)

Subjective description A description that contains value judgments (*a saintly person,* for example). Whereas objective language is distanced from an event or object, *subjective language* is involved. A subjective description focuses on the author's reaction to the event, conveying not just a factual record of details but also their significance. Subjective language may include poetic or colorful words that impart a judgment or an emotional response (*stride, limp, meander, hobble, stroll, plod,* or *shuffle* instead of *walk*). Subjective descriptions often include *figures of speech*.

Summary The ideas of a source as presented in one's own words. Unlike a paraphrase, a summary conveys only a general sense of a passage, without following the order and emphasis of the original.

Support The ideas that explain and expand your thesis or argument. They might include reasons, facts, examples, or statistics. The support helps to convince your readers that your thesis is reasonable.

Syllogism A basic form of deductive reasoning. Every syllogism includes three parts: a major premise that makes a general statement ("Confinement is physically and psychologically damaging"); a minor premise that makes a related but more specific statement ("Zoos confine animals"); and a conclusion drawn from these two premises ("Therefore, zoos are physically and psychologically damaging to animals").

Symbol A person, event, or object that stands for something more than its literal meaning.

Synonym A word with the same basic meaning as another word. A synonym for *loud* is *noisy*. Most words in the English language have several synonyms, but each word has unique nuances or shades of meaning. (See also **Connotation**.)

Synthesize Blending your own ideas and interpretations with those of your source material. It is important to make sure that your own ideas dominate the discussion and that any information from outside sources is cited correctly.

Thesis An essay's main idea; the idea that all the points in the body of the essay support. A thesis may be implied, but it is usually stated explicitly in the form of a *thesis statement*. In addition to conveying the essay's main idea, the thesis statement may indicate the writer's approach to the subject and the writer's purpose. It may also indicate the pattern of development that will structure the essay.

Topic sentence A sentence stating the main idea of a paragraph. Often, but not always, the topic sentence opens the paragraph.

Toulmin logic A method of structuring an argument according to the way arguments occur in everyday life. Developed by philosopher Stephen Toulmin, Toulmin logic divides an argument into three parts: the *claim*, the *grounds*, and the *warrant*.

Transitions Words or expressions that link ideas in a piece of writing. Long essays frequently contain *transitional paragraphs* that connect one part of the essay to another. Writers use a variety of transitional expressions, such as *afterward, because, consequently, for instance, furthermore, however,* and *likewise*. See the list of transitions on page 55.

Understatement Deliberate de-emphasis for effect: "The people who live near the Mississippi River are not exactly looking forward to more flooding"; "Emily was a little upset about failing math." The opposite of understatement is *hyperbole*.

Unity The desirable attribute of a paragraph in which every sentence relates directly to the paragraph's main idea. This main idea is often stated in a *topic sentence*.

Warrant In Toulmin logic, the inference that connects the claim to the grounds. The warrant can be a belief that is taken for granted or an assumption that underlies the argument. (See also **Toulmin logic**.)

Writing process The sequence of tasks a writer undertakes when writing an essay. During *invention,* or *prewriting,* the writer gathers information and ideas and develops a thesis. During the *arrangement* stage, the writer organizes material into a logical sequence. During *drafting and revision,* the essay is actually written and then rewritten. Finally, during *editing and proofreading,* the writer puts the finishing touches on the essay by correcting misspellings, checking punctuation, searching for grammatical inaccuracies, and so on. These stages occur in no fixed order; many effective writers move back and forth among them. (See Chapters 2–5.)

ACKNOWLEDGMENTS

Sherman Alexie. "Indian Education," from *The Lone Ranger and Tonto Fistfight in Heaven*. Copyright © 1993 by Sherman Alexie. Reproduced with permission of Grove/Atlantic, Inc. and Nancy Stauffer Associates. Any third-party use of this material, outside of this publication, is prohibited.

Aaron Bady. "Public Universities Should Be Free," from *Aljazeera America*, November 19, 2013, from http://america.aljazeera.com/opinions/2013/11/public-universitieshighereducation.html. Copyright © 2013 by Aaron Bady. Reproduced with permission of the author.

Joshua Barro. "Here's Why Stealing Cars Went Out of Fashion," from the *New York Times*, August 12, 2014. Copyright © 2014 by The New York Times. All rights reserved. Reproduced with permission and protected by the Copyright Laws of the United States. The printing, copying, redistribution, or retransmission of this Content without expressed written permission is prohibited. https://www.nytimes.com/.

Suzanne Berne. "Where Nothing Says Everything," from the *New York Times*, April 21, 2002. Copyright © 2002 by The New York Times. All rights reserved. Reproduced with permission and protected by the Copyright Laws of the United States. The printing, copying, redistribution, or retransmission of this Content without expressed written permission is prohibited. https://www.nytimes.com/.

David Borgenicht and Ben H. Winters. "How to Build Monster from Spare Parts," from *Worst-Case Scenario Survival Handbook: Paranormal*. Copyright © 2011 by David Borgenicht and Ben H. Winters. Reproduced with permission of Chronicle Books, LLC, San Francisco. Visit ChronicleBooks.com.

Judy Brady. "I Want a Wife," first published in *Ms.* magazine, 1972. Copyright © 1972 by Judy Brady. Reproduced with permission of the author.

Matt Breunig. "The Case against Free College," from the *New Republic*, October 5, 2015. Copyright © 2015 by The New Republic. All rights reserved. Reproduced with permission and protected by the Copyright Laws of the United States. The printing, copying, redistribution, or retransmission of this Content without expressed written permission is prohibited. https://newrepublic.com/.

José Antonio Burcíaga. "Tortillas." Reproduced with permission of the Estate of José Antonio Burcíaga.

Rachel Carson. "Obligation to Endure," from *Silent Spring*. Copyright © 1962 by Rachel L. Carson. Copyright renewed © 1990 by Roger Christie. Reproduced with permission of Houghton Mifflin Harcourt Publishing Company and Francis Collin, Trustee. All copying, including electronic, or redistribution of this text is expressly forbidden. All rights reserved.

Bruce Catton. "Grant and Lee: A Study in Contrasts," from *The American Story*, edited by Earl Schenck Miers. Copyright © by U.S. Capitol Historical Society. Reproduced with permission.

Soraya Chemaly. "What's Really Important about 'Trigger Warnings,'" from *Huffpost*, May 20, 2014. Copyright © 2014 by Soraya Chemaly. Reproduced with permission of the author.

Amy Chua. Adapted excerpt from pages 3–5, 29, 50–54, 60–63, circa 2,471 words [the *Wall Street Journal* 1/8/2011] from *Battle Hymn of the Tiger Mother*. Copyright © 2011 by Amy Chua. Reproduced with permission of Penguin Press, an imprint of Penguin Publishing Group, a division of Penguin Random House, LLC. All rights reserved.

Judith Ortiz Cofer. "The Myth of the Latin Woman: I Just Met a Girl Named Maria," from *The Latin Deli*. Copyright © 1993 by Judith Ortiz Cofer. Reproduced with permission of University of Georgia Press.

Simon Cottee. "What Motivates Terrorists?" from the *Atlantic* magazine, June 9, 2015. Copyright © 2015 by The Atlantic Media Company, as first published in the *Atlantic* magazine. All rights reserved. Distributed by Tribune Content Agency, LLC.

Junot Díaz. "The Money," from the *New Yorker*, June 13, 2011. Copyright © 2011 by Junot Díaz. First published in the *New Yorker* and reproduced with permission of Junot Díaz and Aragi, Inc.

Sophie Downes. "A Misleading Attack on Trigger Warnings," from the *New York Times*, April 11, 2016. Copyright © 2016 by The New York Times. All rights reserved. Reproduced with permission and protected by the Copyright Laws of the United States. The printing, copying, redistribution, or retransmission of this Content without expressed written permission is prohibited. https://www.nytimes.com/

Lars Eighner. From "On Dumpster Diving," an excerpt from *Travels with Lisbeth*. Copyright © 1993 by Lars Eighner. Reproduced with permission of St. Martin's Press. All rights reserved.

Stephanie Ericsson. "The Ways We Lie," from the *Utne Reader*, 1992, also appeared in *Companion into Dawn: Inner Dialogues on Loving*, published 1997 by HarperCollins Publishers. Copyright © 1992 by Stephanie Ericsson. Reproduced with permission of Dunham Literary as agent for the author.

Stanley Fish. "Getting Coffee Is Hard to Do," from the *New York Times*, August 5, 2007. Copyright © 2007 by The New York Times. All rights reserved. Reproduced with permission and protected by the Copyright Laws of the United States. The printing, copying, redistribution, or retransmission of this Content without expressed written permission is prohibited. https://www.nytimes.com/.

Martin Gansberg. "Thirty-Eight Who Saw Murder Didn't Call Police," from the *New York Times*, March 27, 1964. Copyright © 1964 by The New York Times. All rights reserved. Reproduced with permission and protected by the Copyright Laws of the United States. The printing, copying, redistribution, or retransmission of this Content without expressed written permission is prohibited. https://www.nytimes.com/.

Henry Louis Gates Jr. "'What's in a Name?'" from *Dissent*. Copyright © 1989 by Henry Louis Gates Jr. Reproduced with permission of the University of Pennsylvania Press.

Linda Hasselstrom. "A Peaceful Woman Explains Why She Carries a Gun," from *Land Circle*, Anniversary Edition. Copyright © 1991 by Linda Hasselstrom. Reproduced with permission of Fulcrum Publishing.

Shirley Jackson. "The Lottery," from *The Lottery*. Copyright © 1948, 1949 by Shirley Jackson. Copyright renewed © 1976, 1977 by Laurence Hyman, Barry Hyman, Mrs. Sarah Webster, and Mrs. Joanne Schnurer. Reproduced with permission of Farrar, Straus, and Giroux, LLC.

Donald Kagan. "On Patriotism," from the *Yale Review*, 2011, Volume 99, Issue 4. Copyright © 2011 by Donald Kagan. Reproduced with permission of John Wiley & Sons, Inc.

Marina Keegan. "Stability in Motion," from *The Opposite of Loneliness*. Copyright © 2014 by Tracy and Kevin Keegan. Reproduced with permission of Scribner, a division of Simon & Schuster, Inc. All rights reserved.

Olga Khazan. "The Three Types of Happiness," from the *Atlantic* magazine, April 18, 2016. Copyright © 2016 by The Atlantic Media Company, as first published in the *Atlantic* magazine. All rights reserved. Distributed by Tribune Content Agency, LLC.

Vinod Khosla. "Is Majoring in Liberal Arts a Mistake for Students?" Copyright © by Vinod Khosla. Reproduced with permission of the author.

Martin Luther King Jr. "Letter from Birmingham Jail." Copyright © 1963 by Dr. Martin Luther King Jr. Copyright © renewed 1991 by Coretta Scott King. Reproduced with arrangement with the Heirs of the Estate of Martin Luther King Jr., c/o Writers House as agent for the proprietor, New York, NY.

Jamaica Kinkaid. "'Girl,'" from *At the Bottom of the River*. Copyright © 1983 by Jamaica Kincaid. Reproduced with permission of Farrar, Straus, and Giroux, LLC.

David Kirby. "Inked Well," from *The American Interest*, November 1, 2006. Copyright © 2006 by David Kirby. Reproduced with permission of the author.

Maggie Koerth-Baker. "Sure You Saw a Flying Saucer," from the *New York Times*, May 26, 2013. Copyright © 2013 by The New York Times. All rights reserved. Reproduced with permission and protected by the Copyright Laws of the United States. The printing, copying, redistribution, or retransmission of this Content without expressed written permission is prohibited. https://www.nytimes.com/.

Ellen Laird. "I'm Your Teacher, Not Your Internet Service Provider," from the *Chronicle of Higher Education*, January 3, 2003. Copyright © 2003 by Ellen Laird. Reproduced with permission of the author.

Jennifer Medina. "The Literary Canon Could Make Students Squirm," from the *New York Times*, May 18, 2014. Copyright © 2014 by The New York Times. All rights reserved. Reproduced with permission and protected by the Copyright Laws of the United States. The printing, copying, redistribution, or retransmission of this Content without expressed written permission is prohibited. https://www.nytimes.com/.

Arthur Miller. "Get It Right: Privatize Executions," from *Echoes Down the Corridor: Collected Essays, 1944–2000*, edited by Stephen Centola. Copyright © 1992, 2000 by Arthur Miller. Reproduced with permission of Viking Books, an imprint of Penguin Publishing Group, a division of Penguin Random House, LLC.

Janice Mirikitani. "Suicide Note," from *Shedding Silence*. Copyright © 1987 by Janice Mirikitani. Reproduced with permission of Celestial Arts, an imprint of the Crown Publishing Group, a division of Penguin Random House, LLC. All rights reserved.

Jessica Mitford. "The Embalming of Mr. Jones," from *The American Way of Death*. Copyright © 1963, 1978 by Jessica Mitford. All rights reserved. Reproduced with permission of the Estate of Jessica Mitford.

Moisés Naím. "The YouTube Effect," from *Los Angeles Times*, December 20, 2006. Copyright © 2006 by Moisés Naím. Reproduced with permission of the author.

Bich Minh Nguyen. "Goodbye to My Twinkie Days," from the *New York Times*, November 17, 2012. Copyright © 2012 by The New York Times. All rights reserved. Reproduced with permission and protected by the Copyright Laws of the United States. The printing, copying, redistribution, or retransmission of this Content without expressed written permission is prohibited. https://www.nytimes.com/.

George Orwell. "Shooting an Elephant," from *A Collection of Essays*. Copyright © 1946 by Sonia Brownell Orwell. Copyright © renewed 1974 by Sonia Orwell. Reproduced with permission of Houghton Mifflin Harcourt Publishing Company. All rights reserved.

Karen Miller Pensiero. "Aylan Kurdi and the Photos That Changed History: The Devastating Images of a Dead Syrian Boy Were Preceded by Pictures from the Depression, the Civil Rights Movement, and the Moon," from the *Wall Street Journal*, September 11, 2015. Copyright © 2015 by Dow Jones & Company, Inc. Reproduced with permission from The Wall Street Journal. All rights reserved.

Richard A. Posner. "On Plagiarism," from the *Atlantic*, April 2002. Copyright © 2002 by Richard A. Posner. Reproduced with permission of the author.

Henry Reed. "Naming of Parts," from *New Statesman and Nation*, Volume 24, No. 598, August 8, 1942. Copyright © 1942 by New Statesman. Reproduced with permission.

Deborah L. Rhode. "Why Looks Are the Last Bastion of Discrimination," from the *Washington Post*, May 23, 2010. Copyright © 2010 by Deborah L. Rhode. Reproduced with permission of the author.

Heather Rogers. "Hiding in Plain Sight," excerpt from *Gone Tomorrow: The Hidden Life of Garbage*. Copyright © 2005 by Heather Rogers. Reproduced with permission of The New Press. www.newpress.com.

Naomi Rosenberg. "How to Tell a Mother Her Child Is Dead," from the *New York Times*, September 4, 2016. Copyright © by The New York Times. All rights reserved. Reproduced with permission and protected by the Copyright Laws of the United States. The printing, copying, redistribution, or retransmission of this Content without expressed written permission is prohibited. https://www.nytimes.com.

Carolyn Foster Segal. "The Dog Ate My Flashdrive, and Other Tales of Woe," from the *Chronicle of Higher Education*, August 11, 2000. Copyright © 2000 by Carolyn Foster Segal. Reproduced with permission of the author.

Bonnie Smith-Yackel. "My Mother Never Worked." Copyright © 1975 by Bonnie Smith-Yackel. Reproduced with permission of the author.

Brent Staples. "Cutting and Pasting: A Senior Thesis," from the *New York Times*, July 13, 2010. Copyright © 2010 by The New York Times. All rights reserved. Reproduced with permission and protected by the Copyright Laws of the United States. The printing, copying, redistribution, or retransmission of this Content without expressed written permission is prohibited. https://www.nytimes.com/.

Brent Staples. "Just Walk On By: A Black Man Ponders His Power to Alter Public Space," from *Harper's Magazine*, December 1986. Copyright © 1986 by Brent Staples. Reproduced with permission of the author.

Geoffrey R. Stone. "Free Expression in Peril," from the *Chronicle of Higher Education*, October 2016. Used with permission of the Chronicle of Higher Education, copyright © 2017. All rights reserved.

Maia Szalavitz. "Ten Ways We Get the Odds Wrong," from *Psychology Today*, January 1, 2008. Copyright © 2008 by Maia Szalavitz. Reproduced with permission of the author.

Amy Tan. "Mother Tongue," first appeared in the *Threepenny Review*. Copyright © 1990 by Amy Tan. Reproduced with permission of the author and Sandra Dijkstra Agency.

Deborah Tannen. "Sex, Lies, and Conversation," author's own adaptation of text from *You Just Don't Understand*. Copyright © 1990 by Deborah Tannen. Reproduced with permission of HarperCollins Publishers and ICM Partners.

Zeynep Tufekcioglu. "Why the Post Office Makes America Great," from the *New York Times*, January 1, 2016. Copyright © 2016 by The New York Times. All rights reserved. Reproduced with permission and protected by the Copyright Laws of the United States. The printing, copying, redistribution, or retransmission of this Content without expressed written permission is prohibited. https://www.nytimes.com/.

Ocean Vuong. "Surrendering," from the *New Yorker*, June 6, 2016. Copyright © 2016 by Ocean Vuong/The New Yorker. Reproduced with permission.

Timothy Wheeler. "There's a Reason They Choose Schools," from *National Review*, October 11, 2007. Copyright © 2007 by National Review. Reproduced with permission.

E. B. White. "Once More to the Lake," from *One Man's Meat*. Copyright © 1941 by E. B. White. Reproduced with permission of ICM Partners.

"Why Our Campuses Are *Not* Safer without Concealed Handguns." Copyright © 2008 by Students for Concealed Carry. Reproduced with permission.

"Why Our Campuses Are Safer without Concealed Handguns," June 20, 2013. Copyright 2013 by Students for Gun-Free Schools. Reproduced with permission.

Leon Wieseltier. "Perhaps Culture Is Now the Counterculture," from the *New Republic*, May 28, 2013. Copyright © 2013 by The New Republic. All rights reserved. Reproduced with permission and protected by the Copyright Laws of the United States. The printing, copying, redistribution, or retransmission of this Content without expressed written permission is prohibited. https://newrepublic.com/.

Amy Wilentz. "A Zombie Is a Slave Forever," from the *New York Times*, October 31, 2012. Copyright © 2012 by The New York Times. All rights reserved. Reproduced with permission and protected by the Copyright Laws of the United States. The printing, copying, redistribution, or retransmission of this Content without expressed written permission is prohibited. https://www.nytimes.com/.

Isabel Wilkerson. "Where Did the Great Migration Get Us?" from the *New York Times*, February 14, 2016. Copyright © 2016 by The New York Times. All rights reserved. Reproduced with permission and protected by the Copyright Laws of the United States. The printing, copying, redistribution, or retransmission of this Content without expressed written permission is prohibited. https://www.nytimes.com/.

Juan Williams. "Songs of the Summer of 1963 . . . and 2013," from the *Wall Street Journal*, August 26, 2013. Copyright © 2013 by Dow Jones & Company, Inc. All rights reserved worldwide.

Andrew Wilson. "Why I Wouldn't Go to the University of Texas Law School," from the *Nation*, May 5, 2016. Copyright © 2016 by The Nation. All rights reserved. Reproduced with permission and protected by the Copyright Laws of the United States. The printing, copying, redistribution, or retransmission of this Content without expressed written permission is prohibited. https://www.thenation.com/.

INDEX